SPORT, PEACE AND DEVELOPMENT

KEITH GILBERT AND WILL BENNETT

Common Ground

First published in Champaign, Illinois in 2012
by Common Ground Publishing LLC
as part of the Sport and Society series

Library of Congress Cataloging-in-Publication Data

Sport, peace, and development / edited by Keith Gilbert and Will Bennett.
    p. cm.
Includes bibliographical references and index.
ISBN 978-1-61229-086-7 (pbk. : alk. paper) -- ISBN 978-1-61229-124-6 (pdf)
1. Sports--Sociological aspects. 2. Peace-building. I. Gilbert, Keith. II. Bennett, Will.

GV706.5S73556 2013
796.01--dc23

2012036823

Table of Contents

Foreword

Mr. Wilfried Lemke, Special Adviser to the United Nations Secretary-General on Sport for Development and Peace

Sport is indisputably one of the world's most popular leisure activities and it describes a fascinating phenomenon: people from all over the world play, attend, watch, listen to, talk about and experience sport at all levels of performance from amateur to elite. Sport is often described as a language that everyone in the world can understand and indeed sport can bring together and unite groups and communities. On an individual level, sport has the capacity to develop people's skills and faculties. In addition, sport has the power to attract large audiences and can play a major role in communicating positive awareness messages on key issues and assist in driving social change.

That is why the United Nations, governments, NGOs, development agencies, sport federations and social entrepreneurs have increasingly been harnessing the power of sport as a low-cost and high-impact tool in their humanitarian, development and peace-building efforts. The deliberate use of sport, physical activity and play as delivery mechanisms in social and humanitarian work has experienced a significant increase in scope and recognition over the past decade or so. In September 2000, the UN Millennium Summit brought together the largest gathering of world leaders in history. In the Summit's final declaration, signed by 189 countries, the international community committed to eight objectives, known as the Millennium Development Goals (MDGs). In 2003, the UN Inter-Agency Task Force on Sport for Development and Peace published their report entitled "Sport for Development and Peace: Towards Achieving the Millennium Development Goals." The report explicitly stated that "well-designed sport-based initiatives are practical and cost-effective tools to achieve objectives in development and peace" and that "sport is a powerful vehicle that should be increasingly considered by the United Nations as complementary to existing activities."

Today, sport can no longer be considered a luxury within any society but rather it is an important investment in the present and the future, particularly in developing countries. Not only are sport and play fundamental rights that need to be respected and promoted worldwide but sport is also a promising medium to use for social transformation and peace-building. The ever-growing number of projects, initiatives and organizations in the field of Sport for Development and Peace testifies to the usefulness and flexibility of the tool that is sport. At the same time much policy work on national and international levels as well as research has been undertaken. However, resources need to be available; monitoring and evaluation should be mainstreamed in all programming and project work; and research activities need to be further connected. I therefore consider publications such as the present one with its impressive volume of contributions from numerous perspectives to be essential for the consolidation and increase of the know-ledge and evidence base that should underpin all policy and field work.

Since I was appointed the UN Secretary-General's Special Adviser on Sport for Development and Peace in March 2008, I have been visiting a number of developing countries and communities, and witnessed first-hand how sport is used in development and peace projects to bridge divides, foster youth and promote education and development. I have been impressed by many good examples and I am convinced of the great potential of sport, which can be leveraged even more. Therefore, I continue to urge key stakeholders to promote, use and invest in sport for human development. On behalf of the United Nations, I would like to encourage all actors within the Sport for Development and Peace movement to keep researching and harnessing the unique power of sport with the goal of effectively using it to achieve sustainable international development and peace-building.

Preface

Sports diplomacy: A lever for sustainable peace

Joel Bouzou (President L'Organisation pour la Paix par le Sport)

Let's applaud the authors for their initiative of this book that approaches the vital question of the effective contribution that sport can make to development, social cohesion and peace in a methodological and rigorous way. Through relevant illustrations from the field, which give weight to the hypothesis, the diverse texts bring to the fore what for me has been a certainty for more than 30 years: the construction of peace through sport is not a mere "myth"; it covers a multiplicity of realities.

Sports diplomacy is one of the essential facets of any reflection on the use of sport to create peace, because its activation is an integral part of a holistic approach of the subject, and because it can give a lasting stimulus to effective field actions. On a political level, the establishment of peace above all comes from the improvement of relations between States. It is therefore legitimate to question which tools can be effective, and sport is undeniably one of them.

It is in fact difficult to assess the boundaries of sports diplomacy. Indeed, few academic works specifically focus on this concept and its empirical rendition. In reality, sports diplomacy covers multiple fields of application: strategies to develop a country's international policy, potential paths to foster reconciliation between hostile countries or communities, and the use of sport as a sounding board to criticize certain political situations. Although by no means a description of a defined methodology for sports diplomacy, these few words will seek to explain its multi-faceted character and to identify the modalities of action so that sports diplomacy can serve peace-promotion in more ways than simply symbolically.

A traditional approach to sports diplomacy is to analyse its contribution in terms of enhancing the influence and image of countries eager to be recognized on the international stage. Diplomacy is, amongst other things, the art of persuasion. A prerequisite for persuasion is recognition, visibility and prestige; sport can serve such a purpose. The use of sport as a tool for advocacy is one interpretation of the concept of *"soft power"* in international relations. It is the idea that nowadays the power of a State depends not only on its ability to impose itself internationally by coercion, but also by its ability to influence through its power of attraction, in many areas ranging from the economy to culture. Sport is one of these tools for "soft power". In this perspective, sports diplomacy is a vehicle for a State to make known or consolidate its reputation. This notably results in the increasing importance placed on hosting major international sports competitions, especially events such as the Olympic Games, the football World Cup or the Athletics World Championships. In this, sport plays a role in integration and recognition in the concert of nations.

Let's take the example of sports diplomacy in Qatar, which is one of the main pillars of Qatar's international strategy. In recent years, the country has imposed itself on the international stage through various means and its influence is growing in the region, where it is increasingly taking on the role of mediator, becoming a crossroads for communication, as well as a cultural interface. Sport is part of this influential initiative. In 2022 the country will host the football World Cup and attaches great strategic importance to this event which will bring unprecedented worldwide visibility. In addition to the opportunity to be prominent, Qatar also uses sports diplomacy to advance its aim to be a recognized meeting place for peace through sport and to take a pioneering role in this area. For this reason, in November 2011 Doha hosted an original sports meeting which revived the concept of ping-pong diplomacy. Players from India, Pakistan, North Korea, South Korea, Japan, America, China and France competed in doubles matches and diplomats from their respective countries were among the spectators. The crux of this event was organizing mixed doubles matches between teamed pairs of athletes from hostile countries, which demonstrated the power of a sports meeting to bring valuable rapprochement. Where intergovernmental forums sometimes have difficulty in getting representatives from antagonistic countries (South Korea and North Korea, India and Pakistan, etc) to sit round the same table, here sport allowed them to support the same team! This event also provided a place for diplomats to meet in a neutral environment. Exchanges between diplomats are usually characterized by fixed attitudes, a pre-established agenda, well-defined protocol, and possibly a few prejudices... In this case the meeting was apolitical, with no fixed agenda or communication protocol. Thus at its own level, the unifying banner of sport forges links and conveys meaning.

Sports diplomacy as a tool for reconciliation between antagonistic, competitive or rival countries is not new. We often evoke the iconic example of ping-pong diplomacy between China and the United States in the early seventies, which helped to reconcile the two countries - at the time a strategic priority for Washington. Lately much has been said about cricket diplomacy between India and Pakistan in 2005 and 2011, and football diplomacy between Turkey and Armenia in 2009. In both cases, sport brought together the Heads of Government of the competing teams, and thus the highest level of political representation, which gives a significant symbolic weight to these events.

However, we cannot hold false illusions as to the real political impact of these meetings. Sports diplomacy can certainly pass messages and can signify a wish for appeasement or reconciliation; but initiatives may be short-lived if they are not extended beyond the widely-publicized event itself and the official photo.

The political message must find ways to be applied at a local level in order to become inscribed into sustainable logic. In the India-Pakistan and Turkey-Armenia cases cited above, this could entail organizing "Friendship Games" in frontier regions to encourage grassroots communication between hostile communities. This concept of "Friendship Games" was initiated in 2007 by the Haitian Olympic Committee and the Dominican Republic Olympic Committee to bring together communities from both sides of the border. The model was then duplicated in 2010 in the Great Lakes region in Africa, between Burundi and the Democratic Republic of Congo where the event made a very strong local impact and greatly mobilized local populations. By creating an environment of trust between the communities, it also helped to boost cooperation between border authorities (logistics, security, transport, etc.). In this way, sports diplomacy acts at a local level and can then create a virtuous circle. Indeed, rallying populations around events such as these can inspire political authorities and encourage them to invest (themselves) in this momentum.

Another aspect to sports diplomacy is the role of the athletes. Are they ambassadors for their country or ambassadors for peace? They are in fact both. On the one hand, they help to enhance their country's reputation when they win international competitions and contribute to the sense of national cohesion that only sport is able to generate from great victories. On the other hand, they are ambassadors for peace because they are united by the universality of the rules of their sport and by the neutrality of the place where they compete. Athletes have considerable influence on youth, which goes even further as it can be exercised very directly on political decision makers. They are therefore influential spokespeople on multiple levels. Mobilized in development projects or peace initiatives, they can facilitate the transmission of messages and permanently mark mentalities around the values and contribution of sport.

Sports diplomacy at the service of sustainable peace inevitably involves concerted reflection from all actors involved. Transmitting best practices to implement programs based on sport, in the field and in the political arena, are paramount. Whatever the level of action considered, mediation is capital to communicate best practices. To do this, it is necessary for stakeholders involved in cooperation (Governments, sports movement, civil society, etc.) to have a neutral meeting place to encourage communication and reconciliation initiatives, identify intermediaries and think up joint projects. This kind of initiative for cooperation and the role of intermediary surely constitute another variant of sports diplomacy.

This book gives numerous examples of best practices of using sport for peace, development and social cohesion in the field, particularly to achieve the Millennium Development Goals. Sports diplomacy is another pillar, at a more "macro" level to leverage the power of sport as a tool. Thus, in parallel to operational cooperation in the field, priority must also be given to the continuation and strengthening of efforts to raise awareness among political elites and decision-makers about the enormous and largely untapped potential of utilizing sport for peace and reconciliation.

Acknowledgements

We believe that the development of this book provides a much needed addition to the practical and research literature surrounding the relationship between sport, peace and development. As this book is the first of its kind we hope that it is used as an initial baseline text to further stimulate research and practice into this association.

In particular we would like to take this opportunity to thank *Mr. Wilfried Lemke, Special Adviser to the United Nations Secretary-General on Sport for Development and Peace* for providing the 'Forward' to this book and *Mr. Joel Bouzou who is the President and Founder of the organisation Peace and Sport* for writing the 'Preface'. We are grateful for their insightful comments, support and time.

However, there is no doubt that without the support of the authors in this text that it would not have come to fruition. In this respect we would like to take this opportunity to thank each individual author as we know that many interrupted their own work schedules in order to be able to provide the chapters for us. We understand the current problematics placed on academics, practitioners and writers who labour in sport for development and peace programmes and in higher education across the world. Indeed, we realise that for some the development of a chapter for this book was a herculean effort as many pressures had been placed on them in their own separate work environments. Again we thank the authors for their efforts and hopefully we have set the seed for them to join us and be involved in writing for a further text in five years time to review the research on the sport, peace and development. Also our thanks go to the authors who we called upon later in the piece who happily assisted us with chapters which have strengthened and allowed us to broaden the scope of the text and give it a truly international flavour.

There have been others who have kindly spent time and effort supporting the development of this book. One such person is Kathryn Otte the enthusiastic editor from Common Ground Publishing who has been supportive and with us every step of the long and often arduous process towards maturity of this text. Since Kathryn's retirement we have been supported admirably by Stephanie Turza and as such thank her for her insightful ideas and suggestions.

Our thanks go to our respective organisations – the University of East London and Right to Play – and the individuals, to many to mention within them who have provided library, statistical and financial research support for the fine tuning of the book. Without this constant backup and support from our own organisations research work of this kind would not be possible. We thank the academic staff and also the many postgraduate students and the many practitioners who have influenced our thinking and caused us to redirect our thoughts and ideas.

Finally, it would be remiss of us not to thank our respective partners Dr. Yuen Ching Ho and Grace Boyle who provided us with moral, psychological and academic support and advice through the development of this book.

Keith Gilbert & Will Bennett [8th June 2012]

Chapter 1
Restructuring Lives through Sport
Keith Gilbert & Will Bennett

Introduction

This book has been constructed in order to plug a perceived fissure in the literature regarding issues related specifically to the continually evolving and emerging movement of 'sport, peace and development' in university and fieldwork settings around the world. As such we have 'taken on board' the concepts of *theory* and *practice* as they correlate to the excellent work which is currently being produced in various high impact zones[1]. In the growth of this book we were cognizant of the fact that these high impact zones of conflict, war, natural disaster and tension are global, and ever changing in time and place. Furthermore that each case of humanitarian support, utilizing the medium of sport, needs to be taken in isolation and dealt with systematically with strong philosophical and conceptual understandings and exemplary monitoring and evaluation practices. We hasten to add here that the quality and quantity of these programs, of course, are dependent on and relate to the amount of aid and the support provided by the established and rapidly developing new world orders. Never-the-less, from the outset we argue that the emerging areas of sport, peace and development as research

---

[1]. Impact zones in the context of world-wide areas of greatest need for development progams.

discipline and as practical phenomenon are relatively new and yet in such a short time period of ten or twelve years have impacted positively on many people's lives in many countries across the world. Indeed this world-wide network of fragmented and disparate organisations has expanded quickly into a vast, multi-layered, politically sensitive web of support for people living in different countries and diverse cultures. The 'Sport for Peace and Development International Working Group'[2] argued that:

> 'Sport and physical activity are rapidly gaining recognition as simple, low-cost, and effective means of achieving development goals. Over the past decade, agencies, international sport federations, international and national non-governmental organizations (NGOs) and national governments have been using sport as a tool for development and peace'. (2007 p. 3)

We agree with this statement and recognise that in the university sector there have recently been a plethora of excellent journal articles and books which have attempted to deal with the paradigms relating to 'sport, peace and development' (Hoglund & Sundberg, 2008; Sugden, 2008; Coalter, 2007; Donnelly, 2010, Giulianotti, 2011; Giulianotti & Armstrong, 2011; Darnell, 2012) and the role of sport as a solution or panacea to huge problems of humanitarian concern. Indeed, we categorically state, that unlike some other suppositions, that sport cannot be the sole change agent or the device which changes the entire world for the better. Sport is not a panacea and does not exist purely in some utopian society and this is supported by the comments of the UNOSDP (United Nations Office for Sport, Development and Peace) who state that, 'Sport is not a cure-all for development problems. As a cultural phenomenon, it is a mirror of society and is just as complex and contradictory'[3] and similarly by the Swiss Agency for Development and Co-operation in their 1985 report on 'Sport for Peace and Development which comments that: 'As great as its potential may be, sport is not a cure-all for all development problems. As a cultural phenomenon, it reflects society in all its complexities and contradictions' (p.16). However, sport when combined with other development ideas does contribute greatly to the well-being of individuals in disadvantaged societies.

With these previous thoughts in mind we changed the wording of this book from the recognised 'sport, development and peace' to 'sport, peace and development'. We argued this point through carefully and feel that development cannot truly occur unless there are certain aspects or types of peace present even in limited areas after conflict, war, or disaster has struck the particular community. This is supported by the comments of Galtung (1998) when he argues that peace is about the negation of different forms of violence and the subsequent attempts through development for societ-

---

2. Please see (http://www.un.org/wcm/content/site/sport/home/unplayers/membersta-tes/pid/6229) for more information.

3. Please refer to the UNOSDP website http://www.un.org/wcm/content/site/sport/ for further information and details regarding the United Nations involvement and perspectives on Sport, Development and Peace.

al re-building, re-habilitation, re-structuration and re-culturation (Galtung, 1998). This comment again assisted us in our thinking regarding the title changing slightly from the recognised 'sport, development and peace' to 'sport, peace and development'. We also feel that the term 'sport, peace and development' is essentially very broad as there are several types of sport, several types of peace and several types of development. Thus in order to conceptualise the 'movement' what follows is an attempt to review the different definitions of sport, peace and development. More-over, in the past few years, we have been asked for our conceptualisation of sport, peace and development and as such what follows is an attempt to define certain aspects and conceptualise this world-wide movement.

Towards a Conceptualisation of Sport, Peace and Development

Conceptualising the notion of 'sport, peace and development' is not an easy task. In order to start we asked ourselves two questions: What are the separate definitions of peace and development which best suit the development and peace initiatives? And secondly, what is the definition of sport? In regard to the definitions we decided it was important to initially have an idea of the latter question in which we agree with Meier's, (1981) assessment where he noted that:

> 'There are few words in the English language which have such a multiplicity of divergent meanings as the word sport. A detailed scrutiny of the substantial sociology of sport literature indicates that the problem of definition is one of the most basic and extensive, if highly contentious issues are to be found in the field. Despite the importance of the problem, debate continues, inaccurate and contradictory statements abound, and consensus is largely absent'.

This is still the case today and only a cursory look at the definition of sport, for example, will support this statement. Comments by the Oxford Dictionary (2012) provide us with a classic definition by describing sport as '...an activity involving physical exertion and skill in which an individual or team competes against another or others for entertainment'. This is similar to the definition by (Britannica Micropaedia Ready Reference, Number 2) which argues simply that sport may be defined as a 'recreational or competitive activity that involves some amount of physical strength or skill'. Both the previous definitions don't exactly 'fit the bill' as far as we are concerned however, we like the definition as espoused by Jay Coakely (2012) which is more detailed and widely used in the sport science fields. In his book *Sport in Society* (2012) he describes sport as 'an institutionalized competitive activity that involves vigorous physical exertion or the use of relatively complex physical skills by individuals whose participation is motivated by a combination of intrinsic (e.g., self-satisfaction that comes with competition) and extrinsic (e.g., money and public adoration) factors'. Unfortunately, Coakley's definition again differs from the UN Inter-Agency Task Force on Sport for Development and Peace who define sport, for the purposes of development, as '....*all forms of physical activity that contribute to physical fit-*

ness, mental well-being and social interaction, such as play, recreation, organized or competitive sport, and indigenous sports and games'. We prefer the latter as sport for development and peace in most cases does not have an extrinsic orientation and is more intrinsically motivated towards achieving self-satisfaction, skill and fitness development. Thus for the purposes of this book we intend to utilize the definition put forward by the UN Inter-Agency Task Force on Sport for Development and Peace. However, definitions aside, sport has been documented as an essential human right and this fact sometimes eludes the definition writers. As Beutler (2006) mentions sport has been established as a human right since '...the Declaration on Human Rights of the Child (General Assembly resolution 1386 (XIV) of 20th November 1959)'. Nevertheless, nowhere in the definition of sport literature are the words 'fundamental human right' utilized. We argue here that those are the only three words which are required to define the term sport and development and all are relevant to this book. Perhaps we could add them to the UN definition along with the words development so that it reads:

> 'Sport is a fundamental human right and involves all forms of physical activity that contribute to the development of physical fitness, mental well-being, and social interaction, such as play, recreation, organized or competitive sport, and indigenous sports and games'

However, the definition of the term 'development' is a little more complex than anticipated and as such has numerous definitions such as those described simply by (Dictionary.com 2012) as 'The act or process of developing' or even '....to bring from latency to or toward fulfilment' (The free dictionary online, 2012) and the one which we are more aligned is provided by the (Business dictionary, 2012) who describe development as:

> 'The process of economic and social-transformation that is based on complex cultural and environmental factors and their interactions'.

In actuality, the above three definitions appear simplistic as according to Volger (2010, p.102) 'Development debates in the UN system have always reflected a multitude of development perspectives, definitions and theories'. He provides the following reasons for this phenomenon, '....the large number of member states, the growing number of civil societies, the growing number of civil organizations......the diversity of and disparities among countries, as well as the fact that governments are not unitary factors and government delegations often have to represent the concerns of various constituencies'. Consequently there are many and various definitions of the term 'development'. In fact over the past twenty years the United Nations has been referring to 'sustainable development' which it first defined in the United Nations, Brundtland Report (1985) which included what is now one of the most extensively acknowledged definitions:

> 'Sustainable development is development that meets the needs of the present without compromising the ability of future generations to meet their own needs'.

There is another definition for development which relates specifically to 'empowerment' and of individuals taking control of their lives and this equates to economic growth and the raising of social capital. This definition refers to humans capacity '...to lead long and healthy lives, to be knowledgeable, to have access to the resources needed for a decent standard of living and to be able to participate in the life of the community' which has been endorsed by the overseas volunteering agency 'Comhlamh'. However again we feel it is far too simplistic. The definition which we finally settled on is related specifically to human development and reads as follows:

> *'Human development can be defined as a process of enlarging people's choices and building human capabilities (the range of things people can be and do), enabling them to: live a long and healthy life, have access to knowledge, have a decent standard of living and participate in the life of their community and the decisions that affect their lives'.*
> (S. Burd-Sharps & A. Perez 2005)

The defining of the term peace is also not without its problems because: 'In the UN charter, peace is not explicitly defined. Instead, it is implicitly a negative definition of peace (the lack of war) and not a positive definition (the lack of war plus just institutions, structural equality, etc.)'. This quote from the 1998 United Nations resolution[4] as argued by the authors 'does not cover the notion of civil war' and this creates a problem in the definitions which have been put forward and as such peace is difficult to define as there are various forms and levels of peace. In the process of building the definition for sport, peace and development there is however a need for a definition of peace per se. Peace has thus been defined in several ways and the following are two of the most popular:

1. the state existing during the absence of war or other hostilities[5]

2. Peace is a state of harmony characterized by the lack of violent conflict. Commonly understood as the absence of hostility, peace also suggests the existence of healthy or newly healed interpersonal relationships, prosperity in matters of social or economic welfare, the establishment of equality, and a working political order that serves the true interests of all[6].

---

4. In our literature search for the definition of peace we came across many descriptions of the term but no specific definition. However, the 'culture of peace' was defined by the following: 'A culture of peace is an integral approach to preventing violence and violent conflicts, and an alternative to the culture of war and violence based on education for peace, the promotion of sustainable economic and social development, respect for human rights, equality between women and men, democratic participation, tolerance, the free flow of information and disarmament'. (http://www.un.org/en/ga/documents/index.shtml).

5. For the short definition of 'peace' please see (http://www.thefreedictionary.com/peace) or any other reputable dictionary.

6. Definition of Peace taken from the Oxford Dictionary online (www.oxforddictionaryonline.com)

Others have described peace as a 'cessation or absence of war' (Fomerand, 2007, pp. 1771) or '....the condition of survival, the vital requirement of the technological era' (von Weizsacker, 1963, pp. 12) and that 'it must include those positive factors that foster cooperation among human groups with ostensibly different cultural patterns so that social justice can be done and human potential can freely develop within democratic political structures' (Sandy and Perkins, Jr. 1994, p. 1). However, again for the purposes of this book we have decided to utilise the following definition of peace as discussed by Czempiel (1984)[7] as it best suits our 'sport, peace and development' needs. He notes that: *Peace can be defined as a 'process-orientated pattern of the international system, which is marked by decreasing violence and increasing distributive justice'.*

The comparatively recent intensification of the 'sport, peace and development' movement has heralded a new era in which sport as part of a global structure of development can be organised as a means to engage in positive capacity building and become a resource to support human life after instances of violence, poverty, infectious disease, health problems, genocide, gender discrimination, terrorism and environmental problems caused by natural disaster or war between and within states. The use of sport in this context has been described by Ban Ki-moon the United Nations Secretary General where he notes that:

> 'Sport is increasingly recognized as an important tool in helping the United Nations achieve its objectives, in particular the Millennium Development Goals. By including sport in development and peace programmes in a more systematic way, the United nations can make full use of this cost-efficient tool to help us create a better world'[8]
>
> (SPD Platform, 2012)

In fact Kofi Annan (former United Nations Secretary General) has long argued that 'People in every nation love sport. Its values – fitness, fair play, teamwork, and the pursuit of excellence – are universal. At its best, it brings people together, no matter what their origin, background, religious beliefs or economic status' (Beutler, 2005, p.7) and that sport has been linked significantly with the peace process over many years. We only need to cite the legendary[9] football matches on Xmas day between the warring Germans and English during the First World War, the football matches in the Second World War prisoner of war camps, the Chinese – U.S. table tennis matches or the apartheid situation in South Africa or more recently the visits made by famous sportsmen and women to people in disadvantaged areas of the

---

7. Please see Volger, H. (2010). A Concise Encyclopaedia of the United Nations, 2nd revised edition – Martinrs Nijhoff Publishers, Boston U.S.A.

8. Please refer to the website of the International Sport, Development and Peace platform for an excellent and detailed analysis of the role of sport, development and peace (http://www.sportanddev.org/).

9. This is legendary as some historians disagree with the fact that football matches occurred between troops during Xmas day truces over the period of the First World War. In other words this is a debatable point.

world which are supported by organisations such as 'Peace and Sport' (L'Organisation pour la Paix parle Sport[10]) where the H.R.H. Prince Albert of Monaco echoes the comments of Ban Ki-moon and Kofi Annan. He mentions that 'Sport has a unique and irreplaceable capacity to unite people, going far beyond ethnic, religious or social differences. I am convinced that sport can be at the long-term service of peace'[11]. Interestingly and recently the International Olympic Committee, since becoming attached to the United Nations have made some enlightening comments regarding sport, peace and development through the office of Jacque Rogge the President of the IOC who has commented:

> 'We seek change through sport — and the promotion of peace and development has been at the centre of the Olympic Movement since its inception'.

And,

> 'Our founder, Pierre de Coubertin, believed deeply that the unifying power of sport could help lead us to a more peaceful world. Sport cannot solve all of the world's ills, but it can contribute to meaningful solutions. Sport provides a common language. It breaks down barriers and brings people together. It is a magnet for young people that can be used to teach positive values and valuable life lessons'.
>
> Rogge, J. 2011, Plenary, UN 2nd International Forum on Sport for Peace and Development, United Nations, Geneva[12].

Even politicians are getting involved in the philosophy of the 'sport, peace and development movement. For example former United Kingdom Prime Minister Tony Blair's among other positive statements comments that 'Sport today is far more important that just sport itself' (Blair, 2010). For once he is right and there is no doubt that the 'sport, peace and development' movement does pay a role in the thinking of some major United Nations organisations, the International Olympic Committee, and some members of royalty and world leaders.

With the previous thoughts in mind we have put together our own conceptualization of 'sport, peace and development' by utilising the three previous definitions as a base for our final conceptual statement. We understand that this may be controversial and not for everyone's needs but we are happy for you to change and alter the conceptual perspective to suit your own requirements as an organisation or individual researcher or developer of programmes.

---

10. Please see the following website for detailed analysis and descriptions of the organisation Peace & Sport. http://www.peace-sport.org/

11. HRH Prince Albert of Monaco has been for a long time been a supporter of sport, peace and development initiatives.

12. Please see the following for more details (http://www.olympic.org/ioc-unforum) re the forum.

The movement 'sport, peace and development' is conceptualised by the authors as:

The utilisation of sport from a human rights perspective, including play, games and leisure activities which best support the peace processes and contribute towards human development and capacity building after cessation of forms of hostility, conflict, war, famine, terrorism, poverty, natural disaster and combating HIV/AIDS. This can be used as an effective tool in human empowerment and in a culturally sustainable manner by supporting the mental and physical healing processes in rebuilding the human spirit.

We hope this conceptualization will spark more discussion and thought provoking research so that the sector can grow and develop within a clear philosophically defined and grounded framework.

The Sport, Peace and Development Movement

Others have conceptualised 'sport, peace and development' in similar ways. Indeed, the sport, development and peace 'sector' according to (Sekulić, Massey and Hodson, 2006) '...deploys sport as a socio-cultural tool to re-duce social tensions and promote reconciliation and reconstruction, not-ably in post-conflict contexts' and as argued by Giulianotti (2011 p.208) SDP (sport, development and peace) is 'largely driven by Global North agen-cies, much SDP work is conducted in the Global South' such as sub Saha-ran Africa and South America. Interestingly Giulianotti (2011, p.208) a lead-er in the field of sport, development and peace research, goes further by providing examples of the key institutions within the Sport, Development and Peace sector. These include 'nation states, non-governmental organisa-tions (NGO's), inter-governmental organisations, international federations, transnational corporations (especially through corporate social responsibil-ity programs) and grassroots community based organisations[13]'. Increasingly there are other not for profit organisations getting involved in the processes of sport, peace and development. Here we worry about the quality of the programs and the evaluation and monitoring of the programs and also the possible misuse of funding and we deal with this further in the final chapter. However, in order to support the conceptual framework for 'sport, peace and development' the UN has provided a goals oriented skeletal structure for 'sport, peace and development'.

---

13. Please see the excellent introduction to the paper by Giulianotti (2011) Sport, Peace-making and Conflict resolution: A contextual analysis and modelling of sport, devel-opment and peace sector. *Ethnic and Racial Studies*, Vol. 34 No. 2 pp 207-228.

The United Nations goals of sport, development and peace

The goals of sport, development and peace programs[14] have been demarcated by the United Nations in the following manner as they relate specifically to the MDG's (Millennium Development Goals):

Goal 1

Eradicate extreme poverty and hunger

Providing development opportunities will help fight poverty. The sports industry, as well as the organisation of large sports events, create opportunities for employment. Sport provides life skills essential for a productive life in society.

Goal 2

Achieve universal primary education

Sport and physical education are an essential element of quality education. They promote positive values and skills which have a quick but lasting impact on young people. Sports activities and physical education generally make school more attractive and improve attendance.

Goal 3

Promote gender equality and empower women

Increasing access for women and girls to physical education and sport helps them build confidence and a stronger social integration. Involving girls into sport activities alongside with boys can help overcome prejudice that often contribute to social vulnerability of women and girls in a given society.

Goals 4 & 5

Reduce child mortality and improve maternal health

Sport can be an effective means to provide women with a healthy lifestyle as well as to convey important messages as these goals are often related to empowerment of women and access to education.

14.*Source: Concept – Education, Health, Development, Peace (2005), United Nations Office for the International Year of Sport and Physical Education, Geneva 2005*

Goal 6

Combat HIV/AIDS, malaria and other diseases

Sport can help reach out to otherwise difficult to reach populations and provide positive role models delivering prevention messages. Sport, through its inclusiveness and mostly informal structure, can effectively assist in overcoming prejudice, stigma and discrimination by favouring improved social integration.

Goal 7

Ensure environmental sustainability

Sport is ideal to raise awareness about the need to preserve the environment. The interdependency between the regular practice of outdoor sports and the protection of the environment are obvious for all to realise.

Goal 8

Develop a global partnership for development

Sport offers endless opportunities for innovative partnerships for development and can be used as a tool to build and foster partnerships between developed and developing nations to work towards achieving the millennium development goals. Goal 8 acknowledges that in order for poor countries to achieve the first 7 goals, it is absolutely critical that rich countries deliver on their end of the bargain with more and more effective aid, sustainable debt relief and fairer trade rules for poor countries – well in advance of 2015.

As mentioned previously the above goals, of course, cannot be viewed in isolation and relate specifically to the United Nations Millennium Development Goals[15] (Hereafter MDG's), which we discuss in more detail in the final chapter.

Clearly, for sport to be able to support all the above goals and to function effectively within the context of peace and development programming there needs to be much more funding for research and practical work so that we can continue to be able to understand the issues and difficulties arising within this complex area. In this way we hope this book will go some way towards solving some of the problems and highlighting the issues in the sport, peace and development movement. Indeed, because of the complexity of the issues involving sport we have come to understand that sport is just one of the tools which can be used to deliver support for peace-making, peace-keeping, future development and eventual peace. In this respect we also acknowledge that there is an increasingly important role for the Un-

---

15. Please see: United Nations Development Goals available at www.un.org/millenium-goals/ (accessed 1st May 2012).

ited Nations to play in this regard and that the UNOSDP (United Nations Office of Sport Development and Peace) we believe should have more of a regulatory role in the future monitoring and evaluation practices. These and other issues we discuss with the assistance of the chapter authors in the final chapter of this book. What follows then is a chapter anthology which provides a part by part, chapter by chapter review and critical précis of each of the authors work.

Chapter Anthology

This book 'Sport, Peace and Development' provides an anthology of chapters which when viewed as a whole constitutes some of the most up-to-date writings on the relationship between Sport, Peace and Development. The chapters have been written by 42 practitioners and academics from across the world and as such the work is global in its reach and framework. We have attempted as much as possible to integrate original research with sociological underpinnings by providing practical examples of the torrid relationship between sport, peace and development. As such what follows represents varied views, opinions and ideas which have come together in this period of time to represent an anthology which we hope will become the starting point for further practical implications for research into the social, political and comparative aspects of the role which sport plays in the drive for peace and further development.

This book is the first of its kind by incorporating theory and practice in the area of sport, peace and development. In this task we have been supported admirably by our peers and colleagues who have never failed to respond to our many and varied requests for further information, slight changes in chapter outline and in some cases total rewrites. However, due to their professional commitment we have been able to organize chapters herein into six distinct parts in order to further simplify the task and to enable sense and structure to be made of the contents of the book. The parts are:

Part I - Historical Perspectives
Part II - Sport and Peacemaking
Part III - Sport and Reconciliation
Part IV - Sport and Development
Part V - Case Studies of Sport, Peace and Development
Part VI - Reflections on Sport, Peace and Development

These are the separate parts which make up the backbone of the book and throughout these parts are dealt with in a highly sensitive manner by the authors and the writing which follows is a credit to their work and their determination to assist and bring their experience to shaping the lives of others.

Part A, *'Historical Perspectives'* has been developed in order to place the constructs of sport, peace and development and their relationships into an historical cascading framework which is nation state and trans-nationally grounded in order to draw comparisons between issues of Sport, Peace and

Development from an historical perspective. This section 'jump starts' the book with Chapter 2 titled *'Sport for Development and Peace'* written by Michael Kleiner who in the early years was arguably a major force in the expansion of the United Nations Sport for Peace and Development sector. This chapter makes a major point in that the great danger has always been the over estimation of sport and its ability to reach further goals than those reached by traditional means of development and peace promotion. Indeed, sport per se is no panacea and only one small component of the United Nations peace and development goals and is an important point made by many authors in this book. Furthermore in this chapter Kleiner takes a close look at the UN traditions, the work of U.N.E.S.C.O the I.O.C. and in particular the 2005 UN objectives when promoting the 'Year of Sport and Physical Education'. In the conclusive section he argues that 'sport remains the only language spoken by people from all continents and walks of life' and 'this global network of people and groups using sport as a means to achieve development and peace remains immensely active, diverse and fertile' and should be maintained. In contrast in Chapter 3 Eric Dienes also takes an historical perspective but a more contemporary viewpoint. His chapter *'How Sport can Contribute to Peace-building: Perspectives of the United Nations on sport as a tool for promoting peace'* clearly sets out the current United Nations institutional framework and its development over the years. His work discusses the 'UN Millennium Development Goals' and the place of sport in the grand scheme of the United Nations. In particular he promotes the office of UNOSDP [United Nations Office of Sport, Development and Peace] and describes its role in 'peace-making'. He puts forward a series of four perspectives which makes some sense of the difficult issues related to the use of sport as a tool for macro and micro peace building. He also provides clear examples of successful programmes which were supported by the UN and walks us through the specific target objectives in the practical application of sport to peacemaking. This is a well written and well thought through chapter and in the final section Dienes pulls it all together by arguing that sport is a multifaceted tool which can be used effectively to enhance the peace building process. His final statements argue for a thematic working group to be formed which gathers data and uses research on the ground to fully harness the power of sport as a peacemaking tool.

Part B *'Sport and Peacemaking'* is a strong section in the book which captures the essence of 'Sport, Peace and Development' by highlighting the importance of sport for peace and reconciliation, capacity building, reintegration and networking in global contexts. This section begins with Chapter 4 *'Adapted Equipment and Practices: A tool for popularizing Sport for Peace'* by Ludovic Hubler in which he argues for new and inventive ways of promoting sport for peace. He takes a close look at the four issues of funding, equipment, training and facilities which he argues are the four most important aspects which require work and provide access to sports for all. Ludovic goes further by providing examples and a case study of the use of minor games and adapted equipment for the development in Columbia.

Throughout he highlights the work of the organisation 'Peace and Sport' thereby providing clear ideas of their work and their successes overtime in various parts of the world. In his conclusive statements Hubler discusses the use of adapted equipment and how major business, the IOC and ministries for sport should be supporting development by means of imagination and creativity in order to use sport in the service of peace. In the beginning of chapter 5: *'We Don't Play War Anymore: Sport and the Reintegration of Former Child Soldiers in Northern Uganda* Dean Ravizza provides an interesting narrative of an official football match for peace in Uganda involving two rival teams and also rivals after the civil conflict which turned into a fracas. His writings then follow the specifics of the exploitation of children of conflict and war and in particular the functions performed by the children in the conflicts in northern Uganda. Ravissa provides excellent research into their development through the use of sport and games and refers to the psychological benefits of sport after conflict and war for children. He highlights some interesting characteristics which occur when child soldiers return home and their often non acceptance by their communities. He follows this with a lively discussion regarding the building of inclusive communities through the medium of sport and capacity building to support reintegration issues of children who were subjected to the terrors of war. In chapter 6 Bob Munro deals with the following topic: *'Sport for Peace and Reconciliation: Young Peacemakers in the Kakuma Refugee Camp and Mathare Slums in Kenya'.* This is an excellent chapter describing two case studies of the MYSA youth in the Kakuma refugee camp in north western Kenya and in the Mathare area in Nairobi, one of Africa's largest and poorest slums. In the chapter he discusses the issues of peace, justice and sport and provides a theoretical and conceptual framework for his work based on the 17th century Dutch philosopher and pantheist Baruch Spinoza who bluntly asserted that 'peace is not an absence of war'. He provides a summary of the background to the problems in Kakuma and highlights the events in the Kakuma camp which still sees some sectarian violence. Within the context of the chapter Munro provides us with a means to break down the barriers and goes further by describing the collapse of gender barriers which allows girls and women to play sport in the camp. In another comment, re the dependency syndrome shown by some youngsters, he argues strongly for external evaluation and the linkage with sport and the community environment thereby tackling social and health problems for youth. This is a really interesting chapter drawing principally on the personal experiences of the author and providing us with ideas and examples of good practice for the future. The next well written academic piece, chapter 7 by Glenn Laverack is titled *'Building Community Capacity through Sport, Development and Peace programmes'* and follows on nicely from the previous chapter's issues of capacity building. In summary this chapter discusses the key characteristics of community capacity and a 'tool' that can be used to build and measure this concept as a key component of sport, development and peace (SDP) programmes. Throughout

Glen provides concrete examples of positive programmes such as the Saskatoon 'In Motion' initiative and its impact on the building of community capacity. He works through the academic 'domains' of 'community capacity' thereby providing baseline notions which can be utilised by anyone in the field. Lavarack further develops the themes of improved participation, local leadership, organisational structures, increased problem assessment, community questioning, resource mobilization and others and by providing examples drives home the importance of capacity building over time. In conclusion he argues that capacity building is the single most important element in the promotion of sport, development and peace programming. Marion Keim in chapter 8 really drives home the importance of *'Networking for Sport and Peace'.* With her great experience within the area she was able to refer extensively to 'community based organisations' (CBOs) and their importance in the development of youth engagement in sport and physical activity. Like Lavarack and Munro she argues for a strong theoretical structure to any development programmes. In her chapter she writes extensively regarding network theory and actual networking and the power of strong networks with multi-sectorial stakeholders. Interestingly she is able to develop these themes to provide some answers for the relationship between 'network theory and its application to sport'. Throughout Marion provides numerous examples of strong networking and highlights in particular the Western Cape Network for Community Peace and Development. She further argues through the challenges which face many organisations and strongly supports the notion of networks and their positive benefits to the local communities. This is a well-developed chapter grounded in both theory and practice which leads us nicely into the following section of the book.

Part C *'Sport and Reconciliation'* is a section which we developed over time and did not immediately jump off the paper as a theme for this book. However, on reading the series of five chapters which follow we were struck by the absence of reconciliation matter in the rest of the book. What follows then are chapters which we feel might lead towards a reconceptualization of a future research and theoretical area titled sport and reconciliation. Chapter 9 written by Bojana Blagojevic and titled *'Sport and Peacebuilding: Healing the Wounds of War'* is a well written personal tale which provides a conceptual framework for understanding the potential positive role of sport in building peace in ethnically divided, war-torn societies. Her research work is centred on her survival of the war in Bosnia-Herzegovina and as such she provides a graphic account of the influences of war on society and further argues through this utilizing a 'quality of value' framework. Later in the chapter Bojana discusses the movement of individuals from sport to peace through to human development and the rebuilding and reconciliation of communities with the use of sports. This chapter is followed by another interesting and challenging piece of writing from Andrei Markovits titled *'Can This Really Be? America as a Model of Progress: Why Physical Violence, Racist Invectives, Abusive Language and Behavior among Spectat-*

ors of North American Major Team Sports Are Much Rarer and Less Salient than in Europe' and is chapter 10, which bye the way is by far the longest title in the book and perhaps some sort of world record. Nevertheless we really enjoyed this chapter and the context of the work is excellent and captures the problematics of the 'American Situation' in sport which he argues is entirely different when contrasted with Europe. Andrei puts forward a feasible hypothesis for the absence of fan violence in the U.S.A. and promulgates eight reasons for the differences in thinking, for example, about racial integration and sport. In his conclusions Markovits argues that his theory 'reinforces his broader argument that hegemonic sports constitute an important force within popular culture' and that he supports strongly the notions of 'good will and peace'. The following chapter 11 which is titled *'Sport and Recreation as Educational and Diagnostic Means: Don Bosco's vision and the Salesians' mission in Eastern and Southern Africa'* by Clemens Ley and Maria Rato Barrio delves deeply into the theoretical structure and religious perspectives of Don Bosco's visions for Salesian Missions in Africa and more importantly the relationship between sport and the development of the missions. The chapter is written in traditional style with theoretical considerations and results sections and their findings are thought-provoking and worthy of note. They refer to 'diagnostic means and moments', and the 'combination of educational means' in order to analyse the holistic approach of Don Bosco and the Salesians in Eastern and Southern Africa. In conclusion they identify 11 key factors which came out of their research which can be easily transferred to other aspects of sport, peace and development scenarios. Gary Armstrong and Emily Vest provide us with a rare look at the inner workings of the post-conflict situation in Bosnia-Herzegovina. Titled: *'Defending and the Faith: Reflections on Football in Post-Conflict Bosnia-Herzegovina'* Chapter 12 critically analyses the role of football in the reconciliation process after the trauma of war in the Balkans. Personal examples and data drawn from qualitative interview and personal comments are utilised to highlight football hooliganism, protection of the faith and the building of a post conflict civil society. This is a really enjoyable read and highlights the benefits of 'getting out there' and doing the research on the ground. Finally they argue that 'Football should not disturb its enthusiasts or the by-stander with the possibility of death – it should exist to entertain and engage'. We argue that sadly no one listens to the argument put forward as exemplified in the postscript by Gary and Emily. The chapter by Armstrong and Vest begins to start us thinking about sport and reconciliation from differing perspectives and is a great prelude to chapter 13 titled *'Potentialities and Challenges of an Intervention Model to Promote Intercultural Processes in Post-conflict Contexts'* written by Maria Rato Barrio and Clemens Ley. In this chapter they discuss the important perspectives which they have developed through utilising an 'intervention model'. They spend some time explaining the model which that used in researching in the Guatemalan context and discussing the sequence of intercultural phases in the intervention process which they further enunciate in the research design for their study. As emphasised in their conclusive section the '...results of the research show a significant improvement in the affective, cognitive and behavioural elements of tolerance; and a positive change in categories such as a decrease in prejudices; increased knowledge and better understanding of *the other cultural group* involved in the programme; the building of an atmosphere of trust between them; the value of diversity as something positive and enriching; the cooperation and positive interaction between the participants from different cultural groups'. All in all this is a landmark study which sets the scene for further research in the area and leads us perfectly into Part D of Sport, Peace and Development.

Part D *'Sport and Development'* contains 11 chapters which jointly become a focal point for this book *Sport, Peace and Development*. The first chapter number 14 in this section by Oscar Mwanga titled *'Sport for Addressing HIV/AIDS: Examining rationales'* provides a fine example of the type of work which needs to be done in examining the rationales that underpin sport for addressing HIV/AIDS interventions in sub-Saharan Africa. It argues that there are two core assumptions which are just that 'unproven assumptions' which individuals apply to work in SSA without critical examination of their meaning and outcomes. Further into the chapter he discusses the sensitive issues of sport for moral development, sport as a positive diversion, sport as an attractive hook, sport as a means to empowerment and improvement of health. He completes the chapter by referring to sport as an essential tool for addressing HIV/AIDS and argues just stating that sport can combat HIV/AIDS is dangerous as it is a blanket statement which underestimates the complexity sport and also of the HIV/AIDS virus. Indeed, from Mwanga's perspective there can be no quality sport, development and peace programmes without the rigor of theoretical underpinnings and of strong partnerships between theory and practice. In Chapter 15 Australian Kylie Bates continues where Mwanga finished in the previous chapter by discussing the notion of partnerships for sport and development. Her chapter *'Creating Win-Win Partnerships for Sport and* Development' carefully unpicks the relationship between sport, peace and development and the corporate world. Bates discusses the manner in which various agencies leave partnerships and provides examples of the structure required for partnerships to occur. In completing this task the author manages to delve into several areas of partnership development such as: the structure of a partnership, the principals of partnerships, the notions of equity and respect, transparency as it leads to trust and the mutual benefit for all parties concerned. This chapter is full of interesting and relevant diagrams covering issues as important as the 'sport for development continuum' and 'shared objectives' which add to the chapter and highlight the importance of documenting and continually adjusting the partnership and its internal micro-politics. In conclusion she poignantly states that if dealt with carefully and professionally then overtime the impact of equity, transparency, and mutual benefit will be significant and importantly lead to *sustainable partnerships* in the area of sport, peace and development. Chapter 16 by Will Bennett asks some important and provocative questions which are reflected in the title: *'What Stigmas Exist within Communities in Kigali affected by a high prevalence of HIV and AIDS, and how does Right to Play's Sport for Development programmes address them? : A Case Study.'* In this piece he continues the theme of Mwanga and argues through the notion of stigma within communities of HIV/AIDS sufferers in Kigali which is a region in Rwanda. In this chapter Bennett takes the viewpoint of the 'Right to Play' organisation and its research into HIV/Aids in the region. He describes the research, outlines the methodology and rationale being the task and delves into the case study method of data gathering and analysis to document the outcomes of the research. It is a well thought through chapter with viable outcomes and acts as a model for anyone who is interested in researching in the sport peace and development area. In the results section he discusses social exclusion, social stigma, loss of rights and confidence, coping strategies, and the inaccessibility of services or employment for those with the sickness. Bennett blames lack of education, poverty, actual location and fear as major factors in the stigmatization of the people who play sport in the area. He comments on the societies increasing awareness and acceptance of HIV/AIDS positive individuals in Kigali and that sport is beginning to instil hope through confidence building, self-belief and community understanding through education. This is followed admirably by the chapter 17 of Pelle Kvalsund which is titled *'Sport as Response to Emergencies and Disasters'.* This is a moving well written chapter where he brings his own vast experience of working in the sport, development and peace area to the context of some of the problems associated with emergency and disaster. He is careful to set the scene and uses an interesting vignette from his own experience before strengthening his arguments with clarification of terminology and text. The primary theory of his chapter is that: *'the development of resilience in children and youth is essential in order for them to better cope with some of the hardship they are facing during and post disaster'.* He argues that the development of resilience can in itself develop and assist in maintenance of inherent factors such as competence, empathy, problem-solving skills, critical and creative thinking, and finally a sense of purpose and connectedness to each other and society. He explains the benefits of sport and play to survivors all-the-while promoting the common-sense perspectives of 'time and transition' from one phase of their life to another. These building blocks he argues are important for restructuring of lives and cultures after disaster strikes. Chapter 18 titled *'Ensuring Human Rights in Sport: Constructing a Human Rights Sport Monitoring Checklist'* by Mary Hums, Eli Wolfe and Amber Morris defines the concept of 'human rights', 'sport' and the two dimensions of 'sport and human rights'. It then delves into the codification of sport and human rights and identifies from the ensuing discussion a 'sport and human rights checklist' which refers specifically to the areas of social rights, health and safety rights, sport as employment rights, justice in sport rights, environmental rights and financial rights. They then break down each of these heading by providing examples and ideas as to how they should be utilised in differing sport, peace and development contexts. Indeed, the authors take a very interesting and theoretical stance to the notion of sporting rights and in conclusion argue that guides and checklist are only useful if sports administrators can successfully implement them as building blocks and living documents and geared towards local, national and international bodies. Chapter 19 *'Inclusive Sport for Development'* by Amy Farkas , Valerie Karr, Anna Lachowska and Eli Wolffe is a well-designed chapter which discusses people with a disability and sport for development. They argue throughout for inclusivity and inclusive sport development and develop this theme by targeting models of disability including the medical and social models and their benefits or lack there-of support within the development community. As did the previous chapter by Hums et. al. they also argue for an understanding of human rights in sport, but widen their remit to include recreation and play and an understanding of human rights within the context of the MDG's. Later in the chapter they write significantly regarding the relationship between the MDG's and inclusive development for individuals with a disability which they clarify by offering suggestions for how sport-based activities can contribute to the MDG's. In conclusion they strongly develop the notion of the 'right to sport for all' and this includes inclusivity for individuals with a disability. The following chapter 20 by Emma Colluci titled *'Entertainment-Education and sport for development: New frontiers'* is an intellectual piece which challenges the nature of what we are really trying to do with sport and development and the role of media in 'the process of designing and implementation' of the programmes. In this chapter she discusses the theoretical basis of entertainment, the idea of choice, new avenues of communication and of course the relevance of sport. In this chapter Colluci uses 'soccer' as a universal language and as a tool for communication and support her ideas by utilising the theoretical constructs of Paulo Freire (2007) in order to press home her interesting and controversial perspectives regarding 'soccer' in particular 'Grass Roots Soccer' and its role in development. In conclusion she discusses the issues of social modelling and the consequences of bad life choices and the positive aspects of the sporting experience which she argues has great potential and is vast but often underestimated. In the next chapter titled *'Sport for the Disabled as Social (Re) education and a (Re) builder of Lives'* Ian Brittain delivers a stinging argument for the inclusion of people with a disability in the sport and development process in conflict zones. The chapter highlights the 'role of sport for disabled in non-violent conflict transformation/peace-making through its ability to change perceptions and structural barriers. The chapter is grounded in Galtung's (1990) Triangle of Violence theory which follows the concepts of 'direct violence', 'visible violence', invisible violence' and 'extermination, abortion, euthanasia and ridicule'. This is an interesting perspective to take and when combined with the concepts of 'cultural violence' and 'structural violence' becomes a powerful tool for the analysing of sport and development in the disability context. It briefly describes the medical and social models of disability before launching into the above concepts and relationship between sport, peace, development and disability. In his conclusive statements Brittain discusses the medical model and its influence within the violent aspects of the Galtung's theory and that hopefully disability sport and development will become more prevalent in the constructs within the sport, peace and development circles worldwide. Following this excellent chapter from Brittain is the work of Ian Pickup. Chapter 22 *'Sport as an Educational Trojan Horse'* explores the manner in which the potential of sport can best be utilised as a 'tool' in the educational context. This chapter challenges the commonly held belief that sport is a panacea and brings us 'down to earth' in our thinking about the true benefits of sport as a tool in the area of peace and development. Pickup rightly argues that 'if sport is to play a prolific role as an educational tool across the world, then an immediate focus on a human process is required. Indeed much of his chapter focusses on the practical processes and considerations regarding how this humanistic dimension can be developed, highlighting mechanisms and concepts through which integration across various sectors can be achieved. Throughout Ian stresses the point that there is a fundamental misconception in society regarding sport and education and that simply by participating in sport (and by merely providing sporting opportunities) then broad educational benefits will follow. We now know that this is untrue. Pickup discusses the notion of the need to 'move' in order to learn and of the physical context of sport and highlights this point further by discussing the principles relating to the programme STTEP (Space, Time, Task, Equipment and People). He completes the chapter by arguing for a form of *'organic coaching'* which takes into consideration the environmental factors associated with sport, peace and development. We were very impressed by the chapter of Daniela Preti (Chapter 23) titled *'Monitoring and Evaluation: Between the Claims and Reality'* where she basically deconstructs the debate on quality and effectiveness of sport, development and peace programmes across the world. In her own words 'this chapter discusses the claims of finding common and universally applicable indicators and monitoring tools in the field of S&D against the backdrop of its actual transferability into practice. The subsequent deliberations synthesise theoretical considerations with practical experiences made by the Swiss Academy for Development (SAD) through various pilot projects, research and capacity building of grassroots organisations in Asia, South America, the Middle East and Africa in the last years'. Daniela achieves this by describing the theoretical approaches to project planning, monitoring and evaluation. We found this interesting as many programmes require constant evaluation and argue that they are monitoring effectively but in actuality this is not the case in practice. What she argues in this chapter is the need for theory to inform practice and for 'outcome mapping', 'creativity' and increased awareness that monitoring and evaluation of sports programmes is highly relevant in the building of social capital in areas which are culturally sensitive. The following chapter 24 by Ryan Wright, Lori Hanson and Karen Chad is the final chapter in the Part D *'Sport and*

Development' and they provide an interesting and thoughtful piece titled *'Building Community Capacity through 'Sport Development' Usability of the Domains Approach'.* In their analysis they discuss the work of RTP (Right To Play) the respected sport for development agency which works on many projects in under-developed regions and the notion of 'community capacity building' in the sport for development context. This work principally centres on the Kibondo district of Tanzania and the refugee camps therein. There is an excellent theoretical section of the chapter which principally reviews the building of community capacity and its development over the years. They argue that community members must be listened too as they often have extensive knowledge of the problems within their community and effective action requires the involvement of communities directly in sport and development schemes. Much of their work is centred around the implementation of the 'Domains Approach' (Lavarack, 1999) and its nine criteria for success. They go through this theory carefully and highlight the relevant parts as it relates to the work of Right to Play and the work in Tanzania. Conclusions are drawn which recommend use of the 'domains approach' in community capacity building and building of a 'sense of community' through sport and development activities. This excellent chapter leads us into Part E of the book titled *'Case Studies of Sport, Peace and Development'.*

Chapter 25 *'Sport as a Tool for Participatory Education: Exploring the Grassroots Soccer Methodology'* enables Emma Colluci to literally kick off Part E of this book titled *'Case Studies of Sport, Peace and Development'* which we found to be highly significant in that it concentrates on the pressures of running quality programs and their difficulties and successes over time. In this chapter Emma takes a close look at the issues confronting UNAIDS in sub-Saharan Africa. She confronts the problems and provides statistics which highlights the importance of provision of information and education to communities in the sub- Saharan region. After this initial section Colluci cleverly weaves the social theories of Paulo Freires (1985) 'banking model of education' into the text to provide a solid foundation and grounding for the remainder of the chapter. In this she argues that 'education is suffering from narration sickness' and that one of the keys to success in sport, peace and development programming for people with HIV/AIDs is 'participatory learning'. A term which has been around physical education circles for many years. This learning by consensus is highly suited to the work of 'grass roots soccer' that provides 'African youth with the knowledge, skills and support to live HIV free'. She emphasizes the importance of 'dialogue and action' used in a combined manner in order to stop such risky behaviors as unprotected sex and drug abuse. Finally Colluci provides case examples from personal qualitative interviews and highlights the importance of using participatory education for lifelong learning in the area of health and particulary HIV/AIDS prevention. Chapter 26 by Clemens Ley and Maria Rato Barrio titled *'Active Learning and Self-supporting Processes through Sport, Games and Participatory Activities with Women who Suffered Violence'* is a strong chapter highlighting the plight of women in society and the use of sport as a tool for recovery. In this chapter these two young researchers develop the notion that sport is not all positive and is not the panacea which we all want it to be. The research is geared to work which they did in post conflict Guatemala and the discrimination and racism suffered by the Mayan population. They discuss the development of the intervention program 'psychosocial activity through movement, games and sport for women' (APM) which was also grounded (like the previous chapter) on participatory learning theory. In the chapter they specifically focus on the intervention processes which they highlight in the research design of their study. These results are extensive and well written and they provide case study literature to support their claims. The issue of local facilitation of programs seems to run throughout their work and in the conclusion section Ley and Rato Barrio discuss the benefits of utilizing a combined approach of sport, games, participatory activities and group discussion as the main tools for success of the program. Finally, they provide concrete examples of their work and the benefits of facilitation and the support of the women in the research process. Chapter 27 by Geoff Thompson titled *The Social and Human development of Antisocial and Disaffected Young People through the Bidding and Hosting of Major Games in the UK'* provides interesting reading. In it Thompson argues that the great changes seen in sport in the United Kingdom and its associated legacies can perhaps have a positive rather than negative impact on disadvantaged youth. He provides a brief history of bidding and its impact on society an in particular the British youth and then launches into the main argument of his chapter which develops the theme of 'A Spirit of the Streets – Legacy of Hope'. In this section Geoff equates the bidding and winning of the Olympic Games with on-going social behavior in various post bid cities across the world. There are also vignettes or case studies of different and poignant examples of programs which were successful. He then discusses the importance of the programming and policy initiatives of the projects and recognizes the role that sport plays in the engagement, motivation and inspiration of young people. Thompson then discusses the important issues of 'personal and social development', 'multi-agency policy development', 'advocacy', 'connection of communities' and 'social and human development'. Throughout these theoretical concepts are supported by case studies and challenges and opportunities for the future. These are interesting perspectives and can be applied to most situations across the world. Overall this chapter is steeped in experience and linked specifically to the notion of legacy and by that very fact to the concept of sustainability of programming. This leads us nicely into chapter 28 written by Chiaki Okado and titled *The Redevelopment of Sport in Cambodia: Reflections on a Football Player who Survived the Khmer Rouge Regime'.* This chapter is essentially a life history project which reports on the life of Ouk Sareth, a talented Cambodian footballer, who has survived the war and has survived the corruption and re-development of sport in his country. The chapter takes a two pronged attack on the subject. It firstly describes the career history of Ouk Sareth and the second section covers considers the prospects for sports development in Cambodia. We feel that more work needs to be attempted in genre as living sport through other people's lives is an important concept which we still do not fully understand and the notion of researching sport, peace and development through the eyes of the recipients over time is important for us to fully gain the benefits of our programs and outcomes. Chiaki takes us on a journey where she discusses the life of Ouk Sareth in terms of 'living with sports', 'sports and the war', 'reconstruction through sport' and 'the road to development of Cambodia'. Throughout this chapter is highlighted by examples of the football players life and Okado brings to life his experiences and difficulties throughout wartime and now in the relative calm of peace. Chapter 29 titled *Japan's Assistance to Developing Countries in the Field of Physical Education and Sport* by Kazuhiko Saito discusses the promotion of physical education and sports in the role of character building. In doing this is highlights the role which Japan has played in this process over the years and clarifies the trends in the dispatch of Japan Overseas Volunteers who have played a central role in the development of physical education and sport across the world since the inception of the program. The chapter categorizes these achievements and graphs them along with other results of the research and proposes the doubling of the number of Japanese volunteers in the system over the next few years. It is a very interesting chapter with ideas which are novel and innovative and has blossomed in relation to the greater importance placed on education by the Japanese policy makers. It remarks rather poignantly about the need for the volunteers to be based at home since the Japanese earthquake and subsequent nuclear power plant meltdown. We were very impressed with the idea of integration of theory and practice which flowed from chapter 30 from Ben Weinberg and Sebastian Rockenfeller titled *From Theory to Practice: Scientific Support and the Design of a 'Sport-in-Development' Program in Bukoba, Tanzania.* This chapter refers specifically to the theoretical perspectives on 'Sport-in-Development' and illustrates how theory translates into practice. The study is based around the Bukoba district in Tanzania where they argue the Jambo Bukoba project is a prime example of taking theoretical assumptions into consideration when designing programs. This chapter provides an excellent example of the theoretical background underpinning sport, peace and development and provides some interesting 'interim conclusions' before delving into the actual Jambo Bukoba project itself. The main one being the concept of the development of 'Life Skills Coaching' and its importance in the psychological processes involved in development projects. They touch on aspects of 'implementation' and the importance of 'baseline studies' along with the 'design of the physical education teacher workshops' and the 'fundamentals of workshop implementation'. They provide solid ideas of the outlook for the future and suggest that the workshop which they introduced 'Life Skills Through Games' has been very successful but they worry about its sustainability. Finally, they provide five clear recommendations for the future development of such programs in the context of individual countries and cultures. The following chapter 31 provides a really down-to-earth discussion and explanation of the work of *'Streetfootballworld'*. Indeed it is titled *'Streetfootballworld: Development through Football'* and is written by two individuals with much experience and interest in the sports for development field. Vladimir Borkovic and Mia Wyszynski argue from the outset that football is unique in its capacity to change lives for the better. They further highlight the amazing power of their organization and how it reaches out to hundreds of thousands of young people on a yearly basis. It begins with a description of the relationship between football and development where they discuss aspects of 'psychology', 'shared belief' and 'positive social change' through the medium of football. Later they branch into eight specific thematic fields which are constructs of the football and development process. These are: health, social integration, peace building, gender equality, employability, youth leadership, education and environment. These broad fields are discussed and are very important however, we feel they may add the notions of race and disability to the themes to make a stronger case for the inclusivity of football. We will discuss this and other issues later in the book. Vladimir and Mia go on to discuss in depth the potential of football and by highlighting examples from the above list provide us with an excellent appraisal of the 'power of football'. They are cognizant of the limitations of football and do not shy away from this aspect of their work which is commendable. Later in the chapter they relate specifically to capacity building and the important role of evaluation and monitoring of their achievements through football. Indeed, to this end they provide good examples and a case study (Moving the Goalpost) to back up their writing. Finally they provide strong examples of future directions and support for girls and women through the 'Streetfootballworld' agenda. This is an interesting practically written piece which is symptomatic of the type of quality work being produced out in the field. Chapter 32 by Kristina Bohnstedt and Marc-Andre Buchwalder continues with the football frame of reference and their chapter titled *'How Professional Football Clubs can Contribute to Sustainable Development: Scort and 'The Football Club Social Alliance'* really contributes to this book in an original way. Firstly, they delve into the relationship between prosperous football clubs and poor, disadvantaged, underprivileged people who are in need of assistance and support from a corporate social responsibility provider. In this case football clubs. They argue for the football clubs to be more proactive in this way and to be more sustainably proactive in their thinking and to this end they highlight the 'The Football Club Social Alliance' which is a Swiss based organization known as the Scort Foundation. This is a concept that focuses on multi-stakeholders and share funding principle where all parties (clubs) involved can contribute to their interest according to their expertise and budget. In their chapter they highlight the expertise required to link these groups and also the theoretical basis of the 'multi-stakeholder approach' to development through sport. They found it important to emphasis that the programs needed to be sustainable initiatives through intensive co-operation and participation by the clubs, coaches, trainers, and instructors. The notion of 'initiative' is very strong in their philosophy as are the issues which keep arising from monitoring and evaluation by the partners involved in the overseas initiative. Kristine and Marc-Andrew work carefully through the implementation and development of their projects with Scort and put forward many ideas to support their cause which are helpful for other like-minded individuals. In conclusion they argue strongly for social engagement by clubs and coach education programs in order to supplement the lives of young people in socially disadvantaged areas around the world. Chapter 33 on the other hand by Jamie Bull and James Beale is all about reducing the impact factors of anti-social behavior through the 'Fight for Peace' project in the East of London. As such their chapter is titled *'A Qualitative Insight into the Impact of a Community Based Project on Antisocial Behavior within a Deprived Urban Area: The case of 'Fight for Peace'* and as the title suggests is based around the sport of boxing. In this chapter Jamie and James discuss their ideas re sport peace and development from a qualitative viewpoint. They begin with a careful analysis of the use of sport as a preventative method in antisocial behavior after which they delve into describing the 'Fight for Peace' project. They argue through the five pillars of 'Boxing and martial arts training and competition', 'Personal development', 'Mentoring and Youth support programs', 'Job training', and 'Youth Leadership'. They then provide an excellent methodological perspective in relation to the qualitative research which they put into place within the study and within this category they argue strongly for the use of phenomenological frameworks. Their study is well documented as are the comments from individuals and this leads to Bull and Beale's concepts which are detailed within the 'future research' section. This is an excellent chapter, well written and brings some important aspects to research in the sport, peace and development area. For example their final words are highly relevant – 'Involvement in the 'fight for peace' program gave the individuals a positive way out to reduce aggression and perhaps most importantly positive role models that provided social support in other areas of the boxer's life'. *'Able in Sport: Able in Life'* is the title of chapter 34 by Steffi de Jong and Pierre Bataille. In this chapter they discuss the development of the sport, peace and development agency specifically for persons with a disability, which they started, called 'PlayAble'. Initially this chapter refers specifically to the historical underpinnings related to the events leading up to the birth of 'PlayAble'. In this section they argue that sport can be a cost effective way of rehabilitation, and provide psychological and social benefits for people with a disabilities caused from disaster or fighting and its aftereffects. This chapter provides an excellent example of how to go about setting up and organizing an NGO and de Jong and Bataille provide examples of lessons learned and the reasons behind their decisions in organizing the charity. They finish by providing countless examples of the reasons why they are where they are today and these include: outputs and impact, their many awards, and the fact that there is still plenty of work ahead of them in this area. Chapter 35 by Serena Borsani is a classic example of a success story born out of determination, hard work and persistence in the field. It is titled *The Impact of Sport Interventions in Rift Valley Kenya after Post Election Violence: A Case Study'* and provides a fitting end to the section on 'case studies' in this book. Borsani writes of mass displacement, ethnic violence, gender based brutality, extensive looting and destruction of property and of mass deaths and injuries which occurred over a short period of time in Kenya. In her chapter Serena really gets us to understand the nature of sport and its use for trauma healing, reconciliation and long term social change. All of these observations re sport and development are grounded in her experiences in the field and add weight to her resounding success in this area of the world. Throughout she provides examples of the work and the work of others and the importance of evaluation of the projects undertaken. Serena dives further into the evaluation processes and highlights the use of focus groups, analysis of questionnaires and the interpretation of their results which she provides in graphical format throughout. Finally Borsani discusses the theory of Galtung[16] (1998) and how it relates to the '3Rs' of reconstruction of people and places, reconciliation of relationships and resolution of issues and animosities. With this theoretical perspective in mind the chapter suggests and recommends some important principles which can be followed in developing sport and reconciliation programs and that more importantly 'healing is the first step to re building relationships that contribute to wider social change, and sport is proven to be a very adept tool to achieve this difficult goal'.

Part F of this book titled *'Reflections of Sport, Peace and Development'* consists of Chapter 36 which is titled *'Contemplating a Moral World'* and *'Diversion, Tranquility and Advancement: The Outlook'* by Keith Gilbert and Will Bennett provides a meta-synthesis of the previous work and attempts to sort through and document the problems, difficulties and solutions for future practical work and research in the area of sport, peace and development.

It is essential that all people working in the area of 'sport, peace and development' read this book as we hope that – in their most complex form – innovative 'sport peace and development' initiatives can be gleaned from its pages. Also, in actuality, rather than the marginalized being left to their own devices, that as a collective group of people working and researching in the area of sport peace and development, we become empowered to inspire individuals and provide the best possible support for the marginalized in the most optimal manner.

---

16. For further work on the three phases of a conflict, see Johan Galtung, Conflict Transformation by Peaceful Means, Geneva: United Nations, 1998, pp. 6-13.

References

Beutler, I. (2006) (Eds.), *Report on the International Year of Sport and Physical Education 2005,* United Nations, Geneva.

Blaire, T. (2010). Sao Paulo seminar for businessmen and athletes. Available at: (http://celiasan.edublogs.org/2010/10/28/blair-to-rio-olympic-organizers-focus-on-legacy/), (Accessed on 1st May 2012).

Brittanica Micropeadia (2012). Available at: (http://books.google.co.uk/books/about/The_New_Encyclopaedia_Britannica.html?id=BAqtQQAACAAJ&redir_esc=y). (Accessed 1st May 2012).

Burds-Sharps, S. & A. Perez (2005). UNDP Support Package for (HDR's) and other Development Reporting. Available at: (http://hdr.undp.org/en/media/SupportPackage_eng.pdf). (Accessed 1st May 2012).

Business Dictionary (2012). Available at: (http://www.businessdictionary.com/). (Accessed at 1st May 2012).

Coakley, J. (2012). Sports in Society: Issues and controversies, 11th edition, McGraw-Hill, U.S.A.

Coalter, F. (2007). A Wider Role for Sport: Who's keeping the score? Routledge, London.

Czempiel (1984). Democracy in the Age of Globalization, Springer, Dordrecht, Netherlands.

Darnell, S. (2012). Sport for Development and Peace: A critical sociology, Bloomsbury books, London.

Dictionary.com (2012). Available at: (http://dictionary.reference.com/). (Accessed on 1st may 2012).

Donnelly, P. (2010). Sport for Development and Peace: A public sociology perspective; paper presented at the 'sport and International Development: Mainstreaming Sport into development Studies' conference, Department of International Development Studies, Dalhousie University, 20-21 may 2010.

Formerand, J. (2007). Historical Dictionary of the United Nations, Scarecrow Press, Plymouth, U.K.

Free Online Dictionary (2012). Available at: (http://www.thefreedictionary.com/). (Accessed 1st May 2012).

Freire, P. (1985). The Politics of Education: Culture, Power, and Liberation, Greenwood Publishing Group, Santa Barbara, U.S.A.

Galtung, J. (1990). Cultural Violence. *The Journal of Peace Research*, Vol. 27(3) pp. 291-302.

Galtung, J. (1998). After Violence - 3R, Reconstruction, Reconciliation, Resolution: Coping with Visible and Invisible Effects of War and Violence, United Nations, Geneva.

Gilbert, K. (2006). The Wrong Way Around, In Wolff. E.A. & M.A.Hums (2006). Sport & Human Rights, the Bulletin, Special Edition, *Journal of Sport Science and Physical Education*, pp 55-57.

Gilbert.K. (2006). Sport, Peace and Development, unpublished keynote address, Johor Baru Sports Council, [July] Johor Baru, Malaysia.

Giulianotti, R. (2011). Sport, peace-making and conflict resolution: a contextual analysis and modelling of the sport, development and peace sector. *Ethnic and Racial Studies*, Routledge, 34:2, pp. 207-228.

Giulianotti, R. & G. Armstrong (2011). Sport, the Military and Peace making: History and possibilities, Third World Quarterly, 32: 3 pp.379-394.

Hoglund, K. & R. Sundberg (2008). Reconciliation through sports? The case of South Africa. *Third World Quarterly*, vol. 29, no. 4.

Laverack, G. (1999). Addressing the contradictions between discourse and practice in health promotion. Unpublished doctoral dissertation, Deakin University, Melbourne, Australia.

Meier, K. V. (1981). On the Inadequacies of Sociological Definitions of Sport. *International Review of Sports Sociology*. Vol16, No 12. pp. 79-102.

Oxford Dictionary (2012). Available at: (http://oxforddictionaries.com/ words/the-oxford-english-dictionary). (Accessed on 1st May 2012).

Rosenaus, N. & E.O. Czempiel (1986). Governance without Government: Order and change in world politics, Cambridge University Press, Cambridge, U.K.

Sandy, L.R. & R. Perkins Jnr. (1994). The Nature of Peace and its Implications for Peace Education. Available at: (http://oz.plymouth.edu/ -lsandy/peacedef.html), (*Accessed on 1st may 2012).

Sekulić, Massey and Hodson, (2011). Factors of socio-economic Uncertainty in the Bosnian War, Micro-Con research working papers 44, March 2011.

Sekulic, D., G. Massey and R. Hodson (2006) 'Ethnic Intolerance and Ethnic Conflict in the Dissolution of Yugoslavia', Ethnic and Racial Studies, 29 (5): pp. 797-827.

Sport for Peace and Development Working Group (2007). Report of the SPD/WG. Thomson Building, Suite 1900, Toronto, Canada.

Sugdan, J. (2008). 'Anyone for Football for Peace? The challenges of using sport in the service of co-existence in Israel'. *Soccer and Society*, vol. 9, no. 3.

The Brundtland Report (1987). Our Common Future, Oxford University press, Oxford.

Volger, H. (2010). A Concise Encyclopedia of the United Nations 2ns revised edition, Martinus Nijhoff Publishers, Boston, U.S.A. pp 102 – 106

von Weizsacker, C. (1963). Definition of Peace in H. Volger, (2010).A Concise Encyclopedia of the United nations 2nd revised edition – Martinrs Nijhoff Publishers, Boston U.S.A. p. 514.

Part I
Historical Perspectives

Chapter 2

Sport for Development and Peace

Michael Kleiner

In the Beginning

From 'Ping-Pong diplomacy', melting the frozen international relationships between China and the USA in the mid-seventies to 'Cricket diplomacy' still at work to this day between India and Pakistan, the noble use of sport to achieve goals of development and peace promotion have often varied in forms and shapes but have always come down to one same end: sport, with all its power of attraction, globalized informality, ability to mobilize endless energies, uncertainty of the result and accessibility to all, remains a universal and irreplaceable worldly language, able to help resolve most complex and sometimes even hopelessly blocked situations.

When things become 'too' complicated and issues pile up, obscuring any available solution, the resort to sport as an apparently simple and relaxed way of communicating has already often proven its capacity to help opponents see new opportunities, associate with winning sides and come to terms with losses and defeats that become acceptable in sport but are less acceptable in real life situations.

It is not only a matter of communication as some would over-simplify. There is more to the use of sport than sending messages to the world, using prestigious sportswomen and men to attract attention to forgotten issues or organizing spectacular encounters in unusual settings. These are often one shot initiatives that have a tendency of overshadowing the day to day benefits of long term uses of sport in a variety of projects or programs. Sport can also represent a proper change of perspective, a totally different and equally respectable way of interacting as would be diplomatic discussions. Of course, sports encounters are easier to show on television and easier to understand by the public than the working sessions between politicians often held behind closed doors. But if used wisely and with the proper coaching, sport can lead to a creative culture of dialogue through play and fun instead of sterile meetings and expensive receptions.

It is also interesting to notice that it is not only politics, i.e. politicians, diplomats and other public servants who are willing to make use of sport to achieve their goals. Sport itself has come forward to offer its services to propose solutions and offer its support. In cases of natural catastrophes, humanitarian emergencies or regular conflicts, sports associations, clubs or individual sportswomen and men have regularly taken initiatives as sportspeople, aware of their influence, of their power and social responsibility. It is also encouraging to realize that such initiatives bring more satisfaction to the ones being helped as well as those providing assistance if they take place in the longer term and allow for follow up, evaluation and correction if necessary.

Within the United Nations system of organizations, agencies and programs, there are many examples of such cooperation between teams or individual sportswomen and men willing to help achieve global goals of development and peace promotion, each starting with one small step on a sports field.

However, the great danger has always been the over estimation of sport and its ability to reach further goals than those reached by traditional means of development and peace promotion. It was my mission and remains that of the office of the Special adviser to the Secretary General of the United Nations (UN) on Sport for Development and Peace, from the first day until today, to always insist that sport would not save the world as a tool of last resort. Sport cannot be the global panacea and be used in any situation and without clear rules and a well-established frame of reference. Maybe the greatest lesson learned of all is that sport cannot and must not be corrupted. If one wishes to see positive impacts on further issues, one has to respect what makes the interest in sport. The fundamental rule is that sport must remain sport. Sport, in all its complexity must be respected. This may seem contradictory as sport is certainly among the most accessible means of interacting between humans – give two young children a ball and they will invent a game, establish their own rules, perhaps fight and definitely compete and eventually accept defeat and manage the ephemeral side of victory. However, there is no guarantee that they will not also fight without finding the positive aspects of their game and leave without the will to continue to play. That is where the frame has to be established, a frame of which international sports organizations are the custodians and promoters. In this frame, rules have to be accepted and enforced. Sometimes, referees are necessary when the stakes become too high for both sides to administer themselves. The uncertainty of the issue of any sports competition is maybe the most difficult aspect to come to terms with. However well-organized sport may be, uncertainty and spontaneity remain aspects that do not fit well into the predictable and smooth world of international relations. This uncertainty is the very essence of what keeps sport interesting. People will watch football game after football game; the same 90 minutes spent watching two teams of 11 players running after the same ball on the same field. Why? Because the end result is always different. Because the scenario is always renewed, the game finds new twists and allows new combinations. However, this uncertainty is also a difficult element to manage for diplomatic reasons. Sometimes, it would be important to see the weaker one win over the favorite or stronger one. And sometimes the weaker one does indeed win! But it cannot be planned or organized in advance without clearly affecting the nature of sport and the very values that make sport such a powerful tool.

UN traditions

In early 2001, the United Nations Secretary General, Mr. Kofi Annan realized that sport was often used by a variety of United Nations (hereafter UN) entities (agencies, programs or funds). Sometimes, initiatives were aimed solely at communication and fund raising. Quite often initiatives took place in the field, in developing countries or countries at war, together with influential athletes, clubs and teams, willing to bring their contribution. Occasionally, initiatives were organized for pure fun and relaxation, to find a different mode of interaction and make new friends of old enemies. Kofi Annan was seeking a way to bind the strings together and provide some coherence to this variety of means and uses. He created a new function within the UN, directly attached to his executive secretariat. He appointed the former president of the Swiss Confederation, Mr. Adolf Ogi, as his Special Adviser on Sport for Development and Peace. Suddenly an old concept, an ever older idea, became a real function and was impersonated by a high level and respectable person within the world body. This development deeply changed the way the United Nations system approached sport, a new common language was elaborated, partnerships were built and lasting relationships were given a new luster and recognition.

The first steps of sport within the UN were made before the UN was even created. One of the first international organizations, the International Labor Organization (hereafter ILO) was looking at means to limit the exploitation of workers and allow them to enjoy other activities. With the revival of the modern Olympic Games in 1896 by then International Olympic Committee President Pierre de Coubertin, the ILO adopted a resolution at a conference that year to reduce the number of working hours to a maximum of eight per day and to re-orient the time of the workers to social activities which would include recreation and physical education[1].

As mentioned in UN General Assembly resolution 58/5 adopted in November 2003[2], sport was first formally included in activities of the United Nations system at the first international conference of ministers in charge of sport and physical education, organized by UNESCO in Paris in 1976. This led to the establishment of an Intergovernmental Committee for Physical Education and Sport, as well as to the adoption of the International Charter of Physical Education and Sport in 1978. The Charter recognized 'physical education and sport as a human right for all'[3]. Since that time many entities of the United Nations system have engaged in one or several relationships with sports organizations, including the International Olympic Committee and other members of the Olympic Movement, international sports federations, sports clubs and other sport-related non-governmental organizations.

One of the first activities undertaken by Mr. Ogi was to bring together the personnel of the various UN agencies, programs and funds in contact with sports organizations, clubs, teams and athletes. It was necessary to make an inventory of the immense variety of interactions between the sports world and the UN world. In October 2003, the Secretary-General published the report of the United Nations Inter-Agency Task Force on Sport for Development and Peace, entitled *Sport for Development and Peace: Towards Achieving the Millennium Development Goals*[4]. In many aspects the report constituted the basis for General Assembly resolution 58/5 and represents a synthesis of the long-standing relationship between the world of sport and the United Nations system.

The 2003 report recognized that sport presents a natural partnership for the UN. By its very nature sport is about participation, inclusion and citizenship. It brings individuals and communities together, highlighting commonalities and bridging cultural and ethnic divides. Sport provides a forum to learn skills such as discipline, confidence and leadership and it teaches core principles such as tolerance, cooperation and respect. Above all, sport teaches the value of effort and the necessity to work to achieve results.

The UN General Assembly resolution 58/5 continues: When the positive aspects of sport are emphasized, sport becomes a powerful vehicle through which the UN can work towards achieving its goals. The practice of sport is vital to the holistic development of young people, fostering their physical and emotional health and building valuable social connections. It offers

---

1. Fact sheet on ILO and sport at website of UN Office on Sport for Development and Peace www.unosdp.org

2. Link to UN General Assembly resolution 58/5

3. UNESCO International Charter for Physical Education and Sport

4. Link to UN Task Force report

opportunities for play and self-expression, beneficial especially for those young people with few other opportunities in their lives. Sport also provides healthy alternatives to harmful actions, such as drug abuse and crime. Within schools, physical education is an essential component of quality education. Physical education programs promote physical activity and studies have shown that such programs can improve academic performance.

In its 2003 report, the United Nations Inter-Agency Task Force on Sport for Development and Peace found that well-designed, sport-based initiatives were practical and cost-effective tools to achieve objectives in development and peace. Sport can cut across barriers that divide societies, making it a powerful tool to support conflict prevention and peace-building efforts, both symbolically at the global level and practically within communities. When applied effectively, sport programs promote social integration and foster tolerance, helping to reduce tension and generate dialogue. The convening power of sport makes it additionally compelling as a tool for advocacy and communication.

Sports organizations themselves have been increasingly aware of their social responsibility and role. They have taken many initiatives of their own. The International Olympic Committee for example took a number of initiatives ranging from supporting the creation of Olympic Games for physically handicapped persons (Paralympic Games were held for the first time in Rome in 1960 following the traditional Olympic Games) to the revival of the Olympic Truce, calling for conflicts to cease during the Olympic Games or the creation of an internal Commission dealing with environmental issues, including the environmental impact of Olympic Games. The IOC considers the environment as the third dimension of Olympism, alongside sport and culture[5]. The year 1994, was proclaimed the International Year of Sport and the Olympic Ideal by UN General Assembly resolution 48/10, celebrating the centenary of the founding of the International Olympic Committee.

More recently, other non-governmental organizations (hereafter NGOs) have specialized in the use of sport and physical activity to achieve goals of development and peace promotion. They have become strong partners for governmental and international organizations playing a key role in the practical implementation of a variety of programs In 2002, the NGO "Olympic Aid", founded by the speed skating Olympic champion Johann Koss, organized an international conference at the Salt Lake City Olympic Games, calling for a more organized and coherent approach to sport by the United Nations. Olympic Aid is now known under the name Right to Play and defines itself as an athlete driven international humanitarian organization. Apart from its work in the field, active in refugee camps together with the United Nations High Commission for Refugees (UNHCR), Johann Koss' organization has been particularly helpful in bringing structure and recognition to

---

5.International Olympic Committee (2005), Factsheet : Environment and Sustainable Development, http://multimedia.olympic.org/pdf

a UN-wide approach to sport. This has helped the UN in dealing with initiatives that have been taken on all continents and touching on a large variety of aspects of sports.

In 2003, UN Member States felt there was a need to better grasp the potential of sport and to offer sport a well-deserved recognition as a means to assist achievements in development and peace. In the General Assembly resolution 58/5 adopted that year, they proclaimed 2005 as the International Year of Sport and Physical Education. The year 2005 was used to clarify and establish the links between sport and development issues and peace promotion. International conferences and forums on issues such as health, doping, education, peace, environment protection or gender equality allowed for the constructive search of common grounds and the publication of some strong recommendations which paved the way for a better recognition and provided support to a proper implementation.

2005 UN Objectives

The objectives of the United Nations system for the International Year of Sport and Physical Education in 2005 can be summarized as follows:

1. Encourage governments to promote the role of sport and physical education for all when furthering their development programs and policies, to advance health awareness, the spirit of achievement and cultural bridging to entrench collective values;

2. Ensure that sport and physical education is included as a tool to contribute towards achieving internationally agreed development goals, including the Millennium Development Goals (MDGs) and the broader aims of development and peace;

3. Promote sport and physical education-based opportunities for solidarity and cooperation in order to promote a culture of peace and social and gender equality and to advocate dialogue and harmony;

4. Promote the recognition of the contribution of sport and physical education towards economic and social development and encourage the building and restoration of sports infrastructures;

5. Encourage sport and physical education to be used, on the basis of locally assessed needs, as a means for health, education, social and cultural development;

6. Strengthen cooperation, coherence and partnerships between all stakeholders, including sports organizations, athletes, multilateral organizations and the United Nations system, bilateral development agencies, Governments across all sectors, the armed forces, NGOs, the private sector, the sports industry, research institutions and the media,

7. Disseminate scientific evidence about the value of sport and physical education for development and peace in order to mainstream sport in governmental development policies.

The International Year of Sport and Physical Education in 2005 was an opportunity to promote the value of sport as a serious partner for the achievement of development and peace goals. The perception of 'sport' not so much by the general public but rather by governments and local authorities was to be broadened to include the notion of 'sport for all'. This is a particular issue for developing countries where the promotion of elite sport and the achievement of results at international sports competitions are considered a way of promoting national unity and a country's value and competitiveness. However, the access to the regular practice of sport was not necessarily seen as a priority. The International year of sport and physical education demonstrated that a fraction of the resources allocated to elite sport can have a significant impact on the general health conditions and well-being of a large portion of a nation's population. The need to fight discrimination with sport and allow access for all to sport was also highlighted in 2005.

The International Year illustrated the importance of sport for a balanced education. Though an essential component of quality education and an integral part of lifelong learning, physical education is still losing ground in formal education systems. The neglect of physical education reduces the quality of learning, with negative future effects on public health and on health budgets. Given that rates of physical activity tend to decrease from adolescence on, it is considered imperative that young people gain an appreciation of sport at school in order to ensure lifelong active and healthy living.

Closing statements

It is interesting that the sport-related private sector (the sports industry) and international sports federations have also grown more interested in human development and peace-building issues. This was achieved partly by the development of numerous partnerships with the United Nations agencies, programs and funds as well as with NGOs and remains an ongoing effort. Initiatives have been encouraged to use sport as a means of promoting intercultural, post-conflict and peace-building dialogue. Such efforts have brought invaluable lessons from countries and territories such as Israel and Palestine, India and Pakistan. The lessons are being disseminated to new potential users with the hope that they will have the courage to apply innovative solutions.

As Mr. Adolf Ogi said, looking back at the International Year of Sport and Physical Education; the fundamental principles of sport, respect for opponents and rules, teamwork and fair play, are consistent with the principles of the UN Charter and reflect the basic rules of a well functioning society living in peace. This global network of people and groups using sport as a means to achieve development and peace remains immensely active, diverse and fertile. Sport remains the only language spoken by people from all continents and walks of life. Let us continue to speak it for the benefit of all.

Chapter 3
How Sport can Contribute to Peace-Building

Perspectives of the United Nations on Sport as a Tool for Promoting Peace

Eric Dienes[1]

Introduction

Sport has been increasingly recognized and used as an innovative low-cost and high-impact tool in humanitarian, development and peace-building efforts, not only by the United Nations (hereafter UN) system but also by other regional and international organizations, governments, armed forces, development agencies, non-governmental organizations (hereafter NGOs), sport federations, and the private sector, just to name a few. Media and academic interest in the concept of Sport for Development and Peace (hereafter SDP) and its uptake by development practitioners, as well as the number of SDP - NGOs have been continuously growing, creating a 'movement' as some have described it. This Chapter will first briefly outline the institutional framework within the UN as it relates to SDP. As a second step it will expand on why the UN considers sport as an important tool and field

---

1.Note: *The views expressed herein are those of the author and do not necessarily reflect the views of the United Nations.*

to engage in. In the third and final step the different forms of utilization of sport in the development and peace-building work of the UN system are described, with a focus on sport as a tool for promoting peace.

The UN institutional framework

Following the inception of the mandate of the Special Adviser to the UN Secretary-General on Sport for Development and Peace in 2001 many further milestones[2] have contributed to the strong institutionalization of SDP with the UN and internationally, such as the 2003 report by the United Nations Inter-Agency Task-Force on Sport for Development and Peace, *Towards Achieving the Millennium Development Goals*, the creation in 2004 of the Sport for Development and Peace International Working Group, International Year of Sport and Physical Education in 2005, the granting of UN General Assembly permanent observer status to the International Olympic Committee (hereafter IOC), as well as the establishment of a pattern of resolutions of the UN General Assembly on SDP and the Olympic Truce.

However, the utilization of sport in the efforts of the UN dates back prior to 2001 when the first Special Adviser took office. The various agencies of the UN system have long made use of sport in their projects and programmes, albeit to a varying extent and regularity, often in an ad-hoc or one-off approach. On the institutional level, as early as 1922, the IOC and the International Labour Organization (hereafter ILO) established institutional cooperation, which was later complemented by partnerships with other UN agencies. The vastly positive experiences that had been made in the utilization of sport in projects and programmes were increasingly discerned and recognized, leading to then UN Secretary-General Kofi Annan's decision to establish the position of his Special Adviser on Sport for Development and Peace. The position has since been maintained, and consequently, in April 2008, UN Secretary-General Ban Ki-moon appointed Mr. Wilfried Lemke, of Germany, as his Special Adviser on Sport for Development and Peace. He succeeded the first Special Adviser, Mr. Adolf Ogi, a former Swiss President.

The mandate of the Special Adviser comprises three main elements: to serve as an advocate, facilitator and representative of sports' social impact in a development context. As an *advocate*, the Special Adviser leads and coordinates the efforts of the UN system to promote understanding and support amongst UN Member States and other actors for sport as a tool to attain humanitarian, development and peace-building objectives. In addition to supporting systematic, coordinated and coherent approaches that use sport as a tool to address challenges in these areas, the Special Adviser aims to foster the inclusion of sport on international and national development agendas and the inclusion of a social development perspective

---

2. For a detailed history and list of key milestones in Sport for Development and Peace, see http://www.un.org/wcm/content/site/sport/home/sport/history/pid/19908

on sports agendas worldwide. A special focus is placed on sport's contribution to the Millennium Development Goals (hereafter MDG's), which inter alia comprises of poverty reduction, universal education, gender equality and promotion of women and girls, prevention of HIV/AIDS and other diseases, and environmental sustainability. Additional priorities are sport's roles in the inclusion of persons living with disabilities, peace promotion and conflict resolution. Being a *facilitator*, the Special Adviser raises funds for programmes and projects, encourages and initiates dialogue, collaboration, knowledge sharing and partnerships in and around sport between the UN and its Member States, international and national sports organizations, civil society, the private sector, academia and the media. And lastly, as a *representative*, the Special Adviser represents the Secretary-General and the UN system at important global sports events and other key meetings.

While performing the manifold tasks of the mandate, the Special Adviser is assisted by the United Nations Office on Sport for Development and Peace (UNOSDP). The Office, based in Geneva and supported by a Liaison Office in New York, provides the entry point to the UN system with regard to SDP, thus bringing the worlds of sport and development closer together. The Office usually does not run large-scale or long-term SDP programmes in developing countries directly, but rather supports implementing UN agencies through a variety of services, such as contact facilitation, communication, outreach and advocacy, as well as technical and programmatic advice. Occasionally UNOSDP is involved in the distribution and management of external grants and funds and organizes short-term projects such as the UNOSDP Youth Leadership Camp. Moreover, the Office holds a variety of outreach and policy events and international conferences such as the joint UN-IOC International Forum on Sport, Peace and Development.

UNOSDP also hosts the Secretariat of the Sport for Development and Peace International Working Group (hereafter SDP IWG). The SDP IWG is an intergovernmental body which aims to build capacity and expertise of governments. It consists of five Thematic Working Groups: 'Sport and Child & Youth Development', 'Sport and Health', 'Sport and Gender', 'Sport and Persons with Disabilities', and 'Sport and Peace'. The SDP IWG supports governments to mainstream SDP and integrate the concept into their national and international aid and development policies, strategies and work plans. The SDP IWG also provides a forum for governments to benefit from each other's experiences, share best practices and develop recommendations. Involving many partners such as representatives of UN agencies, sport federations, NGOs and academia; it supports the implementation of policy and programme recommendations. Since its inception in 2004 the work of the SDP IWG has sustained momentum with regard to governments' interest in and use of sport as a catalyst for social change. The report of the 2004-2008 term entitled "Harnessing the Power of Sport for Development and Peace: Recommendations to Governments" was a major step in the formulation of policy advice informed by scientific evidence of sport's effectiveness as development and peacebuilding tool.

Sport in the United Nations' efforts for development and peace

There are a number of reasons why the United Nations attaches great importance to sport in its policies and programmes. Two major perspectives on sport can be described. It should be noted that these two vantage points do not exclude each other but are rather two sides of the same coin. Ideally they complement each other in a development and peace-building context.

First of all, sport, play and physical activity are fundamental rights for all - a status that has been enshrined in several international legal documents, which have been developed under the umbrella of the UN. Most notably, sport as a right for all has been proclaimed in the International Charter of Sport and Physical Education, the International Convention on the Rights of the Child, and the International Convention on the Rights of Persons with Disabilities. Correspondingly, sport is also an essential part of education in the form of physical education in schools, which should be free, mandatory, regularly offered and inclusive. In this connection, extra-curricular sport-related projects can be seen as providing individuals and communities with the opportunity to exercise their right to sport and access it. Given the lack of sporting opportunities, facilities and equipment, as well as discrimination of groups and individuals who want to practice sport - phenomena that can be observed in many parts of the world - even a basic sport offer without additional objectives represents progress in its own right, promoting health, equality and self-expression.

In a second perspective, sport is seen and used as a flexible tool, not as a means in itself but to another end, serving superordinate development and peace objectives, such as the MDG's and specific peace-building goals. Here, the difference between development *of* sport and development *through* sport is relevant, giving priority to the latter purpose. In this more recent perspective, the UN puts sport's unique advantages, benefits and assets at the service of development and peace. The following four major areas of opportunities are important.

First, the world of sport, on all its levels, including grassroots community and professional organizations, provides many opportunities to create valuable partnerships. The UN has been collaborating more and more over the past decade with the private sector. UNICEF's and UNESCO's partnerships with professional football clubs and UNHCR's cooperation with Nike, and the alliances between the IOC and many UN agencies are just some examples of the potential of new partnerships that can be forged with sport organizations and corporations for human development. These players offer unique expertise, knowledge, resources and outreach capacity which benefits many joint programmes and initiatives all around the world. Moreover, several UN agencies have enrolled world-renowned athletes as Goodwill Ambassadors who help promote programmes and missions and reach out to various groups.

Second, sport and sport events as mass gatherings, both at the community and global level, provide unique platforms for outreach, public information and communication. At the community level, sport events are used to disseminate information to the public on the UN's mission, objectives and programmes in a given community or country. In post-conflict settings for example, campaigns and public service announcements (PSA's) are run around sports events and festivals. Educational seminars and workshops on human rights or particularly children's rights are offered to drive social change and impart important information. Major international sport events such as the Olympic and Paralympic Games and the Football World Cup create extraordinary worldwide media focus and considerable passion in large groups in society. Thanks to cooperation around these events with the official organizing committees, local and national stakeholders, important audiences have been reached at various levels, both through media and on the spot communication. For example several UN agencies had representation at the Inaugural Youth Olympic Games in 2010, reaching out to and educating young athletes about important issues. At the same time the UN is working with the organizers and key stakeholders to enhance the social legacy impact and environmental sustainability of the mega sport events.

Third, sport's considerable appeal and popularity all around the world, especially among the younger population, are harnessed as a powerful means to attract target groups and beneficiaries of a programme. A sporting component in a programme - which does not necessarily need to take a central place in the intervention - is an enjoyable and enticing element and can thus increase enrolment and retention rates of participants. This effect has also been documented for schools that offer sport and physical education as regular subjects or activities. Thus sport, through its convening power, can help to reach out to persons in remote areas or to those individuals and communities that may have been inaccessible or unwilling to take part in traditional development and peace-building initiatives and project designs.

Fourth and similarly, sport is used as a programmatic component in an intervention, building on and promoting sport's positive characteristics, norms and ideals, such as teamwork and team spirit, solidarity, cooperation, communication, fair-play, respect for the competitor and the rules, equality, leadership, resilience, determination, discipline, regularity, and physical activity. While in some instances such programmatic activities may lead to the development of sport as a side-effect, the primary desired outcome is to contribute to overall development via sport-related projects. Accordingly, sport and games as socio-cultural constructs can even be adapted and modified in order to take into account local social and cultural contexts and, in particular, serve the intervention's set objectives. Hence in such settings, sport is not seen in a purist way but rather as a flexible means of cultural and physical expression and social interaction.

The UN system has sought to utilize these advantages to positively impact on the promotion of education, professional skills, health, and the social inclusion and re-integration of disadvantaged and marginalized persons and groups.

Sport as a tool for peace – the macro and micro level

Although peace is not an MDG, it is one of the main ambitions of the UN to make, keep and build peace. Peace forms a necessary condition for sustainable social and economic development and vice versa. The growing recognition and use of sport as a force in the promotion of peace concerns two levels, the macro and micro levels.

At the macro level, sport can be a factor to promote friendly and peaceful international relations or even contribute to the reduction of tensions between states and their peoples through encounters in competitions and major events of organized sport. This set of goals is shared by the United Nations and the Olympic Movement, which promotes the Olympic Ideals (excellence, participation, peace, friendship, respect), through the organization of the Olympic Games and related activities. The recognition of the IOC as a Permanent Observer to the UN General Assembly since 2009 is a recent manifestation of this common ground. The idea of the Olympic Truce is a further key concept on the macro level. Since 1994, on the occasion of each of the Olympic and Paralympic Games, the UN General Assembly has urged Member States to observe the Olympic Truce. Despite continued efforts, especially in the area of education, the universal compliance with the provisions of the resolutions remains a challenge in a world of protracted and emerging armed conflicts. Mega sports events bring athletes and fans from all around the world together and act as powerful agenda-setters in the international public sphere. International sport thus contributes to the formation of global identities, cultures and transnational spheres. It is a realm in which personal friendships between athletes can function as powerful symbols for change, for example the cordial gesture between a Georgian and a Russian shooting medallist on the podium of the 2008 Olympic Games in the wake of a military conflict between their home countries, or the demonstration of fair-play and friendship between long-jump competitors Jesse Owens and Lutz Lang at the 1936 Olympic Games in Berlin against the backdrop of racist ideology.

International sport has also proven to be a positive force for political change in the form of 'sports diplomacy'. The ping-pong diplomacy between China and the USA in the 1970s, or the international cricket matches between Pakistan and India, at which informal political contacts between the political leaders have led to an improvement of the general political atmosphere, at least temporarily, created opportunities for or facilitated formal negotiations and rapprochement. Recognition of national sport associations of newly independent countries by international associations or even athletic success of young states can be important driving forces for peaceful nation-building. Conversely, in the case of the widely followed international sport boycott of South Africa under the apartheid regime, the sport-specific isolation contributed together with other means of international pressure to ending apartheid. However, it should not be omitted that international sport and sport in general have also been the arena of unethical or controversial behaviour, abuse and exploitation. Instances of undue political interference of governments in independent sport administrations, boycotts of sports events - not only during the Cold War - and intentional amplification of hostilities between states through sport rivalries have led to questions as to the role of sport as a progressive force. Among the negative examples, the so-called "Football War" between El Salvador and Honduras of 1969 and the violent clash between the Russian and Hungarian water polo teams ("Blood in the Water" match) at the 1956 Olympic Games are often cited. Further problems such as racism, discrimination, doping and exploitation of young athletes have to be addressed with the same rigour and vigour as in all other parts of society. The UN and several of its agencies such as UNICEF, UNESCO and OHCHR are actively engaged in addressing these challenges, generally as well as specifically with regards to sport.

Yet both the positive and negative incidents and phenomena must be critically and scientifically assessed and put into their broader context in order to prevent illusions about what sport can and cannot cause and achieve in the framework of international relations. Neither should unfounded underestimation nor overestimation of the role of sport based on insufficiently examined anecdotes guide the judgment, contextualization and practical use of sport for peace promotion. Not least because international sport is nowadays dominated by professional high-performance sport representing relatively exclusive domains to which access is barred by a number of socio-economic factors; activities on the micro level, i.e. community-centred or grassroots level are critical if sport is to unfold its full potential as a tool for peace. With a post-Cold War changed relation of inter-state to intra-state conflicts, today the potential of sport is more needed for peace-building and prevention of violence in countries in a state of internal conflict than between states in conflict. Consequently, actions on the micro level are the main focus of the UN's concrete application of sport for peace.

On the macro level, sport is mainly employed as an instrument to support peace-building in its various facets at the community level, i.e. to (re-)build social relationships, advance reconciliation, tackle prejudices and stereotypes and teach non-violent conflict resolution, social and life skills in programmatic interventions. Particularly in post-conflict situations sport is systematically used as a "door opener" to, inter alia, bring together former opponents, rebuild trust and re-humanize negative perceptions and reduce stereotypes that have fuelled the conflict. Where violence takes place intra-communal, community sport programmes can be used to teach a culture of peace and give an incentive for youth to leave gangs and prevent others from joining them.

Efforts on this level are usually less symbolic and more didactic and pedagogically-oriented as sport for peace activities on the macro level. This being said, interventions on the micro level may also build on events with certain symbolic meanings, such as in the use of rituals or one-off events involving dignitaries, celebrities or representatives of important groups within a society. Since the macro-micro distinction is not a differentiation of international/local, micro level interventions can have an international dimension too, for example in the form of international, regional or cross-bor-

45

der friendship tournaments or youth exchanges. For instance UNESCO organized the "International Friendship Encounter: Sports for a Culture of Peace" bringing together youth from all over the world for peace education around sport activities. A more differentiating attribute between typical sports for peace actions on the two levels is that in a micro level project the achievement of excellence and high performance are usually not intended. The focus lies rather on inclusiveness in the sense of non-elite Sport for All and accessibility for all persons, regardless of their economic status and ability, including marginalized and disadvantaged groups and individuals. Elements of competition can nonetheless be included in the project design, as it is an essential part of sport, its experience and appeal. Healthy and fair competition, especially if it is framed in a protective project environment with experienced managers, leaders or coaches and a didactic curriculum does not need to automatically lead to rivalry between competitors or groups.

In carefully designed and implemented projects, encounters and interaction on the sporting field are used as the opening and basis for further dialogue, intercultural and interethnic exchanges and new friendships. As a first and powerful "ice-breaker", sport - especially team sport and when mixed teams are formed - provides participants, supported by coaches, with the opportunity to get to know each other, learn to understand and respect the points of view of others, thus paving the way for a more peaceful co-existence. Sport programmes on the micro level can also assist in reconciliation and conflict transformation efforts between communities who were involved in violent conflicts or victims of previous structural violence which caused damage to the social fabric in various ways. Such programmes have a strong therapeutic foundation and involve experts or psychologically trained coaches.

As far as the type of sport, game or play is concerned, the appropriate choice depends on a variety of factors such as socio-cultural norms, technical feasibility and popularity among the target group. In order to reach and serve beneficiaries adequately, gender, age and ability have to be taken into account. Although the popularity and the easy implementation of football is unmatched in many countries and contexts, various other sports and forms of physical activity are used in different programmes such as capoeira, dance or indigenous and traditional games to reach targeted groups effectively.

With a view to gender equality, women's sport and mixed sport activities provide excellent platforms to foster leadership skills of girls and women, promote female role models, break down gender barriers, tackle discrimination and change stereotypical perceptions. Sport and play can teach skills and values that are important for girls, given that in some countries and contexts they have fewer opportunities than boys for education and social interaction outside of the home. Through and in sport, girls and young women are given the chance to be leaders, make connections, form networks, and improve self-confidence and self-esteem.

Examples of UN activities in the area of peace-building through sport

Many UN funds, programmes, and specialized agencies have used and continue to use sport in their projects and programmes to achieve their objectives. Together with their implementing partner organizations such as government institutions, sport federations and NGOs, they have implemented sports-related development and peace-building projects in many parts of the world, from Gaza to South African townships. Sport is also utilized in both traditional UN peacekeeping operations and multidimensional, integrated peace-building missions.

The specific targets and objectives of projects and programmes that include sport as a tool for peace promotion are very diverse. They are based on the assessed and identified needs in the country of operation as well as the mandate of the particular UN agency. As a result, sport for peace projects across the UN system can differ tremendously even if some of the projects are implemented together with the same partner organization or if recognized good practices are taken into account. The range and form of sport's uses are as diverse as the environments in which the projects are operating in and the targets that they aim to achieve. In the following, some examples shall highlight the various practical applications of sport in programmes of UN system entities[3].

To promote post-conflict reconciliation, UNDP Sri Lanka carried out a one-year pilot project implemented between 2006 and 2007 in partnership with sport federations at the national level and with the sport and zonal education offices at the district level. The project contributed to peace-building at the inter and intra-community level. It used sport to bring different ethnic communities of Sinhalese, Tamil and Muslim children and youth to play, connect and celebrate together, thus overcoming political, cultural and linguistic boundaries. The primary focus of the project was the development of conflict transformation and life skills of youth affected by the civil war and the tsunami. It also strengthened the capacity of sport coaches in their roles as active mentors for youth, using sport as a medium for trauma relief and reconciliation. The project included sport activities in conflict-prone communities; twinning of schools and sport clubs throughout the districts; youth exchanges and guided exposure visits; and full day workshops on 'Trauma Counselling and Reconciliation'. The project also attached great importance to including and involving persons with disabilities in its sports activities. Moreover, it improved sport infrastructure. Due to the success of the S4P pilot project, the S4P activities were integrated in the subsequent Communities for Peace and Communities for Progress (C4P) programme cycles, which run to this day.

In order to reduce and prevent community violence among youth, the UN peacekeeping Operation in Haiti, MINUSTAH, in cooperation with the NGO Viva Rio, uses sport (football, capoeira and traditional dance)

3.Information about further examples can be found at http://www.un.org/wcm/content/site/sport/home/unplayers/fundsprogrammesagencie

in diverse community programmes in Port-au-Prince's most violent neigh-bourhoods. The programmes' activities include teaching mechanisms for conflict resolution between "bases" (territorial groups with some armed in-dividuals), and the empowerment of women, among other things. Guided sport activities help to dismantle gangs and prevent youth from joining them. Promoting a culture of peace, annual festivals are held at which peace accords between rival gangs are renewed in a ceremonial setting. During the 2010 Football World Cup, the palpable enthusiasm was seized as a setting conducive to spreading messages of non-violence through the organization of a mini world cup between 32 neighbourhoods of Bel Air and the broad-casting of PSAs in public viewing areas.

Sport is also used in programmes for the reintegration and rehabilitation of ex-combatants, in particular ex-child soldiers. UNICEF and UN peace-keeping operations have played a key role in dozens of countries in advocat-ing and securing the release of children from armed forces and other com-batant groups as well as facilitating their demobilization and re-integration into society with the help of sport. In this context, sport offers a space to play; giving children back a part of their childhood while providing an outlet for channelling and controlling potential aggression. Team sports al-low these young people to build positive connections with peers and adults, create a sense of belonging that is essential for forming a positive iden-tity, a feeling of self-worth and overcoming trauma. Stereotypes about relo-cated ex-child soldiers held by members of the receiving community can be tackled by including these vulnerable individuals in sport activities. By shar-ing a common denominator and passion, group sporting activities help re-humanize the negative image of ex-child soldiers.

Using football matches and tournaments to focus on important issues that play a role in conflicts, in 2009 UNICEF conducted a programme in Côte d'Ivoire to raise awareness of the importance of, and provide inform-ation on birth registration, whose rates vary throughout the country along geographical, ethnic and socio-economic lines. Birth registration, which can be requested until the child has reached a certain maximum age, is con-sidered vital to ascertain civil status and ensure access to formal education through valid documentation. The programme which reached out to par-ticipating children and their parents thus contributed to peace-building by promoting the rights of disadvantaged groups and helping them to integrate fully into society.

UNOSDP, the IOC and UN peacekeeping operations have cooperated for the organization of sport for peace programmes and games. To promote the reconciliation process in the Democratic Republic of the Congo, the UN peacekeeping operation MONUC, UNOSDP and the IOC partnered together in 2006 to organize the two-week long "Jeux de la Paix" (Peace Games), which included a variety of sport competitions and brought to-gether youth from all parts of the country. It was intentionally and success-fully implemented in a critical period of national elections, with the major objective of promoting a peaceful and non-violent atmosphere, reinforced by the strong symbol and nationwide attention that the event created. In

Liberia, with the peacekeeping operation UNMIL as the implementer, they teamed up again in 2007 to implement the country-wide four week long "Sport for Peace" programme with the goal of fostering peace in the aftermath of the civil war and educating youth about HIV/AIDS issues.

Sport is also used to promote friendship and reconciliation between armed forces that are or have been pitted against each other. For example, also in Cote d'Ivoire in 2009 the UN peacekeeping operation UNOCI organized a football tournament bringing together members of the armed forces of the FAFN rebels and the government-controlled national forces (FDS) to promote reconciliation and unity. The event was a contribution to support the implementation of the peace agreement in place at that time.

Sport as part of a multifaceted approach to peace-building

Peace-building is a continuous process ranging from early recovery and targeted efforts to prevent violence to the long-term reconstruction of society and the State through capacity building. To be successful, this demanding work towards sustainable peace requires a high level of involvement and commitment of all parts of society, including government and civil society, in many sectors and on all levels. It is evident that in such scenarios sport alone cannot bring about peace. Neither is its employment as a tool in social programmes a one-size-fits-all solution for the manifold challenges faced in a post-conflict setting. But it is an efficient, flexible and multi-versatile instrument in the larger toolkit of peace-building and reconciliation measures.

Programmatic peace-building interventions in post-conflict situations are difficult and sensitive undertakings, which require utmost caution, social, cultural and historical awareness, appropriate planning, adequate human resources and sufficient capacity. The same applies for sport for peace programmes. Therefore, and in order to ensure the intended impact and local capacity building, UN projects are mostly implemented in cooperation with local, national or international non-governmental or civil society partner organizations or governmental agencies. However, due to budget cuts, lack of resources and funds, and the absence of solid policy mainstreaming, sport for peace events and projects are far too often one-off activities. While it is clear that sport cannot always be integrated in peace-building efforts, it is important to ensure that activities that are implemented only for a limited period are designed in such a way that local ownership, self-sustainability and the chance for multiplication are maximized.

Sport for peace programmes and events and their social, cultural and psychological effects have the biggest impact when they are part of a multifaceted and multi-sectorial approach, together with more traditional activities and measures of peace-building, i.e. security sector and judicial reform, compensation of and justice for victims, addressing economic and structural inequalities such as solution of land and property issues, etc. which as a whole tackle the transformation of the root causes of the conflict. While it is clear that sport alone cannot solve these issues, in the social domain it can assist in a wide range of peace-building interventions, complement more conventional approaches, and be utilized in the peace-building process at various stages, such as for conflict prevention work, reconciliation efforts, the promotion of a strong culture of peace, and in public outreach campaigns.

Conclusion and future steps

The UN uses sport for development and peace in two different perspectives, the fundamental rights-based and the tool-based point of view. Both purposes can be fulfilled at the same time, thus making sport a powerful agent of social change. When using sport, positive developments are not automatic. It requires a professional, well-designed and socially responsible intervention which is tailored to the respective social and cultural context and employs knowledgeable, socially skilled and psychologically trained practitioners, coaches and project leaders. As a cultural phenomenon, sport is a mirror of society and is just as complex and contradictory. Negative phenomena such as violence, hooliganism discrimination, racism, nationalism, doping and corruption have to be addressed and prevented. Successful SDP programmes work to realize the right of all members of society to participate in sport and leisure activities. Effective programmes intentionally give priority to development objectives and are carefully designed to be inclusive.

To enable sport to unleash its full positive potential, emphasis must be placed on curriculum refinement and effective monitoring and evaluation. The research and evaluation of sports' distinctive impact in peace-building is especially challenging but not impossible. Monitoring and evaluation of projects and programmes should be conducted continuously and on a long-term basis, using quantitative and qualitative research methods. Peace can be fragile, and sometimes post-conflict countries relapse into full-blown violence within a short period. Positive changes brought about by sport for peace programmes or, for that matter, by any other type of measure, can be lost or reversed, which does not mean that they were ineffective. Moreover, research, monitoring and evaluation should not only be conducted to be accountable vis-à-vis a donor, to raise funds, or worse, to justify its use per se, but essentially to increase efficiency and effectiveness, improve models and gain knowledge about how lessons learnt and best practices can applied in other contexts. Therefore NGOs, governments, development agencies and other programme implementers need to put sufficient resources at the disposal of comprehensive data collection and solid monitoring and evaluation.

Furthermore, networks and partnerships in all sectors, including practitioners and the academic branch are important. Especially in a research area such as SDP that is still developing, it is necessary to create networks and collaborate in order to learn from each other, share research models, data and evidence, as well as to coordinate to fill gaps in research. Interdisciplinary cooperation and multi-sector networking in the field of SDP are thus crucial. Here, the Sport for Development and Peace International Working Group, including its Thematic Working Group on Sport and Peace has an important role to play by gathering good practices and research results for the development of evidence-based recommendations to fully harness the potential that sport has to offer.

References

Sport for Development and Peace International Working Group (2008). *Harnessing the Power of Sport for Development and Peace: Recommendations to Governments.* Available at: http://www.un.org/wcm/content/site/sport/home/resourcecenter/publications, (Accessed 12th March 2012).

United Nations Inter-Agency Task Force on Sport for Development and Peace (2003). *Sport for Development and Peace: Towards Achieving the Millennium Development Goals.* Available at: http://www.un.org/wcm/content/site/sport/home/resourcecenter/publications, (Accessed 12th March 2012).

UN system-wide web platform "Sport for Development and Peace – The UN system in Action": Available at: http://www.un.org/sport, (Accessed 12th March 2012).

Part II

Sport and Peacemaking

Chapter 4
Adapted Equipment and Practices

A Tool for Popularizing Sport for Peace

Ludovic Hubler

Introduction

In countries or regions that are economically disadvantaged, lacking social cohesion or suffering the consequences of armed conflicts or natural disasters, local stakeholders often identify similar obstacles to their development. With regards to using sport for development and peace, consultations with youth leaders, sports clubs, national federations, national Olympic committees or Ministries of Youth and Sport generally reveal short-comings that fall into four categories. These are:

- Funding
- Equipment
- Training
- Facilities

Throughout the world, regardless of the individual social problems encountered from one continent, country or community to another, these four categories of needs remain immutable and absolute. Although the financial need is often the first expressed and the one which represents the main challenge for stakeholders in the field, lack of funds should not prevent the poorest communities having access to sport.

By way of illustration, since 2007, Peace and Sport, "*L'Organisation pour la Paix par le Sport*", has been working around the world to use sport as a tool for peace education and social integration of the most vulnerable youth. Its scope of action lies in post-conflict areas and regions lacking social cohesion or suffering from extreme poverty. From the many projects the organization supports worldwide, concepts and models for 'best practices' have been built, with the aim of duplicating them everywhere across the world where they may be appropriate.

One such best practice to emerge is the use of adapted exercise and equipment. This innovative concept, developed in collaboration with International Sports Federations, aims to give access to structured sport and the values of sport to the most disadvantaged communities throughout the world. Behind this objective lies a conviction: It is simplistic to believe that playing sport in a structured way is limited to having adequate equipment or dedicated facilities. Sport is defined primarily by the respect of rules that are unique and common to all. Football is no less football if it is played without spiked shoes. Athletics just as strongly transmits the value of efforts, pushing one's own limits and perseverance when it is practised with alternative equipment.

Sport is a flexible tool that can be practiced in all kinds of geographical environments (urban, rural, wastelands, a woodland environment, etc.) and socio-economic environments (wealthy areas, disadvantaged regions etc.). If the rules of the World Championships are unique and very strictly controlled by each International Federation, they now seek to develop parallel activities with softer, less restrictive rules and with fewer standards, to enable sport to be practiced by the greatest possible number of people. This approach by International Federations may be motivated by a legitimate desire for development; that is to say as a preliminary step, a springboard for enticing newcomers in areas with a strong potential for growth, such as Africa, Asia, or Latin America. It can also come about as a result of the International Federations better understanding the pioneering role that they can play in the global construction of sustainable peace and development through sport. However, the reality is probably a mixture of both.

The rules of each sport adapt differently to take into account the wide diversity of environments where they can be played. The IRB (International Rugby Board) for example today seeks to promote "Touch Rugby" as an "adapted practice" of rugby with 7 or 15 players: basic rugby with more limited equipment, which can be safely played on bumpy or stony ground, therefore more accessible to deprived communities. AIBA (International Boxing Association) now recognizes "educational boxing" as a discipline in its own right with its own rules, which encourage understanding and anticipating adversaries, rather than confrontation. The UIPM (International Federation of Modern Pentathlon) a few years ago developed "Biathle", a discipline with only 2 (swimming and running) of the 5 traditional Modern Pentathlon events, leaving aside shooting, riding and fencing which are difficult to implement in remote environments as they require the use of expensive equipment that is complicated to acquire and maintain. "Biathle" competitions were held recently in cross-border areas of the Democratic Republic of Congo and Burundi, on the shores of Lake Tanganyika: a way to ease inter-ethnic tension in this troubled region using the natural resources available. The ICC (International Cricket Council) promotes "Street cricket" which it has implemented in sensitive neighbourhoods of Lahore in Pakistan. FILA (The International Wrestling Federation) wants to develop "Beach Wrestling" requiring less facilities and equipment; a discipline which is strongly expanding, especially in Africa.

This adapted sports practice enables a maximum number of people to enjoy wrestling without social or economic discrimination. Once placed in an educational context, these practices can effectively act to socially integrate the most vulnerable populations and to encourage reconciliation between divided communities. They help to popularise sport with a view to building peace and fostering development. But beyond adapting the rules of such and such a sport, it is also interesting to note the launch of the concept of "adapted equipment".

On the ground, it is common that local actors supported by Peace and Sport (managers of NGOs, community leaders, young people, members of national federations, Ministries of Youth and Sport, etc.) believe that it is not possible to practice structured sport without importing equipment, a costly process, which can be very long (purchase, transport, customs, human resources, etc.) and this is not a sustainable process. Is it really necessary to have access to the latest equipment to play sport in a structured environment? The answer is no, and Peace and Sport, in collaboration with International Federations, intends to demonstrate that this is the case. Creating adapted equipment enables local actors at the centre of the process to become empowered and self-sufficient instead of falling into the classic pitfall of waiting for donations of equipment. This strategy promotes independence above dependence on financial providers or donors – and with it ownership and sustainability. Limits to the widespread implementation of sport should not be money, or equipment donations... but creativity, inventiveness and imagination. Some people are becoming experts in the matter.

For example, in Timor Leste, a small independent country barely 10 years on from decades of wars, young people in volatile areas of *Bairo Pite*, *Comoro* and *Becora* now look at waste in a different way. Once dumped onto roadsides in the capital city Dili in the absence of garbage cans, plastic bottles, tyres and soda cans are now recycled and transformed into sports equipment, allowing thousands of young people to be supervised through teaching them adapted athletics, gymnastics, or softball, at very little cost. Surrounding natural resources can also be used: shot putting with coconuts and pole-vaulting with bamboo are enjoying great success among Timorese youth.

The words of José de Jesus, Director of the small NGO "Action for Change Foundation", perfectly summarize this idea:

> "Until a few weeks ago, I was deeply convinced that I could not give young people in my community the possibility to participate in structured sports activities; although I am frequently asked to do so. Importing sports equipment to Timor-Leste is very expensive and small neighbourhood NGOs such as ours working at the heart of communities are generally not able to afford this type of thing. I've learnt that by being more creative and using our common sense, it's possible to offer sports training... And this is even becoming a source of revenue for our centre [...] Adapted equipment therefore fosters the sustainability of our actions." Coconut, bamboo, plastic bottles and used tyres are indeed plentiful in Timor – as there are in many other developing countries[1].
>
> Jose de Jesus (2011)

Of course, no one will pretend that we will produce national or international champions with plastic bottles or sports equipment built using banana leaves or bamboo, but the responsibility of sport goes far beyond elite performances; it also means contributing to the 'well-being' of the greatest number and developing human beings able to propagate a culture of peace in communities considered high risk through the intrinsic values of sport: respect for the rules, for others, for the environment, tolerance, discipline, team spirit, etc. Adapted equipment is not supposed to be a long-term solution, but rather a step for citizen action and an awareness that can be gradually replaced by better quality material, as used in more developed countries.

Adaptation of sports equipment is therefore an up-and-coming activity and International Federations understand this, whether they are an Olympic federation or not. They see it as a way to recruit new members, including countries where they traditionally have few followers. In November 2011, the IAAF (International Association of Athletics Federations) won an award for being 'The International Federation of the Year to have most promoted Peace through Sport', which it did through an educational program of this type aimed at children from 6 to 12 years old. Dubbed "Kid's Athletics", this program offers adapted athletics activities that are fun and attractive, accessible to all without discrimination. Translated into 6 languages, it uses adapted equipment made from waste, local materials and natural resources available in the immediate environment. During the presentation of the award, Mr. Lamine Diack, President of the IAAF explained that this award was *"the fruit of important work carried out by [his] Federation to popularize athletics"*. What other Federations will follow the IAAF in this initiative? FIG (International Gymnastics Federation), with its "Gymnastics for all" program and FITA (International Archery Federation), which has experts teaching people how to make bows and arrows from bamboo, are among the leading International Federations in this field.

---

1. Author interview data.

Peace through sport is regarded by some as a utopia, like an unattainable dream, or even as a waste of time, energy and money. But experiments carried out in the field, with or without adapted equipment, prove that, by its intrinsic values, sport can play a significant role in the education of vulnerable youth in targeted areas. Indeed, today at the practitioner level it is important to have places for exchanging best practice, as well as the tools for evaluation to measure the long-term impact of programs with regards to their developmental impact on the lives of young people concerned. However, in the short-term, simple empirical observation in the field lets us see some positive effects. For example, the village of Luvungi in the province of South Kivu in the East of the Democratic Republic of Congo, once violent, has become much quieter since the development of a big 'peace through sport program' launched in 2009. According to local officials, many young people were not embroiled in post-election violence because they were too busy playing football, volleyball and table tennis! In East Jerusalem, five years after introducing sport for development and peace programs it is apparent that the easily transferable behavioural codes and rules of sport have helped bring a framework of citizenship to hundreds of young people from areas where the words 'police' or 'laws' are only present on paper. In Timor Leste, inter-neighbourhood conflict in Dili has decreased in areas where the presence of the sport has increased: "young people are now recruited by sports clubs instead of gangs" we are used to hearing. In Colombia, employment prospects for youngsters participating in programs run by local NGOs and supported by Peace and Sport have increased as a result of teaching the rules of life in society through sport.

Conclusive Statements

Adapted practices and alternative equipment can potentially be used by all kinds of local actors, youth centres and sports clubs via National Federations, national Olympic Committees and Ministries of Youth and Sport. National Federations and clubs, traditionally driven by a competitive vision, have taken more time to build on the concepts of wider sport for development aims. As a result the situation is gradually changing. For example, in Colombia, the International Gymnastics Federation, with help from Peace and Sport, has worked with the National Federation to develop a training program for 'Peace through Sport' primarily using an adapted practice via the program "Gymnastics for all". Chila Dominguez, President of the National Federation testifies to his experience:

"Colombia is a violent country, and the Colombian Federation of gymnastics would like to participate in peace-building in our country. Through training programs, we have become aware of the benefits that we can offer to help reach this goal. First of all we want to develop a pilot project and then a

59

national program to use gymnastics as a tool for peace. The basis of this program will expand on partnerships with existing youth centres across the country to teach gymnastics for all"[2].

Chile Dominguez (2011)

Importantly, in developing countries, adapted equipment and practices can be used equally effectively in the development of the sport, as in development by sport. Actually *making* sports equipment can go much further than serving education and sport. It can also promote employment, generate activities for revenue, or even in some cases help environmental protection; thus serving society as a whole. In Kinshasa, Peace and Sport has recently started working with a local NGO to produce a large amount of adapted sports equipment to commercialise in the future. Through the provision of machine tools, judo mats will soon be built from tyres, canoes from trees and bicycles from recycled plastic bottles. Selling adapted equipment is undoubtedly still in its very early stages, but the potential is fantastic.

Boosted by these developments, Peace and Sport wishes to continue to work to enable structured sport to be available in extremely remote locations so that it can contribute to building sustainable peace. To this effect, Peace and Sport is currently working on a manual entitled "*Adapted practices and equipment:The road to popularizing sport at the service of peace.*" This manual will sum up the best practices using alternative materials identified throughout the world, enabling the mentoring of vulnerable youth. The organization also wants to launch the first pilot multi-sports centre accredited with an "Adapted practices and equipment" label in the South Kivu region in Democratic Republic of Congo: A centre which will 100% operate on imagination and creativity. There are many initiatives and best practices that can be modelled and transmitted to legitimate local stakeholders and duplicated to popularize the use of sport at the service of peace. Although the specific needs identified by local actors will always remain, adapted equipment will in all cases provide at least a temporary solution.

2.Author interview data.

Chapter 5

We Don't Play War Anymore

Sport and the Reintegration of Former Child Soldiers in Northern Uganda

Dean M. Ravizza

Introduction

In August 2005, I sat in the shade under a mango tree within a rural school-yard in Northern Uganda and listened to Simon[1] a 15 year-old boy who returned from abduction by a rebel group during a civil conflict lasting over two decades. After concluding his involvement in a football[2] match, we spoke about his involvement in a school sport program. Excitedly, he stated: "I love playing football with the other boys in my class. I am a good player... and the others think so too... I hope to play on the school team in tournaments". When I asked him if sport played any significant role in reintegration within his community, he replied:

---

1. Pseudonyms were used to protect the identity of all of the children and youth who participated in this research project.

2. The term football is used to describe what is also known as the sport of 'soccer'.

"I still get mad when some players try to provoke me into arguments...I know they are testing me to see if I will argue or strike them...I have had enough of conflict...I want to show them I am strong player and not a rebel. When I play, I can forget about all of those bad things that happened to me in the bush...playing football is something I should be doing, not hurting people".

(Simon, 2005)

When most people in Western societies think of youth sports, they envision children and youth in their colorful uniforms bounding about gymnasiums or playing fields engaged in organized sporting competitions as parents and bystanders cheer them on from the sidelines. Schoolyards, parks, playgrounds, and open fields are crowded with children and youth seeking the opportunity for self-expression through play with siblings and friends often seen emulating the moves of their favorite sporting stars. Our images of children participating in sport rarely intersect with the topic of war, and even less with child soldiers. Yet, conversations such as that above have become more commonplace as globally children and youth are recruited or abducted into fighting forces.

Children of War

The worldwide exploitation of children as weapons of war is an abhorrent characteristic of recent conflicts. It is estimated that tens of thousands of children are involved in armed conflict in government forces or non-state armed groups in all regions of the world (Coalition to Stop the Use of Child Soldiers 2008). They are recruited and join armed forces within failed states where a lack of access to economic and educational opportunities is prevalent and within breakdowns of society and traditional protective structures (Singer 2005, Wessells 2006). Some armed groups use forcible abduction, often in large numbers of children, to bolster their fighting forces. Systematically, children take on various roles within an armed group other than combatants including serving as porters, spies, messengers, and servants (Machal 2001). They are exposed to heinous levels of violence including killing, maiming, rape, and raiding and torching villages. The role of child soldier has devastating consequences according to gender. Girls constitute a significant number of child soldiers within particular armed groups (McKay and Mazurana 2004). They are routinely branded as sex slaves or 'wives' and prone to sexual violence. Others are victims of brutal mutilations such as amputation to arms, legs, ears, and lips, and the gouging of eyes. They face the added challenge of re-building their lives with a permanent physical disability. International laws such as the Optional Protocol (2002) to the Convention on the Rights of the Child (1989) and the Paris Principles on Children Associated with Armed Forces or Armed Groups (2007) prohibit governments and non-state armed groups from using children under the age of eighteen in armed conflicts. Despite these international standards, the practice of child soldiering still exists.

The conflict in Northern Uganda is a harsh example of the use of child soldiers in armed conflict. Since 1986, the people of northern Uganda have fallen victim to the conflict between the Lord's Resistance Army rebel group (hereafter LRA) and the government forces of Uganda. Throughout the conflict, LRA leader Joseph Kony created his army primarily through the violent abduction of children. International agencies estimated that nearly 30,000 children were abducted by the LRA. However, recent research places that number at more than 65,000 children and youth abducted for periods ranging from a few days to many years (SWAY 2007). As a consequence of widespread insecurity throughout the region, hundreds of thousands of people were forced into camps for internally displaced people (IDPs). These were characterized by overcrowding, disease, and abject poverty, and as such left children vulnerable to exploitation and abuse. The lack of civilian protection throughout the region created the phenomenon of 'night commuters', when tens of thousands of children walked for miles to sleep in town centers for greater protection. International peace talks produced a cessation of hostilities beginning in late 2006, bringing a measure of stability to northern Uganda that remains intact to date despite an implementation of any peace agreement. Large numbers of these internally displaced people continue to leave the camps for the uncertainty of rebuilding their lives in the war-torn region.

Research in Northern Uganda

While the evidence base on child soldiers continues to grow, research on the use of sport as a tool for reintegration and long-term social inclusion of former child soldiers is limited. In order to contribute to the body of knowledge, we began a long-term research project on the impact of sport on the reintegration of former child soldiers in the conflict-affected region of Northern Uganda in 2005. The aims of our research were to assess the role of sport in the psychosocial adjustment and social reintegration of former child soldiers. An initial eighteen-month period was utilized for observational research. Through informal conversations, semi-formal interview protocols with local key stakeholders, and field observations throughout the Gulu and Kitgum districts, we discovered that sport was a significant recreational pursuit in the lives of the children and youth living amidst the conflict.

As we concluded the initial research phase, local Ugandan government officials requested we expand the research to include "more children of war, not just the formerly abducted," stated one official. We fulfilled this request in order to understand the views of those who have a profound effect on the rates of community stigma experienced by former child soldiers within their respective communities, and to compare and contrast the impact of sport on their non-abducted peers. In order to do so, we conducted a mid-scale survey among children and youth (n=411, 51.3% males, 48.7% females) ages 12-22 in twenty-two sub-counties in the Gulu and Kitgum districts of Northern Uganda in June/July 2009. For this survey, former abductees made up slightly over thirty percent of the respondents. A team of locally-trained research assistants from Northern Ugandan conducted the surveys in both English and *Luo*, the local language.

Large numbers of children participated in sport while at school, where they were much more likely to engage in formalized competition than within community-based programs. Children who participated in some form of sporting activity while failing to attend school did so through informal play within their respective villages and open spaces within the community. Reasons for non-participation in sport included no access to sports activities/lack of equipment, sickness/poor-health/injury, must work/make money, and family obligations/chores. Former abductees were less likely to participate in sport than their non-abducted peers due mostly to poor health or injuries obtained while abducted and a strong need to make money to support themselves and family members. Some female former abductees revealed that they lacked the ability to participate in sport in order to raise a child or children born while in captivity.

Sport and games are one of several components of reintegration programs to address the psychosocial needs of former abductees at interim care centers in Northern Uganda (see Allen & Schomerus 2006 for background information on programming at interim care centers in Northern Uganda). At the Gulu Support the Children Organization (GUSCO) center, staff engaged children and youth in games and sport to promote teamwork and cooperation, build trust, and rekindle in them a spirit of enjoyment lost while associated with the rebel group. Boys participated in football games while girls engaged in netball activities outside of the guarded walls of the center, on a large open field adjacent to a local secondary school. Interview data from center officials and staff here and at other interim care centers revealed sport was an important component of psychosocial programming. When asked why sport is factored into the daily routine of the children and youth at the center, their responses focused mainly on the immediate effects of sport. They described sport in the following ways:

> "Sport has a calming effect on former abductees," stated one social worker. "It makes them less aggressive."

> "Playing sport tires them out," remarked another social worker. "It helps them sleep better at night."

> "When they play sport after returning from the bush...they can focus on something positive...it helps them forget the past," declared one center director.

No scientific studies have yielded data to support these stated causal relationships between sport and the traumatic effects of war on former child soldiers. Nor is there empirical evidence to support the immediate effects of sport on returnees and the effectiveness of sport as a psychosocial intervention at interim care centers (Ravizza 2007). Yet, it is not short-sighted to believe that former child soldiers experienced the building or re-building of socially acceptable behaviors through sport within the closed environment of an interim care center with the aim of transferring such behaviors to their communities upon reintegration (Ravizza 2010b).

When Child Soldiers Return Home

The re-introduction of former child soldiers back into the community is a difficult process and is sometimes unsuccessful. They often incur periods of testing or 'provoking' by other members of their communities who view them as unconditional threats to peace (Singer 2005; Wessells 2006). How they navigate this transition from active participants to contributing members of society impacts the peace and stability within their communities (Boothby 2006, Sommers 2005). Our findings indicated that large numbers of non-abductees felt it was not acceptable to exclude former abductees from participating in sport. One male non-abductee replied:

> "Many of the youth from northern Uganda were victims...When they are back from captivity; we should welcome them to participate among us. Isolating them is no good".

However, follow up interviews revealed conditions for participation within some of the responses. One female non-abductee stated:

> "I would include former abductees... because it is good for them to play among nonviolent players so that they may learn more about playing peacefully."

But, she went on to state:

> "They [former abductees] should be removed from the activity if they are too aggressive or knocking other players, and counseled...until then, they should not return."

In addition, significant numbers of former child soldiers felt accepted by their families and other children immediately or after a brief period of time following their abductions. But, many faced a longer period of time before being accepted by members of their community. A significant number of former child soldiers reported that participation in sport with other children was a main factor in their acceptance among peers. One 16 year old male former abductee replied:

> "I played a lot of sports with my friends and schoolmates before I was abducted...football, volleyball, and athletics. When I returned from the bush I wanted to play and they welcomed me back...and now I play during and after school with them...I am accepted in the same way done to those who are non-abducted".

Efforts to provide interventions on behalf of former child soldiers expose the importance of operating within the perspective of a *social ecology* relevant to children of war (Betancourt 2008, Kostelny 2005), that is, according to Betantcourt (2008):

> "the nurturing physical and emotional environment that includes and extends beyond the immediate family to peer, school, and community settings as well as the operant cultural and political belief systems" (p. 139).

Understanding the root of community stigma aimed at former child soldiers is essential to planning and implementing culturally relevant and contextual interventions to aid in long-term social inclusion (Betancourt 2011). In the case of sport, providing opportunities that facilitate the unique needs of former child soldiers applicable to their current situations is necessary to make social inclusion possible. In 2010, our team conducted focus group interviews with key community stakeholders following the completion of the survey process. Additionally, our team identified a panel of survey respondents that included former abductees who both passed through interim care centers and self-reintegrated without any formal assistance (n=42; males=25, females=17) and non-abductees (n=30, males=16, females=14) to participate in more in-depth interviews to better understand the impact of sport on the process of reintegration through multiple lenses within the community.

I spent several afternoons speaking with a young boy named Daniel whose story was told to me by one of the research assistants. Daniel was 12 years old when he was abducted by the LRA rebels while returning from working in the fields one evening. For a period of approximately 20 months, Daniel faced heinous levels of exposure to violence while looting and torching villages and abducting other children. He quickly rose among the ranks to positions of greater responsibility which included overseeing large numbers of children and planning raids and abductions. He explained to me how another soldier, disgruntled over a minor dispute, told the commanders that Daniel was plotting his escape. As a result, the rebels took him further into the bush and amputated his left arm just below the elbow leaving him bleeding to death. The government army came upon him when positioning troops in the area. They transported him to a local child protection unit who transferred him to the hospital where he received medical care for his injuries. Upon recovery, Daniel was taken to the World Vision Children of War interim care center where he began the transition to life outside of the rebel group while awaiting reunification with his family.

Daniel learned of his parent's death during his three months at the center. Upon reintegration he went to live with his maternal grandmother and younger sister. This caused difficulties with the paternal grandmother who felt the children should live with her. In addition, local villagers were not pleased to have him return to their community and tried to provoke him into arguments which was a source of stress for Daniel. In addition, he became involved in a dispute over land previously owned by his deceased father but now occupied by strangers.

Daniel was able to return to a local primary school where he quickly garnered attention as the top athlete. He participated in a number of local football tournaments where he excelled in competition and earned small amounts of money which he promptly used to pay him and his sister's school fees. His athletic prowess despite his physical disability and strong leadership skills - that we came to learn were developed while abducted - earned him the peer-elected title of sport prefect at his school, a position given to the student who assists the games teacher in the organization and facilitation of the school's sporting activities. When asked why they chose Daniel for this position, the students commented on his strong athletic skills in addition to his ability to organize them with little difficulty and quickly resolve the minor disputes that arose while participating in sport. During my last interview with Daniel, he stated how he wished to continue playing sport at a boarding school away from his village after some members of his community broke into his family's modest home and stole items including his only pair of shoes.

The case of Daniel exposes the many complex layers of acceptance experienced by former child soldiers that need to be addressed upon return from fighting forces. Sport was a positive factor in Daniel's acceptance among his peers and the re-establishment of a positive identity (Erikson, 1968) with his peers as evidenced by his elected position of responsibility. Sport alleviated the family conflict he experienced by supporting his and his sibling's education with the earnings from his participation in football tournaments, and thus easing the burden on elderly family members. However, sport failed to address the community stigma he experienced in his village, and could not solve his land dispute. This story represents just one case of the critical need of individual assessment of former child soldiers prior to employing programmatic interventions, and magnifies the dangers of viewing sport on a panacea-like level that leads to inadequate programming and systems of support.

Building Inclusive Communities through Sport

Children of war are at increased risk for a range of mental health problems (Betancourt 2009), and face a multitude of conflicts, making nonviolent conflict resolution a high priority in psychosocial support (Wessels, 1998, 2006). Just as sports can be a building block for peace and stability, they provide opportunities for conflict and physical confrontation. Competitive sports can produce violent behaviors that circumvent peace-related objectives. For former child soldiers, engaging in taunting and fighting on the very public stage of sports can further community stigma leading to social isolation.

By way of inductive analysis, our research revealed that the children and youth engaged in conflict in sport at four levels: *disagreement, argument, physical, and harmful*. The *disagreement* level is characterized by conflicts that involve two different views about a particular play or call. For example, the ball goes out of bounds during a football match. Opposing players believe it to be their possession. A decision is made directly for immediate resolution. The *argument* level is an extension on a disagreement and beyond an immediate resolution. For example, two players run down the field with the ball and both end up on the ground. They argue as to whether a foul was committed and who is the one responsible. A simple statement of forgiveness will not settle this situation prompting the players to refer to the rules or seek outside assistance. At the *physical* level, a player displays an instantaneous physical reaction to an event. For example, a player is accidentally knocked down during play and responds immediately with a push to the opposing player. The physical aspect is often impulsive and even emotional, and is in need of a conversation between the two players to come to a peaceful resolution. The *harmful* level is characterized by delayed retaliation to a previous occurrence. It may or may not be preceded by the physical level. The player who seeks retaliation does not always seek resolution. For instance, a player involved in this level of conflict may be pushed accidentally while playing and wait all game seeking revenge. The player may also attack the opposing player after the game. Conversely, issues external to the sporting premise may also cause a player to cause harm to another. For instance, a dispute that originated between players within the community may extend to the playing field causing physical harm to those involved necessitating an appropriate intervention to prevent further violence.

Children and youth engaging in sport may present qualities of one or several of these levels. However, the levels are not necessarily progressive; children and youth engaging in sport may exhibit behaviors reflective of a lower level of conflict without displaying those in a higher level and vice versa (Ravizza & Matonak 2011).

Our research revealed both former abductees and non-abductees put in place strategies to resolve their differences on the playing field through peaceful means such as talking, referring to existing rules, and seeking outside help, thus attempting to avoid resolving conflict violently in ways such as arguing and fighting. Whether sports is a useful means for promoting psychosocial growth for former child soldiers depends upon the means in which they are conducted (Wessells 2006). Strategies for resolution to conflict that arises during participation in sport are essential to creating an environment that fosters understanding and tolerance without resorting to verbal abuse or physical violence. If ground rules are established prior to the start of play as a reference point for potential conflict, they can serve as a reminder of the rules for players who temporarily forget the rules during intense play. Recognizing that conflicts can be part of sport, taking preventative measures, and responding in pro-social ways to resolve them is an initial step towards building inclusive communities.

Concluding Comments

Despite the many uses of sport as a means of psychosocial support for the reintegration of former child soldiers, many questions are still left unanswered. Does participation in sport foster long-term social inclusion? Do sport interventions ease the trauma-related symptoms of former child soldiers? What are the long-term holistic effects of sport on former child soldiers? Can sport contribute to long-term peace building objectives within regions affected by armed conflict? This research does not claim to answer all of them. It does, however, seek to provide insights into the practical application of sport and contribute to the evidence base on child soldiers. It is intended to better define priorities for programming, to build local capacity for delivering programs that may address critical reintegration issues, and to raise wider issues relating to the role of sport interventions in the reintegration and social inclusion of young survivors of war.

List of References

Allen, T., Schomerus, M. (2006). A hard homecoming: Lessons learned from the reception center process on effective interventions for former 'abductees' in Northern Uganda. USAID: Washington, DC.

Betancourt, T.S. (2008). Child soldiers: Reintegration, pathways to recovery, and perspectives from the field. *Journal of Developmental & Behavioral Pediatrics*, 29 (2), 138-141.

Betancourt, T.S. (2009). A qualitative study of mental health problems among children displaced by war in Northern Uganda. *Transcultural Psychology*, 46, 238-257.

Betantcourt, T.S. (2011). *Sierra Leone's war-affected youth: Using evidence from a longitudinal study to develop a Youth Readiness Intervention (YRI).* Presentation made at the World Bank, Washington, DC.

Boothby, N. (2006). *What happens when child soldiers grow up? The Mozambique case study. Intervention, 4(3), 244-259.*

Coalition to Stop the Use of *Child Soldiers. (2008). Child soldiers: Global report.*Available at: http://www.childsoldiersglobalreport.org/. (Accessed 12th March 2012).

Erickson, E. (1968). Identity: *Youth in crisis.* New York: W.W. Norton.

Kostelny, K. (2006). A culture-based integrative approach: Helping war-affected children. In N. Boothby, A. Strang, & M. Wessells, *A world turned upside down: Social ecological approaches to children in war zones.* Bloomfield, CT: Kumarian Press.

Machal, G. (2001). *The impact of war on children.* London: Hurst & Company.

McKay, S., & Mazurana, D. (2004). *Where are the girls? Girls in fighting forces in northern Uganda, Sierra Leone, and Mozambique:Their lives during and after war.* International Center for Human Rights and Democratic Development, Montreal.

Ravizza, D.M. (2007). *At play in the fields of young soldiers.* Working paper. Available at: www.sfcg.org/programmes/children/pdf/ravizza-sport-conflict.pdf. (Accessed 12th March 2012).

Ravizza, D. M. (2010a). The uses of sport for children in armed conflict. *Journal of Sport Science and Physical Education, Sport and Globalization issue, 59, 14-18.*

Ravizza, D.M. (2010b). We played war, now we play peace: Findings from the field on sport and the reintegration of former child soldiers in Northern Uganda. Sport and *Peacebuilding Symposium,* United States Institute for Peace, Washington, DC.

Ravizza, D.M., & Matonak, E. (2011). *Peaceful play: Strategies for resolution to conflict in sport*. Manual: Salisbury, Maryland.

Singer, P.W. (2005). *Children at war*. New York: Pantheon.

Sommers, M. (2005). *Youth and conflict: A toolkit for intervention*. Washington, DC: USAID.

Survey of War-Affected Youth (SWAY). (2007). *Making reintegration work for youth in northern Uganda*. Available at: http://sway-uganda.org/SWAY.ResearchBrief.Reintegration.pdf, (Accessed 12th March 2012).

Wessells, M. (1998). Children, armed conflict, and peace. *Journal of Peace Research, 35, (5), 635-646*.

Wessells, M. (2006). *Child Soldiers: From violence to protection*. Harvard University Press: Cambridge, MA.

Chapter 6
Sport for Peace and Reconciliation

Young Peacemakers in the Kakuma Refugee Camp and Mathare Slums in Kenya

Bob Munro

Introduction

This chapter describes two case studies on how, by "Giving youth a sporting chance" which is the motto of the Mathare Youth Sports Association (hereafter MYSA), it is also possible - as John Lennon famously wrote and sang - to "Give peace a chance". Both case studies focus on the work of the MYSA youth in the Kakuma refugee camp in north western Kenya and in the Mathare area in Nairobi, one of Africa's largest and poorest slums. This chapter is based on the two case studies as well as similar examples highlighted in United Nations and other reports over the last decade.

Peace, Justice and Sport

One commentator with a sense of humour described peace as "the empty white space between the chapters in history books". But the 17th century Dutch philosopher and pantheist Baruch Spinoza bluntly asserted that "peace is not an absence of war". Instead, Spinoza emphasized that peace "is a virtue, a state of mind, a disposition for benevolence, confidence and justice".[1] Spinoza's final focus on justice is critical. Over a century earlier, German theologian and reformer Martin Luther examined the critical link between peace and justice and concluded that "peace was not made for the sake of justice but justice for the sake of peace".[2]

Over four centuries later, in 1971 the American philosopher John Rawls published his pioneering re-thinking of The Theory of Justice. While confirming that the first principle of justice required equality in basic rights and duties, Rawls insisted the second principle of justice is that "social and economic inequalities are only just if they result in compensating benefits for everyone and in particular for the least advantaged members of society."[3] Fifteen year later, Rawl's second principle of justice was concisely re-stated by another American philosopher, young Calvin in the globally syndicated Calvin and Hobbes cartoon strip. In the first frame, as his father reads a book, Calvin confronts him with a universal declaration that every parent has heard many times: "Why can't I stay up late? You guys can!" In the second frame, Calvin protests loudly that "It's not fair!" In the third frame, Calvin's father solemnly shares his worldly wisdom and proclaims that "The world isn't fair, Calvin". In the last frame, Calvin marches off indignantly while stating on behalf of billions of people on our planet that "I know. But why isn't it ever unfair in my favour?"[4] Calvin said what Spinoza, Luther and Rawls all meant. As long as our unfair world is not unfair in favour of the poor majority of people and countries, then peace will remain elusive.

What follows in this chapter then as previously mentioned briefly describes two case studies on how, by "Giving youth a sporting chance" which is the motto of the Mathare Youth Sports Association (MYSA), it is also possible - as John Lennon famously wrote and sang - to "Give peace a chance". Both case studies focus on the work of the MYSA youth in the huge Kakuma refugee camp in north western Kenya and in the Mathare are in Nairobi, one of Africa's largest and poorest slums. Both examples demonstrate in two quite different situations the crucial role played by youth and sport in reducing communal tensions and contributing to peace and reconciliation.

Summary background on the Kakuma refugee camp

As some summary background, the Kakuma refugee camp was established in 1992 under the management of the United Nations High Commis-

---

1. Spinoza, Baruch, 1670, *Tractatus Theologico-Politicus*.

2. Luther, Martin, 1530, *On Marriage.*

3. Rawls, John, 1971, *A Theory of Justice*, Harvard University Press.

4. Watterson, Bill, 1996, *Calvin and Hobbes*, International Herald Tribune, May 6, 1996.

sioner for Refugees (UNHCR) in cooperation with the World Lutheran Federation (WLF). By 1999 the camp was home to over 70,000 refugees. Nearly 70% of the refugees were from southern Sudan. The remaining 30% were from seven other countries: Somalia, Ethiopia, Democratic Republic of Congo, Uganda, Rwanda, Burundi and Eritrea. The different nationalities, as well as the different clans among the southern Sudanese, largely lived together in their own distinct parts of the camp.

Over two-thirds of the 70,000 refugees were youth under 25 years old. Nearly one in three were unaccompanied minors. In the early 1990s the camp managers initiated a basic sports programme for the parentless kids and other youth. By 1998 there were 200 teams playing football, basketball and volleyball. However, those teams were largely ethnically-based teams and, as there were no organized leagues, less than a third of the teams actually played frequent matches. Although there were over 20,000 girls under 25 years old in the camp, there were no organized sports activities for them.[5]

Events in the Kakuma refugee camp

It was at night. I heard people chanting war songs. They were from my community. I recognized the dialect. I only remember fleeing the camp with my family as all hell broke loose. There was fighting and screaming everywhere. I didn't see much. It was very dark. But I was shocked at what I saw the next day.

(Ismael Lazarus)

That was the traumatic reaction of Ismael Lazarus, a Sudanese exile in the Kakuma refugee camp, as quoted by a Kenyan journalist in his news report on "The day hell descended on a refugee camp".[6] That experience demonstrated yet again that the violence which Ismael and the over 70,000 other refugees had tried to escape too often still followed them even into the camp. In late 1999, after hearing on their radios that SPLA soldiers from Ekitoria region had reportedly raided their home area, the Dinka and other smaller Sudanese communities in the camp retaliated by burning and looting the thatched homes of refugees from Ekitoria. Armed with guns and other crude weapons, that outburst of inter-ethnic violence left six dead and over 30 injured.[7]

Start of the new sport and development programme

At the request of the UNHCR and WLF and with the financial support of the Dutch government through the Netherlands National Olympic Committee/National Sports Federation and Royal Netherlands Football Association (KNVB), in early 1999 some MYSA youth leaders and two Dutch

---

5. Kessels, 2000, 15.

6. Saronge, Joseph, 2000, 4.

7. Ibid, 54

volunteers went to the camp to help start new self-help youth sports and community development programmes similar to those pioneered by MYSA over the previous decade in the Mathare slums. As an indication of the priority MYSA attached to this new initiative, the MYSA Executive Council appointed a founding member of MYSA who was also a previous top striker for Mathare United FC and a former MYSA Director, 26-year old Peter Serry[8], who moved to the camp to launch and head the new programme.

By mid-2000, only 18 months later, there were over 12,000 youth playing on 940 basketball, football, netball and volleyball teams, including over 1,800 girls on 184 teams. Also included for the first time were sports activities in the primary and secondary schools in the camp as well as the neighbouring town of Kakuma and also for over 400 disabled youth who played volleyball, wheelchair basketball, table tennis, darts and other more sedentary games such as dominoes and chess.

Breaking ethnic barriers

The first major challenge and key aim of the new Kakuma sports programme was to break through the ethnic barriers which divided the camp and dominated the previous sports activities. Despite resistance by some elders in a few ethnic groups, that was achieved by dividing the camp into eight zones which cut across the different nationalities and ethnic areas plus Kakuma town as a ninth zone. Each zone had its own ethnically diverse Sports Council and also appointed ethnically diverse representatives to the overall Supreme Sports Council. The Technical Committees for each sport also consisted of representatives of the different ethnic groups. All teams in the under-16 years and older age categories had to be multi-ethnic but, for reasons of language and transportation, exceptions to this requirement were allowed for the under 14 and younger teams.

Breaking gender barriers

A second major challenge was to break through the gender barriers as there was initially a lot of cultural resistance to allowing girls to participate in sports activities, including objections to allowing girls to wear the usual playing uniforms for matches. Consequently, in some sports the girls wore

---

8. Among other later achievements, Peter studied at the Royal Netherlands Football Association (KNVB) Academy where he earned a UEFA-B coaching license, became a top instructor for the joint KNVB/MYSA sport and development courses in Africa and Asia, set up the Kenya Institute for Soccer Education (KISE), became the new CEO of Premier League club, Tusker FC, and in 2008 helped lead the hugely successful 2010 FIFA World Cup/African Cup of Nations campaign as the Team Manager of the Kenyan Harambee Stars national team. Tragically, Peter was among the over 30 Kenyans who died in the devastating fire in a large supermarket in downtown Nairobi in February 2009 and is greatly missed by his family and many friends in and outside MYSA and Kenya.

trousers rather than shorts.[9] But even the girls themselves did not believe they could play a traditional boys sport like football until a team of top MYSA girls football players were flown to the camp, formed mix teams of both MYSA and Kakuma camp girls and then played a special tournament together.

There was also some reluctance from some boys and parents even to allow girls in the sports programme committees. However, that was also a basic requirement from the outset of the new sports programme. For example, in the nine zones at least three of the eleven members of each Sports Council had to be girls. On the overall Supreme Sports Council, at least one girl also had to be included among the three representatives from each of the nine zones.[10]

Breaking the dependency syndrome

A third major challenge was breaking through the dependency syndrome which is easy to adopt when you have spent a decade or more of your life as a dependent refugee living in a camp in a foreign country. But the founding principle of MYSA was also applied from the beginning of the new sports programme: that "if you do something, then MYSA does something; but if you do nothing then MYSA does nothing". Like MYSA, the new Kakuma Sports Association and programme was not done for the youth but was done with and largely by the youth in the camp and nearby Kakuma town. In the new sports programme and structure there were only two paid coordinators in each of the nine zones. All except three of the paid staff were refugees. In addition there were over 600 volunteer youth leaders, coaches, trainers and referees who were all refugees from all the different countries and ethnic groups. During the first 18 months, those volunteers received special training in a series of over 20 workshops in the different sports and functions lasting 1-2 weeks each.

The first external evaluation in mid-2000 concluded that "a strong organizational structure for the sports programme has been established, people have been trained according to their tasks and functions in the system and decentralization of responsibilities and tasks did take place. An administrative system and computer database are in place to register information. Training of sports facilitators is on-going and has to continue as the programme is still expanding and the level of play is increasing."[11] In sum,

---

9. Kakuma Sports Programme Manager Peter Serry noted that "We've also succeeded in getting the girls involved in the programme. In the beginning we had problems because they couldn't be seen in certain clothing. And often the games began just at the moment they had to collect water. We've taken both things into account are more and more girls teams are now being set up.", Broere, Marc, 2001, 150.

10. Kessels, 2000, 18-19.

11. Ibid, 2000, 23.

within 18 months one of the major objectives had already been achieved as the new sports programme was largely owned, staffed, led and managed by the young refugees themselves.

Linking sport with community and environmental improvements

Another challenge in breaking the dependency syndrome was to implement another MYSA principle that "if you get something from the community than you must put something back into the community". As in the Mathare slums a decade earlier, that was achieved by linking all sports activities and teams to new community and environmental improvement projects in the camp and nearby Kakuma town.

Some of the new community service activities were directly linked to the sports programme (e.g. washing and repairing sports uniforms and equipment, clearing rubbish and bushes on and near sports fields, etc.). But more importantly, the community service included a new Youth for Environment Programme which, with the support of the German Technical Cooperation Programme (GTZ), focused on involving all teams in the creation of new "green belts" in the area, including the building of small dams to provide water for tree-planting projects in and around the camp, as well as the clearing of garbage throughout the camp and parts of the nearby town.[12]

Over 150 members of sports teams received special training for organizing and implementing the community service activities. Like in MYSA, the community service activities were fully integrated with the sports leagues. The community and environmental improvement activities were included in the same schedule as the match fixtures and all teams received extra points in the league standings for completing their community service projects.

Tackling social and health threats to youth

A fifth challenge, as in the Mathare slums, was to link the sports activities to social and health risks facing the young refugees and especially to new initiatives on reproductive health issues such as family planning plus AIDS awareness and prevention. Initially, over 30 supervisors and volunteers were trained as a core group of peer educators and leaders for the new information and awareness campaigns on these issues. The first group were all males but the training later extended to include female peer educators and leaders as well. The programme also included the distribution of free condoms.[13]

---

12. Ibid, 26-27.

13. Ibid, 27.

Integrating the disabled in the sports activities

A sixth challenge was to integrate youth with physical and mental disabilities into the sports activities as they had been neglected and largely ignored previously. New sports activities, facilities and equipment such as crutches and wheelchairs were included in the programme from the beginning.

For example, within 18 months over 400 disabled youth, including 51 females, participated in over 300 official matches in different sports every month in addition to their training sessions and friendly matches. To ensure their views and interests would continue to be respected; representatives of the disabled boys and girls were also added to the overall Supreme Sports Council.

The evaluation in mid-2000 concluded that "the sports programme is much appreciated by the disabled. They are excited about the fact that they are given the same opportunities as the non-disabled people. They regard sport as very important as it makes them focus on what they are still able to do and on improving this ability .... It changes the view of the disabled about themselves and by the outside world of the disabled. It makes them happy and proud."[14]

Sport, peace and reconciliation in the Kakuma refugee camp

In only 18 months, the new self-help youth sport and community development programme in the Kakuma refugee camp and town succeeded in breaking down barriers and prejudices between the different nationalities and ethnic groups, between boys and girls, between the disabled and non-disabled youth and between the refugees and Kenyan youth in the nearby town. An evaluation report in mid-2000 concluded that the new programme:

"played a role in changing the mentality of society members. According to many people, including the UNHCR head of sub-office, the community leaders and police officers, the project has a very positive influence on the Kakuma society, especially on the young people in the camp and in Kakuma town. Sport keeps the youth busy so they are less bored and have less time for wantonness ... It is obvious there are less tensions since the programme started. And if problems occur, they will be solved in a less violent way. People know each other from the sports field and, secondly, they have learned to respect each other and to solve problems other than by fighting ... as people are brought together and get familiar, there is more understanding for each other's problems."[15]

---

14. Ibid, 19-21.

15. Ibid, 31.

The evaluation also reported that the UNHCR head of the Kakuma refugee camp stated that he considers the programme:

> "as the most cost-effective project in the camp. With a relatively modest budget the impact is enormous in the sense that there is less violence and destruction, this less protection and restoration is needed. The programme makes people aware of their responsibilities and opportunities. The community service done by sports volunteers such as the cleaning of living areas and tree planting would otherwise be very costly or not done. There is also some income generating for the population as part of the sports materials are locally produced."[16]

A later and separate evaluation concluded that:

> "multi-tribal and multi-national teams are competing in the Kakuma Sports Association leagues. Before teams were competing on tribal and national lines. Sport has helped to reduce crowd and opponent violence during matches. It has provided a unifying forum. The Kakuma all-star team is also a multi-national team. The local Turkana Community and the refugees also now interact freely. The supreme Sports Council is multi-national with members elected from all the nationalities living in Kakuma .... The stepping up of sports activities in the camp has kept a lot of youths very active helping to reduce the tension in the camp. Given stable conditions, sports have gone a long way in promoting peace and harmony in the camp."[17]

The Kakuma sports programme also helped raise the self-esteem and confidence of many young refugees. For example, David Bai, a 23-year old Sudanese who had been a refugee half his life and had not seen his family since he was 8 years old, was the best volleyballer in the camp and was also a top leader, referee and coach for six volleyball teams and twelve football teams. David spoke for many when he said "I've become an important person in the camp. I notice that I am respected by everyone. If you have been a refugee for as long as I have and you're apart from your family, that respect is incredibly important."[18]

Peter Serry, the MYSA leader and overall head of the new Kakuma sport and community development programme, added one of the more compelling anecdotes on its immediate impact and early success: "The most important thing is that the tensions in the camp have lessened. People have something good to do since we set up these sporting activities. From four o'clock in the afternoon you hear match whistles going off across the camp. The atmosphere has become more lively and pleasant. The director of the camp recently said jokingly to me "If there's ever an uprising against the UN personnel, the sports development workers would be spared".[19]

The importance of sport in promoting peace and also helping achieve the Millennium Development Goals is highlighted in the 2003 report of the United Nations Inter-Agency Task Force of Sport for Development and

---

16. Ibid, 31-32.

17. Lindoe, 2001, 58.

18. Broere, 2001, 151.

19. Ibid, 150.

Peace. "The chief finding" of the Task Force was that "well-designed sport-based initiatives are practical and cost-effective tools to achieve objectives in development and peace". The Task Force then concluded and recommended that "sport is a powerful vehicle that should be increasingly considered by the United Nations as complementary to existing activities."[20] The validity of that conclusion and recommendation is certainly demonstrated and reinforced by the achievements of the Kakuma sport and community development programme as well as in many other similar projects since then in refugee camps and in post-civil war and even post-disaster situations around the world.[21]

Following the refugees home

Many of those who benefited and excelled in the sport and community development training programmes in the Kakuma camp were refugees from southern Sudan. As an extension of that programme in the camp, it was agreed that when they returned home, they would provide a nucleus and network of trained expertise for starting similar self-help youth sports and community development projects in southern Sudan. It was also agreed that MYSA would try to help them get the funding needed to start and expand such projects when they returned home.

In 2005, after the successful peace talks and signing of eight protocols earlier that year, MYSA started a pilot project in the town of Rumbek in southern Sudan which was then the administrative capital. Some of the key youth leaders involved in the Kakuma sport and development programme were from Rumbek and they as well as SPLM leaders wanted to test the MYSA approach in a pilot project which could then be adapted and expanded to other communities in southern Sudan. Another reason for focusing on Rumbek was that it was "at the centre of the Child Soldiers Demobilisation Programme in 2001 that saw over 3,000 children demobilized and placed in a child care centre in Rumbek for orientation and reintegration into civil society. The child soldiers underwent a programme aimed at reintegrating them into civil society through education, psycho-social support and vocational training".[22] Those youth were part of defending their communities in southern Sudan and deserved the chance to help re-build them. That project in Rumbek is still continuing.

---

20. Sport for Development and Peace: Toward Achieving the Millennium Development Goals, Report of the United Nations Inter-Agency Task Force of Sport for Development and Peace, August 2003, Executive Summary, v.

21. See the 2005 Swiss Agency for Development and Cooperation (SDC) report on "Sport for Peace and Development" and the 2006 United Nations report on "Sport for a Better World".

22. Sudan Transition and Recovery Database (STARBASE): Rumbek County, UN Office of the Resident and Humanitarian Coordinator for the Sudan, March 2004, 4.

Young peacemakers in the Mathare slums

The Mathare and neighbouring areas constitute one of the largest and poorest slums in Africa and are home for well over half a million people from different ethnic groups. From the outset in 1987, the MYSA leaders, committees, teams and staff have always been ethnically neutral and been composed of youth from all ethnic groups.

Today MYSA is likely the largest self-help youth sports and community development organization in the world. MYSA now has over 21,000 boys and girls actively participating in its over 120 leagues in 16 zones as well as its linked slum garbage/environmental clean-up, AIDS prevention, drama, music, dance, photography, jailed kids, slum libraries and study halls, leadership awards and other community service activities.

The MYSA leaders are elected by the youth from the zonal right up to the top decision-making body: the Executive Council. On the Executive Council, the average age of the elected member is 17 years old and the oldest member is 21 years old. Of the several hundred elected leaders and decision-makers in the 16 zonal committees and overall Sports, Community Service and Executive Councils, 49.3% are girls. That governance structure is the main reason why MYSA has been so successful over the last two decades. MYSA is really owned and run by the youth themselves and conforms to the classic democratic prescription for good governance "of the people, by the people and for the people[23]". But in the case of MYSA "the people" are the youth in the Mathare and neighbouring slums. During the first two decades of MYSA's existence, it was a source of comfort and pride that when there were periodic outbreaks of inter-ethnic violence in other slums and areas in the country, that inter-ethnic violence did not occur in the slum areas where MYSA was working. Sadly, that illusion of inter-ethnic harmony and peace in the Mathare slums was tragically shattered twice, first with the Mungiki vs. Taliban clashes in the Mathare slums in early November 2006 and again during the post-election violence which erupted throughout the country in January 2008.

(a) Mungiki vs. Taliban clashes in the Mathare slums

The first outbreak of violence was in early November 2006 and was initiated by two ethnically-based gangs, the Mungiki consisting of Kikuyus, and the Taliban consisting of Luos, who started fighting over territory and the right to collect protection and other fees from the poor families and small

---

23. "Bob Munro may have kicked off MYSA but much of the organization has long outgrown him. It now has hundreds of leaders, most of whom came up the ranks of MYSA, first as players on youth teams then on scholarships for helping to organize tournaments. It has just opened a brand new training centre for its teams on the edge of Mathare. It has offices, meetings halls, a video production studio, a weight room and fitness centre." Hill, Declan, 2008, p.309.

businesses in the Mathare slums.[24] As the inter-gang clashes escalated with serious injuries and deaths on both sides, Mungiki members were also accused of the gruesome murders of two policemen. In retaliation, the police flooded into the Mathare slums and killed 22 youths who allegedly were Mungiki members.[25] Two days later, another major police operation was carried out and 11 more allegedly Mungiki members were killed.[26] As the death toll and looting and burning of homes and small businesses escalated, that triggered an exodus of thousands from the Mathare slums consisting largely of innocent mothers and their children.[27] Some found refuge with family or friends in other slum areas. But several hundred of the poorest families had no option except to flee and camp on small pieces of open ground outside the nearby Chief's Camp and the Kenyan Air Force base near the MYSA Eastleigh Zone office. In most cases the displaced mothers and children only had the clothes they fled in and lacked shelter, blankets and food. As these were reported largely as local clashes between two rival gangs against each other and the police, the innocent women and children forced to camp in the few open spaces were largely ignored by the United Nations and other humanitarian aid agencies except for UN/Habitat which stepped in a few days later and provided financial support for the Mathare youth efforts.

Response of the MYSA leaders and youth

In one of my proudest moments in MYSA over the last two decades, the day after those women and children started camping near the MYSA Eastleigh Zone office, the MYSA Executive Council met, assessed the crisis situation and decided to take the funds allocated for celebrating MYSA's 20th Birthday the following month and instead use that money to provide tents, food, clothing and blankets for the displaced families. All other MYSA activities were also suspended so the over 60 MYSA staff members could focus entirely on helping the displaced and traumatized families. Over the next two weeks, MYSA worked in close cooperation with the staff of the Jamii Bora Trust, a major micro-finance organization which also had thousands of affected family members in the Mathare slums, were able to assist over 8,000 people, including 6,662 children. In addition to providing tents, food, cloth-

---

24. Kipkoech Tanui, "Gangs take over but officialdom isn't moved", Standard, November 10, 2006, p.12.

25. "Massacre in the slums", front page headline and feature in the Daily Nation, November 6, 2006.

26. "Eleven more killed in hunt for Mungiki", front page headline and feature in the Daily Nation, November 8, 2006.

27. "Thousands flee their homes as slum death toll goes up: Women and children spend night in the cold", front page headline and feature in the Daily Nation, November 9, 2006.

ing and blankets, the MYSA staff also organized special sports activities for the children, not only because the kids needed some healthy activities and distractions from their plight but also because their mothers needed to search for new housing and make other arrangements for their future.

Over the next few weeks the violence decreased, some semblance of law and order returned and the families gradually moved back into the slums. Normal MYSA activities also gradually resumed. However, the brilliant cartoonist for the Daily Nation, Gado, published an editorial cartoon with the caption "The situation in Mathare is back to normal". In his cartoon, some women are standing beside their shacks in the slums as one says "Yes, back to normal unemployment, poverty, diseases, hunger..."[28]

Was this truly an inter-ethnic clash in the Mathare slums?

Was this truly an inter-ethnic clash in the Mathare slums? One editorial commentator made the following observations:

> "As is usual in Kenya, the tribal card is used to explain all the catastrophes that beset this nation. Politicians and media analysts have consistently been blaming ethnic differences between the Mungiki - a quasi-religious sect comprising dispossessed youth from the Kikuyu tribe - and the Taliban, a self-styled vigilante gang made up mostly of youth from the Luo tribe - as one of the main reasons for the violence that erupted in Nairobi's Mathare slum last week. Even the New York Times claimed that: like so many of Africa's conflicts, this one has an ethnic dimension"

What most people seem to be forgetting is that: "when you are dirt poor, when you wonder if there will be food on the table tonight, or when you share a tiny 10x10 foot shack with your three siblings and your parents, tribe is the last thing on your mind."[29] In a concluding remark that foreshadowed the next outbreak of violence just over a year later, the commentator added that: "in such circumstances it is much easier for a cunning politician or a greedy businessman to make you believe your problems are a result of your genetic makeup or religion, not social injustice".[30]

What is clear in this first sad outbreak of violence in the Mathare slums in two decades is that it is the innocent and the poorest who suffer first, suffer the most and, as many lost their homes and few possessions, suffer the longest.[31] But the first and for nearly a week the only ones to respond were also the poorest who were the staff and members of MYSA and the Jamii Bora Trust. The good news is that a few key donors and many individuals,

---

28. Gado, editorial cartoon in the Daily Nation, November 11, 2006, p.8.

29. Rasna Warah, "Want and deprivation know no tribe", Daily Nation, November 14, 2006, p.9.

30. Ibid, 9.

31. The editorial cartoon was published in the Daily Nation on November 11, 2006.

especially friends of MYSA in Norway, donated additional funds so the MYSA youth were still able to celebrate their 20th Birthday in December 2006.

(b) Inter-ethnic post-election violence in early 2008

For the first few months of 2008, in Kenya the whole country was divided and convulsed by inter-ethnic conflict and violence after the disputed presidential elections in late December. Sadly, the Mathare slums were no exception. However, this time the international community and donor focused on the problems and responded from the outset to the shelter, food and other basic needs of the several hundred thousand internally displaced people (IDPs) countrywide, including hundreds of displaced families in the Mathare slums.

Response of the MYSA leaders and youth

As usual, it was the innocent and poorest who suffered first and most. In the TV clips and news photos of the marauding mobs, one stark reality was that they did not include women and children except as victims of the violence. In mid-January 2008 while widespread rioting and inter-ethnic clashes were still rampant, the ethnically diverse MYSA leaders and staff remained united and quietly started organizing regular friendly matches among the youngest kids who, by playing together on the same ethnically diverse teams, sent a clear message of tolerance to their older brothers and fathers. In addition, the MYSA leaders and staff interviewed the displaced mothers and kids in the IDP camps near the Mathare slums. As the international humanitarian agencies were already catering for their basic shelter, food and health needs, the next but unmet priority of the mothers was ... school shoes and uniforms which had been lost or destroyed during the riots. As their kids could not attend school without them, MYSA concentrated its limited funds on buying and distributing new school uniforms and shoes for over 200 boys and girls. MYSA also changed its sports programme plans for 2008 and reallocated its funds to support more inter-zonal friendly matches and sports events in order to promote greater MYSA-wide solidarity in support of peace and reconciliation.

Sport as part of the healing process for national unity

During the post-election period last year, sport also played a major role in reinforcing the healing process and national unity. In early May 2008 the Kenyan Ministry of Youth Affairs and Sport indicated that with the emergency reallocation of government funds to help the hundreds of thousands of displaced people in camps throughout the country, there were no funds for the upcoming campaign starting in late May of the national Harambee Stars for the initial series of qualifying matches for the 2010 FIFA World

Cup and African Cup of Nations. Soon afterwards, officials of the Kenya Football Federation (KFF) also announced they lacked the funds needed to support the national team.

In one of my proudest moments in Kenyan football, I chaired a meeting on May 10th of the 16 Kenyan Premier League clubs who, after only a few minutes of discussion, unanimously agreed that our country needed the national team to play those matches as part of the national healing process. The clubs then also decided unanimously to risk the grants needed to ensure their own financial survival later that year and instead use those funds to finance the national team. At the start of that campaign, Kenya was ranked 120th in the world. Within a few months, the whole nation was excited as the Harambee Stars kept winning points against higher ranked national teams such as Guinea and Zimbabwe. Kenya then rose a remarkable 52 places in the FIFA World Ranking, achieved the highest ranking worldwide in Kenyan football history (68th) and qualified for the final round for the 2010 FIFA World Cup and African Cup of Nations.

That national Harambee Stars team included 11 former or existing MYSA/Mathare United players. The national coach, Francis Kimanzi, and the national Team Manager, Peter Serry, were both former top players, leaders, coaches and even overall managers of MYSA.

Lessons learned

What were some of the lessons learned in these two case studies, especially regarding youth and sport for peace and reconciliation? The lessons confirmed or learned include:

1. That sport provides healthy challenges and lessons for kids which help them cope better with life, even in the tough social, psychological and physical conditions in slums and refugee camps;

2. That sport helps keep kids away from drugs and out of trouble and helps them learn lessons in self-discipline, teamwork and respect for rules which then helps stay them out of trouble;[32]

3. That kids are not born with the ethnic, religious, cultural or other prejudices of their parents;

4. That kids playing together, especially in team sports, are largely blind to the ethnic and other prejudices of their parents;

---

32. For example, Mathare Senior Chief Charles Nyambisa stated that "as a result of MYSA's activities, crime in Mathare reduced tremendously". Chief Nyambisa noted that it also changed the attitudes of those in and outside the slums: "Mathare people and Kenyans now have a changes attitude and belief concerning slums where the majority believed nothing good can come out of Mathare and other slums in the city. This myth has been changed.", Lindoe, Preben, 2001, p. 97.

5. That when their kids are playing on the same team, the ethnic and other differences which divide their older siblings and parents become more difficult to sustain and they are less inclined to hate the relatives of the teammates passing the ball to their own kids;

6. That sport provides kids with new and often better role models in the community;

7. That in times of conflict, kids can themselves become the examples and role models in helping reduce ethnic tensions and communal violence;

8. That in times of peace, the participation of kids in team sports is a significant factor in helping maintain peace and prevent new ethnic tensions and communal violence;

9. That the laws of the game, like the rule of law in society, help promote fair play, justice and peace on and off the field when applied to all equally.[33]

To conclude with a bold statement based on these two case studies on the young peacemakers in the Kakuma refugee camp and Mathare slums as well as similar examples highlighted in United Nations and other reports over the last decade[34], no other social activity has the same potential and power as ethnically-diverse team sports for kids in reducing ethnic prejudices and tensions, promoting reconciliation and maintaining peace.

After playing with your neighbours on the field, it simply becomes harder for kids to develop or sustain ethnic and other prejudices off the field. It also becomes harder for their parents to sustain their ethnic and other prejudices off the field after cheering their own kids and their ethnically diverse teammates and friends on the field.

---

33. For example, see Henley, Robert, 2005, page 22: "Don't change the rules! She [a project field worker] felt this was true as a general statement in using sport with people trying to overcome disaster trauma but found this was specifically important in her work with street children. She found the street kids [in the Ivory Coast] to be eager for structure and predictability in their lives and that the commonly understood rules in football were of particular benefit, readily accepted as a structure and never challenged."

34. Ibid, page 21: "People are now starting to return to their villages [in the Ivory Coast] but there is great suspicion and fear due to past widespread violence, often between neighbours, along with much theft and destruction of property ... [The researcher] found sports to be a particularly important and useful tool because it gives people from different ethnic backgrounds a reason to gather and meet, as sports provides a safe and neutral ground to participate together. For other examples, see the 2005 Swiss Agency for Development and Cooperation (SDC) report on "Sport for Peace and Development" and the 2006 United Nations report on "Sport for a Better World".

References

Broere, Marc and Houwen, Pieter van der, (2001). Unlikely Heroes: The Dynamics of African Sports, Amsterdam, Netherlands: BV Uitgeverij De Arbeiderspers.

Henley, R. (2005). Helping Children Overcome Disaster Trauma through Post-Emergency Psycho-social Sports Programs, Biel, Switzerland: Swiss Academy for Development (SAD).

Hill, D. (2008). The Salvation of Soccer, Epilogue in The Fix: Soccer and Organized Crime, Toronto, Canada: McClelland & Stewart Ltd, pp. 302-314.

IOC/UNEP (2005). Report of the 6th World Conference on Sport and Environment on the theme "Sport, Peace and Environment" held on November 9-11, 2005 in Nairobi, Kenya sponsored by the International Olympic Committee (IOC) and the United Nations Environment Programme (UNEP).

Kessels, P. (2000). Mid-Term Review of the Kakuma Sports Development Project: Report for the Netherlands National Olympic Committee/National Sports Confederation, The Hague, Netherlands: NOC-NSF.

Lindoe, P. (2001). Making Dreams Come True: Sport and Community Development in the Mathare Valley Slums, Oslo, Norway: Forfatterne og Compendius Forlag.

MYSA, (1999). Report on the Mathare girls programme at the Kakuma Refugee Camp in December 1999, Nairobi, Kenya: Mathare Youth Sports Association (MYSA).

Nyabuga, G. (2000). "Kakuma a conundrum: They are all running away from a civil war", East African Standard, June 19, 2000.

Osewe, G. (2003). Strengthening Local Community Structures through Sports: The Kakuma Sports Development Project, Report to the International Sports Experts Conference held on November 11-15, 2003 in Amsterdam, Netherlands.

Saronge, J. (2000). "The day hell descended on a refugee camp", East African Standard, June 19, 2000.

SDC (2005). Sport for Peace and Development, Zurich, Switzerland: Swiss Agency for Development and Cooperation.

United Nations (2003). Sport for Peace and Development: Toward Achieving the Millennium Development Goals, Report of the United Nations Inter-Agency Task Force on Sport for Development and Peace, New York, USA: United Nations.

United Nations (2006). Sport for a Better World: Report of the International Year of Sport and Physical Education, New York, USA: United Nations.

Chapter 7
Building Community Capacity through Sport, Development and Peace programmes

Glenn Laverack

Introduction

This chapter discusses the key characteristics of community capacity and a well developed 'tool' that can be used to build and measure this concept as a key component of sport, development and peace (SDP) programmes.

In recent years there has been considerable interest in physical activities and sports as interventionist approaches to promote health, peace, reconciliation and sustainable development (Giulianotti, 2010). Agencies such as the United Nations, international sport federations, Non-Governmental Organizations and government bodies have engaged in such programmes. The purpose of these programmes, beyond promoting physical activity, have included attempts to resolve differences between religious groups (Sugden, 1991), between different cultural groups (Barrio and Ley, 2011) and for the personal empowerment of people with disabilities and of women (Collins, 2002). Sport alone cannot prevent poverty, reduce conflict or empower others, but it can be a catalyst for mobilisation and capacity building towards people gaining more control over their lives. Examples of how sport has strengthened civil society in this way include facilitating youth groups to engage in public action in Brazil (Butler and Princeswal, 2010) and sports clubs in Finland (Kokko, Kannas and Villberg, 2006) and Australia (Dobbinson, Hayman and Livingstone, 2006) to promote a healthy environment. An example of a programme that has successfully combined physical activity and capacity building is the Saskatoon 'In Motion' Initiative in Canada.

The Saskatoon 'In Motion' Initiative

The Saskatoon 'In Motion' Initiative was a 5 year project designed to unite the strengths of public, private, academic and industry efforts into a collaborative alliance to inspire the residents of Saskatoon, Canada to lead physically active lives. The capacity building element involved other community-wide changes and outcomes as a result of the implementation of the initiative. The nine 'capacity domains' (discussed later in this chapter) were used as indicators for the measurement of community capacity. The partners of the alliance maintained a commitment to the initiative for over five years and new stakeholders in the community were engaged. Resources were mobilized and communication with the community was strong. Leadership continued to be developed and sustainable organizational structures were formed. Other spin-offs in community processes as a result of the initiative included the planning for a new neighbourhood and the establishment of a primary health care site both giving consideration to physical activity needs. The initiative also demonstrated a positive impact on physical activity. In Saskatoon 57% people surveyed said that they had seen, heard or read about the 'in motion' programme. 18% said that the 'in motion' messages had led to them definitely thinking more about physical activity and 30% said they had become more active (Bell-Woodard et al, 2005).

Interpreting Community Capacity

It is important to think beyond the customary view of a community as a place where people live, for example, a neighbourhood, because these are often just an aggregate of non-connected people. Communities have both a social and a geographic characteristic. In practice, geographic communities consist of heterogeneous individuals with dynamic social relations who may organize into groups to take action towards achieving shared goals or pursuing shared interests. Within the geographic dimension of a 'community', multiple other communities can exist as interest groups. Individuals may belong to several different interest groups at the same time. Interest groups include social and sport clubs or else are formed to address a local concern, such as a local action group focussed on gaining better access to public recreational facilities. People who participate in, for example, sports clubs, are termed as forming a 'community of interest' and these can be an integral part of an SDP programme as part of its target group or intended beneficiaries.

There is a broad body of literature in regard to the definition of community capacity, for example, Labonte and Laverack (2001a, p. 114) define capacity building as the 'increase in community groups' abilities to define, assess, analyze and act on concerns of importance to their members'. Community groups in this context can be communities of interest or the community that is created by a Sport Development and Peace (Hereafter SDP) program (referred to as the 'community'). The community includes the intended beneficiaries (many of whom will be part of communities of interest involved in sport) and other stakeholders during its implementation such as non-government and government bodies and funding agencies. Community capacity is also seen by several authors (Goodman et al, 1998; Bopp et al, 1999) as a process that increases the assets and attributes that a community is able to draw upon. Community capacity is not an inherent property of a particular locality, or of the individuals or groups within it, but of the interactions between both. The task for agencies promoting SDP is not to create a new programme called 'capacity-building'. Rather, the task is to examine how it can support the development of capacity-building as a process by which the end result is achieved through increasing the knowledge, skills and competencies of the community involved in the programme.

The 'Domains' of Community Capacity

The process of community capacity is influenced by several 'domains' that significantly contribute to its development. The capacity domains provide a useful means to build and measure this concept (Labonte and Laverack, 2001b). They represent those aspects that allow people to better organise and mobilize itself, are robust and collectively capture the essential qualities of a capable community. Community capacity is built such that the SDP programme:

1. Improves participation;
2. Develops local leadership;
3. Builds organisational structures;
4. Increases problem assessment capacities;
5. Enhances the ability of the community to 'ask why';
6. Improves resource mobilization;
7. Strengthens links to other organisations and people;
8. Creates an equitable relationship with the agency;
9. Increases stakeholder control over programme management.

The following is a brief description of the capacity domains including some examples to illustrate their relevance in SDP programmes:

Improves participation

Participation describes the involvement of individuals in the SDP programme and who are able to influence its direction through their participation. This can be based on representation as it is not usually possible for all members to be actively involved. It is necessary to carefully consider who the legitimate representatives of a community are. Those individuals who have the energy, time and motivation to become involved in programme activities may, in fact, not be supported by other community members and may be considered as acting out of self-interest. In these circumstances, a dominant minority may dictate the community needs unless adequate actions are taken to involve everyone. The example of a programme that benefited from participation is the Safer Parks Scheme in New Zealand.

The Safer Parks Scheme in New Zealand

The Christchurch Council following many complaints about crime in municipal parks preventing patronage by the public. These open areas provided facilities for people to do exercise such as walking, jogging and cycling but were not being used because of the fear of attack. The Safer Parks Scheme invested in employing more park wardens and honorary rangers to patrol the areas, installing cycle ways and play equipment for children to make access easier. The Scheme encouraged public participation through its 'adopt a park' initiative and volunteers helped to raise sponsorship money, to provide preservation and protection work and to report any problems that they encountered in the parks. As a result park patronage and physical activity increased (Gee, 2008).

Develops local leadership

Without a formal leader who takes responsibility for getting things done, deals with conflict and provides a direction, the community can become disorganised. Participation and leadership are therefore closely connected because just as leaders require a strong participant base, participation requires the direction and structure of strong leadership (Goodman et al., 1998). In a SDP programme the leaders may be employed as external organizers such as programme managers, because they are seen to have the necessary expertise. Such leaders can play an important role at the beginning of the programme. However, local leaders, such as volunteer coaches, team leaders and youth workers, are often selected by the members of the community for historical or social reasons. If the agency ignores this selection it can have an adverse effect on the outcome of the programme. Equally, an agency may decide to use a model of promoting the vision and personal leadership of one local charismatic individual. This local leader may be effective but this keeps the potential leadership small and leaves the community vulnerable. Once such charismatic leaders have gone, the vision is not shared by the other members because the programme tends not to address their needs and consequently impetus is lost. Mechanisms must exist to ensure leadership continuity and this can be best achieved through the programme by building the skills necessary for effective management and leadership within the community. This includes skills training in problem assessment, conducting effective group meetings, fund raising, and budgeting, and human resource management and evaluation techniques.

Builds organizational structures

Organizational structures include committees, sports clubs and associations. These are the organizational elements which represent the ways in which the community members come together in order to share their interests and to address their concerns. They are also the way in which people come together to interact and to connect, for example, to organise sporting events. In a SDP programme, it can also be the way in which people come together to identify and to achieve the objectives of the programme. The characteristics of a functional organisation have been found to include a membership of elected representatives that meet and participate on a regular basis. The members have an agreed membership structure (chairperson, secretary, core members and so on) that keeps records such as previous meetings and financial accounts. A functional organisation is also able to identify and resolve conflict quickly and its members are able to identify the resources available to them to achieve their goals (Jones and Laverack, 2003).

Increases problem assessment capacities

Problem assessment involves the identification of problems, solutions to the problems and actions to resolve the problems. The success of a SDP programme depends to a great extent on the commitment and involvement of the community. People are more likely to be committed if they have a sense of ownership in regard to the problems and solutions being addressed by the programme. This means that the problems being addressed need to be identified by the community concerned rather than by an agency promoting SDP. The point is that the services available through the agency should not be imposed over the expressed needs and concerns that reside amongst community. The best approach is to use a 'facilitated dialogue' between the community and the agency to allow the priorities of both to decide an appropriate direction for the programme (Laverack, 2004). An example of community engagement by a programme to find the most appropriate solution to local sports needs is the Asian Women's swimming Project in England.

The Asian Women's swimming project

The Asian Health Forum in Liverpool, England identified a large number of cases of depression and isolation amongst Asian women in their area. Discussions with Asian women to identify their needs for sport resulted in a request to approach a local leisure centre about the possibility of arranging swimming lessons solely for Asian women. This would ensure privacy, for example, windows would be blacked out and the swimming lessons run by a woman. The leisure centre was able to organise weekly lessons and to secure funding for a female instructor. The lessons were very popular and continued throughout the summer with about 20 women per session. Slowly the interests of the Asian women moved to other sports activities and they requested that the leisure centre make available other physical activity choices to Asian women (Jones and Sidell, 1997) such as yoga and aerobics classes.

Enhances the ability of the community to 'Ask Why'

Generally, sports groups focus inwards on the needs of their members. But, as they develop into broader organisations they must be able to look outwards to the environment that creates those needs in the first place (Goodman et al. 1998). Fundamentally, 'asking why' is a process of discussion, critical reflection and collective action. The key term here is 'critical' where the community takes a long, hard and analytical look at its situation. It is also the ability of the community to develop strategies to bring about personal, social and political change based on an understanding of their own circumstances. This is achieved through group dialogue to share ideas and experiences and to promote critical thinking by posing problems to allow people to uncover the root causes of inequality and powerlessness. Once they are critically aware, the community can then begin to plan actions to change the circumstances that influence their lives (Freire, 1973). An example of a programme that used sport with youth groups to promote critical thinking and public action in Brazil.

The engagement of youth in the public sphere through sport

In Brazil, community organizations, cultural groups and social movements have used sports teams to promote participation in youth groups. The purpose was to increase the critical awareness of youth about their day-to-day role in public action and political engagement. This is based on the work of educationalist Paulo Freire whose concept of 'critical consciousness' used education and reflective thinking to increase peoples awareness of the underlying causes of their poverty and powerlessness. Tools for critical consciousness use information and communication and visual prompts such as photographs. This type of an approach is used in discussion groups created by, for example, youth when they come together to pursue their interests in sport, as a means to systematically raise awareness (Butler and Princeswal, 2010) about a particular issue such as the role in public action.

Improves resource mobilization

The ability of the community to mobilize resources from within and to negotiate resources from beyond itself is an indication of a high degree of skill and organization. Resources that the community might be expected to mobilize include voluntary employment, materials, local knowledge, land and infrastructure, as well as some financial contributions. The community can use a variety of ways to mobilise resources such as sponsored walks, runs and swims, subscription to sports clubs, social fund raising events such as events such as fetes and public auctions of crafts and personal items.

Strengthens links to other organizations and people

Links with other people and organizations include partnerships, coalitions and alliances. These relationships demonstrate the ability to network, collaborate, co-operate and to develop relationships that promote a heightened inter-dependency amongst its members. They may involve an exchange of services or the pursuit of a joint venture based on a shared goal. Partnerships, coalitions and alliances have become a popular theme but it is implicit that the process is fully participatory and that the SDP agency does not merely consult with the community. People should be involved in the decision making processes of the SDP programme from planning through implementation and evaluation. The example of an alliance that used sport with ethnic minority groups in England to resolve conflict is provided below.

The 'Aik Saath Project'

The 'Aik Saath Project' was started to address inter-ethnic tension and outbreaks of conflict between the Sikh and Muslim youth in Slough, UK. The programme created an alliance between a non government agency, the government and the youth. The role of locally recruited and trained facilitators in conflict resolution played a major role in reducing tensions, such as the number of playground fights between Sikhs and Muslims, and in building a working relationship with street gangs. The Project also used local conflict resolution groups and activities such as sport in schools to identify and address the key issues causing the tensions. Sport provided a controlled venue in which the different groups could interact. The approach provided an important entry point into the school and into the issues facing youth on inter-ethnic conflict (renewal.net, 2008).

Creates an equitable relationship with the agency

Outside agencies that run SDP programmes have an important role to link the community to resources or to assist them to mobilize and organise themselves. This can be especially important at the beginning of a programme when the capacity of the community is low and the role of the agency is essentially one of developing the knowledge, skills and competencies of the community, for example training in conflict management (Laverack, 2004). Agencies that have been involved in developing SDP programmes include Right To Play, United Nations Inter-Agency Task Force on Sport for Development and Peace, Sport for Development and Peace International Working Group and Saskatoon-in-motion Community Alliances for Health Research.

Increases stakeholder control over programme management

At the heart of management is who controls the way in which the SDP programme is designed, implemented, managed and evaluated. As programme management becomes more sophisticated the agency is less willing to transfer responsibility and skills to the community which is perceived as having poor capacity. To build capacity, the community must first have a sense of ownership of the programme and the agency should increasingly transfer responsibility as a systematic part of the design (Laverack, 2007). In practice, the SDP programme is conventionally managed and monitored by an agency and commonly includes a period of identification, design, implementation, management and evaluation. The basic question planners and practitioners need to ask themselves is: How has the programme also helped to increase community capacity in each of the nine 'domains'?

Next a participatory tool (referred to as 'the tool') that uses the nine 'capacity domains' to build community capacity in a programme context is discussed.

Building and Measuring Community Capacity

The tool is used to strengthen the capacity of communities of interest involved in the SDP programme. It is delivered as a workshop and the participants are members of the community and other key stakeholders. Participants are usually selected by the community as their representatives and in this way the representatives from more than one community of interest can be included in the workshop (Laverack, 2004).

How is the 'tool' implemented?

The tool is implemented in three phases as a part of the programme:

1. Preparation (1-2 days);
2. Measurement of each domain (1 day) and;
3. Developing a strategic plan for community capacity (1 day).

Phase 1 involves the use of simple qualitative techniques. Phases 2 and 3 are implemented as a participatory workshop. Figure 1 provides an overview of the design of the 'tool' for building and measuring community capacity.

Phase 1: Preparation

A period of observation and discussion is important to adapt the 'tool' to the social and cultural requirements of the participants in the programme. For example, the use of a working definition of community capacity can provide all participants with a more mutual understanding of the programme in which they are involved and toward which they are expected to contribute. The meaning of each domain can be discussed with the participants in the programme to ensure that they are understood.

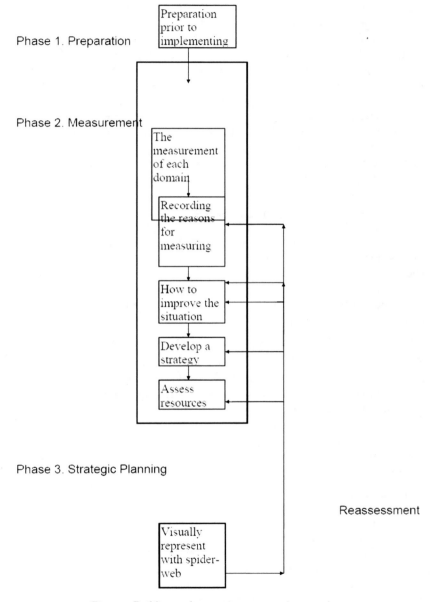

Figure 1: Building and measuring community capacity

Phase 2: A measurement of each domain

Using the nine domains (whose meaning can be altered if the context under phase 1 warrants this action), the participants of the workshop firstly make a measurement of the community's capacity. To do this, they are provided with five generic statements for each domain; each written on a separate sheet. The five statements represent a description of the various levels of capacity related to that domain (see Laverack, 2005, pgs. 99-101). Taking one domain at a time, the participants are asked to select the statement which most closely describes the present situation in their community. The statements are not numbered or marked in any way, and each is read out loud by the participants to encourage group discussion. The descriptions may be amended by the participants, or a new description may be provided to describe the situation for a particular domain. In this way, the participants make their own measurement for each domain by comparing their experiences and opinions.

Recording the reasons for the measurement

It is important that the participants record the reasons why the measurement for the domain has been made. First, it assists other people who make the re-measurement and who need to take the previous record into account. Second, it provides some defensible or empirically observable criteria for the selection. The 'reasons why' include verifiable examples of the actual experiences of the participants taken from their community.

Phase 3: Developing a strategic plan for community capacity

The measurement in Phase 2 is in itself insufficient to build capacity as this information must also be transformed into actions. This is achieved through strategic planning for positive changes in each of the nine 'domains'. The strategic planning for each domain consists of three simple steps: i) a discussion on how to improve the present situation; ii) the development of a strategy to improve upon the present situation and; iii) the identification of any necessary resources.

A discussion on how to improve the present situation

Following the measurement of each domain, the participants will be asked to decide as a group how this situation can be improved in their community. If more than one statement has been selected, the participants should consider how to improve each situation. The purpose is to identify the broader approaches that will improve the present situation and provide a lead into a more detailed strategy. If the participants decide that the present situation does not require any improvement, no strategy will be developed for that particular domain.

Developing a strategy to improve the present situation

The participants are next asked to consider how, in practice, the measurement can be improved. The participants develop a more detailed strategy based on the broader approaches that have already been identified by: Identifying specific activities; sequencing activities into the correct order to make an improvement; setting a realistic time frame including any significant benchmarks or targets; and Assigning individual responsibilities to complete each activity within the programme time frame.

Assessing the necessary resources

The participants assess the resources that are necessary and available to improve the present situation, for example, technical assistance, equipment, finance and training. This includes a review of locally available resources and any resources that can be provided by an agency.

The Visual Representation of Community Capacity

As discussed in Phase 2, a set of descriptors are identified for each domain and a rank assigned for each descriptor from 1 (low) to 5 (high). The assessment of each domain then provides a set of rankings which can be quantified and plotted, in this case, onto a spider web configuration. The visual representation can be used to make comparisons of the domains at different times in the programme. Figure 1 provides an example of a spider web that was used to visually represent community capacity over a six month period, from the first to the second measurement.

A plan of action, detailed in phase 3 of the 'tool', can then be more accurately determined by the community members on how to strengthen the weakest domains over a specific timeframe. The domains are re-assessed every six months and a strategic plan developed for the weakest domains. In this way the capacity of the community is gradually built and the assistance of the agency involved is clearly detailed in the strategic plan.

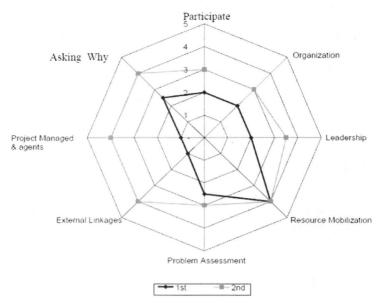

Figure 2: Measurement of community capacity

Conclusions

Building and measuring community capacity using the nine 'domains' offers a workable tool that is suitable for SDP programmes. The tool allows the community to scrutinise the achievements that it, often in partnership with an agency, has identified as being important. It also enables the community to measure programme effectiveness in terms of achieving capacity building and uses an innovative method of visual representation; the spider-web configuration. The approach enables people to participate, to better organise themselves and to critically reflect on their individual and collective circumstances. More importantly, it enables people to strategically plan for actions to resolve their problems, and to measure and visually represent this process as outcomes that demonstrate success in building community capacity.

References

Barrio, M. R., and C. Ley (2011) Interculturalism through physical activity and sports in cooperation for development. *Journal of Sport and Society*. Vol 1 (1): pp.271-284.

Bell-Woodard, G., Chad, K., Labonte, R., and L. Martin (2005). Community capacity assessment of an active living health promotion program - 'Saskatoon in Motion'. University of Saskatchewan (unpublished)

Bopp, M., Germann, K., Bopp, J., Littlejohns, L. B. and N. Smith (1999). Evaluating Community Capacity for Change. Calgary: Four Worlds Development.

Butler, U. M., and M. Princeswal (2010). Cultures of participation: young people's engagement in the public sphere in Brazil. *Community Development Journal*. Vol 45 (3): pp. 335-345.

Collins, L. H. (2002). Working out the contradictions. Feminism and aerobics. *Journal of Sport and Social Issues*. Vol 26 (1): pp.85-109.

Dobbinson, S. J., Hayman A. J. and P.M. Livingstone (2006). Health Promotion International. Vol 21 (2): pp.121-129.

Freire, P. (1973. Education for critical consciousness. New York: Seabury Press.

Gee, D. (2008). Park Scheme seeks more 'friends'. The Christchurch Press. Available at: www.bush.org.nz/library/934.html. (Accessed 12th March 2012).

Goodman, R., Speers, M., McLeroy, K., Fawcett, S., Kegler, M., Parker, E., Rathgeb Smith, S., Sterling, T., and N. Wallerstein (1998). Identifying and defining the dimensions of community capacity to provide a basis for measurement. *Health Education & Behaviour, 25, pp.*258-278.

Giulianotti, R. (2010). Sport, transnational peacemaking and global civil society: Exploring the reflective discourses of "sport, development and peace" project officals. *Journal of Sport and Social Issues*. Vol 35 (1): 50-71.

Jones, A. and G. Laverack (2003). 'Building Capable Communities within a Sustainable Livelihoods Approach: Experiences from Central Asia'. Available at: http://www.livelihoods.org/lessons/Central Asia & Eastern Europe/SLLPC. (Accessed 12th March 2012).

Jones, L. and M. Sidell (1997). (Eds). The Challenge of Promoting Health. Exploration and Action. London: MacMillan.

Kokko, S. Kannas, L. and J. Villberg (2006). The health promoting sports club in Finland-a challenge for the settings-based approach. Health Promotion International. Vol 21 (3): pp. 219-229.

Labonte, R. and G. Laverack (2001a). "Capacity Building in Health Promotion, Part 1: For Whom? And For What Purpose?" *Critical Public Health* 11(2): 111-128.

Labonte, R. and G. Laverack (2001b). "Capacity Building in Health Promotion, Part 2: Whose use? And with what measure?" *Critical Public Health* 11(2): 129-138.

Laverack, G. (2004). Health Promotion Practice: Power and Empowerment. London: Sage Publications.

Laverack, G. (2005). Public Health: Power, Empowerment & Professional Practice. London. Palgrave Macmillan.

Laverack, G. (2007). Health Promotion Practice: building empowered communities. London. Open University Press.

Renewal.net (2008). resolving differences-building communities and Aik
    Saath: Conflict resolution peer group facilitators. Renewal.net
    case studies. Available at : http://www.renewal.net/Documents/
    RNET/. (Accessed 12th March 2012)..

Sugden, J. P. (1991). Belfast united: Encouraging cross-community relations
    through sport in Northern Ireland. Journal of Sport and Social Is-
    sues. Vol 15 (1): 59-80.

Chapter 8
Networking for Sport and Peace

Marion Keim

Introduction

The objective for many initiatives of None Governments Organizations (NGOs) and Community Based Organizations (CBOs) donors, tertiary institutions and government departments in the field of youth development through sport in Africa is to promote lifelong engagement in sport and physical activity as it can lead to wellness, health and socio-economic advantaged, as recently outlined in the Millennium Development Goals. The challenge for many of these well-meant efforts and initiatives is very often meaningful collaboration and local sustainability. Difficulties comprise lack of stakeholders' participation and cooperation and, consequently, the implementation of planned initiatives. In addition, the role of governments in Africa in support of collaborative approaches to youth development and lifelong engagement in sport is underutilized and linkages between existing voluntary initiatives and policy development are lacking.

This chapter attempts to define the concept of collaboration and networking and to raise awareness for the importance of finding a better understanding of the multitude of possible partnerships in collaboration in the area of youth development through sport, be it with partners in the South or collaborations between southern and northern partners. Thirdly it draws on various theories and practical examples including a case study of a

South African network. These models look at challenges and fears but also successes of network partners hoping to create a better understanding on how effective collaboration can help overcome the challenges of good project implementation and thus raise the awareness for youth development through sport and subsequently ideally lifelong engagement in sport and physical activity

Theoretical Orientation

Collaborative approach - Good Practice Networks

Social networking has been playing a significant role in creating awareness and mobilizing support for different kinds of issues and programmes often initiated by civil society. What better way than to use this remarkable tool for life long engagement in sport and physical activity in Africa and globally?

Defining 'collaboration'

For the purposes of this chapter a collaborative approach is defined as a collectively guided independent network of two or more organizations sharing knowledge and learning and working together with common goals and values where all parties are equal. The terms 'collaboration' and 'partnerships' are used interchangeably in the following to refer to 'networks.'

Perceptions of Networks

According to a study of the Resource Development Foundation (RDF) conducted in 2006, organizations are involved in different profiles of networks: Formal and informal networks; multi-sectoral stakeholder networks; focus or issue-based networks; or campaign-based networks. Social networks and best practice networks can be added to this open list. I would, however, like to mention my concern about the use of the term of 'Best Practice Networks' as I think it is a bit presumptuous to claim that our networks are the best, and instead that I strongly believe in 'Good Practice' Networks. My view is that, if we present good practice networks which motivate others to join in or to start something similar then we have achieved a lot. Finding what works best is something that we must all constantly reach for - together.

We can increasingly see a global trend for collaborations and networking. United Nations Children's Fund in its Executive Board Annual Session 8th-10th June 2009 discussed as Item 5 of the provisional agenda* UNICEF strategic framework for partnerships and collaborative relationships and has prepared a report on UNICEF partnerships and collaborative relationships. An accompanying document (E/ICEF/2009/11) contains a mapping of the organization's current engagements with partners. The purpose of the UNICEF strategic framework for partnerships and collaborative relationships is to outline the future approach of UNICEF in a consistent and strategic way and to ensure that partnerships and collaborative relationships contribute to the best results for children and promote their rights. The framework also analyses the organization's current engagements, aiming to foster a common institutional understanding of what partnerships and collaborative relationships are, which modalities they can take, how they contribute to positive outcomes for children, and how UNICEF responds to the opportunities and challenges they present[1]. Similarly UNESCO *has shown* a growing interest in the *role* that *social* networks could *play* in poverty reduction and other social issues. In its latest Report on Poverty Reduction and Social Capital, 'Which Role for the Civil Society Organizations and the State?'. Michael Woolcock discussed the multi-dimensionality of social relationships. According to Woolcock the different existing types and combinations spans the neighborliness of primary groups (bonding), to business and social contacts through secondary groups (bridging), to the formation and participation in formal organizations (linking).[2]

Network Theories

Various theories look at networking in a social context. One of the social theories relating to collaboration and peacebuilding is Lederach's web-approach where he encourages strategic networking or 'web-making' as he calls it as an important intervention for building relationships in the civil society sector. NGO's and CBO's are ideally located to weave dialogue, exchange ideas, resources and knowledge and create a web of sustainable relationships: (Lederach, 2005 : p. 83).

Network theory per se provides the theoretical framework as well as the methodological approach that assist to examine the nature of relationships. Initially, network theory was developed in Northern Europe as a framework of ideas around a focus of business to business relationships. Only recently has the application of network theory been extended to new domains one of which being sport as it is seen as a global phenomenon with major commercial potential.

Network theory and its application to sport

According to Wolfe et al (2002): "No research study, to date, has sought to examine the evolving relationship patterns in the sports network or the phenomenon of power in the relationships between the actors". The authors argue that their research showed that the network approach can provide insights as a well a strategic map for organizations to help them cope with challenges in the sport environment, and that sport has "a pervasive presen-

---

1.See (http://www.unicef.org/corporate_partners/files/N0928210(1).pdf)

2.See (www.unesco.org/most/soc_cap_symp.pdf).

ce in contemporary social reality in both the developing and developed world..." (ibid: p. 612). The authors further believe that, "the network perspective can bring significant insights in the management of sport today."[3]

Agostini (1995: p.60) stated, with regards to relationships, that "sport is a social institution in which a number of actors and groups interact in its shifting daily constitution". The development of relationships instils commitment to a network, and this should ensure that sports bodies, sponsors and media are better positioned for strategic development. Recently a common ground has developed, moved by common drivers who see major benefits in collaborative approaches and are aware that the success, growth and positive development of each of the collaborating actors is dependent on the relationship between them. International initiatives, such as those by the Swiss Academy for Development (SAD) or the International Council of Sport Science and Physical Education (ICSSPE) which highlight the importance of international collaboration promote the exchange of information and *interdisciplinary* research in the field, facilitate organizations to build partnerships and promote networking in various cultural and educational contexts.

In 2009 the Beyond Sport Initiative started with its first summit in July in London with the aim of bringing together international projects, young people, political leaders, private sector actors, social entrepreneurs, sports industrialists and global media representatives to discuss the power of sport to change people's lives. Subsequently both the new networking sites Beyond Sport and Beyond Sport World were launched to create a network of change agents in sport and facilitate their interaction and exchange.

More regionally, Care International recently introduced a network approach within its initiative Sport for Social Change in East Africa, an initiative which believes in the power of sport to create lasting individual and social change. A local model of a coordinated approach of a multi-stakeholder collaboration has been in existence in South Africa since 2005: The Western Cape Network for Community Peace and Development presently has 40 member organizations in its Sport for Peace Programme. This community sport programme, of which Archbishop Emeritus Tutu is the patron, won the 2010 International Beyond Sport Award in Chicago for best project in the category Conflict Resolution and Sport with its Kicking for Peace Project.

Case Study: Western Cape Network for Community Peace and Development

The Western Cape Network for Community Peace and Development is a unique model of a coordinated approach of a multi-stakeholder collaboration, consisting of government, tertiary institution and civil society using sport as a tool for peace building and youth development with its Sport

---

3.Ibid.

for Peace Youth Programme. The Sport for Peace Programme is a success-ful grassroots youth sport cooperation of multiple partners from civil so-ciety, government and tertiary institutions engaging with local communit-ies. Kicking for Peace, one of the Sport for Peace projects is using soccer as a tool for social transformation, peace-building and development in 13 local communities. A focus of Sport for Peace is to use sport as a tools to teach life skills (conflict transformation, communication, problem solving and leadership among others) to the youth, their parents and other commu-nity members and to promote the livelong engagement in sport as a vehicle for health and well-being. The further objective of Sport for Peace is to build new confidence, respect and trust among youth and adults using sport as a vehicle. Operating the project through a broad-ranging, multicultur-al network is the best way to achieve that objective. One of the criteria for its success in Chicago in 2010 was, according to the judges, that it is a local community development initiative which is successful thought vari-ous stakeholders in society (civil society, government and a tertiary insti-tution) working collaboratively with the aim to build more peaceful com-munities and thus to contribute to social transformation, integration and social change.

A survey on the challenges and benefits of collaborative approaches was conducted in 2009 and 2010 with, as it was then, all 35 Network members organizations at the University of the Western Cape, South Africa, taking into consideration the beginnings and development of the Network since 2005. In the following the Network will serve as a case study to highlight challenges, fears, differences and successes of networking as well as import-ant lessons learnt.

Challenges

Many factors challenge organizations to collaborate effectively and to im-plement good projects that promote lifelong sport and physical activities among youth. Difficulties include, the lack of stakeholders' participation and cooperation and, consequently, the under implementation of planned initiatives. It is also worth considering the fact that governments in Africa are under used in terms of supporting collaborative approaches to youth and sport development, and that linkages between existing voluntary initi-atives around lifelong engagement in sport and policy development are lack-ing. Collaborative processes are dependent on the participation and cooper-ation of different organizations or individuals based on the principle that ef-fective action for a specific purpose brings together a range of stakeholders "for certain reasons". (RDF 2006). The main challenge for many of the well-meant efforts and initiatives of NGOs, CBOs, donors, tertiary institutions and government departments in the field of sport and youth development is very often forging meaningful collaboration and sustainability locally.

Challenges for a collaborative approach

The following table outlines the challenges that member organizations of the Western Cape Network for Community Peace and Development have identified in the process of starting and developing the Network (a process from 2005-2010) as a collaborative approach:

Differences and Diversities:	Different understanding of and approaches to development, community development, youth development and sport development (South-South and North-South)
	Different visions of different partners
	Different languages (content and speech North- South)
	Different organizational and leadership styles
	Different cultural, socio-economic backgrounds
	Different expectations. What do we want to get out of the network? What are we prepared to put into the network?
Fears	Fear of "the other"
	Fear of sharing
	Fear of jeopardizing funding, loosing donors
	Fear of new organizations challenging long existing ones with similar aims and objectives
Deficiencies	Lack clarity about own aims and objectives
	Lack of clarity about own strength and weaknesses
	Lack of clarity of aims and objectives of network partner organizations
	Lack of resources of beneficiaries and some partner organizations
	Lack of access to resources by beneficiaries
	Lack of trust
	Lack of network experience
	Lack of communication skills
	Lack of conflict resolution and mediation skills
	Lack of recognition of the historical and present injustices against women and girls
	Lack of knowledge of effective monitoring and evaluation tools, impact assessment and performance indicators
	Lack of clarity regarding concepts of development, community development, youth development, sports development, sustainability (be on the same page)*
External setting	Volatile communities (crime, especially rape and murders gangsters, drugs, alcohol)
	Discrimination of women and girls which still manifests itself in terms of structural and infrastructural barriers which prevent women and girls from equal opportunities in sport
	Political arena: Local government vs national government
	NGO- State: How do we work with government? How does government work with us?

*Quite a big challenge regarded the lack of clarity of the respective concepts and of different understandings of development, community development, youth development, grassroots, and sustainability within organizations with functioning North-South partnerships. It was found that there is some disparity between the North and the South understanding of concepts. It is therefore important to create better appreciation around this issue. According to Galtung we sometimes find a situation where counties from the North are "producing scientific reports on the development situation of any non-western country." However, the Northern concept of and approach to development, and youth development, grassroots approaches at times differ with local African ways and desires. Galtung warns of the large challenges that foreign development assistance can bring to local grassroots initiatives. Foreign assistance according to Galtung can bring "resources to the recipients, setting off competition, even fights for a slice of the pie, making the winners corrupt and the losers lazy victims of the degradation of their own culture." (Galtung. 1996:134)

Through the formation, joint work and continuous exchange of the Network we continuously try to counter these kinds of challenges through **LDDI**: Locally Developed and Driven Initiative(s).

Steps taken by the Network to address the challenges

Building a foundation of trust

To build a foundation of trust, the members needed to identify and clarify common values which would provide a platform for the Network to work from (including the definitions and concepts of sport and youth development and sustainability). Today all Network members share common values and recognize them as binding principles. They include empowerment, youth development, peace building, conflict management, democracy, sustainable development, human dignity, diversity, integrity, transparency, accountability and non-discrimination. The Network feels that these common values help to create conflict free and sustainable communities.

Active efforts were made to get to know one another by attending regular meetings every six weeks and regular subcommittee meetings and by taking turn in terms of meeting venues so that all members have the chance to see the venues and organization of the other members and find out more at site about the challenges and strength and learn about the different programs of different network partners.

Democratic process

The Network worked for one year jointly on a constitution which was acceptable for all. It includes the values of the network and clarification of legal and membership requirements. From the start a democratic process is followed for instance regarding the application and selection procedure of new members interested in joining the network and on clarifying their motivation for joining the Network. Democratic process is also followed regarding the continuous reflection and assessment of past and present initiatives and outcomes and regarding operational and strategic planning.

Regular joint activities

Joint activities as a Network or as partners within the Network have been proven highly effective. Various organizations now train each other and share their skills and knowledge. For the first time NGOs and a university worked together to develop course material and offer accredited training courses to NGOs and CBOs including youth groups and parents. The accredited joint training initiatives are run by the Network and with the University of the Western Cape as a partner (see below). Further joint activities include shared calls for funding and developing a joint network strategy including marketing materials).

Working with Academia

The University of the Western Cape (UWC) was one of the founder members of the Network in 2005. UWC is an engaged university with a rich sporting tradition and a strong focus on sport and development. Outreach, capacity building and community engagement through sport form a big part of UWC's role as an engaged university for the communities it serves. The establishment of the Interdisciplinary Centre of Excellence for Sports Science and Development at the university in 2009 is a response to a need in South Africa, Africa and beyond and has the potential to have a much bigger impact in this crucial area nationally and on the continent and globally. ICESSD's vision is to become Africa's leading interdisciplinary centre of excellence promoting sport as a powerful tool for development, health, wellbeing and social change through high quality research and combining the areas of sports and health sciences and community development and wellness.

Over the years there has been a vital exchange between UWC/ICESSD and the Network which resulted in joint organisation of annual international and African conferences to address crucial issues such as for example xenophobia, leadership, healing, sport and social transformation with various stakeholders from civil society, government and academia. Examples of such exchanges hosted by UWC/ICESSD were: the International Nelson Mandela Seminar on the Role of Universities in Conflict Transformation, Reconstruction and Peace Building in Africa, University of the Western Cape in 2005, (Keim, 2007); the African Conference on Leadership, Social Transformation and Healing in cooperation with the Nelson Mandela Foundation, UPEACE Africa Programme, Western Cape Network for Community, Peace and Development, UWC 4-6 June 2008, (Keim, 2010); the Gandhi Seminar with Prof. Rajmohan Gandhi on "Carrying Gandhi's Legacy forward for Peace and Development in South Africa's Communities" UWC, 25th March 2010 in collaboration with the Network and the National Peace Alliance; and last but not least the International Sport and Development Conference – Beyond 2010 with over 300 participants from 15 countries hosted by ICESSD in collaboration with the Network, the Western Cape Department of Cultural Affairs and Sports, United Nations Office on Sport for Peace and Development, International Council of Sport Science and Physical Education (*ICSSPE*), Jacobs Foundation, EFSA Institute, VLIR, and Western Cape Provincial Sport Council.

Additional joint initiatives of the Network and UWC/ICESSD include trainings, seminars, workshops, community projects including youth development and sport projects such as Sport for Peace, as well as research initiatives in the field of Sport Development and Peace with the support of ICESSD, various local government departments, African foundations, City of Cape Town, the German Consulate, Cape Town and the Office of the Premier, Western Cape. Another addition to address the challenges of effective monitoring and evaluation tools, impact assessment and performance indicators was the establishment of the International Research Working Group on Sport and Development by ICESSD in March 2010 with in-person session once a week, virtual sessions and the annual young researcher's day.

Outcomes to date

So far this unique collaboration between civil society and academia has had significant impact on communities, sport federations and NGOs. In 2009 ICESSD conducted a 6-month training for the Network including 28 community leaders from 14 communities on using sport for conflict management and social transformation. In addition, an outreach seminar for 100 NGO representatives and another for 30 representatives from 25 sport federations was conducted to share knowledge, raise awareness, and create partnerships. In 2010 ICESSD trained 150 sport leaders in conflict transformation and leadership for the City of Cape Town's 2010 Sport Leadership Programme, which gives youth leadership skills to build their communities during and after the 2010 FIFA World Cup. These trainings where attended by Network youth and have a potential impact on 50 communities, each with approximately 300,000 inhabitants, fostering tolerance, building understanding, and nurturing cooperation. The training provided the 150 youth (18-35 years old) the possibility to acquire capacities in the area of sport, leadership and personal empowerment, including contents in Sport and Event Management; Training and Coaching; Leadership; Conflict transformation; Community Development through Sport; Personal Empowerment; and Leisure and Outdoor Recreation. It is a great opportunity for the youth from the historically disadvantaged communities to get input from tertiary institutions and to build up community projects throughout the acquired knowledge and accompanying processes. Their graduation which will take place 20 May 2011 and will be a highlight for

ICESSD, Network members and their communities alike. A participatory research study was conducted to establish the effectiveness of the training and the concept of the Sport Leadership Academy as a replicable model. The results will be published in 2011.

Lessons learnt

The strength of this particular collaboration of civil society, government and academia as a provincial network lies in its common values, regular exchange, mutual assistance, continuous participatory research of its sport programme and joint initiatives as the Network. In addition, the close link to a tertiary institution and to continuous participatory research is a core component of its sport programme. Further strengths of the Network are its diversity, its rich experience in various fields, and disciplines, its cultural and geographical representatively, the fact that the majority of its members are grassroots organisations which provide an entry point into communities in all eleven districts of the Western Cape and at the same time facilitates capacity building and sustainability. The objectives of the Network which, namely, are capacity building, the building of stronger relationships, active exchange of ideas and resources, joint initiatives, using sport as a development tool, and to create a replicable model, are all centered around the goal of joint youth development and community development and sustainable skills and training transfer/capacity building.

[a] Joint Youth Development

In all the Network's sports initiatives youth learn about fair play and about managing conflict and communicating through sport. They regularly interact with youth, coaches and trainers from different backgrounds. Their capacity for trust, love and dedication grows as they develop respect for themselves and others. Inclusion of youth from all groups into the project to ensure a sense of belonging, acceptance, security, relationships, gender equity, values, recognition, self-worth, identity, and achievement. These are core elements will contribute to lifelong engagement in sport. The project's planned long-term impact is on South Africa as a whole, building a nation free of prejudice and violence in which all people matter.

[b] Sustainable skills transfer

To address the issue of capacity building of civil society and the sustainability of skills and training of coaches, the participating civil society organisations were asked to identify youth, parents and teachers who are actively involved with NGO and youth projects in the community to participate in training programmes run or organized by the Network. Coaching workshops were held accredited by the South African Football Association (SAFA) as well as short courses in life skills, conflict transformation and sport, peace and development. The first coaching workshop was held in September 2007 for thirty potential soccer coaches from all participating communities. The multicultural group consisted of players, parents and teachers. After completing the workshop, the successful participants were expected to serve a minimum of 30 hours in their NGOs or CBOs (community based organisation) before they could apply via their NGOs or CBOs for the follow up coaching course. Additional coaching follow ups courses have been presented in 2008 and 2009 though DSB and in the form of Futsal. In 2010 twenty-five community leaders from twelve different communities graduated from a six month, sixty credit course in conflict management and transformation offered jointly by the Network, InWent (Germany) and the University of the Western Cape. In 2010, 150 young network members took part in the above described leadership training as part of the Sport Leadership Academy of the City of Cape Town and in 2011 trainings are being offered to community Network members, parents, grandmothers, teachers in the field ofLife Skills and Community Peace Building (level 4), Sport, Development and Peace (level 4) Introduction to Sport and Recreation for Community Development. (level 4) and Participatory techniques in facilitation, need assessment and evaluation (introductory course).

Recommendations for collaborative initiatives

Based on experiences since the beginning of the Network, the following recommendations for starting and developing a network are offered:

▶ clear understanding of concepts such as community, sport, and youth development as well as engagement in sport activities for funders, organisations in development aid and beneficiaries
▶ clear understanding that the concept of 'partnerships' in a collaboration does not only mean one organisation in the North partnering with one organisation/NGO in the South, it can be local NGOs working together at grass roots level where there are no dependencies and relationships marked by power inequities
▶ clarify and define common values of participating organisations
▶ promote a collaborative approach of NGOs, CBOs and other partners in the field→ formation of local networks
▶ inclusion of an educational/ tertiary institution fro training and participatory research
▶ add a holistic skills development/training including life skills, leadership skills, conflict transformation and peace building and diversity issues
▶ accredited training in the field of youth development (and sport)/accreditation of offered training by educational institutions/universities
▶ inclusion of youth in all aspects to ensure a sense of belonging, acceptance, security, relationships, gender equity, values, recognition, self-worth , identity and achievement
▶ formation of a holistic, value based support net for youth development including families, civil society organisations, schools etc.
▶ local networks and regional centres of excellence in sport and development
▶ participatory research for engagement in sport,including civil society, youth and academics

▶promote CSR (cooperate social responsibility) initiatives by connecting needs with resources

▶support LDDIs (Locally Developed and Driven Initiatives)→ greater chance for sustainability and ownership.

It is hoped that the case study of the Network as a collaborative approach of an LDDI will create a multiplier effect of good practices. It is also hoped that organisations in other regions and countries will be motivated to undertake similar initiatives so that that a continent-wide platform can be created to exchange and discuss good practices around collaborative approaches and address challenges and lessons learnt the field of engagement at all ages in sport and physical activities.

Conclusion

If we want to use sport as a tool for community and peace building in our societies, a multi-stakeholder approach with the virtues of partnership and participation is crucial. Life-long activities in sport and physical activity is a vision to which we can all aspire. To plant the seed and make it grow undoubtedly starts with our children and youth. Young people today have a range of needs which cannot be met by individual organizations or approaches. We believe that programmes for productive youth development and lifelong engagement in sport should aim to address these needs through honest, beneficial and sustainable partnerships so that young people are given the opportunity to develop to their full potential.

The Western Cape Network for Community Peace and Development believes that a collaborative holistic development approach including engagement in sport and physical activity is the most appropriate strategy to address the current needs of young people in South Africa, Africa and beyond.

The role of academia is highlighted using the example of UWC/ ICESSD and its contributions to sport and development through outreach, capacity building and teaching as well as advancement of knowledge through applied research activities and community orientated approaches. Together we can increase the impact of our respective community sport, recreation and physical activity programmes, and to youth development and community peace building in general. Through collaboration we can learn from each other, assist with resources, share information, ideas and good practice models.

Together we can advocate for the interests of our communities by putting youth development, peace and health issues, including lifelong engagement in sport and physical activities for health and wellness of our communities on the agenda of media and business as corporate social responsibility initiatives but also on the national agendas of our countries.

'Alone we can do so little; together we can do so much'.
[Helen Keller 1880-1968].

References

Agostini M. Media monsters on the prowl for Olympic flesh. The Sydney Morning Herald. 1995;70 (20th May).

Galtung, J (1996). Peace by Peaceful Means: peace and conflict, development and civilization. Oslo: International Peace Research Institute, Part III, Development Theory, 127-195.

Keim, M. (2009). Building Peace through Sport: A Model of a University - Civil Society Collaboration in South Africa. African Conflict & *Peace Review Journal*, January 2009, Addis Ababa, Ethiopia: UPEACE.

Keim, M. (2007). (Eds.) The Role of Universities in Conflict Transformation, Reconstruction and Development. Uitgeverij Lannoo Press, Leuven.

Keim, M. (2010). (Eds.) Leadership, Social Transformation and Healing, Sun Media, South Africa.

Lederach J. P. (2005). The Moral Imagination: The Art and Soul of Building Peace. New York: Oxford.

Wolfe, R., Meenaghan, T. & P. O'Sullivan (2002). The Sports Network: Insights into the shifting balance of power. *Journal of Business Research*, Vol. 55 issue 7, July 2002:pp. 611-622

RDF (2006). - Resources and Development Foundation unpublished report. RDF, Stellenbosch.

Electronic sources: UNICEF 2009 Available at: http://www.unicef.org/corporate_partners/files/N0928210(1).pdf (Accessed 12th March 2012).

UNESCO 2009: Available at: www.unesco.org/most/soc_cap_symp.pdf (Accessed 12th March 2012).

Part III
Sport and Reconciliation

Chapter 9

Sport and Peacebuilding

Healing the Wounds of War

Bojana Blagojevic

"When the country I was born in was forcibly landing us and dislanding we were cheering each other up by contemplating the championship strategy........to get the maximum out of ourselves for the World Cup which was just out of the earshot of the guns; going on without us". (Skenderija, 2009)

Introduction

When we live in normal, peaceful circumstances, our lives have a carefree quality which becomes apparent especially after it is taken away. War is a tragedy that robs people of the normality associated with being safe and being able to have some control over what happens to them, their loved ones and their environment. Engaging in activities that enhance a person's quality of life is often impossible in the midst of a war, as people's existence transforms into a mere fight for survival. Opportunities for human beings to grow, develop, dream and achieve are thwarted by the violence and, in many cases, literally destroyed. War dehumanizes individuals through physical and psychological harm. Those who are fortunate to survive a war physically intact carry the burden of invisible, emotional and mental wounds. Rebuilding lives after a war is a daunting, complex, multi-faceted task. In that context, I argue that integrating sport into the overall peacebuilding process can play an important role in restoring the well-being of individuals and communities by fostering human development. The reason for writing this chapter is personal. As a survivor of the war in Bosnia-Herzegovina, I was fortunate to have an opportunity to find refuge in a place that provided many opportunities to rebuild my life. One opportunity, which I found and turned to instinctively, was recreational sport. Playing a sport for fun competition yielded many physical and emotional benefits. Many survivors of war, unfortunately, do not have the same opportunities. Long-term inclusion of sport in peacebuilding efforts should be expanded and strengthened, so more individuals and communities can engage in "healing through play".

This chapter provides a conceptual framework for understanding the potential positive role of sport in building peace in ethnically divided, war-torn societies. The conceptual connection between sport and peace is framed in terms of its relationship to human development. Two levels of impact are discussed. At the individual level, it is argued that organized physical activities can promote self-empowerment and wellbeing, often shattered by the trauma of war. At the community level, the chapter tries to understand how sport can encourage constructive inter-personal interactions that can positively affect and transform relationships amongst and between belligerent groups. The actual effect of sport on peacebuilding is framed in terms of the proposed "principles of application." As noted by the Sport for Development and Peace International Working Group (SDP IWG, 2007), there is a need for more literature that frames sport in peacebuilding concepts and theories (p. 161). The goal of this chapter is to contribute to the efforts to both conceptualize and apply sport as an instrument for peace.

Sport and Peacebuilding: A Conceptual Analysis

In recent history, we have witnessed an increase in internal conflicts that manifest at the level of organized hostilities. These conflict situations are violent pursuits of incompatible goals by different ethnic groups (Reychler, 2001, p. 5; also see Bloomfield, 1997, pp. 99, 101-2; Kaufmann, 1996, p. 138; Coser, 1956, p. 8). Ethnic conflicts are unique because they often take place *within* countries, *within* communities. In conflicts such as in Bosnia and Rwanda, people who once coexisted peacefully become transformed from neighbors to bitter enemies. Communities are torn apart and destroyed by people who themselves are its constituent parts. Therefore, ethnic wars can be defined as the violent self-destruction of societies. War is approached as a zero-sum game – for someone to win, someone else has to lose. In reality, the aggression, violence, destruction and the exclusion of "others" through intolerance leads to a lose-lose outcome. Individuals and communities on all sides of the war suffer the loss of life, and physical and psychological harm. The "victorious" terms of any peace agreement are usually achieved after tremendous defeat for human development at both individual and collective levels.

For the purposes of this chapter, sport is defined as "all forms of physical activity that contribute to physical fitness, mental well-being and social interaction, such as play, recreation, organized or competitive sport, and indigenous sports and games" (SDP IWG, 2007, p. 4). Such a broad conceptualization of sport, encompassing a variety of leisure and recreation activities, ensures that sport is, by definition, inclusive, as it implies accessibility to individuals and groups of various cultural backgrounds and levels of ability. Dutch historian, Johan Huizinga (1971), argues in his book *Homo Ludens: A Study of the Play Element in Culture*, that play is intrinsic to who we are. Human beings are players of games ("homo ludens"). According to him, play is a repetitive, orderly, voluntary activity. It is a stepping out of 'real life' within set limits of time and space "accompanied by a feeling of tension, joy and consciousness that is 'different' from 'ordinary life'" (as cited in Moore, 1966, p. 24).

But, what effect can sport have in a context where individual lives and inter-group relationships were destroyed through the violence of war? Does playing a sport automatically lead to wellbeing and reconciliation? As Sugden (2005) notes, "Sport is essentially neither good nor bad. It is a social construct and its role and function depends largely on what we make of it and how it is consumed" (as cited in SDP IWG, 2007, p. 176). Realizing the peacebuilding potential of sport depends on *how* we construct and apply it in various contexts. Sport can have qualities in common with both war (e.g. aggressive competition) and peace (e.g. cooperation). War is the ultimate zero-sum competitive "game," in which winning is equivalent to a physical and psychological destruction of the opponent. Sport, like war, is competitive. It is a "physical contest between people or teams with different goals" (as cited in Kvaslund, n.d.). The contest can be war-like: belligerent, violent, destructive. Or, it can embody cooperative, constructive qualities that benefit everyone. In this sense, sport can help by providing a structure within which the opposing groups can (re)learn how to relate to each other in a positive way. If we conceptualize war and peace as "games," we should apply the game qualities and values of peace to the way we design and implement sport (and other) peacebuilding programs in post-war societies at both, individual and collective levels. These values can be termed *principles of application*. Table 1 illustrates the game qualities of war and peace that can be embodied through sport.

Table 1: "Game" Qualities and Values of War and Peace

WAR	PEACE
Win-lose	Win-win
Aggression, Violence, Dehumanization	Cooperation, Teamwork, Respect
Exclusion (us v. them)	Inclusion
Harm, Hostility	Well-being, Tolerance

The main focus of sport for peace programs should be on promoting the wellbeing of participants and their communities. Personal and collective progress can be achieved outside the "win or lose", "all or nothing", "success or failure" framework. The emphasis should be placed on the values of mutual gain, cooperation, teamwork, and respect toward others. The quality of inclusiveness is essential. If a sport program privileges one group over another, it is, in effect, reinforcing the structures of exclusion that fuel and perpetuate the dynamics that work against both development and peace. Sport for peace programs should be designed, accessible and safe for everyone in a post-war community, regardless of their ethnicity, gender, age or level of ability.

The concept of *peace* refers not only to the absence of physical violence, but also to abolition of structural violence - the dynamics of oppression and domination within a society (Galtung, 1976, pp. 282-304). Peacebuilding is a complex, multi-level process that "facilitates the establishment of durable peace and tries to prevent the recurrence of violence by addressing root causes and effects of conflict through reconciliation, institution building and political as well as economic transformation." (Paul H. Nitze SAIS, n.d., para 1). It is a process whose goal is "the construction of a new environment" (Boutros-Ghali, para 57) and as stated in the "Supplement to an Agenda for Peace" (1995), "the creation of structures for the institutionalization of peace" (para 49). The process can be both formal and informal, involving a variety of actors.

To build peace means to facilitate development at physical (infrastructural), political, economic, and social levels of post-war societies. All four dimensions of the peacebuilding process are interdependent and overlapping, as illustrated in Figure 1. Success or failure in one aspect of peacebuilding affects all peacebuilding efforts. If we accept that individuals and communities are the foundations of any country, restoring the individual and collective social fabric of war-torn societies through individual and community empowerment can be conceptualized as the *heart* of peacebuilding. While sport can stimulate development at all levels of peacebuilding, it can have the most direct impact at the social level through empowerment of individuals and transformation of relationships among groups. Its success at this level of peacebuilding is interdependent with the effectiveness of other peacebuilding efforts at all levels of the process. For example, to establish a successful sport program, it is necessary to have government support (political dimension), financial capabilities (economic dimension) and a safe space where the program will materialize (physical/infrastructural dimension). In turn, sport can fortify the social foundation on which all other aspects of peace can be materialized.

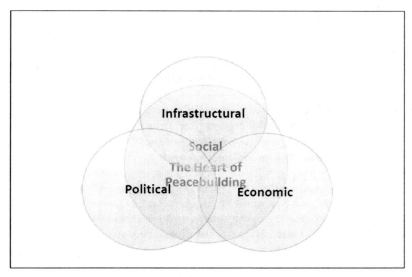

Figure 1: Dimensions of Peacebuilding

From Sport to Peace through Human Development

Sport contributes to the peacebuilding process by fostering human development. The concept of *development* is usually understood as the process of increasing economic growth of a nation. Such conceptualization of development is insufficient to characterize complex peacebuilding needs of ethnically divided, war-torn societies. In the words of Amartya Sen (1999), development can be seen as "a process of expanding the real freedoms that people enjoy" (p. 3). That is people-centered, *human* development. According to Mahbub ul Haq (n.d.), founder of United Nations Development Programme's Human Development Report,

> "The basic purpose of development is to enlarge people's choices…People often value achievements that do not show up at all, or not immediately, in income or growth figures: greater access to knowledge, better nutrition and health services, more secure livelihoods, security against crime and physical violence, satisfying leisure hours, political and cultural freedoms and sense of participation in community activities. The objective of development is to create an enabling environment for people to enjoy long, healthy and creative lives".
>
> (UNDP, The Human Development Concept)

Sport can facilitate human development by expanding people's opportunities to satisfy leisure time and participate in community life. By improving the quality of life at both, individual and community levels, sport can have a direct impact on people's *health*, one of the key indicators of human development. The World Health Organization (1946) defines health as "a state of complete physical, mental pand social well-being and not merely the absence of disease or infirmity" (WHO, p. 1). The other two indicators of human development are knowledge and decent standard of living. Human development is measured by the Human Development Index (HDI), which is determined by calculating a country's life expectancy, education, and Gross Domestic Product (GDP) indices (UNDP, What Is Human Development Index).

Intrinsic to the concept of human development is the concept of "capabilities." Amartya Sen (1985) argued that, in order to successfully understand human well-being and deprivation, we must focus on human capability to achieve valuable functioning. According to him, "Functioning is an achievement of a person: what she or he manages to do or be" (as cited in Clark, 2005, p.4). Capability, then, refers to a person's ability to "do" or "be" something. Sport, as a peacebuilding tool, enhances people's ability to lead a better life by facilitating development and realization of their potential. As Patsy Neal (1972) articulates, "Sport gives one a space and tools for being and becoming. It brings together the actuality of the person, and the action necessary to be more" (p. 83). According to Martha Nussbaum (2000), the ability to *play* (enjoy recreational activities) is one of the central human capabilities which are essential for living a quality human life. Other core capabilities, discussed by Nussbaum, that we could relate to the benefits of sport are: ability to live a normal length of life, have good health, express emotions, and live in affiliation with others through social interaction.

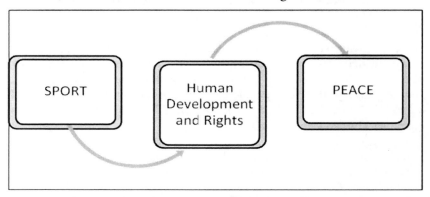

Figure 2: Human Development: The Bridge from Sport to Peace

Sport, as a peacebuilding tool, can have two levels of impact. These are:

1. Empowering individuals by promoting physical, emotional and mental well-being
2. Rebuilding communities through reconciliation - transformation of relationships.

The two interrelated levels are illustrated in Figure 3.

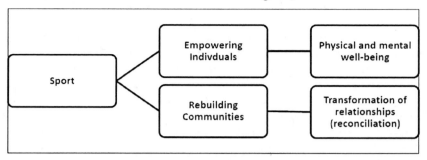

Figure 3: Sport and Human Development: Levels of Impact

Empowering Individuals: Sport and Well-Being

This concept is argued strongly though the following quote:

> "Through sport and physical education, individuals can experience equality, freedom and a dignifying means for empowerment. The control over one's body experienced while practicing sport is particularly valuable for girls and women, for people with disabilities, for those living in conflict areas, for people recovering from trauma".
>
> (International Year for Sport and Physical Education, 2005, para 3).

If constructed appropriately, sport can provide a safe structure for promoting self-empowerment and healing of distress caused by the trauma of war. Participation in sport activities can help individuals build a new sense of self and confidence by countering the effects of dehumanization and rebuilding a sense of dignity and control over one's body, life and surroundings. Literature linking leisure and physical activity to health supports this proposition (SDP IWG, 2007, p. 4). In her review of literature on leisure and health, Linda L. Caldwell (2005) discusses evidence that leisure contributes to physical, social, emotional and cognitive health. The therapeutic benefits of leisure are attributed to "protective factors" derived from leisure activities such as: competence and self-efficacy, being self-determined and in control, feeling relaxed and disengaged from stress, finding continuity in life after a negative event, etc. (p.17). Participating in sport and other recreational activities can help restore a feeling of "normal" life in post-war contexts (Ehrenreich, 2001, p.60). As Douglas A. Kleiber et. al. (2002) argue, leisure, including physical activity, can help individuals, not only "cope" with problematic circumstances by lessening physical and/or psychological stress associated with their situation, but it can also ultimately facilitate a restoration and transformation of one's life. Leisure can provide a context for "post-traumatic growth" that includes a change in perception of self, inter-personal relationships, and a more positive attitude toward life (pp.220-221).

Physical activity has been linked to enhancing mood, self-esteem and promoting restful sleep and relief in symptoms of anxiety and depression (Landers, 1997). In his book, *Sport and Mental Health*, Robert A. Moore (1966) discusses various theories that explain why sport promotes wellbeing. According to the recreation theory, play is "a means of re-creating energy or refreshing the person so he can again pursue the more serious responsibilities of life" (p.22). The recreational aspect of play can be very beneficial to a person who endured war and is struggling to rebuild a normal life in the post-war environment. Energy spent on survival can be renewed and re-channeled through recreational play. Play can also be seen as an opportunity to express emotions that a person would not be comfortable expressing otherwise due to social pressures (catharsis theory). Self-expression theory holds that play allows a person to express themselves through mastery of a skill. The functional pleasure aspect focuses on the physiological and biological benefits of physical activity. As Moore states, "The pure joy of unrestricted movement, the freedom of large muscles to stretch to their limits is a luxury once tasted that can be addictive" (p.29).

Sport provides an opportunity for people who were exposed to prolonged danger of losing their life or being injured to feel empowered in their bodies. According to Patsy Neal (1972), "While participating in sport, one cannot help but be conscious of the body...The body becomes the means to achieving a purpose, belonging uniquely to the individual, and allowing him to perform the wishes of the mind and soul" (pp. 83-4). What we feel, who we are and who we are in contact with become interconnected parts of our experience (pp.23-24). Sport can help individuals transition from being a victim to becoming a survivor. While the victim is or feels powerless, a survivor can "take an active role in efforts to help his community and himself recover from the disaster" (as cited in Ehrenreich, 2001, pp. 8-9).

It is very important that sport peacebuilding programs be designed and applied in a way that will empower rather than re-traumatize victims of war. Drawing upon the expertise of psychologists and recreational therapists is essential. According to a sport development worker, Anneke van Drimmelen, who worked on a project for disabled persons in Tanzania, "I have had little professional preparation and certainly not in terms of how to deal with young people who had been traumatized...My job was really aimed at sport for sport's sake and little attention had been paid to the role sport can play in overcoming trauma" (W.J. H. Mulier Instituut, 2005, p. 7). Careful consideration should be given to the context, appropriateness of activities and the manner in which they are implemented. The focus should be on nurturing the individual and how the positive effects of play can be maximized.

Rebuilding Communities: Sport and Reconciliation

"The activities could bridge ethnic divides; far from simply improving health and strength, sport can also promote crucial values such as the importance of dialogue and interaction".
(Participants of an inter-ethnic sporting event in Burundi, Insight on Conflict).

In war-torn, ethnically divided societies, sport can be used as either a tool to promote hostilities or a tool to promote peace. Depending on how it is applied in a post-war society, it can either cause further divisions or restore the society through positive transformation of broken inter-ethnic relationships. The process that leads to ethnic conflict involves *ethnification*, a process in which "the social, psychological, and political importance of ethnic identities rise relative to other identities," (Somer, 1997) and a reconstruction of social categories of inclusion and exclusion based on ethnicity. To be "excluded" means to be "denied access to the social, economic and political rights afforded to others" (UNDP, 2007, p.16). The society becomes divided into "us" and "them." This dichotomous, competitive relationship is strengthened through the violence of war. Dehumanization plays an important role both in the process leading to ethnic war and in its aftermath. The "other" is stripped of their humanity through propaganda in order to facilitate and justify violence directed against them. Mutual intolerance, as well as direct and structural violence, facilitates the perception of the "other" as less worthy, less than human (Stanton, 1998; also see Blagojevic, Spring 2010). In this context, both before and after ethnic conflict, sport can be used by political entrepreneurs to further solidify inter-ethnic divisions by promoting single ethnic identity and demonstrating how "we" ("our" group) are better and more human than "them." This way of employing sport in a society is equivalent to what Robert A. Moore (1966) calls "military attitude" of sport, used "during preliterate society where play was a preparation for hunting and making war" (p.5). A modern example of using sport in militaristic, divisive manner would be in Nazi Germany. Croatian and Serbian fans fighting at the Australian Open in 2007 in show of "support" for the players from their ethnic groups provides a more recent example of sport-related inter-ethnic violence (New York Times, January 15, 2007). An alternative to the military attitude toward sport is the "social attitude" which "assumes that sports are an opportunity to learn about living competitively with others and in alliance with others through teams" (Moore, 1966, p.14). Unlike the military attitude, this approach toward understanding and applying sport is more conducive to reconciliation and peaceful coexistence.

The word reconciliation is derived from the Latin word *conciliatus*, which means to come together, to assemble, and it refers to a positive transformation of broken relationships (Assefa, 1993, p.9). Similarly, Johan Galtung (2001) interprets reconciliation as "the process of healing the traumas of both victims and perpetrators after violence, providing a closure of the bad relation. The process prepares the parties for relations with justice and peace" (in Abu-Nimer, p.3; also see Lederach, 1997, p.151; Brecke and Long, 2003, p.1). Undertaking peacebuilding through a reconciliation approach in ethnically divided societies means integrating transformation of relationships into each dimension of peacebuilding: infrastructural, political, economic, and social. At all levels, peacebuilding actions and processes should be designed to break down, rather than reinforce, the dynamics of ethnic hostilities and intolerance. The aim is to achieve cooperation, equality and non-discrimination, not by forcing groups to like each other, but by working together toward common goals (Blagojevic, 2007, p. 555; 2004).

For a war-torn society to begin to function effectively again, all parts of the social fabric (individuals and groups) must be able to participate freely in the social/cultural, political and economic processes through which the society achieves human development. As Rusmir Mahmutćehajić (2000) explains:

"Social efficiency...is based on the human capacity for association, and its development in accordance with set goals, depends...on the capacity to recognize, within a culture, reasons to put one's trust in others who are part of the same community or society". (p.95).

Sport can serve as one of the peacebuilding structures through which the social fabric of society can be rebuilt. It can provide a venue where people can participate in their community and engage in constructive inter-personal interaction. In other words, sport can be used as a tool for what Lederach (2005) calls, "web-making" or building of relationships. According to Lederach, "The goal is to create a web that has a capacity to receive blows and even structural damage to one part without those points of damage destroying the rest of the web" (p.170). Building a network of sustainable relationships at the social level of peacebuilding strengthens the core "muscle" of the society – the people. It facilitates a conceptual shift from "us" v. "them" dichotomy to a framework of inclusiveness and interdependence across divides.

Conclusion

Sport has a powerful potential to empower individuals and rebuild communities in post-war, ethnically divided societies. To promote human development, sport for peace programs should embody the principles of mutual gain, cooperation, inclusiveness, respect, supported by knowledge of the local context, inter-group relations, and the effects of trauma. To be truly transformative, recreation and play opportunities should be systematically extended to all victims of war, regardless of ethnicity, gender, age, or level of ability. My hope is that the conceptual framework presented in this chapter will contribute to our evolving understanding of how sport can help heal the individual and collective wounds of war.

References

Assefa, H. (1993). *Peace and Reconciliation as a Paradigm*. Nairobi, Kenya: Nairobi Peace Initiative.

Blagojevic, B. (2010). Causes of Ethnic Conflict: A Conceptual Framework. *Journal of Global Change and Governance, 3(1)*.

Blagojevic, B. (2007). Peacebuilding in Ethnically Divided Societies. *Peace Review: A Journal of Social Justice, 19(4)*, 555-62.

Blagojevic, B. (2004). Ethnic Conflict and Post-Conflict Development: Peacebuilding in Ethnically Divided Societies. PhD diss., Rutgers, the State University of New Jersey.

Bloomfield, L. P. & Moulton, A. (1997). *Managing International Conflict: From Theory to Policy (A Teaching Tool Using CASCON)*. New York: St. Martin's Press.

Boutros-Ghali, B. (1992, June 17). An Agenda for Peace: Preventative Diplomacy, Peacemaking and Peace-keeping. United Nations Document: A/47/277-S/24111.

_____(1995, January 3). Supplement to An Agenda for Peace. United Nations Document: A/50/60-S/1995/1.

Brecke, P. & Long, W.J. (2003). *War and Reconciliation: Reason and Emotion in Conflict Resolution*. Cambridge, Massachusetts: The MIT Press.

Caldwell, L. L. (2005, February). Leisure and Health: Why Is Leisure Therapeutic?. *British Journal of Guidance and Counseling, 33(1)*, 7-26.

Clark, D. A. (2005). The Capability Approach: Its Development, Critiques, and Recent Advances. Global Poverty Research Group, Economic and Social Research Council. GPRG-WPS-032. Available at: http://www.gprg.org/pubs/workingpapers/pdfs/gprg-wps-032.pdf, (Accessed 12 March 2012).

Coser, L. (1956). *The Functions of Social Conflict*. Glencoe, IL: Free Press.

Ehrenreich, J. H. (2001, October). Coping with Disasters: A Guidebook to Psychosocial Intervention, Mental Health Workers without Borders. Available at: http://www.toolkitsportdevelopment.org, (Accessed 12th March 2012).

Galtung, J. (2001). After Violence, Reconstruction, Reconciliation, and Resolution: Coping with Visible and Invisible Effects of War and Violence. In M. Abu-Nimer. (Ed). *Reconciliation, Justice and Coexistence: Theory and Practice*, Lanham: Lexington Books.

Galtung, J. (1976). Peace, War, and Defense: Essays in Peace Research. (Vol. 2). Copenhagen: Christian Ejlers. Not available

Huizinga, J. (1971). *Homo Ludens: A Study of the Play Element in Culture*. Boston: Beacon Press.

Insight on Conflict. Community Reconciliation through Sports and Culture. (n.d.). National Olympic Committee, Burundi. Available at: http://www.insightonconflict.org/conflicts/burundi/peacebuilding-organisations/national-olympic-committee/ (Accessed 12th March 2012).

International Year of Sport and Physical Education. (2005). Available at: http://www.un.org/sport2005/a_year/ayear_for.html (Accessed 12th March 2012).

Kaufman, C. (1996, Fall). Possible and Impossible Solutions to Ethnic Wars. *International Security*, 21(2).

Kleiber, D. A., Hutchinson, S. L. & Williams, R. (2002). *Leisure Sciences, 24*, 219-235.

Kvalsund, P. (n.d.) Sport and Peace Building. Available at: http://www.toolkitsportdevelopment.org/ (Accessed 12th March 2012).

Landers, D. M. (1997). The Influence of Exercise on Mental Health. *President's Council on Physical Fitness and Sports (PCPFS) Research Digest*, 2(12). Department of Health and Human Services. Available at: http://www.fitness.gov/publications/digests/mental-health.html (Accessed 12th March 2012).

Lederach, J.P. (2005). *The Moral Imagination: The Art and Soul of Building Peace*. Oxford: New York.

Lederach, J.P. (1997). *Building Peace: Sustainable Reconciliation in Divided Societies*. Washington, DC: United States Institute of Peace Press.

Mahmutćehajić, R. (2000). *The Denial of Bosnia*. University Park: The Pennsylvania State University Press.

Moore, R. A. (1966). *Sports and Mental Health*. Springfield: Charles C. Thomas.

Neal, P. (1972). *Sport and Identity*. Philadelphia: Dorrance & Company.

Nussbaum, M. C. (2000). *Women and Human Development: The Capabilities Approach*. Cambridge: Cambridge University Press.

Paul H. Nitze School of Advanced International Studies (SAIS). The Conflict Management Toolkit. (n.d.). The Johns Hopkins University. Available at: http://www.sais-jhu.edu/cmtoolkit/approaches/peacebuilding/index.htm (Accessed 12th march 2012).

Reychler, L. & Paffenholz, T. (Eds.). (2001). *Peacebuilding: A Field Guide*. London: Lynne Rienner Publishers.

Sen, A. (1999). *Development as Freedom*. New York: Anchor Books.

Sen, A. (1985). *Commodities and Capabilities*. Oxford: Elsevier Science Publishers.

Skenderija, S. (2009, April). Spasić (More than a Game). *Spirit of Bosnia Online Journal*, 4(2). Available at: http://www.spiritofbosnia.org/volume-4-no-2-2009-april/spasic-more-than-a-game/ (Accessed 12th March 2012).

Somer, M. (1997). Explaining the Hardly Predictable: Causes and Consequences of Ethnification. Working Paper, Center for International Studies, USC.

Sport for Development and Peace International Working Group. (2007). Literature Reviews on Sport for Development and Peace. Commissioned by SDP IWG Secretariat, Toronto, Canada. University of Toronto, Faculty of Physical Health and Education. Available at: http://iwg.sportanddev.org/ (Accessed 12th March 2012).

SportDev.Org: The International Platform for Sport and Development, Available at: http://www.sportanddev.org/ (Accessed 12th March 2012).

Stanton, G. H. (1998). The Eight Stages of Genocide. Genocide Watch. Available at: http://www.genocidewatch.org/aboutgenocide/8stagesofgenocide.html (Accessed 12th March 2012).

Sugden, J. (2005). Sport and Community Relations in Northern Ireland and Israel. In A. Bairner (Ed.), *Sport and the Irish: Histories, Identities, Issues*. Dublin: University College Dublin Press.

Tennis: Croatian and Serbian Fans Fight. (2007, January 15). *New York Times*, Sports Section.

Toolkit: Sport for Development. (n.d.) Available at: http://www.toolkitsportdevelopment.org (Accessed 12th March 2012).

United Nations Development Programme. (2007). National Human Development Report. Social Inclusion in Bosnia and Herzegovina.Available at: http://hdr.undp.org/en/reports/nationalreports/europethecis/bosniaherzegovina/BOSNIA_AND_HERCEGOVINA_2007_en.pdf (Accessed 12th March 2012).

_____The Human Development Concept. (n.d.). Available at: http://hdr.undp.org/en/humandev/ (Accessed 12th March 2012).

World Health Organization (WHO). (1946). Preamble to the Constitution of the World Health Organization as adopted by the International Health Conference, New York. Retrieved from http://apps.who.int/gb/bd/PDF/bd47/EN/constitution-en.pdf

W.J. H. Mulier Instituut. (2005, April). Trauma and Sport for Development: A Toolkit for Sport Development Workers. Available at: http://www.toolkitforsportanddevelopment.org (Accessed 12th March 2012).

Chapter 10

Can This Really Be? America as a Model of Progress

Why Physical Violence, Racist Invectives, Abusive Language and Behavior among Spectators of North American Major Team Sports Are Much Rarer and Less Salient than in Europe

Andrei S. Markovits

Introduction

Like the editors of this volume, I believe that sports on balance have performed an enlightening function in human history, that precisely, by dint of their inherently competitive and agonistic nature, they foster a profound meritocracy and cosmopolitanism that few other venues in social life have. By virtue of these integrative qualities, sports enhance intercultural tolerance and understanding. However, just like in most realms of human activity, so too in sports do cosmopolitanism and inclusiveness meet with resistance by forces that Kwame Anthony Appiah has so aptly termed "counter-cosmopolitanism".[1] Newcomers, immigrants, "alien" languages and cultures

---

1.Kwame Anthony Appiah, *Cosmopolitanism* (New York: W.W. Norton, 2007), pp. 137-153.

are met with ridicule, as well as hostile, even violent reactions by entrenched forces and institutions. Since cultural changes inevitably imply some threat to established identities, such changes exact tensions and defensive responses. This is evident in sports, since adversity; opposition; contest; and thus conflict are their most essential markers. By their very nature, by demanding winners and losers, sports feature a zero-sum essence that extols tensions, rewards the victors and punishes the vanquished.

Counter-cosmopolitanism's ugliest expression is resilient racism and random violence against "others". However, the quantity and quality of such counter-cosmopolitan activities varies over time and space.

This contribution argues that at least over the past four decades, there exists perhaps no greater difference between American and European hegemonic sports culture (i.e. sports that attract a mass following well beyond its actual producers and most immediate fans) than in the expression of counter-cosmopolitanism. While in America, overtly racist taunts accompanied by violent acts against players and viewers have all but disappeared and lack any kind of legitimacy in contemporary sports, this, alas, is not the case in Europe. Soccer grounds have become perhaps the last bastion in contemporary Europe in which the worst kind of racist, sexist, anti-Semitic, xenophobic – i.e. counter-cosmopolitan -- language and behavior have not only been tolerated but actually extolled. But it is not the activities of a committed counter-cosmopolitan minority in European venues that differentiates the European case from its American counterpart but rather what the majority on each continent tolerates as acceptable discourse and behavior.

The American Situation

In contrast to Europe, violence is a very marginal occurrence in present day American sports culture, and open racism is practically taboo and socially sanctioned in the stands and among players. While discrimination and racism undoubtedly remain major issues in American sports and society, overt racism has for all intents and purposes been banned from contemporary American sports. In fact, any of the racist remarks and gestures that remain commonplace in many European stadiums (even where fan violence has been contained if not eliminated over the last few years, as in England), have virtually disappeared from all major league and college-level sports venues in the United States. Moreover, the rare cases of fan violence that have existed in America have had a different substance and tone from their European counterparts. Thus, violence at American sports venues rarely constitutes a premeditated, organized activity, implemented by a small group of well-trained street fighters whose primary, perhaps sole, purpose is to engage in fights and cause havoc rather than watch the game.

Philip Goodhart and Christopher Chataway observed that in America, "a land so often characterized as a land bubbling with violence, sporting hooliganism, apart from racial disturbances, seems to be largely unknown".[2] By far the most prevalent forms of violence in connection with any sports in America belong to the category best described as "celebratory violence" or "celebratory riots". Typically, this involves unruly, and often inebriated, fans celebrating their team's victory by rioting in the streets, burning cars, igniting garbage cans, and fighting the police. Interestingly, it is exclusively fans of the winning teams that engage in such behavior, never the losing teams'. This was the case following the Tigers' World Series triumph in Detroit in October 1984; in Chicago after the Bulls' championship victory in June 1992; in Los Angeles after the Lakers regained their title in June 2009 and then defended it one year later with both occasions witnessing crowd-induced violence immediately following the title-clinching games; in October 2004 in Boston when the hometown Red Sox overcame a three-game deficit to beat their hated long-term tormentor New York Yankees in the series by 4 games to 3; in November 2002 in Columbus when Ohio State fans stormed the field after their team had defeated archrival Michigan on the last play of the game. In each of these cases, the victories released pent-up frustration by the winners' fans. The Boston Red Sox had not only won their series in a manner never achieved by any sports team in the history of major league baseball, professional football, and basketball (down three games to none in a best-of-seven series and winning it by triumphing in four must-win games in a row) but they did so against the very team that was their relentless tormentor and nemesis since 1918, the last time the Red Sox had won the World Series.[3] Ohio State had been dominated by Michigan throughout much of the 1990s and the Buckeyes had just concluded an entire "Beat Michigan week" on campus that preceded the game and catapulted students into a frenzy. But even in these instances, one needs to differentiate between the "celebratory riots" that occurred immediately following these victories, largely in and around the venues themselves, and subsequent physical assaults and lootings, that were only tangentially connected to the sports events. Moreover, unlike in Europe, where virtually all of the violence in and around the stadiums is premeditated, prepared, and designed before the actual games, "celebratory violence" at American venues

2. Chataway, *War without Weapons* (London: W.H. Allen, 1968), p. 144. The "racial disturbances" to which Goodhart and Chataway refer are the fights between black and white youths that led to a temporary ban on high school night matches in parts of the United States. In an early, yet methodologically controversial study, Jerry Lewis observed 312 incidents he classified as "riots" at American sports events between 1960 and 1972; 97 in baseball, 66 in football, 55 in basketball, and 39 in hockey; quoted in Allen Guttmann, *Sports Spectators* (New York: Columbia University Press, 1986), p. 119.

3. The Toronto Maple Leafs of 1942, the New York Islanders of 1975 and the Philadelphia Flyers in 2010 – all of the National Hockey League -- were the only teams in the history of major North American sports to have been down by three games to none in a best-of-seven series and still managed to win.

occurs spontaneously and in an improvised, ad-hoc fashion. Above all, these riots are not directed against the fans of the opposing teams, as much as they are random acts of destruction against whatever constitutes their immediate surroundings. In perhaps the greatest contrast to its European counterparts, these American instances of fan violence had not been accompanied by racial hatred, overt racism or anti-Semitism. Jeering the New York Yankees and deriding the Michigan Wolverines with vulgar language might not be pretty, but it constitutes a different category than spewing hatred and venom against Jews, blacks, and other nonwhite minorities as has remained commonplace in Europe's stadiums since the 1970s. Jerry M. Lewis, expert on fan violence in North American sports, summarizes the situation: "For North America, and particularly the United States, the data on fan violence at the collegiate and professional levels of competition are clear. The typical rioter is likely to be a young, white male celebrating a victory after a championship or an important game or match".[4]

While I do not mean to downplay the ugliness of occasional fan violence in the United States caused by these "celebratory riots", it is noteworthy that European-style spectator-led violence never emerged at American sport venues and events. Why has this been the case? Why has fan violence largely been absent from American team sports, when by any measure the United States suffers from a much higher level of violence in virtually every other aspect of its society than do most countries in Europe?

Tentative Hypotheses for the Absence of Fan Violence in America

1. America is a country of continental proportions. Massive distances inhibit travel to accompany one's team for an away game. In addition, there is less of a tradition in following one's team across the country for a regular season or even play-off game than in Europe. Only year-end bowl games in college football, traditionally played on neutral sites, and the March Madness tournament in men's college basketball also played in neutral arenas strewn across the land, witness American sports fans traveling in large numbers to follow their teams. Rivalry games (or derbies, to use British parlance) constitute exceptions to the American norm. And sure enough these emotionally charged encounters sometimes create fan violence before and after the games in bars and streets near the stadiums, occasionally even during the games themselves, particularly in the bleacher seats. These altercations are invariably quelled quickly by surrounding spectators, and the authorities also subdue matters promptly. But fights happen at these emotionally charged games. With the exception of the rivalry games, however, American sports venues feature few visible "enemies" or outsiders. This drastically reduces the chance of clashes between large groups of opposing fans. By

---

4. ibid., p. 209.

contrast, European soccer matches are more local affairs, and there is a tradition of clubs traveling with a large coterie of fans even to distant games. Geographic proximity in team sports breeds rivalries, which in turn foster contempt and hatred that then increase the likelihood of violence.

2. Many European cities have traditionally featured a bevy of clubs in close proximity, which intensifies rivalries and mutual hatreds: Vienna once furnished ten soccer clubs in Austria's top-level league of twelve teams well into the 1960s and continues to have three or four to this day; Budapest has had six; Bucharest, Istanbul, and Moscow four; London still boasts five clubs in the English Premier League's 2010-11 season; and many cities have at least two. Because American sports teams began as businesses with their owners explicitly disallowing the establishment of any rivals in their territory, no cities other than New York, Chicago, and Los Angeles have more than one team per sport. In those rare cases where cities have multiple teams per sport, they originated in different leagues (as in baseball) and came to lead parallel though rarely overlapping existences. Or, they arose at vastly disparate time periods (as in basketball and hockey), which also mitigated rivalries. Still, the intense mutual dislike on the part of Giants and Dodgers fans in baseball hails precisely from their proximate histories in New York City, where they played each other repeatedly in the very same league. Their antipathy stems not from their post-1958 West Coast incarnation, representing Northern and Southern California respectively. The bad blood between New York Rangers fans and their counterpart supporters of the New York Islanders and the New Jersey Devils in ice hockey also attests to the ubiquitous phenomenon in all competitive team sports that proximity breeds competition and hatred, not respect and harmony. Distance may not foster affection but it most certainly decreases the acerbity of conflict. And the larger distances of America's spaces -- sports and geography -- contribute to a less-violent atmosphere in American sports compared to their European counterparts.

3. In contrast to European clubs, many of which to this day sport strong political identities, sports teams in the United States – tellingly called franchises – possess virtually none of this. In Europe, clubs have often been close to political parties or movements, which in turn reflect often bitter social, economic, religious, ethnic, and linguistic cleavages that divide people. And thus any contest, even a football match, between a team representing one subculture confronting its rival identified with another, becomes a de facto showdown between these two antagonistic "pillars".

    Crucially, American sports have virtually no national dimension to them. There are no national baseball, basketball, football, and hockey teams that represent the country on a regular basis in contests with neighboring countries. Americans are not familiar with the emotionally charged identification with a national team commensurate to what the Brazilians experience for their selecao, Germans for their National-mannschaft, Italians for their squaddra azzurra, or Argentinians for their albiceleste. Of course, there are "Team USA's" participating in quadrennial global competitions such as world championships and the Olympics, but these are far away and few in number and have virtually no relevance for Americans' emotional investment in their sports and teams. American sports and the accompanying emotions are completely inner-directed and insular, in that they exist in an intercity and intra-country environment in which international dimensions are secondary at best.

4. Furthermore, in contrast to the emotional investment in soccer's dom-inant monoculture in Europe, the multiplicity of America's hegemonic sports culture tends to spread a fan's emotional involvement over three, possibly four, teams, thus easing the pain and frustration accompanying a lost game or, an entire season. If, as a New Englander, one is (very likely) a passionate Red Sox fan, and a season goes badly, there are always The New England Patriots, the Celtics, and the Bruins to hope for. Ditto in other American cities and regions in which a multiplicity of teams representing the Big Four American sports share the fans' emo-tional capital, thereby lowering passions and fanaticism. This is less the case in sparsely populated areas with no major professional teams, where a single college or even high-school team assumes a fan base of quasi-European proportions. Indeed, being a Cornhusker fan in Nebraska is more similar in its intensity and commitment to being a European soc-cer club's supporter than that of an American professional team While sports as a whole are much more popular and prevalent in American than European culture, the distinct history of soccer's club and national team cultures in Europe have, as a rule, created deeper ties and long-term local attachments by communities with "their" clubs than exists between American franchises and their fans. For one thing, American professional sports teams have regularly moved from location to loca-tion, even from league to league, unthinkable in the European context.

5. Professional leagues, club authorities, and owners in American sports have increasingly assumed major responsibility in violence prevention and commonly play an active role in an effective, spectator-friendly se-curity system[5] that comprises programs to eliminate hostility among fans --in contrast to their counterparts in European soccer, at least until recently. The constant modernization of the venues in America, a priori in better condition than their European counterparts, and the reshaping

---

5.Major League Baseball and the National Basketball Association participate in TEAM (Techniques for Effective Alcohol Management), which is a program for training everyone from vendors to ushers in handling people who have had too much to drink. Available at www.teamcoalition.org.

of the sports themselves that renders a stadium visit a more congenial experience to the general public, coincides with the search for new solutions to minimize fan violence in the United States. With excessive alcohol consumption posing the biggest problem in terms of fan violence and unruliness, many arenas have come to stop the sale of beer either in its entirety or after a certain period in the game, such as the seventh inning in baseball.[6]

6. If violence does occur among fans of the North American Big Four, it is not articulated in racist language and activities. I am not arguing that racism has disappeared from American sports, let alone among spectators, culture, and society. Far from it! What I am saying, however, is that overt racist taunts have become unacceptable in the vernacular of American sports in the major leagues and on the college level. The reason for this, I am convinced, lies in the fact that in sports and other realms of public life, "the United States has worked harder and gone farther than any other advanced majority-white nation in confronting and righting the wrongs of its racist past."

This is much less the case with "classism." Thus, in sports, various "classist" taunts continue unabated; nor have misogynist slurs disappeared, though they too have become rarer as the number of women as athletes, spectators, and viewers has consistently increased since the 1980s. Any offensive language, let alone action, directed toward a collective that is perceived to be disempowered and/or a minority -- blacks, Latinos, or women -- has been effectively banned from American sports at the top level, though less so on their lower rungs.

Racist songs, slogans, and banners, let alone Nazi salutes -- that have become commonplace in Europe's football stadiums -- are unthinkable in contemporary American sports. It is not only because the authorities would not allow such behavior and punish it promptly and severely, but much more important, because the fans would never countenance it. I regard such massive change in language and behavior in contemporary America -- including its male-dominated sports culture -- as one of the many success stories that the civilizing agents of the 1960s and early 1970s (mostly, of course, the women's and the civil rights movements) wrought to enhance institutional and cultural inclusiveness and thus augment the country's democratic cosmopolitanism.

---

6. In basketball and football, where the universities took the lead, African Americans found earlier access than in the exclusive, resilient, and stubborn world of baseball. It took racial slurs by the New York Yankees outfielder Jake Powell in 1938 to lay bare the game's racism and break the silence that protected segregated baseball until then; see Chris Lamb, "Public slur in 1938 Laid Bare a Game's Racism," *The New York Times,* July 27, 2008, p. Sports 5. The first African American football player was active for the University of Michigan in the 1890s. And virtually all Jewish football stars had their breakthrough because they attended a college.

Moreover, size matters! When there were very few black players on the sports fields and in the stands, racist language and behavior flourished. The same pertains to Latinos, when only a few of them plied their trade in baseball's major leagues in the 1950s and 1960s. But with the proliferation of both among the ranks of top-level players -- to the point where African Americans comprise nearly 80 percent of all NBA players and close to 70 percent of the NFL's; and when Latinos exceed 30 percent of major league baseball players -- racism by necessity fades into the background.

7. Lastly, in notable contrast to Europe, in which most countries until recently had few, if any, sizable nonwhite populations, it was American sports that played a vanguard role in the progress toward racial equality and color-blindness in the country. Beginning with Jackie Robinson's integrating America's pastime in 1947 by joining the roster of the National League's Brooklyn Dodgers, the changes toward more inclusion and diversity in America's sports world regularly preceded and facilitated similarly inclusive changes in other cultural, social, and political spheres. Such inclusive reforms in sports were necessitated not by the enlightened and egalitarian inclination of its practitioners but rather by the inherently meritocratic, competitive, result-oriented, and profit-seeking nature of major-league professional team sports, where winning wasn't everything but the only thing. The stardom of African Americans in the sports world helped expand the social acceptance of blacks and thus constituted the precursors to Barack Obama's presidency. Though racial discrimination in American sports has certainly not disappeared -- the paucity of black team owners, front-office leadership, coaches, as well as managers corroborates this point -- the environment for racism has become socially taboo. Black athletes, as well as some coaches and managers, have achieved so much that it is now much harder for the exclusionary counter-cosmopolitans, who have most certainly not disappeared from American society and sport, to spew their racist venom openly. Above all, their surroundings no longer countenance it. I agree with Orlando Patterson that the remaining pernicious racial divide in contemporary America pertains much more to our private than our public lives.

8. Just as in matters of diversity and racial integration in sports, so, too, has America been ahead of Europe in terms of the presence of women as spectators at major sporting events. With the presence of women hovering around 40 percent of spectatorship in American stadiums, and reaching 50 percent in college sports, the threat of violence has been substantially reduced. More important still, women and families constituting a significant percentage of spectators in American sports has raised the threshold of shame for exhibiting violent behavior and voicing

racially offensive language in sports venues. The role of women as civilizing agents, as active carriers of cosmopolitan thought and behavior, of curtailing men from behaving badly, should not be underestimated as major contributors to the reduction of violence at sports events.

There is one remaining fault line that neither the United States nor Europe has been able to reduce, let alone eliminate, from its respective hegemonic sports cultures: homophobia. Not only are homophobe taunts by spectators still acceptable on both sides of the Atlantic, more important still is the fact that virtually no active player of any stature in any of these sports has openly admitted to being gay.

Conclusion

I believe that the comparative study of sports-related racism and violence confirms and reinforces my broader argument that hegemonic sports constitute an important force within popular culture and facilitate cosmopolitan change. Compared to other social spheres, hegemonic sports provide relatively easy access to (and for) immigrants and ethnic minorities in the global age. In the long run, ethnic minorities are able to enhance their visibility, gain respect and social recognition through sports in increasingly multiethnic postindustrial societies. Despite the continued threat by counter-cosmopolitans in societies in which immigrant sports heroes have acquired considerable standing over time, sports' merit-based cosmopolitanism has furthered progressive developments in culture, society, and politics. Thus, as I said at the beginning of my contribution, I amply share this project's premise that sports constitute on balance an agency for tolerance, good will and peace.

References

Appiah, K.A. (2007). *Cosmopolitanism*, New York: W.W. Norton pp. 137-153.

Dubner, S.J. (2007). "Why Aren't U.S. Sports Fans More Violent? *Freakonomics*, February 9, Available at: http://freakonomics.blogs.ny-times.com/2007/02/09/why-arent-us-sports-fans. (Accessed October 30th, 2008).

Goodhart, P. and C. Chataway (1968). *War without Weapons* London: W.H. Allen p. 144.

Guttmann, A. (1986). *Sports Spectators*, New York: Columbia University Press, p. 119.

Lamb, C. (2008). Public slur in 1938 Laid Bare a Game's Racism, *The New York Times,* July 27 p. Sports 5

Patterson, O. (2009). "Race and Diversity in the Age of Obama" in *The New York Times Book Review*, August 26th 2009.

Chapter 11
Sport and Recreation as Educational and Diagnostic Means

Don Bosco's Vision and the Salesians' Mission in Eastern and Southern Africa

Clemens Ley & Maria Rato Barrio

Introduction

In the year 1841 Don Bosco already practised in his oratory (a meeting place for youth with mostly educational and recreational activities, like a youth centre) and in schools a holistic approach combining sport and recreation with social-educational activities. He wrote:

> "Give them [the youth] ample liberty to jump, run, make a din as much as they please. Gymnastics, music, declamation (of poems, etc.), theatricals, hikes, are very effective methods for getting discipline; they favour good living and good health. One must only ensure that the plot, the characters and the dialogue are not unsuitable".

> (J. Bosco, 1877, p. 3).

But how does he assure that sport and recreation are suitable and beneficial for the youth? What are the key factors in his preventive system that the Salesians of Don Bosco are implementing still nowadays?

Methods

To get answers to these questions was a further factor of motivation to travel on various occasions between 2004 and 2009 to Eastern and Southern Africa. While assessing and developing sport projects together with the Salesians of Don Bosco, we (the authors) analysed their working approach and how they implement sport and recreational activities. Since 1859, the Salesians of Don Bosco offer, in the spirit of Don Bosco's preventive system (*formal* and *informal*) education, professional/vocational training, spiritual activities, and sport and recreational activities for youth (Ley & Rato, 2007).

Therefore, we conducted field visits to 24 different centres of the Salesians Family in disadvantaged areas of Eastern and Southern Africa, some in urban and some in more rural areas of South Africa (2); Lesotho (2); Mozambique (2); Tanzania (3); Kenya (3); Uganda (2); Southern Sudan (1); Ethiopia (8); and in a Refugee Camp in Kenya (1).

In the following, we present a summary of the results from the observation in the field visits (captured in field notes and diaries), the open interviews with youth, leaders, trainers, teachers and Salesians (recorded or alternatively captured by extensive field notes) and group discussions (group products, extensive field notes or recorded). The qualitative data was analysed regarding the emerging themes and afterwards compared to the literature review about Don Bosco's and Salesians' relation to sport and recreation.

Results

Facilities: where is the sport and recreation?

In all 24 centres, sport and recreation were always part of Salesians' specific and holistic programmes of social-educational activities and professional training. In total, the most common sports and recreational activities we encountered in the centres were: music, dancing, acting, acrobatics, cultural groups, hiking and outings, football/soccer, volleyball, basketball, netball, traditional sports and small games. Indeed:

> "Not even one Salesian school has been conceived that does not have at least, on a complementary level, recreative and sports initiatives".
>
> (Vecchi, 2006, p. 9).

In fact, we found in all centres sport and recreational facilities beside educational infrastructure, youth centres and churches. The sport and recreation facilities (football field/s; multi-purpose sport ground with lines and goals/baskets for at least basketball, netball, volleyball and 5-a-side football;

multi-purpose hall with a stage) were mainly in good shape, built in a solid and functional but welcoming open way. They were mostly strategically well located in order to give easy access to all interested youth from inside and outside the compound. The well-selected location of the sport and recreational facilities on the Salesians' compound indicate towards the high importance they attribute to sport and recreation for their students and for participants of other activities. At the same time, providing direct access to the sport and recreational facilities (at least in the afternoon and over the weekend) for the broader community indicates towards the important role of sport and recreation to attract, involve and recreate the youth in general. Being close to the community and especially to the youth is a main principle of Don Bosco and the Salesians. For example, in the Refugee Camp the Salesians of Don Bosco was the only organization (at least in 2004 and 2006) that was living directly with the refugees in the camp (and not in one of the big security compounds outside the camp).

Participants: who is taking part?

The Salesians are dedicated to supporting the youth. Therefore, most participants, especially those who take part in the sport and recreational activities, are young people.

Although spiritual guidance is one of the pillars of the Salesians and is offered for those who are interested, religion is not at all an exclusion criteria or issue for youth to take part in the educational, recreational and sport activities. For example, in the Refugee Camp (Kenya) we found that:

> "there are regular sport and recreational sessions and internal tournaments for the students of the professional training programmes and, of course, there is the oratory/youth centre, open for all refugees, whether they are Moslem or Christian or have any other belief system or not. The important thing is to share cheerfully experiences in sport and recreation and to use meaningfully any free time, independent of religion or any social-political inclination. And free time is in abundance in the camp due to a general lack of jobs and recreational possibilities"
>
> (Field diary 2004).

In Ethiopia, the Salesians invited the other religious institutions to send their youth to play together in order to promote interaction among the co-existing religions in the area. Therefore, "you can observe the children playing in different dress codes. Meanwhile pastoral care, as for example the bible reading group, is offered to those who are interested, religion seems not to be a topic or exclusion criteria for their educational, recreational and sport activities" (Field diary 2007). In various centres, individuals from other religious groups were working with the Salesians, for example, in Tanzania, the coordinator for basketball was a Muslim.

The Salesians are offering a great range of different sport and recreational activities in order to reach out to as many as possible, and to provide that everybody has the opportunity to choose his/her favourite type of activity.

In the selection of the activities they follow the motto '*If you love them you should love what they love*' (J. Bosco, 1884). For example, in the Southern Sudan, we noted that:

> ".....they are using traditional and cultural activities, especially dance, games and music, preserving and promoting cultural identities of the different ethnic groups living in the village. They exchange knowledge of other cultural groups and promote friendships and an intercultural way of living together [in the context of forced migration]. Using their cultural activities helps the Salesians to come close to the youth and to start working together from what they like".
>
> (Field diary 2004).

Although quite a number of the Salesians' youth clubs have strong sport teams playing in the respective regional or country's highest leagues, they have always a wide range of teams with different skills levels. For example, in Uganda, they are trained by the first team players as their contribution to the youth development. Meanwhile having the opportunity to develop their talents for high level sports, all players have to take part in educational and communities activities in order to develop holistically and to contribute to the development of others. For example, in Tanzania we noted that:

> "In the hall of the youth centre their basketball teams train every day, except when the hall is used for income generating activities or for special events. (...) They have all kind of age groups of boys' teams and also some girls' teams. Some of their basketball teams achieve great success in the highest leagues of Tanzania and even in Eastern Africa. The team player is not paid any salary but transport to official games, official registration fees and educational opportunities are provided. The main aim is not becoming the best team, but having good teams make the centre attractive and a lot of youngsters come to see and to play. In this way, they get involved and participate in further activities"
>
> (Field diary 2006).

The centre also has a small but busy football pitch and an art group that is involved in training and performing cultural dances (for example *Ngoma*, a traditional mixed performance of dancing, drumming, singing and acting), dramas, theatre and film acting, life skills and HIV prevention programs, spiritual guidance, a place to study, additional educational support and seminars. Sport and recreation seems to play an important role to include youth at risks of exclusion. For example, in Ethiopia, the Salesians try to reach out to "youth who might not want to play football, basketball or any other team sports, by offering weightlifting and a self-constructed gym (recycling old car and bicycle parts)" (Field diary 2009).

In Tanzania, group discussions with youth leaders in 2004 and with young girls as seminar participants in 2006 showed that some girls and young women are not allowed to come to play, as some parents consider sport a waste of time. Some even are considered lazy and irresponsible when they become involved in sport and recreation. Others cannot get the transport money to come to the centre. Meanwhile some boys are walking very long distances to come to the centre, and often the way is not always safe for girls. In addition, some cannot find the time due to their duties at home, such as cooking, getting water, caring for their brothers and sisters or even working out of home from an early age. In this context, the Salesians offer sport and recreation according to the time table of the girls (e.g. directly after school) and combine them with a place for study and educational support, giving them in some cases an "excuse" to come to the centre and to get involved also in sport and recreation. Apart from awareness creating activities at sport events and in communities, the youth leaders expressed that training and education of female leaders, animators and coaches are crucial in order to set up more teams that will attract more girls and women for regular training and education. They should act as role models and become 'multipliers' creating awareness in their living area. In 2006, a new netball court and separated changing rooms with toilets were built to improve the girls' participation in the centre, due to the lack of intimacy while changing from school to sport clothes. Seminars were organised with girls, including life skills and leadership training, discussion about gender (in-) equality and sport training contents. This aimed to improve opportunities for girls and young women.

Interaction: Playing and learning together

In most of the centres, we found the Salesians physically present on the sports grounds, either playing together with the youth or sharing observation and conversation. At one interview we wrote the following:

> "It is true that even conflicts can take place in the sports field, it can turn into fighting, but when we are present with them there, it is not so easy for them to involve in fighting, drugs, etc. When we are playing with them, they will not fight; it is not so easy for them. They become, more and more, friends; they come to play around football and actually it becomes more and more, a social gathering; and then slowly, slowly the conversion takes place. (...) We always insist that the teacher is with them, not only observing, but also playing with them"
>
> (Interview with a Salesian in the Refugee Camp in 2006).

In some centres and important moments and times, we observed that the number of Salesians and their duties and tasks inhibited their personal presence on the playground.

However, youth leaders were shown to have a key role in the activities. Therefore, the Salesians put a lot of efforts in a holistic development of their skills, e.g. by being close to them, giving them own responsibilities, providing them opportunities for the development of their own initiatives, offering additional training and educational opportunities. In several interviews the Salesians explained that they demand from their educators and youth leaders to participate and engage actively with the youth on the playground. In the same way, Don Bosco argued that:

> "The teacher who is seen only in the classroom is a teacher and nothing more; but if he joins in the pupils' recreation he becomes their brother. If someone is only seen preaching from the pulpit it will be said that he is doing no more and no less than his duty, whereas if he says a good word in recreation it is heard as the word of one who loves".
>
> (J. Bosco, 1884, p.3).

In general, we observed the Salesians approaching youth in a friendly, undemanding and open way, making jokes, etc. and following the principal of *"first you have to build up a friendship and then you can influence them through education"*. Regarding the way of how the director, educators and students interact, Don Bosco distinguishes his preventive system from the opposite repressive system:

> "The preventive system (...) excludes all harsh punishment and tries to limit even light punishment.' (...) Director and assistants act as loving fathers: they talk, guide, counsel and lovingly correct. The student does not feel disheartened. He becomes a friend, for he sees in the assistant a benefactor who wants his good, sparing him sorrows, punishment and dishonour. The educator, having gained the heart of his protégé, will be able to follow him even after leaving, still counselling and even correcting him".
>
> (T. Bosco, 2003, p. 235).

In all 24 centres, having fun and enjoying sport and recreation was not found contradictory to serious commitment of the participants to their studies or to social-educational activities. For example, in the Refugee Camp in 2006, in an interview, a Salesian pointed out that: "sport and recreational activities boosted the motivation in the educational activities and reduced the drop-out rate in the professional training".

Sport and recreation: Using diagnostic means and moments

> "We are with them, we play with them. Once you have played with a boy you know him better, he really shows himself in the field, he cannot hide, because it [the affections in sports, like shouting, anger, etc.] is something natural which comes out of him, and then, we help him to grow".
>
> (Interview with a Salesian in the Refugee Camp in 2006).

Also Don Bosco was using the time on the playground to observe their problems, needs and motivations. He considered that on the playground you really get to know each other, because in sports people do not hide behind their masks. They rather show spontaneously their real motivation and attitudes (Vecchi, 2006). In August 2004, in Southern Sudan, where most people have experienced violence or/and were forced to use it during the long conflict, we observed the following on several occasions in sports being played:

> "Militant authoritarian conducts shown by players, dictation of individually self made rules and harsh games. Very little interaction took place between team players: In volleyball they were playing directly over the net like tennis; in football and in basketball a player was trying to beat all others on his own, all were running behind the ball; there was little cooperation between players; everybody was on his/her own"
>
> (Field diary 2004).

We had the impression, that there was also little sense of confidence and trust between them and in fact:

> "Everybody was looking 'only' after him/herself. Without doubt, in sport and recreation you get faced with personal and social behaviours, and these might have been learnt during the conflict as strategies to survive and to protect oneself, or as a reaction to violence they suffered".
>
> (Field diary 2004).

As the above quoted Salesian expressed, through sport and recreational activities you can get to know the problems of the youth, but you can also work on their problems. However, in Southern Sudan, in 2004 there was a limited number of well-prepared trainers, educators and leaders, making it difficult to use sport and recreation for personal and social development.

Sport and recreation: Combining educational means

As Bosco remarks:

> "We lack something else. Young people should not only be loved, but also should feel that they are.' 'But don't they see that all we do is out of love for them?' 'No.' 'What's needed?' 'That on seeing themselves being loved in the things they like, they begin to love things they like less, like discipline, study and self-control. I'll explain myself: look, look closely at the boys in recreation".
>
> (J. Bosco, 1884, n.p.).

Meanwhile, sport and recreation are attracting youth to the Salesians' centres, this is an ideal place and moment for offering them further educational activities. Therefore, apart from the *"diagnostic means"* (Panampara, 1977, p.126). Don Bosco also used the time on the playground to teach life skills and values, to take aside a boy advising him to be more punctual or responsible and listening to his thoughts (Panampara, 1977; Vecchi, 2006). "For him it therefore became an element of reflection, observation, organization and of guidance" (Vecchi, 2006, p.6) and of "improving personal health, interpersonal relationship, satisfy the need for acceptance by the companions, and win their respect, friendship and admiration" (Panampara, 1977, p.126). He combined cheerful activities with serious learning.

The intentional use of the time at the playground and the positive canalization of sport and recreation are important for the Salesians. These are important reasons for them to be with the youth at the playground. In 2006, in an interview a Salesian in Tanzania explained:

> "For sure, young people have a lot of energies, so they need healthy leisure activities. From that perspective, I do believe that sports, theatre, music and other arts play an important role". However, "clubs or groups left to themselves in sports, in dance, or in performing cultural activities, is also dangerous, (...) if it is not provided that there is someone, an adult, who directs them. (...) It's not rare and it's actually common that you find drug abuse among them, early sexual activities, let me say risky behaviours. A lot of young people, who are involved in cultural activities, especially dance and music [especially when taken out of their traditional context], easily get swayed away by the current fashion and the western culture, a sort of a leisure culture".

He considered guidance and well prepared youth leaders and trainers as crucial. In addition:

> "I don't satisfy myself just by providing a playground; I need to put in place certain things, in terms of formation programmes, even sometimes some rules for the player: Yes you are coming to play basketball. Yes, fine, but can you spend at least one hour a week for formation? If you don't want to do that, make a choice. We don't want to provide you all these facilities just to get you spoilt in the society. We want you to contribute to the society. We want you to enjoy your life, to celebrate your life'. That means there is something more than sports alone. So a problem is that we often do not invest enough in that formation".

At the moment of the interview, apart from the existing regular educational and religious activities, the centre offered a life-skills programme of one hour a week to all the players and actors. Highlighting the importance of combining sport and educational interventions, he suggested that "sport festivals should go hand in hand with some sort of formation programme. (...) So, they go back to the same environment, but they are better equipped to face their environment".

A Salesian at the Refugee Camp explained in an interview in 2004 that sport and recreational activities are used together with educational activities and leadership training to bring people together and to teach them to resolve conflicts and to promote peace. According to him the experiences and capacities gained during these activities would also help the refugees in a peaceful reconstruction of their home countries once they are able to return.

In addition, we observed the Salesians using sport and recreation as a healthy and meaningful occupation of the free time of the youth, intending to prevent them from drug abuse, crime and risk behaviours. At the same time, sport and recreation were attracting youth to the centre and this was an opportunity to reach out to them and to offer education. Salesians, educators, youth leaders and sport coaches mostly functioned as role models on the playground, meanwhile their engagement with the youth around the sport fields gave them the opportunity to address them in an informal way, offering advice and involvement in further activities, such as HIV education, life skills and leadership training.

Conclusion

Regarding the initial question about how we can assure that sport and recreation are suitable and beneficial for youth, in this chapter we have analysed the holistic approach of Don Bosco and the Salesians of Don Bosco in Eastern and Southern Africa. I it clearly understandable how in middle of 19th century used sport and recreation as diagnostic and educational means. We conclude that the Salesians of Don Bosco are following the example of their founder and are using sport and recreation as basic elements of the preventive system, combining them with the other two main pillars, education and professional training, and spiritual activities. We identified as key factors, the following aspects:

1. In all 24 visited Salesians' centres in Eastern and Southern Africa we found solid sport and recreation facilities, mostly strategically well-placed for the open access and benefit of the interested youth from inside and outside their compound.

2. Efforts for inclusion of all youth is done by offering a great variety of sport and recreational activities. Youth are encouraged to get involved with activities they like. Some strategies for addressing specific groups of populations were exemplified, e.g. providing a gym with self-constructed apparatus.

3. In addition, high level sport teams were found to be attractive for youth to get involved in the centres. However, inclusion of the players in further educational activities, community activities and leadership training is considered paramount.

4. In most of the centres, we found the Salesians physically present on the sports grounds, playing together with the youth, sharing observation and informal conversation or providing guidance or information about further educational activities.

5. In addition, youth leaders, trainers and teachers are expected to take an active role on the playground, be role models and engage meaningful with the youth. Therefore, the Salesians provide them additional training and opportunities for their holistic development.

6. In general, youth are approached in a friendly and informal way. The Salesians follow the principal of "first you have to build up a friendship and then you can influence them through education". In all 24 centres, having fun and enjoying sport and recreation was not found contradictory to serious commitment of the participants to their studies and to social-educational activities.

7. Sport and recreation can be diagnostic means. The Salesians are using the time on the playground for getting to know the youth and observing problems, capacities, motivations and behaviours of them.

8. At the same time they might prevent possible violence and unsocial behaviours on the playground through their personal participation or that of their leaders and teachers.

9. Sport and recreation are used as a healthy and meaningful occupation of free time, for learning by playing and improvement of personal and social resources, among other objectives. They are used for a holistic development of the youth.

10. Sport and recreation can support meaningfully other interventions, like education, professional training, intercultural living together, post-conflict rehabilitation and peace building. Often the Salesians combine sport and recreation with life skills and leadership training, and other social-educational activities.

11. Don Bosco and the Salesians show that our concern in education, sport and recreation should be focused on the relationships between the people. The impact of an activity highly depends on the human and social interaction between the educators, trainers, leaders and youth. The personal contact and being close to the youth are essential. Sport and recreation can have an important influence on this interaction through promoting friendships, ludic moments, team processes and abilities to collaborate, fair play, responsibility and self-control, and sharing joy and spontaneity.

References

Bosco, J. (1877). The Preventive System in the Education of the Young. Regulations for the Houses of the Society of St Francis of Sales. (Critical edition by P. Braido, translation and notes by P. Laws). Turin, Italy: Salesians of Don Bosco.

Bosco, J. (1884). Letter from Rome. Rome, 10 May 1884. Available at: www.sdb.com. (Accessed 27th October 2006).

Bosco, T. (2003). Don Bosco. Nairobi, Kenya: Paulines Publications Africa.

Ceria, E.; Castelvecchi, L.; Mendl, M. (Eds.) (1989). Memoirs of the Oratory of Saint Francis de Sales from 1815 to 1855. The autobiography of Saint John Bosco (translated by Lyons, D.; with notes and commentary by Ceria, E., Castelvecchi, L. and Mendl, M.). New Rochelle, New York: Don Bosco Publications.

Ley, C., & Rato Barrio, M. (2007). Deporte y recreación en el sistema preventivo de los Salesianos de Don Bosco. IX Congreso Español de Sociología. CD de ponencias del congreso. Barcelona: Federación Española de Sociología (FES).

Panampara, A. (1977). A Glimpse into Don Bosco's Educational Method in the Light of Modern Guidance and Counselling. Tirupattur, India: Sacred Heart College.

Vecchi, J. E. (2006). Youth Ministry and Sport. Roma, Italy: PGS - Polisportive Giovanili Salesiane.

Chapter 12
Defending and the Faith

Reflections on Football in Post-Conflict Bosnia-Herzegovina

Gary Armstrong & Emily Vest

Introduction

The deceased 23 year old was a student by occupation and a religious hybrid by virtue of a Catholic father and a Muslim mother. He was murdered by gunshots fired by an ethnic Croat ostensibly defending the honour of the predominantly Croat town, Široki Brijeg. This long-standing trading town with a population of 26,500[1] had been designated as a regional H-Q in the Bosniak[2] - Croat Federation, under the political structure of post-conflict

---

1. According to the 1991 census 99.2% of the town's 26,437 residents claimed Croat ethnicity. No census has been undertaken since the conflict so it isn't possible to accurately say how the war changed the demographics of the region.

2. The preferred name used by the Bosnian Muslims to describe themselves is 'Bosniak'. They point out that the Croats are not referred to as Catholic nor the Serbs as Orthodox, and they believe that the description 'Bosnian Muslim' carries religious connotations that do not necessarily accurately reflect their people, many of whom are not actively practicing.

Bosnia-Herzegovina[3]. Its Croat citizens resented this status considering it as one imposed by a central government they did not recognise. Whilst a long way from the front-line of the Balkan conflict of 1991-95, during WW2 the town controlled by the *Ustaša* (a Croatian facist separatist movement, with Nazi connections) holds a reputation for atrocities committed in that epoch. Most notably 4,000 ethnic Serbs were captured by the *Ustaša*, killed and buried in mass graves in ways that preceded what was witnessed across Bosnia some 50 years later. The town's historical legacy remains evident today, their football club, Široki Brijeg NK, supporters group nickname is the '*Škripari*' meaning Cave Dwellers a title which carries a reference to the towns *Ustaša* support and its guerrilla-warfare resistance to the anti-Nazi forces and later the post-war communist government. Today, when supporting the club locals pride themselves on not taking too kindly to 'invaders' of any type - but were particularly hostile to those celebrating their Muslim credentials even if they were loaded onto a pre-existing football rivalry[4].

Fans of all clubs in Bosnia-Herzegovina (BiH) know of the Croat pride ingrained in NK Široki Brijeg supporters; specifically their fearsome home game reputation. Reputations exist to be challenged, particularly when evidenced or proclaimed amongst football supporters groups. Thus the FK Sarajevo supporters group, the notorious and self mythologising *Horde Zla* (Hordes of Evil), were a part of the 500 or so visiting fans that travelled the 140km to Široki Brijeg on October 4th 2009 and disembarked their coach transport several hours before the scheduled kick-off. In the mass disorder that ensued missiles were thrown, people were hurt and eventually a gun was aimed. Receiving several bullets fired from a weapon owned by a police officer was the 23 year old student and FK Sarajevo supporter, Vedran Puljić who bled to death in 20 minutes. The football match he had travelled to watch was cancelled.

---

3. The General Framework Agreement for Peace in Bosnia-Herzegovina better known as The Dayton Peace Accords (sometimes referred to as the Dayton Peace Agreement) was agreed in Dayton, Ohio in November 1995 by Slobodan Milosevic, the Serbian President, on behalf of the Serb Republika Srpska, Franco Tudjman, the Croatian President, and Alija Izetbegovic the Bosniak leader . The treaty –signed in Paris in December 1995-brought the Bosnian conflict to a close dividing the country into two Entities; the Serb Republika Srpska and the Federation the latter being an uneasy alliance between the Croats and Bosniaks. The Federation is divided into 10 cantons, generally of one ethnicity or another and political power is concentrated at this level, essentially ensuring that each group is governed by their own ethnicity. Government structures at the national level and at the Federation level are weak, ensuring that smaller regional HQs are disproportionately influential politically given their size.

4. Although the municipality of Široki Brijeg saw little violence during the 1992-95 conflict the Southern Herzegovina region, of which Široki is a part, witnessed bitter clashes between the Croats and Bosniaks, most evident in the city of Mostar, some 45km away.

The disorder was not purely about football. Since the cessation of the violent conflict in 1996 football games in Bosnia had regularly witnessed mass-disorder between fans. On this occasion however the numbers involved and the level of disorder that preceded the death was not anticipated. Prior to the game officials of FK Sarajevo had informed their opponents and police that the Sarajevo team's following would be negligible and most of the regional police officers were absent from the town at the time of the disorder; deployed instead to police the notoriously confrontational Mostar derby[5] some 45 km away.

The death brought nationwide shock. Death is no stranger to the Balkans - an estimated 250,000 lost their lives in the wars following the collapse of Yugoslavia in 1991- but death around football was unknown in the post-conflict milieu. The murder strengthened prejudices. To their detractors the Croats were - as ever - murderers. To their critics Bosniaks remained the antagonists who - as ever - claimed their innocence. Not all blame was collective; some Catholic Croats dismissed the dead man as a traitor to his Fathers religion. Why, they asked, was he associating with the Muslims of Sarajevo?

It was not a police officer who pulled the trigger but a 32 year old man believed to have belonged to the Croatian Defence Force paramilitary group that went by the name of *Kažnjenička Bojna* (Punishment Troop). During the civil conflicts of the 1990's this gathering was renowned for its particular cruelty towards Bosniaks. In this 2009 football-related disorder he had reputedly grabbed the gun off a local policeman, shooting and killing the 'invader'. Arrested and charged with murder the accused escaped from custody, despite the presence of 7 police officers, and fled to neighbouring Croatia where he lay low for weeks before eventually turning himself in to the Croatian authorities. Like many Bosnian Croats he held dual Croatian and Bosnian nationality and could not be extradited to the nation where the crime was committed, remaining at liberty. The 7 police officers were suspended from duty and investigated for their part - if any - in his absconding.

Puljić's funeral was preceded by a peaceful demonstration by his fellow fans in Sarajevo. Days later a demonstration in Široki Brijeg saw local Croats demanding outsiders stop accusing them of being fascist in politics and murderers by association. A TV chat show soon after the death involving representatives of the two clubs, officials from the Bosnian FA and police representatives dissolved into bitter mutual blame. Two narratives dominated: For the Croats the visitors had arrived in a mob to randomly attack their town and people and the locals acted in self-defence. By contrast the Bosniaks believed that they had once again been the victims of an unprovoked attack. Concerns were raised about the possibility of further outbreaks of violence between the two towns but instead fortuitously the

---

5. The Mostar derby is notable for its political and national tensions. Played between the Bosniak team of Velež and the Croat team of Zrinjski, the fixture is regularly accompanied by high levels of supporter violence and the authorities were expecting there to be violent clashes in Mostar that day.

hatred was reduced to simmering mutual insults and threats on football-related web-sites. The fixture was finally played in November 2009. The evening kick-off attracted a crowd of just 3,000 who sang Croatian nationalist songs throughout. There were no visiting fans.

Football is a secular world loaded with quasi-religious connotations enacted in local cultures encompassed in a framework of trans-national possibilities. It is a near-universal idiom which delights in its simplicity. Inevitably those aspiring to build peace in arenas of conflict may see in such qualities an innocence that could be utilised to their cause of bringing enemies together via a mutual enthusiasm. The game in its aesthetic is enchanting and intensely human. The collective endeavour required for victory makes it intensely appealing to those seeking to rebuild civil society from the ruins of slaughter and destruction. As a past-time with enthusiasts across religious and racial divides, the game is seen by many as harnessing the potential for building upon a joint passion. Football's global tournaments are quick to proclaim the game's capacity to build a sense of shared humanity. The ambassadorial role of its key players stress the game's potential for peace and understanding. At the level of the apparatchiks of FIFA and UEFA the game is ever-accompanied by claims around peace-making and the promotion of human rights. Certainly, football has its evangelists.

Others, however, refute the game's abilities to offer solace or hope in theatres of conflict and post-conflict. The man herein who articulates upon the capacities for the game is actually tasked and paid to promote the philosophy of football as salvation. His days of fighting for the city where his office in the Bosnian-Herzegovina Football Association (*Nogometni/Fudbalski*[6] *Savez Bosne i Hercegovine* N/FSBiH- known colloquially as 'Savez') is now located may bring a sense of perspective to those organisations that proselytise the game's capability for bringing peoples together. Just possibly the structural fault-lines of the society are too great for anything other than resentful toleration. Or perhaps the man who has seen too much death cannot see the innocent potential the game offers.

Employed as the Savez Officer for International Development Velid Imamović travels widely, speaking with high officials of UEFA, FIFA and a variety of NGO's. The politics integral to such a role do not faze this striking man. Well built, tall and with flowing hair and beard, Imamović is in his mid-40s and is confident as he walks in the Ottoman district of his adopted city. Having fought on the streets of Sarajevo for 3½ years as part of the Bosniak infantry against their Serb equivalents, Imamović now claims the city he defended as his and enjoys the victory he was part of and the fact that he had seen death and cheated it. He comments:

> "There were 20,000 of us (Bosniak fighters) maybe 3,000 'real' soldiers. I fought 3 ½ years for this city. You love every day as a soldier. I am not afraid of death..."

---

6. Nogometni is the Croatian word for Football, leading to the Croat abbreviation of NK for many Croat Football Clubs. Fudbalski is used by Serbs and Bosniaks, their clubs are usually demarked by the FK abbreviation.

Born in Vitez, some 55km from Sarajevo, Imamović arrived in Sarajevo in 1981 to study civil engineering. As a child and teenager his sporting passion was basketball. The War interrupted his studies and seeking post-conflict employment he utilised 'good connections' to acquire the position of National TV Head of Foreign Film. In his three years in this role he claimed to have achieved "good results" and concomitantly mastered the English language. Entering politics with the SDA[7] Bosniak Political Party he left when "seeing injustice". He also left his job at the TV station when it was sold off "unofficially" to what he considered "USA interests." In 1998 he was offered a job in Savez by virtue of his abilities in the English language and, when spoken with in late 2009, was in his 11th year of employ. His introduction leaves a listener in no doubt that politics and football were no strangers in this region:

> "Under Communism the heads of sporting organisations were political activists; hence positions were 'political'. When Savez began in 1992 all appointments were political maybe with a small (p)'.

Admitting that he was a political appointment as the organization sought to represent the Bosniak, Croat and Serb ethno-nationalist demographics he assumed the title 'Head of International Development', a position without a job description or mandate. On assuming office he was one of 18 full-time officials. By 2009 that number was 30 and he stated unequivocally not all appointments were made on merit.

The football organisation he is employed by remains factional, a product of a forced alliance between the three Associations originally created in 1992 as Bosnia disintegrated[8]. Even today the Football Association representing the Republika Srpska (FSRS) harbours a not so secret ambition to eventually be recognised by FIFA and UEFA and continues to strive to have its 'national' team recognised and to play 'international' matches[9]. This situation, Imamović believes, was exacerbated by a conspiracy of football's wider and international ruling bodies.

---

7. *Stranka Demokratske Akcije* (Party for Democratic Action) was founded in May 1990 by Alija Izetbegović, the war time Bosniak leader .The Party represents Bosniaks.

8. N/FSBiH was founded in 1992 in Sarajevo and claimed to represent Bosnia as a whole opening their membership to all ethnicities. This was the reason given why it was this Bosnian FA and not the Serb or Croat FAs that were recognised by FIFA and UEFA. The acceptance of N/FSBiH by international bodies meant until 2000 it was predominantly Bosniak teams that competed in Europe. The Bosnian Croats created the Herceg-Bosna Football Federation which finally joined N/FSBiH in 2000 and the Bosnian Serbs created the Football Association of the Republika Srpska (FSRS) which joined in 2002. N/FSBiH is responsible for running the national team and the Premier League only, at lower levels the 3 organisations remain very divided, split along ethnic lines.

9. The RS Football Association continues to press for recognition by FIFA for 'international' matches, claiming the situation with the England, Scotland, Wales and Northern Ireland FAs sets a precedent for UEFA and FIFA to follow. To date neither FIFA nor UEFA have offered such recognition to the RSFA.

FIFA have banned their members from playing matches against the Republika Srpska because it's one step towards recognising their independence. But they know there's too many teams already from the region: us (BIH), Croatia, Serbia and Montenegro.....

The position Imamović holds is, in his words, "frustrating". He sees his role as ceremonial and tokenistic rather than facilitating the power to implement actual change. Furthermore, he argues, those who wish to change things are hamstrung by the structure of Savez and the absence of funds. The Savez organisation relies on monies from FIFA and UEFA and gate income from domestic leagues and international fixtures. Monies from the Government of BiH are limited towards funding flights and accommodation for players and officials for national team fixtures. The fundamental problem however is the absence of government scrutiny. This has seen Savez officials run things to their own advantage. According to Imamović corruption in Savez is "endemic." In his estimation over the decade 1999-2009 some 10m Euros had been stolen from its coffers.[10] At the time of his being interviewed the debts of Savez were reported to be 4m Euros. Such a state of affairs is tolerated by the organisation being controlled by an alliance of governmental officials and what Imamović calls "the Mob." The issue was complex yet reducible to a formula:

> "Don't see the issue as one of ethnic nationalism.... It's about crime and politics".

It was not always thus. In Imamović's opinion the decent and honest men who once sat on Savez were "cleared [and] replaced by too many evil groups". Today the former are to be found doing "low jobs." In this milieu he sees hope only in some distant future:

> "Where there is poison the cure has to come from the same place. The hope for change is here [Bosnia]... our young people are becoming better educated".

The years of armed conflict are evident throughout contemporary Sarajevo. The pock-marked walls of buildings remind the passer-by of the millions of bullets expended. Monuments to the estimated 12,000 or more that died in Sarajevo (a further 50,000 were wounded) litter the city and rows of white wartime gravestones are visible in every direction. The years preceding the fall of the first missiles saw many incidences of fans of Croatian and Serbians teams fighting around football fixtures[11]. According to Imamović the disin-

---

10. Shortly after the interview with Imamović, the General Secretary of Savez, Munib Ušanović and the Finance and Marketing Secretary Miodrag Kures were found guilty of evading taxes on turnover of products and services, as well as of illegal misappropriation of the NFSBiH funds. Each were sentenced to 5 years of jail. An accountant at the trial said that the accounting practices at Savez were the worst she had seen during her 20 years of practice in the profession.

11. Most famously the match between the Croatian Dinamo Zagreb and the Serbian Red Star played in May 1990, a few weeks after Croatia's first multiparty elections had resulted in a strong victory for those parties favouring independence from Yugoslavia. The riots started before the game, which was abandoned within minutes and hundreds were estimated to have been injured.

tegration of civil society was represented by football-related disorder. But the stakes went higher; mass murder was to follow and some of the protagonists of football-related trouble became notorious leaders of paramilitary groups and they recruited directly from the terraces[12]. The hitherto peaceful citizen Imamović was motivated to take up arms as the missiles fell on Sarajevo, fired from the surrounding hill-tops by Serb militia in positions built by the Serb personnel in the Yugoslav Armed Forces years before the civil war began. Whilst the conflict may have had its omens in football-related disorder what ensued remains, in Imamović's logic, impossible to articulate, justify or even explain. Reflecting on some of those former citizens he had fought against he asks but cannot answer:

> "Why would you leave a good job, and leave behind a neighbourhood to walk up a mountain and bomb the city you lived in?".

Regardless of causation the ensuing conflict became in his opinion an issue of global significance and to this day inspires his thoughts and actions:

> "The city was a battleground for Christians and Muslims. They considered us (Muslims) halfway to Taliban... their bombing was a gesture to warn off those elsewhere who were considering adopting Islam".

The Islam of Imamović is Sufi *"it's not about praying at the mosque it's about thinking about the meaning and profundity of one's actions."* The profundity he pursues permits him to speak openly of the organisation that pays his wages. In his opinion only three "good men" (he is one) are employed by Savez and because of the situation he does not enjoy attending games or even watching TV broadcasts of the game beyond that required of his duties His Sufi inspired integrity saw Imamović turn whistle-blower on the Savez procedures and inform Michel Platini, the French General Secretary of UEFA, that its monies were being stolen by Savez officials. Such monies were then suspended and remain so two years later. If anyone in Savez suspected Imamović of whistle-blowing they kept their suspicion to themselves:

> "They said nothing to me... but I know they know. When others wanted to speak out some threatened to kill members of the other good guys' family....".

But not yours?

> "They daren't... I'm not scared of them. I fought daily for 3 ½ years in these streets. What can I be scared of....? I told Platini that if they killed my family I would kill the Savez officials who allowed it... That's maybe why they stopped the money".

The core of the problem is, in Imamović's opinion, that football in Bosnia does not attract those with the best of intentions:

> "People come into football because there is money to be made in transfers and getting into Europe. Such considerations come before political ambitions...".

12.Most famously the leader Željko Ražnatović, whose Serb paramilitary group known as the Serb Volunteer Guard, but better known as Arkan's Tigers, were recruited from the terraces of the Belgrade's Red Star club. Some of the leading protagonists of this entity have been charged with grave breaches of the Geneva Convention including ethnic cleansing actions across Northern and Eastern Bosnia.

But for all their duplicity the men in Savez seeking to make money from football had little financial acumen. A television right deal signed in 2006 to cover domestic league games to cover the years 2010-2014 with the Hamburg-based *Sports 5* company brought just 10m Euros into the Savez coffers. According to Imamović, those in Savez who signed the deal each made 500,000 Euros for their own accounts. For those seeking monies (legitimately or not) the amounts promised from football's governing bodies were considerable for a nation with massive unemployment and little by way of public service. In 2006 Savez stood to receive 5m Euros from FIFA's GOAL! and UEFA's Hat-Trick schemes. The plan was that 4m Euros would go towards the building of a new stadium (Imamović was to be Project Manager). The remaining 1m Euros would go to a variety of 'development projects' for established clubs in Bosnia. This however had brought problems of integrity and accountability:

> "The three Presidents and the General Secretary had done a deal to line their own pockets... FIFA agreed to stop the funding to protect the money...".

This was the situation that prompted Imamović to blow the whistle. The FIFA monies were at the time of the interview ostensibly being held in reserve until Savez cleaned up its act and were due to be released a month after Imamović was spoken with. Those facing the inquiry were in the meantime still in the paid employ of Savez. Such a scenario provoked his contempt for FIFA and UEFA: *"They changed nothing; they were worse than us."*

For a man employed by an organisation that exists to administer and promote football Imamović does not sell the product very well. His knowledge of the way things are combined with his integrity paints a bleak picture of the game and what it might do in a post-conflict context. So, he was asked, does the game as some believe assist in the processes of post-conflict reconciliation? He answers in the negative and cites his own duplicity in such a belief:

> "Not for me and my people. We didn't start the war. Those who perpetrated the mass killings have to live with their actions...How can something as pure as reconciliation be achieved by something like football that is rotten to the core? UEFA promoted reconciliation projects in Sarajevo some years ago. Their officials asked me what I thought of such schemes. I told them publicly I will say 'all is good'; privately I think these programmes are bullshit".

Would the entry of Bosnia-Herzegovina into the (forthcoming) 2010 World Cup Finals[13] be good towards building a sense of nation?

> "No... people are afraid to come and watch us because of what their Serb and Croat neighbours might say...Getting to the Finals would just strengthen the position of the Savez Committee. They will obtain big monies; but out of this 10% will go to the Federation, 30% to the players and 60% to the pockets of the Committee men".

---

13. Bosnia qualified for the World Cup Play-Offs and were drawn to play against Portugal. They lost both games 1-0.

During the final qualification game, when Serbia had already qualified and Croatia was already out of the competition, there was a sense, for the first time, of Serbs and Croats supporting Bosnia in the Play-Off against Portugal. But their loss led to bitter claims of players throwing matches because of their ethnicity[14], particularly in the Bosniak media.

Beyond institutions and football-related programmes do footballers have a role to play in the pursuit of a peaceful co-existence? The answers of Imamović suggests the players place their own interests above that of the nation and that such a pursuit was not the desire of footballs governing bodies:

> "Players at some clubs sometimes go six months without pay. They have no alternative but to carry on training and playing – they have no other job. Some of these players when playing at international level have 'sold' Bosnian matches. A European Finals Qualifier against Denmark saw us need only a draw to get through... we lost 1-0... UEFA didn't want us there anyway- Serbia and Croatia had already qualified..."

Does the presence of a genuinely national Bosnian organisation and players from a variety of ethnic backgrounds playing for the national team offer symbolic hope for wider societal integration? This apparently is not the case and is reflective more of a forced union:

> "The [Bosnian] Serb and [Bosnian] Croat joined the Bosnian-Herzegovian FA only because they were told to by FIFA. They were both afraid to join and didn't want to...".

Is selection for the national team thus ever made with a desire to be all-inclusive?

> "No... forget ethnicity! Players are selected according to their ability to bring in money. International fixtures are a shop window; international selection adds to their transfer window...".

That said politics and ethno-religious affiliation seem to have been instrumental in deciding the position of national team manager. In 2008 Meho Kodro was fired from such a position having stated his unwillingness to take the national team to play a friendly fixture in Iran immediately prior to important World Cup qualification matches. Due to their shared Islam Iran had been the most generous donor to post-war BIH. One argument from Kodro was that the monies BIH would earn from the game were to be paid in cash. Fearing such monies would not reach their rightful destination he resigned. What is Imamović's take on this?

> "National team managers select line-ups, they do not decide fixtures..."

---

14. The Bosnian national team's influential co-captain, Zvjezdan Misimović, is a Bosnian Serb who was widely seen to be instrumental in their qualifying campaign. The play-offs saw him have two substandard games leading to accusations from many, including the manager, that he had deliberately thrown the matches as for Bosnia to qualify would be a disaster for the Republika Srpska (for a more detailed synopsis of the argument between manager and player see http://en.wikipedia.org/wiki/Zvjezdan_Misimovi%C4%87)

Yet Kodro was popular with the players (19 of whom effectively went on strike refusing to play in matches organised by Savez) and the fans, who vigorously demonstrated against his dismissal and associated corruption in Savez. The latter responded by hiring the Bosnian Croat manager Čiro Blažević (manager of the very successful Croatian 1998 World Cup team), who publically stated his team selection would be based on footballing ability and not to satisfy ethnic quotas. The national team started to put together a string of good results muting the effectiveness of the protests. Herein lays a paradox: For the Bosnian Croats and Bosnian Serbs to support Bosnia, their results must be at least the equivalent of those of Croatia and Serbia. But good results have cemented the positions of those in power, shielding corrupt officials.

In the absence of clubs, players and officials making a difference through football, would football fans be a more fruitful demographic in pursuing processes of reconciliation and peace? The murder described in the opening paragraph does not suggest that this is feasible. For Imamović the visiting FK Sarajevo supporters involved in the incident were both misunderstood and treated in a cowardly manner. Additionally, the forces of civil society had little by way of motivation to intervene:

> "The traveling Sarajevo fans did not carry weapons. The Sarajevo fans were on their way after the game to Mostar – some 45 minutes driving time – to join Muslims to enjoy a celebration. Their hosts had Kalashnikovs, such people needed guns – they could not fight the invaders on their terms....".

And,

> "There are no laws pertaining to football hooliganism in Bosnia. There are no laws addressing racism either: There is no political will... it means people can get away with anything.... Police earn 250 euros monthly- they make more money stopping vehicles 'discovering' a violation and asking for 2 Euros to allow the driver to continue...".

The 'BH Fanaticos' fan group are the fan-face of Bosnia – Herzegovina's national team, and actively campaign against corruption in Savez. Founded by the Bosnian diaspora in Sweden the fan movement had thousands of members who follow the national team home and away. Such a group promoted its inclusivity but was Imamović equivocal in locating them as a force for good?

> "They have donated monies to humanitarian causes. But many of them are not 'good guys'. They bring disorder – they protested outside the offices of Savez, but they knew the top four officials – the ones they were protesting against – were not in the building. Why attack the receptionist and the police sent to restore order? In an international match in Belgium we had to stop some of them attacking home supporters in the streets".

For Imamović the future for BiH is bleak and football is a distraction from larger processes.

"The 1995 Dayton Agreement was Treason. They said Bosnia should be two parts: Bosnia-Herzegovina and the Republic of Široki Brijeg. The sub-text is that the latter will one day become Croatia...The war will start again in Europe. The issue is defeating Islam. Football is the last thing we should be trying to build in this society".

Bosnia faces particular challenges of not only moving from a communist to post-communist society, with the development of democracy and civil society, but also from a centrally controlled to market economy at the same time as developing a post conflict society. The type of civil conflict seen during the 1990s led to fracturing of societal norms and traditions, causing people to identify more strongly with their more localised 'clans' and the concomitant ties of religion, history and an imposed sense of ethnicity. This strengthened sense of identification has been reinforced by the political system imposed on the country through the Dayton Peace Accords. With each of the three groups guaranteed a certain number of representatives at each level of government, political parties must seek to ensure they secure their own national vote; there is nothing to be gained from appealing to others of a different ethnicity. Effectively the Accords created a system where although elections in Bosnia are generally considered to be free and fair, the politicians campaign on a basis of what they will do to protect 'national' interests, creating an atmosphere of fear and encouraging people to vote for what they know now, 'people like them'. Politicians have always been known for their abilities to work around the system. Post conflict, most of the personalities remain the same, either because of pre-war political status or because their ability to operate effectively in a conflict economy left them well placed to take advantage of the economic situation post Dayton. Bosnia is not a 'gangster state' but it is not far off. State mechanism, notably education, politics, borders and customs exist, but procedures are slow and the state's influence is often too weak in the face of local people of influence.

Progress in attempts to build a sense of post-conflict civil society exists. Sometimes football can illustrate this. In the first five years following the end of the war football games were dangerous occasions, even though most matches were played between teams of the same ethnicity. In 1998, a Sarajevo vs Banja-Luka football fixture would have been unthinkable[15], but by 2002 a national Premier-league had been established amalgamating the regional system that had emerged post-war. It still exists today – not without problems – but it is the main reason for people to travel in large numbers

15. Banja Luka is the capital of the RS, Sarajevo the capital of the Federation. Prior to 1998 travelling to the other Entity was like travelling to a different country. There were border posts and cars had different licence plates which clearly identified visitors. There had been little or no return of refugees to their pre-war homes and the sense of the 'other' remained a potent force. Very few would want to travel between the two. Gradually the differences have faded, licence plates are now the same, there are no border posts, Bosnian money is widely accepted throughout the country and there has been widespread refugee return.

to visit the people 'over the hill'. In such journeys they take with them football traditions (and hatreds, occasionally stretching back half a century or so) alongside ethno-religious traditions and differences. The game has been present in the region for over 100 years and for some 55 years (1945-90) was part of the Communist system. The clubs had a state-dictated rationale and statutes which separated their purpose from any ethno-religious affiliation. In the post-conflict context when many pre–existing kinship and community networks have been destroyed by violence, some people have utilised the game and the loyalties it provides to create a new identity network. Loyalty to a club combined with ethnic affiliation, combined with a layer of religion topped off with a pursuit of masculine credibility and former warlord operators is a lethal combination. Ethno-nationalist hostilities remain in BIH, but they are for the most part sublimated to the vocal or the fleeting chance to punch or kick an opponent-sometimes around football matches. In the eyes of many, football has been abused by individuals with political objectives who hope to promote - and play on- ethno-nationalist sentiment and fears. Such Machiavellian politicians-cum-club-owners are accused of using the game and associated spectator disorder around specific fixtures to enact ethno-political antagonisms. The game's massive media profile brings publicity to a cause or issue. Fear of the perceived rivals encourages voting polarized on ethnic lines.

Football at its best might help some parts of some communities start to bridge a divide. At its worst, as Imamović recognises, it reflects the rotten body politic and perpetuates the fracture lines of that society. The game in Bosnia Herzegovina needs to achieve that level of innocence to be of any use in the processes of post-war reconciliation.

Post-script

In April 2010 FK Sarajevo drew 1-1 when playing hosts to Siroki. Hoping for a victory to commemorate their murdered colleague the disappointed home fans after the game turned on the police who had been present in large numbers protecting the sparse number of visiting fans. Of the 40 people reported injured in the clashes 17 were police officers. Rumours circulated amongst the fans and throughout the Bosnian game that club management of SK Sarajevo had 'sold' the game.

Chapter 13

Potentialities and Challenges of an Intervention Model to Promote Intercultural Processes in Post-conflict Contexts

María Rato Barrio & Clemens Ley

Introduction

Sport (understood in a very broad sense) is fast becoming more accepted as an effective and efficient tool within the cooperation for development field. In spite of evidence of the positive effects of sport in various cases and intervention areas, we cannot deny its ambivalent nature, as sport can also provoke negative effects (Coakley, 2007; Coalter, 2007; Giulianotti, 2004; Keim, 2003; Rato Barrio & Ley, 2009; Rato Barrio, Ley, & Durán González, 2009, etc.). Thus it becomes necessary to use this tool according to certain carefully chosen methodological models and applying clearly defined and concrete strategies according to the specific objectives stated (Gieß-Stüber, 2005; Gieß-Stüber & Blecking, 2008; Henry, 2009; Ley & Rato Barrio, 2009; Rato Barrio & Ley, 2011, etc.). Thereby, it is also essential to evaluate the processes and results derived from that programmes to raise awareness not only about the good practices but also about the challenges we face (e.g. Engineers without borders - Canada, 2009, 2010). This information might contribute to a learning process and to an increase of useful knowledge in this field, which could lead us to modify our practices accordingly, and as such improve the quality of our action.

In 2007-8, the sport project *Psychosocial, community and intercultural action in the Guatemalan post-conflict context* was implemented in Guatemala by the Group for Cooperation DIM (Sports, Territorial Engineering and Design) based at the Technical University of Madrid (*Universidad Politécnica de Madrid*), in Spain. This project included many 'programmes + researches' with different objectives. One of this 'programme + research' was the Intercultural Programme through Sports (PIDE), whose first evaluation ended in June 2009. The whole project cycle of PIDE can be consulted in Rato Barrio (2009). The purpose of the study was to evaluate the intervention model, its applied strategies and the impact of the PIDE Programme with regards to the promotion of intercultural relations among the different *ethnolinguistic groups*[1] involved in it.

In this chapter we introduce the intervention model designed to promote intercultural living together through sport, based on a theoretical framework with specific goals, strategies and activities, and its evaluation in the PIDE programme, which was run both in *formal* (programmes at schools) and *informal* (community programmes) educational settings, with a hundred of constant participants in the intervention group and another 557 in the control group.

Methodology

Intervention model

In designing the PIDE's intervention model we have first articulated two theoretical models advanced by the Spanish anthropologist Giménez Romero (2000a, 2003a, 2003b; Malgesini & Giménez Romero, 2000) and the French social psychologist Cohen-Emerique (1997, 2004) and secondly we made a physical-sportive adaptation of the resulting model. In it, we maintain the three progressive phases propounded by Cohen-Emerique (*Ob. Cit.*), which we didn't consider as closed compartments but overlapping phases (see graphics 1 and 2):

---

1. We use the category "ethno-linguistic groups" because of being the one utilized locally (in the region where the project was implemented) in the discourses related with the otherness.

* 1st Phase: Developing *decentring* processes.

This refers to a process regarding oneself. It includes taking awareness, acquiring knowledge and critical reflection about your *own cultural* references and trying to observe your *own culture* from *outside* in order to get *certain cultural neutrality*. Neutrality is obviously impossible to get; however, the aim is to get the highest degree each one can achieve. This phase also includes the researcher starting to deconstruct ones' own prejudices and stereotypes. In this phase it is important to emphasise on increasing the knowledge with regards to cultural and identity issues, focusing on the convergences found among the *different cultures* and identities identified.

* 2nd Phase: Developing comprehension

This refers to a process regarding *the Other*[2]. Once we have *neutralized our own cultural* references up to *a certain degree*, and we know the 'rules and practices' of the diverse ethno-linguistic groups involved in the programme, by emphasizing the convergences – i.e. what we share with *Others* - we can gradually generate certain degrees of *identification* with *the Other*. Thus we can gradually work on the divergence as richness - but without neglecting the common aspects. In this phase the curiosity and openness are very important qualities to develop, as well as empathy, mutual understanding, trust, and other important issues we emphasize along the whole process.

* 3rd Phase: Developing negotiation skills

This refers to a process regarding the relationship. It includes mainly non-violent conflict management, conflict resolution, critical self-analysis, mediation and communication skills.

---

2. We don't intend to naturalise nor accept this old dichotomy between *We* and *the Others* (McLaren, 1995 etc.), which emphasizes the divergences stressing clear cultural limits who differentiate *We* and *the Others*. So we will write in italic those words which refer to the otherness, emphasizing our distance with this dichotomy. But due to the size limitations of this chapter and in order to schematize this methodological model, we consider these terms useful to simplify the explanation. In this chapter, we use these terms, while taking into account, that the otherness is done explicit not because of its real existence but because of the perceptions and interpretations of most of our participants, emerging when they are in interaction with *Others*. In their interaction, verbalization, discourses, etc, this otherness is done explicitly. So, we find its important to work with that, emphasizing always the convergences rather than the divergences to gradually get an identification with those persons considered, embodied, experienced as *the Others*, in order to steadily blur this barrier among *me/we – he/she/they*.

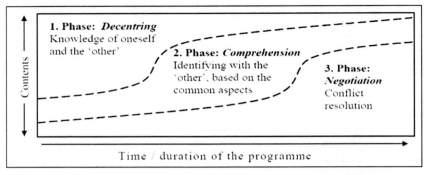

Graphic 1: Sequence of the intercultural phases in the Intercultural Program through
Sports PIDE (Rato Barrio, 2009)

It is very important to remember that these three phases are overlapping. So, we don't finish one day the 1st phase starting the 2nd the next day. In every session we provide some contents of all the three phases, but varying the quantity and the emphasis completed in those contents depending on the moment of the process which we are in. For instance, as we can see in the graphic 1, at the beginning of the process we work especially about *decentring* contents, and in addition, in a minor proportion about *comprehension* and *negotiation*. E.g. at the beginning of the process (in the *decentring* phase) it is very important to train communication skills (which are *typical* content of the 3rd phase), taking into account that we work within interactive processes.

Throughout the programme we used different kinds of sports, games, movement exercises, dynamics, creative and participatory activities, dramatizations, popular theatre, verbal reflections, discussion groups, group presentations, etc., always adapted to the specific goals of each session and to the corresponding intercultural phase (See: graphic 2).

For instance, as part of the first phase the participants represented some elements of *their own culture* (as they perceived it) through role playing and acting, and afterwards, while interest increased from *the other* ethno-linguistic groups, each group also had the option to explain themselves verbally. As a result, a very interesting debate and reflection within the group emerged.

An example within the second phase is the participatory action-research process which was carried out by the participants in their communities. They aimed to research about *their traditional* games and sports. At the end of the process we played some of the sports, learning from the values and cultural aspects which are embedded (e.g. the Mayan ball game) but reflecting about the syncretism as well and some common aspects we can see in some of those games and sports. Also, we modified movement tasks and rules of games and sports (e.g. playing football with four teams and four goals at the same time; or '*hand-basket*', playing at the same time with the rules of basketball in one half of the court and of handball in the other half, etc.), to experiment and train the ability of adapting oneself to different circumstances, materials, ways of playing, interactive processes, etc., and to experience and deal with feelings of strangeness (Bröskamp, 2008; Gieß-Stüber, 2005; Gieß-Stüber & Blecking, 2008; Gramespacher, 2008; Leineweber & Kloock, 2005; Noethlichs, 2005a, 2005b; Rato Barrio, 2009)

As an example of the third phase we used, some games which might provoke a minor conflict of interests and we analysed the way they tried to solve the problems in and through the game; for instance, searching for alternatives and solutions utilizing different team strategies, different movements or changing the way of interaction, the position towards *the other*, the roles, the perspectives, etc.

We always combined verbal and non-verbal expressions. The bodies were in movement and in interaction with each other, mainly intermediated by different materials (diverse balls, hula-hoops, pieces of fabric, etc.). Therefore, the learning process was very experiential and active. The experiences gained were discussed afterwards (in a specific moment we kept after every activity to reflect about what they observed and/or experienced in it) or during specific breaks within the activity. First, the participants had the possibility to express their experiences and knowledge or to raise questions among themselves. However, we also previously prepared specific questions to ask them during and after each activity, to direct their attention to the concrete goals of the activity, session and phase, as well as to facilitate making transferences of the experiences and knowledge they gained in and through the activities, to their daily life situations, to the experiences and situations outside of the protected and directed *playground*. In such a way the *playground* was offering a protected space for learning and experiencing.

PHASE	GENERAL OBJECTIVE OF THE PHASE	SPECIFIC OBJECTIVES AND CHARACTERISTICS OF THE CONTENTS	TRANSVERSAL ISSUES
1st PHASE	DEVELOPING DECENTRING PROCESSES	* Agreeing upon **rules** of *living together* to assure mutual acknowledgement	* **Mutual acknowledgement**. Respect * Emphasise **convergences** * Discussion and debate * **Positive interaction** / Exchange / Mutual learning * Generating and maintaining a **sustainable space** for inter-ethnic gatherings * Promote 'living together'
1st PHASE	DEVELOPING DECENTRING PROCESSES	* **Knowing each other** on a personal basis, like "Mary", "Lewis", "Teresa"	
1st PHASE	DEVELOPING DECENTRING PROCESSES	* Developing one's own **identity**	
1st PHASE	DEVELOPING DECENTRING PROCESSES	* Developing awareness of *other cultures*	
1st PHASE	DEVELOPING DECENTRING PROCESSES	* Attention to the **experience of discrimination** and **deconstruction of stereotypes**	
1st PHASE	DEVELOPING DECENTRING PROCESSES	* Acquisition of **communication skills**	
1st PHASE	DEVELOPING DECENTRING PROCESSES	* Developing **constructive criticism** ability, including **self analysis**	
2nd PHASE	DEVELOPING COMPREHENSION	* Emphasis on generating **empathy** among participants	
2nd PHASE	DEVELOPING COMPREHENSION	* Emphasis on developing **trust** between participants	
2nd PHASE	DEVELOPING COMPREHENSION	* Emphasis on **cooperation** between participants	
2nd PHASE	DEVELOPING COMPREHENSION	* Attention to the richness derived by **divergences** (without neglecting convergences)	
3rd PHASE	DEVELOPING NEGOTIATION SKILLS	* Developing **skills** for peaceful **conflict resolution**	

INTERCULTURAL PACIFIC 'LIVING TOGETHER'

Graphic 2: Scheme of general objectives and contents of the intercultural phases in the Intercultural Program through Sports (PIDE) (Rato Barrio, 2009)

Note: Within each phase, the contents are dealt with simultaneously, with the exception of the consensual rules of living together, which should be done in the first place. The order shown on this chart – within each phase – is totally arbitrary. Also the order of the transversal issues is arbitrary and they should all be present in each phase.

Research design

The hypotheses and the variables of analysis of the research were formulated based on the model (graphic 2), following the goals and contents of the three phases and the logical models used (see: Rato Barrio, 2009). The corresponding research has been approached via multiple cases study, combining quantitative and qualitative methods and techniques to triangulate the obtained data, using tools such as questionnaires, sociometric tests, field diaries of the participants and involved researchers, audiovisual material, projective techniques, *etc.* (for further information on the design of the evaluation and on the instruments used, see: Rato Barrio, 2009).

All the participants of the four intervention subgroups as well as of the control group gave us their written consent to participate in the research.

Results

We obtained data from 100 regular participants in total (see Table 1), and from another 557 in the control group. The majority of the participants were between 15 and 19 years old. 62% of the participants were female[3].

Table 1: Information about the four intervention/*experimental* subgroups of the Intercultural Programme through Sports - PIDE

Subgroup	Place and Time	Participants	No of regular participants	Duration	Frequency
"A"	*Non formal* educational community facilities. Programme in the weekends	Youth	25	77 hours	14 sessions of 5hrs. 30m; every 15 days
"B"	*Non formal* educational community facilities. Programme in the weekends	Youth	16	120 hours	14 sessions of 8hrs. (incl. cine forum) every 15 days. + 8hrs. of research task (PAR)
"C"	School. Programme in working days.	Female students to become teachers	33	40 hours	20 sessions of 2hrs. once or twice a week
"D"	School. Programme in working days.	Students of technical studies	26	40 hours	20 sessions of 2hrs. once or twice a week

From the three intercultural phases as illustrated in (graphic 2), we obtained many results that we summarize as follows (for further results, see: Rato Barrio, 2009):

---

3. The results obtained show no significant differences in any variable with regards to the sex of the participants.

169

1. The PIDE programme promoted to a large extent the process of *de-centring*. The aspects that have improved the most are the decrease in prejudice and the awareness of the other participants and their respective ethno-linguistic groups. Awareness and assessment of the *own culture* improved, particularly in the "A" and "B" PIDE subgroups. Certain improvement was also noted, more in some participants than others, with regard to communication skills, ability of self-analysis and awareness of the existing convergences among the different ethno-linguistic groups.

2. PIDE programme improved to a large degree the variables related with the *comprehension* phase. The aspects that improved the most are cooperation and positive interaction among the participants as well as positive assessment of cultural diversity, with very positive and visible changes in the rich data obtained from the different evaluation instruments, such as questionnaires, field diaries and sociograms (Rato Barrio, 2009). On the other hand, an important improvement is also noted in the trust among the participants.

3. The improving of *negotiation*, focusing on the acquisition of conflict resolution skills, has been dealt with only from the qualitative point of view. The participants stated to have acquired certain skills in that area, and they have been able to achieve development in theory, but implementation of these skills has not been evaluated, other than in an abstract manner in some drills carried out among them in the sessions with hypothetical conflicts.

In addition, the results of this research show an improvement in the affective, cognitive and behavioural elements of tolerance through significant changes in the second and the forth scales of the questionnaire about the attitudes towards cultural diversity in Guatemala (Rato Barrio, 2009; To compare: Díaz-Aguado Jalón, Martínez Arias, & Baraja, 1992; Díaz-Aguado Jalón, Royo García, Segura García, & Andrés Zuñeda, 1996).

The PIDE programme improved respect towards others (Rato Barrio, 2009), as a transverse aspect necessary to develop the intercultural process in an interactive manner. In general, significant awareness is produced concerning the respect we deserve as human beings, regardless of characteristics such as *culture of reference*, ideology, religious/spiritual beliefs, etc. (idem). In this regard, the dynamic of agreeing upon rules of living together at the beginning of the course was of immense help.

The results obtained showed that the four types of *activities and processes* evaluated (content, methodology, active participation and work environment) received positive scoring by the participants. The highest rated aspects, both quantitative and qualitative, were the methodology used and the work environment. In general, they very much appreciated the use of games and sports related to different educational aspects and the corresponding discussions afterwards (idem). For instance, regarding the question what they liked most in the programme, participants expressed: "The creation of games. Another way of explaining topics" (AB1)[4]; "Games with comments at the end [the reflections done afterwards]" (AJ4). "Above all I liked the methodology used for being very interesting and useful as it was like learning by playing" (PA3); "I found very interesting to get to know that games are a very efficient means to interrelate with the others and to make friendships" (FP4).

Content also reached a high level average with regards to all of the aspects evaluated. Content assessment included games and the time dedicated to them, interest in the subject, content of the subject given, and time dedicated to it, and the socio-cultural adequacy of the content. Active participation, evaluated only qualitatively, received a positive rating, although it obtained some comments from the participants expressing their desire that those who were not so active should also involve themselves more and provide their opinions as well (*Ob. Cit.*).

The participants rated the sessions as being very positive and significant, both regarding the usefulness of what was learned and its possibilities for being duplicated in the future with other groups of population. The degree of the expectations accomplished was also rated very positively, in some cases surpassing them. E.g. "This course exceeded all my expectations because they gave us the tools and important knowledge for developing our own leadership" (PA3).

Finally, the *recovery* of traditional games by the participants, in addition to being considered an *output* in itself, was highly valued by many participants of the programme, affirming that it had helped them to better appreciate their respective cultures. For example, a participant expressed: "Sport is a way of learning to interact in new ways and to relate ourselves in any other organization; to appreciate that we, the indigenous Mayas also had our games before plastic things arrived and that we have to promote that we organize ourselves to recover traditional games of my people" (PT4).

All these aspects can be considered as potential elements and benefits of a programme like PIDE. However, we also found some limitations of the intervention and challenges, such as the following:

• Irregular participation of some persons. In the intervention area, one of the biggest challenges we faced were the difficulties of some people to engage in long term processes. They are used to participate in punctual events with short duration, but not so much in longer processes, due to the instability of their daily life activities, among other factors. This was also noted by other organizations working in the area. Although we provided transport, a few participants participated in an intermittent way. This made their inclusion in the research difficult, thus reduced the sample size.

4.Names were coded to guarantee anonymity. For further details, please see Rato Barrio (2009).

- The facilities. Once the local leaders and mayors agreed, we utilized the local available community facilities in order to promote their use also once the project finished and in that way to make the activities of the PIDE sustainable. These facilities were simple, but sufficient for our purpose. However, the participants perceived them less luxurious and sophisticated than the facilities they were utilizing within other activities carried out by several NGOs working in the region. This situation provoked certain degrees of disappointment in a few participants. We would like to suggest further reflection among organizations carrying out these kinds of programmes, about the adequacy of utilizing *luxury* facilities that are not accessible for the public use. Mostly one has to rent these kinds of facilities as maintenance is costly and this might difficult the use of them, and as such the sustainability once the external support has finished. In addition, we experienced a tendency within organizations in paying for several extras for increasing the participation (transport, food). Sometimes this is needed, but other times it could be counterproductive, promoting a participation more motivated on these extras than on a real interest in the programme goals and contents. We feel a huge difference in the programmes we carried out at in the area in 1999 (Nicaragua), 2000 (Guatemala)... when people carrying with them simple maize "*tortillas*", walking from the surrounding communities to the programmes which took place in very simple settings, showing real interest in participating in programmes. Nowadays, it seems like that if the organization doesn't offer everything (food, transport, etc.) they associate it with a low quality programme. Although it seems attractive offering everything to everyone to increase the participation in a context where long processes are difficult to achieve, it can be really counterproductive in some cases. In our specific context, we suggest further reflection and to search for alternatives that provide access to everybody and promote the participation of vulnerable people, while avoiding paternalistic practices that can have counterproductive repercussions.

- The duration of the programme. In only one year it is difficult to have a high impact in all the indicators involved in this kind of intercultural process in a post-conflict context. This needs without doubts a longer process. PIDE was a pilot intervention, linked to a research which aimed to find out if sport could have a meaningful impact in this kind of processes. Once there is evidence about the short and medium term effects that sport can provide in this area, it is important to enrol with other local institutions in a long term programme with long term effects.

- Influence at a *micro* level. This programme had a very positive impact, but just at a group level. In order to achieve a *real* impact in the intercultural relationships sphere in Guatemala, it would be needed to have a bearing on macro educational and sportive levels of the national structure, e.g. in the national educational curricula, reaching more people and in a more sustainable way. In addition, it is very important to have an influence in other essential sectors that contribute to changes in the socio-economic and socio-political structure. This seems to be the only way to have a bearing on the causes which add difficulty to the real and sustainable intercultural processes and thus, the living together. So, PIDE doesn't intend to contribute to a simulation or a false feeling of social *normalization* through these kinds of projects. It is however, necessary to be aware of the importance of getting a change at a *macro* level, these *micro* interventions provide the participants with specific tools to exert their own leadership and influence themselves at the *macro* situation.

Conclusions

The results of the research show a significant improvement in the affective, cognitive and behavioural elements of tolerance; and a positive change in categories such as a decrease in prejudices; increased knowledge and better understanding of *the other cultural groups* involved in the programme; the building of an atmosphere of trust between them; the value of diversity as something positive and enriching; the cooperation and positive interaction between the participants from different cultural groups. On the other hand, it has been noted that there was a tendency towards a positive change in other categories such as an increase in awareness about the convergences that exist between the different cultural groups in Guatemala; respect towards others; the ability for self analysis; the improvement of communication and conflict resolution skills.

In the Guatemalan context, the history of racism and discrimination, suffered particularly by the *Mayan* population, has been put behind them in its most brutal and overt form (for example, the systematic massacres in the 1980's during the civil war); however it still exists in more subtle forms. For this reason, it seems likely that over a longer period of time even better results could be obtained, especially regarding the change in attitude and awareness that would enable each person to make more positive assessments of cultural diversity, while steadily increasing positive interaction between the different cultural groups in a process that should end up in an acceptable degree of peaceful living together (see graphic 2).

With regards to the factors responsible for the improvements and the theories of change, there is a directly proportional relationship in the improvement of the following aspects: inter-ethnic interaction, communication, trust, awareness of others and their cultures, the appreciation of one's own culture, awareness of convergences, appreciation of cultural diversity, and reduction of prejudice – all important objectives in the methodological model used in PIDE programme (see graphic 2). On the other hand, the results show a certain structure in these associations, as follows: interaction continues and communication increases trust. These aspects facilitate improvement in the awareness of the other persons, of oneself, of each other's cultures (awareness that is built based on the relationship) and the convergences that exist between them. All of this fosters a more positive attitude towards diversity and a reduction of prejudice.

As a final consideration, it can be said that the Intercultural Programme through Sports PIDE has great potential to promote intercultural relations and peaceful living together. In spite of some limitations of intervention (duration of programme, irregular involvement of some participants, facilities, *etc.*) and research (small sample size of some subgroups, *etc.*) as mentioned before, the intervention model, the plan of the three intercultural phases, the corresponding strategies and activities planned upon this model (as highlighted in graphics 1 and 2) and the use of sports were found to be very consistent, appropriate and effective, both in *formal* and *informal* educational settings. Through the evaluation of the whole process, we discussed not only the results or *outcomes* of the programme, but also the structure and processes (trainers, facilities, interaction, atmosphere, contents, methodology, etc.). This kind of evaluation approach permits the analysis of key activities and strategies and responsible factors for the changes, as discussed before.

In spite of using different research methods, qualitative and quantitative, and the data triangulation process, due to the specificity of the context and of research, it must be taken into consideration that the results can not be generalised, and that the same strategies applied in another context might not have the same results. As in this programme, the activities must be adequate to the specific context. Having said this, we conclude that in this study there is a propounded model of intervention, theoretically based, with a positive impact shown in certain variables, with examples of specific strategies, which could be of great use in other studies and intercultural projects, as the ones carried out in pluricultural societies within cooperation for development field as well as migrations.

References

Bröskamp, B. (2008). Bodily strangerhood(s) revisited. In P. Gieβ-Stüber & D. Blecking (Eds.), *Sport - Integration - Europe. Widening Horizons in Intercultural Education* (pp. 213-228). Baltmannsweiler: Schneider Verlag Hohengehren.

Coakley, J. (2007). *Sports in Society. Issues and controversies.* New York: McGraw-Hill.

Coalter, F. (2007). *A wider social role for sport. Who's keeping the score?* London & New York: Routledge.

Cohen-Emerique, M. (1997). La negotiation-mediation, phase essentialle dans l'intégration des migrants et dans la modification des attitudes des acteurs sociaux chargés de leur integration. *Hommes et migrations.*

Cohen-Emerique, M. (2004). Incidentes críticos. Un modelo para la comunicación intercultural. *Dossier para una educación intercultural*. Madrid: CIP - FUHEM.

Díaz-Aguado Jalón, M. J., Martínez Arias, M. del R., & Baraja, A. (1992). *Educación y desarrollo de la tolerancia*. Madrid: Ministerio de Educación y Ciencia.

Díaz-Aguado Jalón, M. J., Royo García, M. del P., Segura García, M. P., & Andrés Zuñeda, M. T. (1996). *Programas de educación para la tolerancia y prevención de la violencia en los jóvenes. Instrumentos de evaluación e investigación*. Madrid: Instituto de la Juventud, Ministerio de Trabajo y Asuntos Sociales.

Engineers without borders - Canada. (2009). *Learning from our mistakes. A collection from Overseas Volunteer Staff* (National Conference 2009) (p. 34). Toronto (Canadá): Engineers without borders - Canada.

Engineers without borders - Canada. (2010). *Learning from our mistakes.* (National Conference 2010 No. 2nd issue) (p. 16). Toronto (Canadá): Engineers without borders - Canada.

Gieß-Stüber, P. (2005). *Interkulturelle Erziehung im und durch Sport*. Münster: Lit Verlag.

Gieß-Stüber, P., & Blecking, D. (2008). *Sport - Integration - Europe. Widening Horizons in Intercultural Education*. Baltmannsweiler: Schneider Verlag Hohengehren.

Giménez Romero, C. (2000a). *Guía sobre interculturalidad. Fundamentos conceptuales* (Vol. 1). Guatemala: Proyecto Q'anil B. Retrieved from internal-pdf://Guía sobre interculturalidad I-1448789506/Guía sobre interculturalidad I.pdf

Giménez Romero, C. (2003a). *¿Qué es la inmigración?* Madrid: RBA.

Giménez Romero, C. (2003b). Pluralismo, multiculturalismo e interculturalidad. *Educación y futuro: revista de investigación aplicada y experiencias educativas*, (8), 11-20.

Giulianotti, R. (2004). Human Rights, Globalization and Sentimental Education: The Case of Sport. *Sport and Society, 7*(3), 355-369.

Gramespacher, E. (2008). Dealing with strangeness through play: A practical lesson. In P. Gieß-Stüber & D. Blecking (Eds.), *Sport - Integration - Europe. Widening Horizons in Intercultural Education* (pp. 243-248). Baltmannsweiler: Schneider Verlag Hohengehren.

Henry, I. (2009). Estrategias de deporte e integración social: el uso del deporte para la integración social de refugiados y solicitantes de asilo. *Jornadas "Actividad Física, Deporte e Inmigración. El reto de la Interculturalidad". Libro de comunicaciones*. Madrid: Consejería de Deportes de la Comunidad de Madrid. Próxima publicación.

Keim, M. (2003). *Nation Building at Play. Sport as a Tool for Social Integration in Post-apartheid South Africa*. Sport, Culture & Society. Oxford: Ed. Meyer & Meyer Sport.

Leineweber, H., & Kloock, B. (2005). "Fussball einmal anders" – Ein Projekttag mit der lessing-Förderschule und der Turnsee Grund- und Hauptschule. In P. Giess-Stüber (Ed.), *Interkulturelle Erziehung im und durch Sport* (pp. 146-157). Münster: Lit Verlag

Ley, C., & Rato Barrio, M. (2009). Análisis de las opiniones y conocimientos sobre el Deporte para fomentar el Interculturalismo. In J. Durán González (Ed.), *Actividad Física, Deporte e Inmigración. El reto de la Interculturalidad* (pp. 133-148). Madrid: Dirección General de Deportes de la Comunidad de Madrid.

Malgesini, G., & Giménez Romero, C. (2000). *Guía de conceptos sobre migraciones, racismo e interculturalidad*. Madrid: Catarata.

McLaren, P. L. (1995). Collisions with otherness: "Travelling" Theory, Postcolonial Criticism, and the Politics of Ethnographic Practice - The Mission of the Wounded Ethnographer. In P. L. McLaren & J. M. Giarelli (Eds.), *Critical Theory and Educational Research* (pp. 271-300). Albany, USA: State University of New York Press.

Noethlichs, M. (2005a). Die Sensitivität gegenüber Frendheit (STS) und Interkulturelles Lernen im Sport. In P. Giess-Stüber (Ed.), *Interkulturelle Erziehung im und durch Sport* (pp. 38-47). Münster: Lit Verlag.

Noethlichs, M. (2005b). Judo, ein konstruktiver Weg im Umgang mit Fremdheit. In P. Giess-Stüber (Ed.), *Interkulturelle Erziehung im und durch Sport* (pp. 76-81). Münster: Lit Verlag.

Rato Barrio, M. (2009, June). *La Actividad Física y el Deporte como herramientas para fomentar el Interculturalismo en contextos postbélicos, en el marco de la Cooperación para el Desarrollo. Un proyecto en Guatemala (Centroamérica)* (European PhD). Universidad Politécnica de Madrid, Madrid (Spain). Retrieved from http://oa.upm.es/1674/1/MARIA_RATO_BARRIO.pdf

Rato Barrio, M., & Ley, C. (2009). Análisis crítico sobre proyectos de Deporte e Interculturalidad en la Cooperación para el Desarrollo. In J. Durán González (Ed.), *Actividad Física, Deporte e Inmigración. El reto de la Interculturalidad* (pp. 149-170). Madrid: Dirección General de Deportes de la Comunidad de Madrid.

Rato Barrio, M., & Ley, C. (2011). Interkulturalität und Sport in der Entwicklungszusammenarbeit. In K. Petry, M. Groll, & W. Tokarski (Eds.), *Sport und internationale Entwicklungszusammenarbeit*. Köln: Sportverlag Strauss.

Rato Barrio, M., Ley, C., & Durán González, J. (2009). Derechos Humanos y Cooperación para el Desarrollo en y a través del Deporte. In J. A. Moreno & D. González-Cutre (Eds.), *Deporte, intervención y transformación social.* (pp. 13-58). Río de Janeiro: Shape.

Part IV

Sport and Development

Chapter 14
Sport for Addressing HIV/AIDS

Examining Rationales

Oscar Mwanga

Introduction

Sport has long been identified as a cultural practice that holds the capacity for development. Within recent times sport has been utilised as an instrument to allay social phenomena such as poverty, disease, conflict, and gender discrimination; essentially, there is a belief that sport can facilitate international development (Beutler, 2008). Indeed, in 2008 the United Nations General Assembly passed resolution 63/135 asserting its recognition that sports can provide 'a means to promote education, health, development and peace' (UN, 2008, p.1). This recognition, together with the belief it expresses, signifies a more general movement, by the name of sport for development and peace (SDP), asserting sports capacity to contribute to the achievement of the millennium development goals (MDGs) (Kidd, 2008, p. 370). Of particular interest to the current chapter is SDP's contribution to achieving MDG number six, which aims to 'halt and begin to reverse the spread of HIV/AIDS' (Rigg, 2008, p. 31). While the suitability of MDG number six is heavily debated (does the goal account for the full reality of the epidemic?) this chapter's objective is to analyse the rationales that underpin the contributions of SDP, as exhorted by the movement itself, to the recorded gains made in the passing decade of the epidemic (Rigg, 2008). Indeed, UNAIDS has claimed that 'since 1999, the year in which it is thought that the epidemic peaked, globally, the number of new infections has fallen by 19%' (UNAIDS, 2010, p. 9). Of this percentage, what part has SDP played in reversing the trend? While an exact figure is impossible to provide, the fact that SDP initiatives abound within sub-Saharan Africa (hereafter SSA), in which the epicentre of the epidemic is to be found and thus where a large proportion of the 19% figure would be attributed to, an analysis of the rationales SDP claims for contributions in this reduction of infections seems warranted. Additionally a discussion concerning the types of evidence used to prop such rationales is also provided.

Therefore, this chapter will attempt to identify and critically examine the selected rationales that underpin sport for addressing HIV/AIDS interventions in SSA. The chapter's approach aligns with the research agenda put forth by Delva and Temmerman (2006), positing that the current evidence base regarding the socio-cultural and political appropriateness of sport programmes for HIV/AIDS prevention is limited, particularly where the epidemic is most severe, SSA. I provide this examination as much as a sub-Saharan African who has been directly affected by the epidemic and a SDP activist of the last decade – what Jarvie (2006 p. 384) refers to as the 'public intellectual'. According to Jarvie (2006 p. 384) public intellectuals are 'those who speak the truth to power – or at least expose silences', but their work never ends with exposing the truth. It seeks to promote social justice and transformation where opportunity presents. For the past 15 years, I have been actively involved in a number of HIV/AIDS related SDP initiatives, some of which are discussed in this article. During the past decade, I was the founding chairman of both the KAO network and the EduSport Foundation, a Zambian SDP organisation. Finally, I also provide this analysis because of the deafening silence of alternative (non-western) voices in the formal SDP discourse. Even only for the last reason, I feel justified enough to present this analysis.

The rationales of sport for addressing HIV/AIDS

The rationales underpinning SDP initiatives can be categorised into two core assumptions. The first is that participation in sport automatically contributes to the atomistic development of transferable and socially desirable personal characteristics, such as self-discipline, teamwork and fair play. The second assumption is that sports inherent properties can be manipulated for developmental purposes. In the following sections, I present and critically examine the rationales seen below vis-a-vis sport for addressing HIV/AIDS initiatives in SSA:

- Sport for moral development;
- Sport as a positive diversion;
- Sport as a hook;
- Sport as a means to foster empowerment;
- Sport as a means to improve health for People Living With HIV/AIDS (PLWHA).

Sport for moral development

This hypothesis holds that sports participation per se directly socialises an individual to acquire socially desirable attributes such good moral values. In the last decade, slogans such as "sport stops AIDS; Kicking AIDS Out; Sporting AIDS Out" were standard sport tournament themes. This thinking was so pervasive that it became the core underpinning rationale for our successful funding proposals, particularly those we presented to sport development funders. However, those we sent to traditional HIV/AIDS funding bodies were on the whole less successful. We attributed this failure to our lack of convincing traditional HIV/AIDS funding bodies and as evidence of a conspiracy against SDP organisations by the wider HIV/AIDS policy community. Today, these conspiracy 'theories' we once believed have become a laughing matter as many of us better appreciate the theoretical flaws and limited sophistication that was contained in our proposals.

The main flaw in this hypothesis is the assumption that all participants coming into the SDP programmes represent a homogenous group as it were. Diversity is ignored, with focus given to selected participants who possess the desired attributes as anecdotal evidence to support the claims that sports participation builds the life skills needed to curb the spread of HIV/AIDS. We must bear in mind that the opposite is equally true i.e. sports participation may work against the 'normal' development of skills needed to prevent against HIV/AIDS. For example, it is normally alleged that young people who participate in community sports programmes that lack adult supervision and guidance have poor HIV/AIDS life skills compared with those of religiously rooted programmes. Moreover, this assumption of participant homogeneity also implies that a particular sport (and programme) is experienced in much the same way. To compound the problem further, there is a lack of consensus on this issue within leisure and sport research. For example, Nichols (2004) and Sandford et al (2006) have demonstrated evidence for the attainment of intended outcomes, whereas others have contended that sport programmes fail to empirically demonstrate intended outcomes (Long and Sanderson 2001; Moris et al, 2003). Furthermore, Christine (2008) demonstrated that empirical studies do in fact show that sport participation may impede the development of desirable social behaviour. In Zambia this rationale is still championed by some sports federations. However many SDP organisations such EduSport Foundation and Sport in Action have devised more sophisticated approaches to explain the processes and outcomes that lead to the acquisition or none acquisition of HIV/AIDS life skills for programme participants. Such approaches suggest that the HIV/AIDS life skills developed through sport can come through the process of a participant's subjective interaction with coaches, leaders, teammates, parents, friends, and organizations. For example, social support through mentorship programmes together with peer support go hand in hand with all sport programmes run by EduSport Foundation and Sport in Action.

Sport as positive Diversion

This hypothesis is based on the idea that sport provides an opportunity for young people to do something positive with their time and energy that would otherwise be spent on unprotected sex or behaviours that accentuate the likelihood of unprotected sex occurring (e.g. alcohol and drug consumption). This hypothesis is strikingly popular in SSA communities and has strong community backing of key community stakeholders who consider the time spent in sport as literally time spent away from sex. One danger of applying the diversion rational is that it becomes difficult to identify the flaws of sport itself. For example, in Zambia we hear numerous cases where girls, and in rare cases boys, who are sexually abused by male sport leaders exposing them to a higher risk of HIV/AIDS infection. Nevertheless, some practitioners take moderate and realistic views in the application of the diversion hypothesis. They do not take this hypothesis as a sole rationale for developing and delivering SDP programmes. For example, the EduSport Foundation's Go Sisters10 programme includes school sponsorship and micro financing as a core part of the strategy in using sport to empower girls, while additionally using sporting activities as positive diversion. In my opinion the dancing and singing associated with many SSA sport programmes also makes the sport experience more interesting and attractive, increasing the efficacy of sport as a positive diversion mechanism. However, such assertions require more rigorous investigation.

Indeed, critics have challenged programmes solely based on the diversion hypothesis. Guest (2005) contends that merely distracting people provides only a provisional solution which should not account for development per se. Also, programmes underpinned with this rationale may reenforce negative stereotypes, learned helplessness and false hope. Guest (2005) further argues that negative stereotypes lead to participants being perceived as impulsive and therefore not empowered enough to manage their own behaviour to the point that they need some kind of diversion through external help. In international development aid programmes, the helper is usually 'a westerner'. It can also be argued that the HIV/AIDS problem is simplified through the belief that diversion programmes are sufficient interventions. For example, parents who send their children to diversion programmes are likely to assume that they have done all it takes to help their children to develop HIV/AIDS life skills. At any rate, it must be accepted from the above examination that providing "diversion programmes may be useful but not sufficient by themselves" (Green, 2009, p. 135). But there is hope for a diversion programme when it is incorporated as part of an intervention. Given the limited scientific evidence to support the efficacy of positive diversion programmes (Hartmann and Depro, 2006) our aim should be to develop investigative strategies that disinter the specific circumstances sport provides for effective diversion in the SSA HIV/AIDS context.

Sport as an attractive hook

The popularity of sport to participants and spectators of all ages across the world in general (and SSA in particular) is undeniable. In many SSA communities, all it takes is a ball to gather multitudes of children. KAO partners and other sport for addressing HIV/AIDS initiatives that apply this hypothesis use sport as bait to attract young participants to provide core HIV/AIDS services, such as voluntary HIV testing and HIV/AIDS life skills education.

The KAO partnership utilises sport to attract young people via using interactive movement games, leagues and motivated leaders to deliver HIV/AIDS life education www.kickingAIDSout.net. However, many practitioners agree that it is what you do with the target group(s) once you have them 'hooked' that determines programme successes. For example, you need programme designers and instructors who can create the right motivational climate and strike the balance between sport activity and HIV/AIDS life skills education (Green, 2008; Banda and Mwaanga, 2006; Mwaanga, 2001).

In recent years, non-sport rewards such as T-shirts and international trips (e.g. Norway cup) are increasingly being used to attract young people in the global south, a trend that is common in the global north. One major drawback of **sport as an attractive hook** comprises the creation of attitudes towards sport of expectation. Especially for young people, non-sporting aspects of SDP programmes become the principal reason of participation. More than once, I have had parents of young participants in Zambia express their expectation of payment for their children getting involved in SDP programmes. However, while many SDP practitioners are realising the initial and intuitive appeal of sport, sports' enjoyable essence for the target group should be respected and protected. Non sport rewards and HIV/AIDS life skills education programmes must be cleverly integrated so that the right balance between the sport, life skills education and non-reward is always effectively maintained.

Sport as a means to foster empowerment

This rationale postulates that sport has inherent properties that facilitate empowerment. The focus in on how sports participation increases perceptions of empowerment, physical capacities and wider social control. A number of studies have supported the link between sports participation and increased physical capacities together with positive psychological conceptions (self-efficacy and perceived competence) (Pensgaard and Sorensen, 2002; Dinoigi, 2004). Moreover, some qualitative research is emerging with support for the notion of empowerment gains for HIV/AIDS risk young people in SSA who participate in SDP programmes (see Mwaanga, 2003; Hanne, 2007).

However, it is important to note that empowerment at a personal level is a subjective experience and hence it is not the case that all sports participation will automatically lead to personal level empowerment. Secondly, in as much as sport possesses empowering properties, it equally possesses the opposite i.e. disempowering properties (Mwaanga, 2003). By applying theory, it is clear how we can systematically organise activities that help to facilitate empowerment while debilitating the processes that lead to disempowerment. Thirdly, many young people report that they have felt stronger because of sports participation. While it excites many, it has been a cause of concern for me because it reduces sports empowerment to simply a business of feeling stronger, or "pseudo-empowerment" (Weissberg, 1999, p. 29). Weissberg (1999 p. 29) reminds us that is it not enough simply to feel empowered because "pseudo-empowerment triumphs". Using my empowerment theoretical insights, I have always questioned what feeling empowered means to a HIV positive person, or, poverty stricken youth coach in need of food or employment, as is the reality in SSA cultural context. Sports empowerment should never be promoted only as a matter of feelings (or perceptions) of inner strength to the detriment of addressing how a group's increased access to resources may assist in addressing the poverty surrounding poverty.

Sport as means to improve health for PLWHA

The research evidence and academic consensus supporting the idea that physical activity positively impacts both physical and psychological health for the 'normal' population is strong (Coalter, 2005; Zuka et al, 2007). Qualitative evidence suggests that the greatest gains from involvement in physical activity relate to psychological health and increased feelings of well-being (Coalter, 2005). Zuka et al (2007) posit that the strong link between physical activity and the reduction in non-communicable diseases (e.g. cardiac heart disease, chronic respiratory disease, diabetes, some forms of cancer) present sports as a viable strategy that countries from the global south should consider. Like the research evidence on the HIV negative population, research evidence on the health benefits of sport and physical activity for PLWHA looks promising. I cite a few studies and examine their implications in the following paragraph.

A number of reviews regarding exercise training in HIV infection, which were carried out before the era of Highly Active Antiretroviral Therapy (HAART), found exercise to be beneficial (Smith et al., 2006). For example, a study by Mustafa et al. (1999) found that engaging in physical activity three or more times per week has been associated with a slower progression of AIDS. In addition, aerobic exercise interventions were found to be safe and leading to improvement in cardiopulmonary fitness in adults living with HIV/AIDS (Nixon, 2002). O'Brien et al. (2004) found that progressive resistive exercise, or a combination of progressive resistive exercise and aerobic exercise, appears to be safe and may be beneficial for adults living with HIV/AIDS.

The risk, however, from this consensus on the health benefit of physical activity and health outcomes is that it feeds the somewhat evangelistic discourse that 'essentialises' sport and physical activity as the panacea for a healthy life for PLWHA, almost to the disregard of other more important factors; such as diet, medication and healthy environments. Therefore, when applying this knowledge in SSA countries it must be stressed that benefits only occur in combination with other factors, such as good facilities and good nutrition. Another crucial aspect of the sport and health benefits for PLWHA discourse is its silences on the subjective voices of PLWHA themselves. Gillett et al. (2002, p. 370) argue that "despite the growing interest in the therapeutic value of sport, limited attention has been devoted to understanding the meaning that individuals attribute to their use of physical activity as complementary therapy". Having dialogue around theory within the SDP community can be useful in searching the philosophical and theoretical perspectives that value the voices of end programme users.

Another criticism worth underscoring is that sport and physical activity vary in types and thus there are vast differences in the biophysical requirements and effects of different activities (Zaku et al, 2007). For example, scientifically monitored cardiovascular training effects resulting from the strenuous aerobic demands of Nordic skiing on a HIV+ youth in that part of the world are significantly different from those on a HIV + youth in SSA playing a game of football, where players only exert themselves for brief moments during the game. The benefits of sport and physical activity have serious contextual implications in that benefits will only be accrued to individuals and populations in certain environments and under particular combinations of factors. Nieman (2001), writing with reference to immune functions, underscores the need for a well-balanced diet, minimal life stresses, avoiding chronic fatigue, adequate sleep and the avoidance of rapid weight loss. But in places where people live in poverty, as is the case for many SSA countries, achieving a balanced diet or minimal life stress is highly inconceivable.

On the question relating to types of sport, duration and intensity that are required to optimize the claimed health benefits for specific target populations, Coalter (2005) remarks that among sports participants, the frequency of activity is often less than that required to achieve and sustain health benefits. Rankinen & Bouchard (2002 p.2) support this notion when they note that different "health outcomes do not respond in the same manner to an increased level of physical activity". Coalter's review also underscores the issue of definitions and their practical implications. Accordingly, he argues that much of the research evidence relates to the health benefits of physical activity, rather than sport per se. He notes that among many of the least active and least healthy groups, the promotion of an 'active lifestyle' may be a more useful strategy than the promotion of sports (Coalter, 2005). An important implication within the SSA context based on this analysis is that there are opportunities for physical activity than there are for participating in sport for PLWHA, but culturally, people do not seem to be able to differentiate between the two. For example when we have encouraged PLWHA to be physically active their response has always been that they don't have access to sport.

Evidence discourse

At a more fundamental level of discussion, while the rationales of particular SDP programmes may be explicit, the measurements of the effectiveness of a programme, or, what counts as evidence of sports' contributions to a particular programme's intended objectives, are implicitly entwined in particular unequal power relations. In other words, evidence should not necessarily be viewed as representing 'facts' but more so as representing particular viewpoints. Indeed, numerous commentators have drawn attention to the positivist tradition of research that currently dominates the evidence-based scene of SDP (Kay, 2009). What this dominance tends to achieve is a mitigation of alternative voices and types of evidence within the SDP movement, particularly stemming from those who, as it were, occupy the nadir of the SDP hierarchy (Nicholls, 2009). Nicholls et al (2011) argue that this subjugation of alternatives inevitably results in a less nuanced evidence base for the SDP movement, thus effectively limiting the scope of real progress for the programme users. What is needed is a recasting of the categories; in other words, allowing the arena to be opened up to the plurality of types of evidence that actually exists within the SDP movement (Mwaanga and Barron, *in press*).

Conclusions and Recommendations

Two concluding remarks are worth highlighting. Firstly, an essential point worth recognising in exploring the capacity of sport as a tool for addressing HIV/AIDS is that the power of sport is not found in sport per se but the people involved in sport, especially the leaders. Sport experiences have the potential to contribute towards the development of HIV/AIDS life skills, empowerment of PLWHA and building strong advocacy on HIV/AIDS issues; however, the choice often depends upon the nature of the sport experience and the care that leaders put in the designing of programmes. It is always useful to remember that some form of a rationale always underpins our programmes. Therefore, research must focus on understanding the nature of SDP programme experiences and the underpinning programme rationale(s) and less on whether or not sport can address HIV/AIDS.

Secondly, to claim that sport can combat HIV/AIDS is not only to overstate the limited capacity of sport but to dangerously ignore the complexity of HIV/AIDS. In stating the complexity of HIV/AIDS Whiteside, cited in Lawson (1997: 4), asserts:

"AIDS is the end result of an HIV infection and it is a health issue. But HIV/AIDS are both symptoms rather than causes. They are symptomatic of past injustices, dislocations and inequalities. I think when one looks at the AIDS epidemic one has to look both upstream at the causes – like poverty, the violence, the position of women – and downstream at the consequences. So the relationship between AIDS and development is a very complex one".

However, possibilities do exist within sport to provide some effort and resources within a world ravaged by what is now called the disease of 'endless tears'. The fundamental question that confronts us i.e. SDP activists, practitioners and academics: is how can we better understand the interplay between sport, with its limited capacity on the one hand, and HIV/AIDS, in its full complexity, on the other. I don't see how we can systematically respond to this question without evoking theoretical analysis of our intervention rationales, plans, delivery evaluations together with the evidences of SDP's contributions for addressing HIV/AIDS. If we agree that the rationale has an important place, then the next challenge is how we proceed designing and implementing theoretically informed sport for addressing HIV/AIDS interventions while creating evidence that is, while being robust, representative of the plurality of the movement.

To respond to changing opportunities and current conditions that present themselves in SDP now and in the future, it is clear that we need to be sophisticated in the way we approach our work, being consciousness about the role of theory in our practice; doing both is a good place to start. Encouraging theoretical dialogue and theory based research and practice will most certainly give a nudge in the right direction. Theory driven research and practice can however be intimidating to those outside the academic world, thus why I stress the need to encourage collaborative community research were SDP activists, practitioners and academics collaboratively develop research programmes that are theoretically rigorous (academics' input), culturally relevant (practitioners' input) and in tune with wider HIV/AIDS and sport priorities (activists' input). For example, at the time of writing this chapter we just completed the signing a Memorandum of Understanding between Southampton Solent University and the Network of Zambian People Living with HIV/AIDS (NZP+). This is a three year agreement that will see the two organisations working together within the principles of participatory research to develop a sport programme that meets the needs of the target group while being theoretically rigorous. The process of developing this partnership is another issue, but what is important here is that we shall need a total shift in the way we approach SDP research.

Notes

1. Sport has diverse meanings, however, within SDP research an accepted definition involves sport as being viewed as: "all forms of physical activity that contribute to physical fitness, mental well-being and social interaction, such as play, recreation, organized or competitive sport, and indigenous sports and games." International Working Group on SDP (2003)

2. Kicking AIDS out (KAO) is an international network of sport for development NGO's, organizations and national sport structures working as a collective to raise awareness about how sport and physical activity programmes can be adapted to promote dialogue and education about HIV and AIDS and to facilitate life skills training. KAO is also concept and methodology. Kicking AIDS Out is almost entirely dependent on Norwegian Agency for Development Cooperation (NORAD) funds. NORAD through the Norwegian Olympic and Paralympic Committee and Confederation of Sports (NIF) have been the leading 'Northern' Sub – Saharan African SDP movement financier and support in the decade.

3. Global South is sometimes referred to as developing economies or the third world or Low – and middle-income countries (LMIC). These terminologies are is contentious. The article applies the term generally to all SSA countries mostly located in the southern hemisphere. I acknowledge the economic and cultural diversities of these countries in SSA.

4. Go Sisters is an EduSport Foundation programme that uses sport and other SDP interventions for girls empowerment.

References

Banda Davies and Oscar Mwaanga, (2008). HIV/AIDS education through Basketball movement games and drills. St John York University.

Bjertnæs H, (2007). Playing to win or playing for empowerment? An analysis of a Namibian team participating in the Norway Cup-project. MA Thesis in Peace and Conflict Transformaiton, Faculty of Social Science, University of Tromso

Bopp, C., Phillips, Fulk, L., Dudgeon, W. Sowell, R. & G. Hand (2004). Physical activity and immunity in HIV-infected individuals. *Journal of AIDS Care* .16.3 387-393.

Cashman, R. (1995). Paradise of sport: The rise of reorganised sport in Australia. Oxford: oxford University Press Australia

Clammer, J. (2005). Culture, development, and social theory: On cultural studies and the place of culture in development. The Asia pacific journal of Anthropology, 6 (2) 100-19

Coalter, F. (2005). *The Social Benefits of Sport: An Overview to Inform the Community Planning Process.* Edinburgh: SportScotland.

Cowen, M. and R. Shenton (1996). Doctrines of Development. New York: Routledge.

Delva, W., and T.Temmerman (2006). *Determinants of the Effectiveness of HIV Prevention through Sport.* Sport and Development.

Dionigi, A. R. (2004). *Competing for Life: older People and Competitive Sport.* Unpublished PhD thesis. University of Newcastle: Australia

Donnelly, P. (1993.) Democratization Revisited: Seven Theses on the Democratization of Sport and Active Leisure, *Loisir et Société/Society and Leisure* 16(2): 413– 434.

Gillett, j., Cain, R., and Pawluch (2002). Moving Beyond the Biomedical: The Use of Physical Activity to Negotiate Illness. *Sociology of Sport Journal* 19, 370 -384

Grant, B.C. (2001). *You're never too old. Beliefs about physical activities and playing sport in later life.* Aging and Society, 21 (6) pp. 777-798

Green, (2008). Sport as an Agent for Social Change and personal development. In Girginov, V. *Management of Sports Development.* Butterworth-Heinemann, Oxford

Guest, A. M., (2005), "What exactly does sport do? Thinking both critically and positively about development through sport "University of Portland, US; Available at: www.sad.ch (Accessed 12th December 2008)

Hartmann, D. & B. Depro (2006). Rethinking sports-based community crime prevention: A preliminary analysis of the relationship between Midnight Basketball and urban crime rates *Jnl of Sport & Social Issues* 30:2, 180-96, Available at: http://www.kickingaidsout.net (Accessed 11th January 2010)

Kay, T., (2009). Developing through sport: evidencing sport impacts on young people. *Sport in Society* [online], 12(9), pp. 1177-1191. Availableat : www. InformaWorld (Accessed 12th March 2010).

Kidd, B. and P. Donnelly (2007). *Literature review of sport for development and Peace.* Sport for Development and Peace International Working Group (SDP IWG). Toronto: Canada

Jarvie, G. (2006). Sport, Culture and Society. An introduction. Oxon: Routledge

Lawson, L. (1997). *HIV/AIDS and Development.* A Project of SAIH and INTERFUND. Yeoville: Teaching Screens Production.

Long, J. and I. Sanderson (2001). The social benefit of sport: where's the proof? In *Sport in the City: The role of sport in economic and social regeneration* - C. Gratton and I.P Henry, (eds). London: Routledge, pp. 187-203

Moris, L., Sallybanks, J., Willis, K., and T. Makkai (2003). *Sport, physical activity and anti social behaviour in youth. Trends and issues in crime and criminal justice, April. Canberra:*

Mustafa,T., F. Sy,F., C. Macera, C., Thompson, S, Jackson, K., Selassie, A. & L. Dean (1999). Association between Exercise and HIV Disease Progression in a Cohort of Homosexual Men. *Annauls of Epidemiology* 9: 127-131

Mwaanga. O. (2001). Kicking AIDS Out Through Movement Games. Norwegian Development Agency.

Mwaanga, O. (2003). *HIV/AIDS at risk adolescent girls empowerment through participation in top level football and Edusport in Zambia*, Master Thesis in Sport and Exercise Psychology, Norwegian University of Sport and Physical Education, Oslo

Nichols, G. (2004). Crime and punishment and sport development. *Leisure Studies*, 23, 177-95

Nicolls, S., (2009). On the backs of peer educators: Using theory to interrogate the role of young people in the field of sport-in-development. *In*: R. Levermore, and A. Beacom, eds. *Sport and International Development*. Palgrave, MacMillan, New York: US, pp. 156-175

Nicholls, S., A.R. Giles, and C. Sethna (2010). Perpetuating the 'lack of evidence' discourse in sport for development: Privileged voices, unheard stories and subjugated knowledge. *International Review for the Sociology of Sport* [first published online], pp. 1-16. Available at: www. SageOnlineJournals (Accessed 23rd February 2011).

Nixon, S., O'Brien, K.., Glazier, R., and A. Tynan (2002). Aerobic exercise interventions for adults living with HIV/AIDS. In: *The Cochrane Library*, 2. Oxford: Update Software

Rankinen, T. and C. Bouchard (2002). Dose-Response Issues Concerning the Relations Between Regular Physical Activity and Health. *Presidents Council on Fitness and Sports 3*(18).

Sandford, R.A., Armour, K.M and P.C. Warmington (2006). re-engaging disaffected youth through physical activity programmes. *British Educational research Journal*, 32, 251-71

Smith, E., Crespo, C., Semba, R., Jaworowicz, D., D. Vlahov, Ricketts, D., Ramirez-Marrero F., and A. Tang (2006). Physical Activity in a Cohort of HIV-Positive and HIV-Negative Injection Drug Users," *Journal of AIDS Care* 18(8) 1040–1045.

Pensgaard, A.M. and M. Sorensen (2002). Empowerment Through the Sport Context: A Model to Guide Research for Individuals With Disability, in Adapted PhysicalActivity Quarterly, Vol. 19, 2002, Human Kinetics Publishers, Inc. Available at: http:www.sport-anddev.org (Accessed 17th January 2010).

Warburton, D., Nicol, C. and S. Bredin (2006). Health Benefits of Physical Activity: The Evidence (Review), *CMAJ* 174(6) 801–809.

Weissberg, R. (1999). *The politics of empowerment.* Westport CT: Praeger Publishers.

UN AIDS (2008). Report on Global AIDS Epidemic (Available at: http://www.unaids.org/en/KnowledgeCentre/HIVData/GlobalReport/2008) (Accessed 11th January 2010)

Unitied Nations (2005). Millennium Development Goals (Available at: http://www.un.org/ millenniumgoals) (Accessed 11th January 2010).

Zuka D, Njelesani, D, and S. Darnell (2007). *Literature Reviews on sport for Development and Peace.* International Working Group (SDP IWG) Secretariat Toronto, Canada

Chapter 15
Creating Win-Win Partnerships for Sport and Development

Kylie Bates

Introduction

Sport, as a tool for community development, naturally brings the development and sport sectors together. As such sport convenes and connects people making it a powerful communications platform[1]. Its universal popularity and its potential to inspire, empower and motivate creates a powerful brand that is attractive for both corporate and development agencies. The sport sector and the agencies that specialize in using sport as a development tool see benefit in using the networks, delivery systems, innovation, marketing skills and resources of the corporate and development sectors. In addition, most of the agencies involved in the sport for development industry

---

1. *Right to Play on behalf of the Sport for Development and Peace International Working Group (2008) Harnessing the Power of Sport for Development and Peace: Recommendations to Governments*

value partnerships because they uphold the development principles out-lined in the Paris Declaration for Aid Effectiveness - ownership, alignment, harmonization, results and mutual accountability[2].

Identifying the right partner/s, establishing a solid foundation to work together and then maintaining a partnership that will achieve successful outcomes requires specific skills and commitment to an agreed process as well as investment and effort. As partners share more decision making and accountability responsibilities, they need to also make a greater investment into managing the partnership itself as well as the activities that are gener-ated by the partnership. This chapter aims to discuss why sectors choose to partner with each other. It highlights some of the principles that can be ap-plied to establish effective partnerships as well as a process for partnership development.

Getting in the Game - Why agencies start and leave partnerships

While partnerships provide a vehicle for achieving an impact that an agency cannot achieve alone, they also require effort, resources and often, com-promise. Along with resources for a shared activity, agencies bring their own values, culture, politics and idiosyncrasies. While some partnerships dis-solve in a deliberate way that opens up new opportunities, breakdowns or limitations on the success of the partnership are often due to the failure to resolve conflicts or for the partnership to meet expectations. Some reasons why agencies start and leave partnership are outlined in boxes 1 and 2:

> **Box 1: Nine reasons agencies start a partnership**
> Some opportunities that attract agencies to partnerships include:
> 1. Get leverage from a partner organisation's capacity, credibility or visibility in a particular field or amongst a target audience.
> 2. Share knowledge and generate learning opportunities that result in developing new ways of addressing old issues and complex challenges
> 3. Expand or enhance delivery systems, especially in rural areas

---

2. These principles in the Paris Declaration for Aid Effectiveness are:

a. *Ownership: Developing countries set their own strategies for poverty reduction, improve their institutions and tackle corruption;*
b. *Alignment: Donor countries align behind these objectives and use local systems;*
c. *Harmonisation: Donor countries coordinate, simplify procedures and share information to avoid duplication*
d. *Results: Developing countries and donors shift focus to development results and results get measured.*
e. *Mutual accountability: Donors and partners are accountable for development results. In Paris Declaration for Aid Effectiveness. Viewed online (20 June 2011) see: http://www.oecd.org/document/15/0,2340,en_2649_3236398_35401554_1_1_ 1_1,00.html#Paris*

4. Connect directly with new audiences
5. Maximise impact whilst not using resources unnecessarily
6. Attract new funders or access new funding streams
7. Promoting organisational agendas (for example, a rights based, inclusive approach to working with communities or and innovative, fast moving business development approach) among more organisations
8. Draw on a wider pool of specialists, technical expertise, experience, skills and networks
9. Improve program stability by decreasing reliance on a single resource source.

Box 2: Nine reasons agencies leave a partnership

Some of the reasons agencies leave partnerships include:

1. Partners are unable to establish a culture of trust due to lack of transparency, competing organisational cultures and values or unclear shared objectives.
2. Partner's organizational priorities result in the focus shifting to incompatible areas which exclude the shared partnership objectives.
3. Partners are focussed on what they can gain from the other agency (for example funds or branding) rather than considering the value the partnership brings to both agencies.
4. Management, comfort with risk and accountability practices, including the speed with which processes take place, are not compatible.
5. Partners have relationships with other agencies that have practises that do not align with other partners.
6. Partners address issues that are a high priority to the other partner in an inauthentic or token way
7. Partners fail to involve people at all levels of an organisation's hierarchy in the partnership.
8. The activity undertaken as part of the partnership is complete and there is no reason to continue working together.
9. The partnership has opened up new opportunities for the program and the existing partnership is no longer required.

Understanding the Rules – Structure and Principles for Partnerships

Structure of a Partnership

A partnership should be structured in a way that best supports the achievement of its objectives. One type of partnership is not judged on being more effective than another, rather partners should have the opportunity to identify the kind of collaboration that best meets their organizational goals, and the shared objectives. If there is a mismatch between the needs of the project or benefits an organization wants from the partnership and the realities of the actual collaboration, then a more accurate assessment of the structural relationship may improve the effectiveness and efficiency of a partnership[3].

The structure of partnerships falls along on a spectrum identified by The Partnering Initiative as The Relationship Spectrum Tool (diagram 1)[4]. A transactional collaboration is characterized by a one-on-one "principal-agent" relationship where the dominant party largely determines the work plan and obligations for services. While the "receiving" agency may contribute to this process, they have limited opportunity to assert terms and conditions. At the other end of the spectrum, a transformational partnership is characterized by a work plan shared by all parties, reciprocal obligations, and partners that work closely together and prioritize the principles of equity, transparency and mutual benefit[5].

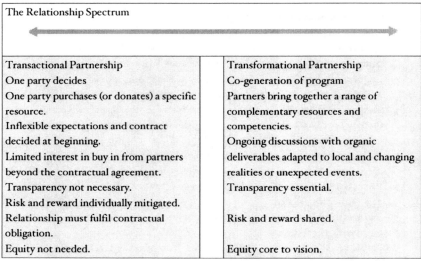

The Relationship Spectrum	
Transactional Partnership	Transformational Partnership
One party decides	Co-generation of program
One party purchases (or donates) a specific resource.	Partners bring together a range of complementary resources and competencies.
Inflexible expectations and contract decided at beginning.	
Limited interest in buy in from partners beyond the contractual agreement.	Ongoing discussions with organic deliverables adapted to local and changing realities or unexpected events.
Transparency not necessary.	Transparency essential.
Risk and reward individually mitigated.	
Relationship must fulfil contractual obligation.	Risk and reward shared.
Equity not needed.	Equity core to vision.

Diagram 1: The Relationship Spectrum Tool

Principles of Partnerships

Rules of sport are established to promote shared understanding of what people are doing on the field and for every player to have a fair chance for

3. Bobenrieth, M. E., Stibbe, D, *Changing Trends in Business-NGO Partnerships. A Netherlands Perspective.* The Partnering Initiative and SOS Kinderdorpen, July 2010

4. Viewed online: http://www.thepartneringinitiative.org/ (accessed 13th February 2012).

5. Bobenrieth, M. E., Stibbe, D, *Changing Trends in Business-NGO Partnerships. A Netherlands Perspective.* The Partnering Initiative and SOS Kinderdorpen, July 2010

success. In a similar way principles such as the three developed by The Partnering Initiative[6], guide the development and implementation of successful good partnerships:

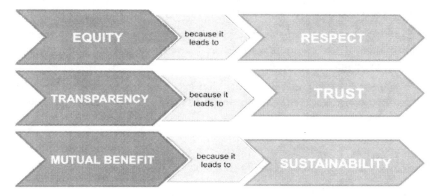

Diagram 2: Issues Related to Partnering

This section explores the application of these principles for establishing partnerships that use sport as a tool for development.

Equity... because it leads to Respect

"As an NGO you must come to the table with a clear value proposition regarding the 'equity' you bring to a partnership. Equality is about the quantity of your contribution, and equity is about the quality. Most lasting and effective partnerships for development are based on 'equity' and find ways of re-enforcing and re-invigorating the roles, values, and primary activities of the different sectors, contributing to the strengthening rather than undermining society and societal structures".

(Maria E.Bobenrieth, Executive Director, Women Win)

Equity in the partnership context refers to fair distribution of decision-making power and accountability. It is not always in proportion to the resources that each party contributes, or the public profile of the organization. Critical activities for establishing equity include:

• Identifying all assets that agencies bring to the partnership; including networks, experience, knowledge, delivery systems, opportunities for growth and relevance with the target audience.

• Creating formal and informal opportunities for individuals to contribute ideas, give feedback and discuss issues in environments that support open sharing.

6.Online: http://www.thepartneringinitiative.org/about_us.jsp (Accessed 20th June 2011).

- Ensuring that each agency has the capacity to invest time and effort into activities to contribute to the shared objectives of the partnership.

- Describing roles clearly and ensuring each partner agrees the responsibilities are fair and equitable for the investment required.

- Building in mechanisms for the partner to provide feedback on the performance of the partnership itself not just the activities undertaken as part of the partnership.

- Consider reporting arrangements that avoid having one partner reporting to another. Instead, issue joint reports to an external group such as an advisory group.

Transparency...because it leads to Trust

"The keys to the NBA relationship, and true for any of the league-level relationships, are transparency and shared expectations: transparency begets an understanding of where objectives overlap, where the value-add lay, and what asks are and are not feasible."

(Joshua Harvey, Officer, Integrated Partnerships at U.S. Fund for UNICEF)

As well as bringing different assets to a partnership, agencies also bring different organizational cultures. Organizational cultures impact accountability requirements, priorities, work standards, time frames and flexibility. Transparency, and thus trust, can be promoted by developing a shared understanding about:

- Each partner's core business, ideologies, values and the basis for entering into a relationship, including the reasons why one partner might be funding the partnership.

- What each partner hopes to gain from the relationship, noting that the shared objective may not be the prime motivator for each partner.

- Each partner's ability to support the core function of the other organization, as well as the activities specific to the partnership.

- The available resources and the likelihood of more or less resources being allocated in the future.

- Willingness to disclose corporate information that is not directly relevant to the partnership activities but could influence the future of the partnership

- Processes for disclosing issues and difficulties as well as successes.

- Ways the partners will work together to minimise risks and solve problems.

Mutual Benefit...because it leads to Sustainability

"When we were talking to organizations about why they were considering Magic Bus as a partner, we wanted to know what was in it for them. Why have they chosen us to talk to? What did they really want out of it? What were they going to require from us? Some organizations in our position think that asking those questions is like biting the hand that feeds them but if we were going to be able to be effective partners, as opposed to simply recipients of funds, we needed to know what the expectations are. We want long term relationships with partners and we know for that for that to happen, they have to see value in working with us. It's better to have the honest conversation at the beginning so there are surprises down the track".

(Matthew Spacie, Founder and Director, Magic Bus, India)

If all partners are expected to contribute to the partnership they should also be entitled to benefit from the partnership. Benefit derived by one party but holds very little interest for the other party is also a legitimate product of a partnership. In order for a partnership to have mutual benefit, agencies should consider:

- Do the organizations both have something to gain from working together?
- Do they have strengths that will foster a complementary rather than competitive working relationship?
- Is the potential gain from a successful partnership worth more than the potential negatives of a failed association?

Pre Game Preparation

Knowing your team: Assessing Capacity and Compatibility

Whether the partnership is set up by an outside party or the agencies are going through a process of exploring mutual benefit, agencies should identify both what they bring to the partnership and what they need from the partnership. The types of information that should be shared include[7]:

- What is the vision you would you like to see the partnership contributing to?
- What is your organisation's core business?
- What values guide the work of your organisation?
- What are the strengths of your organisation?
- What resources will your organisation bring to the relationship (e.g. money, knowledge, networks, influence or labour)?

7.*Adapted from: Australian Agency for International Development, Pacific Leadership Program, Partnering Handbook, Version 2, January 2009*

- What limits the ability of your organisation to achieve the vision outlined above?
- What are the benefits to your organisation of us working together?
- What are the risks to your organisation of us working together?

After sharing this information, partners should assess their compatibility and decide on the most important types of activities for the partnership to work on first.

Understand the conditions: The Sport for Development context

Sport for development is a continuum based on what outcomes the activities aim to achieve[8]. At one end of the continuum the primary objective is to promote *sports activities* and/or the *development of sporting organizations* because participation in sport is understood to have inherent positive benefits for individuals and communities. At the other end, "plus sport", sport is simply a tool used to achieve a *non-sporting development outcome*, usually related to the achievement of the Millennium Development Goals[9].

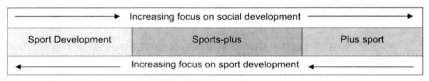

Diagram 3: Sport for Development Continuum

Partners will often be selected by where their core business falls on the continuum. For example, if a corporate agency is interested in increasing its appeal to a particular target audience they may partner with organizations that deliver large scale sport development activities to that particular audience. If the corporate agency is more interested in contributing to a particular community where it has commercial interests then it may seek a partner that is committed to social development through sport

Having a Game Plan - Developing Shared Objectives

"Partnerships usually work best when organizations trial working together on small activities first. It takes time and some shared experiences to really understand the personalities, informal agendas, capabilities and other things – good and bad – that are not always clear in a formal exploration process. Having the opportunity to get to know each other before leaping into a large or long term commitment gives an understanding of what is really possible and not possible".

(Erin Hatton, Sport for Development Advisor, Australia)

---

8. Australian Sports Commission and Australian Agency for International Development. Australian Sports Outreach Program - Joint Partnership Strategy (2006)

9. Information about the Millennium Development Goals can be found at: http://www.un.org/millenniumgoals/

Most partnerships start because organizations believe they could achieve more if they worked with another agency. For the agencies to enter into a partnership that is likely to be successful, they need to be able to agree on a shared purpose for the partnership and have full commitment to it. While this shared purpose may relate directly or only indirectly to the partners' core business, it is essential that each partner is fully committed to the partnership objectives. Ensuring adequate investment in the exploration phase to establish if this is the case is crucial.

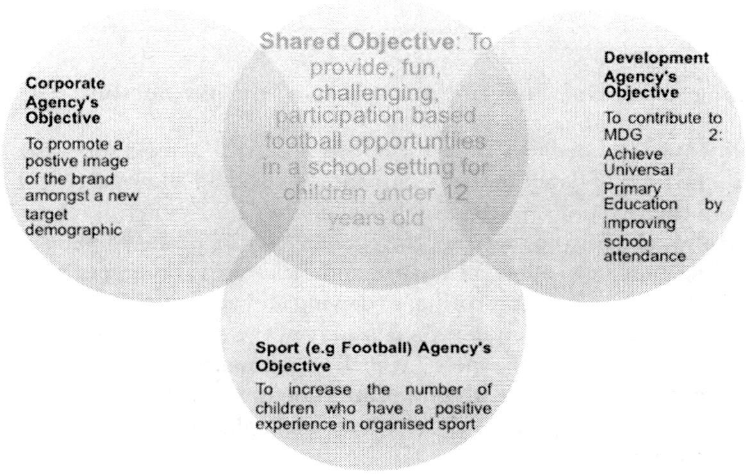

Corporate Agency's Objective

To promote a postive image of the brand amongst a new target demographic

Shared Objective: To provide, fun, challenging, participation based football opportunties in a school setting for children under 12 years old

Development Agency's Objective

To contribute to MDG 2: Achieve Universal Primary Education by improving school attendance

Sport (e.g Football) Agency's Objective

To increase the number of children who have a positive experience in organised sport

Diagram 4: Example of a shared objective that contributes to the specific objective of each partner agency

---

Box 3: Preventing mission shift: Successful organizations have core values and a core purpose that remain fixed while their strategies and practices endlessly adapt to a changing world9. Some organizations and their programs have core ideologies that are more compatible than others however none are exactly the same. While organizations might be able to alter their strategies and practices for the sake of the partnership, in almost all cases, their core ideology and values will be constant. For a partnership to be effective, organizations need to be able to reach a shared objective that is consistent with each partner's ideology and values.

Organizations therefore need to:

a. Know and *be able to communicate* their core ideology and values,

b. Decide which (if any) areas of their strategy and practices they are willing to compromise in

c. Be clear about the ideology, values, strategy and principles they are looking for in a partner.

> "The more dependent a project is on one financial source, the more vulnerable they will be to shifts in policy, economic marketplace and commercial factors.... so diversify streams that fund a project. The more partners you have, the less influence one donor can have, the less likely one partner can force you to take a certain route".
>
> (Ned Wills, Laureus Sport for Good Foundation and Edwin Moses, Laureus World Sports Academy)

Keeping score: Documenting and adjusting the partnership

Documentation needs to reflect the dialogue and agreements that take place. The level of detail in the documentation should allow partners to understand their responsibilities and be accountable for undertaking tasks. It should also take into the account the evolving nature of the partnership and be flexible enough to allow for change and maximising emerging opportunities. The capacity for monitoring, reviewing and adapting the partnership, not simply the activities undertaken as part of the partnership, needs to be included in all agreement types. Typically documents include an overarching partnership agreement which outlines the long term values and objectives of the partnerships and a shorter term work plan which can be easily revised and adjusted.

Post-Game Analysis - Scaling up, transforming or moving on

The nature of partnerships can range from a relatively informal relationship between the parties, to a more formal agreement that involves transfer of resources. Many relationships with a partner organization will change over time and in reaction to a specific situation. For example, a partnership that may have been initiated for the purpose of a specific event may continue after that event but have different objectives. In order for the partnership to evolve effectively, partner organizations need to continually invest in the development of the partnership itself.

 While considerable attention is given to partnership initiation, often less attention is given to evolving the partnership or moving on from some aspects of the partnership. Disbanding or changing aspects of a partnership is not always an indication of failure. Often, it is actually an indication of success as it means a task has been completed or opportunities have opened up to explore new possibilities. Opportunities for scaling up, transforming or moving on can be identified by the following:

- Trialling activities for a 6 to 12 months and then meeting to review the effectiveness of the partnership and make the required adaptations before continuing the partnership.

- Bringing the organisations together regularly to reflect on the activities, share lessons and decide on the course of future activities

As partnerships naturally evolve and change as the organizations get to know each other, other areas for possible collaboration may arise and objectives may alter during the course of the partnership. While not all partnerships can been sustained, there is often the potential for informal relationships to continue.

Summary

Partnerships are often described with the analogies of dating, marriage and divorce. What these analogies fail to do is acknowledge the wide variety of partnerships that organisations enter into. Partnerships are not always unilateral nor are they cross sectorial. Some organisations have a long and lasting association without having a formal agreement. Some agencies (for example, departments in the same government) form associations that are possible due to the similar cultures if not because of their similar objectives. Often partnerships form between several organisations not all of which have direct agreements or shared objectives but have become partners by association. Not all partnerships follow the same course or have the same structure as a traditional marriage and nor would it be appropriate if they did. However, this chapter asserts that if agencies are clear about their own identity and the reason for entering the partnerships, apply the principles of transparency, equity and mutual benefit and follow good partnership development process, then the impact of the partnership can be significant and long lasting.

Chapter 16

What Stigmas Exist within Communities in Kigali Affected by a High Prevalence of HIV and AIDS, and how does Right to Play's Sport for Development Programmes Address them?

A Case Study

Will Bennett

Introduction

Stigma[1] can prevent people living with HIV and AIDS from full participation in the community, be it through social exclusion, forced or self-enforced reclusiveness or economic marginalisation. On an individual level, stigmatisation erodes a person's sense of hope and worth, and on a national level it deprives the state of a full working force, ultimately undermining its economic capacity. The organisation 'Right To Play' strives to discover how

---

1.Goffman. E. (1990). *Stigma: Notes on the Management of Spoiled Identity*. Penguin Books, London. [For further reading this book by Erving Goffman is recommended and provides a detailed account of the notion of 'stigma' and its relationship to marginalised individuals].

to best prevent these consequences, because to do so will have positive effects for all participating children, their wider communities and, in this case ultimately, Rwanda as a whole. As such this chapter reports on a Rwandan study which was intended to provide 'Right To Play' with a deeper understanding of how stigma manifests itself and how it can be addressed. It is hoped that the results from this case study will provide a baseline from which 'Right To Play' can expand and develop further studies and programme improvements both in Rwanda and globally.

Policy Implications of the Research

Although the findings of a case study are by definition specific rather than general, this case study provided 'Right To Play's' policy and programming teams and external organisations some transferable data to inform policy direction and in actuality assisted them in understanding the following three questions:

- What stigma can arise in areas with a high prevalence of HIV/AIDS?
- How Right To Play tackles stigma attributed to HIV/AIDS?
- What improvements can be made to better build community knowledge and understanding elsewhere?

In Rwanda, the relevance of the data was obviously particularly acute, and as such this chapter also seeks to provide some general lessons and recommendations for program improvements globally.

Rationale

'Right To Play' was also interested in gathering multiple sources of data on HIV/AIDS related stigma in order to develop a comprehensive a picture of its manifestation and implications. The case study method was decided to be the most appropriate for this research because of its ability to produce reliable, deep, qualitative results steeped in rich testimony that allows the researcher get to the root causes of problems. The researchers could investigate stigma within its actual context, in a far more organic way than other data collection methodologies.

Rwanda and Kigali were chosen, in particular, for a few reasons. These were:

- Infection rates in Kigali were dropping, yet previous studies had identified stigma was still an issue[2,3]
- The Right To Play office in Kigali works regularly with children and youth living with HIV/AIDS and could provide access to them
- The Right To Play office in Kigali has a great deal of experience in facilitating external evaluations
- The two districts of Gasabo and Nyarugenge were chosen because collectively, the participants attending the schools and health centres come from all across the city, helping to make the study as useful as possible
- Furthermore, Right To Play has a very strong working relationship with the Centre de Santé (which has a dedicated HIV/AIDS unit) in Gasabo, the strength of which gave unprecedented access to PLWH

Research Methodology

The case study employed a diverse array of data collection methods including focus groups, individual and small group interviews, photo elicitation, video elicitation, drama workshops, mapping exercises, creative drawing, researcher observations, and games. The study lasted six weeks and consisted of a pilot study followed by data analysis, utilising grounded theory, and open coding to inform and guide a subsequent main study.

The researchers visited schools and health centres in two districts in Kigali, Nyarugenge and Gasabo, the attendees of which come from across the three districts in Kigali. Data collection was carried out in Kinyarwanda by locally trained 'Right To Play' programme staff who were supervised by the head researcher. There were four data sources/groups of participants:

- Children and youth in Right To Play programs living with HIV/AIDS at the Centre de Santé
- Parents or guardians of the children and youth in Right To Play programs living with HIV/AIDS

---

2. Nault. A. (2010). Discrimination, HIV/AIDS and International Law in Rwanda: A Case Study of Life Insurance Contracts. Montreal: International Clinic for the Defense of Human Rights (CIDDHU). Retrieved from http://www.ciddhu.uqam.ca/documents/Discrimination%20(english%20v.).pdf

3. Jean-Baptiste, R. (2008). HIV/AIDS-related Stigma, Fear, and Discriminatory Practices among Healthcare Providers in Rwanda. *Operations Research Results*. Published for the U.S. Agency for International Development (USAID) by the Quality Assurance Project. Bethesda, MD: University Research Co., LLC. Retrieved from http://pdf.usaid.gov/pdf_docs/PNADM901.pdf

- Children and youth in Right To Play programs with unknown/mixed
  health status at Solidarity Academy Right To Play coaches

As with most forms of research full ethics approval and consent was given by
all participants before they took part in the study. The study was explained
to them in Kinyarwanda and they were asked to read and sign a consent
form approved by the Rwanda National Ethics Committee, The Rwanda
National AIDS Control Commission (CNLS), Right To Play Rwanda, and
The Rwanda National Centre for Research on AIDS, Malaria, Tuberculosis
and other Epidemics (TRAC). Participants were free to withdraw at any
time during the study without repercussion.

Pre-Study Preparation

The full methodology was designed by the researcher with input and approval of the Steering Committee. This included data collection tools, target participants, ethical considerations, questions and timelines.

Once in Rwanda with the country office staff, the researcher identified
a pilot group with whom he conducted an initial study. Pilot study participants were chosen to closely mirror the main study participants, as envi-
sioned by the researcher and steering group. Research was carried out by
a team consisting of the researcher and country staff, comprised to negate
any potential age and gender biases. The pilot group assisted with the development of interview guides and other methodologies through feedback,
and their answers helped identify the themes or codes upon which the main
study was built. They also piloted the photo and video data collection methods. The data collected from the pilot group was shared and analysed by the
researcher, the steering group, and the country staff in preparation for the
main study.

Data Collection

Methodology and Toolkit

The methods and tools used for collecting data were purposefully diverse
and creative so as to provide as many paths as possible for people to express
themselves and share very sensitive information. This also provided an opportunity to better triangulate the data. The following methods of data collection were used:

- Focus group discussions
- One-on-one and small group interviews
- Photo elicitation
- Video elicitation

- Drama workshops
- Researcher observations
- Mapping exercises
- Drawing exercises
- Games

It is very challenging to get children and youth to open up in front of their peers in focus groups, particularly around sensitive areas like stigma. The arts-based methods used in this study helped considerably to prompt discussion. In the focus groups, the study used Stigma Mapping and Relationship Mapping exercises from the HIV Alliance 'Tools together now' toolkit[4] to encourage full participation.

Box 1: The format for each focus group session

1.	The purpose of the study was clearly explained to the participants at the beginning of each session. Consent forms were explained and handed out to be signed and returned.
2.	Participants were then given the choice of which arts or games activity to take part in, so that they felt more comfortable to participate in what we know is a very sensitive subject.
3.	At the end of that session we held a discussion and talked about the thought processes behind their activities, while asking the focus group questions.
4.	In the discussion we used various methods to elicit responses to ensure the participants were engaged and comfortable, such as individual or group mapping exercises.
5.	All activities were carried out in Kinyarwanda by trained RTP programme staff. Right To Play coaches were also on hand.
6.	The head researcher observed throughout and intervened as necessary."

The research team spent a single two to three hour session with each group both during the pilot and the main study. This applied to both youth/child and parent/guardian groups. In this time the researchers conducted as many of the data collection tools as time would allow and the participants were comfortable with. As participants took part in different activities there were also break out interviews, smaller focus groups and one-on-one interviews. Each participating coach was interviewed once, lasting one hour. Questions were asked in Kinyarwanda by trained Rwandan staff, recorded, and subsequently translated.

---

4. International HIV/AIDS Alliance. (2006). Tools Together Now! 100 Participatory Tools to Mobilise Communities for HIV/AIDS. Published for the U.S. Agency for International Development (USAID) and the and the Bill and Melinda Gates Foundation. Retrieved from http://www.aidsalliance.org/includes/Publication/Tools_Together_Now_2009.pdf

Sampling

To garner in depth responses and verify them through triangulation, a small
sample size was entirely necessary and perfectly suited to this qualitative
study. Inclusion criteria for the study were specific to the data source and
type of participant. The participants were invited to take part by Right To
Play coaches who had been briefed to form groups with equal numbers of
boys and girls aged 14 to 18. Participants from the pilot study were not
permitted to take part in the main study. **The inclusion criteria were** as
follows:

- **Youth with unknown health status:** A focus on youth aged 14-18 years
  old; each group session sought to evaluate 10-14 people maximum at a
  time, and each group ideally consisted of equal numbers of boys and girls.
  There were no other criteria for youth participation.

- **PLWHA at the Centre de la Santé:** A focus on youth aged 14-18 years
  old; each group session sought to evaluate 10-14 people maximum at a
  time, and each group ideally consisted of equal numbers of boys and girls.
  Participants had to be PLWHA. There were no other criteria for youth
  participation.

- **Right To Play Coaches:** In-depth interviews with 4-6 Coaches; these
  coaches were ideally half men, half women; there was no other criteria for
  coach participation.

- **Parents:** Up to 10 parents or guardians of youth attending the Centre
  de la Santé were asked to participate; an equal gender split was desired;
  there was no other criteria for parental/ guardian participation.

The number of participants who took part in the pilot study and main study,
which were mutually exclusive, is detailed below in Table 1. Although the
researcher invited participants according to the requirements set out by the
inclusion criteria, the number of actual participants differed slightly. Two
girls with unknown/mixed health status were unable to participate in the
main study. Due to limited time and resources, arrangements could not be
made to replace these participants. For interviews with coaches, the single
male participant in the pilot study was determined to satisfy the gender requirements, given the difficulty travelling between sites to recruit additional participants.

Table 1: Right to Play Case Study Participants

Category of Right To Play (RTP) Participants	Number of Participants			
	Pilot Study		Main Study	
	Total	Gender Split	Total	Gender Split
Child/youth in RTP program living with HIV/AIDS	10	5 male 5 female	10	5 male 5 female
Child/youth in RTP program with unknown /mixed health status	14	7 male 7 female	8	5 male 3 female
Parent or Guardian of child/youth in RTP program living with HIV/AIDS	5	1 male 4 female	7	2 male 5 female
RTP Coach	1	1 male	3	3 female

Target Information

Based on previous evaluations, five key questions were identified for exploration in this study. Data from these five questions were to answer the overarching case study problem. These questions are presented in Box 2, below.

Box 2: Guiding questions used in pilot study

1. After identifying the nature of stigma (e.g. stemming from lack of knowledge, fear of casual transmission, shame and blame etc.), how can we best address this?
2. What are the factors that are influencing the level of stigma in Kigali?
3. Do parents' attitudes affect children most strongly, or do children affect their parents' attitudes?
4. What are the implications for improving the effectiveness of our intervention strategies?
5. What are the personal experiences and perceptions of PLWHA in the target areas?

However, following the pilot study, it became clear that these were not the best questions to be asking. For example, point 5 above, instead became the principal vehicle for trying to understand the preceding four points, along with personal experiences of youth attending Right To Play programs with unknown/mixed health statuses, parents and guardians of PLWHA, and Right To Play Coaches. For the main study, the research team used more succinct questions to uncover the personal experiences and perceptions of PLWHA in the target areas, included in Box 3 below.

Box 3: Revised guiding questions used in main study

1.	What types of HIV/AIDS related stigma have participants, coaches, or parents of participants experienced or seen in their communities?
2.	What factors or environments influence the prevalence of such stigma in their communities?
3.	Does Right To Play tackle stigma, and how?
4.	How can Right To Play do more, and what would be the implications?

The information targeted by each of these above questions was approached using various methods of data collection. In the Table 2 below, each data collection method is listed on the left, with the corresponding target information on the right, numbered 1 to 4 depending on which guiding question from Box 3 the collection method sought to investigate.

Table 2: Data collection methods to extract target information

Data collection method	Target Information
Interview questions	1, 2
Focus Group: Children and youth living with HIV and AIDS	1, 2, 4
Focus Group: Parents of PLWHA	1, 2, 3, 4
Focus Group: Coaches	1, 2, 3
Focus Group: Children and youth on Right To Play programs with unknown/mixed health status	1, 2, 4
Photo elicitation	1, 2
Video elicitation	1
Drama skits	1, 2
Games	1, 2
Creative writing and drawing	1, 2, 3, 4
Researcher observations and notes	1, 2, 3, 4

Data Analysis

Once collected, data was organised and prepared for review to give the researcher a sense of the whole. It was also shared with the Right To Play Steering Committee. The data was then coded to generate a description of the setting and people as well as the themes for deeper analysis. Stories and powerful narratives were then explicated from the interconnection of these themes. These are presented in the **Results** section. The final stage was interpretation, for example: *what has the study discovered and what are the repercussions of these findings?* These are presented in the **Conclusions and Recommendations** section.

The Results section uses a variety of five standard devices in order to present, describe and analyse the data obtained from the grounded theories methodology. These five different core devices used to present and describe the qualitative data are:

  i. Directly quoting interviews, focus groups, drama workshops, games feedback
 ii. Summarising events by constructing readable case studies
iii. Describing events and acts while providing a description of places and space
 iv. Using photographs, drawing, maps and videos to visually display these case studies, spaces and events
  v. Summarising the findings in a variety of ways that are suitable to inform donors, national offices, in country staff, volunteers, and head office policy and programming teams

Challenges

Bureaucracy

This was the biggest challenge this study faced. The government process for securing ethical clearance was long, multi-layered and incredibly time consuming. This unfortunately took away from some of the time allotted for data collection.

Timing

This was difficult to manage on occasion. These were long sessions, but the data was very sensitive and it was impossible to rush through data collection methods. As a result some data collection methods were not as fully explored as they would have been had more time been possible. In particular photo elicitation involving walking around a community taking photographs and talking about it was too time-consuming to prioritise. Instead, mapping exercises were used to get a feel for the community and stigma within it, and cameras were provided for participants to use to capture the drama skits or games.

Successes

Training

The extra time afforded for study preparation was very useful. By having fully trained national staff, the study really negated the language barrier between the researcher and the participants. The RTP Rwanda staff assisting with data collection in Kinyarwanda knew what questions to ask to gather the results needed to answer the study question at hand.

Staff Capacity Building

The Rwandan team now have the experience of case study research methodology to potentially carry out similar studies independently in the future.

Data Collection

Aside from the time constraints mentioned above, this interactive methodology was very successful. It allowed people to discuss a taboo subject comfortably, creatively, and in a way that engaged participants.

Translation

This was carried out both internally by RTP staff, and externally by a highly experienced translator who understood the needs of the study and greatly assisted with local nuances.

Results

Organisation of Results

The variety of data collection methods allowed researchers to collect a rich and robust set of data. This data has been combined and analysed in order to identify common themes for presentation. These themes correlate to four key lines of questioning derived from the pilot study findings outlined in Box 4, below.

Box 4: Key lines of questioning

1. What types of HIV/AIDS related stigma have participants, Coaches, or parents of participants experienced or seen in their communities?
2. What factors or environments influence the prevalence of such stigma in their communities?
3. Does Right To Play address stigma, and how?
4. How can Right To Play do more, and what would be the implications?

Each of the four questions from Box 4 are individually highlighted below to organise relevant themes that have been identified in the data. In this Results section, this combined data will provide answers to the question under investigation as a whole.

1. What types of HIV/AIDS related stigma have participants, coaches, or parents of participants experienced or seen in their communities?

Social Exlusion

Being ignored, barred from social or work situations, and suffering from **social exclusion** were the most common manifestations of stigma. A large number of participants confirmed that once people know a person is living with HIV/AIDS "people don't visit you again" and "you lose friends." This type of isolation is **externally inflicted (social stigma)**:

> "We see people scared of sharing food with us thinking that they will get HIV. At work, in my family at home, at the hospital, at church, at the market, at school, in weddings, people discriminate against me and my child."
>
> - Parent of a child in a RTP program, Nyarugenge district

At school, a series of drama skits created and performed by children and youth corroborated this finding. They depicted PLWHA being excluded from playing, and expanded on their opinions in a subsequent focus group:

> Q: Where did we see stigma in the play?
> A: When they were playing.
> Q: How?
> A: When they [PLWHA] came to play with other kids, they didn't want to play with them. Instead they kicked them away, and when they were going home from school they kept on telling them that they were sick and people shouldn't get close to them.
> Q: Is that the way our society treats people with HIV?
> A: Yes.
>
> Drama skit by PLWHA

In addition to this forced exclusion and social stigma, there was a large amount of evidence confirming how stigma led to **self imposed exclusion/isolation (self stigma)**. One skit dramatising a doctor and a patient by a separate group of children (with unknown health conditions) went as follows:

> Doctor: I am going to ask a simple question. What if you find yourself HIV positive, what will you do?
> Patient: I will lock myself in my house and never go back out.
>
> Drama skit by youth with unknown health status

One skit included the line "*I am HIV positive but don't tell anyone or they will hate me.*" Another girl, aged 16, said in an interview that "*only when we teach people how harmful stigma is will everybody share that they are HIV positive.*" Indeed the dangers of social exclusion and fear of confronting the virus in public were very evident from the study. "*I don't go to take my medicines because I meet people on the way who will know I am HIV positive,*" said one 16 year old girl in Gasabo district.

Loss of Rights

This exclusion and suffering in silence is closely linked to perceptions of lost rights for PLWHA, and speaks of an absence of representation, be it actual or self-perceived:

Q: How do you think stigma shows itself?
*A: Not getting your rights, people discriminating against you and sometimes hating
you.*

Focus group with PLWHA

Mapping exercises encouraged children, youth and parents living with HIV
and AIDS to draw and describe challenges faced by PLWHA who are stig-
matised. Their answers included: **having no care; being alone; losing
rights; and losing the freedom of choice regarding jobs, houses, and
partners.** Children and youth participants with unknown health conditions
also drew maps conveying similar challenges:

> *"We are denied so many things. There are even places you ask for a house to rent and
> when they know that you are HIV positive they don't give it to you."*

> - Parent of a child in a RTP program, Nyarugenge district

Loss of Confidence

This loneliness, lack of rights, and paucity of opportunities leads PLWHA
to **lose confidence** or hope. Mapping exercises consistently raised this
point, and it is little wonder when *"neighbours start telling their children people
with HIV/AIDS are **enemies**...and want nothing to do with you." "You can't even
borrow anything from them"* said one youth, *"just in case."*

For those unable to build coping strategies or find support networks, loss
of confidence is a worrying, devastating stage, and **reinforces self-stigma**:

> *"I don't go to school because there is nothing I can do in my life. I don't take medicine
> because I will die." -* Girl, 17, Gasabo district

> *"People think since you have HIV you are done in society, and that you can't do any-
> thing for the community."-* Boy, 16, Nyarugenge district

For those that are able to build **coping strategies** to overcome a loss of
confidence, people carry on and try to remain hopeful. In the face of prejudice and discrimination, some individuals are able to maintain focus on the
things that matter most. The effects of stigmatisation lead to uncertain prospects and opportunities, and it takes considerable strength and determination to remain focused on the future.

> *"I keep on doing my job. Once I am sick I go to the hospital like others, I think about my
> future and follow the doctor's instructions. I don't think about the families that discrim-
> inate against me; I think of the future of my children." -* Parent of child in a RTP
> program, Gasabo district

Inaccessibility of Services or Employment

For the community too, this dejection, withdrawal and hopelessness reinforce beliefs that PLWHA have little or nothing to contribute. Results
highlighted that social stigma led to **inaccessibility of services or employment** for PLWHA. In this drama skit, youth in were asked to create a play
depicting HIV/AIDS in the workplace:

Soldier: Sir I am going to tell you my problem but I don't know how you will react. I am HIV positive.

Captain: This is a big problem. I don't want to see you again here. Take off your uniform and go away- when a fruit is bad you have to take it out lest it contaminates the whole barrel.

Drama skit by youth with unknown health status

Mapping exercises showed that **stigma made it hard to get jobs,** but in instances where they did have them, parents of children on Right To Play programmes were able to expand more on how having HIV/AIDS affects your work life. In doing so, they give an insight into the stigma awaiting their children once they leave education.

"At work when people know [you are HIV positive] they start to avoid you. Whenever you come across them they start leaving." - Focus group with parents of children in RTP programs, Gasabo district

"At the market, when people notice changes in your body, they stop buying from you." Focus group with parents of children in RTP program, Gasabo district

> 2. **What factors or environments influence the prevalence of such stigma in their communities?**

Education

All responses from all participants deduced that **education was central to eradicating stigma.** There is a fear of HIV/AIDS which drives stigma, and this fear emanates from misconceptions regarding transmission, confirmed by these youth.

Q: Why do people discriminate?
A: They do it because they don't know HIV
A: Yeah, it's ignorance
A: Some people discriminate against you thinking they are protecting themselves.

Focus group with PLWHA

In places where someone of authority is present and delivering this education, such as on Right To Play programs, stigma is less prevalent. There were many examples of this. One comes from the end of the drama skit with the soldiers mentioned above. It ends with the General restoring the moral order, undoing the injustice, and even wielding some Shakespearian retribution:

General: What's all the fuss here?
Captain: You see General, he [the Soldier found to be HIV positive] is contaminated, weak and can't do anything more for our country.
General: You think since he is HIV positive he can't do anything anymore?
Captain: Yes, sir.
General: I am removing you from your position. You are a private now. Reinstate this man [pointing to the HIV positive soldier] as Captain in your place.

Drama skit by youth with unknown health status

Other supporting testimony from coaches said parents have an important
role to play in education and authority, too.

> Q: What is the role of parents in contributing to stigma, both positively and
> negatively?
> A: *A negative role parents have is when they stop their children going to see people
> whom they know or think have HIV/AIDS.*
> A: A positive role is when those parents teach children how HIV is transmit-
> ted and that it's wrong to discriminate against those who are HIV positive
>
> Interview with coaches, Gasabo district

An interview with a girl of 17 in Gasabo district also made similar conclusions about the centrality of responsible, informed parenting.

> *"When a child discriminates against you, you can report him to his parents who can
> punish him."*

Another interview with a boy aged 15 in Nyarugenge highlighted that the
converse is true in places lacking authority.

> *"At the playground children talk and discriminate a lot because there is no authority
> there."*

Poverty

Poverty also exacerbates the likelihood and severity of stigma surrounding
HIV/AIDS. "*When you are poor you see a lot of stigma*", was heard from a number of participants. The majority of PLWHA are low income, replete with
tighter living conditions, less education and harder lives. Given that poverty
alone is the target of substantial stigmatisation, this effect is amplified by
HIV/AIDS. "*Improve the abilities of people living with HIV,*" researchers were
told, "*because it's when you are poor that you experience a lot of stigma.*"

Location

Twenty-five participants were asked to draw arrows leading out from each
place on their map. The length of the arrow intended to show how prevalent
stigma was in that place, with longer arrows signifying a greater amount of
stigma. The following graph in Figure 1 uses the experimental probability
equation (Box 5) to show where participants felt stigma was most prevalent.

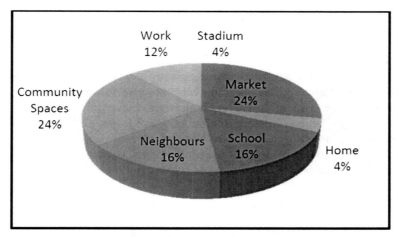

Figure 1: Where is stigma most prevalent?

Box 5: Experimental probability equation

Experimental Probability = Number of categorised answers
Total number of responses

As is similarly illustrated in Figure 1 above, two places consistently regarded as free from stigma were the hospital and the church.

> *"At hospital they don't discriminate a lot because the doctors understand. At church there is no stigma because they are people of God- even if they know you are HIV positive they cannot discriminate. They approach you, talk to you and even pray for you."*
> - Girl, 16, in a focus group, Nyarugenge district

A doctor in a drama skit by children in Gasabo was very supportive, showing the sort of understanding that is lacking in mainstream society.

> *"Let me tell you that when you are HIV positive life does not stop. There are medicines you can take, and if you follow the doctor's directions then life goes on, you can continue to do your job, live with your family."*

This sharply contrasts with other places common in young peoples' lives. For example at school:

> *"At school you can find a lot of stigma because sometimes someone will tell friends they are HIV positive and they tell the whole school."* - Boy, 14, Gasabo district

> *"At school some children don't want to play with people who are infected and won't go close to anyone who is."* - Boy, 16, Gasabo district

> *"In class, students might tell you to sit by yourself."* - Girl, Nyarugenge district

However some participants in this research saw school as more tolerant than others- *"at school it's not that much"* said one boy, adding that in fact stigma is much more prevalent in public spaces. This wariness of public spaces was a view commonly shared:

> *"Where we collect water people discriminate a lot. Sometimes they even tell people with HIV to be quick and go because they don't want them to stay and infect them."* - Boy, 14, Gasabo district

> *"Where we fetch water lots of people sit and talk and gossip about everyone and we see
> a lot of stigma."* - Girl, 14, Gasabo district

---

3. Does Right To Play address stigma, and how?

In the current case study, participants, coaches and parents of PLWHA described how Right To Play programs **increase awareness of HIV/AIDS,
provide a safe and inclusive environment, increase acceptance, let
young people become agents of change, instil hope, and build confidence.** All of these do much to sensitise and educate people on issues surrounding HIV/AIDS in an effort to reduce stigma. In the following section,
quotes and anecdotes are used to support these findings.

Providing a Safe and Inclusive Environment

The programmatic focus on tolerance, communication, understanding and
cooperation regardless of any inequality or difference, be it real or perceived, creates **an environment geared towards eradicating the prejudice and fear** that can consequently lead to stigma.

> *"We see people scared of sharing food with us thinking that they will get HIV. At
> work, in my family at home, at the hospital, at church, at the market, at school, in wed-
> dings, people discriminate against me and my child. But on Right To Play programmes,
> we are treated the same as everyone else. Even for just an hour it's such an empowering
> feeling."* - Parent of a child in a RTP program, Nyarugenge district

A Right To Play coach said how he worked with a local organisation providing Antiretrovirals (ARVs). There was a lot of self-stigma and fear among
PLWHA regarding taking this life saving medication in public. So Right To
Play sensitised people in the school to the drugs and created safe places for
children and youth to take them.

> *"One student, after we spoke about stigma, came to me and told me he was HIV posit-
> ive but was scared to take his ARVs provided by WE ACT in public. So I started to
> let him use the privacy of my office to take his medication. In time he told his friends,
> we spoke about it, and they supported him. He stayed healthy and went on to finish sec-
> ondary."* - RTP Coach, Nyarugenge district

Increasing Awareness of Hiv/Aids

Under-education and awareness of how HIV/AIDS is transmitted and develops was tackled head on by Right To Play programming.

> *"Some people think since you have HIV you can't do anything for the community.
> People talk about you a lot, ignore you, and you lose friends. They do it because they
> don't understand HIV/AIDS. Right To Play educates against this ignorance, and we
> can see things changing here."* - Girl, 17, Nyarugenge district

> *"Before, once they knew that you were HIV positive they started to refer to you as 'that
> bad kid who is HIV positive.' They would ignore me and I was always alone. But then
> Right To Play coaches educated people here and that stopped pretty quickly."* - Boy, 15,
> Gasabo district

This report finds that coaches are equipped with the skills and confidence to create HIV/AIDS awareness and anti-stigma messaging far beyond the playground or classroom.

"Right To Play have given me the ability and confidence to stand in front of a crowd and educate them about HIV/AIDS. That is so valuable in a community like mine where a whole generation missed out on formal schooling." - RTP Coach, Nyarugenge district

Perhaps equally if not more encouraging is that the children and youth on the program fan information out from Right To Play programs too.

"We play games that help people understand HIV/AIDS and stigma surrounding it; the really amazing thing is the way the kids go and teach other kids in their villages afterwards." - RTP Coach, Gasabo district

Increasing Acceptance

This demonstration of increased understanding and compassion is crucial as it leads to increased acceptance of PLWHA. Not only that, but Right To Play programs increase the acceptance by PLWHA of coping with the virus. This reduces the chances of social exclusion and loss of confidence. Encouragingly, acceptance was echoed in children and youth on Right To Play programs throughout the study.

Q: Would you be ashamed if you knew that someone in your family was HIV positive?
A: No, I would talk to him so that he won't feel lonely

Girl, 14, Nyarugenge district

This contrasts with the views of participants concerning compassion, or lack of, in wider society amongst people who have not attended Right To Play programs. *"When you are ill, neighbours say you are going to die. They start talking about you as if you weren't there anymore,"* said one parent of a child on Right To Play program in Gasabo district. *"Even neighbours discriminate against you because they think you will contaminate them,"* said another parent in the same focus group.

These are both examples of stigma arising from fear of "contamination" as it was called in some drama skits. Right To Play coaches do a great deal to ensure that this fear based stigma is tackled and eventually reversed.

"When we started games here the students would discriminate against any other student who had any sign of HIV/AIDS. There was even a case of one student they knew well and suddenly they didn't even want to sit close to him. But with playing and teaching through Right To Play they started to become close again and even started to support each other, aware of how difficult it was to live with the disease." - RTP Coach, Gasabo district

"Q: How do you explain stigma in your programmes?
A: We talk about stigma after we finish playing games about HIV and AIDS. We talk about how it's not acceptable and how unfair it is; we tell them that even if you are HIV positive you still have a life to live and a lot to contribute to society. We instil hope and empathy."

RTPCoach, Gasabo district

Instilling Hope and Building Confidence

With this support from coaches working to undermine both projected and received fear, Right To Play helps cultivate hope for the future.

> *"I talked to my children about the virus and we all discuss it freely. Right To Play has given them hope- they even have dreams for the future, big dreams."* - Parent of a child in RTP program, Gasabo district

A coach supported this, saying,

> *"You see that they [PLWHA] are growing up knowing that they are like the other kids and they can do something with their lives."* -RTP Coach, Gasabo district

> *"The games help us learn the truth about HIV,"* said one girl aged 15. The games and sessions create a support system for people who would otherwise risk being marginalised. A coach summed it up well:

> *"For me I think games help a lot. When the children know that somebody created a game thinking about them it encourages them. You explain to them what Right To Play does and they then know that there are people from high places that think about them. Can you imagine the confidence it gives them?"* - RTP Coach, Nyarugenge district

In addition to benefiting the participants, **the coaches themselves greatly gain from their role** and the training Right To Play provides:

> *"There is a lot that their teaching has helped me with in my life, because Right To Play was the first institution to teach on HIV and other sexual transmitted diseases."* - RTP Coach, Nyarugenge district

---

4. How can Right To Play do more, and what would be the implications?

There was a strong, generalised call for expanding Right To Play programming in an effort to spread educational messages as far as possible. *"Make public announcements,"* said a number of participants; *"Invite more children to attend, because the more you teach the better things get;"* or

> *"Go to every district, teach everyone about HIV/AIDS and stigma."*

There were some more specific recommendations that support the evidence regarding stigma levels differing from environment to environment.

> *"Hold sessions at watering holes so more people can see your work."*

The loneliness that comes with society not sharing anything with PLWHA was a huge and common concern. Right To Play was strongly encouraged to work towards correcting this type of social stigma.

> *"Trainings! More trainings! Some people still think that they can get HIV from sharing food from you, you need to educate them."*

> *"Kids need to know that there is no problem playing or sharing food with people who have HIV."*

Coaches spoke of needing more staff *"because they are outnumbered."* They also echoed parents in their concern that Right To Play may not be reaching the poorest, most uneducated, most needy recipients:

> *"Many families are very poor- you may find that some of the children don't go to school, don't learn, and that's when some of them start doing bad things."*

Discussion and Conclusion

*Summary of Key Findings and Recommendations

The study deduced that stigma surrounding HIV/AIDS in the districts of Nyarugenge and Gasabo in Kigali is extensive but manageable. The most prevalent theme that arose was fear of infection, which develops from lack of understanding how HIV is transmitted. This fear is amplified in environments where people are in close proximity, with a higher chance of interaction, such as school or the community watering hole. The effects of this fear and stigma towards people living with HIV and AIDS (PLWHA) are social exclusion, loss of confidence and hope, social barriers regarding employment, under-education, limited access to services, and loss of rights. For society, unwillingness to fully integrate with PLWHA results in disjointed communities and the emergence of marginalised minority citizens. The study also found that Right To Play helps to address these negative effects of fear by encouraging participation of all children and youth in programs and activities, regardless of health status. This method strives to mitigate perceived inequalities by fostering cooperation and education in a fun and relaxed setting. There is trust and communication on Right To Play programs: Coaches are role models and provide support and integration opportunities for PLWHA. This builds both self-belief and hope among PLWHA, and empathy and understanding from the community as a whole.

It is clear that Right To Play has given Coaches transferable skills that positively affect their behaviour and the perceived impact they can have on fighting stigma in their communities outside of Right To Play. They talk of having more confidence, being role models and trusted members of society, more knowledgeable, and able to influence the behaviours and opinions of others. With this influence comes an opportunity to break down stigma outside of Right To Play programmes too.

Right To Play's work is successful at reducing the frequency and severity of stigma. It promotes understanding, interaction and dialogue between children and youth. Participation in programs, and the friendships developed through social interaction, foster hope for PLWHA. These programs also lessen the chances for exclusion and marginalisation by educating and sensitising those without HIV/AIDS to its realities, from transmission to living with the virus. There is a call for Right To Play, however, to carry out more visible work, especially in public community spaces where stigma is most prevalent. Both participating youth and coaches reported wanting more training opportunities, more coaches, and more youth-led initiatives in order to encourage wider dissemination of Right To Play's educational messages. There is also a concern by parents, coaches and children alike that Right To Play's close work with schools, whilst universally praised by participants in the study and regarded as vital, also means a risk of missing some of the most marginalised children and youth.

Results indicate that stigma is revealed most frequently through **avoidance of those believed or known to be suffering from HIV/AIDS.** For example, children or youth suspected of suffering from HIV/AIDS were on occasion avoided at school, and peers would often not play with them. An extension of this avoidance is that many participants spoke of an **unwillingness by community members to share with PLWHA**, be it food, water, cutlery, clothes, or even space.

This avoidance arises from fear of contracting HIV/AIDS because of a lack of education of HIV is transmitted. These types of stigma indicate that PLWHA are considered **social deviants** by many members of their communities. As a result, this social stigma is magnified by self-stigmatisation among PLWHA, which arises from lack of confidence, fear of greater reprisals, or a perceived lack of self worth. Participants spoke of the manifestations of stigma manifesting for PLWHA in four principal ways: (1) Social exclusion; (2) Loss of rights; (3) Loss of confidence; and (4) Inaccessibility to services or employment.

Social stigma, rooted in a **fear of transmission**, is indicative of deep misunderstandings and under-education. This fear contributes to communities that are less cooperative, **less tolerant of differences, and subject to divisions and discrimination** that extends into the school, workplace, markets and community spaces. This study found that stigma emerging from fear was also present in PLWHA: the **fear of being marginalised or ostracised** as a result of carrying the virus. Indeed there were incidences of stigma being negative enough that **PLWHA did not want to publically reveal their health status.** However, this behaviour was not omnipresent and many participants spoke about the importance of compassion for PLWHA and more education about HIV/AIDS in order to eradicate stigma.

Right To Play was universally seen to be contributing positively to lessening both the types and prevalence of HIV/AIDS related stigma in a number of ways: the sport for development programmes themselves built knowledge of and tolerance for PLWHA, programme participants shared what they learned with peers and relatives outside of Right To Play programmes, and the wider community impact of Right To Play's well trained coaches were cited as important for taking messages of social acceptance beyond the confines of the programmes. There was almost unanimous support for Right To Play to provide more activities, more programmes, more education through trained coaches, and more visible work in busy community spaces to maximise messaging. Offering more or better services to children not attending school was seen as a priority.

Strengths

Education Sessions

Well-led, positive, informative education sessions can break this mould and change behaviours. Children and youth in Right To Play programs, as well as parents associated with them, testified that they are in an environment where they feel safe and accepted rather than socially excluded. Regardless of their health status, children and youth play and learn together and coaches encourage everyone to think positively about themselves, their peers, and their futures. Play and sport are perfect mediums for addressing the fear behind stigma. Through the necessary communication and co-operation that comes with these activities, as well as sharing and touching components of the games, misinformation regarding transmission is undermined. Not only were participants of Right To Play programs benefiting, but this study found that children and youth were taking these lessons back to their communities. It also found that coaches used their knowledge and influence outside of Right To Play programs, and had the confidence to change behaviours and perceptions through discussions in their local communities.

Grassroots Support

Right To Play seems to have adequate grassroots support to expand in Rwanda, as made evident from this study.

Data Collection Model

The implementation of data collection methods elicited responses that go some way to answering all the strands of a complex study question and must therefore be considered a success. The data collection model itself worked very well and provided enough variation in its collection methodology to let people feel comfortable about discussing a sensitive subject that could otherwise be taboo. Mapping exercises and drama skits followed by group discussions were the most successful in providing the data to answer the study question. They allowed the participants to share their perceptions and experiences in a relaxed environment. For participating parents and guardians, mapping exercises were useful for starting discussion, but they then talked more readily about stigma without the need for further games or drama etc.

The Rwandese research assistants were very well trained and experienced in both facilitating sessions and providing feedback to improve the study. All the data collection materials were sensitive to the issue and, after explaining how they worked, largely participant lead. This meant there was an enthusiasm in each session.

Limitations

While the results provide much optimism of the role of Right To Play in reducing stigma, there are limitations to these results and drawn conclusions.

Time

Bureaucratic interventions and the need to secure ethical clearance from more than four committees meant the researchers were not afforded much time between the pilot and main study for the organisation and coding of data. Although the researchers are confident that the coding correctly reflects the content of the data, more time would have been ideal.

Data Collection and Participation

Although the study design and training of the research staff were strong enough to ensure the methodology worked very well, collection methods could have been adapted depending on the participants. Having the resources and questions on hand to probe the issues of stigma depending on how participants responded would have enriched the types of accounts collected in this study. Also, some of the activities were very time consuming. As such all data collection methods were not fully explored, photo elicitations in particular, and were substituted for more intense mapping exercises.

One common feeling among researchers was that stigma was most acute in public spaces, and consequently much could be gained by holding Right To Play sessions more visibly. Poverty was also shown to be a multiplier of stigma, and there was concern Right To Play was missing the poorest children and youth who could not afford to go to school. Additionally, the lead researcher could have been a more vocal participant in the data collection sessions with participants if he were able to speak the language used in the collection of data.

Generalisability of results

It must be remembered that case study data is collected in a single socio-cultural context and thus, conclusions made cannot be generalised to other situations. While this information is critical in informing future studies and Right To Play programs in Kigali and elsewhere, the roots of stigma nor this study's findings are uniform. Instead, they have been rigorously collected and diligently analysed, triangulated (cross verification of findings to increase the credibility and validity of the results) and presented with one heavily contextualised case study question as the focus.[5]

Recommnedations for Right to Play

Future Studies

1. More preparation ahead of the study regarding what necessary ethical and governmental clearances may be needed.
2. Allow more time for all the data collection methods, especially photo elicitation.
3. Use this study as a guide to conduct other studies in other locations with a high prevalence of HIV/AIDS to understand the nature of stigma there too.

---

5. Des Jarlais, Lyles, C., & Crepaz, N. (2004). Improving the Reporting Quality of Nonrandomized Evaluations of Behavioral and Public Health Interventions: The TREND Statement. American Journal of Public Health, 94(3), 361-366.

4. Use the data collection methodology to conduct similar qualitative studies into different research topics. Rwanda staff described the methodology "as innovative, entertaining, and revealing for the participants and the facilitators."

Future Programs and Trainings

1. Coach recommendations for programme improvements included: more coaches, preparing competitions of sketches that talk about stigma, and more games that address the issue.
2. Use some of the study methodologies (such as drawing, mapping or drama) on programmes to further connect children and youth with stigma. "*It let them express themselves*" said a Right To Play Coach, "*they had fun- they were just free.*"
3. More visible work in public spaces, such as community watering holes, schools, and markets, to increase Right To Play's messaging around stigma.
4. Work with the poorest children and youth, i.e. those not able to attend school and others who may be severely under-educated to teach them about HIV/AIDS and stigma.
5. Training of national staff to carry out future in-country qualitative case studies independently.

Conclusion

The initial project design sought to provide Right To Play with a deeper understanding of how stigma manifests itself and how it can be better addressed in communities with a high prevalence of HIV/AIDS. As such, researchers looked to provide a method from which Right To Play could expand and develop further studies and program improvements both in Rwanda and globally. The researchers suspected that stigma would present social barriers arising from discrimination, but wanted to find out exactly how and why; only then could Right To Play discover how best to negate them.

The study discovered that stigma is deeply rooted in the selected communities in Kigali. For PLWHA stigmatisation leads to social exclusion, lack of opportunities, diminished rights, and a loss of confidence or hope. At these deep roots is under-education which results in irrational fear of transmission. This fear dissuades people from fully accepting PLWHA into their communities. This can manifest itself in a refusal to share, touch, or even be in the proximity of someone living with HIV/AIDS. This type of social stigma is well defined as "an acute social disapproval of or personal discontent with a person on the grounds of their unique characteristics distinguishing them from others in society."[6] This study not only supports this sentiment, but also surmises from participant accounts that stigma is a social construct founded in the "otherness" of PLWHA. This dichotomy causes an individual to be mentally classified by others as an undesirable, rejected stereotype rather than accepted as a 'normal'. Erving Goffman noticed this forty years ago, defining stigma as "the process by which the reaction of others spoils normal identity,"[7] calling it an attribute, behaviour, or reputation which is socially discrediting in a particular way. In the communities researched in Kigali, this social stigma leads to fear among PLWHA as well as the fear of being ostracised. This shows itself through self-stigma and self-removal from society, and further reinforces community divisions.

The report deduced that stigma surrounding HIV/AIDS in the studied districts of Nyarugenge and Gasabo in Kigali is extensive but manageable. The study also found that Right To Play helps to address these negative effects of fear by encouraging participation of all children and youth in programs and activities, regardless of health status. This method strives to mitigate perceived inequalities by fostering cooperation and education in a fun and relaxed setting (Box 2). There is trust and communication in Right To Play programs: Coaches are role models and provide support and integration opportunities for PLWHA. This builds both self-belief and hope among PLWHA, and empathy and understanding from the community as a whole.

6.Goffman, E. (1990). Stigma: Notes on The Management of Spoiled Identity. London, UK: Penguin Group.

7.Goffman, E. (1990). Stigma: Notes on The Management of Spoiled Identity. London, UK: Penguin Group.

Chapter 17
Sport as a Response to Emergencies and Disasters

Pelle Kvalsund

Vignette

The sun is getting low; it is late afternoon before the game begins. The local sport authorities in Makamba, a town and a province in southern Burundi, have organized a 'peace-game' of football between a local club and a team of returning refugees from neighboring Tanzania. We have been invited to watch the game together with officials from the local football association and other local authorities. I am part of a small team assessing the feasibility of starting a sport for peace project in Burundi, initiated by the Burundian President Hon. Pierre Nkurinziza. His Excellency is well known for his passion for sport, and was educated as a physical education teacher at the faculty of Sport and Physical Education at the University of Burundi. He even has his own football team, *"Halleluja Football Club"*, in Bujumbura City, where he plays several times a week. The peace-game in Makamba has started, and despite a number of good chances for both teams it remains goal-less. The energy level is high, however, and it is clear that the players have not come here to lose neither game nor face to their opponents or supporters. The first half ends with the score at 0 - 0 and as the second half starts you can clearly feel that the intensity has increased further; and with it some tension and aggression. There are a couple of players in particular that are not holding anything back, and the referee has to step in to control some of the tackles. The spectators are also becoming more involved, loudly cheering their own teams and discouraging the others. A bad tackle ends up in a scrap between the two feistier players. Four others join, then eight and finally about thirty-five people from both teams and the sidelines seem to be violently involved in the peace-game. Luckily the police are present and manage to control the crowd, albeit with the use of whips and sticks, and, after a fifteen minute delay the peace-game can continue. The game ends goal-less to the displeasure of both teams and spectators. To our relief however, it does end peacefully.

Makamba Burundi June 2007

Introduction

The percentage of us who share the world's prosperity is decreasing. It is today estimated that over a billion people go hungry every day, including over 15 million in "developed" countries. In addition, natural disasters and conflicts have increased in frequency and affect more of us. It is currently projected that close to 1 percent of our close to 7 billion people are currently displaced due to forms of forced resettlement[1]. About 80 percent of them are estimated to be women and children. The children are naturally the most vulnerable in these situations and, as the risk levels rise, fewer escape the consequences of their adverse environments. When a disaster strikes, whether man-made or natural, thousands of children are often left alone and requiring quick interventions in order to safeguard their protection.

Sport and play have long been recognized as valuable contributors towards the enhancement of a child's development. There is also, according to researchers, compelling practical, anecdotal and theoretical evidence to suggest that psychosocial sport and play programs can be helpful with children who have experienced severe stress or trauma, although there is little empirical evidence proving it.[2]

Post-disaster interventions using sport are therefore challenged by a number of skeptics arguing that sport is neither a need, nor a priority. They argue that sport interventions are competing for funds better spent providing shelter or rebuilding broken education and health systems, and that sport in some cases might in-fact add trauma to already distressed children and youth. Many humanitarians and academics are questioning sports value and role in a post disaster situation; and I am glad that they do. It is in fact much needed that we all question our contributions when responding

---

1. Statistics from Office for Co-ordination of Humanitarian Affairs 2009

2. Henley R., Schweizer I., C., de Cara F., and Vetter S. (2007). How Psychosocial Sport & Play Programs Help Youth Manage Adversity: A Review of What We Know & What We Should Research . International Journal of Psychosocial Rehabilitation. 12 (1), 51-58

to disasters, as the interventions are intended to address very sensitive situations in areas decimated infrastructurally, socially and economically, and where as a result, the potential for even more damage is very high.

This chapter is not intended as an academic documentation of sports' ability and shortcomings to improve communities in post-disaster environments, and it might not provide answers to some of the questions posed by the readers. It is rather a number of reflections based on observations and experiences from the field. It is also worth noting that many of my statements are also based on assumptions that I have developed from play and conversation with children and youth, from dialogue with local people, cultural and political leaders, sport coaches and administrators, and from humanitarian workers' experiences around the world.

The Context

Before I continue, please first allow me to qualify clarify some of the terminology I am using. The word disaster is commonly used in this chapter to describe *'serious disruptions to the functioning of a society, causing widespread human, material or environmental losses that exceed the affected society ability to cope using only its own resources'*[3]. This includes natural disasters and emergencies such as hurricanes, floods, earthquakes and tsunamis, but it also includes human caused or man-made disasters like conflict, war and terror. The levels of complexities following a disaster are many: Sometimes two or more forms of disasters coincide, adding difficulty to the response; and in some instances, for example in Sri Lanka after the Tsunami, this overlap of disasters might even lead to the creation of a temporary unity where populations in conflict join forces to overcome a larger common threat.

My work is based soundly on a few theories and models developed by more competent people than myself. The primary theory of this chapter is that *'the development of resilience in children and youth is essential in order for them to better cope with some of the hardship they are facing during and post disaster'*. The simple core of the theory is that the level of resilience is a result of protective and risk factors, and that a resilient child should be able to say:

> "I AM a loveable person, I CAN find ways to solve problems, and I HAVE people I trust and care for.[4]

This comment goes hand in hand with what John Clifton Waring, a clinical psychologist, presents in his three building blocks for resilience development'[5]. These are:

---

3. Moving Forward Toolkit, A Guide for Practitioners in the Field of Sport for Youth in Emergencies, P 52 (2008)

4. Grotberg, E. (1997) 'The international resilience project.' In M. John (1997). (ed) A Charge against Society: The Child's Right to Protection.

5. Presentation: Raising Resilient Children, J. Waring, (2006).

1. A sense of security, whereby the child feels a sense of belonging and being loved.
2. Good self-esteem, leading to an internal sense of worth and competence.
3. A sense of self-efficacy, that is, a sense of mastery and control, along with an accurate understanding of personal strengths and limitations.

In addition, research has shown that building resilience among survivors of high-risk environments can help develop and/or maintain: social competence, empathy, caring, problem-solving skills, critical and creative thinking, task mastery, and a sense of purpose and social connectedness. Problem-solving skills are a particularly strong predictor of improved resilience in children and youth in the long-term, as improved problem-solving skills can enhance the possibility that future life challenges will be resolved successfully[6].

There are however, fully developed, recognized and useful scales measuring both resilience, such as Connor's and David's Resilience Scale, and self-efficacy, for example the General Perceived Self-Efficacy Scale by Ralf Schwarzer & Matthias Jerusalem. However, the most challenging part is to actually be in a position to accurately measure a baseline once you have decided to start with your sport interventions. Indeed, Rolf Schwery, a Swiss sport and development professional with considerable experience of sport interventions in post disaster areas argues that:

> "......the four first weeks after a disaster is an intensive resilience training for the children and youth affected by the impact. Interventions started and measured after this might therefore not quantify a significant change in resilience".

This difficulty of measuring impact makes it challenging for us as believers and professionals in the field of sport response, and we often find ourselves in a clutch, jammed between the child protectionists' and psychologists' knowledge and advice, as well as the researchers' need for evidence and the humanitarians' fight for funds. Some organizations therefore choose to do little while we are waiting to find the hard proof, while luckily some choose to respond.

For the affected population, stress caused by disasters may lead to serious readjustment problems. It is clear that a disaster provokes a reaction in everyone, but these reactions and their outlets can vary vastly depending on the person's nature, situation and level of resilience and network of support. Many children, particularly in areas where daily hardship has shaped them into survivor experts, may cope well in these situations. Others may appear to be coping well with adversity, but may be internalizing their reactions and showing 'apparent resilience'[7].

---

6. Vetter et al., Impact of resilience enhancing programs on youth surviving the Beslan school siege Child and Adolescent Psychiatry and Mental Health (2010) 4:11

7. Suniya S. Luthar Ph.D., Vulnerability & Competence: A Review of Research on Resilience in Childhood (1991)

The reactions to stress are commonly divided into physical, social, emotional and cognitive. We as coaches or mentors in sport activities are usually not trained to assess or deal with severe reactions, and furthermore, access to health professionals during and after a disaster are generally very limited. It is therefore wise to be aware of some common signs (of stress reactions) that we should be attentive to during play with children. Following is an (incomplete) list of behaviors:

The child:

- Is avoiding certain activities
- Has trouble concentrating
- Has difficulty relating to other participants
- Is showing regressive behavior or 'clinging' - fear of being left alone
- Is unusually irritable or angry
- Is showing self-destructive behavior
- Is easily startled or frightened
- Is hearing or seeing things that aren't there

Once you observe "out of the ordinary" reactions during the activities you are offering it is also important to have an idea of what you should do, or should not do as a coach/mentor. It is believed that the one thing that sport practitioners can do is offer our time to listen to anyone that would like to talk and to share their experiences. We do not have to make the conversation into a debriefing session, but just give them a chance to express themselves once they are ready to do so. We mustn't try to be psychiatrists. We as coaches are generally not qualified to deal with post-traumatic stress, and once you realise that participants show severe indications of stress and the problem is beyond your capability and level of training, you should refer to professionals that might offer qualified help. It is also important to inform the person concerned about your intentions, and what infrastructure and staff are in place to continue to support him/her.[8] It is important that you as a coach are prepared that these conversations might lead to reactions, and that you have considered how to deal with these.

Organizing Structures

"Do-as-little-additional-harm-as-possible"

Luckily quite a few organizations choose to respond to disasters, but for those that do, the common principle of *do-no-harm* should be adapted to *do-as-little-additional-harm-as-possible,* and guide the entire process starting with the preparations and the assessment of potential interventions. It is hard to imagine the stress people are and have been experiencing during a disaster and presence does not automatically decrease this.

---

8. For more info see; Psychological Support: Community-based Psychological Support Training manual. International Federation of Red Cross and Red Crescent Societies, 2002

It is therefore important to research and utilize all resources and previous knowledge about the area, the situation and the affected population. You are usually and most likely not the first outsider to enter the disaster area. A comprehensive overview of the general situation and the sport specific situation is key, as is knowledge about existing goals, plans, programs/ projects and sport structures in addition to human, technical and financial resources is a very important starting point. Many assessments might have been already made: access them before bothering the population with more questions and "promises".

"Standards for operation"

As the program evolves, the activities must be fused with other minimum standards of operation. The Inter-Agency Network for Education in Emergencies (INEE) is a global network that are working together within a humanitarian and development framework to ensure the right to, and minimum standards for education in emergencies and post-crisis reconstruction[9]. The Sphere Project outlines a number of minimum standards that humanitarian organizations must consider when entering into disaster response- for example the principle of ownership. Project ownership in all parts of the intervention is very important to ensure positive results. This means that the disaster-affected population should actively participate in the assessment, design, implementation, monitoring and evaluation of the program.[10] An example on where this is working well is on a project called Thailand Burma Border Football. This project on the Thai/Burma border was established in 2006 and aims to provide leisure opportunities for the young population in two Karenni refugee camps. The refugee settlement has been "warehoused" in these camps for years, some for over fifteen years, as a result of a long conflict between the Burmese military regime and ethnic minorities on the Thai border. Although the initiative was started by the UNHCR, the project has been designed, planned and implemented by the refugees, including budgeting and financial management. As consultants, our role in this project was merely to facilitate and guide, and to assist applying for funds, not to spend or to dictate the use of the resources. This approach was not been without its challenges. Encouraging refugees to take responsibility for direct and active involvement was not easy after years of living in isolation. They have been surviving on donations and support, and to a certain extent been at the mercy of humanitarian organizations, so independence and freedom of action were not naturally adopted.

---

9. INEE, *Minimum Standards for Education in Emergencies, Chronic Crises and Early Reconstruction*, 2004, ISBN 1-58030-034-0

10. Sphere Handbook, *Chapter 1: Minimum Standards Common to All Sectors, Common standard 1: Participation*, Edition 2004

Another program called the Sphere Project recommends that humanitarian assistance or services are provided equitably and impartially, based on the vulnerability and needs of individuals or groups affected by disaster.[11] This can at times be very challenging to ensure, particularly in conflicts where ethnic division has led to a Government and its governing sport bodies being ruled by one ethnic group. The same often goes for other minority issues, such as those regarding gender or people with disabilities. The selection of partners here is very important, and the mix of governing sport bodies and civil-society partners must be rigorously assessed.

There have been attempts to develop certain standards in general sport and development work, such as the *ICES*[12] project lead by the UK Sport. However, when it comes to sport specifically responding to disaster there are no international standards agreed upon. A number of key documents[13] have been developed to elaborate and promote the rights of children in humanitarian emergencies, but there is limited agreement or discussion on the best ways to support children's healthy development following a disaster. "The Moving Forward Toolkit"[14] developed in 2008 addresses in detail issues regarding design of sport as response projects, but best practices from this field have yet to be specifically incorporated into international humanitarian standards. Both UNICEF and UNHCR are in the process of developing their own guidelines and manuals for this work, too.

"Sport and Play"

In 2003, the UN Inter-Agency Task Force on Sport for Development and Peace defined sport, for the purposes of peace and development, as "all forms of physical activity that contribute to physical fitness, mental well-being and social interaction, such as play, recreation, organized or competitive sport, and indigenous sports and games."[15] I believe that a definition of sport for the purpose of peace and development would benefit by being more specific with regards to the important methodology we should use when implementing the activities. We all know the negative sides of sport like bad winners and losers, doping, physical and mental injuries, and hyper-competitive coaches for whom desire to win overshadows the more im-

---

11.Sphere Handbook, Chapter 1: Minimum Standards Common to All Sectors, Common standard 4: Targeting, Edition 2004

12.http://www.uksport.gov.uk/pages/ices/

13.ICSSPE (2008). Sport and Physical Activity in Post-Disaster Intervention. A Handbook Prepared in Conjunction with ICSSPE's International Seminar. 2nd edition SAD and Schwery Consulting (2007). Considerations in Establishing Sport Programs for Youth in Disasters and Complex Emergencies. Landscape document.

14.Moving Forward Toolkit, A Guide for Practitioners in the Field of Sport for Youth in Emergencies (2008)

15.United Nations Inter-Agency Task Force on Sport for Development and Peace, Sport for Development and Peace: Towards Achieving the Millennium Development Goals (Geneva: 2003) at 2, online: United Nations <http://www.un.org/themes/sport/task.htm> [UN, Towards Achieving].

portant right for all to participate in sport based and show skill and desire. Dr. Stuart Brown, founder of the National Institute for Play in California defines play, one of the UN's definitions central components, as: 'an apparently purposeless voluntary activity with inherent attraction. The activity is free for time and diminishes the participants' consciousness of one self. It also possesses a potential for improvisation and a continuation desire'[16].

He cites sport as a form of play, but also says that not all forms of sport fit the definition. Maybe this is why there seem to be quite different understandings, concepts and views of sport and play in our field. A common perception by humanitarian and development agencies is that sport and play are two different things, where play possesses the more serene and positive elements that are easier to control, and that might lead to positive learning and social change. On the other hand it is often held that sport, with its necessary competition and subsequent winners and losers, should be avoided in programming addressing sport in response to disasters, and especially in conflict areas as it might lead to increased tension: for example in Makamba. It is felt this might also lead to a large number of participants who, by not winning, mastering or achieving, will perceive the activities negatively and feel discouraged to continue.

The reality is that performance and achievement are natural parts of sport and other forms of play. It includes, amongst other, measuring and mastering skills and showing your abilities off to other participants and significant others. The Persian word for "sport" is based on the root "*bord*," meaning "winning"[17], and it is my personal view is that competition should continue to be a natural component of sport and play in programs also responding to disasters. Competition helps us learn to set goals and manage the process of achieving them. It also makes us strive for improvement and provides challenges and obstacles for us to overcome, and it can be a healthy part of our personal development. But, it is important to be *constantly* aware of the potential negatives of conflict. When working with programs dealing with sensitive situations and populations it is very important that one adapts a methodology that takes into considerations some of the issues your activities might lead to. Let me give you an example from a project that I was fortunate enough to observe closely in 2004 - "The Open Fun Football Schools". The OFFS is a humanitarian initiative using games and the pedagogical "Fun Football Concept" as tools to stimulate peaceful co-existence, gender equality, tolerance and social cohesion in countries and communities affected by war and ethnic conflict[18]. I had the opportunity to attend both their training of trainers' sessions and the 'football schools', and the methodology used for the activities of the project is based on a very well thought through child-centered philosophy. They focus on the playful

---

16. Stuart Brown, M.D., PLAY, p 17 (2009)

17. http://en.wikipedia.org/wiki/Sport

18. (Available at:http://www.ccpa.dk). (Accessed 03.11.2010)

aspects of the activities where all the fun is derived from simply playing. Competition is a normal part of most of the games, but they often personalize the results to fit the children's need for individual success.

"OFFS Methodology"

The "football" activities at the OFFS's provides many 'diverse exercises' and small games designed to make everyone feel successful regardless of their abilities and skills. Exercises like rope skipping, tug of war, handball and juggling, some designed for individuals, some for small groups and some for teams. This diversity ensures that the activities preserve the appropriate level of competition or challenge needed to satisfy the personal desire for experimentation and test.

Another important and challenging methodical element when using sport and play to respond to disasters is to balance the activity level and the energy/time used to address social-developmental challenges faced by the participants. In order to retain the participants and prevent them from losing interest it is imperative that the activities offered are perceived attractive and fun, and this was a main challenge for the group of young coaches I observed and trained in Sri Lanka in 2009. The goal of the organization they represented (Future Peace) was to use sport and play activities to address local conflict and to cultivate peaceful dialogue. The group was a mix of remarkable Singhalese and Tamil young men and women, none of whom had a sport coach background. Similar to other observations I have made in both Africa and South East Asia, the combination of several (too many) development goals often makes the activities complicated, boring and time-consuming. The organization of the activities becomes difficult and inefficient, often leaving the children standing in lines and circles waiting to touch the limited accessible sport equipment, or otherwise be involved in the game. This is not a criticism of the young coaches from Sri Lanka, they in fact did very well despite their limited training, but an attempt to address issues that have been observed for years and still need attention.

Added to this are a few more examples of best methodological practices that I would recommend:

- The guarantee of and access to safe (physically and psychologically) and conducive play space for the activities. Many children will feel generally unsafe and needs assurance that they won't be harmed in any way.

- Selection of appropriate activities that don't exclude any participants due to the nature of the game. Activities like aggressive ball games might scare some participants that want to avoid excessive physical contact and/or exposure.

Transition

Another assumption underpinning this chapter is that lasting (long term) regular sport and play activities is a central goal for organizations working within the field of Sport, Development and Peace. It is well documented that regular organized and controlled physical activity leads to obvious health benefits and opportunities for development and learning of basic skills, processes and emotions that could benefit the participants in their day-to-day lives. Sporting activities can also provide a good support network for children and youth. For example an organized and well-driven sport club can provide a safe space where people can come on a regular basis to have fun together with peers, get support from significant others and address issues that affect their lives. This, one assumes, must be particularly important for children and youth in areas affected by disasters, and where previously existing social networks have been damaged. The regular weekly gatherings provide a stable venue where we can "positively" influence the participants for years to come. Once these networks or activities stop most of the above mentioned benefits will eventually do the same. Therefore, one of the mayor challenges for sport programs responding to emergencies is to make the shift from a short-term humanitarian intervention to a long-term (several years) development program.

In 2005 over a decade of civil conflict in Burundi ended. Four years later a sport project focusing on stabilization and unification was launched, mandated by the Ministry of Youth Sport and Culture and partnering Right To Play and the Norwegian Olympic and Paralympic Committee and Confederation of Sport (hereafter NIF). The approach is a two-pronged mobilization and capacity development project and builds on the strengths of both the local and the external partners. Right To Play use a bottom-up approach to mobilize the youth at the grassroots level through civil-society partners accessing the local population, including thousands of returning refugees from neighboring countries. At the other end, NIF is focusing on the governing bodies of sport, partnering with the Ministry of Youth Sport and Culture, the Paralympic Committee and national sport federations. The idea is to strengthen their capacity to govern sport on a national level whilst, at the local level, enable them to assume their duties and absorb the increased number of participants.

The hypothesis is that through regular long-term participation in "well run" sport and play (see the methodology section) the project will contribute to stability and long-term relationship development. The project addressed important peace-building elements such as equal access to services, rebuilding capacity and infrastructure, strengthening of civil society, and possibly fostering unity amongst the participants through local ownership of activities. The transition from peace games primarily offered by NGO's filling the gap of the non-existing sport structures in affected communities, to national or local structures like supported sport clubs offering regular activities is the biggest challenge in this and other projects. In Bosnia and Croatia the Open Fun Football Schools have taken years to finally receive endorsement by the National Football Associations.

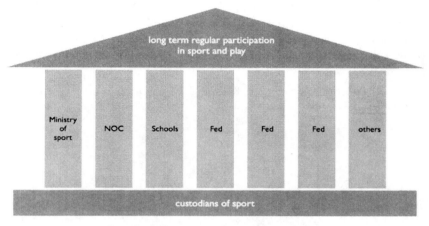

Fig.1: Long Term Participation in Sport & Play

Figure notes: Others include social sport clubs, gyms and fitness centers, NGOs or private initiatives.

Figure 1 illustrates a typical "well functioning" sport system in a "stable" environment where long term regular (weekly) participation in sport is the goal. This includes competitive sport as well as recreational sport and play opportunities for children, youth and adults that would just like to partake in physical activities for health benefits, socializing, or pure fun based on their own time, level and abilities. Many countries lack such systems, or have developed this only for a very small fraction of the population. After a disaster, or for many countries around the world, this system usually looks more similar to the illustration in figure 2, characterized by low participation and broken support systems and governing sport bodies:

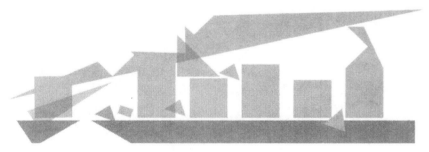

Fig. 2: Low Participation and Broken Support Systems

The custodians of sport, illustrated in the purple pillars, have been destroyed (or are not developed) together with other parts of society, and regular organized participation (the roof) in sport has vanished. The rebuilding

239

phase is naturally often very complicated and challenging. There are some-times, depending of the "popularity" of the disaster, a number of S&D ini-tiatives and almost always very limited coordination by the governing sport bodies. This can lead to a number of parallel systems being built who all have the potential to collapse without local buy-in and support. It is important that the NGO's and projects that aim to support don't take over and as-sumes roles and responsibilities that the custodians of sport should own.

Fig 3: Gradual Rebuilding of Systems of Sport

In figure 3 NGO's have moved in and filled the gap of the broken sport pil-lars to maintain a service to the people. Selection of partners is another is-sue that needs serious consideration. The same goes for access to baseline information and plans, and the level of recognition and support the initiat-ives are able to foster from governing bodies to mention just a few. At the same time, the rebuilding phase presents a fantastic opportunity for posit-ive change, building on areas that were functioning well and abolishing the parts that don't work to improve the total delivery of youth sport for all. There is no blueprint to how this is done, but there are many previous initi-atives to learn from.

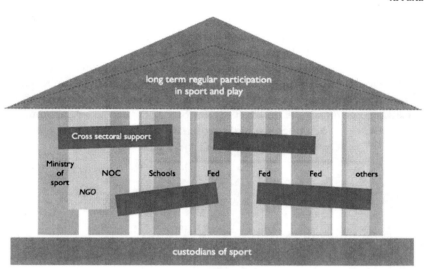

Fig 4: Long Term Regular Participation in Sport & Play

Figure 4 indicates a situation where there has been a shift back from a system ran by gap-fillers to a state where the natural custodians of sport have regained their position, roles and responsibilities, and some of the Sport Development and Peace NGO's have moved on or assumed natural roles in partnership with national or local sport organizations. Importantly it also shows (the cross bars) where cross sector support from other Ministries and NGOs are supporting and using sport to develop the communities and support the youth population. There are obviously a number of coordinating tasks that the national sport leaders must undertake as well, and, in addition political buy-in and recognition must be translated from lip-service into concrete plans, agreed upon strategies and tangible actions, and be reflected in financial plans and resources. The list, sadly, is long.

Appeal

In Makamba in 2012, the situation is calm, and despite many people struggle to reclaim lost land and the day–to-day scramble for resources to make a living the returnees and the people whom stayed behind live in relative harmony. Sport and play in Makamba, as in Burundi at large, play an important role in the lives of children and youth as well as adults. Promoted by the Ministry of Youth Sport and Culture in Burundi, training is provided in club formation and capacity development of local sport leaders in order to increase regular participation in sport, and to promote unity and peaceful coexistence in the provinces. Sport and play as response to disasters can to a certain extent be compared to what, unfortunately, many education systems around the world refer to as a "non-essential subject," much like art, music and physical education in public schools. As the conventional education systems struggles with resources these non-essential subjects are the first to be cut. This is similar to what is often viewed as happening to sport and play as part of the psychosocial programs of organizations providing humanitarian support and relief after a disaster. But as neuroscience is continuing to build the recognition for play as an important factor for growth, flexibility, the development of optimal learning capabilities, normal social functioning, self-control, and other executive functions, it is sincerely hoped that more organizations in the near future chose action rather than reluctance and become involved at a greater levels of participation.

Chapter 18

Ensuring Human Rights in Sport

Constructing a Human Rights in Sport Monitoring Checklist

Mary A. Hums, Eli A. Wolff & Amber Morris

Introduction

Sport for development and is a multi-faceted topic, and this book covers a range of topics and authors herein are sharing theoretical and practical perspectives throughout the text. This is good as sport for development and peace takes many forms, but intertwined with its many forms is the notion of sport and human rights. Indeed as argued by the United Nations Office for Sport, Development and Peace: "Successful Sport for Development and Peace programmes work to realize the right of all members of society to participate in sport and leisure activities" (UNOSDP, n.d., Path to Success section).

Sport administrators working in all types of sport organisations should keep in mind the notion of sport and human rights. However, the discussion about sport and human rights is new to many sport administrators and they may not be familiar with how their organisations stack up in this regard. One way to help them is through use of a human rights checklist, since checklists are commonly used tools in sport organisations. The human rights in sport checklist clearly outline the rights of all sport participants. When used as a tool to raise awareness about the current status of human rights in sport, sports organizations as well as third parties can use this instrument to better understand the spectrum of sport and human rights by looking at the strides sport has made as well as areas that may need improvement. The 2008 press release announcing the development of the checklist stated:

> People who recognize the influence and power of sport can step to the forefront of the international movement to ensure human rights for all. The development of this checklist will help policy makers define and quantify human rights issues for organizations which are leading the way and will provide guidance for organizations wanting to do better...

This checklist goes hand in hand with the work that sport and development groups have been doing. Different organizations have been focusing on the ways sport can be used as a tool to improve human rights around the globe, but sometimes looking at the status of participants in sport and their rights is forgotten. That is why we created this checklist (Sport in Society, 2008, p. 1).

This checklist offers the sports community and to human rights organizations a guideline for every sport, every organization, and every team to examine and reflect on the status of these rights within themselves and each other. The checklist was established within the framework and guidelines of international treaties and conventions addressing human rights in sport.

The rights delineated here are meant to be a guideline for organizations and third parties to consult while examining the state of human rights in sport. We envision through this checklist gaining a better understanding of the accomplishments in the field of human rights within sport as well as areas that may need more focus and direction. We hope to be able to highlight which of the following rights are flourishing and which may need a helping hand. We would also like to note that when we refer to sport we are referring to not only professional and amateurs sports, but also all forms of physical activity that contribute to physical fitness, mental well-being, and social interaction, such as play, recreation and indigenous sports and games.

This chapter will discuss the development of such a checklist and its application to sport for development and peace. Before getting to the checklist, we must establish some basic definitions of three terms used in this chapter – human rights, sport, and sport and human rights.

Definition of Human Rights.

Defining human rights is a complex undertaking. The United Nations High Commissioner for Human Rights (2011, pp. 1-2) uses the following definition:

> 'Human rights are rights inherent to all human beings, whatever our nationality, place of residence, sex, national or ethnic origin, colour, religion, language, or any other status. We are all equally entitled to our human rights without discrimination. These rights are all interrelated, interdependent and indivis-

ible. Universal human rights are often expressed and guaranteed by law, in the forms of treaties, customary international law, general principles and other sources of international law. International human rights law lays down obligations of Governments to act in certain ways or to refrain from certain acts, in order to promote and protect human rights and fundamental freedoms of individuals or groups'.

Definition of Sport

Before we can discuss human rights in sport, a baseline definition is needed for what is meant by sport in this context. What is meant by "sport?" For purposes of this chapter, sport includes "all forms of physical activity that contribute to physical fitness, mental well-being and social interaction, such as play, recreation, and or competitive sport, and indigenous sports and games" (United Nations Inter-Agency Task Force on Sport for Development and Peace, 2003, p. v).

In other words, sport is not limited to its elite level professionalized forms, but rather is much more inclusive.

Sport and Human Rights - Two Dimensions

When thinking of sport and human rights, it is important to remember two important dimensions of sport and human rights:

1. Sport as a human right
2. Using sport to promote human rights

How is it then that sport would be considered a human right? Certainly when thinking of human rights, issues which come to mind first include participating in a political system, being free from torture, or having access to safe and clean drinking water. However, sport and physical activity allow us to be more fully human, just as art or music allows us to be more fully human. In addition, sport and physical activity helps to promote healthy living as well as equity and inclusion. These notions are consistent with the United Nations Millennium Development Goals (MGD), which focus on gender equity, children's health, maternal health, and preventing HIV/AIDS. "Beyond its physical and health dimensions, sport contributes to comprehensive and harmonious development and fulfillment of the human being" (African Union, 2008, p. 9).

Using sport to promote human rights, on the other hand, entails the use of sport to draw attention to societal issues and ways to deal with those issues. Two examples are worth noting here. First there is the iconic image of Tommie Smith and John Carlos on the medal stand at the 1968 Mexico City Olympic Games, gloved fists raised in the air as a symbol of protest over the treatment of African-Americans in the United States. A second example involved the protests by groups such as Team Darfur surrounding the staging of the 2008 Summer Olympic Games in Beijing, China because of that country's questionable record of human rights for its citizens.

Codification of Sport and Human Rights

The notion of sport and human rights has been codified in numerous documents, including several emanating from the United Nations (United Nations Inter-Agency Task Force on Sport for Development and Peace, 2003). Numerous United Nations documents deal to some degree with sport, including:

1. Convention on the Elimination of Discrimination Against Women (CEDAW)
2. Convention on the Rights of the Child (CRC)
3. Convention on the Rights of Persons with Disabilities
4. UNESCO, International Charter on Physical Education and Sport
5. Declaration of the Rights of the Child
6. Geneva Conventions Relative to the Treatment of Prisoners of War
7. Universal Declaration of Human Rights
8. International Convention Against Apartheid in Sports, G.A. Res. 2396
9. The International Covenant on Economic, Social, and Cultural Rights
10. UNESCO, Convention Against Doping in Sport

A sampling of the wording from these documents as they pertain to sport and human rights follows.

First is the language from the Convention on the Elimination of Discrimination against Women (Office of the High Commissioner for Human Rights, 2007a), which reads:

> 1. States Parties shall take all appropriate measures to eliminate discrimination against women in order to ensure to them equal rights with men in the field of education and in particular to ensure, on a basis of equality of men and women: The same opportunities to participate actively in sports and physical education
>
> 2. States Parties shall take all appropriate measures to eliminate discrimination against women in other areas of economic and social life in order to ensure, on a basis of equality of men and women, the same rights, in particular: The right to participate in recreational activities, sports and all aspects of cultural life

The Convention on the Rights of the Child (Office of the United Nations High Commissioner for Human Rights, 2007b) contains the following:

> 1. States Parties recognize the right of the child to rest and leisure, to engage in play and recreational activities appropriate to the age of the child and to participate freely in cultural life and the arts.
>
> 2. States Parties shall respect and promote the right of the child to participate fully in cultural and artistic life and shall encourage the provision of appropriate and equal opportunities for cultural, artistic, recreational and leisure activity.

The Convention on the Rights of Persons with Disabilities contains the most extensive language dealing with sport and human rights of all the UN Conventions. Article 30.5 Participation in Cultural Life, Recreation, Leisure and Sport (United Nations, 2006) states:

1. With a view to enabling persons with disabilities to participate on an equal basis with others in recreational, leisure and sporting activities, States Parties recognize the right of persons with disabilities, on an equal basis with others, to participate in recreational, leisure and sporting activities..."

2. To encourage and promote the participation, to the fullest extent possible, of persons with disabilities in mainstream sporting activities at all levels.

3. To ensure that persons with disabilities have an opportunity to organize, develop and participate in disability-specific sporting and recreational activities, and to this end, encourage the provision, on an equal basis with others of appropriate instruction, training and resources

4. To ensure that persons with disabilities have access to sporting and recreational venues.

5. To ensure that children with disabilities have equal access to participation in play, recreation, and leisure and sporting activities, including those activities in the school system.

6. To ensure that persons with disabilities have access to services from those involved in the organisation of recreational, tourism, leisure and sporting activities (United Nations, 2006, Section Article 30.5).

In addition to these policies and documents, a number of sport organisation documents refer to human rights, including, for example:

1. The Olympic Charter
2. International Olympic Committee Sport for All Commission mission.
3. European Charter for Sports
4. Draft Sport Policy Framework for Africa (2008-2018)

For example, the Olympic Charter, which is the governing document for the International Olympic Committee (IOC) reads:

> "The practice of sport is a human right. Every individual must have the possibility of practicing sport, without discrimination of any kind and in the Olympic spirit, which requires mutual understanding with a spirit of friendship, solidarity and fair play. The organisation, administration and management of sport must be controlled by independent sports organizations."
>
> (International Olympic Committee, 2010, p. 11).

Additionally, the IOC's Sport for All Commission has as part of its mission, which suggests that: "Sport for All is a movement promoting the Olympic ideal that sport is a human right for all individuals regardless of race, social class and sex. The movement encourages sports activities that can be exercised by people of all ages, both sexes and different social and economic conditions" (International Olympic Committee, 2009, p 3).

Development of the Sport and Human Rights Checklist

The idea for the human rights in sport checklist idea evolved from work in four inter-related areas (a) sport for people with disabilities, (b) sport and human rights, (c) sport for development, and (d) sport and social change.

Sport managers use checklists all the time, for example, the scripting of pre-game activities, ensuring the safety of patrons at a match, or keeping track of team equipment.

Over several months, a team of international sport and human rights experts, compiled a detailed list of human rights for participants of sports including players, coaches, officials, and others. The checklist was established within the framework and guidelines of international treaties and conventions addressing human rights in sport. Through our research, we discovered that although human rights have been a subject long studied, there has not been a comprehensive look at the state of human rights in sports. This checklist will be a tool to fill that gap. We created the checklist as a tool to study sports organizations, and it can easily be tailored to review government programs, grassroots programs, and a country's overall system.

This idea emerged from discussions with individuals with Amnesty International, an organisation which routinely uses checklists to assess the state of human rights around the world. Consequently, an Advisory Group of individuals sharing an interest in this area was assembled. These individuals included:

Kate Mardel- Ferreira, Amnesty International
David McArdle, University of Stirling
Paolo David, UN Office of the High Commissioner on Human Rights
Janet Lord, Blue Law International
Kathy Guernsey, International Human Rights lawyer
Ann Peel, Havergal College
Eli Wolff, Center for Sport in Society (now at Brown University)
Amber Morris, Center for Sport in Society
Mary Hums, University of Louisville

The structure for the Checklist grounded in other Human Rights checklists which assessed the rights of Victims of Torture, Women Prisoners, Victims of Enforced or Involuntary Disappearance. Several individuals took the lead in developing the content of the checklist, which was then sent out for comment from Advisory Committee, as well as selected United Nations agencies and Human Rights groups. As a result of this process, the Sport and Human Rights Checklist took shape.

The Sport and Human Rights Checklist

After going through this extensive development process, the resultant checklist contained the following major headings:

1. social rights
2. health and safety rights
3. sport as employment rights

4. justice in sports rights
5. environmental rights
6. financial rights

Each one of these rather major headings can be further broken down to provide illustrative examples of what me be covered in each of the different rights.

Social Rights

Non-discrimination/Equity in Sporting Participation

1. The right to be free from discrimination based on the following reasons

   a. Racial/Ethnic
   b. Gender
   c. Disability
   d. Sexuality/Sexual Identity
   e. Political/Cultural Affiliation
   f. Religion
   g. Age
   h. Birth status/legitimization

   This is includes the right to equal opportunity to sport including access to facilities, equipment, medical care, education, employment opportunities, development, financial opportunities, etc.

2. The right to be recognized as a person under the law and all rights and duties associated with it

Right to Physical Education

1. The right to physical activity and instruction on sport, hygiene, and exercises as part of a school curriculum

Fair Play

1. The promotion of the rules of the game and good sportsmanship as defined by the governing bodies of the sport including the absence of cheating and biased actions

Inclusive Facilities and Equipment

1. The right to have adequate activity, playing, and changing facilities for all ages, genders, and abilities including availability of bathrooms for both genders as well as accommodations for disabled people, equal ability to use playing fields, equipment, and training facilities.

Self-Determination

1. The ability for each participant to make decisions for himself including, where to live, which participate in play, whether to play or work professionally in sport and which organisation to play or work with, etc without pressure or coercion from outside forces including governments and private citizens
2. No one may be forced into an association
3. No person should be arbitrarily separated from his/her parents, guardians, or family except under competent authority or court ruling including for the purpose of training for sport.
4. Should a person be separated from his/her family, that person has the right to regular communication and contact with his/her parents
5. No person should be transported abroad against their will even for the purpose of training or playing sport
6. No person should be forced to remain in one country for the purpose of playing sport, people have the right to determine which country they wish to live in and play for

Health and Safety Rights

Right to Health, including doping

1. The right to proper nutrition to promote a healthy body and mind for sport
2. The right to develop a healthy active body including access to proper nutrition and the absence of drugs of all types but performance enhancing drugs in particular
3. The right to be physically active and participate in the enjoyment of sport

Protection Against Abuse and Violence

1. The right to play free from any physical, emotional, or verbal abuse or violence from the opposition, fans, grounds staff, or officials

Safety and Security

1. The right to play in a safe environment free of structural defaults and environmental hazards including safe air quality and clean playing surface
2. The right to play free of fear or threat of bodily injury, harassment, anxiety, or danger.

Injuries and Rehabilitation

1. The right to proper medical care upon injury
2. The right to proper protection from injury through training and supervsision
3. The right to proper training on how to avoid injury and care for injuries
4. The right to retain a playing contract after injury
5. The right to compensation for being dismissed because of injury

Sport as Employment Rights

Sport-related Labor Conditions

1. The right to a safe working environment
2. The right to just and favorable conditions of work
3. The right of protection against unemployment
4. The right to proper compensation for work including the right to equal pay for equal work
5. The right to time off, including limited periodic paid vacation

Employment and Hiring Practices

1. The right to form a players association as a collective bargaining unit to protect and uphold labor laws
2. The right to be free from discrimination in the hiring process on the basis of race, religion, gender, ethnicity, national identity, sexual orientation, age, political affiliation or disability
3. The right to be free to create a contract and a working relationship with whomever

Justice in Sport Rights

Right to Due Process

1. The right to an independent hearing and an effective remedy for complaints
2. The right to challenge a decision in either arbitration or the court system
3. The right to the process of law as stated under the local, national, and international law as well as the laws of the game
4. The right to confront all complaining witness against you

Access to Information

1. The right to view all documents pertaining to your complaint including evidence and witnesses against you
2. The right to view your contract at any time and to have it examined
3. The right to access to the rules and information regarding sport including the process for securing proper playing areas and equipment

Freedom of Speech

1. The freedom to express your opinion publicly barring bringing the game into disrepute
2. The freedom to hold opinions without interference
3. The freedom to impart information and ideas through any media channel and regardless of frontiers

Right to Privacy

1. The right to be free from arbitrary intrusions of a person's privacy including family, home, and correspondence

Environmental Violations

1. The right to protect and maintain the environment during the creation of new sporting facilities, major sporting events, and in general industrialism so as to promote better health of the planet and the participants.
2. The right to proper building codes to as protect the environment
3. The environment should be protected from degradation or destruction due to sport related events including but not limited to the building of facilities, the training of players, and the occurrence of major sporting events

Financial Rights

Displacement of Persons

1. The right to adequate and fair compensation for any governmental land seizures for the purpose of sport
2. The right to be free of arbitrary seizures of personal property
3. Every person has the right to his nationality and shall not be deprived of his nationality arbitrarily

Access and availability of resources/Financial Spending

1. The right to not be denied financial spending or resources on the basis of gender, race, ethnicity, religious affiliation, national identity, disability, or sexuality
2. The right to apply for resources and financial support

Concluding Thoughts

Guides such as the Human Rights in sports checklist are only useful if sport administrators can successfully implement them. Wolff and Morris (2009) offer some thoughts on this. First, a checklist is really a building block, and one which can be easily implemented. As a living document, the checklist serves as a first step as its use will result in adding coverage as different rights emerge for consideration. Also, the checklist is written in such a way as to be used by sport organizations at different levels – local, national, or international. This flexibility allows sport managers to assess their organizations' level of respect for human rights. According to Hums, Moorman, Wolff, Morris, & Lyras (2009, p. 337), "The rights delineated here are meant to provide guidelines for organizations and third parties to consult while examining the state of human rights in sport. The authors envision use of the Checklist will help sport organizations gain a better understanding of the accomplishments in the field of human rights within sport as well as areas that may need more focus and direction."

References

African Union. (2008). Draft sport policy framework for Africa (2008-2018) Available at: http://www.africaunion.org/root/au/Conferences/2008/october/sa/sport/Sport_Policy_Framework_en.pdf , (Accessed 12th March 2012).

Hums, M.A., Moorman, A.M., Wolff, E.A., Morris, A., & Lyras, A. (2009). Monitoring human rights in sport: How a human rights in sport checklist can assist with best practices. In H. Westerbeek, & P. Fahlström, *Conference proceedings EASM 2009* (pp. 336-338).Nieuwegein, The Netherlands: ARKO Sports Media.

International Olympic Committee. (2010). Olympic charter. Available at: http://www.olympic.org/Documents/olympic_charter_en.pdf, (Accessed 12th March 2012).

International Olympic Committee. (2009). Sport for All Commission. Available at: http://www.olympic.org/sport-for-all-commission, (Accessed 12th March 2012).

Office of the United Nations High Commissioner for Human Rights. (2007a).

Convention on the Elimination of all Forms of Discrimination Against Women. Available at: from http://www2.ohchr.org/english/law/cedaw.htm, (Accessed 12th march 2012).

Offic of the United Nations High Commmissioner for Human Rights. (2007b).

Convention on the Rights of the Child. Available at: http://www2.ohchr.org/english/law/crc.htm, (Accessed 12th March 2012).

Office of the United Nations High Commissioner for Human Rights. (2011). What are human rights? Available at: http://www.ohchr.org/EN/Issues/Pages/WhatareHumanRights.aspx, (Accessed 12th March 2012).

Sport in Society. (2008, August 16). Sport in Society introduces groundbreaking human rights in sport checklist. Available at: http://assets.sportanddev.org/downloads/human_rights_in_sport_checklist_press_release.pdf (Accessed 12th march 2012).

United Nations. (2006). Convention on the Rights of Persons with Disabilities. Available at: http://www.un.org/disabilities/convention/conventionfull.shtml, (Accessed 12th march 2012).

United Nations Inter-Agency Task Force on Sport for Development and Peace. (2003).

Sport for development and peace: Towards achieving the millennium development goals. Available at: https://www.un.org/wcm/webdav/site/sport/shared/sport/pdfs/task%20force%20report%20english.pdf, (Accessed 12th March 2012).

Wolff, E.A., & Morris, A. (2009, May). Promoting human rights in the Olympic

Movement: The development and implementation of a human rights in sport checklist and athletes' bill of rights. Presented at Olympic Reform–A Ten Year Review, Toronto, ON, Canada.

Chapter 19
Inclusive Sport for Development

Amy Farkas, Valerie Karr, Eli A. Wolff & Anna Lachowska

Introduction

With its universal popularity and ability to transcend linguistic and cultural barriers, sport is an ideal tool for raising awareness, addressing stereotypes and fostering the inclusion of people with disabilities in society. The growth and popularity of the Paralympic Movement and Special Olympics have shown that people with disabilities have the abilities to excel in sport and recreation. Sport is also increasingly being recognized for its valuable role in creating social change and contributing to broader development objectives, such as the Millennium Development Goals (MDGs). This is the concept of *sport for development* (hereafter S4D), using sport and recreation as a means to achieve social objectives, which is very different from the development of competitive sport or athletes. It draws on the fundamental values of sport and recreation being fun, enjoyable, and participatory, as well as having the convening power to bring individuals and communities together, making it an attractive activity to engage people of all ages and abilities.

There are an estimated 1 billion people with disabilities worldwide with 80% living in developing countries and denied access to basic health, education, and support services".[1] [2] People with disabilities include those who have long-term physical, mental, intellectual, or sensory impairments which in interaction with various barriers may hinder their full and effective participation in society on an equal basis with others".[3] [4] Since 2007 the Convention on the Rights of Persons with Disabilities (hereafter CRPD) has encouraged governments to further acknowledge the human rights of people with disabilities and scale up efforts to address their needs.

Within the broader concept of *inclusive development*, which aims to ensure that all groups regardless of age, disability, poverty, gender, ethnicity or sexual orientation contribute to creating opportunities, share the benefits of development as well as participate in decision-making[5], is the concept of *inclusive sport for development*. Based on the United Nations Development Program' human development approach, *inclusive sport for development* integrates the standards and principles of human rights: participation, non-discrimination and accountability to the field.[6]

This chapter will provide an introduction to basic concepts of disability and sport for development; an overview of sport, recreation and play as human rights; the linkages between disability, the CRPD and the MDGs (Millennium Development Goals); and lastly an examination of how sport can contribute to inclusive development.

Models of Disability

The CRPD, a United Nations human rights treaty entered into force on 3rd May 2008, adopted a broad categorization of people with disabilities (see definition of disability above) and reaffirms that every person regardless of their impairments and disabilities has the same human rights and fundamental freedoms. Prior to the CRPD there was no specific global treaty addressing the needs of people with disabilities, the world's largest minority[7],

1. World Health Organization (2011). World Report on Disability.

2. World Health Organization. (2005). Disability and rehabilitation: Global programing note 2005–2007. Promoting access to healthcare services for people with disabilities. Retrieved January 29, 2006, from http://www.who.int/nmh/donorinfo/vip_promoting_access_healthcare_rehabilitation_v2.pdf

3. UN, http://www.un.org/disabilities/documents/convention/convoptprot-e.pdf, accessed 19 July 2010.

4. STAKES: Label Us Able: A Pro-Active Evaluation of Finnish Development Cooperation from a Disability Perspective. P. 27. www.dfid.gov.uk/pubs/files/disability/dfid-and-disability.pdf

5. http://www.undp.org/poverty/focus_inclusive_development.shtml

6. Ib id

7. UN Secretariat CRPD http://www.un.org/disabilities/default.asp?id=476

but that did not mean they did not have the same rights and fundamental freedoms as their peers without disabilities.

The CRPD has marked a radical shift from the medical approach to the social or human rights approach towards disability. This is outlined in the definition of disability enshrined in the CRPD as a measure of inter-action between an individual's impairment(s) and societal barriers.[8] Under this definition it is not an impairment that limits or disables an individual; rather it is the attitudinal and environmental barriers that limit their parti-cipation in society. These societal barriers must be overcome or removed to enable people with disabilities access to the rights and freedoms allowed to others.

The medical model

Under the medical model of disability, the impairment (e.g. blindness) is viewed as the fundamental issue. As a result, people with disabilities are viewed as a burden in need of special care and services. This model focuses on special health care and education institutions, sheltered workshops and disability specific service agencies. It essentially reduces the value of people with disabilities to lead independent lives, is contrary to the inherent dig-nity and self-worth of people with disabilities as human beings and there-fore discriminatory by design.

The social model

The social model or the human rights model cardinally redefines disability, by viewing it simply as a function of the interaction between the impair-ment and the environment, therefore stressing the need to remove the bar-riers in society - physical, attitudinal, and social - that prevent people with disabilities from enjoying, to the fullest, their human rights. Under the so-cial model of disability, the structures within society are the issue that need to be "cured" (i.e. made accessible), not the impairments. These problems such as the lack of inclusive education, lack of employment, inaccessibility of the built environment, and all sorts of prejudices are actually the barriers that disable people with disabilities.

Therefore, whereas the medical model sees the impairment as the prob-lem, the social model sees the problem as the societal barriers that need to be removed to allow people with disabilities access to their rights that oth-ers take for granted.

Sport, Recreation and Play as Human Rights

Historically it has been a challenge for people with disabilities to fully access their right to sport, recreation and play although it has been clearly artic-

---

8. The CRPD Convention states that people with disabilities "include those who have long-term physical, mental, intellectual or sensory impairments *which in interaction with various barriers may hinder their full* and effective participation in society on an equal basis with others." (Emphasis added).

ulated in numerous international documents. The UN Universal Declaration of Human Rights (1948) states that all people have the right to "rest and leisure", which can be interpreted to include sport, recreation and play. Language referring to these three as human rights is also contained in the Convention on the Elimination of Discrimination against Women (1979), the International Convention Against Apartheid in Sports (1985), the Convention on the Rights of the Child (Article 31, 1989), and most recently, the Convention on the Rights of People with Disabilities (Article 30, 2006). Furthermore, sport is also mentioned as a human right in Article 1 of the Charter on Physical Education and Sport put forth by UNESCO in 1978.

As we examine the intersection between disability, the MDGs and sport, it is most relevant to review the CPRD, but as previously mentioned this does not preclude people with disabilities from the rights outlined in other documents. The CRPD (Article 30) specifically requires State Parties to encourage and promote the participation of people with disabilities in mainstream and disability-specific sporting activities at all levels and to ensure that they have access, on an equal basis with others, to training, resources, and venues. Particular to children with disabilities, the same article mandates State Parties to ensure that children with disabilities "have equal access with other children to participation in play, recreation and leisure and sporting activities, including those activities in the school system".[9] It also promotes and advances inclusion, access and dignity of people with disabilities in sport, recreation and play, and contributes to a broader understanding of the rights in the domain of sport, recreation and play for people with and without disabilities.

These documents provide a foundation and framework placing the responsibility on governments, non-governmental organizations, and sport governing bodies to ensure there is access for all to sport, recreation and play. The recognition of sport, recreation and play as a human right advances and protects the value of these activities to exist as a central element of the human condition. Without an awareness and articulation of sport as a human right within a policy context, sport is not taken seriously, and is not free from protection against discrimination and exclusion. By understanding sport, recreation and play as human rights, there is recognition that the space of sport (including recreation and play) is central to everyone and access, inclusion, dignity and respect in sport must exist for every human. Only through access and inclusion can sport then serve as a vehicle for human development.

9.Convention on the Rights of Persons with Disabilities, http://www.un.org/disabilities/default.asp?id=290

Understanding Disability, Rights and the Millennium Development Goals

The MDGs, an established unifying set of global development objectives adopted at the United Nations Millennium Summit in 2000, were developed to foster collaborative action to reduce poverty, improve health, address educational and environmental concerns, and achieve gender equality reflecting concerns for the world's most pressing development problems. The MDGs are specifically designed to address the needs of the world's poorest citizens and most marginalized populations to achieve the goals of the United Nations and its commitment to promote "human rights and development for all."[10] [11] Strikingly, there were no specific references to people with disabilities in the 18 targets set for 2015 or the indicators to monitor progress when they were developed.

With people with disabilities comprising a significant proportion of the most marginalized and poorest in the world, and having the same rights as their peers without disabilities, it is imperative that disability be included in the efforts to achieve the MDGs.[12] However some progress has been made. *For example, in 2010, the education of children with disabilities was included in the Progress Report for MDG 2 and t*he General Assembly during its sixty-fifth session adopted the resolution 'Realization of MDGs for persons with disabilities for 2015 and beyond'[13]. The resolution articulated how to incorporate people with disabilities in policy development and programming, as well as in monitoring the *MDGs.*[14] *But more still needs to be done.*

A common and initial association between disability and the MDGs concerns the link between poverty, disability and prevention. A major focus of the MDGs is on the eradication of extreme poverty and hunger in all nations by the year 2015 (MDG 1). In 2007, there was a*n estimated 426 million people with disabilities living below the poverty line.*[15] *Further* estimates show that 51% of disability is directly linked to poverty and preventable diseases and at least 20%

10.UN Millennium Campaign, http://www.un.org/millenniumgoals/bkgd.shtml

11.Mainstreaming Disability in MDG Policies, Processes and Mechanisms: Development for All, Report of the Expert Group Meeting*, Organized by the Secretariat for the Convention on the Rights of People with Disabilities, Division for Social Policy and Development, Department of Economic and Social Affairs in collaboration with the World Health Organization, World Health Organization Headquarters, Geneva, Switzerland 14-16 April 2009

12.Enable http://www.un.org/esa/socdev/enable/dissre00.html

13.http://www.cbm.org/article/downloads/54270/65_186_Realizing_MDGs.pdf

14."Millennium Development Goals: mainstreaming disability", to the report of the Secretary- General on the Fifth Quinquennial review and appraisal of the World Programme of Action concerning Disabled Persons, A/63/183, available at: http://www.un.org/disabilities/images/A-63-183.DOC

15.Facts on Disability in the World of Work (Geneva, International Labour Organization, Nov 2007), available at: http://www.ilo.org/global/About_the_ILO/Media_and_public_information/Press_releases/lang--en/WCMS_088028/index.htm

of impairments are caused by hunger alone[16], thereby addressing the root causes of poverty, and can impact the number of individuals living with disabilities. The MDGs also address maternal health (MDG 5) and it is well understood that abnormal pre-natal and per-natal events are a major cause of disability in children.[17] A final example is with MDG 6 pertaining to HIV and AIDS, malaria and other diseases which can be root causes of impairments. Living with *HIV or AIDS can lead to blindness, neuropathy or dementia.*[18] Malaria, and in particular cerebral malaria, can lead to neurological impairments that may result in developmental delays and epilepsy.[19] There is no question that efforts to stop the transmission of these illnesses by 2015 will help prevent more people from acquiring impairments.[20]

However while it is important to address prevention, it is only half the story. The MDGs also provide a framework to ensure people with disabilities have full access to the information and services they need to realize their rights. A few examples of this are:

- *To effectively halve the proportion of people whose income is less than a dollar a day (MDG 1), it is important that we disaggregate data to assess the proportion of people with disabilities with an income of less than a dollar a day and that nations develop policies to include people with disabilities.*

---

16. See 'Overcoming obstacles to the integration of disabled people, UNESCO, DAA, March, 1995. See also Charles Gore, The global development cycle: MDGs and the future of poverty reduction. Paper presented at After 2015: promoting pro-poor policy after the MDGs. Brussels. Available at http://www.eadi.org/fileadmin/ MDG_2015_Publications/Gore_PAPER.pdf. (accessed 10 November 2010)

17. See UNICEF 1980, Childhood Disability: Its Prevention and Rehabilitation, UNICEF Document E/ICEF/L/1410. See also *Margaret C Hogan et al.*, Maternal mortality for 181 countries, 1980-2008: A systematic analysis of progress towards Millennium Development Goal 5, The Lancet, Volume 376, Issue 9745, 18 September 2010, available at: http://download.thelancet.com/pdfs/journals/lancet/PIIS 0140673610605181.pdf?id=e16241398b8eb460:-1b3c8f53:12c6af24f05: -2801290287571028. (accessed 10 November 2010)

18. WHO, United Nations Joint Programme on HIV/AIDS and Office of the High Commissioner for Human Rights Policy Brief, April 2009, available at: http://data.unaids.org/pub/Manual/2009/jc1632_policy_brief_disability_en.pdf. (Accessed, 12 November 2010).

19. See Murphy SC; Breman JG, Gaps in the childhood malaria burden in Africa: cerebral malaria, neurological sequelae, anaemia, respiratory distress, hypoglycaemia, and complications of pregnancy. Am J Trop Med Hyg. 2001 Jan-Feb;64 (1-2Suppl): 57-67. Available at: http://www.ncbi.nlm.nih.gov/pubmed?term=%22Breman%20JG %22%5BAuthor%5D(accessed, 12 November 2010).

20. See *Robert W Snow et al*, Equity and adequacy of international donor assistance for global malaria control: an analysis of populations at risk and external funding commitments, available at, http://download.thelancet.com/pdfs/journals/lancet/PIIS 0140673610613402.pdf?id=e16241398b8eb460:-1b3c8f53:12c6af24f05:-2 8101290287571028 (accessed, 12 November 2010).

- *To achieve full and productive employment and decent work for all (MDG 1), we must address the growth rate of GDP per person with a disability employed. Evidence shows that people with disabilities are more likely to be excluded from the labour force and under-employed. If employed, they are often given the lowest paying and menial tasks[21]*

- *To halve the proportion of people who suffer from hunger by 2015 (MDG 1), we must address the prevalence of people with disabilities who are under weight. People with disabilities are often denied equal access to sufficient amounts of food as available to others[22]*

- *To ensure that children with disabilities are able to complete primary education (MDG 2), we must monitor the number of children with disabilities enrolled in primary education, completion rates, and literacy rates. "Over 90 per cent of children with disabilities in developing countries do not attend school"[23]*

- *To promote gender equality (MDG 3), we must first understand and address the discrepancy and double-discrimination experienced by girls and women with disabilities in relation to education, employment, equal access to program and services, and political participation.*

- *To reduce child mortality rates (MDG 4), we must assess the mortality rates of infants and children with disabilities. Those born with or acquiring disabilities at a young age are often denied medical and rehabilitative care due to neglect and lacking of services[24].*

How Sport Contributes to the MDGs and Inclusive Development for People with Disabilities

Since 2000, there has been a surge in understanding and endorsement for S4D. World leaders at the UN Millennium Summit were the first to officially recognize the power of sport for development and key roles it can play in fostering healthy child development, peaceful communities, and addressing major development challenges such as those outlined in the MDGs. Later the same year the UN Secretary-General Kofi Annan established an Inter-Agency Task Force on Sport for Development and Peace co-chaired by then UNICEF Executive Director Carol Bellamy and Adolf Ogi, the former president of Switzerland who in 2001 had become the first Special Adviser to the UN Secretary-General on Sport for Development and Peace. The task force produced a report titled "Sport for Development and Peace: Towards achieving the Millennium Development Goals," in 2003 which

---

21. http://www.un.org/disabilities/documents/mdgs_review_2010_technical_paper_advance_text.pdf

22. World Bank 2003.

23. UNICEF

24. http://www.who.int/disabilities/media/events/idpdinfo031209/en/index1.html

concluded that sport, from play and physical activity to organized and competitive sport, is a powerful and cost-effective way to advance the MDGs. Since then, there have been major milestones in building a sustainable foundation for S4D including 2005 being declared the International Year of Sport and Physical Education (IYSPE) and the formation of the government-based Sport for Development and Peace International Working Group (SDP IWG) that released a key set of recommendations in 'Harnessing the Power of Sport for Development and Peace: Recommendations to Governments.'

During the same period, the UN General Assembly passed six resolutions (2003-2010) pertaining to this topic. Most recently, a resolution was adopted on 18 October 2010 and entitled "Sport as a means to promote education, health, development and peace" encouraging the use of sport as a vehicle to foster development and strengthen education, prevent disease, empower girls and women, foster the inclusion and well-being of people with disabilities, and facilitate conflict prevention and peace-building.[25]

Furthermore, the UN Office of Sport for Development and Peace (UNOSDP), established in 2001 to support the efforts of the Special Advisor to the United Nations Secretary-General on Sport for Development and Peace in his worldwide activities as an advocate, facilitator and representative of sports' social purposes,[26] has outlined the ways sport can contribute to achieving the MDGs in the following table.

Table 1. CONTRIBUTION OF SPORT TO THE MILLENNIUM
DEVELOPMENT GOALS

1. Eradicate extreme poverty and hunger

- Participants, volunteers and coaches acquire transferable life skills which increase their employability
- Vulnerable individuals are connected to community services and supports through sport-based outreach programs
- Sport programs and sport equipment production provide jobs and skills development
- Sport can help prevent diseases that impede people from working and impose health care costs on individuals and communities
- Sport can help reduce stigma and increase self-esteem, self-confidence and social skills, leading to increased employability

ERADICATE
EXTREME POVERTY
AND HUNGER

2. Achieve universal primary education

- School sport programs motivate children to enrol in and attend school and can help improve academic achievement

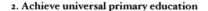

25.http://www.un.org/wcm/webdav/site/sport/shared/sport/pdfs/A%2065%20L.4%20%20%20%20N1058367.pdf

26.http://www.un.org/themes/sport/

- Sport-based community education programs provide alternative education opportunities for children who cannot attend school
- Sport can help erode stigma preventing children with disabilities from attending school

ACHIEVE UNIVERSAL
PRIMARY EDUCATION

3. Promote gender equality and empower women

- Sport helps improve female physical and mental health and offers opportunities for social interaction and friendship
- Sport participation leads to increased self-esteem, self-confidence, and enhanced sense of control over one's body
- Girls and women access leadership opportunities and experience
- Sport can cause positive shifts in gender norms that afford girls and women greater safety and control over their lives
- Women and girls with disabilities are empowered by sport-based opportunities to acquire health information, skills, social networks, and leadership experience

PROMOTE GENDER
EQUALITY AND
EMPOWER WOMEN

4. Reduce child mortality

- Sport can be used to educate and deliver health information to young mothers, resulting in healthier children
- Increased physical fitness improves children's resistance to some diseases
- Sport can help reduce the rate of higher-risk adolescent pregnancies
- Sport-based vaccination and prevention campaigns help reduce child deaths and disability from measles, malaria and polio
- Inclusive sport programs help lower the likelihood of infanticide by promoting greater acceptance of children with disabilities

REDUCE
CHILD MORTALITY

5. Improve maternal health

- Sport for health programs offer girls and women greater access to reproductive health information and services
- Increased fitness levels help speed post-natal recovery

IMPROVE MATERNAL
HEALTH

6. Combat HIV and AIDS, malaria, and other diseases

- Sport programs can be used to reduce stigma and increase social and economic integration of people living with HIV and AIDS
- Sport programs are associated with lower rates of health risk behaviour that contributes to HIV infection
- Programs providing HIV prevention education and empowerment can further reduce HIV infection rates

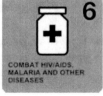

COMBAT HIV/AIDS,
MALARIA AND OTHER
DISEASES

- Sport can be used to increase measles, polio and other vaccination rates
- Involvement of celebrity athletes and use of mass sport events can increase reach and impact of malaria, tuberculosis and other education and prevention campaigns

7. Ensure environmental sustainability

- Sport-based public education campaigns can raise awareness of importance of environmental protection and sustainability
- Sport-based social mobilization initiatives can enhance participation in community action to improve local environment

8. Develop a global partnership for development

- Sport for Development and Peace efforts catalyse global partnerships and increase networking among governments, donors, NGOs and sport organizations worldwide

Note: The source of Table 1 can be found at the following URL address: http://www.un.org/wcm/content/site/sport/home/sport/sportandmdgs

The outcomes mentioned in the table above apply to all people, including people with disabilities assuming they are afforded the same opportunities to participate on an equal basis with their peers without disabilities. Unfortunately, this is not often the case due to prevailing stereotypes, stigma and discrimination and a general lack of understanding of how to communicate with and include them in sport-related activities and programmes. Therefore, it is important to outline some specific ways sport-based activities designed for and including people with disabilities can contribute to achieving the MDGs as well as key considerations when *planning such activities.*

MDG 1: Eradicate Extreme Poverty and Hunger

- Research shows that active and regular participation in physical activity can reduce the incidence of secondary conditions and non-communicable diseases, thus enabling people with disabilities to continue to engage in gainful employment;
- 80% of children with disabilities are out of school[27] and sport can provide unique opportunities for teaching life skills which can lead to employability;
- Images of people with disabilities achieving accomplishments through sport and recreation can lead to changes in perception, particularly related to abilities;

---

27. UNESCO, Education for All Global Monitoring Report 2010: Reaching the Marginalized (2010), p. 181.

- The sport sector can provide employment opportunities for people with disabilities – for example people with disabilities manufacturer wheelchairs for sport and everyday use.

MDG 2: Achieve Universal Primary Education

- Sport can be a learning environment for people with disabilities – community, sport-based programmes can provide alternative opportunities for children not in school;
- Displays of achievements through sport can change perceptions of people with disabilities, thus influencing policy change that could lead to increased accessibility for example;
- School sport programmes can influence the likelihood of people with disabilities engaging and remaining interested in attending school;
- Sport and physical education are essential elements in quality education for healthy child development;
- Sport activities and physical education generally make school more attractive and improve attendance.

MDG 3: Promote Gender Equality and Empower Women

- When girls and women with disabilities participate in positive experiences in sport there is a marked increase in self-esteem, self-confidence, and enhanced sense of one's body;[28]
- Sport provides opportunities for girls and women to learn to be a leader and take on leadership roles – for example women that participated in the leadership trainings offered by the International Paralympic Committee were trained in administration;
- Achievements on and off the field of play can provide opportunities for girls and women to become role models;
- Sport helps address the double (e.g. being female and having a disability) and triple discrimination (e.g. being female, having a disability, and living in poverty) often experienced by people with disabilities.

MDG 4: Reduce Child Mortality

- Through the display of ability and achievement in sport, stereotypes are challenged and the perceptions of children with disabilities can change, thus having the potential to influence negative social norms (e.g. incidence of infanticide);

28.Nancy A. Murphy et al., "Promoting the Participation of Children with Disabilities in Sports, Recreation, and Physical Activities," Pediatrics, vol. 121 (2008): 1057-106.

- Sport-based vaccination and prevention campaigns can help reduce the incidence of child deaths and disability resulting from diseases such as measles, malaria and polio (see MDG 6).

MDG 6: Combat HIV/AIDS, Malaria and other Diseases

- Disability focused sport programmes can be a vehicle to provide key messages in accessible formats to people with disability who are often excluded from accessing mainstream campaigns or messaging;

  Sport can challenge stigma and change perceptions of people with disabilities, potentially reducing the incidence of rape and potential for transmission of HIV.

MDG 8: Develop a Global Partnership for Development

- Athletes with a disability can be spokespersons to disseminate key messages on rights and MDGs;
- Sport can be a means to develop dialogue or bridge various government ministries (e.g. Ministry of Education, Ministry of Youth and Sport, Ministry of Social Welfare);
- Sport provides opportunities for innovative partnerships – for example the London 2012 Olympic and Paralympic Games legacy programme called 'International Inspiration' is a partnership between the world of sport, a UN agency, governments and civil society working towards common objectives;
- Disability specific organizations can be effective partners for governments in providing support to people with disability, supporting their social integration, raising awareness and advocating for their rights.

When designing an *inclusive sport for development* programme, some key considerations include:

- Ensure active and meaningful participation of every participant regardless of their abilities;
- Use *person-first terminology* by naming the person first and the condition second to emphasize that they are first people and the disability is caused by the environment, an example includes people with visual impairments or people living with autism;
- Encourage integrated opportunities for individuals with and without disabilities to play together, recognizing there are situations where separate or segregated activities may also be appropriate to ensure the full participation of people with disabilities;

- Provide specialized training for coaches and managers to ensure they use appropriate language, have a thorough understanding of disability specific considerations for individuals with physical, sensory or intellectual impairments participating in sport, and are familiar with the ways to adapt activities to be truly inclusive.

Conclusion

While *inclusive development* and *inclusive sport for development* are gaining momentum globally, people with disabilities deserve more attention to ensure the realization of their rights and fundamental freedoms. 'Nothing about us, without us', the slogan of the disability rights community, affirms the rights and interests of people with disabilities to participate in the development and implementation of programmes that directly affect their lives.

Recognizing the significance of inclusive sport for development in the context of the MDGs and the CRPD are opportunities to better understand the role and impact of sport for development in promoting equality for people with disabilities. *Inclusive sport for development* is a useful framework for practitioners and policymakers to advance the realization of equality for everyone. *The CRPD reminds us that, as human beings, people with disabilities remain equal in their inherent dignity and self-worth with all other members of society and therefore are entitled to the full enjoyment of all of their human rights. While the CRPD asks us to move from the medical model to the social model of disability, achieving the MDGs goes hand in hand with the realization of the rights enshrined in the CRPD and the principles of inclusive development for all, which includes the right to sport and recreation.*

Chapter 20
Entertainment-Education and Sport for Development

New Frontiers

Emma Colucci

Introduction

As defined by Arvind Singhal and Everett M. Rogers (2004), Entertainment-Education (hereafter E-E) is "the process of purposely designing and implementing a media message to both entertain and educate, in order to increase audience members' knowledge about an educational issue, create favorable attitudes, shift social norms, and change overt behavior" (p. 5). Rather than a communicative *theory*, Singhal and Rogers (2004) describe E-E as a communicative *strategy* directed toward bringing about behavioral and social change. Through E-E, social change is aimed at influencing audience members' awareness, attitudes and behavior regarding a specific issue. E-E also aims to impact upon the audience's external environment, thus creating the proper conditions in which to foster positive social change.

As Srinivas Melkote and H. Leslie Steeves (2001) note, research studies have shown that people prefer entertainment shows rather than educational programs, which reveals the importance of combining education with entertainment. Consequently, more E-E programs have been developed in attempts to capitalize on the universal appeal of entertainment in order to show audiences how they could live safer, healthier and happier lives. E-E interventions were originally found in the form of radio or television dramas, but have now grown to include types of entertainment such as theatre performances, dances, videos, comic books or cartoons, and can be found in countries all over the world.

The Theoretical Basis of Entertainment-Education

E-E embraces a variety of social and behavioral theories that have guided much of the development, implementation and research on the communicative strategy. While many original studies on E-E focused on individual-level behavioral changes, more recent studies have explored in more depth the larger impact that E-E has on the community as a whole. Messages originally aimed at enhancing self-efficacy, whereby a person feels more apt to deal with and control certain situations, are now branching out and aiming to enhance collective efficacy in an effort to increase the abilities of people in a social system to organize and execute actions necessary for the achievement of collective goals (Singhal & Rogers, 2004). E-E interventions can now promote self-efficacy, collective efficacy, or both. These have been amongst the most prominent of E-E theoretical links, and will be the first of three E-E theories explored in this chapter.

Much of Albert Bandura's work has had a direct influence on the development of E-E. Bandura (1995) states that: "People's level of motivation, affective states, and actions are based more on what they believe than on what is objectively the case. This core belief system is the foundation of human motivation and accomplishments" (p. 2). Furthermore, Bandura (2004) notes that, "Among the mechanisms of self-influence, none is more central or pervasive than beliefs in one's efficacy to exercise control over one's functioning and events that affect one's life" (p. 78-79). Gaining a sense of self-efficacy is a vital component to behavior change. The greater the belief in one's ability to create or affect positive change in his or her life, the more likely that person will take the necessary action due to his or her increased sense of personal agency. Research has consistently found that such beliefs in self-efficacy contribute significantly to human motivation and attainments (Bandura, 1995).

Two of the major factors that create and strengthen a person's belief in his or her self-efficacy are mastery experiences and vicarious experiences (Bandura, 1995; 2004). Mastery experiences are based on an individual's acquisition of the cognitive, behavioral and self-regulatory tools necessary for making positive life choices through his or her own successes and failures. The resilience required to overcome obstacles throughout one's life is built through the effective management of personal failure in order to learn from it rather than becoming discouraged and unmotivated to continue. Vicarious experiences, which will be further elaborated on through the following discussion of Social Learning Theory, are the observed experiences of people similar to oneself. By witnessing people exceed in similar situations, an individual increases his or her belief that they too can succeed in comparable situations. The greater the similarity between the individual and the person or people they are observing, the greater the influence will be on their sense of self-efficacy (Bandura, 1995; 2004).

While people's belief in their own efficacy plays a vital role in the creation, organization, and management of circumstances that shape their lives, many life challenges relate to common problems that require the collective efforts of people working together to create positive social change (Bandura, 1995). Collective efficacy is defined as the abilities of people in a system to organize and execute actions necessary for the achievement of collective goals (Singhal & Rogers, 2004). Bandura (1995) states that, "Effective action for social change requires merging diverse self-interests in support of common core values and goals," thus making both self and collective efficacy vital components for life choices and actions aimed at positive social change (p. 37). A lack of self and collective efficacy can create psychological barriers that can often be more demoralizing and debilitating than external factors. E-E focuses on enhancing self-efficacy by equipping individuals with pertinent knowledge that can give them the confidence to make positive life choices. E-E aims at producing collective efficacy by bringing certain issues into the public realm to be discussed, and also by connecting individuals to each other in their common goal of addressing important issues in society.

The second theory that will be discussed explores the way in which people learn from one another by observing and imitating their actions, which is referred to as Social Learning Theory (SLT). SLT parallels the impact that vicarious experiences can have on the creation and increase of self-efficacy. While there have been many scholars in the field of SLT, Albert Bandura's version of the theory is the one most widely accepted and utilized in E-E research (Singhal & Rogers, 2004). Bandura (2004) notes that there are two modes of learning: directly through personal experience, and indirectly through social modeling. Social modeling enables people to observe and learn from the experiences of others. In its most basic form, SLT posits that people learn by observing the attitudes and behaviors of others, as well as the outcome these attitudes and behaviors produce. It is through this observation that an individual forms an idea of how certain behaviors are performed, which later serves as a guide for how that individual chooses to behave (Bandura, 1977).

In E-E programs, the characters serve as the social models from which the audience is to learn. Social learning takes place through instructive, motivational, social prompting, and social construction functions of the model being represented (Bandura, 2004). Social models are instructive in a sense that they transmit knowledge, values, cognitive skills and behavior styles to observers. Observers become inclined to embody and emulate the emotions shown by the social model especially if they can relate to, and see similarities between themselves and that social model (Bandura, 1995; 2004). This enhances the degree to which they learn from observed behaviors. The motivation behind the adoption of new behaviors comes from both the perceived benefits as well as the detriments of the social model's behavior (Rotter, 1982; Bandura, 2004). The behavior of characters in E-E programs also serves as social prompts that activate, channel and support modeled styles of behavior.

The last theory discussed examines the way in which ideas are transmitted through E-E programs. In order to fully explain, measure and enhance the wide scale impact E-E messages can have throughout different societies, one must also examine Innovation Diffusion theory. In its most basic definition, Everett Rogers (1983) defines Innovation Diffusion (also referred to as the Diffusion of Innovations) as the process by which an innovation is "communicated through certain channels over time among the members of a social system" (p. 5). The first element is the innovation itself, which can consist of an idea, object or practice that is deemed 'new' to a certain society. Secondly, there is the channel of communication through which the innovation is disseminated to or within the society, which can range from mass media channels to more interpersonal face-to-face channels. The third element of innovation diffusion is time. This can relate to the time it takes for the innovation to be diffused throughout society as well as the time it takes for the innovation to be adopted by members of society. The last element is the social system in which the innovation is diffused. Vijay Mahajan and Robert A. Peterson (1985) define social systems as "individuals, organizations or agencies that share a common culture and are potential adopters of the innovation" (p. 7). These systems can range in size from a small group of students enrolled in the same course to as large a group as the entire citizenry of a country. Due to its wide range of applicability, the Diffusion of Innovations is one of the most widely studied social phenomena.

One of the earliest studies on Innovation Diffusion was conducted by Paul Lazarsfeld, Bernard Berelson, and Hazel Gaudet (1968) in their book *The People's Choice: How the Voter Makes up his Mind in a Presidential Campaign*. With respect to innovation being an idea, concept, or a new way of thinking and/or behaving, Lazarsfeld et al. (1968) discussed the way in which opinions were more easily changed through interpersonal communication rather than mass media channels. This was known as Lazarsfeld's 'two-step flow of communication' whereby ideas flow from the media to opinion leaders, and then to the general public (Sherry, 2002). An essential component of the adoption of innovations is the reduction of uncertainty about the innovation itself. In this process, the individual must be able to consult the media or inter-personal channel in order to better understand the innovation and decide if it will indeed produce the desired outcome. In a discussion of this two-step flow of communication, John Sherry (2002) states:

"A key message sender variable is the level of homophily (similarity) or heterophily (difference) the sender has with the receiver. Communications in which the sender and receiver are homophilous are more likely to be effective. Due to the mass heterogeneous audience of the media, homophilous relationships are more likely to occur in interpersonal or social system contexts than in the mass media context" (p. 215).

Thus, through the two-step flow of communication, Lazarsfeld et al. (1968) found that innovations were more easily adopted through interpersonal channels rather than wide scale broadcasts. Consequently, it is important for E-E programs to attempt to create characters that audience members can relate to and will be more likely to emulate due to the perceived homophily between the message sender and receiver.

b. Potential Problems with the Entertainment-Education Strategy

E-E has often faced resistance from the message production side, as well as from the message reception side. On the message production side, E-E encounters trouble due to the fact that many commercial media broadcasters fear that entertainment aimed at positive social change might not receive as high ratings as other shows less concerned with the message they are portraying. It can therefore be difficult for E-E programs to compete with popular TV shows such as *The Bachelor* or *Jersey Shore*[1] which are considered forms of 'entertainment-degradation' or 'entertainment perversion' due to the often lewd and/or detrimental messages they portray in the name of high ratings (Singhal & Rogers, 2004). Commercial broadcasters do not want to lose audience members or sponsors due to controversial or educationally charged program content that is often deeply embedded in E-E. This can create a gap between the aims of the producers of E-E and the broadcasters who are responsible for airing the shows.

In regards to the message reception side of E-E, there is no guarantee that the audience will receive the message in the intended or desired manner. As Singhal and Rogers (2004) note, "Audience members selectively expose themselves to E-E messages, selectively perceive them, selectively recall them, and selectively use them for their own purposes" (p. 14). Singhal and Rogers (2004) further note that there is growing evidence that interpersonal rather than broadcast communication of E-E message content can greatly magnify the effects of behavioral change. This notion follows suit with Lazarsfeld et al's (1968) views on the adoption of innovations.

When it comes to messages aimed at behavioral change and enhanced self and collective efficacy, the style in which the messages are conveyed plays a significant role in how they become internalized. Issues of top-down message transmission and lack of audience participation and involvement are often found in E-E messages that are broadcast to large audience groups. Paulo Freire (2007) has been one of the most prominent voices for the importance of participatory communication and learning. Messages are presented and discussed on a horizontal level in participatory communication structures, rather than being transmitted in a top-down style that voids the message receiver of any voice or inquiry on the topic. Freire (2007) refers to this top-down message transmission as the 'banking model' of education. Unlike participatory communication, the top-down communication

---

1. *Jersey Shore* and *The Bachelor* are American reality TV shows that depict negative cultural stereotypes as well as problematic portrayals of love and sexuality.

style projects a sense of ignorance onto the audience as their knowledge base and potential contribution to the learning process are negated.

Being able to participate in the learning process gives those receiving important messages regarding behavior change a stronger sense of self-efficacy. This is due to the fact that they are better able to recognize their potential impact on what they learn and how they can shape their *own* knowledge and behavior, rather than simply having general behavioral guides prescribed to them. This enhances one's ability to think critically and independently, thus providing the individual with more appropriate and effective tools for making suitable decisions in different life situations. A participatory educational methodology is essential for behavioral change as those receiving the messages become more able to perceive, and believe in their abilities to have a positive impact on situations that occur in their own lives.

As Freire (2007) notes, top-down message transmission deems pieces of information as items to be deposited in the audience rather than discussed and investigated on a more contextual level. A more interactive learning process can enhance the internalization of messages portrayed by E-E via interpersonal communication due to the increased opportunity of consultation and discussion between the sender and receiver. This can provide clarity or contextualization of the information for the message receiver. There is also a greater potential for a homphilous relationship between the message sender and receiver on a more interpersonal learning structure. As posited by both SLT and Innovation Diffusion, the greater the homophily and ability to relate between the message sender and receiver, the greater the chances of individuals adopting the behaviours portrayed by the message sender (Bandura, 1995; 2004; Lazarsfeld et al., 1968). This type of interpersonal connection and interactivity is rarely found in mainstream and wide scale media broadcasts.

New Avenues of Communication: Integrating Participatory Learning into Entertainment-Education programs

As Singhal (2004) notes, E-E programs can highly benefit from incorporating participatory processes into their strategy to effectively enhance positive social change. While traditional E-E programs have been based on the benefits of large-scale media broadcasts in order to disseminate important messages to a wide range of audiences, the importance of interpersonal and participatory communication cannot be down-played in regards to its ability to enhance self efficacy and the proper mindset for an individual to follow through with positive behavioural choices. Perhaps an exploration of alternative channels of communication would open new doors with respect to how participation can be fostered more effectively in E-E programs.

Throughout much of the research and implementation of E-E programs, sports have rarely been taken into account. A deeper exploration of the sport world, however, exemplifies its potential as an instrument of E-E, as it can be a powerful and effective communicative avenue for messages aimed at behavioral change. E-E aims to capitalize on the universal appeal of entertainment in order to show audiences how they could live safer, healthier and happier lives. Sports are one of the most universal forms of entertainment, and every country produces both players and spectators on both a local and global level. Furthermore, due to the innate interactive qualities of games and sports, this channel of communication fosters an environment rich in opportunity for participatory and interactive learning structures, as well as the effective enhancement of self-efficacy through Social Learning Theory and the Diffusion of Innovations (all of which are essential components of E-E).

The Relevance of Sport

Sports, like many other activities in life, can act as a major socialization tool for its participants. Throughout the process of socialization, a person is shaped by his or her personal experiences while also being involved in a larger process of cultural production, reproduction and change. While sports can impact both positively and negatively, depending on who is involved and on the nature of their participation, most cultures recognize that sport builds character and improves health and well-being. As Coakley and Donnelly (2009) note, "Socialization occurs through the social interaction that accompanies sport participation. Therefore, the meaning and importance of playing sports depends on a person's social relationships and the social and cultural contexts in which participation occurs" (p. 90). Among the factors important for providing positive sporting experiences are: knowledge-building that goes beyond the playing field; the building of new relationships and social networks; and examples of how lessons learned in sports can be applied to other situations in a person's life (Coakley & Donnelly, 2009). These factors all play an important role in using sport as a tool for positive social change.

Soccer [AKA Football] as a Universal Language

While the appeal of some sports is specific to certain areas, soccer has enjoyed popularity all around the world. Steve Fleming (2009), the co-founder and co-Chief Executive of Kick4Life, which focuses on development through soccer, notes that soccer has become the national sport in 175 of the world's 195 countries. Today, the World Cup is the most widely viewed sporting event by people across the globe. FIFA's 2006 World Cup was watched by roughly 715 million people, and the 2010 World Cup in South Africa was attended by a total of 3,178,856 (Fleming, 2009; FIFA, 2010). The global popularity of this sport has often been a positive force in regards to the game's ability to act as a universal language that breaks cultural and linguistic barriers. As Dennis Liwewe, a Zambian soccer commentator states:

> "[Soccer] is a religion here...It's not easy to assemble 73 different tribes speaking literally 73 different languages together in one unit. And [soccer] has been a catalyst. [Soccer] has played a very important role in putting us together as a people, as a nation" (Hagerty, 2006).

Although national in scope, this statement speaks to soccer's ability to unite people and bring them together under a common interest. While soccer enjoys global popularity, it has also been able to develop throughout the world in different ways due to its rich history, allowing for the diverse integration of the game into different social and cultural contexts (Goldblatt, 2006; Murray, 1998; Wagg, 1995). Furthermore, soccer has the ability to garner the attention of audiences worldwide, while also providing the opportunity for a participatory learning environment through its interpersonal team structure. Although not regarded as a traditional form of communication, a closer examination of the sport of soccer reveals the ways in which it can be used as a communicatory tool that has the potential to foster positive social change.

Grassroot Soccer's Effective use of Sport as Entertainment-Education[2]

Grassroot Soccer (GRS) is an organization that "provides African youth with the knowledge, skills and support to live HIV free" (www.grassrootsoccer.org). The program focuses on educating youth in the community, often by way of school-based programs. Through the use of interactive soccer activities, information regarding HIV and AIDS prevention as well as positive life skills are discussed with the youth in order to combat the pandemic at the community level. GRS games are not only fun and stimulating, but they teach very important messages that the students more successfully internalize due to their active participation in the learning process.

One activity used in GRS sessions, known as 'HIV Attacks,' is designed to illustrate the process by which HIV weakens the immune system, thus allowing germs and diseases to attack the human body (Personal Field Research, 2009, South Africa). In this activity, the students stand in a circle with one student in the middle wearing a sign that says 'Human.' The students on the outside of the circle represent germs and diseases such as the flu, TB, malaria, etc. The 'germs' are armed with a soccer ball that they are to lightly kick at the 'human' in the middle. In the first round, the 'human' in the middle holds an 'Immune System' card that allows the student to move and protect himself or herself from the potential danger of the germs (represented by the ball). After discussing ways in which someone can contract HIV, such as unprotected sex, another student makes his or her way into the middle of the circle wearing a sign that says 'HIV.' This student inhibits the movement of the student wearing the 'human' sign by holding the human's hands behind his or her back. This time, when the 'germs' kick the ball, the 'human' is unable to avoid getting hit as easily, representing the way in which HIV makes the human body defenseless against germs. Rather than just explaining how HIV works, as many traditional top-down styles of teaching would do, GRS involves the students in the leaning process by making them active and essential components in the delivery of the

---

2.This is an introduction to Grassroot Soccer. Its educational methodology and stronger links to participatory education will be discussed in the chapter focused on the Case Study of the organization in this book.

key message. Each activity is then followed by a dialogue session known as a 'team talk' which allows the students to discuss, inquire and interact more personally with the information regarding HIV and AIDS (Personal Field Research, 2009, South Africa).

While traditionally not considered a form of E-E, sport (especially soccer) embodies many theories and principles of the communicative strategy that has mainly been implemented through TV, radio, theatre, and comics. GRS is continually finding ways to tap into the power of soccer, as it is an excellent tool for mass communicating life-changing messages, especially to youth. As stated in the GRS Annual Report (2007), soccer is especially important in Africa: "Every town has a team. Players are heroes and role models. Simply arriving at a field with a soccer ball wins instant friendship" (p. 11). In addition, having the 2010 FIFA World Cup hosted in Africa for the first time heightened the buzz to fever pitch. Soccer can also connect people through its coaching structure, whereby coaches can act as role models (GRS, 2007). Garnering attention and providing role models are two key aspects of the adoption of behavior change. In order to ensure that the program remains culturally appropriate, GRS uses local soccer players as the coaches of their curriculum in the areas in which the program is run. This ensures that the national character of the game remains unchanged while also providing suitable role-models for the students. Thus, youth are more likely to connect to the communicatory structure rather than alienated by a homogeneous and out-of-context avenue of communication, which can often happen with the mainstream global media industry.

Soccer as a tool of communication on an interpersonal level does not have to compete against mainstream media such as TV and radio E-E programs, nor does it need to comply with commercial broadcast standards which could potentially alter or damage important messages in order to increase the entertainment value. While the professional associations of soccer are widely entrenched in the global media industry, soccer at the recreational level gives its participants a much different experience, relatively untouched by global media regulations. By being more interpersonal, E-E through soccer can be more interactive while also having more control over how the audience internalizes the messages being portrayed. Soccer is also more highly accessible to a much greater number of people worldwide than other forms of media, such as TV.

As Freire (2007) states, it is important to find the proper avenue of communication in order to effectively discuss important messages, especially messages aimed at behavioral change and the adoption of life-saving health practices. Soccer ultimately combines the benefits of appealing to the masses through its global popularity with an interpersonal structure. GRS employs a highly interactive curriculum that focuses on shared interpersonal communication, rather than top-down communication that leaves little room for audience participation. While the GRS students are able to have fun learning through soccer and games, they are also able to voice direct questions and concerns about HIV and AIDS during the 'team talk' that is held at the end of each GRS session (Personal Field Research, 2009, South Africa).

Instead of just telling the students what they should or shouldn't do, 100% of GRS participants interviewed in an independent study stated that they felt the GRS program really listened to what they had to say (Personal Interviews, 2009, South Africa).[3] This style of participatory learning enhances the GRS participant's sense of self-efficacy by increasing his or her level of knowledge about HIV and AIDS. Furthermore, by being encouraged to participate in the learning process rather than simply ingesting information regarding healthy life choices, their critical and independent thinking capabilities are enhanced. Students are better able to see and understand their role in the learning process, and ultimately their role in shaping their reality. In this way, the GRS methodology effectively enhances self-efficacy by equipping individuals with pertinent knowledge, as well as the right tools to be able to properly apply that knowledge, thus increasing the individual's confidence in his or her own abilities to make healthy decisions. When implemented properly, this is one of the major aims and benefits of E-E.

Self-efficacy is also enhanced via vicarious experiences offered through a coaching structure where they act as role models to the students. This is due to the notion that the greater the similarity between the individual and the person they are observing, the greater the influence will be on his or her sense of self-efficacy (Bandura, 1995; 2004). If someone in a similar cultural and social context to the youth participants can make healthy life choices to combat HIV and AIDS, the participants will be more likely to believe that they too can take similar action. This also enhances the sense of collective efficacy amongst the youth participating in the GRS sessions, as they are more able to develop strong personal relationships and build a solid social network of positive support. Increased self and collective efficacy can provide an environment for individuals to better address the devastating impact of HIV and AIDS in their on lives and in their communities.

Paralleling the enhancement of self-efficacy through vicarious experiences, as posited by both SLT and Innovation Diffusion, messages are better received and internalized when there is a high level of homophily between the sender and receiver (Bandura, 1995; 2004; Lazarsfeld et al., 1968). Important messages can be more easily internalized by youth within the GRS coaching structure due to the fact that these messages are delivered to them by people who have lived in similar situations, and to whom they can more easily relate. The coaches are encouraged to share their stories and divulge how HIV and AIDS have impacted their lives in order to initiate the process of dialogue. These personal revelations encourage the youth, who see

---

3. A further discussion about my research findings will be discussed in the chapter focused on the Case Study of Grassroot Soccer later in this book.

the coaches as role models, to share their own views and opinions, as well as raise questions and concerns about HIV and AIDS in an open and comfortable environment.

Within the SLT framework, the GRS participants are able to see the positive outcomes of the coaches making healthy life choices, which acts as a motivational strategy for the participants to adopt similar health practices. Through listening to, and sharing personal stories, GRS participants are able to feel strong emotional connections, allowing for more compassion and care in the ensuing discussions. Through these stories, GRS participants are also able to create their own narratives as a way of portraying important messages, rather than simply following the preconceived ones on a TV or radio show.

With respect to Innovation Diffusion, an essential component of the adoption of innovations is the reduction of uncertainty about the innovation itself (Lazarsfeld et al., 1968). The inter-personal communicatory structure of the GRS program allows the students to raise questions and concerns about HIV and AIDS, thus creating a more holistic and contextual understanding of the pandemic. Furthermore, the GRS curriculum provides youth with homework, magazines, and fun games, all of which relate to HIV and AIDS. This gives the students more tools to further diffuse the information they have learned in the GRS sessions to their friends, family and community members. In fact, part of their homework is often to share the messages they have learned (Personal Field Research, 2009, South Africa).

In conjunction with these theories, Pierre Bourdieu (1984) discusses the value of capital not only in an economic sense, but also in a cultural and social context. Someone with high *cultural* capital has individual preferences, lifestyle tastes, choices, intellectual and physical competencies that are highly valued by others, while someone with high *social* capital has strong and supportive social networks, connections and relationships. The GRS coaches have high cultural capital in a sense that they are involved with a universally popular sport that garners the attention of so many youth. This cultural capital gained through their involvement with soccer in turn creates greater motivation for their other tastes and lifestyle choices to be emulated by the GRS students. Once the students have gone through the GRS program, their social capital is increased not only by the closer relationships they have formed with their peers, but also through the friendship and support created between themselves and the GRS coaches, thus increasing their social support networks.

Conclusion: New Frontiers

E-E programs can be particularly effective when it comes to changing the knowledge, attitudes, behaviors and norms regarding public health issues due to their ability to evoke emotions, create role models, stimulate discussion and emphasize the consequences of unhealthy choices. Through its unique educational methodology, GRS has the ability to do all of these things. As Bandura (2004) states:

> "A major advantage of [social] modeling through the media is that it can reach a vast population simultaneously in widely dispersed locales. Video systems feeding off telecommunication satellites have become a dominant vehicle for disseminating symbolic environments. New ideas, values, and styles of conduct are now being rapidly diffused worldwide in ways that foster a globally distributed consciousness," (p. 78).

However, as Singhal and Rogers (2004) note, there is growing evidence that interpersonal communication of E-E message content can greatly magnify the effects of behavioral change, more so than relying on broadcast messages to impact upon audiences. With GRS's interpersonal communicatory style, it is able to foster participatory communication and better instill self-efficacy while still reaching a wide audience base through its use of the universally popular sport of soccer. The GRS methodology capitalizes on social modeling through the use of local soccer players as role models. The information taught through the GRS curriculum is diffused at a high rate through the encouragement of GRS participants to share with and teach others what they have learned in the GRS sessions. GRS also taps into the positive aspects of the sporting experience, as outlined by Coakley and Donnelly (2009), by providing knowledge that goes beyond the game of soccer, building meaningful relationships with coaches and peers, and exemplifying how the knowledge learned through the program can be applied to their daily lives. While traditional forms of E-E aim to enhance self-efficacy via social modeling and imitation of behavir and knowledge seen through (often) mainstream media, a better sense of self-efficacy is created through participatory learning which can only be fostered through a horizontal and interactive communicatory process.

The potential of sport is vast, but is often underestimated. As Roger Levermore (2008) states, there is often a striking neglect in academic research conducted on, and directed toward the field of Sport for Development (S4D) and its potential role in positive social change. Despite the underestimation of sport in the realm of positive social change, it is increasingly becoming a topic of consideration for human development. While the way in which sport can be used is vast, Grassroot Soccer provides an effective example of how the universal popularity of soccer and the inter-personal bonding structure of sport culture can be used to deliver a comprehensive and effective HIV and AIDS prevention strategy. The GRS program has made an excellent case for the positive potential of sport. It is time to consider this potential much more seriously in order to effectively make use of a powerful contributing tool towards achieving positive social change.

References

Bandura, A. (1977). *Social Learning Theory*. New York: General Learning Press.

Bandura, A. (1995). *Self Efficacy in Changing Societies*. Cambridge: Cambridge University Press.

Bandura, A. (2004). Social Cognitive Theory for Personal and Social Change by Enabling Media. In A. Singhal, M. J. Cody, E. M. Rogers & M. Sabido (Eds.), *Entertainment-Education and Social Change: History, Research and Practice* (pp.75-96). New Jersey: Lawrence Erlbaum Associates, Inc.

Bourdieu, Pierre. (1984). *Distinction: A Social Critique of the Judgement of Taste* (R. Nice, Trans.). Cambridge: Harvard University Press.

Coakley, J. & Donnelly, P. (2009). *Issues and Controversies: Sports in Society*. Toronto: Mcgraw-Hill Ryerson.

FIFA (Fédération Internationale de Football Association). (2010). *2010 FIFA World Cup South Africa*. Available at: www.fifa.com/about-fifa/developing/technicaldevelopment/technicalmenreport.html. (Accessed 12th March 2012).

Fleming, S. (2009). *Eleven: Making Lives Better: 11 Stories of Development Through Football*. Brighton: Pitch Publishing.

Freire, Paulo. (2007) [1970]. *Pedagogy of the Oppressed*. New York: Continuum.

Goldblatt, D. (2006). *The Ball is Round: A Global History of Football*. London: Penguin Books.

GRS (GrassrootSoccer). (n.d.). Available at: www.grassrootsoccer.org. (Accessed 12th March 2012).

GRS (Grassroot Soccer). (2007). *Annual Report 2007*. Available at: http://www.grassrootsoccer.org/resources/. (Accessed 12th March 2012).

Hagerty S. (2006). Lusaka Sunrise [Video File]. SmoothFeather Productions. Available at: http://www.youtube.com/watch?v=kyple-f2Hi6Y. (Accessed 12th March 2012).

Levermore, R. (2008). Sport in International Development: Time to Treat it Seriously? *Brown Journal of World Affairs*, Spring/Summer 2008, XIV (2), 55-66.

Lazarsfeld, P., Berelson, B., & Gaudet, H. (1968). *The People's Choice: How the Voter Makes up his Mind in a Presidential Campaign* (3rd ed.). New York: Columbia University Press.

Mahan, V. & Peterson, R. A. (1985). *Models for Innovation Diffusion*. Beverly Hills: Sage Publications.

Melkote, S. R. & Steeves, H. L. (2001). *Communication for Development in the Third World: Theory and Practice for Empowerment*. New Delhi: Sage Publications India Pvt Ltd.

Murray, B. (1996). *The World's Game: A History of Soccer*. Chicago: University of Illinois Press.

Personal Interviews (Emma Colucci). (April, 2009). Port Elizabeth, South Africa.

Personal Field Research (Emma Colucci). (March – April, 2009). Port Elizabeth, South Africa.

Rogers, E. M. (1983). *Diffusion of Innovations*. New York: Free Press.

Rotter, J. (1982). *The Development and Application of Social Learning Theory: Selected Papers*. New York: Praeger.

Sherry, J. (2002). Media Saturation and Entertainment-Education. In *Communicative Theory*, 12 (2), May 2002, 206-224.

Singhal, A., & Rogers, E. M. (2004). The Status of Entertainment-Education Worldwide. In A. Singhal, M. J. Cody, E. M. Rogers, & M. Sabido (Eds.), *Entertainment-Education and Social Change: History, Research and Practice* (pp. 3-20). New Jersey: Lawrence Erlbaum Associates, Inc.

Singhal, A. (2004). Entertainment-Education Through Participatory Theatre: Freirean Strategies for Empowering the Oppressed. In A. Singhal, M. J. Cody, E. M. Rogers, & M. Sabido (Eds.), *Entertainment-Education and Social Change: History, Research and Practice* (pp. 377-398). New Jersey: Lawrence Erlbaum Associates, Inc.

Wagg, S. (Ed.). (1995). *Giving the Game Away: Football, Politics and Culture on Five Continents*. London: Leicester University Press.

Chapter 21

Sport for the Disabled as Social (Re) education and a (Re) builder of Lives

Ian Brittain

Introduction

There is a steadily growing body of work regarding the significance of non-disabled sport within society (Coalter, 2007) and the potential impacts it can have, particularly in terms of developing 'better' citizens in terms of health, behaviour and productivity. There is also a growing body of work regarding the use of non-disabled sport in conflict zones as a means of development and brokering peace. However, there appears to be relatively little work which addresses these issues with regard to the use of sport for the disabled and the role it might play both in the re-integration into society of people with disabilities nor of the impact that high level disability sport e.g. the Paralympic Games can have upon changing perceptions of / (re)educating people within the wider community regarding people with disabilities and thus aiding the re-integration process.

The aim of this chapter is, therefore, to highlight the role of sport for the disabled in non-violent conflict transformation/peace-making through its ability to change perceptions and, therefore, break down perceptual and structural barriers to the inclusion of people with disabilities within mainstream society. It will begin by using an adaptation of Peace Studies scholar

Johan Galtung's triangle of violence to show the various ways, throughout history, that people with disabilities have been victims of various kinds of violence (direct, cultural and structural) throughout the world.

Galtung's Triangle of Violence

Direct Violence

Extermination/ Abortion/ Euthanasia

Ridicule

Visible

Violence

Invisible/ Less

Visible Violence

Cultural Violence

- Fear

- Hatred

- Dismissiveness

- Negative Perceptions regarding abilities

- Pity

Structural Violence

- Unequal access to opportunities/ - services (Education, Health, Employment)

- Inaccessible built environment

- Poverty

- Institutionalisation/ Hiding away by families

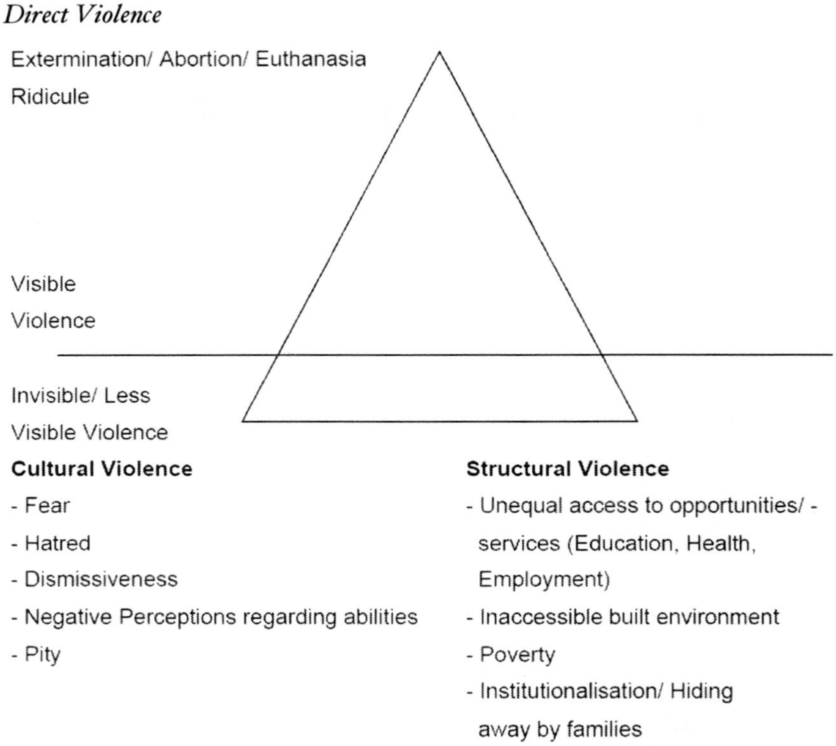

Figure 1: Disability and the triangle of violence (adapted from Johan Galtung, 1990)

The chapter will now briefly touch upon the medical, social and bio-social models of disability and how they relate to the various forms of violence outlined above.

Models of Disability

Briefly, the medical model of disability posits that any problems that arise as a result of disability are due to the particular physical or intellectual impairment and are, therefore, a problem solely of the individual with the impairment. The impairment is also something that needs to be medically 'cured' in order that the individual fits in with societal accepted norms of function and appearance (Abberley, 1993). The overall result of this model is that people with disabilities are perceived by many within non-disabled society as weak, non-contributing members of society who are nothing more than a burden upon the state and the taxpayer (Middleton, 1999). On the other hand, the social model of disability argues that it is the perceptions of non-disabled society regarding people with disabilities and an inaccessible built environment that really 'disables' (Morris, 1991). The bio-social model argues that the real position is a combination of the previous two models in that there will always be times when the actual impairment itself will raise issues that changes in perceptions or the built environment cannot overcome e.g. a blind person's inability to perceive non-verbal cues such as a smile or a frown (French, 1993). Most of the issues outlined in figure 1 arise out of the application of the medical model of disability. The social model of disability can help us understand the manner in which sport for the disabled can help change perceptions within non-disabled society regarding people with disabilities and, thus, negate or at least lessen some of the 'violence' directed, consciously or sub-consciously, against people with disabilities.

With these previous thoughts in mind, I will now attempt to relate the different kinds of 'violence' outlined in my adapted Galtung's Triangle of Violence in particularly to the medical model of disability by using brief examples from a variety of countries and situations. Violence is defined by the World Health Organisation as:

> "The intentional use of physical force or power, threatened or actual, against oneself, another person, or against a group or community, that either results in or has a high likelihood of resulting in injury, death, psychological harm, maldevelopment, or deprivation".
>
> (World Health Organisation website, 2010)

Direct Violence

Extermination of people with disabilities has occurred throughout history from ancient times for a variety of reasons including some religious beliefs that held that people with disabilities were evil, to modern genetic engineers who put a modern spin on the need to exterminate anything that might interfere with ideal or 'normal' development of the human body, for example the atrocities committed by Nazi Germany.

With regard to Ridicule, earlier societies, particularly in the medieval period where many of the court jesters were individuals with different appearances or mental functions (e.g. dwarfs, hunchbacks), were prone to ridicule and taunts were common towards those who were disabled in some way (So called 'Freak Shows' would be a more modern day example of this). Even today individuals with disabilities frequently have to endure rude, ignorant and offensive comments. Our language is full of expressions that have a tendency to poke fun at those with disabilities (for example cripple and retard). Although the more extreme forms of visible direct violence such as extermination may not be anywhere near as prevalent today (although this is not to state that it does not still happen in more isolated areas or individual cases) other forms of visible violence such as abortion and even euthanasia still occur, often legally within society and even though both practices come under heavy criticism from a number of different sources.

Direct Violence and Sporting Participation

In many ways the kinds of direct violence outlined above are manifestations of the cultural violence outlined below. The more extreme forms of direct violence such as extermination are, thankfully, quite rare, but the ridicule of people with disabilities is still all too common. The impact of this ridicule and the perceptions from which it stems can act as a major barrier to sporting participation by people with disabilities. When constantly ridiculed or confronted with negative perceptions about their abilities to carry out tasks that most people take for granted, and also bombarded with images of 'physical perfection' that most of the general public could not live up to, it is little wonder that many people with disabilities suffer from low self-esteem (Hargreaves, 2000). Seymour (1989) sums this up when she states:

> "The body in which I live is visible to others; it is the object of social attention. I learn about my body from the impressions I see my body make on other people. These interactions with others provide critical visual data for my self-knowledge".
>
> (Seymour, 1989 cited in Hargreaves, 2000, p. 185)

This perceived fear of failure and low sense of self-worth can act as a strong deterrent for many people with disabilities, becoming involved in sport. This is especially true when you consider the fact that placing themselves in a sporting context is very likely to exacerbate the visibility of the very physical differences that lead to these feelings and perceptions in the first place. However, if these psychological barriers can be overcome Berger (2008) claims that the benefits gained by participation in sport include improved physical conditioning and a sense of bodily mastery, along with a heightened sense of self-esteem and personal empowerment that spills over into other social pursuits. (Berger, 2008, p. 650). These comments appear to concur with the findings of Sporner et al (2009) who investigated the psychosocial impact of participation in the 2006 National Veterans Wheelchair Games and Winter Sports Clinic for 132 veterans with disabilities. Key findings included that 84% felt that participation in these events led them to a greater acceptance of their own disabilities and 77.1% felt it led to a greater participation in society.

Structural Violence

In addition to the usually reported issues of poverty and an inaccessible built environment there are a number of other issues that come under the heading of structural violence. Up to the early 1900's, it was very common to institutionalise any individual who somehow deviated significantly from the norm. Although this was viewed as the humane thing to do, many acknowledge that institutions were created to protect the non-disabled from those with disabilities.

The hiding away by families of family members who are disabled can occur as a result of a variety of cultural and/or religious reasons. For example Cambodia is a Buddhist nation. The central precept of Buddhism revolves around 'Karma' whereby actions in this life dictate the level of existence in the next. At a conceptual level, this often means that disability is seen as a punishment for bad actions committed in previous lives. Persons with a disability, especially in rural areas are, therefore, often hidden by their families who are afraid for their reputations in the wider community - specifically the very Asian idea of 'losing face'. In Kenya, in the 1980's, 50% of Kenyans with disabilities had no children, compared to the average Kenyan family of six or more children (Crawford, 2005, p.13). Crawford attributes this fact to myths surrounding passing on 'bad blood' combined with perceptions that people with disabilities are 'asexual, unable to care for children, or are medically incapable' (Crawford, 2005, p.13). This concept of 'bad blood', similar to the idea of Karma described above for Cambodia, plays a key part in impacting the way many people with disabilities are treated in Kenya compared to the non-disabled. However, non-disabled family members of people with disabilities may also be deemed to be tainted by the same curse, meaning whole families may be treated differently or even shunned.

Unequal access to services can result from many different situations and not just in relation to what those in the non-disabled section of society receive. For many years' disabled war veterans in Israel have been compensated from a system of benefits that means that they receive far better care and financial reimbursement than Israeli individuals injured as a result of birth defects or traumatic injuries or illness later in life. Indeed, Dr. Yaniv Poria, author of a study on the disabled in Israel stated that 'it is common among disabled people in Israel to say that it is better to become disabled during your army service than as a result of birth or an accident' (Brinn, 2004). Gal and Bar (2005) claim that disabled war veterans are more highly regarded within Israeli society than other disabled due to the fact that they received their disabilities fighting in the name of Israel. Gal and Bar differentiate between the 'needed' and the 'needy' disabled individuals with the 'needed' disabled individuals having much higher status and far better care and remuneration than the 'needy' individuals, due to the sacrifices they made 'in the name of an array of social values' (Gal & Bar, 2005, p.592).

Structural Violence and Sporting Participation

It is the structural violence that possibly has the biggest impact upon all areas of the lives of people with disabilities. Unequal access to opportunities and services, poverty and an inaccessible built environment make affording to participate in sport and gaining access to the requisite sporting facilities and coaching a real problem for many people with disabilities. Crawford

(2004) cites a number of telling statistics that arose from a Kenyan Government survey. These include the facts that: [i] roughly 81% of people with disabilities parents or guardians come from the poorest economic levels (p.12-13) and [ii] 91% live in rural areas where access to facilities such as education, training and employment are very scarce (p.16). One impact of this highlighted by Crawford (2004, pp. 83-84) is that inadequate nutrition for athletes with disabilities is a major problem in Kenya with several coaches cited as being fearful of pushing their athletes too hard for fear they had not even eaten that day. However, in some of the more developed sporting nations athletes with disabilities that reach the elite levels of either Paralympic or World Championships and if successful can now receive funding from their national sports federation on a par with their non-disabled peers. For Example, in Great Britain elite athletes with disabilities can receive World Class Performance funding, which not only helps them pay their day to day expenses, but also gives them access to support services such as physiotherapy and funds to allow them to travel abroad to train and compete. There is also a trend in Great Britain now where a small number of successful athletes with disabilities have achieved a certain level of media celebrity that has enabled them to appear on mainstream television programmes e.g. Eleanor Simmonds (Family Fortunes) and Dame Tanni Grey-Thompson (A Question of Sport) or even carve out a career in the media e.g. Ade Adepitan (TV Presenter). Such exposure on mainstream television can only help in breaking down some of the negative perceptions of disability held by many with the non-disabled society.

Cultural Violence

Emotional responses to disability such as fear, hatred, dismissiveness or pity can have major impacts upon the way people within non-disabled society interact with people with disabilities. Even the reaction of close friends to a sudden acquired disability can cause problems in a previously close friendship as Danny (in Brittain, 2002; p.138) pointed out following the loss of his right arm at the shoulder during a car accident:

> "A lot of them found it very difficult, obviously, to come to terms with it. More so than me. And they found it hard to be around me, friends that I'd had for years".

(Danny, 2002)

The fact that many of Danny's long term friends found it hard to be around him following his accident appears to be in line with Hogan's (1999) contention that an acquired disability signifies a massive change in social status in the eyes of those around them. It is likely that a general lack of understanding of disability and the issues surrounding it were to blame for the difficulty of Danny's friends in accepting his disability, for as Chris (in Brittain, 2002, p.138) so concisely commented:

"They have very little knowledge of people with a disability and instead the attitude is basically if I leave it alone and don't touch them and don't get involved then it's not my problem kind of thing."

(Chris, 2002)

The reaction of Danny's friends to his acquired impairment clearly demonstrates the effect that a lack of understanding and a fear of the difference of anyone who does not conform to societal norms of able-bodiedness can have. Danny is still fully ambulatory with all his visual and intellectual faculties intact. He simply has one arm less than the majority of people.

It might be assumed that negative perceptions with regard to disability are only relevant to non-disabled individuals when dealing with or discussing people with disabilities. However, the power and reach of the perceptions of disability embedded in the medical model discourse are such that they can inform people with disabilities' discourses regarding people with different or more severe impairments in much the same way as they do for the non-disabled community. The following quote from Ina (in Brittain, 2002, p.147) comes from a discussion regarding the type and severity of disability and people's perceptions:

"I think it gives a bad impression when you see these people that, like the ones doing boccia[1]. I think that's just such an embarrassment and you know when we went out there and came back then people were saying oh we're not on the same plane as the boccia lot...it's people like that that give the rest of us a bad name and impression and they seem to class us all together and they only see the really bad ones generally."

(Ina, 2002)

It appears then that 'Ina' is displaying a discriminatory or disablist viewpoint of a group of people more severely disabled than herself. Arguably there is a tendency within society to label all people with disabilities as 'disabled' and attribute the same 'meaning' (usually that of the person with greatest level of impairment) to people with all types of impairment. This then could be why 'Ina' fears being associated with this group. However, in reality the quote from 'Ina' clearly demonstrates a lack of understanding of what it means to have cerebral palsy and also a discriminatory attitude towards their right to be taking part in their chosen sporting activity and being part of the same team as Ina and the others she refers to. This kind of occurrence has also been reported by Hunt (1966 cited in Sherrill, 1986, pp. 23-24) who stated that 'people with less stigmatized disabilities are often quite prejudiced against individuals who are more stigmatized'. This then plays a part in reinforcing and recreating negative perceptions of disability and their continued use within society.

1.A sport on the Paralympic programme played by athletes with cerebral palsy and similar in nature to the French game of boules or petanque.

Cultural Violence and Sporting Participation

Devine (1997) claims that society has a prescribed set of standards by which we are all measured and when someone's biological make-up or function fails to meet these standards they are 'assumed to be inferior and are subject to a decrease in inclusion in society' (Devine, 1997, p. 4). This is equally true for many aspects of life, but in the realm of sport, where one of the key aims is to distinguish between different levels of biological make-up and function through tests of physical strength, speed and endurance, this is especially true. In many ways sport is designed to highlight and revere extremes of bodily physical perfection and, under these circumstances, it is possible to see why, for some people, the idea of elite sport for people with disabilities, and in some cases any sport at all, is an anathema. Mastro *et al* (1988, p. 81) claim that part of the reason for this is that 'there is no culturally recognised need for competition and sports beyond therapeutic programs', which in itself has its roots in the schism between the socially constructed discourse of what sport is and the perceptions of disability embedded in the medical model discourse. By this I am referring to the view of sport as a means of highlighting bodily perfection and the perceptions embedded in the medical model discourse that views disability as a major form of biological imperfection. The outcome of such a situation for potential athletes with a disability is that their dreams and aspirations can be met with scorn or derision, which can then have a huge impact upon their self-confidence and self-image.

This kind of negative reaction to disability is not just restricted to strangers. Even close acquaintances can display this kind of behaviour as Bob (in Brittain, 2002, p.140) describes:

"I was going out with a girl then [1982], she was older than me, and we went to see Chariots of Fire, and I said, "That'll be me one day," and she just laughed at me. "Yeah, right! I don't think so" kind of thing".

(Bob, 2002)

It is clear from Bob's account that the idea that someone with a disability (in this case blindness) could achieve great things in a sport such as running was totally at odds with the girl's own perceptions of sport and disability. However, this attitude does not just relate to elite sport as 'Ina' (in Brittain, 2002, p.140) found when a colleague at work was recounting his recent skiing holiday:

"I remember one guy went skiing once, and he was talking all about this great skiing holiday he'd been on, and I said, "Did they have any disabled skiing facilities?" And he sort of looked at me and said, "No?!" Sort of, what a stupid question to ask! And I've never forgotten that".

(Ina, 2002)

These reflections appear to suggest that physical activity, particularly strenuous physical activity, is not something that people with disabilities are capable of taking part in. Even when they do, it is seen more as a form of physical rehabilitation rather than as something done for an ulterior reason or for its own sake. However, media coverage of events such as the Paralympic Games have gone part way to beginning to change some of these attitudes by highlighting some of the incredible sporting performance athletes with disabilities have proved themselves capable of achieving. By showing that Paralympic athletes are as equally determined, skilled and dedicated as their Olympic counter-parts media coverage of the Paralympic Games has helped to challenge perceptions that people with disabilities are weak and helpless individuals incapable of doing anything for them.

Conclusion

In conclusion, it can be argued that most of the forms of violence outlined above arise out of the application of the medical model of disability. The social model of disability can help us understand the manner in which sport for the disabled can help change perceptions within non-disabled society regarding people with disabilities and, thus, negate or at least lessen some of the 'violence' directed consciously or sub-consciously against people with disabilities. The impact that sport for the disabled can have upon the self-confidence and self-image of people with disabilities and upon the perceptions of those within non-disabled society regarding people with disabilities appear to indicate a potentially strong role in non-violent conflict transformation/ peace-keeping. These conflicts highlighted in the adaptation of Galtung's Triangle of Violence and rooted in the medical model of disability can have a hugely negative impact upon the lives of people with disabilities. There is a growing body of evidence of the potential of sport for the disabled to transform these conflicts into positive experiences for both disabled and non-disabled individuals alike. This is perhaps particularly true of post-conflict zones where non-disabled sport is already being heavily championed as a key element of both peace and development. Hopefully, it won't be much longer before the potential for sport for the disabled in this process will be fully recognised and utilised.

References

Abberley, P. (1993). Disabled people and 'normality'. In Swain, J., Finkelstein, V., French, S. and M. Oliver, (1993). (Eds.) *Disabling Barriers – Enabling Environments.*, Open University, Milton Keynes, pp. 107 – 115.

Berger, R.J. (2008). Disability and the Dedicated Wheelchair Athlete: Beyond the "Supercrip" Critique, *Journal of Contemporary Ethnography*, Vol. 37 (6) pp. 647 – 678.

Brinn, D. (2004). *Israeli athletes strike gold at World Paralympic Games*, Available at: (http://www.israel21c.org/culture/israeli-athletes-strike-gold-at-world-paralympic-games). (Accessed 13th April 2010).

Brittain, I. (2002). Elite Athletes with Disabilities: Problems and Possibilities. *Unpublished Ph.D. thesis.* Buckinghamshire Chilterns University College, UK.

Coalter, F. (2007). *A wider social role for sport: who's keeping score?* Routledge, UK.

Crawford, J. (2005). Constraints of Elite Athletes with Disabilities in Kenya, *Unpublished Masters Thesis*, University of Illinois at Urbana-Champaign, USA.

Devine, M. A. (1997). Inclusive Leisure Services and Research: A Consideration of the Use of Social Construction Theory in *Journal of Leisurability*, Spring Vol. 24(2) pp. 3 – 11.

French, S. (1993). Disability, impairment, or somewhere in between, In Swain, J., Finkelstein, V., French, S. and M. Oliver, (Eds.) (1993). *Disabling Barriers – Enabling Environments,* Open University, Milton Keynes, pp. 17 – 25.

Gal, J. & M. Bar, M. (2000). The Needed and the Needy: The Policy Legacies of Benefits for Disabled War Veterans in Israel, *Journal of Social Policy*, Vol. 29(4) pp. 577-598.

Galtung, J. (1990). Cultural Violence. *The Journal of Peace Research*, Vol. 27(3) pp. 291-302.

Hargreaves, J. (2000). *Heroines of Sport: The Politics of Difference and Identity*, Routledge, London.

Hogan, A. (1999). Carving out a space to act: acquired impairment and contested identity. In Corker, M, & S. French (1999). (Eds.) *Disability Discourse*, Open University Press, Buckingham, UK pp. 79-91.

Huang, C. J. & I. Brittain (2006). Negotiating identities through disability sport: From negative label to positive self-identification, *Sociology of Sport Journal*, Vol. 23(4), pp. 352-375.

Hunt, P. (Ed.), 1966, *Stigma: the experience of disability*, Chapman, London.

Mastro, J.V., Hall, M.M., & M.Y.Canabal (1988). Cultural and Attitudinal Similarities – Females and Disabled Individuals in Sports and Athletics. *JOPERD*, Nov/ Dec 1988, Vol. 59(9), pp.80-83.

Middleton, L. (1999). *Disabled Children: Challenging Social Exclusion*, Blackwell Science, Oxford.

Morris, J. (1991). *Pride Against Prejudice: Transforming Attitudes to Disability*, The Women's Press Ltd. London.

Seymour, W. (1989). *Body Alterations*, Unwin Hyman, London.

Sherrill, C. (1986). Social and Psychological Dimensions of Sports for Disabled Athletes, in Sherrill, C. (Ed.), 1986, *Sport and Disabled Athletes*, Champaign, Il., Human Kinetics, pp. 21-33.

Sporner, M.L., Fitzgerald, S.G., Dicianno, B.E., Collins, D., Teodorski, E.,
Pasquina, P.F. & R.A. Cooper (2009). Psychosocial impact of participation in the National Veterans Games and Winter Sports
Clinic. *Disability and Rehabilitation*, Vol. 31(5) pp. 410 – 418.
World Health Organisation (2010) *Definition and typology of violence*. Available at: (http://www.who.int/violenceprevention/approach/defini-
tion/en/index.html). (Accessed 29th May 2010).

Chapter 22
Sport as an Educational Trojan Horse

Ian Pickup

Introduction

Across the world, sport generates multi million dollar business deals, creates global superstars and flirts with political movers and shakers. In a time of global recession and public spending meltdown, what other industries retain such currency? Whilst people across the world find it increasingly difficult to stay employed, the business of sport continues to trade human resources for millions of dollars. Sure, different sports have more capital than others in some parts of the world and, from time to time, the popularity of individuals can grow and wane (For example: Tiger Woods' recent fall from grace as a case in point). Yet it is this power, this form of capital which holds so much potential for considering sport as an educational opportunity. If we can harness sport's ability to engage, to ignite passions, to foster a sense of belonging, and to inspire, then the true educative value of a sporting world can be realised.

This chapter explores ways in which this potential of sport as an educational tool can be best brought to life, focussing on the human processes of teaching and learning to bring about specific programme objectives. The metaphor of a 'Trojan Horse' is used to reflect sport's potential as vehicle for positive messages, for interaction and engagement that is sometimes difficult in other circumstances. The metaphor allows sport to be seen as a means through which positive educational outcomes can be facilitated and delivered, particularly where other vehicles for learning and teaching have failed. The chapter begins by considering the claims that are made for the educational value of sport in a variety of contexts, before identifying a range of problems inherent in common approaches and possible practical solutions.

Claims of an Olympic Magnitude

Set against the phenomenally successful and media fuelled background of the sports business; it is easy to be seduced into thinking that sport can be the answer to the world's ills. Indeed, much has been claimed concerning sport's educational potential; sport, it is said, can foster peace, rebuild war torn communities and engage the seemingly otherwise hard to engage in pro social activities. There are some who can barely conceal an almost evangelical zeal to spreading good through sport, whether this is through football in Gaza, athletics in Sri Lanka or Boxing in the Bronx. In schools, too, teachers claim that physical education can reach the parts that other subjects cannot. In a comprehensive literature review, Bailey at el (2007) suggested that there has been a tendency to make extravagant claims for the benefits and outcomes of physical education and school sport. For example, the United Nations (2003, 58/5) promoted the 2005 International Year for Sport and Physical Education 'as a means to promote education, health, development and peace', bold claims with questionable realism or for that matter measurable outputs through which the organisers could be held to account.

Claims of this magnitude are neither rare nor new and many international, national, regional and local organisations hold resolutely to the vision that sport can make a difference beyond the immediate confines of the sporting contest. Most famously (and highly relevant to the timing of the publication of this book) Baron de Coubertin saw in the Olympic movement an ideal opportunity to develop a set of universal principles, what have become known as the Olympic Values, that can be applied to education and to society as a whole. These values are reflected today in the mission statements of a variety of organisations that utilise sport as an educational and development tool, as demonstrated in other chapters within this book. For example, Right to Play allude to the 'power' of sport to improve children's lives whilst in the UK, the Youth Charter, a UK-based charity state that:

> "Sport is an order of chivalry, a code of ethics and aesthetics, recruiting its members from all classes and all peoples. Sport is a truce. In an era of antagonisms and conflicts, it is the respite of the Gods in which fair competition ends in respect and friendship. (Olympism). Sport is education, the truest form of education, that of character. Sport is culture because it enhances life and, most importantly, does so for those who usually have the least opportunity to feast on it".

The spirit of such passionate statements is, at least to anyone involved in sport, irrefutable, although legitimate questions are raised: if this vision is really possible, is sport currently delivering against this potential? What needs to be addressed, developed and improved in order for this vision to be realised? The London Olympic Games brought the notion of sporting legacy into sharp focus in the United Kingdom. For some, the substance of legacy is neatly summarised above, yet seemingly for others it is centred on the long term tenancy and sustainability of the iconic Olympic facilities. In London, rival football clubs have presented plans to create new uses for the stadium whilst the Government has dropped one of the original legacy targets for the Olympics, the promise to inspire one million adults in England to play more sport. There has also been a public and somewhat unseemly spat between the British Olympic Association (BOA) and the London Organising Committee regarding the use of profits generated from the Games, casting a further shadow across the bid-time promises of legacy from the 2012 Games and providing a poor comparison with the legacy achievements of the Los Angeles Games of 1984. A tangible outcome of these Games was the creation of the LA84 Foundation, using surplus funds to develop and fund youth sport-based projects. In 2011, 27 years after the event, over 200 million dollars has been invested in sport and education projects through the Foundations' grant making activity.

Back in London, whilst the Board, shareholders and (some) fans of West Ham FC PLC will no doubt be delighted with the prospect of a new post-Olympic home, the media and government activity in relation to legacy remains disproportionately focused on the 'bricks and mortar'. This may well be rooted in the failure seen in previous attempts to utilise public money to develop state of the art facilities and a fear that a 'white elephant' is being created. After all, the nearby Millennium Dome in Greenwich has only recently found a profit-turning niche as 'the 02' within London's entertainment industry. Yet this obsession regarding commercial viability of spaces is at odds with the Olympic values; the 'hardware' (stadium, other venues and infrastructure) is only a small part of the legacy potential; we need, above all else, a clearly articulated and integrated social and human 'software' dimension of sport, brought to life through education *in* and *through* sport. Learning *in* sport explains the processes through which skills, rules, tactics and techniques are learned, whilst learning *through* sport is a reference to the wider and more holistic social, cognitive and affective development facilitated by taking part in the activities. Learning in sport provides the mechanism through which engagement and motivation of participants can be catalysed, whilst learning through sport has greater potential for supporting the achievement of broad educational goals. It is this concept which brings sport and educational philosophies together and provides practical opportunities for realising sport's wider potential.

However, such a vision currently remains fragmented and uncoordinated in public policy, funding and overall effort. On-going fiscal challenges in the UK's public sector have seen cuts made to local authority youth services, the closure of programmes, leisure centres and existing sport based social inclusion programmes. Meanwhile, the young people of London continued to kill each other. On January 21st 2011 Kasey Gordon, aged 15, became just the next young man to lose his life following a fight in West Green Road, a short journey from the newly built Olympic Park. The spirit of friendship, solidarity and fair play seems a very long way from the streets, families and lived experiences of this and many other areas of the UK where opportunities in education, the environment and health are characterised by stark inequality. Learning (and education) in and through sport has the potential to redress this balance, by providing alternatives to anti-social behaviour, by bringing people together to work towards common goals and through creating structures and codes that are vehicles for healthy, socially responsible citizenship. Such activities have enormous educational and developmental potential. There is greatest potential for sport to enhance life in those areas where it is needed most, in those areas of the UK and the world where opportunities are most limited. A multitude of schools, charities and grass roots clubs deliver such activities and achieve remarkable things on a daily basis, often without funding, state of the art facilities or support from public relations firms. The secret of their success can be traced to the commitment of volunteers working as coaches, leaders, mentors, teachers and officials – the software dimension so often lacking in funding, thinking and delivery and which, with a modicum of investment, could lead to the realisation of a real and lasting sporting legacy.

Software Development

So, although the sporting hardware of stadiums, clubs and merchandise is not in short supply, it is the software of teaching, coaching and mentoring which demands a much clearer focus in policy and practice. If sport is to play a prolific role as an educational tool across the world, then an immediate focus on these human processes is required. Without well developed and integrated software, sport may remain blighted with inequality and remain unfulfilled with respect to its potential for making a significant educational, developmental or societal impact. This section of the chapter focuses on practical processes and considerations regarding how this software dimension can be developed, highlighting mechanisms and concepts through which integration across various sectors can be achieved. This section begins by addressing a fundamental misconception regarding sport and education; that simply by participating in sport (and by merely providing sporting opportunities) then broad educational benefits will follow.

Just do it?

The opportunity for children and young people to engage in physical education and sport programmes is recognised as a fundamental human right (UN, 1978). In some cases, just taking part in positive activity of this kind may have a direct and positive impact. For example, diverting children away from crime, bringing people together from warring factions or simply providing an opportunity to escape from the challenges of day to day life. However, it must be recognised that measurable educational benefit will *not necessarily* follow in a linear or causal fashion from participation. Specific learning outcomes must be planned for and supported to ensure that participants' learning and development is enabled through their participation in a sporting programme. Furthermore, this progress must then be observed, assessed, measured and reported in order for learning and development to continue. This on-going planning- coaching/teaching – assessment cycle creates a virtuous circle through which any sports programme can be planned, monitored and adapted to benefit participants and their continued involvement. Effective programme staff make continuous improvements, making decisions regarding the what, where and how of sport sessions to ensure that learning is kept on track. There are parallels in this argument that can be drawn between the historical assumptions made in early year's education in relation to the development of children's movement competence. For a long time it was thought that young children learn and develop physical skills through play and that this is a natural, maturational process without the need for formal, direct teaching by an adult. However, as Pickup (2012) points out, modern, western societies do not necessarily provide children with ample opportunities to play and move, to receive direct and indirect feedback regarding the quality of their movements, and we see many children today without the perceived 'natural' ability to run, jump, skip, dodge, balance and so on. In a similar way, children do not necessarily learn to engage positively with others, to solve problems, to be creative or to listen effectively by simply taking part in sport. It is critical that those charged with planning and delivering sessions understand how to best utilise the sporting environment to support and enhance learning and development, to consider a variety of possible approaches and to reach beyond a pedagogy which assumes that simply providing the chance to play sport is enough to bring about a range of desired, tangible and long-lasting educational outcomes.

Moving to Learn

Moving to learn is an expression borrowed from physical education literature and policy whereby *learning to move* and *moving to learn* are identified as the key features of physical education in school. It is the second term, *moving to learn*, which provides most potential for the use of sport as an educational and developmental vehicle which sees:

> "…..physical activity as a context for and means of learning. It involves a whole range of learning outcomes which go beyond learning how to engage in selected physical activities – social skills; managing competition and cooperation, including use of strategies and tactics; problem-solving; applying moral and aesthetic judgements; and knowing when and why different actions and behaviours are appropriate and effective".
>
> (Association for Physical Education, 2007).

Whilst this definition is designed to be relevant to the curriculum context of physical education and retains a physical reference (even in relation to social and cognitive skills) the use of sport as an educational tool inside and outside of formal educational contexts, and across the lifespan, becomes exciting when learning across all developmental domains is considered in this way. Whilst physical and health benefits are hoped for from all sport sessions, it is those gains made in social, cognitive and affective domains which provide the greatest potential for lasting individual growth and development and societal change. Regardless of the level of physical ability, it is the facilitated pursuit of learning and improvement in these non-physical domains which is most relevant to those wishing to use sport as an educational and developmental tool. The physical, sports-based focus may provide a persuasive hook for initial engagement and motivation for on-going participation, and even persuade governments and corporate organisations to provide the necessary funds, yet learning to cooperate and to solve problems whilst also developing a positive self-esteem are aspects of personal development that can last a lifetime and make an impact beyond the confines of a pitch, court or track.

Figure 1 provides a simple focus for the planning of learning which can be used by practitioners as a starting point for designing programmes and sessions. By reflecting on the desired programme outcomes within each of the developmental domains shown, learning outcomes can be scoped and mapped from the outset as relevant to the individuals and groups taking part and the environmental context within which the programme exists. Physical learning (for example being able to dribble a basketball with both hands; to be able to keep a ball away from a defender; to perform a forward roll) is deliberately shown here as a smaller domain, a conduit through which learning in other domains flows. The physical domain provides the way in – the Trojan Horse. The reader is encouraged here to reflect on the use of sport within their own programmes and to consider specific learning outcomes that are planned for within each of the developmental domains.

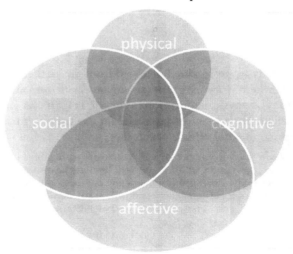

Figure 1: Simple Focus for the Development of Learning

One Size Fits All?

The extent to which sessions and programmes are planned and delivered with due regard to *individual participants* is a further dimension for consideration. An 'off the shelf' or template approach to delivery is misplaced and misguided if the educational outcomes of the sessions are to be fully realised. It is in this way that many sporting (and school based physical education) programmes across the world fall short. It is often assumed that practitioners have limited time to plan and therefore need an immediate, ready to go set of lesson plans to deliver. There are numerous texts and resources for teachers and coaches who provide ample choice from a battery of tasks and activities. This approach suggests that all learners progress at the same rate and that they will all be equally ready to engage with particular tasks. Whilst practitioners will have little problem in filling a session plan with safe and fun activities, and participants may generally enjoy the activities, this approach provides no guarantee that learning will actually take place. In much the same way that individual appropriateness is a key concept of developmental physical education in schools, sport sessions must also be planned thoroughly to include consideration of the relationship between the characteristics of individual learners, the conditions of the learning environment and specific requirements of the tasks. It goes without saying therefore, that football based sessions with rival gang members in an urban setting will need to be planned somewhat differently to volleyball sessions for the survivors of a natural disaster in a less developed country. The starting points for programme and session planning must therefore be a clear notion of participants' learning needs, a good knowledge of the social, economic and physical context within which the learning is to take place and consideration of the tasks to be used to bring about learning. Figure 2 below provides further reflective scope for practitioners to consider the extent to which they are planning and delivering sessions in full consideration of this range of factors.

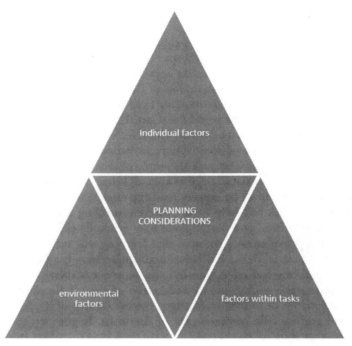

Figure 2: Reflective Scope

Whilst the individual learning needs and environmental factors need to be identified and articulated in relation to the planning process, they are not controllable (at least not in the first instance) by the coach or programme manager. However, the conditions of the learning tasks *are* very much in the hands of the facilitator, who is able to set the tasks in relation to learning needs and contextual factors. It is crucial therefore that the session leader is able to spend some time in getting to know participants and to understand the context in which the activities are to be delivered. Central to the planning and selecting of tasks is also the concept of *differentiation*, through which adaptations are made to tasks to ensure that they are set at an appropriate level for individuals within each group. Physically, tasks can be made easier or more demanding, but skilful differentiation can also create greater variability of demand with respect to non physical domain learning. In general terms, tasks can be adapted through variation of a range of conditions within each task, commonly encapsulated by the STTEP acronym (see figure 3 below).

Figure 3: The principles of STTEP

	SPACE	Make the space larger or smaller
T	TIME	Ask learners to work faster or slower
T	TASK	Change the task itself
E	EQUIPMENT	Vary the equipment
P	PEOPLE	Change the numbers of people

In this way, the space, time, tasks, equipment and number of people can be amended in response to specific learning needs. Efforts made by the practitioner to ensure that sessions are individually relevant will go a long way to enhance levels of motivation, improve chances of success, which in turn will impact on retention within programmes and educational benefits within the affective domain (e.g. increased self-esteem). The ability to use differentiation to carefully match sporting activities to the learning needs of participants and the possible and desirable learning outcomes is crucial to the success of sporting programmes which aim to make significant educational impact. Differentiation of tasks in this way is most commonly thought of in relation to physical learning. For example, young people learning to catch a ball for the first time will benefit from using different sizes and colours of balls which travel at different speeds – the slower the better in the first instance! For social, affective and cognitive learning, it is sensitivity towards variation of the tasks in relation to how people interact that must be uppermost in the coaches' mind.

Organic coaching

The approaches articulated in this chapter are central to the principle of *starting with what the participants can already do*. Planning sessions with individual, task and environmental factors in mind will ensure that sessions and programmes remain focused on the particular, contextualised learning needs of the specific group of participants and that tasks can be varied in response to individuals' progress. This approach once more draws a parallel with kindergarten pedagogy whereby 'starting from the child' is a much heard byword for practitioners. In other words, the entry point for teaching and learning is the existing ability levels of participants (in all domains), not what the coach feels the participants should theoretically be able to accomplish. This sounds very simple, yet so many sport based programmes fall short at the first hurdle by designing programmes that are de-contextualised and irrelevant to particular learning needs. Perhaps programmes are concocted at the head office of a charity or in response to a sponsor's need to see a 'product' such as a manual or teaching pack. To remain true to a developmental philosophy, practitioners need to be confident that they can engage with potential participants in a way which enables an understanding of learning need to develop whilst also building strong and trusting relation-ships. The case study described briefly below exemplifies this approach, but should not be seen as the only approach or as one that negates the need for spending time to plan programmes. The programme managers took time to consider a variety of possible approaches, consulted with a wide range of local people and organisations (including the local police, parents and com-munity leaders) and fully assessed the risks inherent in the approach. The space utilised for the activity was checked and considered safe, the coaches were trained and qualified and the programme learning objectives had been fully articulated with reference to the domains of learning described above. This was a well planned and skilful approach made to look unofficial and 'loose' to support the programme objectives.

Case study

An urban sport based social inclusion project in London adopted an organic approach from the outset. The very first session, during the school holidays and in the middle of one of the UK's largest social housing complexes, was advertised only by word of mouth and recommendation through local char-ities, youth workers and other agencies. Four coaches waited nervously on the grass area, kicking a football to each other and wondering if anyone would turn up. They were in the middle of the housing estate overlooked by high rise flats. Eventually, and long after the publicised start time, a small group of young people arrived and asked the coaches who they were and what they were doing. Some minutes later, jumpers had been put down for goalposts and the coaches were challenged to a game of football by the young people. Other young people appeared, the teams grew in number and two teams became four. Rules were introduced and new friendships were begun. Two hours later, the coaches said they had to go, but that they would be back the following week at the same time and place and that the parti-cipants were all welcome again and they should bring their friends. In this way, a highly organic approach created an opportunity to engage enabled the coaches to begin to foster positive relationships and to consider the various learning needs amongst the group of local young people. Over time the sessions introduced greater levels of structure, friendly matches were organised against other teams, coaching courses were attended by the par-ticipants and some became more engaged in school or employment. The organic approach planted seeds from which more sustainable and clearly structured activity followed. Without taking this approach it was thought that engagement would not have been possible with this particular group of young people in this particular context at this particular time.

Approaches of this kind are not therefore *top down*, pre determined or pre-scribed by 'others' but are organic methods through which programmes are developed from the ground up. Such approaches are highly flexible, looser and less defined from the outset, but should not be seen as less demand-ing than a more rigid, pre planned approach. The practitioners need to be skilful in observing and assessing, building positive relationships with participants, judging the potential of contextual influences on programme outcomes and changing session content where things do not necessarily go to plan. This raises a clear and pressing challenge for those who seek to use sport in such ways in the form of workforce development.

Developing the Workforce

The approaches to planning, teaching and learning introduced here are not revolutionary, and are in large part borrowed from other educational contexts. However, opportunities for sports coaches to think differently, to pursue alternative ways of doing and to clearly articulate outcomes beyond the physical domain are lacking in practice. This is evident in provision made by sports bodies in the UK which tend to have well developed and resourced coaching structures, often with a range of levels of qualification available to the aspiring coach, but which lack a focus for those seeking to utilise the sporting context for broader educational advancement. The majority of coaching courses focus, understandably, on the 'how' of coaching and equip practitioners with a range of physical and technical approaches to improving athletes' abilities. At the entry level, new coaches will often be provided with a range of sample activities, learn where to stand and how to speak to large groups, but receive little encouragement to reflect critically or to consider wider learning. The recruitment and development of staff to deliver sport based educational programmes outside the school context is therefore challenging; although many coaches are qualified to coach specific sports, their ability to utilise sport as an educative conduit are often relatively untested. Programme organisers need to recruit staff who can organise and coach sport-based sessions, but who also understand the wider educational aims and how to facilitate the achievement of these amongst specific populations.

The ideal solution to this workforce issue is the development of a hybrid practitioner, a combination of coach, teacher, counsellor, mentor and social worker rolled into one. In many successful programmes, such staff show empathy and understanding towards participants, borne out of personal life experiences. In some cases, the most successful coaches are produced over time through the programmes themselves, as participants learn and become coaches of younger members of the programme. This development of peers and 'near to peers' is a powerful mechanism through which real learning, anchored in the same life world context can be demonstrated effectively to others. This approach also supports the growth of local capacity and programme sustainability and mitigates an over reliance on external organisations being 'parachuted' in to deliver in a particular context. When funding has been spent and visiting coaches have left, new leaders and coaches have been developed to continue the work. The coach's ability to build trusting relationships in the community, with the participants themselves and in the real-world context is a vital ingredient of successful sport based educational projects. The development of such a workforce is vital for continued growth and success and this must become a clear focus of policy and practice worldwide. Broad educational gains will not be made by simply taking part in sport and the skilful and reflective facilitation of sessions will not materialise by chance. There are pockets of excellence across the world and a community of practice does exists where interaction between coaches, charities, sporting bodies and NGOs takes place, often through web based forums. This is supported by on line dialogue and occasional conferences, yet extensive academic debate or a comprehensive understanding of how to best use sport as an educational Trojan horse, borne out of detailed and longitudinal research remains somewhat elusive. It is this, drawing on theory and practice from different disciplines in education, sport, psychology, health and sociology which must become a priority for policy makers and practitioners alike. Without this integrated social and human dimension of coaching, sport's educational potential cannot be fully realised.

Conclusion

This chapter has discussed the potential for sport to act as a catalyst for education and development and has provided some practical points of reference for those attempting to use sport in this way. The focus has been on the software dimension, the role of people in creating the sporting vehicle through which learning can be facilitated. Whilst the international focus on sport is often dominated by the business and money of sport, it is a foregrounding of the role that people play in maximising sport's educative role that has been lacking. In an Olympic year, with so much promised in terms of legacy, we are not naive to think that sport can make a difference, but we are wrong to assume that this will take place without a significant investment in such a software dimension. We can no longer assume that providing sporting opportunity is enough; we must focus on creating a workforce of people to welcome participants, to build positive and pro social relationships and programmes and to strive towards the ideals espoused by so many organisations. Learning through sport holds the key in this regard and provides a means through which the ideals can be achieved.

References

Association for Physical Education (2008). *A manifesto for a world class system of physical education*, Reading: afPE.

Bailey, R., Armour, K., Kirk, D., Jess, M., Pickup, I., Sandford, R. & BERA Physical Education and Sport Pedagogy Special Interest group (2009). The educational benefits claimed for physical education and school sport; an academic review, *Research Papers in Education*, 24 (10), pp. 1-27.

Bourdieu, P. (1986). The (three) forms of capital, in J. G. Richardson (Ed.) *Handbook of theory and research in the sociology of education*, New York: Greenwood Press.

Pickup, I. (2012). The Importance of Primary Physical Education, in G. Griggs (Ed.) *An Introduction to Primary Physical Education*, London: Routledge.

Right to Play (2011). Webpages of Right to Play, available at: http://www.righttoplay.com/International/about-us/Pages/mission.aspx, (Accessed on 13th September 2011).

Sallis, J., & N. Owen (1999). *Physical activity and behavioral medicine*, Thousand Oaks, CA: Sage.

Stead, R. & M. Neville (2010). *The impact of physical education and sport on education outcomes: a review of literature*, Loughborough: Institute of Youth Sport.

The Guardian (2011). *Police investigate cause of fight that led to fatal stabbing*, London: The Guardian, 22nd January, 2011.

United Nations (2003). *Resolution adopted by the General Assembly: 58/5: Sport as a means to promote education, health, development and peace*, Geneva: UN.

United Nations Educational, Scientific and Cultural Organization (1978). *International Charter of Physical Education and Sport*, Paris: UNESCO.

World Health Organisation (1998). Sports and children: Consensus statement on organized sports for children, *Bulletin of the World Health Organization*, 76, pp. 445–7.

Youth Charter (1993). The Youth Charter Philosophy and Mission, available at: http://www.youthcharter.co.uk/about_philosophy_mission.html, (Accessed on 20th June 2011).

Chapter 23
Monitoring and Evaluation

Between the Claims and Reality

Daniela Preti

Introduction

The Debate on Quality and Effectiveness of Development Cooperation

In the last two decades, the debate on the quality and effectiveness of development cooperation has gained importance and there has been a growing emphasis on the need to measure the results of development interventions. It is no longer sufficient for governments, development agencies and NGOs to simply report on the outputs produced. There is an increasing demand to know how well development interventions achieved their intended objectives and how effectively they contributed to broader development objectives (Bamberger 2009: p.5). The fundamental paradigm-shift from input-output oriented project planning towards a focus on the levels of outcomes and impact has also led to a need for complex and sophisticated monitoring tools and evaluation methods. As a consequence, NGOs are increasingly under pressure to invest more in evaluating their work and measuring its impact.

Especially since the adoption of the Millennium Development Goals in 2000 and the Paris Declaration on Aid Effectiveness in 2005, the development of standardised procedures and instruments for measuring and attributing the results of development cooperation have been playing an increasingly important role (Reuber & Haas 2009: p.3). While this tendency is observable throughout all fields of development cooperation, it might be even more evident in the still rather young and emerging field of Sport and Development (S&D). In 2003, The UN General Assembly acknowledged the potential role of sport in achieving development goals in its resolution 58/5 entitled "Sport as a means to promote education, health, development and peace" and thereafter proclaimed the year 2005 as the International Year of Sport and Physical Education. Parallel to this recognition within the UN body, there has been an increasing demand to provide evidence on the impact the growing number of S&D programmes actually have on the ground. According to the "International Platform on Sport and Development", there is – despite the broadly shared conviction of the added value sport can bring for the development of individuals and of communities – still a lack of substantiated evidence to support the purported potential of sport. Congruently, the 2006 report of the UN Secretary-General "Sport for development and peace: the way forward" stated that mainstreaming Sport for Development and Peace in national and international programmes and policies required comprehensive monitoring and evaluation, and the international community was called upon to "develop and promote common evaluation and monitoring tools, indicators and benchmarks based on commonly agreed standards" (A/61/373:p.17).

Theoretical Approaches to Project Planning, Monitoring and Evaluation

Nowadays, it is almost inconceivable to think about planning and monitoring tools in development cooperation without considering the logical framework approach (LFA). Originally developed and applied in the military and private sector, the LFA was adopted by USAID for development projects in the late 1960s. Subsequently, it was also picked up by European development organisations and by the end of the 1990s, it had become the standard procedure required by many international donor agencies (Hailey & Sorgenfrei 2004: p.7). The LFA is built up as a linear model that includes results chains based on the assumption of objective causal relationships between inputs, outputs, outcomes and impact. The purpose of the model is to illustrate the project's components and how they are logically linked. The results of the logical framework analysis are presented in a four by four square matrix that essentially provides a summary of the specific project: It contains the project's hierarchy of objectives, indicators to assess whether the objectives have been achieved, sources of information for each indicator and a set of assumptions concerning the necessary preconditions needed for a project to succeed. There is a difference between the logical framework approach as such (the overall project planning process including problem analysis, the development of objectives and indicators and the identification of assumptions) and the actual logical framework (the matrix which summarises the main elements of the project and connects them to each other, thus being the result of the analytical planning process). It is import-ant to bear this distinction in mind in order to avoid mistaking apples for oranges when considering the usefulness of the approach.

In fact, despite its widespread use, there is much criticism of the use of the LFA in development cooperation. In 2005, the Swedish International Development Cooperation Agency (SIDA) conducted a review on NGO's perceptions of the LFA. It revealed that the prevailing attitudes on the LFA are that donors insist on it, while NGOs use it under sufferance. "Although the logical framework has become universally known, it is far from univer-sally liked" (Bakewell & Garbutt 2005: p.1). Much of the criticism relates to its rigidity and inability to reflect the complex reality of development pro-jects implemented in multifaceted, at times unpredictable and culturally di-verse environments. "It is a mechanistic idea of cause and effect as if we can turn the key in the engine of development and the wheels start turn-ing" (Ibid.:p.12). Further, it is criticised that the LFA only includes anticip-ated outcomes and cannot take into account unanticipated and unexpec-ted outcomes, be they positive or negative. The study concludes that while managers and donors dealing with multiple projects seem to appreciate the logical framework matrix as useful summaries, those "closer to the messy realities of development are less convinced" (Ibid: p.6). According to Des Gasper, who conducted numerous studies on international development, policy analysis and evaluation, the four recurring failings of logical frame-works have been: (1) the set up of 'logic-less frames', where only an illusion of logic is provided; (2) the 'jamming' of too much information into one dia-gram, (3) the creation of 'lack-frames', which omit vital aspects of a project; and, finally, (4) the elaboration of 'lock-frames', whereby programme learn-ing and adaptation are blocked (Gasper 1999: p.7). In theory, logical frame-work matrixes can and should be revised in the course of a project. In prac-tice, however, this rarely seems to happen and logframes are put to rest once the project begins (Bakewell & Garbutt 2005: p.9). The model thus seems to offer the temptation to engage in rather inflexible "blueprint planning" (Roduner/Schläppi & Egli 2008: p.8).

The described shortcomings of the LFA have led to increased experi-mentation with alternative frameworks and strategies. For instance, the In-ternational Development Research Centre Canada (IDRC) put forth an al-ternative methodology called "Outcome Mapping" (OM) in 2001. In recent years, OM has been drawing increasing interest amongst practitioners. The underlying assumptions of OM are that changes are not one-dimensional but complex and that at its essence, development occurs through changes in the behaviour of people. OM thus places people and learning first and accepts unexpected change as a source of innovation. It moves away from claims regarding the achievement of development impacts, and rather puts the focus on outcomes. Projects planned with OM seek to identify the part-ners with whom to work and then devise strategies to help equip these part-ners with the tools, techniques and resources to contribute to the develop-ment process. This is based on the understanding that a key precondition for successful development is the local ownership and continued responsibility felt by local people and institutions. According to the IDRC, the originality of the OM methodology lies in its shift away from assessing the products of a programme to focus on changes in behaviours, relationships, actions, and/or activities of the people and organisations with whom a development program works directly (Earl/Carden/Smutyo 2001). Practical experiences in working with OM highlight three key advantages: (1) The clear definition of roles and responsibilities of all project actors; (2) Milestones that reflect the process instead of final indicators and (3) Concentration on learning and accountability, since learning from experience and coping with change are key elements of OM (Roduner/Schläppli/Egli 2008: p.15). Generally speaking, however, OM is still evolving as a method for planning, monitoring and evaluating development projects and there are no systematic studies on its effectiveness and efficiency to date.

In their discussion paper put forth in 2008, Roduner et al. present an interesting synthesis model between LFA and OM. The synthesis model seeks to bring together the strengths of both approaches and is based on the argument that whilst the focus on changes in behaviour of partners is fundamental to sustainable development, these changes cannot be an end in itself. If poverty alleviation is the utmost concern, the authors argue, behaviour changes should also induce changes or improvements at a higher level (Ibid.: p.16). Their proposed synthesis model does not see the results-oriented nature of the LFA and the capacity building focus of OM as mutually exclusive, but rather as complementary approaches. Consequently, the logic model presented in the synthesis model contains elements of both approaches. It also deliberately leaves open the possibility of adjusting it to each specific case. According to the authors, debates about whether one approach is better than the other have not proven to be productive and the way forward should rather be to integrate aspects of both approaches (Ibid.:24). To date, however, the synthesis model remains a theoretical model that will need to be tested and adapted based on practical experiences.

In conclusion, despite the previously mentioned shortcomings and the rise of alternative frameworks, the LFA remains the standard used by most multilateral and bilateral agencies.

Experiences from the field

In the last decade, the Swiss Academy for Development (SAD) implemented numerous capacity building projects with grassroots organisations working in the field of S&D in Asia, South America, the Middle East and Africa. Given the current weight of the LFA as an international standard, SAD trained grassroots organisations on how to plan, monitor and evaluate projects using the LFA. This chapter summarises main findings.

A key observation is that measuring and analysing a project's achievements actually remains quite a struggle for many grassroots organisations. Monitoring and Evaluation (M&E) depends on both, appropriate institutional capacity as well as considerable investment of time and effort. In practice, however, limited financial resources often deter smaller organisations from spending sufficient funds on M&E – with the consequence that too little time and insufficient workforce are allocated to the time-consuming process of data collection and analysis. When inadequate funds are allocated, M&E activities run the risk of being perceived as something that adds extra pressure on the organisation, disrupts a project and is too time-consuming for the staff (NSD Concept Paper 2009: p. 18).

Furthermore, different theories and standards about project planning and M&E can create confusion among grassroots organisations. This situation often exacerbates with different donors requiring their separate monitoring and reporting systems, thereby greatly overloading smaller organisations. Application procedures of major donors often require fairly elaborate logframe matrixes as an integral part of project proposals. Grassroots organisations, however, often seem to struggle to define realistic and useful indicators. The tendency is to come up with large lists of indicators that look good on paper, but are completely overwhelming to implement in practice. Furthermore, M&E systems and tools that are imposed unilaterally on organisations are often perceived as manifestations of power from donors or the management. If project staff considers M&E not as a benefit for the organisation but rather as an "evil conducted for the sake of the donors" (Ibid: p.20), there is a high risk of a lack of motivation that ultimately results in poor data and analysis quality.

To avoid that project staff feels alienated from the M&E system, it is crucial to develop culturally sensitive processes and relevant indicators to meet the demands of different contexts. While the awareness of the challenge of transferring models and methodologies to different cultures and contexts has increased, the demand for internationally accepted and comparable systems remains strong: "The transferability of performance measurement systems depends on how far they can be adapted to local circumstances while remaining internationally accepted and comparable" (Hailey & Sorgenfrei: p.22). Another common point raised is that while tailor-made frameworks and context-specific measures can reflect needs of the local culture, they are expensive to design and of limited value in international comparisons (Ibid: p.22). In SAD's experience however, the design of tailor-made M&E systems and the involvement of a broad range of staff members in the definition of indicators and tools have helped significantly to increase local ownership for M&E processes, which in turn has proven to result in higher levels of motivation and openness to learning. A central concern of any M&E system should always lie on the sustainability of the introduced concepts and on contributing to capacity development within an organisation. To achieve this, it is indispensable to follow a realistic and genuinely participatory approach. In workshops, for instance, we have tried as often as possible to invite staff members from both the management and the field. The heterogeneity of the participants always proved to be enriching, since it allowed for different (and at times conflicting) perspectives to be taken into consideration and thereby triggered consensus in defining indicators and processes. Furthermore, it became apparent that these joint discussions between field staff and management were crucial in order to avoid creating a gap between what is desirable in theory and what is actually implementable in practice.

Another lesson learnt regards the choice of data collection tools. Gasper rightly points out that the choice of methods in M&E should be driven by an understanding of the nature of what is evaluated rather than starting from a choice of methods, however prestigious those are (Gasper 1999: p.16). Outcomes and impact in the social and psychosocial sphere often contain so-called "soft outcomes" such as changes in attitudes, perceptions and behaviour. These crucial but fairly intangible factors are quite difficult to measure. In our view, the shift from a focus on activities and outputs to outcomes and impact also requires thinking more in qualitative terms. This is not to spurn quantitative tools. Quantitative methods have numerous important strengths, arguably first and foremost the ability to generalise from a sample to a wider population – therewith meeting the demands for global comparability. "However, from another perspective, these strengths are also weaknesses, because the structured and controlled method of asking questions and recording information ignores the richness and complexity of the issues being studied, the context in which data are collected or in which the programs or phenomena being studied operate" (Bamberger 2009: pp.36/7). Or, put differently, "conventional quantitative monitoring of predetermined indicators only tells us about what we think we need to know. It does not lead us to into the realm of what we don't realise we need to know" (Davies/Dart 2005:p.59).

An approach that is rapidly gaining in popularity is mixed-method research, which seeks to combine the strengths of both quantitative and qualitative designs. It is becoming increasingly acknowledged that the process of triangulation (using a combination of methods, tools and perspectives) is more likely to provide a comprehensive picture of the effects of a project. It is our understanding that another crucial aspect is to design age appropriate M&E tools, since the perspectives of children and youth tend to differ from those of adults. When dealing with children or youth, experience shows that conventional methods are often not suitable, as they tend to be too complex – or simply too boring. Being genuinely interested in the youth's perspectives, we thus tested a variety of creative and youth-friendly M&E methods to complement the conventional tools. The tools used included, for instance, community mapping, self-recording videos, drawings, photo monitoring and story telling. These creative M&E methods not only directly engage the youth and provide them with the opportunity to express their own perspectives; they have also proven to be very motivating and fun for both the participants and the project staff. In our view, this is a very important, but often underestimated factor. The focus of the S&D approach lies on social development and therefore, measurement should be combined with learning whenever possible. Methods that are collective rather than individual can help to enhance learning processes. With groups of youth generating data through discussion (using, for instance, community mapping) consensus finding and teamwork skills can be fostered and peer group relationships promoted. In that sense, collective participatory methods can in themselves contribute to creating cohesion and understanding within a group (Armstrong et al. 2004: p.17). The use of techniques such as storytelling, self-recording videos, drawings or photo monitoring allowed us to grasp unintended outcomes, to move beyond measurement that only focuses on the visible and enabled us, to some extent, to "apprehend those invisible elements that constitute so much of what development is about" (Dlamini 2007: p. 4).

Conclusions

In his book "The White Man's Burden", the economist William Easterly criticises, among other things, that the planning mentality of development organisations often leads to ignoring the circumstances and needs of the people concerned (Easterly: 2008). Easterly raises a very crucial point here. While we do not want to dispute that planning tools can be very beneficial insofar as they force us to carefully think through what we are planning to do and what our basic assumptions are, M&E methods are of very limited use if not adapted to the local context. Attempts to seek for common and universally applicable indicators and monitoring tools tend to neglect local circumstances and run the risk of imposing unsuitable and inappropriate instruments that lack local ownership.

Shifting the responsibility more and more to local organisations is not only justified from a development policy point of view, it is also necessary. Indeed, local ownership and genuine empowerment are imperative to enhance lasting and sustainable development processes. It is our understanding that the same applies to M&E systems. It is crucial to involve a broad range of stakeholders not only to increase ownership, but also to ensure that key knowledge on M&E processes is shared, therewith helping to impede that evaluation skills remain "in the hands of the few" (Bitel 2000: p.2). However, greater stakeholder participation in M&E processes also calls for wider capacity building and training efforts of local staff in analysing the data gathered. It is crucial to bear in mind that participatory approaches to project planning (be it using the Logical Framework Approach or Outcome Mapping or any other tool) involves a major investment in time and resources, since it requires extensive training and support to ensure people know how to use it and buy into it. Fortunately, however, the money spent on that process not only helps to generate valuable data, but also highlights good practice and facilitates organisational learning. The evaluation expert Mark Bitel takes this point even further stating that when ordinary people become involved in evaluation activities, evaluation can also be a tool for building social capital in communities (Bitel 2000: p.2).

Ultimately, the key is not the choice of the M&E framework, but rather its application in practice – "it is essential to make the process as important as the product" (Hailey & Sorgenfrei: p.22). We would like to argue that the way forward in the S&D sector should be to promote the use of practically oriented planning, monitoring and evaluation tools. Grassroots organisations should adapt existing tools to make them suitable for their respective projects and contexts. Whichever tool is used, it should first and foremost serve the purpose of improving the projects – not to please donors, but to increase the benefits to target groups.

Furthermore, measurement should be combined with learning whenever possible. Organisations should be encouraged to think out of the box and to use creative, age- and culturally appropriate tools that not only generate high quality data, but are also motivating and fun to produce, collect and analyse. This also requires an increased awareness that any kind of measurement that seeks to apprehend meaning takes time.

As Albert Einstein remarked: "Not everything that counts can be counted, and not everything that can be counted counts."

References

Armstrong, Miranda / Boyden, Jo / Galappatti, Aananda / Hart, Jason. (2004). Piloting Methods for the Evaluation of Psychosocial Programme Impact in Eastern Sri Lanka. USAID (Ed.) / Refugee Studies Centre, University of Oxford.

Bakewell, Oliver / Garbutt, Anne (2005). The use and abuse of the logical framework approach. SEKA - Resultatredovisiningsprojekt: SIDA.

Bamberger, Michael (2009). Institutionalizing impact evaluation within the framework of a monitoring and evaluation system. IEG. World Bank.

Bitel, Mark (2000). "Taking evaluation to the people? Who wants it?!!". Paper presented by Mark Bitel at the European Evaluation Society Conference, Lausanne.

Davis, Rick / Dart, Jess (2005): The 'Most Significant Change' (MSC) Technique. A Guide to Its Use.

Dlamini, Nomvula (2007). Stories and M&E. In: ONTRAC No: 37: Rethinking Monitoring and Evaluation.

Easterly William (2006): "The White Man's Burden": Why the West's Efforts to Aid the Rest Have Done So Much Ill and So Little Good. New York.

Earl, Sarah / Carden, Fred / Smutylo, Terry (2001): Outcome Mapping. Building Learning and Reflection into Development Planning. International Development Research Centre (IDRC). Ottawa.

Gasper, Des (1999). Evaluating the "Logical Framework Approach" – towards Learning-oriented Development Evaluation. ISS Working Paper, General Series No. 303. The Hague.

Hailey, John / Sorgenfrei, Mia (2004): Measuring Success: Issues in Performance Management. Occasional Papers Series No: 44. INTRAC. Oxford.

NSD Concept Paper (2009): How to Monitor and Evaluate Sport for
    Development Projects. SELA Advisory Group. Copenhagen.
Reuber, Marianne / Haas, Oliver (2009). Evaluations at the Deutsche
    Gesellschaft für Technische Zusammenarbeit (GTZ GmbH) /
    German Technical Cooperation. Eschborn.
Roduner, Daniel / Schläppi, Walter / Egli, Walter (2008): Logical Frame-
    work Approach and Outcome Mapping. A Constructive Attempt
    of Synthesis. Discussion Paper, Agridea & NADEL ETH. Zurich.
UN General Assembly Resolution 58/5 (2003): Sport as a means to promote
    health, education, development and peace. United Nations.
UN General Assembly Report of the Secretary-General A/61/373 (2006).
    United Nations.

Chapter 24
Building Community Capacity through 'Sport for Development'

Usability of the 'Domains Approach'

Ryan W. Wright, Lori Hanson & Karen Chad

Introduction

Recently, physical activity and sport[1] programs have been promoted in majority world[2] communities as a means to promote peace, a participatory tool to create inclusive opportunities for marginalized groups, and as a forum for social mobilization efforts and other health-based initiatives (Sport for Development and Peace International Working Group [SDP IWG], 2008; United Nations Inter-Agency Task Force on Sport for Development and Peace [UNIATF], 2003). In addition, the UNIATF (2003) claims that sport not only increases human capabilities in terms of social and health benefits,

---

1. In this context, sport is defined broadly as "all forms of physical activity that contribute to physical fitness, mental well-being, and social interaction... [such as] play; recreation; organized, casual or competitive sport; and indigenous sports or games" (UNIATF, 2003, p. 2). Notably, elite sport is outside the scope of this definition.

2. Majority world – reference to the poorer and less developed countries where the majority of people of the world live (Crump, 1998).

but also promote sustainable human and community development. Given this latter contention, several international organizations are now promoting sport as a developmental tool in and of itself. The Commonwealth Games Canada, Sports Coaches' OutReach, Mathare Youth Sports Association, and Right To Play (RTP) are examples. Our research focuses on the international non-governmental organization (NGO) RTP, which currently implements Sport for Development[3] programs in countries in Africa, Asia, South America, and the Middle East. RTP's mission is to improve the lives of children, youth, and whole communities by using the power of sport and play for development, health, and peace (RTP, 2008). Thus, RTP works with severely disadvantaged groups including former child combatants; children orphaned due to war, poverty, or disease; and refugee populations (RTP, 2004b).

An objective of RTP programs is to build community capacity (RTP, 2002, 2007, 2008). RTP reports that through the transfer of skills and knowledge to community members as well as the development of sport specific organizational structures such as sport councils/task teams, the organization builds stronger communities and increases the likelihood of community ownership and projects sustained by the local population (RTP, 2002, 2005, 2006). Specifically, the organization believes that training local youth and adults to be coaches and program leaders can foster ownership of RTP programs and project management may be assumed in the long term (RTP 2002, 2005, 2006).

To date, very little is known about the role Sport for Development programs actually play in increasing community capacity. Given that no empirical studies exist regarding this specific objective, the primary purpose of our research was to understand the effectiveness of a RTP Sport for Development program in community capacity building in a refugee camp in the Kibondo district of Tanzania. Our results showed that community capacity was increased in eight of nine 'operational domains' (see Wright et al., 2010). However, because our research incorporated a specific and well-established method of assessing community capacity, a secondary purpose, and the focus of this paper, was to determine in what ways implementation of this participatory workshop methodology was an effective strategy for measuring and building community capacity in a Sport for Development context. The challenges associated with community capacity building in the present refugee assistance system are also discussed.

---

3. Sport for Development is a shortened version of the term 'Sport for Development and Peace'. Sport for Development, or Sport for Development and Peace, is a recently developed stream within the field of international development that utilizes sport as a development tool. These concepts evolved out of a growing belief that well-designed, sport-based initiatives incorporating the best values of sport can be powerful, practical, and cost-effective tools to achieve development goals and peace objectives.

The research context

In 2005, the primary researcher was hired as a project coordinator with RTP. A placement overseeing implementation of four Sport for Development projects in four refugee camps in the Kibondo district of Tanzania provided the basis of this research.

Mtendeli refugee camp

The Kibondo district has long been an asylum site for Burundian refugees because of its close proximity to Burundi. This research was carried out in Mtendeli, which was one of the largest and most destitute camps in the district. At the time of this research, Mtendeli had a population of 25,950 Burundian refugees (UNHCR, 2005a). The refugees in Mtendeli were, for the most part, of the Hutu[4] ethnic group and were predominantly from the Ruyigi, Cankuzo, Karuzi, Makamba, Gitega, and Rutana provinces, which are mainly rural areas in Burundi.

At the highest level, Mtendeli refugee camp was governed by Tanzania's Ministry of Home Affairs. However, refugee assistance was coordinated and administered by UNHCR. UNHCR relied on partnerships with other specialized United Nations agencies and NGOs to provide food, water, shelter, and medical care to the refugee population. The majority of the organizations providing such assistance were Implementing Partners (IPs) who received funding directly from UNHCR. IPs were responsible for specific services such as overall camp management, water and sanitation, community services, education, environmental protection, among others. In addition, UNHCR also had Operational Partners (OPs) who supported UNHCR's work but did not receive financial support from the organization. RTP was one of UNHCR's OPs working in Mtendeli camp.

Program implementation and the research environment

RTP is an organization that aims to build community capacity (RTP, 2002, 2007, 2008). Importantly, the most empowering programs are those that allow identification of, solutions to, and actions to resolve problems to be performed by the community (Laverack, 2001; Smith et al., 2001). Yet a tension often exists between bottom-up and top-down approaches to programming and this fact is crucial to the comprehension of community capacity building in health promotion and community development. Bottom-up programs focus on issues which concern those community members or groups involved in the program and view improvement in those individuals overall power or capacity as the goal of the program (Bopp & Bopp, 1999; Laverack & Labonte, 2000; Raeburn et al., 2007; Simpson et al., 2003). Conversely, top-down programs involve community members or groups in is-

---

4. Modern ethnic typologies often divide Burundians into three different ethnic groups: The Hutu comprise 85% of the population; the Tutsi 14%; and the Twa a mere 1% (Waters, 2003). In most summaries of the history of Burundi, the conflict is presented as an ethnic rivalry between Tutsi and Hutu.

sues and activities that are largely defined by professionals from outside agencies; they regard changes or improvements in behaviour as the important health outcome of the program (Bopp & Bopp; Laverack & Labonte; Smith et al., 2001).

During the researcher's job training and orientation to RTP, numerous RTP staff stressed the importance of using participatory and bottom-up approaches to programming while in the field. Such an approach was also evident in the organization's annual report which stated that "...we [RTP] have learned that local communities can often generate the best responses to local problems" (RTP, 2002, pg. 17). Despite such emancipatory discourse, in the first few months in the field the researcher observed that programming approaches were, to a great extent, top-down rather than bottom-up. Most major organizational decisions and program plans were made by staff working for RTP International in Toronto. Such plans were passed to RTP project coordinators who were responsible for presenting them to the community. To illustrate, community members in Mtendeli discussed how "....when RTP project coordinators come, they come with what they've already planned and they work on that. In addition, programs vary time after time and in accordance with the project coordinators who come to work in our community".

Importantly, this disparity between policy and practice is consistent with Laverack and Labonte's (2000) claim: Many health promotion initiatives continue to exert power over communities through top-down programming but simultaneously claim to address interests and concerns of individuals and community groups.

During the first few months of working in the Mtendeli community the researcher attempted to shift to a participatory approach to program implementation by involving community members in needs assessing, decision making, and program planning. However, a major obstacle faced was negotiating community concerns and issues with the top-down organizational and program decisions made by RTP International. This is consistent with Laverack and Labonte's (2000) discussion of the tension often experienced by health promotion workers when supporting community needs and concerns in top-down programs that usually define the health promoters' job description and/or the program's funding. Thus, the researcher's field position as project coordinator put him between the community and the organization, constantly shifting between and negotiating with these two parties. Specifically, the researcher's focus was to support community ideas and efforts and defend these to RTP managers, while also considering top-down program plans from RTP International. In an effort to solidify participatory and bottom-up programming in the context of a top-down program, as well as assist community members' discovery of their own abilities and competencies in the RTP program, utilizing a well-established participatory approach to building and assessing community capacity was introduced.

Building and measuring community capacity

In the past 15 years, the focus on community capacity has gained increased prominence in community development, health promotion, and population health research as both academics and practitioners "see that effective action requires engaging the community directly and in ways where meaningful decision making power is shared" (Smith, Baugh Littlejohns, & Roy, 2003, p. 11). Community members often have extensive knowledge and understanding of their community's history, its people, resources available, and its strengths and weaknesses (Smith et al.). Accordingly, communities themselves are often fully capable of identifying their assets, needs, as well as the specific issues and problems they face (Bopp, GermAnn, Bopp, Baugh Littlejohns, & Smith, 2000; Easterling, Gallagher, Drisko, & Johnson, 1998; Laverack, 2007; Smith, Baugh Littlejohns & Thompson, 2001). The importance of collaborative and capacity building approaches to programming, research, and development may also be attributed to the realization that the success and sustainability of health promotion and community development initiatives are largely dependent on the commitment and involvement of community members (Laverack, 2007).

Community capacity refers to whether or not a community "has the characteristics, skills, and energy to take on the challenges it will need to face in order to move to greater levels of well-being and prosperity" (Bopp et al., 2000, p. 1). Community capacity building, in turn, is increasing community groups' abilities to define, evaluate, analyze, and act on health or other concerns of importance to their members (Labonte and Laverack, 2001a). Thus, community capacity building can play a major role in increasing group's and communities' abilities to address issues and barriers that directly affect people's health and quality of life (Hawe, Noort, King, & Jordens, 1997; Labonte, Bell Woodard, Chad, & Laverack, 2002). Accordingly, community capacity is promoted as a necessary condition for the development, implementation, and maintenance of effective, community-based health promotion and disease prevention programs (Goodman et al., 1998). Nevertheless, community capacity has proven difficult to evaluate or measure (Ebbesen et al., 2004).

Community capacity assessment reflects a growing understanding of the importance of social context and collective individual and community resources as factors in the effectiveness and sustainability of health promotion programs. Numerous descriptions of community capacity exist (Bopp et al., 2000; Bopp & Bopp, 2004; Bush et al., 2002; Chaskin, 2001; Easterling et al., 1998; Frank & Smith, 1999; Gibbon, 1999; Goodman et al., 1998; Hawe, King, Noort, Jordens, & Lloyd, 2000; Jackson et al., 2003; Laverack, 1999, 2007; Maclellan-Wright et al., 2007; McKnight & Kretzmann, 1996), each includes a collection of domains or influences on capacity. Notably, there is considerable overlap among the various schemas. Within the literature, six of these frameworks comprise a coinciding approach to measurement (Bopp et al.; Bush et al.; Hawe et al.; Laverack; Maclellan-Wright et al.; McKnight & Kretzmann). At the time of our research, Laverack's nine

323

domains seemed the most concise of these approaches, offering a straight-forward way to understand and measure community capacity in a program or community setting[5] As well, the nine domains and the specific method of evaluating community capacity, labeled the 'domains approach' (Laverack, 2003), had been used in numerous health promotion and development projects in various countries and with different cultural groups.

Initially, the nine domains were field tested in Fiji using focus group responses (Laverack, 1999, 2003). The domains were also used in initiatives to improve sustainable livelihoods in rural communities in Kyrgyzstan (Jones & Laverack, 2003) and for improving local community-managed ecotourism in Northern Thailand (Laverack & Thangphet, 2007). Importantly, Laverack's domains have also been used in African contexts with development projects in both Kenya and Malawi (G. Laverack, personal communication, September 10, 2007). Furthermore, Laverack's domains approach has been implemented within a physical activity initiative; specifically with Saskatoon *in motion*™, an inter-sectoral partnership of four Canadian agencies, to promote active living (see Bell-Woodard, Chad, Labonte, & Martin, 2005).

Implementation of the 'Domains Approach'

As mentioned, the nine domains offer a straightforward way to understand and assess community capacity. Such a framework provided a means to operationalize the organizational aspects of community capacity building in the RTP program and determine the extent community capacity was built. To accomplish this, Laverack's (1999) nine domains were used to make an initial assessment of community capacity, transform this information into action by way of strategic planning, and, subsequently, re-assess one year later to determine changes in the nine domains.

Each assessment took place at the community youth centre, occurred over two full days, and was carried out adhering to Laverack's (2003) description of the assessment process. Twelve key stakeholders from the RTP community participated in each assessment[6] Key stakeholders were those people who were directly involved in or had influence on the program; these included Sport Council members, RTP coaches, and program leaders.

Preparation prior to implementation

Since the researcher was unable to speak Kirundi (the language most commonly used by Burundians), un-facilitated discussions were not possible. Workshops, meetings, and other interactions were carried out with the

---

5. The research began in July of 2005. At that time, only five of the six frameworks existed. Maclellan-Wright et al.'s measure of community capacity was not published until 2007.

6. Following Johnson and Johnson (2000), who describe the most effective size of a problem-solving group to be 8-12 people, 12 key stakeholders from the RTP community participated in each assessment. Notably, since completion of our study, Laverack (2007) has discussed how his methodology can accommodate 15-20 people.

help of a hired facilitator/translator (a Burundian living in the camp who was also involved in the RTP program). Prior to assessment, the researcher and the facilitator adapted Laverack's (1999) nine domains in an effort to make them relevant, understandable, and usable in Mtendeli refugee camp (see Table 1).

Table 1: The Nine Domains of Community Capacity

Community Participation – active involvement by stakeholders and community members in setting direction, making choices, and being involved in the Right To Play program.
Local Leadership – ability of Right To Play program/community member(s) to articulate a vision, assess needs, encourage and support others, and engage in legitimate decision-making to produce a high quality valued program as well as community satisfaction.
Organizational Structures – organizational structures in a community include groups such as committees, councils, and church and youth groups. These groups provide an opportunity for people to come together in order to socialize and to address their concerns and problems.
Problem Assessment Capacities – ability of Right To Play program/community members to problem solve related to the Right To Play program.
Resource Mobilization – ability of the Right To Play community to mobilize resources from inside the community (internal) and negotiate resources from outside the community (external). Internal resources are those developed or found in the community such as food, land, money, local knowledge, and the skills of both individuals and groups. External resources are those resources that are brought into the community by an outside agent and may include financial assistance, equipment, new knowledge (training) or technical expertise.
Ability to 'Ask Why' – ability of the community to critically assess the social, political, economic, and other causes of inequalities.
Links with Others – scope and degree of interaction with other individuals and organizations operating in the camp. Links with people and organizations, including partnerships, coalitions, and voluntary alliances may assist the Right To Play community in addressing problems and in mobilizing resources.
Role of Outside Agents – role of Right To Play project coordinators (and possibly other outside institutions or agencies) in initiating and sustaining community action.
Program Management – the involvement of community members in program planning, decision making, program implementation, evaluation, and conflict resolution in the Right To Play program.
The nine domains have been adapted from Labonte & Laverack, 2001; Laverack, 1999, 2001, 2003; Laverack & Labonte, 2000.

Within this framework of assessment, each of the nine domains consisted of five descriptor statements, arranged in an ordinal rating system from one (low level of capacity) to five (high level of capacity). The descriptor statements were adapted from Laverack (1999) and Bell Woodard(2004) and were collaboratively developed by the facilitator and the researcher specifically for the research project. For example, the descriptor statements for the domain 'Community Participation' were:

1. People in the camp are not aware of or engaged in the Right To Play program.
2. People in the camp are aware of the Right To Play program but very few are directly involved with the program or program activities.
3. Many people in the camp are involved in the Right To Play program, but are not involved in making choices or setting direction of the Right To Play program.
4. Many people in the camp are involved in the Right To Play program. Right To Play Coaches are involved in group discussions, making decisions, and planning the future direction of the Right To Play program.
5. Many people in the camp are involved in the Right To Play program. Right To Play Coaches continue to participate in group discussions, make program decisions, and plan the future direction of the Right To Play program. These activities have been maintained for a sustained period of time.

Following development of the descriptor statements, they and the nine domains were translated into Kirundi and cross-checked with three community members who were able to speak English, to determine their community relevance. Both the domains and the descriptor statements were determined to be understandable, culturally appropriate, and suitable for use with the community.

Baseline assessment of the nine domains

Subsequent to adapting the methodology, the baseline assessment of community capacity was carried out two months following the researcher's arrival in the placement community. To ensure all stakeholders had a comparable understanding of the project's past, the assessment was prefaced by a review of the developmental history of the RTP program in Mtendeli. This was followed by descriptions of community capacity concepts and consensus by stakeholders on the nine domains and their definitions. An opportunity to adapt or modify the nine domains was important because the descriptions and indicators of community capacity need cultural and contextual specificity in order to be relevant to community members and the health promotion program (Jeffery et al., 2006). Key stakeholders agreed on the appropriateness and applicability of the domains as they currently existed. Such confirmation recognized the community capacity domains as having cultural and contextual specificity and a determination of being usable in this context.

Laverack (1998, 2003) discusses how creating a culturally relevant working definition of community capacity increases the likelihood that community members will develop an understanding of the concept and how they can contribute to the research process and the overall program. Thus, a working definition of community capacity was developed by participants prior to assessing the nine domains. Key stakeholders specific definition of community capacity was *the actual force, will, and skills of community members to work together to assess critical issues and address problems and concerns with the aim of moving to greater levels of well-being and prosperity*[7] This wording was adopted as the working definition of community capacity and was used throughout the research process.

The assessment was conducted one domain at a time. To assess capacity in each domain, the five descriptor statements were provided to key stakeholders on five separate, un-numbered and un-marked sheets of paper. Each descriptor statement was typed out in both Kirundi and English. To prevent statement selection bias, the statements were randomized and the numerical values attached to the statements were removed so participants were unaware of the rating scale in each domain. As a group, stakeholders collaboratively determined which statement they thought most closely represented the present situation in their community[8] Once participants determined which statement (or statements) best represented the existing level of capacity in a specific domain, they were asked to provide justification for the assessment (i.e., the reasons why they chose that specific statement). Stakeholders then developed strategic plans for capacity building if improvement in that domain was deemed necessary.

Following assessment of all nine domains, a spider-web configuration (Rifken, Muller, & Bichmann, 1998) was created by the researcher, using the numerical values attached to each of the selected statements, to visually communicate the level of capacity in each domain in a simple and straightforward manner (Laverack, 2006)(Figure 1). Both the spider web diagram and the qualitative justification for each selected statement became the basis for further discussion and strategic planning at several follow-up meetings.

---

7. The working definition was largely influenced by Bopp et al. (2000) who define community capacity as "whether or not the community has the characteristics, skills, and energy to take on the challenges it will need to face in order to move to greater levels of well-being and prosperity" (p. 1).

8. The statement selection process was flexible in that the descriptor statements could be amended or added to or a new description could be provided by participants to describe the situation for a particular domain. In addition, more than one statement could be selected by participants if consensus on one statement could not be reached.

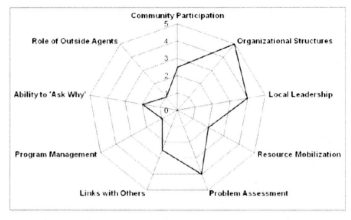

Figure 1: Spider-web Configuration (Baseline Assessment)

Final Assessment of the nine domains

A final assessment of community capacity occurred one year following the baseline assessment. At the second assessment, stakeholders were once more familiarized with the project's historical development, community capacity concepts, and the nine domains. Participants then, using the same tool and procedures from the baseline assessment, again determined which statement best represented the existent level of capacity in each of the domains and provided justification for such assessments. For a second time, a spider-web diagram was created. The spider web diagrams from each assessment were then compared and became the basis for further discussion and strategic planning. Key stakeholders commented on the domains showing the most significant changes and noted the one domain that decreased in capacity (Figure 2).

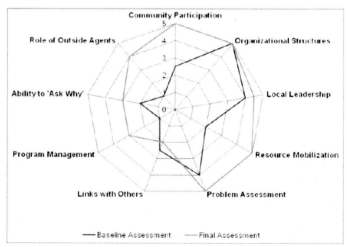

Figure 2: Spider-web Configuration (Baseline and Final Assessments Compared)

Effect of using the domains approach in evaluating Sport for Development

Experiences in Mtendeli refugee camp demonstrate that the domains approach (Laverack, 2003) was an effective tool for evaluating and building community capacity in a Sport for Development program. One of the most notable strengths of this model of community capacity evaluation is its participatory nature. This approach served as a framework for community stakeholders to critically look at the impact of their participation in the RTP program, assess the current level of community capacity, and reflect on the community's strengths and weaknesses. Consistent with the work of Laverack and Thangphet (2007), this process was aided, at each assessment, by use of the spider web diagram (see Figures 1 and 2), which visually illustrated the level of capacity in each domain and allowed all stakeholders (both literate and non-literate) to understand the community's strengths and weaknesses. However, it was the qualitative comments provided by stakeholders defending the descriptor statement(s) selected in each of the nine domains which were most useful for assessing community capacity building; these provided greater insight into actual changes in community capacity because community members were dialoguing in their own terms, rather than in terms of a pre-determined framework.

For example, despite the domain 'Organizational Structures' being rated the same (i.e., rating of 5) at both assessments, key stakeholders believed that capacity in this domain had in fact increased over the one year period. At the final assessment, stakeholders discussed how two seven-member task teams, specific to RTP, had been created to replace the original sport council, which was accountable to an organization responsible for community services in the camp. Workshop participants discussed how the task teams were more actively involved in decision making and program planning compared to the sport council because the task teams were responsible for holding meetings (independent of project coordinators) and developing and submitting their own monthly project plans. In addition, the task teams also submitted project reports based on monthly camp activities, which had not previously been carried out by the sport council. As well, developing two RTP-specific task teams resulted in an explicit focus on sport and play activities for children and youth because the task teams no longer incorporated sport for adults in their program plans. Based on these discussions, key stakeholders concluded that replacement of the sport council with RTP task teams led to increased capacity of the RTP organizational structure.

Not only did the assessment process generate dialogue as well as community interest in critically looking at the impact of community members' participation in the program, but it increased the extent and degree in which key stakeholders participated in the initiative; an essential component of community capacity building. The insight gained from this process allowed community members to transform community knowledge into program planning for collective action. Specifically, strategic plans were developed to build on the community's strengths, to mitigate community weaknesses, and to meet community needs. In addition, many individuals who participated in the assessment process became invested in and committed to carrying out the strategic plans for improvement in the nine domains (Wright et al., 2010). Given this, implementation of the community capacity assessments fostered increased community ownership over the RTP program and was a way of shifting to a participatory and bottom-up approach to programming in the context of a traditionally top-down program.

Consistent with the literature, the assessment process resulted in community capacity building becoming an end goal of the RTP program as well as a means to enhanced program delivery and the achievement of specific program goals (Hawe et al., 1997; Gibbon et al., 2002; Goodman et al., 1998; Labonte et al., 2002; Labonte & Laverack, 2001a; New South Wales Health Department, 2001; Smith et al., 2001, Wright, 2009). In the context of RTP, community capacity building has been presented as an explicit goal and outcome of the organization's Sport for Development programs (RTP, 2002, 2007, 2008). Nevertheless, at the time of this research, no specific model or outline for community capacity building existed in the literature, nor was one provided to RTP project coordinators to use in their program implementation strategies. Implementation of the domains approach allowed community members and project coordinators to create a specific set of community capacity objectives (i.e., strategic plans) which ran parallel to existing RTP program goals in what several authors describe as a parallel track approach to community development programming (Labonte et al.; Labonte & Laverack, 2001a, 2001b; Laverack, 1999; Laverack & Labonte, 2000). Through participation in the assessment process and the deliberate creation of measureable community capacity objectives, community members and project coordinators ensured that community capacity building became an 'actual' or 'genuine' goal of the RTP program.

The findings from our study suggest that use of the domains approach was a promising practice for community capacity building in a Sport for Development program. However, such an approach to community capacity assessment should not be exaggerated for what it does. Despite community capacity increasing in eight of nine domains in the context of the RTP program (Wright et al., 2010), community capacity was extremely constrained by the prevailing refugee assistance system as well as the living conditions in the refugee camp.

Refugee assistance system

Notably, the structure of the refugee assistance system and its associated policies has encouraged the confinement of many refugees in camps or settlements and existing in such a system has caused dependence on relief (Hyndman, 1996; Kibreab, 1989, 1991; Voutira & Harrell-Bond, 1995). This system has been primarily created and designed by non-refugees, with the majority of existing policies and programs being developed during the initial emergency relief phase which focuses heavily on hand-outs (Clark, 1985). This arrangement of hand-outs continues after the initial emergency phase ends and thus deters refugee self-reliance (Clark). This was the case in

Mtendeli camp where the refugees were largely dependent on external agencies (i.e., UNHCR and other organizations) for meeting their basic needs. As a consequence, these organizations had much control over many aspects of the inhabitants' lives. Clark's (1985) description of the refugee assistance structure emphasizes the specific features where such control exists:

> "The refugee assistance system is directly involved in a wide range of areas of refugees' lives, including decisions about what kinds of food people will eat and how much, the kinds of housing they will have, the protection they will receive, their health care and education, their employment opportunities, and many others" (p. 2).

Kibreab (1993) points out how many relief organizations and academics presume that a prolonged reliance on hand-outs fosters a dependency syndrome or dependency mentality among refugees. The refugee dependency syndrome is described as "lethargy; lack of initiative; acceptance of handouts with little attempt at self-sufficiency; [and] frequent complaints, especially about the lack of generous outside help" (Clark, 1985, p. 1). The perception that refugees suffer inertia and lack initiative and ambition is commonly held by relief and aid workers, donors, and government officials (Clark). However, the so-called refugee dependency syndrome has received much criticism (Clark, 1985; Kibreab, 1993; Waldron, 1987) because of its association with victim blaming and failing to challenge the refugee system: itself the likely the source of such dependency. Specifically, Clark discusses how use of this term incorrectly overstates the extent to which refugees are responsible for such dependency, which is more likely attributable to the powerful role the refugee system itself plays in creating and perpetuating this problem.

In consideration of the local context, a participatory approach to building and assessing community capacity was a means to re-build power of community members and resulted in increased community ownership of the program and a more active role in program planning and management (Wright et al., 2010). However, local RTP community leaders were frequently unable to independently make requests of other NGOs and to have such requests approved. To appreciate the workings of this system, the same requests would often be granted if they were made by an expatriate (i.e., a project coordinator). This was emphasized by one community member who explained: "In these organizations, if they see an expert from another organization, an expatriate or a Tanzanian, it is important. His importance is more notable than that of a refugee." This situation is consistent with Jackson et al. (2003) who discuss how the policies and regulations set out by organizations, agencies, and governments can play a key factor in hindering individual or collective action. Importantly, the policies and regulations of other organizations resulted in both Tanzanian and refugee staff working for those organizations being unresponsive to RTP program leaders; this undermined coaches' and community leaders' abilities to solve camp-level problems involving negotiations with NGO workers or other refugees working as staff for those NGOs.

Such a hierarchical system directly hindered community capacity building because it promoted powerlessness among refugees, even among those who challenged the notion of refugee dependence through actions which demonstrated motivation and initiative. Specifically, the system impeded RTP community members from exercising control over the RTP project due to Tanzanian aid workers, as well as Burundians working for various NGOs, unwillingness to recognize other refugees as having any sort of program authority. Moreover, unresponsiveness to requests made by RTP community members also affected the RTP community's ability to mobilize resources in the larger Mtendeli community, since coaches were often not able to acquire resources or assistance from other NGOs without the help of project coordinators. Thus, the RTP community and the researcher were essentially working to build community capacity within a system that focused on aid, care, and maintenance over self-sufficiency and development. Thus, capacity building as a development process faces enormous challenges in the current refugee assistance system.

Lessons learned

Social elements of community capacity

A weakness of the domains approach is that it does not take into account the social or relationship dynamic among participants nor how this might affect assessment within specific domains. Specifically, Laverack's (1999, 2003) model of community capacity does not directly incorporate social elements of community capacity such as community cohesion, sense of community, or relationships among community members. Instead, he and other authors (Laverack & Labonte, 2000; Laverack, 2001; Laverack & Wallerstein, 2001) propose that the organizational elements (i.e., the nine domains) act as proxies for such social elements. Importantly, other models of community capacity (Bopp et al., 2000; Bopp & Bopp, 2004; Chaskin, 2001; Goodman et al., 1998; Hawe et al., 2000; Maclellan-Wright et al., 2007) identify sense of community, or some similar construct, as a domain of influence on community capacity.

At the end of the one year between assessments, a noticeable tension was apparent among community leaders and this rift prevented leaders from collaborating to carry out program activities. Nevertheless, at the final assessment, key stakeholders determined the RTP community to have a high level of capacity in the domain 'Local Leadership'. Understandably, evaluation of leadership proved complicated because a number of the stakeholders present at the assessment were those involved in the aforementioned circumstances. Thus, it would have been difficult for other community stakeholders to assess leadership as low or to examine the existing power struggles when those involved were present. A domain focusing on community social dynamics (e.g., 'sense of community' or 'community cohesion') could be incorporated into Laverack's (2003) community capacity methodology; an essential aspect of this domain would be a culturally appropriate method for resolving conflicts; one that is developed by and agreed upon by community members. This may, in the future, help to prevent or resolve similar tensions.

Shared vision

A second element that was missing from the assessment process revolves around the concept 'shared vision'. Shared vision is defined as a description of a community or program at some point in the future, depicted in a clear enough manner so that all people involved can imagine it (Bopp et al., 2000; Frank & Smith, 1999). At the time of the research, RTP's organizational delivery model involved sending teams of international project coordinators to introduce, develop, and implement Sport for Development programs in majority world communities – the aim of these programs was that local volunteer coaches would then provide continuous and regular sport and play opportunities for children and youth in the community. However, this overall objective was not mutually defined. In fact, it is not clear whether project coordinators and community members collectively developed and agreed to any shared vision for the program. The words of my colleague exemplified the challenges that stemmed from a lack of a mutually defined shared vision:

> "I think part of the problem is that our expectations of what we want coaches to do and their understanding of what they're supposed to be doing, I don't think these are synonymous. I don't think their interpretation matches our expectations. Maybe our expectations of them haven't been set out clearly enough by us. I think there is a disconnect between what we expect them to do to meet community needs and what they think they should be doing to meet those needs".

Both Smith et al. (2001) and Smith et al. (2003) discuss how having a shared vision is crucial to the success of health promotion initiatives and increased community capacity. Other community capacity building approaches (Bopp et al.; Bopp & Bopp, 2004; Frank & Smith, 1999) confirm the importance of shared vision and incorporate it in their methodology as a domain that influences capacity building. A collectively defined and agreed upon shared vision may have emphasized expectations of the program and the responsibility of both community members and project coordinators in contributing to its success. This, in turn, may have increased accountability to one another and may have made continued community participation, community ownership, and program sustainability achievable in the long term. Authors who advocate the importance of shared vision (Bopp et al; Bopp & Bopp; Smith et al., 2001, 2003) would likely argue for the incorporation of this domain into Laverack's (2003) methodology for assessing and building community capacity. Still, important questions remain: should collectively developing a shared vision happen? If so, at what point should developing this shared vision take place? And is this something that needs to be evolving and updated continuously over time?

Conclusion

The findings from our research suggest that the domains approach was an effective tool for assessing and building community capacity in the context of a Sport for Development program. By way of the domains approach community members were able to critically look at the impact of their participation in the RTP program, determine the current level of capacity in each of the nine domains, and generate knowledge and awareness regarding the community's strengths and weaknesses. This process was greatly aided by use of the spider web diagram, which was useful for visually illustrating changes in community capacity. However, focus on the qualitative data provided by stakeholders was essential for providing justification for changes in community capacity as well as giving voice to community members. Importantly, the strategic planning that occurred was essential for translating the knowledge gained from the assessments into community-applicable solutions. This resulted in the development of community capacity objectives which ran parallel to the RTP program. For that reason, community capacity building became operational and an actual end goal of the program.

Future use of the model may wish to include 'sense of community', or a similar construct focusing on community social dynamics, as a domain of influence on community capacity. As well, developing a mutually defined shared vision, by both community members and project coordinators, may also be important as it may emphasize expectations of both community members and project coordinators and the responsibility of each in contributing to program success. This is a possible direction for future research. Overall, this research provides one model or outline for community capacity building and evaluation in Sport for Development and may aid RTP, as well as others, in future program implementation and capacity building.

References

Bopp, M., & Bopp, J. (2004). Welcome to the swamp: Addressing community capacity in ecohealth research and intervention. *EcoHealth, 1,* 24-34.

Bopp, M., GermAnn, K., Bopp, J., Baugh Littlejohns, L., & N. Smith (2000). *Assessing community capacity for change.* Red Deer, AB: David Thompson Health Region and Four Worlds Centre for Development Learning.

Bush, R., Dower, J., & Mutch, A. (2002). *Community capacity index manual.* Centre for Primary Health Care, University of Queensland. Available at: http://www.nursesreg.health.nsw.gov.au/public-health/health-promotion/capacity-building/community/comm_cap_manual.pdf, (Accessed 12th March 2012).

Chaskin, R. J. (2001). Building community capacity: A definitional framework and case studies from a comprehensive community initiative. *Urban Affairs Review, 36,* 291-323.

Crump, A. (1998). *The A to Z of world development: A unique reference book on global issues for the new century.* Oxford, UK: New Internationalist Pub.

Cuthbert, M. (1985). Evaluation encounters in Third World settings: a Caribbean perspective. In Patton, M. Q. (Ed.), *Culture and evaluation* (pp. 29-35). San Francisco, CA: Jossey-Bass.

Easterling, D., Gallagher, K., Drisko, J., & Johnson, T. (1998). *Promoting health by building community capacity: Evidence and implications for grantmakers.* Denver, COL: The Colorado Trust.

Frank, F., & Smith, A. (1999). *The community development handbook: A tool to build community capacity.* Quebec, CAN: Human Resources Development Canada.

Gibbon, M. (1999) *Meetings with meaning: Health dynamics in rural Nepal.* Unpublished doctoral dissertation, South Bank University, London, UK.

Gibbon, M., Labonte, R., & Laverack, G. (2002). Evaluating community capacity. *Health Social Care in the Community, 10(6),* 485-491.

Goetzel, R. Z., Anderson, D. R., Whitmer, R. W., Ozminkowski, R. J., Dunn, R. L., & Wasserman, J. (1998). The relationship between modifiable health risks and health care expenditures: An analysis of the multi-employer HERO health risk and cost database. *Journal of Occupational and Environmental Medicine, 40,* 843-854.

Goodman, R., Speers, M., McLeroy, K., Fawcett, S., Kegler, M., Parker, E., Rathgeb Smith, S., Sterling, T., & N. Wallerstein (1998). Identifying and defining the dimensions of community capacity to provide a basis for measurement. *Health Education & Behaviour, 25,* 258-278.

Harrell-Bond, B., Asiku, E., De Lorenzo, M., Lammers, E., & Kayiira, J. L. (2000). *DanChurchAid Evaluation of the Tanganyika Christian Refugee Service (TCRS) Refugee Project in Kibondo District, Tanzania: 5 – 9 January 2000.*

Hawe, P., King, L., Noort, M., Jordens, C., & Lloyd, B. (2000). *Indicators to help with capacity building in health promotion.* Sydney, AUS: Australian Centre for Health Promotion/NSW Health.

Hawe, P., Noort, M., King, L., & Jordens, C. (1997). Multiplying health gains: The criticial role of capacity-building within health promotion programs. *Health Policy, 39,* 29-42.

in motion. (2004). *Community Capacity Assessment: Developmental progress and challenges for in motion.* Presented to the *in motion* Partners, CAHR in motion Research, University of Saskatchewan, SK: *in motion.*

Jackson, S. F., Cleverly, S., Poland, B., Burman, D., Edwards, R., & Robertson, A. (2003). Working with Toronto neighbourhoods toward developing indicators of community capacity. *Health Promotion International, 18,* 339-350.

Jeffery, B., Abonyi, S., Labonte, R., & Duncan, K. (2006). Engaging numbers: Developing health indicators that matter for First Nations and Inuit people. *Journal of Aboriginal Health,* September 2006, 44-52.

Jones, A., & Laverack, G. (2003). *Building capable communities within a sustainable livelihoods approach: Experiences from Central Asia.* Available at: http://www.livelihoods.org/lessons/docs/Kyrgyz_SLLPC, (Accessed 12th March 2012).

Katzmarzyk, P. T., Gledhill, N., & Shepard, R. J. (2000). The economic burden of physical inactivity in Canada. *Canadian Medical Association Journal, 163,* 1435-1440.

Labonte, R., Bell Woodard, G., Chad, K., & Laverack, G. (2002). Community capacity building: A parallel track for health promotion programs. *Canadian Journal of Public Health, 93,* 181-182.

Labonte, R., & Laverack, G. (2001a). Capacity building in health promotion, Part 1: For whom? And for what purpose? *Critical Public Health, 11,* 111-127.

Labonte, R., & Laverack, G. (2001b). Capacity building in health promotion, Part 2: Whose use? And with what measurement? *Critical Public Health, 11,* 128-138.

Laverack, G. (1999). *Addressing the contradictions between discourse and practice in health promotion.* Unpublished doctoral dissertation, Deakin University, Melbourne, Australia.

Laverack, G. (2003). Building capable communities: Experiences in a rural Fijian context. *Health Promotion International, 18,* 99-106.

Laverack, G. (2006). Evaluating community capacity: Visual representation and interpretation. *Community Development Journal, 41,* 266-276.

Laverack, G. (2007). *Health promotion practice.* London, UK: Open University Press.

Laverack, G., & Labonte, R. (2000). A planning framework for community empowerment goals within health promotion. *Health Policy and Policy, 15,* 255-262.

Laverack, G., & Thangphet, S. (2007) Building community capacity for locally managed ecotourism in Northern Thailand. *Community Development Journal, 44,* 172-185.

Laverack, G., & Wallerstein, N. (2001). Measuring community empowerment: A fresh look at the organizational domains. *Health Promotion International, 16,* 179-185.

Leonard, M. (1998). *A sociological perspective of sport (5th Ed.).* Boston, MA: Allyn and Bacon.

Maclellan-Wright, M. F., Anderson, D., Barber, S., Smith, N., Cantin, B., Felix, R., & Raine, K. (2007). The development of measures of community capacity for community-based funding programs in Canada. *Health Promotion International, 22,* 299-306.

McKnight, J. L., & Kretzmann, J. P. (1996). *Mapping community capacity.* Evanston, IL: Institute for Policy Research Northwestern University.

New South Wales Health Department. (2001). *A framework for building capacity to improve health.* Sydney, AUS: New South Wales Health Department.

Rifkin, S. B. (1990). *Community participation in maternal and child health/ family planning programmes.* Geneva, CH: World Health Organization.

Right To Play. (2002). *Every child has the right to play: Right To Play 2002 annual report.* AvILble at: http://www.righttoplay.com/pdfs/annual_report_final.pdf, (Accessed 12th March 2012).

Right To Play. (2005). *When children play, the world wins: Right To Play annual report 2005. Available at: http://www.righttoplay.com/site/DocServer/FINAL_low_res_PDF_of_Annual_Report_05.pdf?docID=358, (Accessed 12th March 2012).*

Right To Play. (2006). *When children play, the world wins: Right To Play annual report 2006.* Available at: http://www.righttoplay.com/site/DocServer/12509_RTP_report_L.pdf?docID=6381 (Accessed 12th March 2012).

Right To Play. (2007). *When children play, the world wins: Right To Play annual report 2007.* Available at: http://rtpca.convio.net/site/DocServer/AnnualReport2007.pdf?docID=9761, (Accessed 12th March 2012).

Right To Play. (2008). *Results: Progress Report June 2008.* Available at: http://rtpca.convio.net/site/DocServer/RTP_Results_Magazine_2008.pdf?docID=9661, (Accessed 12th March 2012).

Schuftan, C. (1996). The community development dilemma: What is really empowering? *Community Development Journal, 31,* 260-264.

Skinner, S. (1997). Building community strengths: a resource book on capacity building. London, UK: Community Development Foundation.

Smith, N., Baugh Littlejohns, L., & Roy, D. (2003). *Measuring community capacity: State of the field review and recommendations for future research.* Red Deer, AB: David Thompson Health Region.

Smith, N., Baugh Littlejohns, L., & Thompson, D. (2001). Shaking out the cobwebs: Insights into community capacity and its relation to health outcomes. *Community Development Journal, 36,* 20-41.

Sport for Development and Peace International Working Group (2008). *Harnessing the power of sport for development and peace: Recommendations to governments.* Available at: http://iwg.sportanddev.org/floor/CMS?&server=iwg&lang=en&item_categoryID=13&item_ID=65, (Accessed 12th march 2012).

United Nations High Commissioner for Refugees (2005a). *United Rep. of Tanzania: 2005 UNHCR statistical yearbook.* Available at: http://www.unhcr.org/statistics/STATISTICS/4641bec90.pdf, (Accessed 12th march 2012).

United Nations Inter-Agency Task Force on Sport for Development and Peace. (2003). *Sport for development and peace: Towards achieving the Millennium Development Goals.* United Nations.

Vuori, I. M. (2001). Health benefits of physical activity with special reference to interaction with diet. *Public Health Nutrition, 4,* 517-528.

Warburton, D., Nicol, C., & Bredin, S. (2006). Health benefits of physical activity: The evidence. *Canadian Medical Association Journal, 174,* 801-809.

Waters, T. (2003). Ethnicity and Burundi's refugees. *African Studies Quarterly,* 68-75. Available at: http://www.africa.ufl.edu/asq/v7/viii.PDF/v7i1a5.pdf, (Accessed 12th March 2012).

World Bank (2007). *Tanzania Country Brief.* Available at: http://web.worldbank.org/WBSITE/EXTERNAL/COUNTRIES/AFRICAEXT/TANZAIAEXTN/0,,menuPK:287345-pagePK:141132-piPK:141107-theSitePK:258799,00.html, (Accessed 12th march 2012).

World Health Organization (1999). *The WHO global initiative on active living.* Geneva, Switzerland. World Health Organization Department of Health Promotion. Available at: http://www.who.int/moveforhealth/publications/mfh_gialwhorev2.pdf, (Accessed 12th March 2012).

Part V
Case Studies of Sport, Peace & Development

Chapter 25

Sport as a Tool for Participatory Education

Exploring the Grassroots Soccer Methodology

Emma Colucci

The HIV and AIDS Situation

While the HIV and AIDS pandemic ranks as one of the major health crises of the human race, its impact has clearly ravaged the world unevenly. Of the 33.4 million cases worldwide, 67% are concentrated in sub-Saharan Africa (UNAIDS, 2009). In 2008, 68% of new HIV infections among adults, and 91% of new HIV infections among children occurred in this region leading to a total of 1.9 million new HIV infections in sub-Saharan Africa (UNAIDS, 2009). This same region accounted for an overwhelming 72% of all AIDS related deaths in that same year (UNAIDS, 2009). In South Africa alone, the number of annual AIDS related deaths went from under 50,000 in 1995, to 180,000 in 2001, and even further to 350,000 in 2007 (GRS, 2007; WHO, 2008). Perhaps the most troublesome aspect of these statistics is that this devastating disease, that continues to kill so many, is 100% preventable.

Though many steps have been taken by various countries to address the *treatment* of the pandemic, UNAIDS (2008) reports that only slightly more than half of the countries impacted by the HIV pandemic have made goals for *prevention* strategies. Such strategies are generally poorly funded and under-emphasized in many countries. However, without proper evidence-based prevention programs, an estimated 60 million men, women and children will become infected with HIV by the year 2015 (GRS, 2007). One major underlying issue concerning HIV prevention is the lack of accurate and complete information regarding ways to avoid becoming infected.

Valuing the importance of information and education, the UN Declaration of Commitment on HIV and AIDS (2001) set a global goal of ensuring that 95% of young people attain comprehensive knowledge about HIV by the year 2010. It is estimated from surveys of 64 different countries, however, that currently only 40% of males and 38% of females in the 15 to 24 year age category have accurate and useful knowledge about protecting oneself from HIV, such as condom usage (UNAIDS, 2008). For instance, in Zimbabwe, an estimated 1.8 million people are living with HIV, yet only 10% of sexually active males and 11% of sexually active females in the 15-19 year age range use condoms (Clark, Friedrich, Ndlovu, Neilands, & McFarland, 2006). These statistics on HIV and AIDS knowledge are troublesome as African youth are especially at risk with 45% of new HIV infection rates occurring between the ages of 15 to 24 (UNAIDS, 2008). Without proper prevention programs, it is estimated that 50% of youth in the southern African region will become HIV positive in their lifetime (GRS, 2007). It is for this reason that new tools for positive social change aimed at HIV prevention require exploration.

Top-down Learning: Paulo Freire's Banking Model of Education

Conveying important messages about healthy behavior in order to prevent HIV and AIDS is of vital importance. The way in which the messages are conveyed, however, has an immense impact on how effectively the healthy behavior will be adopted and implemented by the target audience. In his book *Pedagogy of the Oppressed*, Paulo Freire (2007) discusses the 'banking model' of education and the detriments of a one-way flow of information. Freire (2007) states, "Education is suffering from narration sickness" (p. 71). When information is only narrated, it becomes lifeless and disconnected from reality. Memory rather than critical or independent thinking is what is most highly valued in the banking model of education. This achieves neither true knowledge nor true culture in an education system that, paradoxically, claims to value these two important aspects of our cognitive world. For Freire (2007), only dialogue can generate independent thinking, and only authentic education investigates this way of thinking.

According to Freire (2007), "Human beings are not built in silence, but in word, in work, in action-reflection" (p. 88). The ability to speak and have those words valued should be the right of everyone, not just the privilege of a few. However, in the banking model of education, the one-way flow of information negates the voice and knowledge base of the students. Students do not learn to trust their independent thinking capabilities and thus have less confidence in their own knowledge base. As a result, the development of self-efficacy, whereby a person feels more apt to deal with and control a certain situation, is greatly inhibited. The teacher in the banking model of education also misses what can be learned from the students as the top-down learning structure deems their knowledge base as unimportant.

For Freire (2007), authentic education investigates the process of independent thinking and understands reality as a complex system that is constantly being developed and recreated. Comprehending reality as a process being shaped by one's own thoughts and actions allows people to understand their ability to impact upon the world. However, oftentimes in the banking model of education, only one view of reality is perpetuated as what is "right". This is fed to the students as an objective truth despite its subjective make-up. Thus, students are not taught to critically assess what they learn or think independently about their own realities. The danger in this structure lies in the fact that without the ability to think critically and independently, it becomes difficult to be aware of one's ability to impact upon, or transform their realities, thus further undermining the self-efficacy of the students. This also greatly inhibits the students' creative powers as they are transformed into receiving objects rather than active and conscious beings, or spectators rather than re-creators of the world (Freire, 2007).

During the educational process, Freire (2007) stresses the importance of teachers challenging their students and presenting content as a problem to be worked through and discussed rather than static information to be absorbed. This initiates a dialogical learning structure whereby students are able to discover the answers as part of an independent rather than controlled process. A major component missing from the banking model of education is the act of dialogue. Freire (2007) writes, "Without dialogue there is no true communication, and without communication there can be no true education" (p. 92-93). The importance of dialoguing with people rather than simply telling them what to do or how to think lies in its ability to foster independent thought (Freire, 2007). It is only through critical dialogue and reflection that learning can turn into independent thought and thus independent action by the students. In the banking model of education, however, students develop a somewhat 'submerged consciousness,' which is unable to realize its independent and transformative potential (Freire, 2007).

Participatory Learning: Moving Beyond the Banking Model of Education

Freire (2007) discusses the importance of students developing what he refers to as 'conscientização,' which is the "process of learning to perceive social, political, and economic contradictions, and to take action against the oppressive elements of reality" (p. 35). To be aware of such situations and to be able to transform them, the ability to think confidently, critically and independently is essential. The more a person believes in his or her ability to create or affect positive change in his or her life, the more likely that person will be to take the necessary action. This is due to an increased sense of personal agency, thus making self-efficacy one of the most important factors in the adoption of behaviour change (Bandura, 2004). As discussed previously, the banking model of education does not provide the necessary environment for students to develop critical and independent thought that enhances their self-efficacy. What Freire (2007) posits as the resolution to the implications of the banking model of education is what he refers to as 'participatory,' 'dialogical' or 'problem-posing'[1] education.

An important aspect of the participatory style of learning is the sense of value that is established in the student's voice and knowledge base. Freire (2007) stresses the importance of acknowledging that every perception of something is shaped by background intuitions and experiences, and that reality is a subjective and ongoing entity. Rather than teaching 'facts' that are to be accepted at face value, problem-posing education initiates dialogue with the students whereby perceptions of situations are discussed. Through the classroom dialogue, students are able to voice their thoughts while also building their independent thinking capabilities. This style of education ensures that the students are engaging in the process of reflection and inquiry. Furthermore, this encourages their ability to independently and critically assess reality, thus fostering the first steps of conscientização (Freire, 2007).

Problem-posing education focuses on developing content somewhat *with* the students rather than simply creating the content *for* them without considering their context, input or knowledge base (Freire, 2007). This creates a situation whereby students are better able to address issues pertinent to their own realties. From Freire's (2007) perspective, students are more apt to engage in personal expression of their thoughts in discussions of situations in which they can recognize themselves. Thus, authentic education must investigate the process of thinking and the fact that one's view of the world reflects his or her own situation, thereby making the student view of the world highly important to the process of self-reflection and personal transformation. By thinking and discussing their own views of the world, students are able to gain a feeling of being masters of their own thoughts.

A horizontal relationship with mutual trust between the dialoguers is an essential component to dialogical education. In order to create this horizontal relationship, the educators must understand the conditions in which the student's thoughts and language are framed in order to communicate effectively. Without understanding the conditions in which peoples' realities are formed, education cannot be effective (Freire, 2007). Through dialogical learning, there is a reconciliation of the relationship between teachers and students. While teachers undoubtedly have the task of contributing fundamental subjects and information that have not been addressed by the students, they must always be cognitive rather than simply narrative

---

1. The terms 'participatory education,' 'dialogical education,' and 'problem-posing education' will be used interchangeably throughout this chapter.

throughout the learning process (Freire, 2007). The participatory educator must constantly reform his or her reflections in those of the students in order to foster a system whereby the students become critical co-investigators in dialogue with the teacher throughout the learning process.

One of the most important aspects of problem-posing, participatory, or dialogical learning is the emphasis on horizontal dialogue and discussion rather than top-down information transmission that is found within the banking model of education. Engaging in dialogue not only allows the students a voice in their learning process while better understanding their thoughts and views on reality, but as Freire (2007) stresses, it is an essential component of praxis; an essential component in taking education and reflection and turning them into action. When thinking independently and critically about content through the dialogical learning process, students are able to understand their ability to shape and impact upon their own realities. Students are encouraged to turn knowledge into action by seeing the world as a reality in progress rather than a static entity. The importance of praxis lies in the fact that both reflection and action upon the world are necessary in order to be able to transform one's life. This is how detrimental situations are overcome – by the reflection upon them through the process of discussion, and the understanding and eventual belief in one's power to impact upon that situation. Both reflection and action are fostered through dialogical learning.

The co-investigational character of participatory learning creates an environment conducive to the development of conscientização and self-efficacy through mastery experiences. Mastery experiences occur when an individual's acquisition of the cognitive, behavioral and self-regulatory tools necessary for making positive life choices develop through his or her own successes and failures (Bandura, 1995; 2004). Participatory learning creates an environment whereby students are able to think independently and develop the healthiest thinking patterns through their *own* cognitive abilities that they are able to carry with them throughout their lives. True dialogue, and thus true education, enables a way of thinking that sees reality as a process and not a static entity; a way of thinking that does not separate itself from action (Freire, 2007). By instilling ideas of confidence, critique and action as part of the educational process, behavioral and social change are more likely to develop over time. Through dialogical learning, pedagogy is used as an instrument to encourage independent and critical thought that leads to action and affect upon reality.

Introduction to Grassroot Soccer

Grassroot Soccer (GRS) is an organization that "provides African youth with the knowledge, skills and support to live HIV free" (www.grassrootsoccer.org). The curriculum is taught to the youth by GRS 'coaches,' who are local soccer players from the areas in which the program is delivered.

Through the use of interactive soccer activities, information regarding HIV and AIDS prevention and positive life skills are discussed with the youth in order to combat the pandemic at the community level.

For example, one game often played in the GRS program is referred to as "Risk Field" (Personal Field Research, 2009, South Africa). It starts out as a fun relay race where students form four or five different teams dribble a soccer ball through a line of cones. In the first round, the team that gets through all of the cones first without touching any of them with the ball wins. In the second round, the GRS coaches tell the students that the cones on the field represent risks such as unprotected sex, drug and alcohol abuse, or multiple sexual partners that could lead them to contracting HIV. The students then weave in-between the cones with the ball and are forced to do one push-up for every cone they hit. This represents the personal consequences of risky behavior that may lead to the contraction of HIV. During the third round, for each cone the students hit, their whole team must do a push-up in order to represent the way in which their participation in risky behavior that leads to the contraction of HIV affects not only them, but their friends and family (represented by your team). In the last round, each cone that the students hit forces everyone playing the game to do push-ups, emphasizing the impact on the whole community (represented by the whole class) by their contraction of the HIV virus.

This game is not only fun and stimulating, but it teaches a very important message that the students more successfully internalize as they are active participants in the learning process. Each activity in the GRS sessions is followed by a discussion period known as the 'team talk.' This gives the students a chance to discuss their views, ask questions, and gain more information about HIV and AIDS from the coaches. To better understand the efficacy of GRS's educational methods, and the ways in which the program is both delivered and received, I travelled to Port Elizabeth, South Africa in March of 2009 in order to complete two months of participant observation and interview research on the GRS program.

Participatory Learning and the Grassroot Soccer Methodology

With a focus on providing vital HIV and AIDS information along with guidance for making healthy life choices, Grassroot Soccer takes a unique approach to behavior-changing education. GRS taps into the universal popularity of soccer and the innate interactive qualities of sport to deliver a highly dialogical education structure. Its focus is on providing youth with essential HIV and AIDS information through a style of education that fosters critical and independent thought, and self-efficacy. The GRS program empowers youth to combat HIV and AIDS as they become equipped with essential information along with the confidence and skills to turn their knowledge into action.

Listening to the Students

An essential component of the Grassroot Soccer program is listening to what the students have to say. In the organization's curriculum, referred to as SKILLZ (GRS, 2009), part of the 'Be's' of successful coaching and facilitation is to 'Be an Elephant' due to the fact that elephants have big ears and small mouths. This encourages coaches to first and foremost listen to what the students are saying. The coaches are to facilitate rather than dominate dialogue by asking questions that initiate vital conversations (GRS, 2009). The GRS style of education, as opposed to the banking model of education, allows for material about HIV and AIDS to be presented to students as information to be worked through together, as opposed to information being statically transmitted from the teacher to the student. This invokes Freire's (2007) notion of participatory education and its ability to encourage students to think critically and independently about what is being taught.

An example of how this educational methodology is played out through the GRS curriculum is an activity called 'Fact or Nonsense' (Personal Field Research, 2009, South Africa). The coach will read out statements about HIV and AIDS which then have to be deemed either 'fact' or 'nonsense' by the students. In this activity, the students are lined up facing each other and must run to their partner in order to discuss the statement about HIV and AIDS and why they think it is true or false. The students must then run back to their original spots in order to show they have come to a decision about the statement. The students then discuss their reasons for thinking one way or the other as a group while the coach listens and facilitates without divulging the correct answer. Once the group has debated the topic, the coach reveals whether or not the statement is true, and explains why. This begins the process of shared discourse rather than following a top-down line of communication.

Not only by seeing the program in action through personal research, but also through personal interviews, many benefits of the GRS participatory style of education came to light. In fact, 100% of my interview subjects stated that they truly felt that the GRS program really listened to what they had to say (Personal Interviews, 2009, South Africa). When asked how the GRS program compared to the school style of education, one student stated "When I'm in class I don't feel the same way as when I'm in GRS...I feel too small to talk about those things [HIV and AIDS related topics] with the big people in school" (Personal Interview P26, 2009, South Africa). Another student stated, "If you said something that was wrong, they [the GRS coaches] would give you another chance and not shout at you – they would help you get to the right answer" (Personal Interview P9, 2009, South Africa). This exemplifies how information is presented as something to be worked through rather than simply fed to the students. When asked why she felt the GRS program listened to what she had to say, another participant stated, "Because sometimes they want explanations from us about how we feel about GRS, and also what do you want them [the coaches and program] to change" (Personal Interview P36, 2009, South Africa). The students are able to speak their minds while having their words thought about and considered by the coaches. Furthermore, a GRS staff member and former coach, stated, With GRS, you don't only get to be taught, at the same time you get to talk such that people get to learn from you, so I mean, the participants also get to express themselves...rather than just sitting and being passive (Personal Interview S1, 2009, South Africa). The GRS program truly listens to, and appreciates what the students have to say.

Understanding and Valuing the Student Realities

Unlike the banking model of education's presentation of reality as one objective truth, GRS understands the importance of context, and acknowledges that reality is a process shaped by several different factors in the lives of the students. One way in which GRS is able to get to the root of many issues behind risky behavior amongst youth that can lead to HIV and AIDS is by searching for the 'bottom story.' In a GRS session, the 'top story' would be a key message, such as 'always wear a condom.' This message, however, will only go so far without getting to the bottom of why it is not happening. The bottom, or root of the story is *why* condoms are not being used, which relates to social beliefs and activities in the community. When interviewing one GRS staff member, he stated:

> "The idea is that it [the curriculum] becomes tailored to each group of kids. So, you know, if kids already know about condoms, if you have an hour with kids don't just spend time saying "condoms prevent HIV." Spend time actually discussing what we call the 'bottom story.' Get to what keeps us from using condoms, you know, what the challenges to using condoms are consistently. Within a relationship, if a girl is dating an older guy that doesn't want to use condoms, you know, those are the conversations that need to happen. Quite frankly, my guess is they're probably not happening in schools where it's just a teacher with a book in front of them talking about the biology of HIV".
> (Personal Interview S4, 2009, South Africa).

The way to get to these 'bottom stories' is by listening to the students and encouraging them to speak freely about their lives. When asked if the coaches really listen to what the students are saying, one interviewee responded, "Yes, and then they apply their knowledge to your situation" (Personal Interview P4, 2009, South Africa). This exemplifies the GRS program's recognition of the diversity of student contexts as opposed to traditional singular realities.

In the SKILLZ (GRS, 2009) curriculum, one of the '11 Be's of SKILLZ Coaching' is to 'Be Aware.' This guideline encourages coaches to understand the background of the students, as well as the issues that they face, while also ensuring that each student has the opportunity to participate in the discussions. Furthering this point, Freire (2007) states, "authentic thinking, thinking that is concerned about reality, does not take place in ivory tower isolation, but only in communication" (p. 77). There are a lot of myths about HIV and AIDS that are socially constructed and widely believed. The students are just as valuable a source of information as the coach in the sense that dialoguing with them and learning their social beliefs will provide deeper understanding into their realities and reveal how they can best combat the pandemic in their context. In this sense, the coaches are learning from the participants while the participants are learning from the coaches, creating a co-investigational learning environment.

Placing importance on context also emphasizes that realities are not fixed and can be molded through thoughts and actions. The first step to realizing one's potential to shape his or her reality is to foster independent and critical thinking throughout the whole educational process. Activities such as the previously mentioned 'Fact or Nonsense' not only provide good information about HIV and AIDS, but they get the GRS participants to think for themselves and go through the process of making their own choices without being told the information right away. This is how self-efficacy through mastery experiences develops, leading to a better understanding of one's own cognitive capabilities. When discussing the curriculum, one GRS coach stated: "It makes [the students] think on their own. They are the ones who are coming up with their own issues and their own opinions" (Personal Interview C3, 2009, South Africa). HIV and AIDS facts and behavioral information will only go so far if the students are not trained to think on their own and make their own choices. This style of dialogical learning not only informs the students of important information about HIV and AIDS, but it enables the students to be able to put that information to use in their lives outside the classroom by encouraging them to use their own cognitive capabilities to avoid risky behaviors.

In addition to gaining important information, students also learn their own strengths and abilities to make the right life choices. This is further revealed through activities such as 'Praise Circles' that occur at the end of various GRS sessions (Personal Field Research, 2009, South Africa). The point of the praise circle is for students to stand up in front of the class in pairs and congratulate each other while also acknowledging their own accomplishments. Knowing one's strengths helps to build the confidence GRS students need to be able to use the HIV and AIDS information in the face of pressure to participate in risky behavior. When asked how the students felt about themselves now that they knew more information about HIV and AIDS, one student stated: "I feel proud of myself...I feel very good because I can make decisions now that the first time [around] I couldn't do, but now it's much better" (Personal Interview P36, 2009, South Africa). Another student stated that he felt "so good because now I can take care of myself" (Personal Interview P22, 2009, South Africa). Taking care of oneself not only relates to the information learned, but, as one student stated, "I've learned that you must make your own decisions" (Personal Interview P15, 2009, South Africa). When asked how she felt after the GRS program, another student stated, "I feel like I can cope better with challenges" (Personal Interview P4, 2009, South Africa). Armed with the right information and the right mental capacities and attitudes, GRS students become empowered through their belief in their own capabilities.

349

Dialogue and Action

An essential component of dialogical education is providing an environment where students are able to speak comfortably and freely. One of the biggest concerns with HIV and AIDS is that it is a taboo subject to discuss amongst families and friends, and even in school. One student interviewed during my personal research stated that: "Due to our culture, our parents aren't supposed to talk to us about sensitive issues" (Personal Interview P14, 2009, South Africa). A comfortable speaking environment is especially important when dealing with sensitive issues relating to risky behaviors such as unprotected sex, drug use, etc., that could lead to the contraction of HIV. In order to create this 'safe space' for dialogue in education, the teacher and students must be on the same level. Freire (2007) notes the importance of reconciling the strict vertical teacher-student relationship found within the banking model of education, and maintaining a horizontal relationship based on equal sharing, trust and respect. The SKILLZ (GRS, 2009) curriculum emphasizes this point by encouraging coaches to 'be a team player' through using language the participants can relate to, and also asking for advice or feedback from both the participants and other coaches on what can be improved in the program. The SKILLZ (GRS, 2009) coaches are encouraged to also 'be referees' and let the students laugh or giggle when discussing sensitive topics or vocabulary such as 'penis' or 'vagina,' while ensuring that no one student in particular is being laughed at in order to maintain a comfortable and safe speaking space. The coaches are instructed to never talk down to the students and are encouraged to be able to laugh with the students while ensuring the dialogue stays on track and focused on the key message of the lesson.

When asked how their experiences with GRS differed from their school experience, all of the participants interviewed stated that there was more opportunity to talk and have their voices heard with GRS (Personal Interviews, 2009, South Africa). A more comfortable speaking environment, where teachers (coaches) listened intently to what they said and encouraged them to speak about what was on their minds emerged as the contributing factors (Personal Interviews, 2009, South Africa). One student explained that the GRS sessions and coaches made her feel happy because she was able to talk openly about things she had not been able to talk about before with her parents or other teachers (Personal Interview P24, 2009, South Africa). When asked how the GRS style of teaching differed from the education received in class, one student stated:

> "You see, here at school, we can't tell the teachers about our feelings, but at GRS, you can tell them about your feelings...I won't tell my teacher things because I feel embarrassed, but...I feel comfortable when I speak to GRS".
> (Personal Interview P28, 2009, South Africa).

When asked about her schoolteachers, one student stated, "Some [school teachers] are so aggressive and they shout," however, when asked about the GRS coaches, she said, "I feel very comfortable, because, it's like...[the coaches] don't judge you, they hear what you have to say" (Personal Interview P4, 2009, South Africa). Another student stated that the coaches are very caring and they ask the students a lot of questions to find out how HIV and AIDS has affected them personally, which encourages the students to open up and speak their minds (Personal Interview P9, 2009, South Africa). When asked about speaking in the GRS sessions, 87.8% of the students stated that they were comfortable enough to speak openly about topics covered in the program (Personal Interviews, 2009, South Africa). Many of the students stated that this type of relationship was not the same with teachers in their school classes (Personal Interviews, 2009, South Africa).

In addition to the emphasis on dialogue, mutual trust, and respect, GRS further fosters a deeper empathy between the coaches and the students by hiring coaches that are from the areas in which the GRS program is implemented. In this way, the program maintains cultural appropriateness as the coaches better understand the realities of their students (Botcheva & Huffman, 2004). At the beginning of each new GRS program, the coaches are instructed to share what is referred to as the 'Coach's Story' (Personal Field Research, 2009, South Africa). During this activity, the coaches are instructed to share how HIV and AIDS have impacted upon their lives through a personal story. They are then to discuss how they have taken action against HIV and AIDS while also revealing other ways in which they have bounced back from bad situations in their lives. The coaches act as social models whose positive life choices have helped them deal with the impact of HIV and AIDS in their lives. The goal of the 'Coach's Story' is to testify to the realities of HIV and AIDS, thus creating a safe and comfortable space for the students to discuss similar stories and issues. This builds strong and compassionate relationships between the coaches and the students. In fact, 100% of the students interviewed during my personal research stated that they felt that they could relate to the coaches and that the coaches truly understood them (Personal Interviews, 2009, South Africa). One student stated that the coaches "understand our language" (Personal Interview P1, 2009, South Africa). Another student furthered this response by stating, "[The coaches] teach us very easily because we understand what they talk to us about because they talk the same 'language' we talk" (Personal Interview P14, 2009, South Africa). One of the GRS coaches stated that it was important to break the teacher/student relationship in order to be on the same level and "allow [the students] to be able to speak their language so that they can feel comfortable to talk [about] any issue they have" (Personal Interview C1, 2009, South Africa). This creates an environment in which students can speak to coaches about sensitive issues that they do not feel comfortable discussing with other people.

Grassroot Soccer's Lasting Impact

Important information and discussions about HIV and AIDS do not just end at the GRS sessions, but spark discussion topics for youth to think and talk about with others outside of GRS. As one staff member stated during my personal interviews,

> "I think [the students] have a very huge part because we don't get to reach all the schools, but through the participants we can reach a lot of kids because those kids teach others who didn't get the chance to be in our program. So, they are very important in spreading the message that we're trying to spread".
> (Personal Interview S1, 2009, South Africa).

The participants are always encouraged (often with the help of a copy of a SKILLZ magazine that they take home) to talk about what they have learned and share it with their friends, family, and community (Personal Field Research, 2009, South Africa). The homework that GRS provides allows the students to be able to bring up the topic with their parents or guardians by providing a way to initiate discussions around sensitive subjects. Furthermore, many students enjoy the activities-based learning because they are taught information in a way that they understand and enjoy while also benefitting from the innate interactive style of games and sports. Often, the participants will play the GRS games with their friends. They are able to remember the key messages more effectively because they have learned it through a medium that interests them. All the students interviewed during my personal research stated that they began talking to friends, family members, neighbors and people in their community about HIV and AIDS after their involvement with the GRS program (Personal Interviews, 2009, South Africa). Nineteen of those 33 students stated that they played the games with their friends and family members in order to pass the HIV and AIDS messages along (Personal Interviews, 2009, South Africa).

The philosophy underpinning GRS resonates with the Freirean perspectives on participatory learning. Soccer should be read as a communicative praxis where dialogue (the act of sharing one football) is essential for effective teamwork. Furthermore, action is fostered through the GRS program by using sports and activities as a way to actively involve the students in the learning process. Action and participation are inherent qualities of sports and games. Not only are students practicing the ability to think independently and critically through participatory education, they are also actively involved in learning about and understanding key messages. Rather than just explaining the impact of HIV, as many traditional top-down styles of teaching would do, GRS involves the students in the learning process by making them active and essential components in their own education.

In the GRS program, students become empowered not only by gaining integral information on how to combat HIV and AIDS, but through the development of critical and independent thought as they begin to see their own potential as agents of change. Gaining a sense of self-efficacy, whereby an individual feels more apt to deal with and control a certain situation, is a vital component to behavior change. As Bandura (1995; 2004) notes, the more a person believes in his or her ability to create or affect positive change in his or her life, the more likely that person will be to take the necessary action due to his or her increased sense of personal agency. Being equipped with vital knowledge about HIV and AIDS, along with the right tools to apply that knowledge and also to pass it on to others, made the GRS students feel "happy," "powerful," "proud," "privileged," "honored," and more "capable" to deal with challenges (Personal Field Research, 2009, South Africa).

The GRS educational methodology provides students with vital information about HIV and AIDS as well as the confidence and skills to be able to implement healthy life choices. By developing independent and critical thinking, GRS students are better able to apply the information they have learned to a variety of different situations they may face, thus being able to turn knowledge into action. Students become masters of their own thinking and masters of their own lives through the participatory learning structure implemented by GRS. The potential of sport is vast, but is often underestimated. Grassroot Soccer provides an effective example of how the innate interactive qualities of sport can be used to deliver an effective participatory education system that empowers its participants to be able to live HIV-free.

References

Bandura, A. (1995). *Self Efficacy in Changing Societies*. Cambridge: Cambridge University Press.

Bandura, A. (2004). Social Cognitive Theory for Personal and Social Change by Enabling Media. In A. Singhal, M. J. Cody, E. M. Rogers & M. Sabido (Eds.), *Entertainment-Education and Social Change: History, Research and Practice* (pp.75-96). New Jersey: Lawrence Erlbaum Associates, Inc.

Botcheva, L & Huffman, L. (2004). *HIV/AIDS Education Program: An Intervention in Zimbabwe*. The Children's Health Council, Evaluation Report. Availble at: http://www.grassrootsoccer.org/resources/. (Accessed 12th March 2012).

Clark, T. S., Friedrich, G.K., Ndlovu, M., Neilands, T.B., & McFarland, W., (2006). *An Adolescent-targeted HIV Prevention Project Using African Professional Soccer Players as Role Models and Educators in Bulawayo, Zimbabwe*. Available at: http://www.grassrootsoccer.org/resources/. (Accessed 12th March 2012).

Freire, Paulo. (2007) [1970]. *Pedagogy of the Oppressed*. New York: Continuum.

GRS (GrassrootSoccer). (n.d.). Available at: www.grassrootsoccer.org. (Accessed 12th March 2012).

GRS (Grassroot Soccer). (2007). *Annual Report 2007*. Available at: http://www.grassrootsoccer.org/resources/. (Accessed 12th March 2012).

GRS (Grassroot Soccer). (2009). SKILLZ Coach's Guide.

Personal Interviews (Emma Colucci). (April, 2009). Port Elizabeth, South Africa.

Personal Field Research (Emma Colucci). (March – April, 2009). Port Elizabeth, South Africa.

UN (United Nations). (2001). Declaration of Commitment on HIV and AIDS. Available at: http://www.un.org/ga/aids/coverage/FinalDe-clarationHIVAIDS.html. (Accessed 12th March 2012).

UNAIDS (United Nations program on HIV/AIDS). (2008). *The 2008 Report on the Global AIDS Epidemic*. Available at: http://www.un-aids.org/en/KnowledgeCentre/HIVData/GlobalReport/2008/2008_Global_report.asp. (Accessed 12th March 2012).

UNAIDS (United Nations program on HIV/AIDS) (2009). *Epidemic Update*. Available at: www.unaids.org/en/dataanalysis/epidemiology/. (Accessed 12th March 2012).

WHO (World Health Organization). (2008). *Epidemiological Fact Sheet on HIV and AIDS: Core data on epidemiology and response, South Africa. September 2008*. Available at: http://apps.who.int/GlobalAtlas/pre-definedReports/EFS2008/index.asp. (Accessed 12th March 2012).

Chapter 26

Active Learning and Self-supporting Processes through Sport, Games and Participatory Activities with Women who Suffered Violence

Clemens Ley & Maria Rato Barrio

Introduction

Sport and games are increasingly recognised as effective and efficient tools in the area of inclusion of different population groups, education (both *formal* and *informal*), holistic development, rehabilitation and health promotion, among other fields of intervention. In spite of evidence of their positive effects in various groups and intervention areas, we cannot deny the ambivalent nature of sport that also can provoke negative effects, like injuries, violence, exclusion, etc. (Coakley, 2007; Coalter, 2007; Henley, Schweizer, de Gara, & Vetter, 2007; Keim, 2003; Rato, Ley, Durán, 2009). In addition, evidence is primarily based on studies in western settings. They differ significantly from disadvantaged countries in opportunities and access to physical education and sport, and in regards to lifestyle, cultures, education, state of health, resources, interests, etc. In post-conflict situations these differences might be even higher due to the multi-dimensional impact of violence and conflicts. There is a strong need to enhance and evaluate projects in disadvantaged countries and to investigate appropriate intervention strategies in different social-cultural and social-political contexts (Joachim,

2006; Kay, 2009; Ley, 2009; Ley & Rato, 2010). The increasing research in the sport and development field could contribute to more evidence and better understanding of the responsible factors. However, care must be taken that the research designs are adequate to the local setting and that researchers have deep understanding and knowledge of the social-cultural context. Therefore, to build up research capacities and to promote local research initiatives should be main objectives, especially in University cooperation (Keim, Ley, Jordaan, et al., 2011). The use of participatory approaches, qualitative and mixed methods in research and evaluation are recommended in this field in order to contribute to a better understanding of key aspects of sport and development projects in the specific contexts (Kay, 2009; Ley & Rato, 2010).

The purpose of the research initiatives in Guatemala was to investigate appropriate intervention strategies in different social-cultural and social-political contexts and to contribute to an increase of knowledge and experience that in some way might improve the usage of sport and games in this field (see Ley, 2009; Rato, 2009).

This chapter is focusing on participatory and active learning and self-supporting processes through sport, games and participatory activities with women who suffered domestic violence in Guatemalan post-conflict context. In Guatemala, the history of racism and discrimination, suffered particularly by the *Mayan* population, as for example the 36 years of civil war including systematic *ethnic* massacres, persists still today in a more subtle form. As in many other conflicts, in Guatemala, misuse of power, oppression, violence, discrimination and social-political influences target to control the people, to maintain or obtain more power (over people, natural resources, economy, etc.) and to destroy educational and social-cultural structures, families and lives. In this complex situation, one of the most affected groups of population in Guatemala is the women, especially *Mayan* women in rural areas.

The programme of *psychosocial activity through movement, games and sport for women* (APM) focused, among other health-related aspects, on mutual support in group setting, active learning processes, and coping skills of women *victims* or *survivors* of violence, mainly domestic violence. The APM programme was based upon a specific methodology, including methods and techniques of local experiences (e.g. Belmont, 2006; Grupo de Mujeres Mayas Kaqla, 2004; Ovalle, 1999; PROPEVI, 1999; Proyecto Reducción de la Violencia contra la Mujer, 2002), physical education, sport and movement therapy, active and participatory learning processes, and psychosocial intervention. The main tools were sports, games, (bodily) movement, dance, dramatisation, creative and participatory group techniques and group discussions. The programme was implemented with various local partners in the region of Sololá (Guatemala, C.A.). who were in continuous contact with the participants.

In this chapter, we do not focus on the evaluation of the programme *outcomes*, but more on the intervention *processes*. For further results, we have to refer to other publications (Ley, 2009; Ley & Rato, 2009a; 2009b; 2010, 2011a; 2011b).

Research Design

Among other initiatives, a programme of *psychosocial activity through movement, games and sport for women* (APM) was developed and evaluated in the specific context of Guatemalan rural area. It was part of the project *Psychosocial, community and intercultural action in the Guatemalan post-conflict context* run and funded by the Group for Cooperation DIM (Sports, Territorial Engineering and Design) based at the Technical University of Madrid, Spain (*Universidad Politécnica de Madrid*). To carry out the programme, we (the authors) moved to Guatemala in November 2007, to the intervention area, where we stayed continuously for one year, during which our involvement in the APM programme was over a period of six months.

Quantitative (questionnaires) and qualitative (participatory observation, semi-structured interviews and participatory group techniques) methods have been combined in this research, according to the deepening and triangulation models (Ley, 2009).

From the 56 *Mayan* women of different ages who participated in two parallel groups in the APM programme in the region of Sololá, 33 women participated both in initial (pre) and final (post-test) measurements. As the number of participants increased continuously, more final than initial measurements are available. In one group (APM-Sololá) 12 workshops of four hours, twice a month, were developed and in the other group (APM-Chaquijyá) six intensive workshops of seven hours, once or twice a month, were realized based on the decision of the women. A higher frequency, such as twice a week training, might have improved the impact on physical health, but was not possible due to the local constraints.

In addition to the evaluation of the programme, reference data about the Guatemalan population in general was collected (n= 508, purposely chosen). As a main concept and content of the questionnaire, the *orientation to life questionnaire* (also called SOC scales), measuring the *sense of coherence* in the *Salutogenesis* model of Antonovsky (1987), was adapted to local context working with the local University and social workers, and translated into the local language *Kaqchikel* and back-translated to Spanish. To those who could not read, the questionnaire was read in their language and they made the crosses accordingly.

The data collection of the participatory observation and of the participatory group techniques was carried out by three facilitators using field diaries. In addition, 32 individual semi-structured interviews with women, two with local facilitators and one person from the local organisation took place.

357

The analysis was made according to various categories following the logical model (*context, input, processes, outputs* and *outcomes*) and the *Salutogenesis* model (risks factors, resources and *sense of coherence*) of Antonovsky (1987). In this way, we evaluated not only the changes, but also the whole process from beginning to end, analysing the factors responsible for the change and the role of the different activities and strategies. However, only the last mentioned process evaluation is content of this chapter.

Results and Discussion

According to the data about the *context*, both intervention groups are lacking personal and social resources and are facing a high degree of threads and stressors. The women usually are looking for support in their own families, more than in the community where mistrust is predominant. At the same time, we find a high degree of family problems of the participants of the programme. The women are often alone with their problems, avoiding them and relying on an external or fatalistic control. The low self-esteem, the low education level, the lack of economic resources in order to be independent, the preoccupation of the children, etc. indicate few personal resources, few initiative to solve the problems and to a high degree of vulnerability of the women.

In this context, the programme of *psychosocial activity through movement, games and sport for women* (APM) achieved a very constant and high level of active participation. The number of participants grew progressively, starting with few women – that is also the reason why some women did not participated in both the initial and final evaluation. The participation remained more or less stable once a woman participated the first time. The fluctuation of participation was low and occurred only in certain moments because of conscription problems and some external factors (like demonstrations on the road, occasional violent events, transport problems, etc.). Various activities were implemented to facilitate the participation; e.g. the activities and the methodology were planned to meet the social-cultural context of the women; basic costs were covered; the dates and the duration of the programme were determined by the women. In addition, the privacy of the space, the translation into the local language, the usage of local materials, movements and all daily living activities were very important and consequently they were assessed positively. For example, the confidential and secure atmosphere was evaluated very positive as they appreciated that the programme was not implemented in a public visible location, demanding a private space.

Three phases of the programme were identified:

1. Interaction and integration of the group: Getting in contact and interaction with each other and with oneself, building up security, confidence and trust (stabilisation phase).

2. Expression of experiences of violence, problems and pains: Non-verbal expression through the body in movement and interaction, and verbal reflections regarding the embodied experiences, observations and expressions (confrontation phase).

3. Searching of alternatives and solutions: Promoting creativity, different points of view and alternatives through physical, social and emotional movement and interaction (integration phase of experiences and alternatives).

In all phases, the primordial intervention approach laid on the resources of the women and on their expressions, interpretations and leadership. The activities were planned and adapted to facilitate positive experiences and learning processes that were considered significant by the women and that improved resources from a *salutogenetic* perspective (Ley & Rato, 2011). Among others, the APM programme improved cognitive (perceptions, knowledge, strategies to handle stress situation), and psychological resources (self-esteem, emotional relaxation), e.g. an increased *Sense of Coherence* (n=33; t = 2.49; p =.018) and self-esteem (n=33 ; t = 3.56; p=.001) was found comparing the initial and final measurements (see further details on outcomes in Ley, 2009).

Different kinds of sports, games, movement exercises, stretching, dynamics, creative and participatory activities, dramatizations, role plays, relaxation and respiration exercises, verbal reflection and group techniques, *etc.* were implemented according to the objective of the corresponding programme phase and to the respective specific goals of each session.

> *"We did a dramatization, in which there were several roles: children, husband, mother. The husband hit the mother and he was alcoholic. And then the women felt themselves supported, those who were victims, and then among them they themselves gave conclusions. Among themselves they found out how to denounce this mistreatment and not to keep quiet (...). Anyway, in this way the woman saw herself in her process. This was one of the exercises that I liked a lot"* (Claudia, in the interview).

This example shows how useful dramatization was for the women as well as for the research process. Similar results were obtained by other participatory group activities, such as role playing, games and modified sport. The mutual support among the women through sharing similar experiences and showing up alternatives from their own lives was very strong. Empathy and supporting effects in the group were visible, both while playing and discussing in the programme, and also outside of the programme. For example, the women supported one of them by going to her house, talking to the husband. Both intervention groups were rich in resources that contributed to self-supporting group effects. Thereby, the expressions were sometimes addressed directly, to a women who asked for support, but often the discussion were indirect, not personalised, e.g. an imaginary woman or situation was used to speak about underlying personal experiences.

The search for alternatives and solutions in these situations was lived in an active and participatory process. This process was not limited to a theoretical reflection about the problem and its possible solutions, but, rather, the women experienced it themselves by directly participating in these activities.

> "*Many times, the women are considered guilty that they suffered violence. So, I think, through the games, somehow, they realized or they could identify that they are not the only ones guilty of all what is happening. And also I think that now they can identify, if a similar problem comes up, they maybe can denounce it*" (Federica, local facilitator).

In sport and games, the bodies were in movement and in interaction with each other, mainly intermediated by different materials (balls, rings, textiles, etc.). Therefore, the learning process was valued as very active and participatory, which makes the difference from other more magisterial courses. A facilitator wrote in his field diary:

> "*She told me: 'Sometimes they invite us to a workshop and this is somehow boring and we nearly fall asleep. But this workshop is quite active. We have a lot of fun and forget our problems*" (Field diary - Session 9).

Verbal and non-verbal expressions were combined. The women themselves played and analysed their situation and searched for solutions and alternative 'movements'. The experiences gained were discussed afterwards or during a specific break to examine the concrete aspects experimented or observed. First, the participants had the possibility to express verbally their experiences and knowledge or to raise questions among themselves. In addition, previously prepared specific questions to direct attention to the explicit goals of the specific phase, session and game were sometimes asked. We proposed questions relating to a transfer of experiences and knowledge made in the programme to their 'real life' situations, to the experiences and situations outside of the protected 'playground'.

> "*For me, the course seemed to be very dynamic, very enjoyable, where women, even without knowing how to read, without knowing how to write, talked, participated and commented. (...) This was like a school for me, because it was through games (...); because each game had its reason to be and after finishing a game, the dynamic, there was always a reflection*" (Claudia, a participant and facilitator in another organisation).

Some women showed difficulties in the reflection phase, in expressing their opinions, experiences and feelings. These difficulties declined significantly with growing trust and after a certain period of adaptation to the participative and reflective methodology, bearing in mind that for some women it was the first time that they were asked about their feelings and opinion.

> "*Before, she was not used to talk about her problems, but now she knows that she has to search for support and like that she did*" (Clara, translated by Emma in the interview).

Both the participants and the facilitators assessed the relaxation exercises as very important, especially those based on the body, respiration and movement, like tension-relaxation exercises, Qi Gong and Tai Chi.

> "*All these workshops, they helped me a lot, because they helped me to relax. I had a lot of problems, too much problems, (...). One is joyful for a moment and relaxes herself; the exercises we did at the end [relaxation exercises], they helped me a lot*" (Faustina in an interview).

Relaxation activities were a permanent and fundamental part of each session. They were something completely new to most of the participants and it took them some time to get used to them. These exercises needed to be simple and attention was directed only on a few aspects. Another contributing factor in this context was the perception of the programme as dynamic and enjoyable. This contributed to a high motivation and, at least, a temporary relieve from daily problems. The results were the perception of an increased emotional relaxation and well-being.

Another key factor was the facilitators, especially the local facilitators who knew the local social-cultural codex. Their role was in no way authoritarian, but, rather, motivating and stimulating participation, creativity and leadership of the women, and facilitating opportunities of reflection and discussions. The relationship with the participants was characterised by trust, intention of mutual understanding and respect.

The facilitators were tasked to be flexible and to modify the activities according to the group processes. Good observation skills of the individual and group processes as well as the ability to adapt each activity were found key. Previous knowledge and own experiences in the sport, games and participatory techniques was paramount. However, the group were taking increasingly ownership and responsibility of their own processes. Therefore the promotion of creativity and leadership in sport and games was very important.

The local facilitators, the persons from the local organisation and two participants who are working as facilitators with women in another organisation expressed the utility of the methodology and that they will or are already using the methodology in other workshops.

> "*For myself as well as for working with women; we work with self-help groups of women, who are victims of violence; [the programme] is very appropriate to what we are doing*" (Dora, participant and facilitator in another association).

Local facilitator Federica expressed in an interview that she learned that you can promote learning processes "*through dynamics, and not to make a magisterial speech*".

Conclusions

The type of research and the limited number of participants do not permit a generalization of the results, nor should it be expected that the same strategies can be used without any adaptation in another context. However, in this chapter, the process evaluation of the APM programme was illus-

trated and it showed how active and participatory learning and self-supporting processes can be successfully facilitated through sport, games and participatory group activities with women who suffered violence in Guatemalan
post-conflict context. In the complex situation of oppression, discrimination, violence and social-cultural and social-political conflicts in Guatemala,
women are mainly excluded from social-educational and care programmes.
Their vulnerable situation is characterised by lack of coping skills and cognitive and psychosocial resources, among other challenges.

In this context, the APM programme focused on a participatory and active learning approach and self-supporting processes with women *victims* or
survivors of violence. Sport, games, participatory activities and group discussion were the main tools in the programme, which was structured basically
in three phases (stabilisation, confrontation and integration phase).

The women showed a high level of interest and participation in the programme, in spite of daily problems. In total, a high degree of pertinence and
viability of the activities and the methodology was shown.

We consider several aspects to be key factors for the success of the APM
programme and responsible for positive evaluated changes in the women:

- The methodology of the programme is recommended especially for its
  active and participatory character. That is how it distinguishes itself
  from other interventions in this context. The women were not mere re-
  ceivers of a speech or other passive activities, but participated actively
  and expressed themselves through their body in movement and interaction.
- The perception of the programme as dynamic, attractive and enjoyable
  contributed to a high motivation and to emotional recreation, providing
  at least a temporary relieve from daily problems.
- Paying attention to themselves, their body and relaxation were stimulated by body-centred movement and interaction, and by the relaxation
  techniques at the end of each session.
- Group processes of mutual support contributed to the improvement of
  psychosocial resources (e.g. self-esteem, reduction of isolation).
- Learning by playing contributed to the improvement of cognitive resources (e.g. knowledge, coping skills) that have been made explicit in the
  respective reflection phases.
- The women searched on their own for alternatives and solutions to their
  problems.
- Experiences made in the activities were verbally discussed, starting from
  the reflections of the women and complemented by previously prepared
  questions for guidance. Transfer to real life situation was made.
- Experiences made were perceived as significant and meaningful by the
  women. From a *salutogenetic* perspective, these kind of experiences were
  important to foster the *sense of coherence*, which improved significantly.

- The facilitators accompanied them in their processes, and offered different movement, games and participatory group activities regarding specific relevant topics. The quality of the facilitation and the provision of a secure and confidential atmosphere were crucial.
- Local facilitators confirmed the utility, applicability and relevance of the approach.

Acknowledgement

We thank the *Universidad Politécnica de Madrid* (Technical University of Madrid) for all their support and co-funding of the project *Psychosocial, community and intercultural action in the Guatemalan post-conflict context.* We are also very grateful for the collaboration of *CARE Guatemala* and the *Defensoría Maya Sololá*, professors of the *Universidad San Carlos de Guatemala* and *Universidad Rafael Landivar*, the Group for Cooperation DIM, and of course all facilitators and participants of the APM programme.

References

Antonovsky, A. (1987). *Unraveling the mystery of health. How people manage stress and stay well.* San Francicso, Estados Unidos: Jossey-Bass.

Belmont, N. I. (2006). *Manual de Capacitación: Abordaje de la Violencia de Género contra las Mujeres en el Ámbito Familiar y la Utilización de los Métodos Alternativos de Resolución de Conflictos.* Guatemala: ICCPG - Instituto de Estudios Comparados en Ciencias Penales de Guatemala.

Coakley, J. (2007). *Sports in Society. Issues and controversies.* New York: McGraw-Hill.

Coalter, F. (2007). *A wider social role for sport. Who's keeping the score?* London & New York: Routledge.

Grupo de Mujeres Mayas Kaqla. (2004). *La palabra y el sentir de las Mujeres Mayas de Kaqla.* Guatemala: Grupo de Mujeres Mayas Kaqla.

Grupo de Mujeres Mayas Kaqla. (2006). *La internalización de la Opresión. Una Propuesta Metodológica.* Guatemala: Grupo de Mujeres Mayas Kaqla.

Henley, R., Schweizer, I., de Gara, F., & Vetter, S. (2007). How Psychosocial Sport & Play Programs Help Youth Manage Adversity: A Review of What We Know & What We Should Research, *International Journal of Psychosocial Rehabilitation,* 12(1), 51-58

Joachim, I. (2006). Psychosoziale und psychotherapeutische Arbeit mit Überlebenden sexualisierter Gewalt im Kontext von Krieg und Krisen, in: medica mondiale e.V. & K. Griese (Eds.), *Sexualisierte*

*Kriegsgewalt und ihre Folgen. Handbuch zur Unterstützung traumat-
sierter Frauen in verschiedenen Arbeitsfeldern* (Vol. 2, pp. 375-412).
Frankfurt a.M.: Mabuse.

Kay, T. (2009). Developing through sport: evidencing sport impacts on
young people. *Sport in Society, 12*(9), 1177-1191

Keim, M. (2003). *Nation Building at Play. Sport as a Tool for Social Integration
in Post-apartheid South Africa.* Sport, Culture & Society. Oxford:
Ed. Meyer & Meyer Sport.

Keim, M., Ley, C., Jordaan, G., Rato Barrio, M., Chikwanda, C., Grover,
T., Bouah, L., et al. (2011). Sport and Development from the perspective of University. In K. Petry, M. Groll, & W. Tokarski
(Eds.), *Sport und internationale Entwicklungszusammenarbeit* (pp.
75-96). Köln: Sportverlag Strauss.

Ley, C. (2009). *Acción psicosocial a través del movimiento, juego y deporte en contextos de violencia y conflicto. Investigación sobre la adecuación sociocultural de la 'terapia a través del deporte' y evaluación de un programa
para mujeres en Guatemala.* Doctoral Thesis. Madrid: Technical
University of Madrid. Available at: http://oa.upm.es/1672/ (Accessed 12th March 2012).

Ley, C., & Rato Barrio, M. (2009a). Experiencias "incorporadas" y "movi-
das": expresión de la violencia contra la mujer indígena en Sololá
(Guatemala) en y a través del cuerpo y el movimiento. In SIEG
(Eds.), *Actas del I Congreso Internacional Cultura y Género: la cultura
en el cuerpo.* Elche (España): Seminario Interdisciplinar de Estudios de Género (SIEG), Universidad Miguel Hernández.

Ley, C., & Rato Barrio, M. (2009b). Aspectos socioculturales y espirituales
en la promoción de la salud psicosocial de mujeres indígenas en
Guatemala. El modelo de Salutogenesis como marco de investigación y de intervención centrado en el cuerpo y el movimiento. In
SIEG (Eds.), *Actas del I Congreso Internacional Cultura y Género: la
cultura en el cuerpo.* Elche (España): SIEG, Universidad Miguel
Hernández.

Ley, C., & Rato Barrio, M. (2010). Movement, games and sport in
psychosocial intervention: a critical discussion of its potential and
limitations within cooperation for development. *Intervention, 8*(2),
106-120.

Ley, C., & Rato Barrio, M. (2011a). Movement and sport therapy with women in Guatemalan context of violence and conflict. *Body, Movement and Dance in Psychotherapy: An International Journal for Theory,
Research and Practice.*

Ley, C., & Rato Barrio, M. (2011b). Evaluierung der psychosozialen Intervention APM in Guatemala. In K. Petry, M. Groll, & W.
Tokarski (Eds.), *Sport und internationale Entwicklungszusammenarbeit* (pp. 159-182). Köln: Sportverlag Strauss.

Ovalle, V. J. (1999). Una experiencia metodológica en el abordaje de la violencia intrafamiliar. In ECAP (Eds.), *Curso de especialización en Psicología social y violencia política* (pp. 217-221). Guatemala: ECAP, URL y USAC.

PROPEVI. (1999). *Manual de capacitación sobre violencia intrafamiliar.* Guatemala: SOSEP - Secretaría de Obras Sociales de la Esposa del Presidente. Programa de Prevención y Erradicación de la Violencia Intrafamiliar.

Proyecto Reducción de la Violencia contra la Mujer. (2002). *Manuales para Capacitación Integral sobre Violencia en contra de las Mujeres.* Guatemala: Asociación Mujer Vamos Adelante; Centro de Investigación, Capacitación y Apoyo a la Mujer & Consejo de Mujeres Mayas de Desarrollo Integral.

Rato Barrio, M. (2009). *La Actividad Física y el Deporte como herramienta para promover el Interculturalismo en contextos posbélicos, en el marco de la Cooperación para el Desarrollo. Un proyecto en Guatemala (Centro América).* Doctoral Thesis. Madrid: Technical University of Madrid. Available at: http://oa.upm.es/1674/. (Accessed 12th March 2012).

Rato Barrio, M., Ley, C., & Durán González, J. (2009). Derechos Humanos y Cooperación para el Desarrollo en y a través del Deporte. In J. A. Moreno & D. González-Cutre (Eds.), *Deporte, intervención y transformación social.* (pp. 13-58). Río de Janeiro: Shape.

Chapter 27

The Social and Human Development of Antisocial and Disaffected Young People through the Bidding and Hosting of Major Games in the UK

Geoff Thompson

Cry from the Streets – from Tragedy to Opportunity

The role of sport in the social and human development of young people in communities of disadvantage and disaffection is now a well-established movement that sees a multi-agency range of projects, programmes and initiatives all with the aim of assisting young people to improve their life chances. However, what continued and improved role can sport and social and human development provide in assisting a more effective and efficient benefit with a global framework that can deliver social and human development goals in both the developed and developing world?

The Youth Charter was established in 1993 with the specific intention of developing an approach to promote such a role for sport and cultural activity and the legacy benefits that could be realised through the bidding and hosting of major games. The agency's birth reflected a pre-twenty first century effort in the social and cultural notion of "sport for all". With the advent of social and community based recreational activity identified as a result of the urban riots of the eighties, the role of sport in addressing social and cultural inequalities was given a policy focus and consideration with the

setting up by the then Thatcher Government with a review to look at sport
and recreation in the inner cities. The report "The Review of Sport and
Recreation in the Inner Cities" provided the policy platform in the overall
community sports provision across governmental and non-governmental
organisations.

As the nineties approached, a number of initiatives had been established
with some marked success. However, without a sustainable and integrated
policy approach, another generation of inner city youth, in the main, had
missed the opportunity in benefiting on the holistic role that sport could
have played in their development. There were a number of factors that included the relocation of sport from the Department of the Environment to
the Department of Education and then to its final inclusion of the newly
established department of National Heritage. This was then renamed 'The
Department of Culture, Media and Sport'.

This period of change in sport provided a more stable policy approach
with Sport England (formerly GB Sports Council), which was restructured
as the English based agency for the delivery of community sport. With a
series of re-structuring to accommodate the advent of the lottery windfall
for sport, capital policy thrived with a limited recognition of the revenue
streams required to sustain them. Local Authorities more critically, broke
the covenant of replacing local sport and recreational resources with lottery
bids. This saw a period of potential growth for the social and human potential of sport compromised. In addition to this, the selling off of playing
fields, the loss of goodwill from the teaching profession and the non-encour-
agement of competitive sport conspired to reduce both the impact and appeal to another generation of young people who were now beginning to face
other alternative distractions for their lifestyle choices and time.

However, this period heralded the positive social and human community
benefits of the hosting and bidding of major games, with the Birmingham
1992 Olympic bid[1] providing a legacy that would see the National Indoor
Arena initiate the first integrated approach in the 'participation, development, performance and excellence' policy themes of the then GB Sports
Council. A bidding culture was then established with Manchester bidding
on two occasions. The failed 1996 Bid[2], highlighted the role sport would
play in regenerating a northern city in social, economic and civil pride. This
would see a greater emphasis on the social and economic regeneration of
the city centre and surrounding communities of historic social and cultural deprivation, with a unique multi- agency public private sector relationship. With the Central Manchester Development Corporation providing
the catalytic coordination and much needed investment in to the bid effort,
there was also a unique urban community regeneration effort taking place in
Hulme and Moss Side. With a similar public private sector multi-agency re-

---

1.Birmingham Olympic Bid Document (1992). Available at: http://www.skyscraper-
city.com/showthread.php?t=1064099 (Accessed 12th February 2012).

2.Ibid

lationship developing alongside the Manchester 2000 bid effort, there was still little by way of a truly integrated social and human bid policy and or indeed strategy.

This was to change on January 2nd 1993, with the tragic shooting of a fourteen-year-old schoolboy Benji Stanley. The murder was to bring to national focus the advent of a new and disturbing culture now pursued as a life choice. As a result and with the then Manchester 2000 bid team deciding on a response to the damaging international media attention, the Youth charter for sport was launched at the Recman Conference at Wembley Conference Centre in March 1993.

The philosophy of the Youth Charter was to present the continued need for sport, in its broadest social, cultural, recreational, economic and political benefits and impact to reflect its mission aims "to provide young people with an opportunity through sport to develop in life"[3]. The mission aims were established as part on consultation with the young people and wider community of Moss Side. The Manchester 2000 Olympic bid also provided a unique opportunity to consult, discuss and above all develop a truly collective effort from all aspects of civil society. As a result, a local tragedy and response also saw a global contribution made.

A Spirit of the Streets - Legacy of Hope

This first all-important global link was to be established with the legacy host city of the 1984 Los Angeles Olympic. As the first legacy successful games, with the surplus profits invested for the social and community benefit of South Central LA, the Amateur Athletic Foundation (Now LA84 Foundation) was established to provide a new and pioneering legacy benefit that would contribute to the on-going social and cultural challenges of the community. The 1992 Los Angeles Riots and subsequent re-build LA initiatives provided an opportunity for the Youth Task Force of LA to visit the inner cities of the UK to look at the social and cultural challenges and opportunities faced by their youth counterparts. The group, 'Spirit of the Streets Tour of the UK' were hosted by the Manchester 2000 Olympic Bid. Twenty diverse young citizens from Los Angeles were provided with an opportunity to look at two cities with similar social, cultural and youth and community challenges. Both cities had historic communities of deprivation, and both had had riots as a result. Both cities had also experienced the violence, crime and overall negative impact of a generation of young people who had not channelled their energies in a life-constructive way. Their visit to Moss Side was to have a lasting and far-reaching impact, with issues identified and commonly shared between the many discussions that took place with the young people from across the pond. The common bond and positive impact

---

3. The Role of Sport as a Social Vehicle of Change. Available at: http://www.care.org/careswork/whatwedo/initiatives/sportforsocialchange.asp (Accessed on 12th February 2012).

made by the visiting LA Tour Group inspired an invitation for the youth of Moss Side to visit Los Angeles. The 1994 Spirit of Hulme and Moss Side Tour of LA was born.[4]

CASE STUDY
'SPIRIT OF HULME AND MOSS SIDE TOUR OF L.A.'

The Spirit of Hulme and Moss Side Tour of Los Angeles aimed to engage, motivate and inspire a diverse social and cultural representation of young people who lived in Moss Side, Manchester, Trafford and Salford. The aim was to break down territorial boundaries and to build on the confidence and growing trust that had resulted from the Youth Charter's work in the area to date. The trip was also designed to give the young people of the respective areas a first-hand insight of South Precinct, Los Angeles and how a former Olympic host city and recent riot torn area was meeting the challenges of social, cultural and economic disaffection and the resulting gang related activity.

Identified as a legacy of the failed Manchester 2000 Olympic Bid, a commitment of over 20 public and private sector agencies all participated in the resource and realisation of these Olympic street citizens. The young people were selected on the basis of their cultural, sporting and artistic activity and the difference they would make in the lives of their peers and communities in which they live. The tour group were hosted by the Amateur Athletic Foundation, which was established and funded with the legacy proceeds of the 1984 Olympics.

The Hulme and Moss Side Tour Group Members were exposed to the street realities and impact of gang violence, as well as the positive role that the Amateur Athletic Foundation and other key agencies were contributing in regenerating and rebuilding the area and lives blighted as a result of the continued social and economic disaffection.

The tour group members returned back to Manchester, with eyes opened and horizons broadened, so much so, that IOC member and former Olympian Anita DeFrantz presented each of the tour group members with IOC solidarity citation certificates as part of the IOC Centenary year marking their contributions and efforts. The Anglo-American Youth Culture initiative was also signed by the Mayor of Los Angeles, the British American Chamber of Commerce and Industry, the Consul General and IOC members Anita DeFrantz and Dame Mary Glen Haig. This marked a legacy of endearing and continued spirit that was to see many practical spin offs realised. Most notably was the visit of the NAACP (National Association Advancement of Coloured People) to Manchester

---

4. The Spirit of the Streets Tour of Los Angeles Report. Available at: http://back-streets.com/news.html (Accessed on 12th February 2012).

The Justiceville Cricket Programme (a team of homeless young people who had been given hope, life skills and life opportunities through cricket) was another legacy benefit hosted by the Youth Charter and Lancashire County Cricket Club. The Lord Taverners, Prince Andrew and the English Cricket Board have all seen the support and developments reflected in the Justiceville Cricket project's participation in the 2011 Cricket World Cup. The Spirit of Hulme and Moss Side Tour of Los Angeles led to many other tours by young people in different communities globally. Most notably the Spirit of the Streets Tour of South Africa where again, 20 young people from Greater Manchester provided an immediate legacy opportunity in the social and human potential of major games.

The Youth Charter has hosted youth delegations from approximately 20 countries providing information, tools and experience with student placements and academic studies also facilitated as a result.[5]

Programmes, Projects and Policy Initiatives

The highly successful tour, and the resulting legacy of the visit, provided an all-important platform of growing trust and confidence in the collective efforts of all concerned. This saw the establishment of a multi-agency effort of public, private and community agencies and organisations look at how the aspirations and dreams of the returning tour group members could be brought to fruition. As a result of a number of consultations, the Youth Charter established a "Sports Social Impact Model" and a "Social impact Model through Sport".[6]

These two complementary yet separate approaches recognised the role that sport could play in the engagement, motivation and inspiration of young people, and also the need to have a secondary and integrated approach once the life skills and potential of the young people needed to be employed. The establishment of the community models provided the social and community platform to introduce over 20 projects, programmes and initiatives that would not only impact on the lives of the young people of Hulme and Moss Side, but the lives of young people and communities globally in the areas of education, health, social and civil order, the environment, vocation, training, employment and enterprise. Three examples of the truly global, yet local nature of the many examples of both successes and failures provide the knowledge, experience and best practice in the diverse and changing nature of the social and human development through sport agenda.

---

5. Opportunities for Business report 2011.

6. The 'Sport Social Impact Models' were identified as part of Hulme recreation's leisure strategy for the area.

CASE STUDY
AGORASPACE

The need to establish trust and confidence not only on the streets and the rival gang
territorialism but more importantly the public/private sector engagement with the
young people and wide community was critical. As a result, the Youth Charter engaged with a regeneration company and the Central Manchester Development Corporation. The aim was to refurbish a five aside kick about area that was in a state
of disrepair linked to the Procter Youth Centre and very much seen on the other
half of the gang divide. The Youth Charter sought to realise an improved area for
play, recreation and competition. Establishing a unique public / private sector partnership, the Agoraspace, an already successful European concept was introduced to
the youth club members of Proctor. The project's ability to engage young people in
both the planning, development and running of the facility provided a unique set of
challenges and opportunities as the relationship between young people, government
services and the private sector were established for the first time. The other major
challenge was the Agoraspace's construction materials of wood and Astroturf in the
main. Health and safety concerns were raised as to the project's sustainability with
sceptics predicting only a short-term existence and fears of it being burned down in
a matter of weeks of its completion. The Agoraspace was successfully funded, constructed and opened by the Sports Aid Foundation Trust with the support of the GB
Sports Council, Central Council of Physical Recreation, British Olympic Association
and Business in the Community. The facility was completed within six months and
was opened by British Actress, Susan Hampshire and sporting philanthropist, Sir Ed-
die Kulukundis. Joined by honorary IOC member, Dame Mary Glen Haig and the
Manchester 2000 Bid Chair, Sir Bob Scott, this project established a number of cultural and wider community links that would lead to many attending the opening event
at a time when the area had been likened to Los Angeles and Beirut! The Agoraspace
provided a multi sport environment that was also a meeting place where community
disagreements could be resolved.[7] Agoraspace – meaning – meeting place, a multi usage sports area that can be used for 36 different sports in the one area.

With a confidence established, the young people of the area found a new sense of
pride with the wider community also participating in the establishment of new soccer leagues. The Agoraspace provided an alternative and wide ranging opportunity
of activity that was to see them cut a hole in the fence after the Youth Centres's
closing time and using the nearby motorway fly-over to establish the first recorded
midnight sporting activity in Britain. This powerful statement demonstrated by the
young people of the area showed their willingness to feel safe and active, with the

---

7. Agoraspace: In 1990, AGORESPACE® created the multisports grounds concept
"to bring sports closer to people and people closer to sports". Whether set in the
heart of cities, in the heart of villages or in the heart of life, AGORESPACE®
grounds are local sports facilities. Available at http://www.agorespace.com/en/in-
dex.html (Accessed on 12th February 2012).

Agoraspace identified as a symbol of hope and opportunity. The project's success also helped and contributed to government social regeneration and community policy and to this day sees the facility still used and in testament to its sustainable longevity, it is still in immaculate condition, well maintained and has never been vandalised or damaged.

The key to the Agoraspace success is simple; if you involve young people, establish what they need, involve them in the delivery and then make them responsible for what their needs are with the support of the wider community, long-term sustainability and success can be realised. Many projects locally and globally visited the area to learn, observe and witness the Agoraspace's success as a practical and on-going demonstration of the ability of sport to address the youth disaffection, anti-social behaviour and gang related activity that can blight so many communities.

Further recognition of the project's success saw the corporate fitness chain Forza donate fitness equipment for the benefit of the young people and wider community. Ministerial visits also followed with the realisation of the 1997 Social Centre of Excellence Prospectus.[8]

Youth wise – Personal and Social Development for Life

In the communities in which disaffected young people live, with the ever present political challenges that can see hard earned and achieved trust and confidence lost through ongoing gang violence and continued loss of young life, it was becoming clear that whilst sport could, in its broadest and most beneficial light, contribute to the social vaccine and effect of re-engaging the disaffected, the cultural opportunity, vocation, jobs and employment would provide the only alternative to the life choices being made. A personal social development life skills programme was established to meet the needs of the many community interventions, experiences and needs of both young people and those professionals and volunteers working with young people. Youth wise was launched in 1997 to provide a holistic and complimentary added value and more integrated approach to the existing community based sports and arts interventions of the time.[9]

---

8. Social Centre of Excellence Prospectus (1997).

9. The 'Youthwise Toolkit' was produced in 1998 and was modulated to the benefit of agencies and organisations globally.

CASE STUDY
RUGBYWISE

The sport of rugby is an unusual pastime in its role to engage and above all maintain the interests of young disaffected hearts and minds. Following the highly successful Spirit of Hulme and Moss Side Tour of Los Angeles, the Rugby Football Union invited the Youth Charter to the 1994 England v Wales five nations Grand Slam decider at Twickenham.

At the suggestion of GB Sports Council Chairman, England rugby international and administrator, the late Sir Peter Yarranton, a relationship was established that was to see rugby attempt to make a return back to the inner cities following a 20-year absence. This would not be an easy assignment as rugby was seen as class removed from the areas where the Youth Charter was attempting to make a difference.

In order to really establish the all-important 'buy-in' that was not just seen as a token box ticking exercise, the Youth Charter presented at all levels of the RFU establishment. With many RFU officials serving as magistrates, justices of the peace, barristers and solicitors, police offers and even probation officers, the Youth Charter found an unusually open door in the social and cultural issues presented.

As a result, the Royal Sun Alliance invested in the establishment of the Youth Charter RFU Inner City Social Inclusion programme. This saw rugby clubs encouraged to go into the inner cities with the oval ball and establish social and cultural relationships that had not previously existed. Club officials and many of the rugby club volunteer workforce were encouraged to hear the potential of this new ground breaking initiative.

The Youth Charter was then invited to present to the first generation of Youth Development Officers as the link in establishing a presence in the inner cities. The historic and 'honest discussion' identified the need for a better understanding of the language, culture and appreciation of the challenges ahead. This led to the Rugbywise Toolkit[10] (www.youthcharter.co.uk/rugbywise) being designed to give youth development officers, rugby clubs and the rugby community as a whole a social inclusion, equality and community participation framework that would help shape future policy and deliver future project programmes and initiatives.

The Rugbywise Toolkit was then presented to the Rugby Administrators Conference where, for the first time social inclusion and community rugby became part of a central future policy delivery for the RFU. As part of their 2002 Commonwealth Games contribution, the RFU was introduced as a new Commonwealth Games discipline. Premier Rugby side Sale Sharks hosted a Rugbywise Conference, which presented

---

10. Rugbywise Toolkit - Available at: http://www.youthcharter.co.uk/products_bespoke.php?id_ref=53 (Accessed on 12th February 2012).

the overall approach to an invited audience. This led to the Rugbywise approach being shared as part of the international rugby union family and contribute to the UN High Commissioner for Refugees work.

The Rugbywise toolkit provided an ongoing point of reference in the measurement and impact of rugby as a social vehicle of change. Of the many initiatives that have now been established as a result of the 17 year association, the Southwark Tigers Inner City Rugby Club is of particular note, established following the murder of Damilola Taylor on a Southwark estate. The Southwark Tigers has blossomed in the area as a truly community rich environment. Another unique relationship was established between the two codes of Rugby Union and Rugby League (with the Youth Charter socially brokering and designing the joint project) saw the establishment of the British Asian Rugby Association; established in response to the radicalisation of Asian youth in Bradford and surrounding areas. The Youth Charter arranged a number of visits between the respective youth culture representations in order to reduce potential conflict of both gang related and even terrorist activity. This culminated in the production of the Rugbywise Report[11] which was produced following the shooting of 15-year-old schoolboy, Jessie James, in 2006. The report attempted to provide a further lobby for the challenges faced by government and sporting communities, because whilst considerable resources were being made available, many were tragically not finding their way to the most identified area of need. Challenges were also faced as key personnel within the RFU moved on- and with them the enthusiasm and commitment for the ongoing and invaluable work and relationship to date.

CASE STUDY
SOCCERWISE

The role of soccer as a social vehicle of change is well established within initiatives both globally and locally. The Youth Charter's use of the 'beautiful game' was a major tool in addressing the then rival gangs in Moss Side, Manchester. Following an approach by local youth workers, the Youth Charter facilitated a truce with rival gangs brought together and the Moss Side Amateur Reserves soccer team was born as a result. The team provided a cultural and social focal point for the then distant public and community sector workers and organisations. With a commitment to match their peace on the streets with recognition, reward and respect, a number of global

---

11. Youth Charter – Available at: 2006 Rugby report Available at;: http://content.yudu.com/Library/A1ur55/YouthCharterRugbywis/resources/index.htm?referrerUrl=http%3A%2F%2Fwww.google.ch%2Furl%3Fsa%3Dt%26rct%3Dj%26q%3D%2520rugbywise%2520report%2520%26source%3Dweb%26cd%3D2%26ved%3D0CC4QFjAB%26url%3Dhttp%253A%252F%252Fcontent.yudu.com%252FLibrary%252FA1ur55%252FYouthCharterRugbywis%252F%26ei%3Dnx44-T9DiD4Ol-gbo8pzODA%26usg%3DAFQjCNHIjSIYcwcEaDRz3M5zxY_SCIe3DA (Accessed 12th February 2012).

milestones were realised. In 1995 the SASOL U23 South African Olympic side played their goodwill match in Moss Side, playing against the Moss Side Amateur Reserves at Manchester City's Platt Lane training ground. This all-important game marked the Youth Charter's on-going contribution to the work of the Commonwealth Games movement and the Olympic family.

Other high profile visits were to follow with the Ghanaian World Cup U17 winning side also playing the Reserves. Soccer legend and Youth Charter Vice President, Sir Bobby Charlton provided a continued presence in addition to the two rival Manchester Clubs, Manchester City and Manchester United. As a result, many visits were made by premiership footballers in support of community events that greatly lifted the community spirit.

In 1995 the local effort spread its wings and influence to Europe where the Youth Charter visited AFC Ajax Amsterdam as part of the U.N. Criminal Tribunal visit to The Hague. By this time, confidence continued to grow in the area with the Moss Side Reserves winning leagues, cup doubles and even one treble.

Although soccer was beginning to have an important vaccine effect on the community, the continued loss of life and lack of economic and career opportunities saw one member of the Reserves serve a life sentence.

In 1997, one of the key milestones in demonstrating soccer's ability to change lives was evidenced by the Bafana Bafana visit to the area prior to their historic international against England at Old Trafford. It was a unique visit. For the first time we saw professional soccer players playing five aside football with young men who were already disaffected and simply on the streets. What was more remarkable was the fact that these international players were able to play with these young men just 24 hours prior to a major international.

In 1999 the Nigerian U17 World Cup took place, where social policy and development programmes were presented to an international audience in partnership with the British Council and the Professional Footballers Association.

With the Dutch FA in attendance and with the English FA also participating as part of their own FA Charter, the Youth Charter developed its international programme as part of its continued contribution to the new South Africa. With presentations to the world governing body, FIFA and through a Soccerex conference platform, the social and human potential of soccer was highlighted. As a result, Soccerwise was launched at the 1999 Women's World Cup in Los Angeles. Since its launch, the Soccerwise programme has been presented, shared and contributed to all five of FIFA's football confederations that include the UN Conference 2003, Magglingen 2003 and 2005.[12]

---

12. Youth Charter Issue Document (2005). Available at: http://www.hsrc.ac.za/ HSRC_Review_Article-34.phtml (Accessed online 12th February 2012).

The Youth Charter scroll

(www.youthcharter.co.uk.preview.exa.net.uk/about_ambassadors.html) achieved global recognition when it formed part of the pre-match ceremony with former South African President Nelson Mandela signing the scroll, along with the African Select and FIFA World Select teams.

This workshop was delivered as part of the Youth Charter's contribution to the England 2006 World Cup bid. Further workshops were held in Mali, Cameroon and Cote d'Ivoire. The Youth Charter also uniquely contributed to England's 2006 World Cup Bid providing a continued collaboration between the two nations superseding bid rivalry with the ongoing commitment to the Anglo South African youth culture initiative.

In 2001, as part of the North West trade mission to South Africa, the Youth Charter delivered a milestone social coach workshop at Selekelela High School using a soccer ball to address the issues of HIV Aids and rape. The workshop was an all-important first and helped introduce what were considered highly controversial issues. This historic workshop also saw the introduction of the Youth Charter's soccerwise toolkit, which attempted for the first time to measure the behavioural and overall programme impact of sport and its ability to influence social and human issues.

In same year the Youth Charter produced the Soccerwise Education packs[13] as part of a unique tripartite with Manc thehester United Soccer Club and UNICEF. The programme was introduced locally to address school non-attainment, truancy, bad behavioural issues and racism. The success of the programme saw a global sharing of the curriculum with UNICEF realising a new policy direction as a result. Education packs have also been shared with projects and programmes globally over the past decade. 2002 saw the Moss Side Amateur Reserves receive international acclaim with a Korean World Cup host nation featuring a documentary of the team and their achievements. The culmination of this 18-year effort saw the Youth Charter invited to observe and contribute further to South Africa's Soccer World Cup 2010 and the June 16th Youth Day activities.

In 2011 the Youth Charter contributed to the Future Champions International Youth Tournament, which uniquely provides U23's with football tournament and life experience. The Youth Charter helped in the delivery of a social coach workshop and is now developing the Soccerwise Youth Culture and Community Framework as part of the Brazil 2014 Soccer World Cup.

Eighteen years on, the first generation of Moss Side Amateur Reserves are all alive, are all employed and virtually all fathers. There have now been two generations of Moss Side Amateur Reserves with up to three teams ongoing to this day. The current generation, re-named West Manchester continues to this day with the former team members now heading up the community football effort.

---

13. Soccerwise Education Pack

The Youth Charter has worked with the following soccer teams: Manchester United FC, Manchester City FC, Liverpool FC, Aston Villa FC, Arsenal FC, Macclesfield FC, Stockport County FC, Chester City FC, Stalybridge FC, Orlando Pirates, Kaiser Chiefs, Ajax Amsterdam and others.[14]

Multi-agency Policy Development and Advocacy

With the invaluable contributions made by visiting IOC member countries and other leading international agencies to Manchester, the Youth Charter was able to build a unique insight and opportunity to establish a social and community framework through sport. With the failed Manchester 2000 Olympic Bid consigned to the past, the growth of the Youth Charter's development was to be realised further and with far reaching impact, with Manchester's wish to bid and host the 2002 Commonwealth Games. With the Youth Charter identified as part of the youth culture and community policy strategy of the Bid, the Charter's growth was rapid and challenging in meeting the expectations of young people and the wider global community. The Manchester 2000 Bid's lobbying efforts would also coincide with the efforts and historic changes brought about with the end of apartheid in South Africa.

This saw the Youth Charter contribute to the overall vision, mission and policy development and implementation of the role sport and recreation could play in the re-building and growth of the Rainbow Nation. The Youth Charter South Africa Desk was launched on Youth Day, 16th June 1996.[15] The Spirit of Hulme & Moss Side legacy activity also saw the realisation of the Youth Charter's presentation of its work at the Pre Millennium Forum NGO Conference entitled 'Global Partnership for Children and Youth' in May 2000. As a result, a dialogue was established with UNICEF with a continued introduction of the potential role of sport as a social vehicle of change and the social issues of young people and communities, with the Youth Charter invited to the UN criminal tribunal in the Hague[16] and the establishment of the Youth Charter Netherlands desk in Holland. Other UN agencies the Youth Charter has worked with include UNHCR, World Health Organisation, UNDPI, UN Working Group on Sport and Development, UNESCO, and United Nations Office on Sport for Development and Peace. The Youth Charter also participated in UK trade visits to Cote d'Ivoire, Zambia and South Africa and contributed policy and initiative

14. Soccerwise Report: see (http://www.youthcharter.co.uk/youth_soccerwise.html).

15. The Youth Charter '17' SA Report saw the Executive Summary launched in 2006.

16. Youth Charter as a Contributor to Social Regeneration 17. Youth Charter Commonwealth Report 2006.

advice to the: 1997 FIFA World Cup, 1999 FIFA Women's World Cup, All Africa Games 1999, 2008 UEFA Soccer Championships, 2010 FIFA World Cup.

Connecting Communities

Eighteen years on, the Youth Charter has continued to identify cross boarder and intercontinental approaches that continue to build and take forward the social and human potential of sport as a social vehicle of change through its key themes of education, health, social order and the environment.

The opportunity to bring together local and global project and programme work to date was realised with the 2002 Commonwealth games and the "Connecting Communities" initiative. This ambitious youth cultural programme saw 1000 young people from 10 disadvantaged communities and cities in the UK realise the spirit of the Games. They were also joined by youth delegations from the commonwealth with a diverse experience of games visits and youth culture dialogue in the recently inspired Moss Side Millennium Powerhouse[17]. This saw the then Secretary General Sir Don McKinnon visit the centre and chair the debate. The 'Spirit of the Streets Tour of South Africa' a decade later saw 20 young people from Manchester visit the rainbow nation to explore and experience the social and human developments taking place there. The visit, the experiences and the memories built on the previous 'Spirit of Hulme & Moss Side Tour of LA'. With each tour group member aiming to establish a project that would provide a lasting social and human legacy on his or her community, the 2003 tenth anniversary of the Youth Charter's journey to date provided an opportunity to invite the collective global and local activity toexplore the future. A bonding weekend took place as a social and cultural fusion of activity, debate, celebration and recognition of the challenges and opportunities faced in the issues surrounding policy, delivery, sustainable impact and above all – community empowerment. The resulting contributions saw the Youth Charter again visit the UN in New York where it would co-sponsor a seminar as part of the UN DPI/NGO Conference 2003.

---

17. **Youth Charter Commonwealth Report:** Web Citation; The report that led to the social policy changes that now see more resources invested in young people and communities through sport and the arts. Social inclusion and regeneration projects and programmes, case studies along with invaluable insights into voluntary and agency activity in this challenging but reward. Available at: http://www.youthcharter.co.uk/products_reports.html (Accessed 12th March 2012).

CASE STUDY
DAY OF THE AFRICAN CHILD

The Day of the African Child followed the successful Youth Charter co-hosted work-shop at the UN in 2003 where a New York based community organisation formed part of the 2012 New York Olympic Bid. Day of the African Child was the youth and community element of the bid. With the Youth Charter's commitment to the new South Africa and the launch of its South Africa desk in 1996 as part of the June 16th Youth Day in commemoration of the Soweto uprisings, this opportunity provided an important legacy potential of social and human value within the bid-ding and hosting of major games. As a result, the Day of the African Child was es-tablished as part of a unique videoconference experience between the continents of Africa, America and Europe. Young people from Kenya, Senegal and South Africa joined young people of Jamaica, America and England to discuss the social, cultur-al and economic issues, challenges and opportunities faced as 21st century global cit-izens. The UK delegation was hosted by the British Council as part of the Youth Charter's ten-year relationship. A dialogue was maintained, with the Day of the African Child building a relationship with the Muhammad Ali Institute for Peace & Justice, which was established within the University of Louisville, Kentucky. The In-stitute was formed to provide a contribution to the Muhammad Ali Center, which was opened in November 2005 to build on the social and human legacy of boxing le-gend and greatest Olympian, Muhammad Ali.[18] In 2006, the Muhammad Ali Schol-ars, a unique representation of young people, were selected from the University of Louisville Campus to develop and take forward the Ali ideals of promoting respect, hope and understanding, and to inspire adults and children everywhere to be as great as they can be. The Ali Scholars are also expected to put something back into their community upon their return from their international travels. The 2006 Ali Scholars were hosted by the Youth Charter prior to their visit to Africa and visited the North West of England. The highlight of their tour featured their attendance in Liver-pool at the Anthony Walker Conference and the Race Relations Resource Centre at Manchester University as well as the launch of the Manchester 12 Report[19] at the Moss Side Millennium Power House. In 2008 the Youth Charter was invited to the University of Louisville as part of the Ali in Focus week. This saw the Youth Charter contribute at all levels of the community social and human development ex-

---

18. Youth Charter Manchester '12' – "This ground breaking report charts the early be-ginnings, experiences of the anti-social gang related activity that inspired the Youth Charter's work. Invaluable social, cultural and sporting policy along with facts, fig-ures, case studies and proposed solutions for the ongoing debate of the role of sport as a social vehicle of change". See related website for further information; Accessed 12 February 2012. (http://youthcharter.co.uk/index.php?/products/details/youth_charter_manchester_12_report)

19. Youth Charter Muhammad Ali Report: The report of the 2010 Muhammad Ali Scholars tour of England was built on an exciting global collaboration between the Youth Charter and the MUHAMMAD ALI INSTITUTE.

perience. The highlight was the visit to the International Warrior Arts Federation and the'Champions Aren't Made in the Gym' lecture to an invited audience of student athletes from surrounding colleges and universities.

2009 saw changes in both the institute and the center, resulting in the Youth Charter hosting the 2010 Ali Scholars for their UK tour. Hosted by the Universities of Salford and Roehampton and joined by a group of British Council scholars from the Leasowe Community on the Wirral, the Ali Scholars visited the cities of Liverpool, Bradford, Manchester and London. An itinerary that exposed them to the social and cultural challenges as global citizens was reflected in the social and cultural realities now being faced by local communities of inner cities, urban, suburban and rural in the north and the south of the UK. The tour culminated in its contribution to the Roehampton Legacy Conference *(20)* which discussed the local, national and international legacy challenges and opportunities presented as part of London's 2012 Olympic and Paralympic Games.

As a result a legacy manifesto and recommendations were agreed (www.youth-charter.co.uk.preview.exa.net.uk/olympic_legacy_conference.php) with the 2010 Scholars travelling on to Ghana where they were to contribute to community development and capacity building.[20]

The legacy of the 2010 Scholars tour of the UK has seen an ongoing dialogue with regards to the Youth Charter's global Citizenship in Action initiative and how its contribution can be made to the local young people and communities of Louisville and beyond. The 2011 visit of the Youth Charter to Louisville saw a contribution to the Ideals Festival with other international social and human development through sport activists from other states in the USA and abroad. The Youth Charter presented its legacy cultural framework and community campus as part of the consultation, dialogue and contribution to the 2012 global youth summit, which will hopefully be hosted in London during the Olympic and Paralympic Games.

The legacy of the 2002 Commonwealth Games saw the establishment of the "Citizenship in Action initiative," which would aim to develop the Youth Charter approach in ten communities of the UK and the Commonwealth. The continued challenges and opportunities of sport as a social and human vehicle of change will also be explored within the global social economic and cultural stability and the notion of global citizenship, rights, responsibilities and the need for a more collective and collaborative effort. In 2003 the Youth Charter presented its Citizenship in Action international legacy initiative of the 2002 Commonwealth Games to the inaugural Magglingen Conference for Sport and Peace. In 2005 The Youth Charter presented its social and human development cultural framework and a proposed UN and NGO multi-agency effort.[21]

20.Roehampton Legacy Forum 21

21.Roehampton Legacy Forum 21

CASE STUDY
NAMIBIA

Following the Youth Charter's presentation and contribution to the Magglingen 2003 conference, the Youth Charter was invited to submit a funding proposal to deliver a social coach leadership programme and toolkit for Southern Africa. This opportunity provided a chance to develop an integrated framework and approach in the growing investment being made in the Sport for Peace and social and human development agenda. The Youth Charter had already established a strong and continued fourteen-year presence in Africa and Southern Africa in particular, with UK Trade Missions delivered to Zambia and South Africa. Project programme initiatives had already been contributed to Malawi, Zimbabwe and Namibia. The Youth Charter set about establishing a needs assessment of the social and human activity through sport in the region through its dialogue and contribution to the Zone 6 Supreme Council for Sport as part of the legacy of the 1999 All Africa Games in South Africa.

The Youth Charter then consulted a number of NGOs working as part of an EU sponsored programme initiative in Southern Africa to establish a common framework and respond to issues surrounding South African community sport and development organisations wishing to deliver their own projects and programmes and even design them with a more cost efficient, effective and sustainable benefit.

The Youth Charter responded with a consultation and contribution to a UK Sport and UN ILO hosted workshop in Mozambique. A two-day seminar saw a national youth sports policy and social and human development policy through sport framework agreed and an offer extended to the Youth Charter to deliver the social coach workshop. This overall approach was presented to an international audience at the Magglingen 2005 Conference with preparations made for its delivery. A number of challenges were experienced, resulting in the social coach workshop finally hosted and delivered in Namibia by the Namibian government and Sports Commission. Participation was also forthcoming from Zambia and South Africa with a number of leading NGO's in the region in attendance.

As a result, the Africawise toolkit was designed and developed and established by Africans for Africans and realised for those in the developed world for the developing world.[22] Forty social coaches were in attendance and also saw the first Youth Charter social coach accreditations offered anywhere in the world. The project was independently reviewed and highlighted the need for more sustainable resources as part of the continued ability for the social coaches to utilise their toolkits as the all-important tools in measuring, mapping and tracking the impact of their efforts as part of the collective and integrated Southern Africa contribution to the Millennium Development Goals. Sadly and to date, this has not been possible. However an interactive

---

22. UN Quadrennial Report: Available at: http://esa.un.org/coordination/ngo/new/index.asp?page=quads (Accessed 12th February 2012).

social network facilitation has been developed and efforts are ongoing as part of the legacy contributions to the 2010 South Africa Soccer World Cup and 2012 Olympic and Paralympic Games.[23]

Social and Human Development

The legacy of major games has only recently adopted the socially inclusive and regenerative ability of Olympic, Paralympic Games/major events in the pursuit of social and human development of young people and the wider community. Whilst the 1984 Olympic Games re-established and saved the Olympic movement with the corporate sponsorship that many argue has corrupted the Olympic ideal, what was seen as an ideological legacy of debt to previous host cities was now seen as a profitable vehicle for promoting tourism and global attention within the political and economic interests reflected in the respective bid candidate cities. 20 years on, the Olympic Games in both its summer and winter attraction along with the Paralympic Games are seen as the ideal vehicle in reviving, promoting or reinforcing a host city, national sense of identity and importance in the global community. Even failing bids consider the investment of what can run in to many millions of dollars as worth the effort in promoting a city and national interest. To the winning candidate host city, much can be enjoyed with the benefits as wide ranging as they are narrow within the Olympic contract that is signed as an agreement of ensuring that the Olympic ideal is maintained within all the interests however corporate however political, however social or cultural in the ability to bring the world together and provide a global focus and attention unlike any other.

However, despite the recent recognition by the United Nations that sport can indeed impact on the social and human development of young people and communities and even help the UN achieve its Millennium Development Goals, the 2015 date approaches with the goals under threat in their ability to score a winning opportunity for the African continent. With Africa only now having just hosted the 2010 FIFA world cup, the first major global sporting event hosted on the continent, the ambitions to host a first Olympic Games on the African continent would be a wonderful achievement to coincide with the 2015 Millennium Development Goals milestone.

With FIFA leading the way and with Rio uniquely hosting a FIFA soccer world cup and then Olympic Games, the social and human potential for impacting and improving lives through the Olympic and Paralympic movement have never been greater in their potential and realisation. Indeed, with

---

23.Namibia Report. - Available at: http://www.amazon.de/Reportage-Namibia-Durch-Augen-Geparden/dp/3854529759 (Accessed 12th February 2012).

the 30th Olympiad given to London on the pledge of improving the healthy and active lifestyles of a global youth culture switched off from the Games in favour of the alternative interactive computer games, the interests for the IOC and their ability to maintain its global appeal as well as the ongoing appeal of its sponsors is imperative. Add to this the ability to address crime and community safety with a diverse multiculturalism provides too compelling an argument and case. But with global austerity and disputes between the National Olympic Committee and the Local Organising Committee seeing a court of arbitration in Lausanne having to judge an argument over the legacy profits of the 30th Olympiad, this does not bode well with the legacy pledges made and current efforts to date. The Youth Charter has contributed to: 1992 Barcelona Olympic Games, Nagano 1998 Olympic Bid, All Africa Games 1999, Manchester 2000 Olympic Bid, Commonwealth Games 2002 bid and games, Cape Town 2000 Olympic Bid.

Challenges and Opportunities

The challenge lies in the simple fact that legacy means different things to different people. However, many people believe that the legacy of any games is reflected in the host city's bid document pledges at the final session where the bid is decided upon, and more critically in the acceptance speech once the UN contract is signed. London's efforts to that end cannot be assessed until the Paralympic Flame goes out and the legacy is consigned to memory. Current efforts are fragmented, patchy and uncoordinated. The legacy efforts are confined to the East End corridor and the Olympic Stadium which again sees another publicly funded national symbol of pride handed over to corporate interests with some justification made in the young people and wider community concessions made.

With the 2002 Commonwealth Games Eastland's stadium now owned by the richest premiership club in the world, there are plenty of reminders of how legacy can become a social and human travesty in the life chances and opportunities it provides for the young people and the wider community it was pledged to improve as a result of legacy efforts. However, the potential to build on the legacy potential and effort of late lies in the ability of the Olympic and Paralympic movement to provide a framework that can integrate the games, sports and international development departments of the current IOC structure and deliver something truly sustainable. If this is achieved, then legacy toolkits can be introduced via the National Olympic Committees and help provide added value where applicable in the national and sovereign effort in which they reside. However, with the current issue of social and human development aid at the political level (ie channelled through sovereign state departments of youth, culture and social affairs) being by-passed by the NGO industry and autonomous identity and activities of the National Olympic Committee, the potential for wasted resources exists.

This could also be helped by the UN itself having an integrated multi agency policy approach. With all UN agencies currently using sport to deliver their own respective policies, the competition for the signatures and ambassadorial endorsement by the sportsmen and women who have come from those communities is immense. It must be better coordinated in order to deliver all of the social and human development needs in a holistic and more effectively efficient and integrated way. Current UN sponsored events give the sport for peace and social human development movement an opportunity to provide a truly global framework that can then deliver a sub-regional approach. It can be argued that with the 2010 Soccer World Cup legacy activity, coupled with the Rwanda Genocide remembrance movement, this sub-regional opportunity is currently presenting itself in Africa. The focus on memorial and reconciliation in Rwanda and South Africa, along with South Africa still grappling with the challenges of educational illiteracy, means looking at the existing NGO activity in the region would be of considerable value with regards to achieving the 2015 Millennium Development Goals. Europe is providing an opportunity to look at the continued challenges of youth issues within the 41 member states of Africa through the intercultural cities programme. Again, this provides the opportunity to integrate and culturally map the on-going sport, peace and social/human development policy agenda and effort. The continuing migration fears from the Middle East and Africa, as well as issues surrounding the causes, effects and impact of terrorism will be addressed in the forthcoming UN seminar. This again provides an opportunity to truly integrate and join up existing efforts.

With 2022 Soccer World Cup host nation Qatar hosting the United Nations Alliance of Civilisations and Civil Society Forum in May, and the Sport for Peace Forum taking place in Monaco, the on-going platforms to look at impact to shape best practice are considerable. With the current IOC 'Olympism in Action' initiative and the Sport for All Conference in Beijing in September 2011, twinned with a global youth revolution and the UN International year of Youth, there has never been a greater opportunity for the sport and social and human development movement to collude and provide the youth of the world with an opportunity to develop in life. There also needs to be a global fund specifically established for this purpose, and a solid policy framework for this funding and investment made available to compliment the other lending instruments currently in place. This coherence would remove significant waste and mismanagement.

The argument for providing a truly social and human opportunity for sport for all that can deliver a global youth culture experience replete with healthy lifestyles and realising potential cannot be underestimated. In a time where the world is both uncertain and unpredictable, the need for sport as a vehicle of hope, opportunity and bringing mankind together to develop and foster goodwill has never been greater. We need to deliver a legacy that is truly sustainable and, above all, meets the potential that sport can bring to the development arena.

To do this best will require a global set of *legacy goals* that can build upon the Millennium Development Goals and go far beyond the African continent. The goals can be universal and then locally delivered within the respective sub-regions. It is also worth remembering that the Burkino Faso's and Mali's of this world will not host an Olympic Games any time soon. Therefore it is absolutely critical that present and future legacy efforts fulfil their commitment to improve the conditions and opportunities for the entire world's youth.

Legacy 2012 and Beyond

The Youth Charter will continue to present, develop and share its ongoing work from its Citizenship in Action global initiative. Case study examples will be presented through our current legacy activity and through our Legacy Campus, Cultural Framework and Social Coach Legacy Toolkit. They will show how physical and cultural activity can provide social benefits through the bidding and hosting of major games to address educational disaffection and the unhealthy lifestyle choices that can lead to anti-social, violent, and radicalised young people who continue to face socio-economic and cultural deprivation.

The impact of the Youth Charter's work will also present its contribution and impacts following the 2010 soccer World Cup, and it will look at how the agency can contribute to the ongoing challenges to the delivery of the U.N. Millennium Development Goals, and how sport may be able to assist. The continued challenges and opportunities of physical activity as a social and human vehicle of change will also be explored within the global social economic and cultural stability and the notion of global citizenship, rights, responsibilities and the need for a more collective and collaborative effort. These contributions will hopefully evince the opportunities and benefits of physical activity, and highlight the programmes and policies that show real potential within the 2012 legacy plans. It will also, I am certain, show how a more integrated, efficient and effective use of resources and stakeholder efforts must necessarily be the future if Sport For All is to be realised.

YC Philosophy

"Sport is an order of chivalry, a code of ethics and aesthetics, recruiting its members from all classes and all peoples. Sport is a truce. In an era of antagonisms and conflicts, it is the respite of the Gods in which fair competition ends in respect and friendship (Olympism). Sport is education, the truest form of education, that of character. Sport is culture because it enhances life and, most importantly, does so for those who usually have the least opportunity to feast on it".

Chapter 28

The Redevelopment of Sport in Cambodia

Reflections on a Football Player who Survived the Khmer Rouge Regime

Chiaki Okada

Introduction

The Kingdom of Cambodia is a Buddhist country in Southeast Asia bordered by Vietnam, Laos and Thailand. Although records vary, under the Khmer Rouge Regime in the 1970's, Cambodia experienced extensive slaughter, which decreased the population from 7.5 million to 6 million. This regime ended in 1978, but Cambodians suffered subsequent conflicts until the Paris Peace Accords of 1991. Because of these confusing decades, Cambodia still faces many problematic issues such as serious poverty, high child mortality and lack of social infrastructure. Rebuilding a country, requires the development of human resources in every field, and much development assistance from outside is continued even today. Siem Reap, hometown of Ouk Sareth, the subject of study in this chapter, is among the most seriously poverty-stricken regions in Cambodia (see table 1 below).

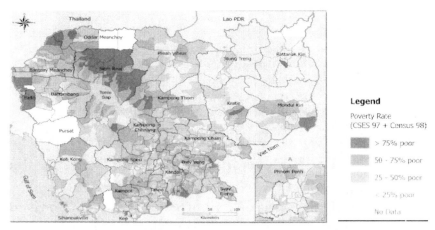

Table 1: Poverty Map of Cambodia - Source: Danida (2006) "The Atlas of Cambodia"

About 53.7 percent of residents in Siem Reap live below the poverty line of 0.32US$ (for urban areas) and 0.27US$ (for rural areas) per capita per day consumption, set by the Cambodian government.

The purpose of this chapter is to record the corruption and re-development of sport in Cambodia through reflection on Ouk Sareth's life and career. After the Khmer Rouge Regime there are very few remaining documents, records or survivors' memories. Accordingly, the development of sports depended entirely on the few persons who used to be concerned with sport. Ouk Sareth is one such person, being involved in and devoting himself to promoting sports. It is hoped that by documenting his history this chapter will contribute to sports development in Cambodia, and set an example for other post conflict societies. This research is based on the results of a life history interview conducted in September 2007 in Siem Reap.

This chapter has two sections. The first describes the career history of Ouk Sareth divided into four periods, and the historical background and sports environment in each period reflecting Ouk Sareth's life. The second section, referring to Ouk Sareth's comments, considers prospects for sports development in Cambodia.

Living with Sports

[1] Until Graduation from High School: from 1947 to 1963 (0-16 Years of age)

Cambodia became independent from France in 1953 and had a peaceful time under the rule of Norodom Sihanouk. Just a few years before its independence, Ouk Sareth was born, May 30th 1947, to be the first boy of eventually the 13 children of Ouk Saly and Svang Rin, at Peamro village, Prey Veng province. He had one elder sister, and was to have nine younger sisters and three younger brothers.

Ouk Sareth's father was a national government official and held several important positions. He was an intellectual person with ability in the French, Vietnamese, and Pali languages, and was killed during the Khmer Rouge Regime. When Ouk Sareth lived in Kampot[1], a Russian football team visited Cambodia for a match in Phnom Penh, the capital city of Cambodia. Ouk Sareth took a cyclo (pedicab) from Kampot and went to the stadium[2] in Phnom Penh to watch the game with his father. He vividly remembers the game and his impression of the appearance of the stadium at the time.

Although Ouk Sareth had good physical abilities in elementary school, his talent appeared when he was in secondary school in Siem Reap. He was slim and only 160 centimeters tall in his first year of secondary school, however, he participated in the national competition for secondary school students representing Siem Reap province in his third grade. He competed in the 100-meter, 200-meter sprint and 4x100-meter relay and won a gold medal in the 200-meter sprint. His parents had not realized he had such good physical ability until that time, but then they started encouraging him to play sport.

Ouk Sareth played football intensively after meeting a physical education teacher, Tan Kiryvuth, at secondary school. He firstly played striker but switched to goalkeeper during high school.

[2] Until the Collapse of the Khmer Rouge Regime: from 1964 to 1979 (17-32 Years of age)

In 1964 Ouk Sareth entered a college in Phnom Penh. Soon after his graduation in 1966 he went to North Korea to learn sports management for three years. In North Korea, while he took his classes, he had training and practiced football three times a day, and ate a lot of food and drank ice coffee with plenty of condensed milk to increase his weight. As a result, he developed muscular strength rapidly and gained seven kilograms in the first four months[3].

When he came back to Cambodia he continued studying at a university until 1973. He had also played football for the team of the Royal Police and contributed to their coming first in the national championship. This led him to start his life as a Cambodian national football team player in 1968, when he was 21 years old. He was selected as a representative for the Cambodian youth team and the national team at the same time. The Cambodian national team at that time was coached in turns by coaches from North Korea, France, Czechoslovakia and China. The team participated in international games many times mainly in Asia, and won third place after Burma

---

1. His family moved to Siem Reap, Phnom Penh and Kampot as his father was transferred for his work.

2. This stadium was called Stade Rambair, named after the French architect who designed it. The stadium can still be seen in Phnom Penh.

3. He was 175 centimeters tall and only 60 kilograms before he came to North Korea.

and North Korea in the Asian Championship in 1971. Ouk Sareth married a Cambodian woman in 1971, who was a national volleyball team player and they had two children.

Cambodia was one of the leading countries for sport in Southeast Asia in the 1960s. Athletes were trained intensively at the national training center as in the other socialist countries, and young sport scholars were accepted from neighboring countries[4]. In Battambang, the second largest city in Cambodia, there was a sport center for the intensive training of talented Cambodian junior athletes aged between 8 and 13[5].

In the 1970's, Cambodia entered a chaotic period, when the country was involved in conflicts between democracy and communism. America and South Vietnam carried out raids periodically against Cambodia. Affected by these airstrikes, internal public safety and the economic situation had weakened in 1969. Under this adverse environment, Ouk Sareth graduated from university in 1973 and joined a team "Force Army National Khmer (FANK)", where he could dedicate himself to playing football in the national football team.

On April 17, 1975 Cambodia's capital Phnom Penh fell to the Khmer Rouge, which severed diplomatic relations with the united Vietnam and had a utopian idea for a new country with unskilled farmers who tamely serve their government. Everyone was forced to immigrate into rural areas and live in designated groups to work under the directions of young farmers. People were starving and many died because of disease and debility by servitude labor or long distance traveling on foot. What is more, intellectual people, questioning the authorities, were slaughtered after horrific torture.

Ouk Sareth was in Phnom Penh the day it fell. He was forced to move to Kompong Speu province and stay in a group in Phnom Srong district. After eight months, he was taken to Sisophon and after that he was moved back and forth several times between Sisophon and Phnom Srok district in Banteay Meanchey province. During this time, he pretended to be uneducated and not able to write. He concealed his name and his career as a football player. He had learned to do this from his experiences in North Korea, to avoid torture and slaughter. Meanwhile, his father, four brothers and sisters, wife, two children, and many of his former teammates in the national team died under the regime.

This tragic period continued for three years, eight months and twenty days. Hun Sen, and Heng Samrin came into Phnom Penh supported by a Vietnamese force at the end of 1978 and put an end to the Khmer Rouge Regime. In May, 1979, Ouk Sareth started walking to Siem Reap, where he had grown up, from the Phnom Srok district in Banteay Meanchey province,

---

4. Chhay Kimsan, current coach of national track and field team, stated in the interview posted on NyoNyum, vol. 36, 2008.

5. Three Japan Overseas Cooperation Volunteers worked in the field of swimming for seven years. Refer to the website: Sports Environment in Cambodia, M. Shibata, http://www.valley.ne.jp/-join/network/kampuchea_sports/kampuchea_spo%20.htm [2008/10/10]

over 100 kilometers away. May is dry and the hottest time in the year, so he rested under the shade of trees during the day time and walked during the night and he was physically weak because of the chronic lack of food. In the middle of June, he arrived at Kralanh Bridge located on the border of Siem Reap and Banteay Meanchey province. He was barely able to walk by that time; however, his earnest desire to go back to his hometown encouraged him to step forward. There was nothing but broken houses and bridges hidden by lots of trees in Siem Reap when he arrived. He walked around looking for his family for about a month and he also asked for them in Battambang and Svay Rieng. Nevertheless, this was, sadly, in vain.

[3] Until the Time Worked as a NGO Staff member: from 1980 to 1996 (33-49 Years of age)

After coming back to Siem Reap in June 1979, Ouk Sareth started to play a guitar on the devastated streets, busking for food. During this time, he took part in cutting down the trees that had grown up over the village, so that it could be rebuilt. He continued this voluntary work and subsistence lifestyle until he could start to work for the Department of Culture, Information and Sport, Siem Reap province, as a sports manager in January 1980. He married his current wife, and they had two sons and a daughter. He formed a football team with some Vietnamese men and started training at the same time as taking up a job in the government. Furthermore in 1982, he returned to the Cambodian national football team. He played in the national team again until his retirement in 1985 at the age of 38, after which he took the position of sports manager in the Department of Education, Youth and Sport Siem Reap province[6], newly established in 1987 as a part of the governmental reform.

After the Khmer Rouge Regime collapsed, Cambodia lacked infrastructure and utilities in every field. Many people suffered from lack of food and housing. Moreover, there was no freedom to travel and no postal or telephone facilities. This situation obstructed the rebuilding of lives and people moved toward refugee camps on the Thai-Cambodian border. While traveling, they always feared landmines and attacks by the pockets of surviving Khmer Rouge forces. The number of refugees increased with time and this revealed, to the international society, what had happened and was happening in Cambodia.

In the 1990s the situation started to improve, when the United Nations became involved in settling the political struggles in Cambodia. The UN assisted in the conclusion of the Paris Peace Accords in 1991, and the first general election was held in 1993. Under the operation of the United Nations Transitional Authority in Cambodia (UNTAC), a turnout of more

---

6. The Department of Education, Youth and Sport was organized under the Ministry of Education, Youth and Sport (MoEYS). The department has three offices under its organization; education office, youth office and sport office. Ouk Sareth headed the sport office. At the time of starting up, however, the operation of youth Office and sport office was not clearly defined.

than 90 percent was recorded, with a power shift from a communist regime to a democracy. Under the new regime, Ouk Sareth temporarily worked as a staff member of a UNHCR[7] - a related NGO from 1994 to 1997. The stadium, located at the center of the city, had been left empty and overgrown with grass, becoming just a playground for children.

[4] After Starting to Work as a Sport Administrative Officer in the Ministry of Education, Youth and Sport: from 1997 to 2009 (50-62 Years of age)

In 1997, finishing his work at the NGO, Ouk Sareth returned to Siem Reap and resumed his work as a sports manager. He located his office at the deserted stadium in the center of the city and started to reconstruct the sports environment from scratch; there were no facilities, equipment, material nor human resources for sports in Siem Reap at that time. No one showed interest in sports, including government department directors, so he had to face all the difficulties with his two colleagues in the sport office; Keo Bunthoun[8], specialized in track and field, and Thu Sam Ang, specialized in volleyball. It took time to change this situation until the fifth director of the department, To Kim Sean, was appointed.

Ouk Sareth set a target for the sport office: to hold the 2000 national competition for secondary school students in Siem Reap and launched efforts to improve the sports environment especially in schools. In particular, his office set up a plan for preparing a field, arrangement of equipment and recruiting of new sports teachers. To forward these plans, he had to collect money by himself because there was no assigned budget from the government. Therefore Ouk Sareth visited the Siem Reap provincial governor, Agriculture Department, Commerce Department and even individuals who seemed to have money to ask for financial support, showing his prepared proposals for sport development. Among them, the provincial governor showed a particular understanding of the plan and provided some funds to implement it. Ouk Sareth bought some tools from the Commerce Department with the funds, and repaired facilities which could be used for sports activities. Furthermore, he raised pigs and got money from selling their meat at a market[9], while he kept some portion of it aside for his family to eat[10]. The income was spent for improving ground areas for sport.

These patient efforts opened the way to holding the 2001 national competition in Siem Reap. As a host province of the games, budgets for building and repairing of fields and offices concerning sport were allocated by Ministry of Education, Youth and Sport (MoEYS), which accelerated the reconstruction of the sports environment in Siem Reap. Sport offices chose

---

7. It is the UN's refugee agency, United Nations High Commissioner for Refugees.

8. He was appointed to a sports manager in 2008.

9. At that time, many athletes gained their expenses by selling products.

10. Officials' salaries being low, he also had trouble making a living.

some large high schools as enhanced base points in each area and prepared improved sports environments by making football fields, volleyball and basketball courts and distributing equipment.

After Ouk Sareth's retirement from the national football team, he devoted himself to promoting sports in Siem Reap, even though he had several requests to be a coach or a government officer in Phnom Penh. He explained that his reason was because most of the national team athletes at the time were from urban areas, and he worried about the poor opportunities for young talented children in the rural provinces. Slayman Salim, Ouk Sareth's former teammate, is one of those people who worked hard by improving the sports environment in rural areas. He used to be the head coach of the Cambodian national football team, coaching the team in Phnom Penh, and at the same time, he worked as a sports manager in Koh Kong province, where he lived. Ouk Sareth and Slayman Salim are good friends and share the same hope for the revival of Cambodian sport.

In 2007, still in the process of reconstruction of the sports environment, Ouk Sareth retired from the department, becoming an advisor and continuing to work until 2009. Even after resigning from this post, there are numerous operations that no one can handle but him, for example: collaboration projects with foreign aid groups, or international competitions. Therefore he is putting all his effort into these operations as well as into the development of the younger generation, without a salary, as of 2011.

Road to Sports development of Cambodia: The comments of Ouk Sareth

Ouk Sareth survived chaos to devote himself to promoting Cambodian sport, although, sport endangered his life with his background as a footballer. Siem Reap is recently regarded as a province successful in sport promotion. A Cambodian governmental sport magazine, which is the only sport-related publication in Cambodia, describes the Siem Reap sport scene as follows "*we can see remarkable activities surrounding sport in Siem Reap. That includes training for athletes, sport activities in and out of school, and developing sport infrastructure. In Siem Reap, it is essential for continuing those activities to gain support from groups and individuals of good will*" (MoEYS: 2008, p.3).

Such development owes much to Ouk Sareth's work for the Siem Reap sport office. The reasons for his successful leadership are his effective ideas, practical hands, and adept understanding of Cambodian children, drawn from his exceptional experiences. The Cambodian society needed such experience for regional and national sport development, and Ouk Sareth tries to develop sport to as high an international level as possible. He avoids using inadequate fields and equipment which would violate the rules and encourages students to wear proper clothes for sports instead of school uniforms. We frequently see sport played without rules, ignored by referees. Ouk Sareth requires the observance of rules by players and referees. It is difficult to demand such levels as a condition for participating in sport in such an area of severe poverty, differing living circumstances and morals. Although over strict regulations may exclude people from playing, they will be the key for achieving sport development in and outside of Cambodia. Ouk Sareth has established a certain level of standards for sport, complying with the realities of Cambodian society. His sense of standards has added to the basic principles for people, although, the globalized modern sporting environment is not without problems itself.

Circumstances surrounding sport has greatly changed in Siem Reap. Until a few years ago, sport was not a common activity. Now, however, some people play sport regularly, especially around the city center. To make these changes more widespread and sustainable, Ouk Sareth has pointed out the importance of the national and local governments' role and people's voluntary participations in sport and commented;

> "The central government can support people's activities instead of ignore them. Meanwhile, the ministry preferentially allocates a budget to some provinces to carry out sport related projects actively. Therefore, we should consider carefully how we plan and manage our activities". He continues;

> "We, the sport office, have ideas but we can't bring them to fruition without people's participation. When I say "people", I mean the players, teams and local people who support the team. When we have certain kinds of competitions, people are willing to take part. The reasons are that they have recognized playing football is good for their health and they like playing it. People who don't participate in a competition are those who don't like football. We can't force them to play football if they don't like it. We want them to play another sport which they like". And furthermore;

> "In sport activities, we are trying to increase the number of people in all positions through the following approaches; we ask retired players to help manage games and coach young players. We also support various companies and NGOs, most of them are involved in the tourist businesses (major industry in Siem Reap), to form a league and play games. Once that is realized, sport in Siem Reap will truly prosper".

(Interview data)

While Ouk Sareth has carried out his responsibility for sport promotion in the province as a sport administrative officer, he has been involved in football training as a coach. He teaches a wide age range, students to amateur players, who can freely ask his advice on any occasion, and he can give comprehensive advice on management, enhancement of competitive abilities, and teaching skills. All are attached to him, calling him "our sports mentor" or "our football mentor". Ouk Sareth is a key person for sport promotion in Siem Reap at governmental and grass-roots levels. Particularly noteworthy are his achievements in promoting sport by encouraging people to participate because he can communicate with every generation and class, not being at the top of a pyramid type organization.

In recent development studies the view prevails that individual happiness should be centered on development, and human development should be the priority when setting development goals. In the capability approach by Amartya Sen, *"the well-being of a person should be measured in terms of what a person can do and can be."* (Sen: 1993) and, Marbub ul Haq set a force of Human development in 1990 by commenting that:

> "Human development is a process of enlarging people's choices. In principle, these choices can be infinite and change over time. But at all levels of development, the three essential ones are for people to lead a long and healthy life, to acquire knowledge and to have access to resources needed for a decent standard of living".

(UNDP:1990).

When viewing Ouk Sareth's activities from the standpoint of current development trends, that is, taking the word "development" as people's voluntary involvement in activities to pursue their own happiness, we can say his approaches are classed as "community development through sport".

Ouk Sareth's words offer us valuable suggestions as they come from his exceptional experiences in sport reconstruction from zero facilities, equipment or players. Cambodia restarted from nothing after the three years and eight months of the Khmer Rouge Regime, when all social activities were prohibited and many intellectuals were killed. All sport related assets such as culture, human resources, facilities, equipment, organizations, systems and documents were lost. It has taken a long time to bring back a sporting culture and tradition, not to mention meeting sports' material needs. Under these circumstances, reconstruction of sport is being carried out only with the memories and efforts of a few related survivors. Although it is minimal, it is lively enough to show us directly the attractive significance of sport.

References

Linton, S. (2004). *Reconciliation in Cambodia,* Phnom Penh, Documentation Center of Cambodia.

Martha, C. N. and A. Sen (1993). *The Quality of Life*, The United Nations University.

Ministry of Education, Youth and Sport, Kingdom of Cambodia (2005).*Education Strategic Plan 2006-2010,* Phnom Penh: Ministry of Education, Youth and Sport.

Ministry of Education, Youth and Sport, Kingdom of Cambodia (2005). *Sport Development Report 2004-2005,* Phnom Penh: Ministry of Education, Youth and Sport.

Ministry of Education, Youth and Sport, Kingdom of Cambodia (2007). *Cambodia Sport Magazine* Vol.30, Phnom Penh: Ministry of Education, Youth and Sport

Ministry of Education, Youth and Sport, Kingdom of Cambodia (2007). *Cambodia Sport Magazine* Vol.32, Phnom Penh: Ministry of Education, Youth and Sport.

Rusten, C. and K. Sedara et al.(2004). *The Challenges of Decentralisation Design in Cambodia,* Phnom Penh, Cambodia Development Resource Institute.

Save Cambodia's Wildlife 2006). *The Atlas of Cambodia – National Poverty and Environment Maps*, Phnom Penh: Danida.

Sonfas, P. (2001). *Kingdom of Cambodia Country Report*, First Asian Conference on Women and Sport.

Sport for Development and Peace International Working Group (2005). *Sport for Development and Peace*, Paper presented at the International Working Group Meeting. New York: Sport for development and Peace International Working Group.

UNDP (2008). *Human Development Report 2007/2008*, United Nations Development Program.

UNDP (2009). *Human Development Report 2008/2009*, United Nations Development Program.

Yamazaki, Y. (2008). *NyoNyum* Vol.36, Aug-Sep, NyoNyom.

Chapter 29

Japan's Assistance to Developing Countries in the Fields of Physical Education and Sport

Kazuhiko Saito

Introduction

The global trend in recent years is for a focus on aid in the social development sphere, and education, in particular, is seen as being the key to all forms of development. A major issue in educational development is the promotion of "physical education" and "sports", with the physical performance so vital for human beings and also the dissemination of information about health playing an important role in character building. This is a field that not only stimulates physical and mental development, but also is an effective force in international exchanges that can inspire and energize a nation. However, in many developing countries there is insufficient physical education in schools due to such causes as lack of trained teachers, insufficient awareness of the significance of this school subject or a lack of facilities to provide physical education classes. In addition, factors such as a lack of coaches and budgetary problems mean that only the financially privileged are able to engage in physical activity and other sporting activities.

Against the backdrop of this situation, for more than 40 years ago Japan
has provided international assistance in the field of physical education and
sports with the Japan Overseas Cooperation Volunteers programme performing the central role in providing this aid. The need for such support
continues to expand and, in line with this, there is a trend for increased
cooperation in the field of educational development. Indeed, as of January
2010, Japan has increased its aid program and dispatched a total of 2,667 volunteers. An even greater need is predicted in the near future and a study of
the policy with regard to such assistance is becoming even more essential.
This chapter is intended to provide a clear overview of the physical education and sports assistance provided by Japan, and to clarify trends in the
dispatch of Japan Overseas Cooperation Volunteers (sometimes known as
JOCV), which has played a central role in this assistance.

Japanese Physical Education and Sports Aid

The principle behind Japan's Official Development Assistance (hereafter
ODA) is to provide support for the self-help efforts of developing countries.
The ODA can be broadly categorized into three forms: (1) bilateral grants
(grant aid and technical cooperation), (2) bilateral loans, and (3) contributions and subscriptions to international organisations.

Japan's largest aid organisation, the Japan International Cooperation
Agency (hereafter JICA) is in charge of technical cooperation within the
area of bilateral grants, and of investigation, implementation and promotion, and technical assistance for grant aid. Cultural grants from amongst
the grant aid, and trainee programmes and Japan Overseas Cooperation Volunteer projects from amongst the technical cooperation, are the main aspects related to physical education and sports. Of these, Japan Overseas Cooperation Volunteer projects have the largest scope, if we take both their
budgetary scale and content into consideration.

The Japanese Overseas Cooperation Volunteers (sometimes referred to
as JOCV) was established in April 1965 as a Japanese state project that
comes under the jurisdiction of the Ministry of Foreign Affairs. It is a programme that "encourages and promotes young people's overseas activities
with the objective of uniting with the people of developing regions and
cooperating with the economic and social development of those regions"
(Article 21 (2) of the Japan International Cooperation Agency Law), and is
characterized by its volunteer spirit and public nature, being a membership-
based aid programme based on popular support. Volunteers are dispatched
after an "Agreement Regarding the Dispatch of Japan Overseas Cooperation Volunteers" has been concluded between the Japanese government and
the government of the country concerned, and once the other government
has made a formal request for volunteers via an official Japanese diplomatic
mission. Volunteers are recruited twice a year in response to such requests.
Those who pass the recruitment examination become trainee volunteers
and are required to undergo approximately 80 days of training before being

sent overseas to their various destinations. The first group was dispatched in 1965, and its 26 Japan Overseas Cooperation Volunteers were sent out to four countries (Laos, Cambodia, the Philippines and Malaysia)[1]. In the 45 years since the Japan Overseas Cooperation Volunteer was established, a total of 34,034 Japan Overseas Cooperation Volunteers (as of January 2010) have been dispatched to 81 countries[2]. The volunteers have worked in more than 250 kinds of jobs and their activities can be categorized into seven sectors: agriculture, forestry and fisheries; fabrication of mechanical and electrical equipment (hereafter, "fabrication"); maintenance, repair, and operations of mechanical and electrical equipment (hereafter, "repair operations"); civil engineering and construction; health and sanitation; education and culture; and sports.

Japan Overseas Cooperation Volunteer in Physical Education and Sports

In this section we will look at trends so far in cooperation activities to do with physical education and sport, analyzing them according to factors such as time period and region, and discuss their characteristics. This analysis of trends and transitions uses a random sampling of data belonging to JICA (JOCV performance tables and various other kinds of data) divided according to decade and analyzed from such angles as time period, occupation and area. Data from the 40 years between 1965 and 2005 was used and analysed.

Trends in Volunteer Programs in the Field of Sport

The number of Japan Overseas Cooperation Volunteers dispatched to each sector is categorized by year and shown in Figure 1 below.

---

1. Japan International Cooperation Agency Japan Overseas Cooperation Volunteers Office (2001). *The History of Japan Overseas Cooperation Volunteers in the 20th Century*, 8.

2. According to tables of JICA data showing dispatch results according to year and country.

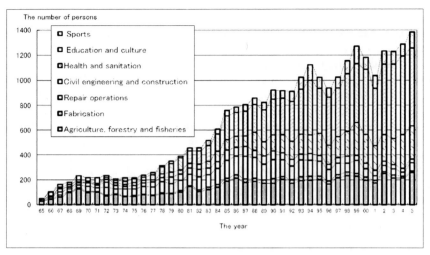

Fig. 1: Volunteers Sent in Each Sector for Each Year (1965 – 2005)

Source: Compiled by the author from JICA data regarding JOCV missions

The first 20 years (from 1965 to 1985) saw a marked increase in the actual number of volunteers dispatched and the tendency of such an increase can be seen in all sectors. There was a particularly dramatic increase in their numbers between 1983 and 1985, a period that coincided with a campaign to "double the number of volunteers in three years"[3]. After 1985 the tendency is for no such marked increase to be shown in sectors such as agriculture, forestry and fisheries, fabrication, repair operations, or civil engineering and construction, and in some cases a decrease can be observed. However, there is a marked increase in the number of Japan Overseas Cooperation Volunteers dispatched in sectors concerned with human development itself, such as health and sanitation, education and culture, and sports. The rate of this increase has been intensifying since the 1990s in the sports sector. It is considered that the number of volunteers dispatched in the sports sector will continue to increase, as will the number of those sent in the health and sanitation and education and culture sectors.

Trends in Physical Education and Sport Cooperation Activities According to Country and Job Category

Trends and transitions so far in the sports sector according to the work undertaken by the volunteers and the country to which they were dispatched are grouped by decade and shown in the following Figures 2 and 3, and Tables 1 and 2.

3.The campaign to "double the number of volunteers in three years" was proposed by JICA President Arita in 1982 and implemented from the following year. The period up until 1982 has been dubbed "the era of system design" when the focus was on Japan.

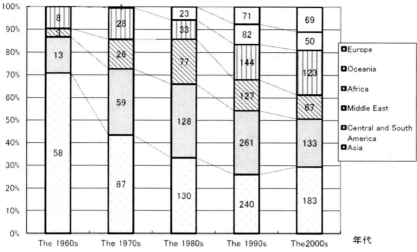

Fig. 2: Transitions in the Dispatch of Sports Volunteers for Each Region

Source: Compiled by the author from JICA data regarding JOCV missions

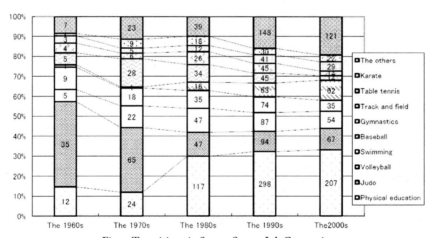

Fig. 3: Transitions in Sports Sector Job Categories

Source: Compiled by the author from JICA data regarding JOCV missions

The mid 1960s (1965 – 1969)

Japan Overseas Cooperation Volunteers were dispatched to nine countries during the five years from the launch of the programme in 1965 to 1969; 58 volunteers were sent to Asia, representing more than 70% of the total number of volunteers dispatched. In terms of numbers, Asia was followed

by Central and South America with 13 volunteers (all to El Salvador), Africa
with 8, and the Middle East with 3. Volunteers had yet to be sent to Oceania
or Europe.

During these five years the country to which the highest number of volunteers was sent was Malaysia, followed by El Salvador. If we look at the
kinds of work to which they were assigned, during the 1960s 13 job categories were represented, and 35 people out of the 82 volunteers dispatched during this period did work that was involved in judo.

The 1970s (1970 – 1979)

The campaign to "double the number of volunteers in three years" was proposed by JICA President Arita in 1982 and implemented from the following
year. The period up until 1982 has been dubbed "the era of system design"
when the focus was on perfecting the recruitment and selection system and
establishing a firm foundation in Japan.

During the 1970s Japan Overseas Cooperation Volunteers were sent to
18 countries. Of the total number of 201 volunteers, 87 were sent to Asia,
59 to Central and South America, 28 to Africa, 26 to the Middle East and 1
to Oceania. The number of volunteers dispatched to Asia and Central and
South America represents more than 70% of the total number. As in the
1960s, the two countries welcoming the highest number of volunteers in the
1970s were Malaysia and El Salvador. A total of 20 sports volunteers were
sent to Malaysia in 1971 but after that their numbers decreased. In addition,
sports volunteers were not sent to El Salvador from 1978 to 1991 due to the
civil war 4). If we look at the job categories, as in the 1960's, work involving
judo is most heavily represented with 65 people; this is followed by work in
the fields of gymnastics, physical education and volleyball. There were 17 job
categories, 4 more than in the 1960s.

The 1980s (1980 – 1989)

In the 1980s the number of Japan Overseas Cooperation Volunteers dispatched overseas increased dramatically due to factors such as the campaign
to "double the number of volunteers in three years" (1983-1985). Asia was
sent the largest number of volunteers (129) but the number sent to Central
and South America also more than doubled to 128, and these regions were
followed by the Middle East with 77, Africa with 33 and Oceania with 23.
The countries who were sent the most volunteers in the 1980s were Peru,
Syria and Paraguay, in that order. Many volunteers had been sent to Malaysia during the 60s and 70s but their numbers declined during this decade
and, as was mentioned earlier, no one was sent to El Salvador. If we look at
the job categories, fewer volunteers than in the 70s were sent for work
involving judo, a field which had dominated previously. The largest group of

volunteers (116) was sent to work in physical education, with the next most numerous categories being those that involved judo, volleyball, swimming and gymnastics. There were 18 job categories, one more than in the 1970s.

The 1990s (1990 – 1999)

The 1990s were a time when the number of sports volunteers increased rapidly. Central and South America had the largest number with 261, followed by Asia with 241, Africa with 144, the Middle East with 127, Oceania with 82 and then Europe with 69. The dispatch of Japan Overseas Cooperation Volunteers to Europe began in 1993. The country that received the most volunteers during this decade was Zimbabwe, which had not been sent anyone before the 1990s. The dispatch of volunteers to Zimbabwe began in 1992 and as many as 85 people were sent in the next eight years. "Physical education" volunteers were particularly numerous, making up 53 of the total 85. In terms of numbers, the next countries were Syria, Guatemala and then Ecuador. If we look at the job categories, physical education continued to dominate, as in the 80s. This was followed by judo, volleyball, swimming and then baseball. Volunteers were dispatched for 27 job categories, 9 more than in the 80s.

The 2000s (2000 – 2005)

The increasing dispatch of Japan Overseas Cooperation Volunteers in the education and culture, sports, and health and sanitation sectors of the 1990s has continued in the 2000s and the dispatch of sports volunteers continues apace. Up until 2005, Asia has received the greatest number of volunteers with 183, followed by Central and South America with 133, Africa with 123, the Middle East with 87, Europe with 69 and then Oceania with 50. There was a trend of increased dispatches to Africa and Europe. The country that received the greatest number of volunteers during this decade was Syria, which has seen a lot of activity since the 1980s. In terms of numbers, the next countries were the Maldives, Mongolia, Zambia and then Bangladesh. If we look at the job categories, physical education continued to dominate, as in the 80s and 90s. This was followed by work involving judo, baseball, volleyball and then swimming. At present volunteers are being sent for 26 job categories, almost the same number of categories as in the 90s. Since FY2005 a system of short-term missions has been set up [5]), and the number of Japan Overseas Cooperation Volunteers working in the field of physical education and sport is increasing under this system.

Table 1: The Top Five Destinations for Sports Sector Volunteers

The1960s	The1970s	The1980s	The1990s	The2000s
1. Malaysia(35)	1. Malaysia(41)	1. Peru(33)	1. Zimbabwe(85)	1. Syria(35)
2. El Salvador(13)	2. El Salvador(35)	2. Syria(31)	2. Syria(55)	2. Maldives(29)
3. Cambodia(9)	3. Nepal(18)	3. Paraguay(31)	3.Guatemala(50)	3. Mongolia(25)
4. Laos(8)	4. Philippines(15)	4. Sri Lanka(30)	4. Ecuador(45)	4. Zambia(24)
5. Zambia(6)	5. Kenya(15)	5. Morocco(26)	5. Sri Lanka(34)	5.Bangladesh(22)
6. Philippines(6)				

Source: Compiled by the author from JICA data regarding JOCV missions

Table 2: The Top Five Kinds of Work for Sports Sector Volunteers

The1960s	The1970s	The1980s	The1990s	The2000s
1. Judo(35)	1. Judo(65)	1.Physical Education(116)	1.Physical Education(298)	1. Physical Education(207)
2. Physical Education(12)	2.Gymnastics(28)	2. Judo(47)	2. Judo(94)	2. Judo(67)
3.Swimming(9)	3.Physical Education(24)	3. Volleyball(47)	3. Volleyball(87)	3.Baseball(62)
4. Volleyball(5)	4. Volleyball(22)	4. Swimming(35)	4. Swimming(74)	4. Volleyball(54)
5. Gymnastics(5)	5. Swimming(18)	5.Gymnastics(34)	5. Baseball(63)	5. Swimming(35)

Source: Compiled by the author from JICA data regarding JOCV missions

Characteristics of Sports Sector Missions Demonstrated by Region and Job Category

Japan Overseas Cooperation Volunteers who have been dispatched in the sports sector are categorized according to region in Table 3. So far the region that has received the highest number of volunteers is Asia, while the ratio of volunteers dispatched in the sports sector is high for Europe, the Middle East, and Central and South America. Africa has received many volunteers for all job categories so, although the actual number of sports sector volunteers is high, their ratio of the total number is low. If we compare the regional GDPs, there is a tendency for a higher ratio of sports sector volunteers to be sent to regions with a higher GDP (Gross Domestic Product). It has been reported that international assistance needs place more emphasis on education in lower income countries and that there are an increasing number of requests for cultural and sporting assistance from middle income countries[4], and the above-mentioned characteristics are thought to be connected with this.

---

4. Due to the political instability Japan Overseas Cooperation Volunteers were pulled out of El Salvador in 1979, and missions there recommenced in 1993. JICA (1998). *JOVC Status Documents, October 1998 Revised Edition*, 4

Table 3: Number of Volunteers and Sports Sector Ratio for Each Region (1965~2005)

Region	Sports Sector Volunteers	Volunteers in All Job Categories	Sports Sector Ratio (%)
Asia	698	8195	8.52%
Middle East	300	1893	15.85%
Africa	336	8324	4.04%
Central and South America	594	5948	9.99%
Oceania	156	2278	6.85%
Europe	140	662	21.15%
Total	2224	27300	8.15%

Source: Compiled by the author from JICA data regarding JOCV missions

Physical education and judo are categories that are heavily represented in Asia and Africa, while in the Middle East sports such as volleyball and swimming feature heavily. Many of the volunteers sent to Oceania and Central and South America worked in physical education, but in Europe traditional Japanese sports such as judo, baseball and kendo were heavily represented. Overall, work involving judo dominated when volunteer missions first began to be dispatched but the number of "physical education" volunteers sent started to increase in the 1980s, a trend that still continues today. It is thought that these phenomena are related to the greater awareness of the importance of educational assistance and to the increasing cooperation in the field of education.

The Current Form of Japan Overseas Cooperation Volunteer Missions

Table 4 indicates the types of work for which volunteers have been dispatched so far in the sports sector. During the 90s there was a rapid increase in the types of work for which volunteers in the sports sector were sent and the content of these jobs is currently becoming more diverse. Duties now take many different forms, such as working at primary or secondary schools, physical education teacher training institutions, stadiums, NGOs (non-governmental organizations), or police agencies, or rotating between schools. The level of the requests also varies, ranging from coaching athletes with the national team in mind, through training league or association club coaches and providing guidance for educational institutes, to coaching street children. A closer look at the job type "physical education" reveals that it can take varied forms ranging from primary school PE teachers to university staff and sports coordinators. The form and content of Japan Overseas Cooperation Volunteer missions and developing countries' assistance needs

are tending to become increasingly diversified in recent years, and it seems
that, in developing countries too, sports are widely deemed to be beneficial
within society, not simply within formal education.

Table 4: Current Job Categories in the Sports Sector

Physical Education	Swimming	Basketball	Wrestling
Sports medicine	Synchronized Swimming	Softball	Archery
Aerobics	Water polo	Baseball	Judo
Track and field	Tennis	Handball	Karate
Skiing	Table tennis	Association Football	Aikido
Gymnastics	Badminton	Rugby	Kendo
Rhythmic Gymnastics	Volleyball	Boxing	Weight lifting

Source: Compiled by the author from JICA data regarding JOCV missions

From the perspective of the efficacy of technical assistance, there seems
to be a greater ripple effect for the partner country from activities such as
involvement in the overall planning of physical education with the volunteer employed in a relevant administrative organisation, regional educational institution, or training school for physical education teachers, than when
the volunteer acts as a PE teacher in a school or as a regional sports coach.
However, this does on the other hand present difficulties in the performance of their activities since advanced specialization and language skills are
required of the volunteer in such situations.

It is predicted that the physical education and sports sector needs of developing countries will continue to diversify, and it is considered that the
current composition of mission sectors and job types will be insufficient and
will require further subdivisions to correspond to those needs.

Conclusion

This chapter has analysed the trends in the Japan Overseas Cooperation
Volunteer sports sector missions that have been implemented so far. Initially the missions focused on Asia but gradually expanded to other regions
and countries. This is thought to be linked with the fact that Japan's international assistance started as part of our post-war reparations and initially
focused on Asia, but spread to embrace other countries from around the latter half of the 70s when reparations came to an end. During the 60s and 70s
the sports sector focused on the dispatch of volunteers involved in judo, but
the trend is for an increase in the number of physical education volunteers
from the 80s onwards. This is thought to be connected with the greater importance placed on education and the increasing awareness of the importance of physical education in schools. The activities of sports volunteers
take many different forms and, in recent years, the trend is for an increase
in these different forms, and in the number of volunteers, and it is clear that
the needs of developing countries are also diversifying. Thus, with the current diversification in countries and tasks, there is the possibility that one-

off assistance sent in response to a formal request will, on its own, be unable to cope with the expected continuing diversification in needs from now on.

It is considered that it will be necessary to also send teams and groups that include field coordinators[5], senior volunteers[6] and specialists in addition to Japan Overseas Cooperation Volunteers, and to implement systematic action such as project activities, in response to these diversifying needs. It will also be essential to cooperate more closely with other organizations providing assistance in this sector[7], sports associations and university physical education departments, and to work to secure personnel who are capable of meeting those needs. Indeed, as of April 2011 the recruitment of Japan Overseas Cooperation Volunteers has been halted due to the Great East Japan Earthquake, which took place while this chapter was being written. We can only pray that the situation will return to normal as soon as possible.

---

5. The Japan Overseas Cooperation Volunteer / Senior Volunteer Short-Term Dispatch System was set up in FY2005. Up until then only people with Japan Overseas Cooperation Volunteer experience could be re-dispatched for a short-term mission. The extensive advertising for short-term volunteers under this system has made it easier for people to apply.

6. Saito, M. (1993). An Evaluation of Japan Overseas Cooperation Volunteer Development Cooperation, *Journal of Economics of Chuo University*, 34 (2), p. 101

7. A form of coordinator to provide indirect support for volunteers, established in FY2005.

Chapter 30

From Theory to Practice

Scientific Support and the Design of a 'Sport-in-Development' Program in Bukoba, Tanzania

Ben Weinberg & Sebastian Rockenfeller

Introduction

Despite the fact that the amount of sport-related development projects and interventions has increased exponentially throughout the last few years, the most important question how to actually incorporate sport as sustainable tool into a development context remains untouched or merely superficially reflected upon in academic circles. In fact it has been argued that in some cases a sceptical discussion of the issue might interfere with the "overly romanticised" (Coalter 2010b: 1386) discourse on promoting sport as cost-effective instrument in order to achieve the objectives of the *Millennium Development Goals* which have been formulated by the United Nations in a period of paradigmatic change regarding development issues, i.e. a strategic refinement of international development policies in terms of increased focus on human and social capital. The defining of these objectives corresponds with many of sport's traditional claims about being capable of contributing to personal and social improvement. However, few projects draw upon substantial results regarding the efficacy of utilizing sport. As a matter of fact most rely on intuitive assurance and personal experience. The aspect of how to conceptualize such programmes is therefore as important as monitoring and evaluating the process, output and outcome. Until now few projects have been assessed in accordance with scientifically valuable methods and instruments although it has been frequently emphasised that science is the key to help deconstruct claims on solving broad gauge problems through limited-focus interventions (Coalter 2010a).

This chapter will therefore firstly refer to theoretical perspectives on "Sport-in-Development" to draw upon and in order to secondly illustrate how these recognitions have informed the design and implementation of a programme in Bukoba, Tanzania. The programme of the project, which is called *Jambo Bukoba*, is thought of as example for taking theoretical assumptions into consideration within the practical designing process. The following pages also include a summary of a baseline study, outline the environmental setting of the project and illustrate how this analysis has influenced the initial programme design.[1]

Theoretical Perspectives

As depicted by Groll and Hillbring (2010: p.12 ff.) the policy field of development work contains a certain degree of terminological vagueness that requires definitional explanations. According to Nohlen (1998: p.152) development policy can be broadly understood as sum of all measures taken in order to improve the political, economic and social development of developing countries, while the term development work or cooperation can be regarded as development policy in a narrow sense (Nuscheler 1996). In practice development policies can be mostly divided into financial cooperation on the one hand and technical cooperation on the other hand. While the first concentrates on providing capital and credits for financing specific projects, the latter is characterized through the provision of technical know-how or human resources (Bodemer & Thibaut 1996: p.135). Historically speaking financial cooperation resonates strongly with the concept of modernization (Rostow 1960), which has also been subsumed under the paradigm of development aid. Due to the fact that especially during the Cold War the pattern of development aid was often instrumentalized by the creditors as well as abused by corrupt debtors in order to pursue other political interests the term has been considered to be psychologically inappropriate (Kebschull, Fasbender & Naini 1976: p.27). As from the 1990's and in the context of a neo-liberal zeitgeist major development policy actors have therefore been concerned with reconfiguring their strategies in terms of focussing more on cooperation and collaboration including the increasing participation of non-governmental organisations and companies dealing with

---

1.Further publications on the roles of research and training in "Sport-in-Development" in general and Jambo Bukoba in particular have been produced by Petry & Weinberg (2011) and Rockenfeller & Bauer (2011).

social responsibility issues (Levermore & Beacom 2009b: p.27). Debates on new forms of governance within the development policy sector have also inspired the emergence of the concept of sustainable development, which calls for improving policies with regard to economic efficiency, social justice and environmental sustainability (Bauer 2004: p.52). As one can assume the above-mentioned evolution of policy paradigms has been accompanied by a respective development of the definition of a developing country. In fact socioeconomic factors such as per-capita income or GDP together with mortality or literacy rates remain to be the strongest determinants while sociocultural attributes receive more and more attention but are still difficult to measure (Nohlen 2000: p.221).

As with defining the area of sport-related development policies and finding a general term Levermore and Beacom (2009a: p.9) have suggested calling it "sport-in-development" as opposed to what is mostly referred to as "Sport for Development and Peace" (Kidd 2008: p.370) arguing that the latter transports the illusion of sport as a panacea while the first represents the perception that the use of sport may assist the international development process". More specifically Coalter (2007: p.71) has elaborated on different forms of sport-related projects and programmes differentiating between "sport plus" and "plus sport":

It is possible to divide sport-in-development projects into two broad approaches: Some can be described as sport plus, in which traditional sport development objectives of increased participation and the development of sporting skills are emphasized. (...) The other approach can be described as plus sport, in which social, educational and health programmes are given primacy; and sport, especially its ability to bring together a large number of young people, is part of a much broader and more complex set of processes. Short-term outcomes (e.g. HIV/AIDS education and behaviour change) are more important than the longer term sustainable development of sport. Of course there is a continuum of such programmes and differences are not always clear-cut.

The debate on terminology reflects the fact that the issue constitutes a relatively new field both from a political and from a scientific perspective. As a matter of fact most academic studies have been rather descriptive and only few have conducted theoretical explorations. Meanwhile Levermore/ Beacom (2009b), Hayhurst (2009) and Girginov (2008) have contributed to explaining the matter from a political science perspective through locating the policy field, its politics and discourse in a macro-analytical context. They conclude that "sport-in-development" can be best understood in a neoliberal framework in which notions of deregulation, privatization and individualism have led to a refinement of development policy strategies including an increase of NGOs and private actors that are involved in the formulation and implementation processes. Coalter (2010b) embarks upon these recognitions and employs a theory-led approach including assumptions on social and human capital (s.a. Coleman 1994; Portes/Landholt 2000) when examining the case of the Mathare Youth Sport Association. He thereby illustrates how to complement macro-analytical findings with in-the-field research calling for a process-led approach with regard to designing, monitoring and evaluating programmes while stressing the importance of creating an appropriate setting in order to assess the actual potential of sport as development tool. In this context Coalter also draws attention to the problem of being too optimistic about the development potential of sport and therefore the improvement of social capital against the background of 'hard' facts, i.e. the lack of material resources such as money, infrastructure and education, that cannot be entirely compensated through the enhancement of the collective ability to manage these resources.

Interim Conclusions

When it comes to using sport as a tool within the development context more theoretical knowledge should be considered, rather than merely providing access to sport. The important question is how to create a learning environment within a sport programme to change attitudes and to be realistic with regard to the impact sport can make. But instead of conceptualizing a specific programme, which fits to the actual needs, most projects merely export a 'western' concept of sport to development countries. The question of how these projects should be conceptualized and delivered is as important as the measurement of the outcomes of the project. The success of a project depends on drawing upon a theoretical framework, which guides the project to find the most effective tools for the development process. Initiators of projects should therefore build a bridge between theory and practice.

Programmes aimed at social change cannot easily be transferred from one country to another because of cultural differences and different resources and conditions. Instead of just exporting a western movement culture through the implementation of 'western' sport concepts and programmes, it is crucial to adapt those programs. Cultural sensitivity and recipient-oriented approaches can only be developed through intensive analyses and serious know-how exchange. The biggest challenge of each programme is to create a specific pedagogical setting wherein the achievement of certain development objectives becomes tangible.

One theoretical framework that seems to be suitable for the further implementation process of *Jambo Bukoba* in particular is social-cognitive learning theory; according to Bandura (1999: p.21) it can be assumed that personal factors - such as cognitive, affective and biological processes – and behavioural patterns and societal influences all condition each other. Accordingly individuals are simultaneously both creators and products of social systems. Thus when individuals realize that their own commitments may have an impact and contribute to achieving the objectives formulated by them, the motivation to challenge difficulties of life increases significantly (Bandura 2004: p.144). Bühler and Heppekausen (2005: p.22) state that this theory is highly important for the didactics, techniques and methods of life skills enhancement and has therefore frequently been chosen as basis for health improvement programmes.

In addition it is considered to be useful to refer to the model by Gould et al. (2006; 2007; 2008) on teaching life skills[2] through sport, which constitutes a rare example of creating a heuristic model - considering the general lacuna of theory-led research in this context - on the issue of developing and coaching life skills.

Fig. 1: Life Skills Coaching Model (in reference to Gould et al. 2006: p.6)

As will be depicted in the following passages the programme and the scientific assistance are still at an early stage; hence a theory-led implementation scheme and an evaluation of the learning processes regarding the transfer and acquisition of life skills have to be developed more thoroughly. However, it is important to note that these recognitions about the relevance of applying a specific theoretical model such as developed by Gould et al. (2006; 2008) constitute the conceptual core of the further work of *Jambo Bukoba*.

---

2. Life skills are here understood as "the term to refer to psychosocial skills. Keywords used to describe psychosocial skills [are]: personal, social, interpersonal, cognitive, affective, universal." (WHO 1999: p.3). According to Gatz et al. (2002: p.53) life skills describe those competences that provide human beings to be successful in the environment they live in. Gould et al. (2008: p.60) mention that life skills – while they may be compared to physical techniques that can be acquired through models and trainings sessions – can only be termed as such provided the competences acquired are successfully transferred to other situations in life.

Project Description: Jambo Bukoba

The project was founded by the NGO also called *Jambo Bukoba* in 2008. The founder, Clemens Mulokozi, was born in Tanzania and has had the chance of creating links with Tanzanian actors such as the ministry in the Kagera region. Furthermore the initiative has received technical support from the German Ministry of Foreign Affairs and the *Deutsche Olympische Sportbund* (DOSB) since April 2010.[3] The *Institute of European Sport Development and Leisure Studies* (*Deutsche Sporthochschule Köln*) has also been involved since then through providing scientific support. The primary aim of *Jambo Bukoba* is to develop social skills such as communication skills, trust and fair play and thereby empower children and youth. Sport shall also be utilized for raising awareness on sensitive issues such as HIV/AIDS and gender empowerment. It also contains rather sport-oriented objectives according to which sports programmes, facilities and physical education in schools shall be improved (s.a. Chappell 2007).

Implementation Design: Jambo Bukoba

The basis for understanding the process of designing the programme is the model as depicted in figure 2. It illustrates the relations between resources, conditions, aims, the programme, its outputs ("Life Skills Through Games", P.E. Teacher Training) and its outcomes. It also shows the four phases of the project programme - namely identification, planning, implementation and evaluation - and thus indicates where to locate the important step of conducting the baseline study in the whole conceptualization process and which relevance the study has for the outputs of the programme.

3.The sport expert Sebastian Rockenfeller, one of the authors of the article, was sent to Tanzania to develop the project with the local partners.

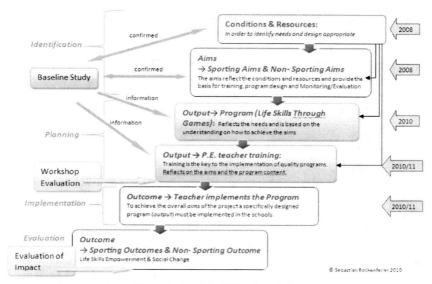

Fig. 2: Project Model *Jambo Bukoba*

The analysis was part of the identification phase in which an examination of the requirements and priorities of the local project partners was conducted. The partners have been an important cornerstone in helping design and implement the first steps. It is intended to build upon their knowledge against the backdrop of the overall objectives of *Jambo Bukoba* in order to facilitate a significant degree of ownership in the long run. Based on the results of the baseline study a special workshop programme for P.E. teachers (contents: physical education, sport and the means of conveying life skills) has been created in correspondence with the local culture, the conditions, needs and available resources.

Baseline Study

According to Bauer (2004: p.38) case studies examining a country's special needs, challenges and perspectives are inevitable for a high-quality design of a project or programme. It requires a long-term planning phase and a thorough analysis of the local situation. Before conducting the workshops it was therefore necessary to understand the cultural, institutional and organizational context that has a direct impact on the implementation process. Accordingly it was crucial to gain insights into the following aspects:

a. The situation of physical education in schools.
b. The situation of girls in this context.
c. The degree of participation in class.
d. The "traditional"/ regional movement culture.
e. The knowledge on HIV/AIDS in connection to sport.

In terms of research methods the study employed various qualitative instruments: observational techniques have been used for assessing the significance of physical education in 18 schools. One "sportmaster"[4] was asked to give a lesson and make a demonstration. Semi-structured interviews with other "sportmasters" and principals of ten different schools were conducted. The interviews were recorded and transcribed. In addition a questionnaire that had been translated into Swahili was distributed and filled out by 154 pupils. The empirical research has led to the following assessment:

a) The situation of physical education in schools

All pupils enjoy doing sports and are generally interested in sport activities. Also the teachers express interest in expanding their knowledge and the principals advocate increasing the importance of physical education as a subject. Most schools do have sporting facilities, which may require some maintenance but generally provide space for practising sports.

A major problem with regard to improving school sport may be the lack of qualified personal. Few teachers have a degree or certificate and most teach without any qualification and also lack motivation. Further deficits are the lack of material, clothes and facilities. There are no dressing rooms or gyms. The pitches are in a bad condition. All this has also do to with the fact that P.E. is generally not considered an important subject because the children move a lot during day due to long ways home or in case they have to help in the household. It is therefore doubtful in how far additional or modified lessons could prove useful or how the parents would perceive them considering they might fear that their children get injured or perform worse in other subjects.

Generally it has become clear during the observation phases that the relationship between teachers and pupils is not very close and that most teachers have a rather authoritarian understanding of teaching. They consider discipline to be one of the most important aspects of an ideal learning environment while not having specific didactic knowledge or expertise on how to convey contents. Some are even not aware of their responsibility and don't act as role models.

b) The situation of girls in this context

It has become clear that girl don't engage in sports activities as often as boys do. This could be explained through cultural norms, low self-confidence or timidity. Moreover the skirts, which are part of the school uniform, interfere with moving freely. In some schools boys and girls are taught separately and no coeducational lessons take place.

---

4. Term used to describe a physical education teacher in Tanzania.

c) The degree of participation in class

The schools visited don't include P.E. as fixed lesson in their timetables. Girls are as mentioned above not as actively involved as boys. The extracurricular sports lessons are mostly tailored according to boys' interests. During the breaks and after school hours the pupils tend to get organized themselves provided they can get hold of a ball.

d) The "traditional"/ regional movement culture

Traditional rhythmic games and dances play a very important role in the region, however they are rarely part of the school lessons. The locals also don't regard them as equivalent to the dominating sports such as football. The girls prefer netball, which is similar to basketball.

f) The knowledge on HIV/AIDS in connection to sport

Initially the teachers who were interviewed could not see a connection between fighting HIV/AIDSand sport and only few had heard about concepts as such. After they had been introduced to the concept and had seen some possible integrative exercises they expressed interest in the idea: "Sports can do that! [...] I didn't know that good training, it's nice! I can do that [...] immediately, I can promote it."[5] A significant amount of teachers said in the interviews that they would be interested in a workshop that addresses the concept of "sport-in-development" and that they would like to learn more about it.

The Programme Design of the P.E. Teacher Workshops

The results obtained from the observations and interviews allow drawing conclusions regarding the design of the workshops. The following chart (fig. 2) draws upon the results of the study and demonstrates the causal connection to the programme design of the workshops.

Fig. 3: Correspondence between Baseline Study and Programme Design

Results of the Baseline Study	Programme Design
a)The Situation of Physical Education in Schools	
Lack of Qualification	Know-how transfer regarding planning, organisation and Implementation of a lesson including easy games.
Lack of Material	Although the trained teachers receive two balls for their school within the project concept, it is essential to teach them exercises, which can be realized with a limited number of balls or local/ self-made equipment. ($\rightarrow$ sustainability)

5.Excerpt from an interview with a teacher from Mugana Secondary School.

Lack of Clothes (especially girls)	Introduce games/exercises for which the clothes are not a problem anymore and the girls don't feel embarrassed (skirts).
Lack of Sport Budget	Free participation in workshop.
High Activity Level (the learners have long distances to go to school; have to work after school, which means they are very active)	No exercises which are too exhausting; breaks between the activities.
Dangerous Grounds (glass, sharp rocks on the ground)	Integrate a "pitch clean up game" as part of the programme.
Many Pupils per Class	Include activities where many learners can be active at the same time
Language (poor English skills)	Use Swahili languages anytime to be able to speak about sensitive issues and to ensure that they understand and learn.
Discipline (discipline is one of the most important values in Kagera's schools)	Integrate games, which teach discipline but also offer activities which offer fun, enjoyment and relaxation.
No close Relationship between Teacher and Pupils	Games which integrate the teacher; Pupils against teachers or mixed.
b)The Situation of Girls in this Context. *c)The Degree of Participation in Class.*	
Low Girl's Participation	Include games, which are preferred from girls, invent new rules, where a girl must be part of a team.
Low self-confidence of girls	Empowerment, no embarrassment; games to gain self-esteem; provide positive experiences.
d)The "Traditional"/ Regional Movement Culture	
Traditional/ Regional Games	Use local, traditional games (also dance), adapt the roles to achieve your learning outcome; these games are accepted in the community.
Boys like soccer; Girls like netball	Modification of rules; draw upon enthusiasm; apply to training scheme.
e)The Knowledge on HIV/AIDS in Connection to Sport	
Lack of Knowledge but Interest in the Concept	Games that incorporate awareness raising techniques.

It is noteworthy that the programme design is based on preliminary results and with regard to creating further concepts for the incorporation of HIV/AIDSand gender issues more studies have to be implemented. Therefore the current programme design can only provide first step measures and practical advice. Accordingly the first workshop phase is focussing on conveying social and life skills based on the assumption that the transportation of values such as tolerance, team spirit, fair play and trust can forms a basis for personal and social development. Teachers shall therefore learn how to convey these skills through adopting modified games and acquiring didactic competences.

Fundamentals of the Workshop Implementation

In order to ensure a successful outcome it is generally necessary that the local partners are capable of conducting the training without external support. The workshops have to become an integral part of the teachers-training schemes to guarantee a degree of sustainability. It is crucial to not only adopt the concept but to understand it in order to identify with its contents and thereby foster ownership, especially if the teachers have to explain the new concept to the pupils or the parents or other colleagues. Furthermore it should be avoided to make use of extraordinary equipment or teaching materials such as laptops or electronic presentations. Due to financial constraints the budget should be kept as minimal as possible. So far the *Institute of European Sport Development and Leisure Studies* has been involved in creating curricula for the workshops; accordingly Sebastian Rockenfeller has trained local staff on how to implement and organize the P.E. teacher training without the support of an external facilitator. This "Help for Self-help" approach helps creating ownership, which is needed for the success of the project. So far 130 teachers in the Kagera Region were trained in four workshops including theoretical sessions on the basics of "Sport-in-Development" and practical sessions introducing the teachers to specific games that are mainly aimed at trust-building and conveying tolerance and fair play.

Outlook and Future Agenda

The programme as outlined above has been titled *"Life Skills Through Games - Introductory Course"* and it has been applied in four workshops. Initial evaluation results indicate a high acceptance and interest. The teachers were able to implement the theoretical contents in the practical sessions and exams. It is unclear though in how far they will integrate the knowledge into everyday teaching. Whether the workshops will have a sustainable effect remains to be uncertain and is probably a matter of time, particularly with regard to the identification process.

Since the baseline study and the workshops have demonstrated that the topic of HIV/AIDSis a very sensitive issue, it is intended to carefully design a specific training scheme that deals with the concept of utilizing sport in the fight against HIV/AIDS. It is therefore necessary to draw upon academic knowledge and existing concepts such as developed by Maro et al. (2009) and Mwaanga (2010). In addition it is crucial to frequently reassess the situation of the project in Bukoba because if sport is supposed to become an effective tool the programme has to relate to the cultural setting and social environment. Only if the social context and the available resources are taken into consideration when creating an appropriate learning setting the full potential of sport can be achieved and the negative outcomes can be reduced (Schott & Merkel 2008; Gieß-Stüber 2008). Consequently the major aspects of the necessary measures that have to be taken can be summarized as follows:

- As with elaborating on the incorporation of a theory-led approach it is thought of producing more in-depth research on the applicability and validity of the model designed by Gould et al. (2006; 2008).

- Based on these theoretical underpinnings a highly important aspect that shall be covered is the design and production of a workshop manual and handbook published in English and Kiswahili. It shall contain theoretical and practical recommendations and summaries of the contents of the workshops. It shall also include a collection of methods and games.

- Cooperation with local institutions has to be ensured and expanded. It is vital that schools are included and interested in the programme in order to provide a productive learning atmosphere and access for all pupils. In this context it is crucial to achieve acceptance and commitment by teachers and parents.

- The probably most important objective of the project is to transfer the ownership and implementation of the programme to the local stakeholders and actors. From the perspective of the *Institute of European Sport Development and Leisure Studies* it is regarded essential to share expertise and produce a sustainable transfer of know-how.

- Finally a process-led evaluation scheme (ideally conducted by local stakeholders themselves) shall provide data and information regarding the impact of training the teachers to convey life skills and how these skills are adapted in other situations in life.

References

Bandura, A. (1999). Social Cognitive Theory: An Agentic Perspective. *Asian Journal of Social Psychology, 2,* 21-41.

Bandura, A. (2004). Health Promotion by Social Cognitive Means. *Health Education & Behavior,* 31, (2), 143-164.

Bauer, M. (2004). *Entwicklungszusammenarbeit und Breitensport.* Frankfurt a.M.: Peter Lang.

Bodemer, K., & Thibaut, B. (1996). Entwicklungspolitik. In D. Nohlen (Hrsg.), *Wörterbuch Staat und Politik.* München: Piper, p. 135-142.

Bühler, A. & Heppekausen, K. (2005). *Gesundheitsförderung Konkret, Band 6. Gesundheitsförderung durch Lebenskompetenzprogramme in Deutschland. Grundlagen und kommentierte Übersicht.* Köln.

Chappell, R. (2007). *Sport in Developing Countries.* Surrey: International
Sports Publications.

Coalter F (2007). *Sport a Wider Social Role: Whose Keeping the Score?* London:
Routledge.

Coalter, F. (2010a). Sport for development – Limited focus programmes
and broad gauge problems. In Tokarski, W. & Petry, K. (Hrsg.),
Handbuch Sportpolitik, Band 72 (p. 311-331). Schorndorf: Hofmann-
Verlag.

Coalter, F. (2010b). "Sport-for-Development: Going Beyond the Boundary?" Sport in Society Vol. 13, No. 9, November 2010, 1374–1391.

Coleman, J.S. *Foundations of Social Theory.* Cambridge, MA: Belknap Press,
1994.

Gatz, M., Messner, M.A. & Ball-Rokeach, S.J. (Hrsg.) (2002). *Paradoxes of
Youth and Sport*: State University of New York Press.

Gieß-Stüber, P. (2008). Reflexive Interkulturalität und der Umgang mit
Fremdheit im und durch Sport. In P. Gieß-Stüber & D. Blecking
(eds.), *Sport - Integration - Europa. Neue Horizonte für interkulturelle
Bildung* (p. 234-248). Baltmannsweiler: Schneider.

Girginov, V. (2008). Management of Sports Development as an Emerging
Field and Profession. In: Girginov, V. (Ed.), *Management of Sports
Development,* Elsevier: Oxford.

Gould, D. & Carson, S. (2008). Life skills development through sport: current status and future directions. *International Rewiev of Sport and
Exercise Psychology,* 1, 58-78.

Gould, D., Collins, K. & Lauer, L. (2006). Coaching life skills: A working
model. *Sport & Exercise Psychology Review,* 2, (1), 1-71.

Groll, M., Hillbring, M. (2011). Deutsche Entwicklungszusammenarbeit im
Kontext sportpolitischen Handelns. In: Petry, K. et al. (eds.),
*Sport und internationale Entwicklungszusammenarbeit. Theorie- und
Praxisfelder* (p. 11-28). Köln: Sportverlag Strauß.

Hayhurst, Lyndsay M. C.(2009). "The power to shape policy: charting
sport for development and peace policy discourses", International
Journal of Sport Policy, 1:2, 203 — 227.

Kebschull, D., Fasbender, K. & Naini, A. (1976). *Entwicklungspolitik* (3.
überarb. u. erw. Ausg.). Opladen: Westdeutscher.

Kidd, B. (2008) 'A New Social Movement: Sport for Development and
Peace'. Sport in Society 11, no. 4: 370–80.

Levermore, R. & Beacom, A. (2009a). Sport and Development: Mapping
the field. In R. Levermore & A. Beacom (ed.), *Sport and International Development.* Hampshire: Palgrave Macmillan, p. 1-25.

Levermore, R. & Beacom, A. (2009b). Sport in International Development: Theoretical Frameworks. In R. Levermore & A. Beacom (ed.), *Sport and International Development*. Hampshire: Palgrave Macmillan, p. 26-45.

Maro, Cyprian, Glyn Roberts, and Marit Sorensen. "HIV/AIDS Education in Tanzania: The Experience of at-Risk Children in Poorer Communities." Vulnerable Children and Youth Studies 4.1 (2009):23-36.

Mwaanga, O. (2010). Sport for addressing HIV/AIDS: Explaining our convictions. *Leisure Studies Association (LSA) Newsletter,* No. 85, p. 61-67.

Nohlen, D. (1998b). Entwicklungspolitik. In D. Nohlen (Hrsg.), *Lexikon der Politik* (Bd. 7, Politische Begriffe). München: Beck, p. 152.

Nuscheler, F. (2004). *Lern- und Arbeitsbuch Entwicklungspolitik* (5. völlig neu bearb. Ausg.). Bonn: Dietz Nachfolger.

Petry, K. & Weinberg, B. "Research and Training in the Area of 'Sport-in-Development': Challenges and Demands", in: Petry, K. et al. (Hrsg.) (2011) *Sport und internationale Entwicklungszusammenarbeit. Theorie- und Praxisfelder*. Köln: Sportverlag Strauß, S. 97-104.

Portes, A., and P. Landholt (2000). 'Social Capital: Promise and Pitfalls of its Role in Development'. Journal of Latin American Studies 32: 529–47.

Rockenfeller, S. & Bauer, K. "Die Entwicklung und Durchführung des Projekts *Jambo Bukoba* in Tansania", in: Petry, K. et al. (Hrsg.) (2011) *Sport und internationale Entwicklungszusammenarbeit. Theorie- und Praxisfelder*. Köln: Sportverlag Strauß, S. 147-158.

Rostow, W.W. (1960). *The Stages of Economic Growth: A Non-Communist Manifesto*. Cambridge University Press.

Schott, N. & Merkel, K. (2008). Chancen und Wege der Entwicklungszusammenarbeit im Sport. In: E. Balz & D. Kuhlmann (ed.), *Sportentwicklung: Grundlagen und Facetten* (p. 119-140). Meyer & Meyer Verlag.

WHO (1999). *Partners in Life Skills Education*.

Chapter 31
Streetfootballworld

Development through Football

Vladimir Borkovic & Mia Wyszynski

About Streetfootballworld

Millions of young people around the world are born into a cycle of social injustice. Streetfootballworld believes in the unique power of football to change lives and bring people together behind a common goal. The mission of Streetfootballworld is to strengthen our worldwide network of local organisations that use football to help young people overcome challenges such as poverty, discrimination and lack of education. The streetfootballworld network unites over 80 organisations in more than 50 countries and in 2010 alone they empowered over 600,000 young people. Streetfootballworld strengthens its network members through capacity development programmes, access to funding, opportunities for sharing expertise and the creation of new partnerships—because stronger network members mean better opportunities for the young people who need them most.

No sport in the world generates as much passion as football. Football brings young people into social development programmes: and keeps them there. Football also gets people from all walks of life speaking the same universal language. Establishing common ground is Streetfootballworld's first step toward uniting the global community around a shared goal. Street-footballworld believes that the football industry and the development arena are moving into a new era, where collaboration off the pitch will be as important as competition on the pitch. Streetfootballworld works closely with private and public partners, both in the football sector and beyond, to channel their resources into creating a better future for young people around the world. As a team, streetfootballworld, its partners, and the streetfootballworld network aim to reach out to 2,000,000 young people worldwide every year by 2015.

Development through Football

Issues relating to football appear to psychologically move the worlds fans more than any other sport. All around the globe, organisations driven by local social entrepreneurs and activists use the power of the 'beautiful game'[1] to positively transform their communities. The streetfootballworld network is the product of the shared belief of its members and founders that football can contribute to positive social change if used appropriately in the context of development programmes and activities.

The purpose of the streetfootballworld network is to promote, encourage, facilitate and achieve sustainable development of the communities represented by its members through the use of football. According to the UN Declaration on the Right to Development, the term development encompasses a comprehensive economic, social, cultural and political process which aims at the constant improvement of the well-being of the entire population and of all individuals on the basis of their active, free and meaningful participation in development and the fair distribution of benefits thereof.[2] It is about putting the focus on people and creating an environment in which individuals can develop their full potential and lead productive, creative lives in accordance with their needs and interests. Streetfootballworld supports this definition of development and works to tackle development challenges as defined in the UN Millennium Development Goals through its contribution to social development.

The streetfootballworld network supports local community-based development as the most effective means of achieving the particular development goals most required by communities around the world. This approach is driven by the belief that individuals and communities can themselves best identify the appropriate solutions to address the issues they face. By uniting in effective social enterprises, all kinds of people, especially young

---

1. The following phrase was taken from Wikipedia which argues that: "**The Beautiful Game**" is a synonym for Association Football. The origin or individual who coined the phrase is unknown and it is difficult to verify. Cited on Wikipedia available at: http://en.wikipedia.org/wiki/The_Beautiful_Game (Accessed 13th February 2012).

2. See (www.un.org/documents/ga/res/41/a41r128.htm) for further details of the origin of the term development.

people and women, can make a significant and positive contribution to their communities and beyond through purposeful networking and international partnerships.

Sustainable change can only happen locally, through community ownership and engagement. However, international cooperation and peer-to-peer exchanges have the potential to enhance local development through the creation of truly global partnerships for development. It is the role of the streetfootballworld network and its members to shape and promote this global, participatory approach to development that remains rooted in communities.

The streetfootballworld network and its members are focused on, although not limited to, achieving development in the following eight specific thematic fields:

1. Health,
2. Social integration,
3. Peace building,
4. Gender equality,
5. Employability,
6. Youth leadership,
7. Education
8. Environment.

These broad fields represent innumerable challenges for individuals and communities worldwide, the causes of which cannot be isolated or easily overcome. Within this context, the streetfootballworld network strives to improve the lived experiences, opportunities and conditions of individuals and communities by using football to address these challenges.

The potential of football

We argue here that Football is a uniquely effective tool for development and there are several reasons for this supposition:

Popularity:

The world's most popular sport, football is an international language with local dialects. It is a powerful mobilizing force that easily crosses cultural divides. Football can be used to attract participants to educational activities and community projects and provides an opportunity for spectators and the wider community to mix.

Health:

Participation in sports is intrinsically good for those involved, and using football for development has the added advantage of engaging participants in a healthy activity. Football itself, when played with the right attitude, can have positive personal and social benefits. Experiencing joy and pursuing the activities one loves are essential elements of emotionally and physically healthy growth for any child. Football provides young people all over the world with this opportunity.

Accessibility:

Football can be enjoyed at practically no cost, is easy to learn, and can be played almost anywhere. The term 'street football' (or *fútbolcallejero*, *Straßenfußball*, *fútebol de rua*, etc.) refers to the informal flexibility of rules that allow the game to be adapted the world over. The rules of the game can be manipulated to produce enhanced social outcomes – for example, by using football-related games or modified skills training to raise awareness of specific issues. By emphasizing the traditional idea that sport is a field for developing life skills, rather than an end in itself, the game promotes the life skills most required in contemporary society.

Values:

Football is a fitting analogy for life itself. It is unpredictable, sometimes unfair and often difficult, but through co-operation, teamwork and commitment there are opportunities to succeed, create and inspire. Players learn to cope with winning and losing; they take responsibility for their teams and actively participate in shaping their communities. What they learn in training sessions and matches can be directly transferred to life off the pitch. Football is a team sport and, as such, it carries the values of co-operation, mutual understanding, respect for oneself and others, collaboration, solidarity in defeat, and strength through diversity, and conveys the notion that a functioning team is more than the sum of its parts.

Profile:

Football in general has an unparalleled level of public interest and media attention and, as an industry, generates significant financial involvement from international corporations. This public profile and the amount of financial resources involved in the football sector make it possible to spark interest in development programmes and raise the opportunity of potential partnerships with professional football and the sports industry. Football can serve as a conduit and a platform to communicate and build development and a potential source of income.

Culture:

Football has impacted and is impacted by the cultures of those who play it. Football culture is part of popular culture. Its artistic expressions are born inside and outside the field – from the songs, the flags and the colours to the influence of dance, literature, film, theatre, photography, music and more. The cultural dimension of football is expressed in the social perception of the game and as such constitutes a powerful and coveted political tool. Football culture affects large parts of the population and creates important bonds between people.

The Limitations of Football

Strong development through Football programmes positively impact the lives of participants. However, despite the numerous success stories that are all valid testimonies to football's impact on personal development, there is still a need for scientific assessment that proves the effectiveness of programmes that use football in the community. The limitations of these programmes must also be identified and communicated and as such streetfootballworld is aware that football cannot solve all of today's problems and that 'Development through Football' cannot readily address many of the institutional inequalities that precipitate a range of social problems. However, streetfootballworld network members are committed to improving the lives of as many individuals as possible, and are similarly committed to researching, monitoring and evaluating the impact of Development through Football in order to maximize the outcomes of their work.

The streetfootballworldnetwork and the 'hub' model

All streetfootballworld network members commit to active networking and organisational sustainability when they enter the network. They strive to not only improve their own work, but also to expand the network's collective reach. Streetfootballworld has identified the 'hub' model as a highly effective method of scaling impact without straying from a bottom-up approach.

Hubs are strong organisations that engage with and mentor smaller local organisations, advising them on establishing Development through Football programmes, inviting them to attend events and programmes, and offering training. In this way, hubs can scale the power of Development through Football within existing infrastructures, and without losing direct contact with communities. Hubs also identify and evaluate prospective streetfootballworld network members, and network on national, regional and international levels. Streetfootballworld aims to strengthen network members through capacity development programmes in order to help them become hubs in their communities. In order to achieve this aim, streetfootballworld has created a comprehensive database that focuses on each network member's organisational strength and networking history and capacity. Information is updated annually in collaboration with the network members themselves, and the end result is a clear view of the varying needs of member organisations. Based on these needs, streetfootballworld works with partners such as Sony and Adidas to create capacity development programmes that effectively support network members in creating social change.

Capacity development programmes

Streetfootballworld has increasingly been focusing its strategy on facilitating capacity development opportunities for its network members in order to support them in their efforts to improve their organizational capacity and thus ultimately the effectiveness of their overall operations and programme delivery in their respective communities. A wide range of elements form part of the capacity development strategy:

Exchange programmes:

Streetfootballworld facilitates peer-to-peer knowledge exchange opportunities in collaboration with external experts. The programmes are based on the needs of specific target groups and bring organisations together to exchange experiences, expertise, and ideas, thereby enabling them to gain meaningful insight and support from experts and each other. For example, in the framework of FIFA's Corporate Social Responsibility (CSR) strategy and the flagship initiative 'Football for Hope'[3], streetfootballworld is facilitating the Adidas Exchange Programme[4], which provides local organisations with a unique opportunity to exchange and develop key expertise and capacities that are vital for effective programme delivery and overall operations.

Targeted support:

Targeted capacity development programmes are developed in cooperation with partners and network members. Examples include '20 Centres for 2010'[5], the official legacy campaign of the 2010 FIFA World Cup in South Africa, and the Sony European Graduate and Leadership Development Programmes. TwentyFootball for Hope Centres across Africa are being built through 20 Centres for 2010, each of which addresses local social challenges in disadvantaged areas and improve education and health services for young people. The Sony Leadership Development Programme and the Sony European Graduate Programme engage high-ranking managers and promising young employees, respectively, to work with streetfootballworld network members and channel their expertise toward a specific need identified by the local organisations.

---

3. Football for Hope is an impportant part of the FIFA Corporate Social responsibility programme which has become a flagship for similiar programmes across the world. For more information please see: http://de.fifa.com/aboutfifa/socialresponsibility/footballforhope/index.html (Accessed 12th February 2012).

4. This is a successful programme started in West Africa, details of which can viewed and accessed at: http://de.fifa.com/aboutfifa/socialresponsibility/news/newsid=1325533/index.html

5. A programme put into place in conjunction with the 2010 World Cup in South Africa.

Theme-based webinars:

Through knowledge exchange opportunities via the streetfootballworld website, www.streetfootballworld.org, network members and experts can share their knowledge on an interactive platform.

Funding programmes:

As part of FIFA's Football for Hope programme network members can apply for financial support; those working in Latin America are eligible for additional financial support from the Inter-American Development Bank.

Festivals:

Festivals held around the world are showcases for the effectiveness of Development through Football. Young people from around the world come together for a celebration of the power of football as a tool for social development. The festivals comprise not only a street football tournament but also a cultural programme in order to provide a holistic experience that empowers young attendees. The festivals also offer network members another opportunity to meet and learn from each other.

The holding of Forums:

After the inaugural Football for Hope Forum, held in partnership with FIFA, streetfootballworld will stage the first Beyond Football event in December 2011, in collaboration with Beyond Sport. This unique day will focus on streetfootballworld's motto that it takes a team to win a game, with a diverse range of players in attendance to better understand how everyone can work together toward the same goal: creating positive social change through football.

Evaluating the Development through Football approach

In recent years streetfootballworld has identified the need to further promote systematic monitoring and evaluation among network members. Proving what can be achieved through football is a significant challenge which so far has only been addressed by a few individual organisations and programmes, and there is currently no universally accepted, integrated standard for measuring and evaluating impact.

Streetfootballworld, the Laureus Sport for Good Foundation and Aqumen Social Technologies are developing a monitoring and evaluation (hereafter M&E) service package to increase the impact and efficiency of network members, to gather evidence for what football can achieve, and to communicate the real power of football to the world. It is a practical, straightforward and flexible tool that can be used for programmes in the field of Development through Football.

The service package consists of two components: experts who can provide personalised advice, training, and tools, and online software that helps organisations manage their projects, collect and analyse data, and communicate their impact. It provides holistic support using a tailored approach to M&E and taking into consideration the unique needs of each organisation. All services are participatory, transparent and needs-oriented, and the varied objectives, cultures, locations, languages, local constraints and programming are taken into account at every step.

The M&E system will serve as a simple, useful way of helping organisations capture and communicate their impact, and will offer a clear standard for M&E reporting in the field of Development through Football. Indeed, streetfootballworld network members that demonstrate a strong commitment to enhancing their M&E capacities will not only be able to better manage their own programmes and impact, but also to eventually train other organisations to use the M&E package.

Case study – Moving the Goalposts (MTG) in Kilifi, Kenya

The following case study appears in an extended form on streetfootballworld's online Knowledge Centre[6], and offers insight into the work of just one streetfootballworld network member, including the challenges it faces and the results it achieves. When **Moving the Goalposts (MTG)** began in Kilifi, a small rural village in Kenya, the community was dominated by males. Parents favoured boys and would send them to school; girls were expected to help look after the family and household from an early age. Girls had much higher rates of HIV/AIDS infection and levels of abuse than boys and faced a cycle of poverty that seemed inescapable. Moving the Goalposts Programme Manager Margaret Belawa explains:

> "Across Kenya, girls from birth are often excluded–socially, economically and politically. This absence has had significant consequences for girls and ultimately for society."

As a consequence, girls frequently:

> "....don 't have the skills to challenge the barriers they face, whether it be succeeding at school, finding work, learning life skills, accessing health services, or participating in civil society."

A holistic approach

MTG wanted to correct this imbalance — with football. "We wanted to use football to change the thinking of the girls and the villagers themselves," says Margaret. "It was a tool to change everybody's thinking. When you start taking on a man's game, and then the girls find out they can do it too, they start thinking 'what else can I do?'" MTG works with girls only in order to ensure that girls take on leadership roles, rather than stand back and let boys take over. For MTG, placing young women at the heart of everything means addressing empowerment holistically in order to make a real differ-

---

6.www.streetfootballworld.org/knowledge_centre/ten-years-on-moving-the-goalpost

ence. Over the years, 'Moving the Goalposts' has developed into an organisation that not only get girls playing football, but also teaches them about sexual and reproductive health issues, helps them stay in school and encourages them to take ownership of their financial stability. The streetfootballworld network member has so far reached 3,688 girls from 27 league fields spread across the larger Kilifi District and trained hundreds of coaches, referees, qualified first aid people, counsellors and committee members.

Gaining control

A crucial aspect of empowering girls in the community is ensuring that they are able to make informed decisions about sexual and reproductive health issues. With girls ranging in age from nine to 25, the organisation tailors its approach to reflect the varying needs of the different groups. Topics covered over the three different modules include hygiene and puberty, HIV/AIDS, rape, sexually transmitted infections, abortion, contraception, early pregnancy, decision-making, assertiveness, goal setting, self-esteem, and adolescence. Alice Wekesa, Moving the Goalposts's Executive Director, notes that "a girl's confidence stems from feeling competent and in control of her body, her behaviour and her environment". Through the health modules, girls gain control over their bodies and the decisions they make.

Girls as leaders

A key component of MTG's success lies in its insistence on placing the girls themselves in control. 'Moving the Goalposts' participants take charge of the programmes, whether as peer educators, volunteers or employees. With 80% of 'Moving the Goalposts core staff having once been participants in MTG initiatives, "......it is the girls of MTG that are the engine that runs the programme," says Alice.

Alongside peer education, MTG enables girls many ways of gaining confidence and honing their skills. Exercises range from minute taking and chairing meetings to public speaking. The girls are even required to put this training into practice, representing MTG at stakeholder meetings. Initially, community leaders were unwilling to accepting girls at their meetings with adults. Some even called to insist that an adult come to replace the girls. But MTG stood strong, insisting that the girls knew better than anyone what they themselves needed.

Giving girls a voice

Alice believes that getting the girls to represent the organisation at stakeholder meetings is one of the most important steps they have taken. "It is an incredibly powerful tool that allows a girl to voice her opinion in front of the chief of the village," she explains. Participants such as Lidya Kasiwa are happy with how they are now perceived in the community. She comments:

"In my life I was never given a chance to speak. But now I am respected in my community. They not only listen to me, but they even seek out my opinion! I speak my opinion–respectfully but confidently."

(Lidya Kasiwa)

Getting the community on board

MTG counts parental support as a vital ingredient in its model, recommending that any organisation working with girls actively engage parents early on and seek their consent to their daughters' participation. The organisation also places a lot of importance on building partnerships at different levels, forming relationships with the girls, schools and teachers, communities, the private sector, government and even the international community. In this way MTG has been able to move the role of girls in society from an individual issue to a community-wide one.

A sustainable future

In 2009 MTG began to actively help the girls become economically independent through a range of initiatives, bringing in a new staff member to focus on economic empowerment and networking. As a result girls can receive training and find work through a number of different avenues, owing in part to the reputation they have built for themselves at MTG. "If we recommend a girl, the employer can say 'fine, I know it is an MTG girl, she will be a good worker," explains Margaret a programme developer.

The next ten years

Empowering girls is a demanding job, but MTG knows to stay focused. "Sometimes you get very tired," Margaret laughs. "You feel like you're going forward and then you feel like you're going backwards. Changing attitudes takes a long time. You have to be real patient." The organisation's work spans generations, with older participants taking the reins as their skills develop. Girls will continue to flourish in this part of the country for many years to come. For Margaret, who joined 'Moving the Goalposts' in 2005 and has watched as older participants gain control of their lives and sdupport their peers, the work is challenging, but rewarding. She argues:

"Girls who may have been lost along the way now have a better life, they go to school, they are able to meet their daily demands," she smiles. "We have created opportunities for them to voice their talents in life. Through MTG they go to international forums and they share. We have opened a voice."

(Margaret Streetfootballworld developer)

When Alice looks out her office window and onto a football pitch, she can be sure to have an immediate view of the very core of MTG's work. Alice remarks:

"The girls come down here every day now, unsupervised. It is amazing. They sit in a circle and talk after playing football, all without a teacher or coach. Things have come a long way for the girls in Kilifi."

Football appears to be having a profound effect on the lives of the young girls and women of Kilifi and it is hoped with continued support from sponsors and the communities that this great work will continue to provide fulfilling sporting experiences for the youngsters who through sport are experiencing development to their fullest potential.

Chapter 32

How Professional Football Clubs can Contribute to Sustainable Development

Scort and "The Football Club Social Alliance"

Kristina Bohnstedt & Marc-André Buchwalder

Introduction

When thinking of professional football clubs, at a first glance, their contribution to sustainable international development work is something we would not have in our mind. On the one side, professional football clubs focus on performance and success with elite players living in luxury and filling the newspapers: on the other hand, young, underprivileged people with hardly any chances in life suffering from natural disasters or wars and being dependant on the help of various aid organisations.

Motivation and Problems

The clubs' main focus is on the performance of the first team. So why are professional football clubs interested and motivated to become socially engaged on local, regional but also international levels? Different reasons arise in this discussion: 1. Sometimes an individual person in the top management is convinced that social engagement is just the right thing to do or 2. The social engagement could be part of the club's Corporate Social Responsibility programme. 3. Sometimes clubs are under pressure from their stakeholders (e.g. fans, sponsors) to be socially active or 4. They embed their social engagement in a larger branding strategy which allows the club to represent a certain image in the public. Other reasons can be 5. To generate income for the clubs, especially when the social engagement is implemented in countries with emerging markets or 6. To scout for talent. Whatever the cause motivations are different and vary from altruism and charity thoughts to economical and public relationship interests. Nowadays, more European professional football clubs set up community departments or foundations and run highly successful social programmes on local and regional level, while the 'social engagement on international level is often limited' due to different reasons. The clubs complain about missing funds and a lack of expertise in international development work as the clubs' main target is to invest funds and qualified experts in the success in elite sport, mainly the professional teams and academies. In addition, the clubs also discuss their negative experiences. For example, former international initiatives which did not reach the set targets or were criticized as short-term initiatives. They should perhaps focus on PR to reach new markets or they are shy because they are considered as rather positive expressions for hidden talent scouting. So very often, the professional football clubs are motivated to become socially engaged on international level but are afraid of getting involved in something they cannot control with their existing capacities and know-how. The clubs want to go further than just distributing jerseys and shoes or sending a star to a developing country and returning the next day. They want to realise sustainable development with their existing capacities. But how?

"The Football Club Social Alliance"

To overcome the obstacles for the clubs and their social engagement on international level mentioned above, the Scort Foundation (Switzerland) set up "The Football Club Social Alliance" (hereafter, "Alliance") – a concept that focuses on a multi-stakeholder and shared funding principle where all involved parties can contribute their share corresponding to their interest, expertise and budget. Following the motto "Together we Inspire" the Alliance is a platform for professional European football clubs who jointly want to contribute to sustainable development work in crisis regions. So how is this achieved? What is done and how do we do it?

What? **Inspire** – where we educate and motivate youngsters to become grassroots football coaches and proactive role models.

How? **Together** – working jointly through a strong network of professional clubs and local partners facilitated and organised by Scort.

Figure 1: Scort's official partner clubs and members of "The Football Club Social Alliance" (standing January 2012)

During the initiatives professional coaching instructors of the different participating clubs educate committed young women and men as grassroots football coaches, role models and proactive personalities in society. Due to geopolitical factors or conflicts, freedom of movement can be significantly limited. Young people in crisis regions are confronted with restricted access to international know-how and educational opportunities. Therefore, the international football instructors of Scort's partner clubs work locally in close co-operation with experts of local partner organisations and Scort acts as a facilitator between both sides.

Linking Expertise–the Multi-Stakeholder Approach

"The Football Club Social Alliance", administered and implemented by Scort, uses an innovative multi-stakeholder approach. The programme connects the world of professional football with the international community in order to support a sustainable development approach through sport. It helps professional football clubs to get actively engaged in the Sport for Development and Peace Movement and local partner organisations (e.g. NGOs) to gain access to specific know-how and visibility through the co-operation with internationally well-known football clubs.

The aim of Scort's programme is to link the engagement of well-known professional football clubs and local partner organisations. Each stakeholder is supposed to contribute its share to the initiatives corresponding to the own interest, expertise and budget.

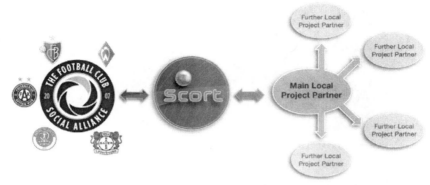

Figure 2: Multi-Stakeholder Approach: Scort's concept of linking "The Football Club Social Alliance" with local development organisations

Professional Football Clubs

F.C. Basel 1893 (Switzerland), SV Werder Bremen, Bayer 04 Leverkusen (both Germany), Hapoel Tel-Aviv F.C. (Israel) and FK Austria Wien (Austria) are permanent partner clubs of the Scort Foundation and full members of "The Football Club Social Alliance". Additionally, Liverpool F.C., Tottenham Hotspur F.C. and F.C. Barcelona supported the Alliance by engaging for individual initiatives. The clubs with their strong brands, professional instructors/experts and social football related know-how can offer the following added value:

- Access young women and men who often cannot be reached through non-sport or non-football related initiatives.
- Motivate involved young people to join year-long educational programmes and to become motivated to get socially engaged in their surroundings.
- Run grassroots football coaching education programmes including the delivery of teaching social skills through football – conducted by coaching education experts of the clubs.
- Cover the costs of their involved personnel.

Local Partners

The local partners in the respective crisis regions can contribute in particular with the following expertise:

- Offer local know-how and coordination.
- Select and supervise participants for the year-long programmes.

- Conduct coaching education in non-football related social topics (life and soft skills) relevant in the respective project region.
- Provide organisational and financial support (mainly by covering local project costs through in-kind support).

Local ownership is one of the key elements within the programme. As the football clubs and Scort do not set up a local office with international staff at the project location/region, the success of the initiatives depend on the expertise and interest of local partners. The local partner organisations mainly support with important inputs during the project development phase, local organisation, co-ordination and contributions with regard to content – in return they gain visibility, international know-how and new networks on local as well as on international level.

Scort Foundation

Within this concept the Scort Foundation acts as facilitator and organiser. During all projects, realised within "The Football Club Social Alliance", Scort coordinates all structural and organisational processes. This includes e.g. the evaluation of potential project locations corresponding to given criteria, the establishment of local and international partnerships with trustworthy and engaged partner organisations and the fundraising on local and international level. We work out the overall project concept based on the inputs of all stakeholders, including the local partners as well as the professional football clubs. In addition, Scort guarantees all organisational aspects (in co-operation with the main local project partner) during the implementation of the projects and takes care of reporting, monitoring, accounting and evaluation. Thas way, the club instructors and staff of local partner organisations can mainly focus on the education of young women and men who are empowered to act as role models for the younger ones in their local communities in the future.

Sustainable Initiatives through Intensive Co-operation

Due to limited time resources on behalf of the involved club instructors, the engagement of "The Football Club Social Alliance" focuses on specific target regions in Eastern Europe, Africa, Middle East and Asia (e.g. Kosovo, Sri Lanka, Palestine, Sudan, and Uganda). All participating club instructors are full time employees so that travel time has to be limited and time used economically when implementing the coaching education programmes.

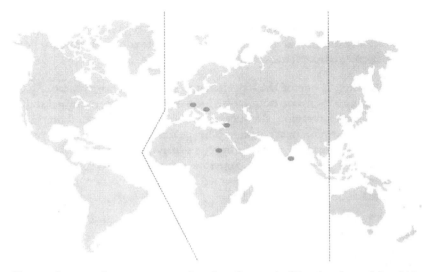

Figure 3: Sector and current target regions (standing 2011) of Scort's partner clubs within "The Football Club Social Alliance"

A minimum of two clubs get engaged in each target region so that instructors of different clubs form the team of instructors conducting the coaching education on the spot. Through this joint engagement of different football clubs within the initiatives a long-term engagement can be realised at the different target regions. While the local partners receive continuous support, the clubs can change project locations. This keeps the projects interesting for the involved staff and the clubs' communication interests.

A long-term initiative consists of different projects and each project of four coaching education modules implemented during a one-year project phase. During each project module young and committed women and men are educated as so called "Young Coaches". These Young Coaches are trained to immediately apply their new learned skills by implementing football activities for underprivileged children in their surroundings.

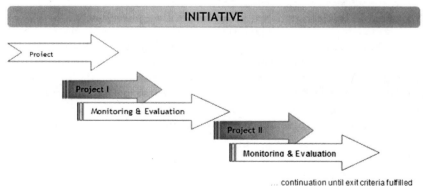

Figure 4: Design of initiatives conducted by "The Football Club Social Alliance"

The clubs engage in a region until evaluation reveals that the overall goal has been achieved or that necessary criteria in the respective region (security, trustworthy partners etc.) do not allow a continuation of the initiative anymore.

The overall goal of any initiative is to educate and motivate a significant number of committed young women and men ("Young Coaches") as role models and grassroots coaches who start working regularly with children in their communities and therefore positively influence the children's development through targeted football activities.

Project Development and Implementation

All projects are composed of a 'project development phase' (6-9 months) and a 'project implementation phase' (9-12 months). Additionally, each year-long project is carefully evaluated (internally and externally) during and after the project phase. The evaluation forms an important basis to adapt ongoing processes and to design follow-up projects corresponding to the local needs. The following chapters will give an overview about some selected aspects during the development and implementation of the projects.

Location

When selecting a new project location the Scort Foundation mainly responds to wishes, suggestions and requests from its official partner clubs within "The Football Club Social Alliance", NGOs, the foundation's board of directors or further interested institutions. Scort considers all proposals and discusses them with the foundation's board of directors and the Alliance's member clubs. The clubs' presidents then jointly decide on their future engagement during their annual meeting. Scort evaluates if the selected project location is suited to stage an international Scort project. The following guiding principles are relevant for the final decision of a project location:

- The potential project location is a crisis region or generally underdeveloped region where the primary humanitarian needs are already covered;
- The project and the participation of the clubs bring a specific added value to the region;
- Guaranteed safety for the international delegation which travels several times to the selected country/region;
- Scort finds a reliable and committed main local project partner who is willing to closely co-operate with Scort throughout the whole year-long initiative and to be responsible for various organisational tasks on the spot;

- Scort finds further committed local project partner organisations who are interested in making a contribution with regards to content, as well as local project supporters who cover at least 20% of the budgeted project costs (particularly local project expenses through (in kind) donations);
- It is possible to access disadvantaged children, youth and young adults in the region.

Bringing an added value to the involved local organisations and the local development in the project region is one of the most important aspects in the establishment of the projects. This must be carefully analysed before but also during and after the projects and adaptations have to be implemented if needed during the course of a project or when designing follow-up projects.

Involved Stakeholders

According to Scort's experience the projects' success is based on the reliance and long-term engagement of various partners who contribute to the projects corresponding to their expertise, interest and capacities. The roles of Scort, the professional football clubs and the local partner organisations were already discussed in the description of the multi-stakeholder approach. These three stakeholders are directly involved in the development and implementation of the projects. The engagement of further stakeholders has to be realised to guarantee the best possible success of the projects. Embassies and partner organisations like e.g. the UN Office on Sport for Development and Peace provide important contacts and information during the development phase of the projects. Apart from cultural and political advises the close contact to the embassies also ensures the safety of the international delegation during the year-long educational programmes.

In addition, local and international supporters which offer (in-kind) donations are of special relevance for the successful implementation of the projects as Scort is an operative foundation that contributes an own share but is also dependant on the support of external donors.

Financing

Since all general administrative (office) and personal costs (project management) of the Scort Foundation are covered by confirmed private donations and corporate partners, Scort is able to ensure that all fundraising and non-financial contributions generated through fundraising can be used exclusively for expenditures concerning directly the projects.

Scort follows the principle of "Shared Funding" in the financing of the projects. All project partners contribute their share to the realisation of the project – of course adapted to the capacities of each involved stakeholder. The aim is that 40% of the budgeted project costs are covered by an own share of the Scort Foundation and the participating football clubs, 20% by local supporters/partners and 40% by international supporters through (in-kind) donations.

Selection of Participants

A crucial element and the basis for the impact and success of the projects is the selection of participants who take part in the year-long educational pro-gramme. Scort cedes this to the local partners who conduct the selection in close co-operation with each other. Generally all participating local partner organisations are allowed to recommend potential participants according to given criteria. The aim is to find young women and men who love football but don't have to be experienced players. It is more important that they are committed to join the whole year-long coaching education programme and willing to work with underprivileged children in their surroundings or the recommending organisations (e.g. NGOs, schools) during and after the coaching education programme. To realise a diversified group of Young Coaches who can set up a network among each other the selection process aims to include both genders and young people with different social, reli-gious, cultural and professional backgrounds. Best possible, the participants should already work with children on a voluntary or professional basis and gain new skills and the expertise to use football as a social tool through the coaching programme. By leaving the selection process to the local partners it is realised that young women and men are selected who are motivated and already showed (social) engagement with children in the past. They know the situation of the children in their communities and organisations as they grew up and live under the same conditions. Based on the needs in the re-spective project regions the local partner organisations have the possibil-ity to recommend young people who profit most from this further training and who will realise the best possible impact in the communities by working with underprivileged children in the future.

Objectives, Content and Methodology

The year-long initiatives, implemented by "The Football Club Social Ali-ance" focus on the following objectives:

1. Education, capacity building and mobilisation
2. Health promotion
3. Communication and mutual respect
4. Setting up local and international co-operations to support children and youth.

Alongside staff of local partner organisations, the professional instructors of the clubs travel to the respective project region four times in a year. They offer a year-long capacity building programme which focuses on edu-cating youth and young adults as grassroots football coaches with specific

443

social competencies. The football club instructors concentrate on delivering know-how on didactical and methodological aspects of grassroots football as well as teaching social competencies through football. Staff of local partner organisations and Scort deliver sessions focusing on non-football related and socially relevant topics corresponding to the needs in the respective project region (life skills and soft skills).

Methodologically, the content is delivered in theoretical and practical sessions by the instructors. A general theoretical introduction is always followed by practical sessions to show the participants how to implement the topics in practice. Afterwards the Young Coaches have to show the international instructors that they are able to implement the new learned skills by working with invited children groups. The instructors offer as much support as needed and demand more and more independent work of the Young Coaches in the course of the project. At the end of each project module the participants of the coaching education have to pass a practical assessment and in between two modules they get the task to organise and implement football activities for children in their private or professional surroundings.

1ST PILLAR	2ND PILLAR	3RD PILLAR
Coaching Education Programme	**Social Competencies through Football**	**Non-Football Related Topics**
• Education as coaches in grassroots football • Theoretical and practical know-how on didactical and methodological aspects of grassroots football	• Education as role models and peer-to-peer educators for younger ones • Convey sport specific values like respect of the opponent, acceptance of rules, teamwork and fairness; handling of aggressions, tensions, victory and defeat	• Teaching socially relevant topics adapted to the local situation and needs on the spot • e.g. reconciliation, first aid, health education, conflict resolution, trauma coping, vocational training
International Instructors of the Clubs	International Instructors of the Clubs	Expert Staff of Local Partner Organisations
Football Development		Development through Football

Figure 5: Content of year-long coaching education programmes

Impact

As every stakeholder contributes its share to the success of the project, each stakeholder should also profit from the involvement and investments in the project. While the participants of the coaching education programme directly and sustainably profit from the acquired know-how and skills also the other stakeholders can report about positive impacts.

Local and international financial supporters can directly and positively impact the development in the respective project region. By investing money, they profit from the rare fact that 100% of the donated money is used exclusively for direct project expenditures as Scort covers all administrative and personal costs (project management) and the clubs cover the costs for their involved personal. In addition, the donors are promoted as project supporters in Scort's PR work and are communicated alongside with the strong brands of the involved clubs.

The local partners gain visibility through local and international project communication realised by all involved partners. The projects are promoted on the clubs' and Scort's websites as well as in local and international media. By recommending young staff of their own organisations the local partners gain new know-how and capacities within their institutions. Being involved in the organisation and implementation of the project this also offers them the opportunity to set up and profit from a network of involved organisations and individuals through the project.

The co-operation of different professional football clubs and their joint social engagement on international level in "The Football Club Social Alliance" offers the following advantages for the involved clubs:

- Sustainable development work while also changing project locations which offer trustworthy social engagement as well as PR opportunities.
- International social engagement corresponding to own interests, expertise and budget.
- Reaching the set targets through a platform coordinated and managed by a professional facilitator.
- Costs are limited and only spent for clubs own expenditures (travel costs of the club's involved experts).
- Exchange with other professional clubs in the field of social engagement.
- No misinterpretation of international social engagement as talent scouting, branding or generating income as initiatives focus on the education.
- Active involvement and identification of the clubs' staff in the projects who forward this to colleagues and friends inside and outside the clubs.

"The Football Club Social Alliance" offers the professional football clubs a framework to become successfully and sustainably engaged on international level without the necessity to set up new structures and hire development or international relations experts within their clubs. Through this network local organisations and individuals in different crisis regions are effectively supported through targeted initiatives. The direct involvement of the clubs' instructors and coaches offers the opportunity to directly identify with the social work. It is not only the youngsters in the respective project region who profit from the educational projects but also all other involved partners. In general, it can be stated that an impact is realised on an individual as well as on a structural level.

Conclusion

Through the joint social engagement with their opponents and by running coaching education programmes focusing on grassroots football and delivering social skills, the clubs show true motivation for international social engagement away from merely talent scouting or economic interests. With

Scort they have a professional facilitator who coordinates and organises their social engagement on international level within "The Football Club Social Alliance". The multi-stakeholder approach offers all involved partners the opportunity to contribute their share corresponding to own interests, expertise and financial as well as human capacities. This way, the best possible impact is realised through co-operation and shared investments. This offers the clubs the opportunities and surroundings to be involved in trustworthy and sustainable social engagement on an international level without any negative side effects. This concept is not based on the involvement of the football stars and coaches of the first teams. This allows the clubs to concentrate on their core business while also becoming more socially engaged. Staff of the clubs – mainly of the academies and social departments or foundations – work on educating local role models in the respective project regions who are more important for underprivileged children in their daily lives than heroes who show up for a day and then never return. The Young Coaches educated by the club instructors know the situation of the local children and offer long-term support by staying and regularly working with them in the future. As local role models they can influence children's lives significantly.

Chapter 33
Able in Sport

Able in Life

Steffi de Jong & Pierre Bataille

Vignette

This chapter is not about demonstrating academic evidence for what PlayAble is trying to achieve. It is the story of the successes and failures of a social business using sports to bring people with disabilities off the sidelines and back into games and sport. You will not find significant statistics or even pre and post-tests results highlighted. However, through this chapter, we wanted to share the story of PlayAble in an honest and transparent manner. We will therefore not only discuss our successes, but also our failures as they are also part of the development of an organization (though unfortunately they are not always valued).

The Beginning

The story of PlayAble starts naturally with its founders. In April 2007, we (Steffi de Jong (The Netherlands) and Pierre Bataille (France)) were two Masters students in the area of Adapted Physical Activity writing our

Master's Thesis on Disability Sport and Development at the University of Stellenbosch in South Africa. There, we coincidentally and by luck met Francis Kimanzi. Kimanzi is a Kenyan alumni of Mathare Youth Sports Association (hereafter MYSA) one of the most successful organization in the area of youth empowerment through football. Meeting him was the very beginning of PlayAble's journey.

One piece of information that Francis gave us stuck in our mind, his organization was delivering sports programs for over 18,000 youths in Nairobi but only one had a disability (a young man with a hearing impairment but who could communicate reasonably well while using his hearing aid). MYSA, state-of-the art organization and pioneer in the area of sports and development was clueless when it came to disability! It was then that we realized that with our knowledge we could bring positive change in the world. We therefore proposed to help MYSA in this area and a couple of months later we hopped on a plane to Nairobi.

No time to waste, a couple of days later we were going to visit people in different slum areas around Nairobi. What we saw was pretty shocking for 21 years old student from Europe who had never seen a slum area. We witnessed people with disabilities literally locked in their home sitting in the dark with no one to talk to. One moment that we will always remember is when we met Chairman. Chairman was a young boy 14 year old with a disability living in Huruma, a slum area in Nairobi. He could not talk or walk and was left alone during the days with no one to assist him in his daily care. The stench in the shelter was so strong that we immediately understood that no one could even assist him to reach the toilet. His mother was helpless, she was a single mom who had to bring money back to the household to feed her kids and send them to school. She loved Chairman but did not see any other way of dealing with the situation.

This was one of the moments were our passion and determination to do something for children like Chairman grew. We were and still are convinced that if Chairman only had access to sport and leisure activities, he would be able benefit in many ways:

• Physically as sport can function as a cost-effective way of rehabilitation,
• Psychologically as sport can help people becoming aware of their abilities which might result in an increased self-confidence
• Socially as sport promotes team work and being out on the field gives opportunities to make friends.

In addition, if the sport would be used as powerful platform to spread awareness about the abilities and right of people with disabilities, it could even function as a springboard to access to schools, health services, employment, etc. After reflecting on different ways of contributing, we found one model to help organizations like MYSA to have a more holistic approach to youth empowerment and community development. Thousands of (sport and development) NGO's have the knowledge and experience of developing programs and finding solutions with and for their communities. We did not see the point in reinventing the wheel by setting up new programs as these organizations are definitely more legitimate to implement activities in their communities than us, Europeans having very limited expertise of the local situation. What we therefore wanted to do, was to assist them a little and push towards inclusive programs by sharing our knowledge and experience. We also helped them design the adaptations in their existing activities and educate inclusive activity coaches needed in order to include people with disabilities within their various projects.

In February 2008, we therefore founded the ancestor of PlayAble: APAID (Adapted Physical Activity International Development) with the aim of enhancing quality of life and promoting social inclusion of people with disabilities through sports. Since that time, we have helped organizations in 4 different countries (Kenya, Uganda, Mozambique & Senegal) to set up inclusive projects. 253 coaches were educated, 1,296 children with disabilities are taking part in weekly activities and awareness was raised among over 21,000 community members. A few examples of the impact of these activities are as follows:

- In Kenya, the coaches and children convinced local leaders and the head teacher of a primary school to open their doors for 20 children with disabilities to give them a change to education.
- The Ugandan national youth football team that participated in the Youth World Cup in South Africa chose a girl with a leg amputation as the captain of team.
- In Mozambique, majority of the children from the special school for children who are deaf have improved their marks as they have never concentrated better in class (more especially on the Fridays when they work very well as they have a sport class when they finish their school work).

Lessons Learned

We may have achieved some great things, but we definitely also learned a lot since the founding. Like many other organizations, we were initially stubborn enough to think that we had found the right solution at our first trial. Over time, we learned to listen to the market response by interacting with our direct and indirect beneficiaries. We have always been trying to measure our impact, but only recently did we understand the importance of also evaluating the process behind it. This made us realize that the concept of "nothing about us without us" was not only relevant in our project implementation but also for us as organizations as we simply could not claim to have found the solution without listening to the feedback and ideas of the organizations and the people with disabilities we were targeting.

They taught us that our initial model was not perfect at all since it was not very sustainable. When we started, we choose a simple charity model: advised our NGO partners (e.g. MYSA) on adaptive strategies, trained coaches and fundraised to pay for the program. This might be considered as one of our first mistakes. Our beneficiaries made us realize that using the charity model was tough because of total dependence on third parties and due to restricted funding. In our view, people are the driving force of any project, organization or business. Many funders however still function as if a ball is going to change the world. They will only fund project costs, but refuse to contribute to overhead costs or salaries. Unfortunately, ideas still come from people instead of basketballs or hula-hoops, so people remain therefore the ones who can change the world using a ball (and not the other way around)! In fact, this attitude of funders made it difficult so that in the first 24 months of our venture, we had not earned a single cent as staff but we had brought many dozens of footballs to our project countries.

Eventually it was the creation of a team and the valuable relationships that it brought which provided us with the changes our approach. We learned that change would not come from two over-motivated APA-students as we pretentiously thought in the beginning (second mistake). What we needed was a strong team with people with different expertise and qualities. Our board welcomed new people with different backgrounds and we set up an advisory board. One of the most important people who crossed our path was Joost de Wit, a successful Dutch entrepreneur and a passionate about start-ups. He has been advising us for the last 3 years on the business approach of our organization and meeting him literally helped us switching from charity model to social business model.

Social business meant for us using market opportunities to positively impact the lives of people with disabilities. With the help of Joost de Wit we created our new hybrid structure that allows us to do exactly that. A for-profit entity (PlayAble Consulting) charges clients such as international NGO's, governments and corporates for our consulting on project design and capacity-building programs. 100% of the profits made by this entity cross-subsidizes the programs serving local NGO's (so they pay only a limited fee for our services) and the persons with disabilities on the ground. In addition, these local NGO's can earn a PlayAble education accreditation when a local trainer is educated. This allows them to "sell" our courses to other organizations and share in the revenue. In this way, we do not only create an income generating mechanism for our own organization but also for our local partners.

Valuable relationship also brought us another change: APAID (choosing a name that is not clear or attractive was a third mistake) became PlayAble. In 2010, we got the chance to meet with over 60 mentors at the Unreasonable Institute, a social business mentorship program in Boulder, Colorado. Among them our current advisors Paul Jerde (Director of the Deming center for entrepreneurship at University of Colorado) and Greg Miller (co-founder of Google.org). All these people contributed to shaping our new look, in terms of communication, marketing and business model.

To summarize, the biggest lesson we learned was to listen to other people who could help us learn from our mistakes. It is only because of all the amazing people that surrounded us both on and off the field, that we were able to take action towards the major improvements in our behavior (from self-orientated to market-orientated), structure (from charity to social business) and branding (from APAID to PlayAble).

Reasons to Dance

Though we did not get it right at first, we are very thankful for all the mistakes we made (luckily none were destructive) because it did help us reach where we are today. And currently, we do have a couple of reasons to dance:

- First of all, the output and impact we have reached in the last 3 years (as described above).
- Global Sport Forum Barcelona Award 2011 (Spain).
- Finalist Beyond Sport Award 2011 (South Africa).
- Jean Bart Trophy 2011 (France).
- Young Professional Award of the International Federation of Adapted Physical Activity (IFAPA) 2011 (France).
- Unreasonable Institute Social Business Fellowship 2010 (United States).
- Ashoka Changemaker winner in 2009 (United States).

Chapter 34

A Qualitative Insight into the Impact of a Community Based Project on Antisocial Behaviour within a Deprived Urban Area

The Case of Fight for Peace

Jamie, E. Bull & James, T. Beale

Introduction

It is thought that antisocial behaviour tends to be concentrated in deprived urban areas (Millie, *et al.*, 2005). Antisocial behaviour consistently occurs in areas of higher deprivation; additionally areas controlled by the metropolitan police were eight times more likely than the national average to have antisocial behaviour occur (Collin and Cattermole, 2004). Crime among young people is a problem in London and more widely in the UK as a whole. Newham, the area in which this research is conducted was among the three most deprived local authorities in the UK in 2004 (Smith *et al.*, 2009) and in 2007 was ranked 6th (Newham 2010). In 2005, two thirds of the population believed that putting preventative measures in place are a superior method of antisocial behaviour prevention than more punitive harsher action (Millie, *et al.*, 2005).

Sport as a Preventative Method of Antisocial Behaviour

Australia recognises sport as a strong preventative method of antisocial behaviour for young people (Morris, *et al.*, 2003). The Australian Institute of Criminology created a project directed towards sport, physical activity and antisocial behaviour in youth (Morris, *et al.*, 2003). Similar established projects exist in East London, the likes of the Leyton Orient Community Sports Project and the current focus 'The Fight for Peace Academy', both use sport as a way of developing young people in deprived areas (Leyton Orient, 2011; Fight For Peace Academy, 2011).

The wider literature on sport as a preventative method for antisocial behaviour has demonstrated a lack of consistency in the findings. When combat sports are taken into isolation the results are far more consistent. The more traditional forms of martial arts are viewed positively, a wide variety of literature has concluded that these forms of martial arts training are a successful method to reduce anti social behaviour (Nonsanchuk, 1981; Trulston 1986; Lamarre and Nonsanchuk, 1999; Bjorkqvist and Varhama, 2001; Daniels and Thornton, 1990; Zivin, *et al.*, 2011). Within the literature there is a belief that participation in boxing is damaging to the individuals and in turn the society, as involvement in the sport is believed to result in fighting outside the gym (Endresen and Olwues, 2005; Bloom and Smith, 1996). Zivin *et al.* (2001) used 60 hostile young males in an urban middle school and exposed them to traditional martial arts on a regular basis. The 60 boys were selected due to the fact that as individuals they were known to have a high risk of violence or delinquency. The sessions were delivered by a master of the specific form of martial arts (Zivin, *et al.*, 2001). The results demonstrated an improvement in antisocial behaviour within the school (Zivin, *et al.*, 2001).

The results of this research were consistent with other finding that examined the impact of martial arts on antisocial behaviour (see, Nonsanchuk, 1981; Trulston 1986; Lamarre and Nonsanchuk, 1999; Bjorkqvist and Varhama, 2001; Daniels and Thornton, 1990)

The literature on boxing and antisocial behaviour/delinquency is sparse, with a limited amount of research examining the topic. Endreson and Olwues (2005) investigated the relationship between boxing, weightlifting, oriental martial arts and antisocial behaviour. The research was a longditudinal intervention, running over 2 years using a sample of 477 boys aged between 11-13 years old. Endreson and Olwues (2005) found that participation in a least two of the sports resulted in increased antisocial behaviour outside of sport. To date with the exception of the current research previous published work has not used participants that are dedicated competing boxers, a vital aspect due to the necessity to engage in the discipline that is within the sport at a competitive level. Previous research has further ignored qualitative enquiry into the social impact of boxing thus not enabling the academic community to have depth of insight into the experiences of those that have been involved in boxing.

The Fight for Peace Project

The fight for peace project uses boxing and martial arts within an academy. These sessions are supplemented with educational sessions and personal development sessions to enable vulnerable young people to achieve their potential. Fight for peace academies are based on 'five pillars', this represents an integrated methodology consisting of boxing and martial arts competition. The five pillars are

1. Boxing and martial arts training and competition
2. Personal development and education: Helping to develop awareness, identity, talents and potential of young people and offering individuals educational opportunities.
3. Youth support: Mentoring, supporting and guiding young people.
4. Job training and Work access: Helping young people gain job related skills and providing key skills for working life.
5. Youth leadership: Young members will exercise authority over themselves or others.

A Qualitative Approach

Currently to the authors knowledge there are no published manuscripts examining the topic of the impact of boxing on antisocial behaviour from a qualitative perspective. This investigation was driven by a strong interest in the individual experiences of those involved in traditional boxing classes and how participants perceive any changes that are taking place as a result of boxing. The previous research aimed at creating an understanding of the relationship between sports and antisocial behaviour used quantitative methods of enquiry.

Qualitative research aims to provide 'rich' and 'thick' descriptive accounts of the phenomenon under investigation, while quantitative research is more generally concerned with counting occurrences, volumes, or the size of associations between entities (Smith, 2008). The aim of qualitative research is to understand and represent the experiences and actions of people as they encounter, engage and live through situations (Smith, 2008). In qualitative research, the researcher attempts to develop an understanding of phenomena under study, based as much as possible from the perspective of the participant (Smith, 2008). Qualitative research involves collecting data in the form of naturalistic verbal reports. The benefits of utilising a qualitative strategy in this type of research was that the investigation was directed through an interpretation of what the text gathered actually meant rather than the numerical properties of the text. Qualitative enquiry is vital to gain an understanding of how and why an individual has been affected by boxing.

In using a qualitative approach this research did not attempt to test a preconceived hypothesis on a large sample, but instead tested a very small sample and tried to understand the individual frames of reference (Smith, 2008).

Phenomenology

Phenomenology was formed as a philosophical framework in the early 20th century (Smith, 2008). Phenomenology focuses on how the world is experienced by the individual, instead of making statements about the world in general (Willig, *et al.*, 2008). Phenomenological psychology aims to clarify situations lived through in a person in everyday life, rather than reducing the phenomenon to a convenient number of identifiable variables (Smith, 2008). Interpretative Phenomenological Analysis (IPA) represents one of the latest developments of phenomenology (Smith, 2008). IPA adopts an inductive approach which is 'bottom up' rather than 'top down', IPA does not go through the process of testing a hypotheses and prior assumptions are avoided where possible (Smith, 2008). In using IPA the goal is to capture texture and quality of individual experience. However the information is presented the way in which the participant has chosen to present it, therefore the researcher can interpret it in many ways (Smith, 2008). The current study utilised the IPA technique as it felt appropriate as a means to captures the experiences of the boxers over the period of time spent with Fight For Peace.

Method

Participants

Three male amateur boxers aged 16 to 18 years old, all of differing ethnic backgrounds were selected to take part in the research. All of the boxers were from East London and were members of the Fight for Peace Academy Amateur Boxing Club. The participants were selected on the basis of having a history of antisocial behaviour and had been involved in the traditional settings of the boxing club long enough for the sport to have had an effect on them. The boxers experience levels ranged from 4 to 6 years.

Procedure

Semi structured interviews were conducted based on the guidelines suggested by Smith (2008) and considered the best method to use with Interpretative Phenomenological analysis. The semi-structured interviews had a schedule comprising of a list of open ended questions which guided rather than dictated the interview. The interviews were conducted in a room that had been designed for such a process. The interviews lasted between 25 and 40 minutes and the interview schedule allowed the individual to discuss areas such as feelings towards past behaviour, personal change, role models and self confidence. Interviews took place at the Fight for Peace Amateur Boxing Club. Interviews were recorded and transcribed verbatim.

Analysis

The first author worked at Fight for Peace and gained a rapport with the group for a period of time prior to the start of the research. The data was analysed using Interpretative Phenomenological Analysis (IPA). IPA is an ideographic approach which involves the process of reading and re-reading transcripts in order to capture the quality and texture of individual experience (Willig, 2007). Whilst using IPA a series of steps were taken that facilitated the identification of themes, which were then integrated into meaningful clusters, first within and then across cases (Willig, 2008; Smith, 2008). The interviews were transcribed from the audiotape recordings. Thoughts and observations were noted on the transcribed interviews and cases were carefully read and then re- read to indentify any emergent themes. Themes were then given to each part of the text and were assigned on the basis that they best characterised the individual's accounts and each section of the transcript. Individual summary tables of themes were produced for each individual's interviews. The themes were then investigated in order to indentify clusters. A final integrated table of themes was then produced on which the superordinate theme and sub ordinate themes were cited with reference to where the themes were in the individual transcripts. Transcripts and summary tables were then viewed independently by another researcher in order to check that the interpretation was an accurate reflection of the original date and to triangulate the date.

Table 1: Summary table of integrated themes

Superordinate Theme: Past Self			
Subordinate themes	Participant 1	Participant 2	Participant 3
• Lack of stimulation	P: 1.L: 11-12 / P 2: L: 71	P: 1. L: 29-30	P: 1 L: 22-28
• Aggression/ violence	P: 2.L: 40	P: 1. L: 41-42	P: 1. L: 5-7
Superordinate Theme: New Self			
Subordinate themes	Participant 1	Participant 2	Participant 3
• Focused	P: 2.L: 55/P: 3.L: 82,110	P: 1. L: 23 / L: 36	
• Purpose	P: 4.L: 136-138	P: 3.L: 102-103	P: 1. L: 30
• Outlet	P: 2.L: 65-68/P: 3.L: 111		
• Increased confidence	P: 4. L: 146	P: 1. L: 24-25	
• Satisfaction	P: 4. L: 144	P: 1.L: 27/P: 3.L:101	P: 2. L: 81
• Reduced Violence	P: 3. L: 82-83	P: 1.L: 44	P: 1. L: 7,.L: 24

Superordinate Theme: Relationship with Coach			
	Participant 1	Participant 2	Participant 3
Subordinate themes			
• Coach impact	P: 2. L: 61/ P: 3. L: 85-87	P: 2.L: 61-67	P: 2. L: 53-54
• Coach as a role model	P: 3. L: 88	P: 2.L: 90-93	P: 2. L: 54
• Respect	P: 3. L: 93	P: 2.L: 66-67	P: 2. L: 68
Superordinate Theme: Perception and views of others			
	Participant 1	Participant 2	Participant 3
Subordinate themes			
• Time exposed to traditions	P: 3. L.108-109	P: 2.L:76-80	P: 2. L: 65-68
• Social support		P: 2.L: 60-70	P: 2. L: 63
• Supportive group of boxers			P: 2. L: 58

Results

Analysis of the transcripts revealed 5 super ordinate themes that are phenomenological in their make up: past self, new self, relationship with coach,
purposeful activity, perceptions and views of others involved.

Discussion/Results

To understand how the participants perceive their experiences of boxing,
it was important to first gain an understanding of how the participants perceived their world before they started traditional boxing classes. When discussing their experiences of themselves in the past, (super ordinate theme
past self) the participants stated that they felt they had a lack of opportunities in the past and any activities they did find were negative and ultimately
lead to them get.

The first subordinate theme within past self was identified as being a
lack of stimulation; the literature suggests that antisocial behaviour stems
from boredom and it is stated that if a young person lacks stimulation and
has little to do they will seek their own, often antisocial, activities, which
is usually the case in underprivileged urban areas (Collingwood et al. 1992;
Coalter, 2008, Allen, 2007). Being part of a gang or being part of an antisocial peer group is seen as a large contributor to antisocial behaviour (Coalter, 2008). The participants spent a large amount of time on the streets and
in gangs in the past as a result of a lack of stimulation. The second subordinate theme that was identified within past self was violence and aggression,
which the individuals believed also occurred due to a lack of stimulation.

> (First author) 'Ok, why do you think the behaviour stopped when boxing star-
> ted' 'I don't know really, it just relieved aggression, and it made me realise I
> was being stupid, it weren't my fault I just had nothing better to do, like be-
> fore I was out on the street, kicking the crap out of somebody's head, since I

have been here its over, I don't fight anymore. I think back then and think like, I was somebody else honestly. I would be worse now, id be smoking more drugs even more violent' (Participant 3. p1: L 18-26).

Participant 3 discusses how his antisocial behaviour stopped, why he feels it has stopped, as well as discussing why he feels it initially occurred. This quotation suggests that he was not stimulated in the past and very aggressive, with this combination he began socialising and fighting with friends on the street. After the reply to this question the first author asked:

(First author) 'Why did you do it?' 'Something to do in a way, I was very bored and we felt like it was important that have a purpose on the street, like the toughest gang' (Participant 3. p1: L 27-30).

With the participants perception being that their antisocial behaviour in the past was linked primarily to boredom, the participants expressed how starting traditional boxing classes impacted positively on boredom. The participants stated that boxing has given them something to focus on and therefore they are no longer on the streets and lacking opportunities. Giving the individuals an activity to focus on seemed to have reduced past boredom and subsequently antisocial behaviour. This is consistent with previous research that stated programmes which have been linked to decreases in antisocial behaviour and delinquency are usually due to reductions in boredom (Collingwood, et al. 1992). Responses to questioning suggest that participants now have a sense of satisfaction through taking part in boxing along with feeling happiness, reduced aggression and enjoyment.

'I just spend time in the boxing gym, relieving aggression' (Participant 3. p1: L 19)

In addition it emerged that the participants felt that all the hard training was for a purpose and they now feel that they have a purpose within boxing. The participants felt that in the past they did not have a purpose and anything they were involved in on the street was pointless, but through boxing they have a life line.

(First author) 'How would you describe your own individual gains from boxing?' 'Boxing has giving me a focus and purpose, a target and has thrown me a life line. If it wasn't for boxing I would be smoking, drinking fighting and would be on the streets all the time' (Participant 1. p4: L 132-140).

When discussing their 'new self', the second superordinate theme, increases in self-confidence was perceived and experienced across all participants and emerged in all of the interviews.

'Has your perception changed at all?' (First author) 'No man, my perception has stayed the same, its done good for my life, it's the best feeling, I am out there on my own winning, its all down to me 'innit', which gives me confidence because I win because of me' (Participant 2. p1: L 22-25).

The participants in this research discussed how boxing was an outlet and any other stressful parts of their lives are put at the back of their mind and forgotten while training. The participants stated that boxing gave them an outlet and discussed how they experienced boxing as a way to relieve anything else that is going on in their world.

' (first author) 'Why do you think boxing is affected you in this way?' 'When
I enter the gym all my problems are left at the door, maybe you could say
that you will take your problems out on the bag. I like to just leave my problems at the door, like if you take your problems into sparring its gonna affect
you bad, you will be all over the place, you have got to leave your problems at
the door. The gym is a sanctuary; it's a place to get away from problems. You
put everything aside; you get away from everything and focus on your training
(Participant 1. p2: L 64-69).

These results mirror the results of traditional martial arts on anti social
behaviour, the traditional martial arts have consistently been found to reduce aggression, violence, hostility and increase self-confidence and self es-
teem (Nonsanchuk, 1981; Trulston 1986; Lamarre and Nonsanchuk, 1999;
Bjorkqvist and Varhama, 2001; Daniels and Thornton, 1990; Zivin, et al.,
2001). The participants in this research found that the nature of boxing
training had a cathartic effect and reduced their aggression. The participants also emphasised the importance of boxing to them as an individual
and cited this importance as a major reason for not fighting outside of the
gym, as fighting outside the gym would put their boxing at a risk. The participants were concerned about becoming injured in a street fight where there
are no rules. Participants perceived boxing to be so important that any risk
that would stop them from being able to participate was avoided.

'If it wasn't for boxing I would be smoking, drinking fighting and would be on
the streets all the time. Like I don't want to risk losing boxing again, like I did
when I got hit with the pole back in the day' (Participant 1. p4: L 138-140).

The result of this qualitative piece differs to the research of Endreson and
Olwues (2005). These differences may be due to differences in the research
approach and other fundamental differences in participants, e.g. the current
study examined competitive boxers and not a combination of sports where
participants were not immersed into the specific sporting environment. In
addition the participants in this research were from an area of deprivation
and experienced boredom and dissatisfaction in the past before starting
boxing with the fight for peace programme. A further important difference
was the fact that the participants in this research were able to discuss the
relationships that they were able to build with the coach. A major factor in
experiencing the traditions of boxing is experiencing the traditions of the
coaches and the discipline that has been handed down over generations of
boxers and their coaches. Respect for the coach was frequently discussed by
participants in this research and may be an additional reason for not using
the skills that the coach has taught them outside of the gym. The subordinate themes respect, coach impact and coach as a role model, occurred within the super-ordinate theme relationship with the coach. A key benefit of
traditional boxing to the participants appears to be their experience of the
boxing coach as all participants perceived their coach as a positive role model and believed that the way their coach behaved, was the correct way.

In terms of how the coach has an impact on the participants, it seems
that in some cases boxers can link any changes they have experienced directly to the coach.

'Wow, if it wasn't for him I wouldn't be how I am now, he is there when ever I need him and he is there making sure that I can be the best that I can be, he is very important in my life' (Participant 2. p2: L 61-64).

This statement by participant 2 links to coach respect and coach impact. Coaches were certainly role models to the participants in this study.

'they set a good example. Like for me anyway I study and love boxing, so anybody that has achieved in the sport is somebody that I will look up to' (Participant 1. p3: L 89-90).

'I just want to be like him he has his head screwed on with everything and plus he accomplished stuff actually as a boxer as well and when somebody close to you shows you that hard work and a good attitude is all it takes to get there you know that's what you want to do' (Participant 2. p2: L 91-94).

The boxers were no longer violent outside of the gym and were no longer involved in gang related crime. The coach behaviour appears positive and could be deemed a major factor in the change in behaviour. Having a positive role model is important as young people will often repeat what they have seen older people or role models doing (Clarke, 2003). The participants in this research also discussed the fact that other club members were seen as role models. Participant responses during the interviews suggested that the way other boxers behave has influenced new participants and other boxers that are competing set an example for boxers who wish to compete:

'I saw the way these guys were behaving in the gym and I found that I started acting the same way you know I found that there behaviour did like, uuuuum influence me I guess, also I would like to get to where team mates are like ability wise. The coach is also somebody to admire as well you know, because he has been there and done it all' (Participant 3. p2: L 65-69).

The participants also discussed how individuals change progressively with the more time they spend in boxing. It appears that time exposed to traditions of boxing could shape individual behaviour. A section of a transcript that was particularly interesting was the perception that a coach should not solely teach an individual to box, as just providing an antisocial individual with the skills is going to lead to them using those skills outside, but instead the coach should mentor the individual and expose to them to the traditions of boxing. This section represents a good example of where qualitative research methodology provides rich information on participant experiences that would likely be missed in more traditional forms of research. The experiences and insights gained through this research creates an image of a member of a traditional boxing club and allows readers to experience a piece of their world, similar to the experiences of Loic Waqcuant who spent three years socialising with and training with more than 50 boxers of a traditional boxing gym in Chicago (Waqcuant , 1992, cited in Coakley, 2007). He also experienced mutual respect in the gym and spoke of the fact that fighting did not take place outside the gym, even though all boxers lived in a deprived and violent area (Waqcuant , 1992, cited in Coakley, 2007).

Future Research

To build on the current research it is suggested that longitudinal research take place where boxers are followed post involvement in boxing. The authors would further recommend that traditional boxers involved in boxing clubs that do not have the educational aspects attached to them be examined to enable an understanding of how experiences differ from when these aspects are removed from the programme. A quantitative comparison between the fight for peace programme and a boxing gym that does not have the educational features attached to it would be of further interest.

Personal Reflection

The first author has eleven years experience in amateur boxing and as well as going through the same system as the participants in terms of sport, the author was born in and has lived in, the same area of East London as the participants in the current study. The interest in this area was ignited by the negative views of boxing that exist in the absence of a qualitative investigation. Having experienced the traditions of a boxing club, the first author was intrigued to investigate the individual experiences of others going through the same system. The results of this study have suggested that boxing can be a successful tool in preventing antisocial behaviour. A factor that needs to be considered is that many boxers stop taking part in the sport between the ages of 15 and 18. With that in mind the boxers may resume the activities that they were previously involved in, but now possessing an enhanced ability to fight and cause damage to others. The advantage of The Fight for Peace Academy is that the club incorporate a 5 pillar methodology. In using their 5 pillar methodology situations such as a young person quitting boxing and returning to crime armed with dangerous skills is less likely. The 5 pillar uses personal development, education, youth support, job training, work access and youth leadership, as well as martial arts and boxing. This type of approach develops the whole person and prepares the individual for a possible life away from combat sports.

Concluding Remarks

Examining the results of this research and how they compare to previous literature, a clearer picture has been provided of how the traditions of a boxing club can positively affect any antisocial behaviour in participants. It can be concluded that being involved in a traditional boxing club provided previously bored individuals with a focus and created an environment where happiness, satisfaction and a sense of purpose was experienced. Boxers self confidence grew through attendance at a traditional boxing club. Involvement in the fight for peace programme gave the individuals a positive way to reduce aggression and perhaps most importantly positive role models that provided social support in other areas of the boxer's life.

References

Allen, C. (2007) *Crime, drugs and social theory: a phenomenological approach*. UK: Ashgate Publishing Limited.

Bjorkqvist, K. and Varhama, L. (2001) 'Attitudes towards violent conflict resolution among male and female kareteka in comparison with practitioners of other sports', *Perceptual & Motor Skills*, 92, 2, pp. 586-588.

Clarke, D. (2003) *Pro-social and anti-social behaviour*. UK: Routledge

Coackley, J. (2007) *Sport in Society: Issues and Controversies. 9th Edn*. USA: McGraw Hill.

Coalter, F. (2008) *A wider social role for sport: who's keeping the score*. UK: T & F Books

Collins, S and Cattermole, R. (2006) *Anti social behaviour and disorder: powers and remedies*. UK: Thomson, Sweet & Maxwell publishers.

Collingwood, T.R., Reynolds, R., Jester, B. and Debord, D. (1992) 'Enlisting physical education for the war on drugs', *Journal for physical education and research development*, 63, 2, pp. 25-28.

Daniels, K. and Thornton, E.W. (1990) 'An analysis of the relationship between hostility and training in the martial arts', *Journal of Sports Sciences*, 8, 2, pp. 95-101.

Endresen, I.M and Olwues, D. (2005) 'Participation in power sports and anti-social involvement in preadolescent and adolescent boys', *Journal of Child Psychology and Psychiatry*, 46, 5, pp.468-478.

Fight For Peace Project (2011) *Five Pillars*. Available at:10/11/11. http://www.fightforpeace.net/default.asp?contentID=3&lang=1 (Accessed 12th March 2012).

Lammare, B.W and Nonsanchuk, T.A. (1999) 'Judo- The gentle way: A replication of studies on martial arts and aggression', *Perceptual and Motor Skills*, 88. pp. 992-996.

Morris, L., Sallybanks, J., Willis, K., and Makkai .(2003) 'Sport, Physical Activityand Antisocial Behaviour in Youth', *Australian institute of criminology: trends and issues*, No. 249.

Leyton Orient LOCSP (2011) Delivering Sport Strengthening communities. Available at: http://www.leytonorient.com/page/LOCSPIndex (Accessed 12th March 2012).

Millie, A., Jacobsen, J., Hough, M. (2005) Antisocial Behaviour Strategies: Finding a balance. UK: Policy Press.

Morris, L., Sallybanks, J., Willis, K., and Makkai .(2003) 'Sport, Physical Activity and Antisocial Behaviour in Youth', *Australian institute of criminology: trends and issues*, No. 249.

Newham (2010) *Joint strategic needs assessment*. Economic ambition.

Nonsanchuk, T.A. (1981) 'The way of the warrior: The effects of traditional martial arts training on aggressiveness', *Human Relations*, 43, pp. 435-444.

Smith, J.A., Flowers, P. and Larkin, M. (2009) *Interpretative Phenomenological Analysis: Theory, Method and Research*. UK: Sage Publications.

Smith, J.A. (2008) *Qualitative Psychology: A Practical Guide to Research Methods*. 2nd Edn. USA: Sage Publications.

Trulston, M.E. (1986) 'Martial arts training: A novel "cure" for juvenile delinquency', *Human Relations*, 39, 12, pp.1131-1140.

Willig, C. (2008) *Introducing Qualitative Research in Psychology*. 2nd Edn. USA: McGraw Hill.

Zivin, G., Hassan, N.G., DePaula, G.F., Monti, D.A., Harlan, C., Hossain, K.D and Patterson, K. (2001) 'An effective approach to violence prevention: Traditional martial arts in middle school', *Adolescence*, 36, pp. 443-459.

Chapter 35

The Impact of Sport Interventions in Rift Valley Kenya after Post Election Violence

A Case Study

Serena Borsani

Introduction

At the start of 2008, Kenya was in the grip of its worst crisis since independence and the violence following the December 2007 election was unprecedented. For over two weeks there were alarming reports of targeted ethnic violence, killing, gender-based brutality, extensive looting and destruction of property, and mass displacement. More than one thousand people were reported dead and thousands more injured, and for a time the unrest seemed to pose a real threat to the unity of the nation. On 7th January the Government of Kenya reported that two hundred and fifty-five thousand people were displaced, and it was estimated that the total vulnerable population was thought to be about half a million people.

The initial spark was the contested presidential result, where the incumbent Mwai Kibaki – candidate of the Party of National Unity (PNU) – claimed victory, and was swiftly sworn in despite claims of widespread poll rigging. However the unrest quickly took on a much more ethnic dimension.

The Kikuyus, who have dominated Kenya economically since independence in 1963, bore the brunt of the violence. As Mwai Kibaki was also a Kikuyu, they were perceived to be the supporters of both him and his Kikuyu-dominated PNU alliance. The worst unrest was around the Northern Rift Valley town of Eldoret where Kalenjins mobilised against Kikuyu, looting and burning their property. Relative calm only returned to the country following the formation of a coalition cabinet consisting of Kibaki's PNU and Raila Odinga's opposition Orange Democratic Movement (ODM) in April 2008, with Kibaki as President and Odinga as Prime Minister.

Sport for Trauma Healing, Reconciliation and Social Change: Experience from the Field

In Kenya, especially in the Rift Valley where youth were believed to have played a major role in the post-election violence, sporting events are increasingly becoming popular forums through which peace and reconciliation messages can be effectively delivered. Sport attracts a large number of people, and in particular the youth, who, to varying degrees, were unquestionably involved in the violence.

There were numerous events and activities carried out by international organizations, local organizations and community based organizations in the immediate post election violence. Almost universally, these were designed to impart positive social values and life skills including leadership, self-confidence, teamwork, conflict resolution, discipline, respect and fair play. This breadth assisted with the research for this paper as it was possible to identify the many different approaches of how to best use sport as a tool for healing and reconciliation. The principal methodologies used and a brief overview of their relative strengths were as follows:

- Single events: an ideal forum for reaching large numbers of people, whether at the event or through subsequent media coverage. One of the most important events was Tegla Loroupe Peace Run, which aimed to spread a message of peace and reconciliation across communities affected by violence.

- Sport based projects like the *"Peace and Reconciliation Project"* by Kesofo and the *"Kenya Youth Sports4Peace & Reconciliation Project"* by Care International. In these cases sport was presented as the main vehicle to achieve sporting and non-sporting aims. Sporting aims might include: expanding opportunities for participation in sport; developing sporting skills; providing opportunities for development; or training sports coaches. Non-sporting aims might be: developing citizenship values and commitment to collective responsibility; healing psychosocial trauma; addressing gender-related issues; building relationships amongst different communities; creating opportunities for dialogue to eradicate the roots of the conflict; developing conflict resolution and conflict management skills; reducing social isolation and tension; and addressing health-related issues, including HIV/AIDS.[1]

- Sport activities as part of a wider project like the *"Amani Football Cup"* organised by International Organization for Migration (IOM). These activities were part of a wider psychosocial support project sponsored by the Norwegian Embassy aimed at assessing the psychosocial needs of IDPs in camps and host communities in the Rift Valley Province. Once assessed, they used sport as part of a wider project to provide psychosocial support to IDPs through both training counsellors and establishing counselling and recreational centres.

Research projects: Sport activities in Child Friendly Space (CFS) – An early evaluation

The IOM, under a psycho-social support project sponsored by Norwegian Embassy, set up two Child Friendly Spaces in Illula in the Uasin Gishu district, and Seregeya in Lugari District, between November and December 2008. Through community mobilization around children's needs, CFS provided regular, structured activities for children, adolescents and parents of young children under the supervision of caring adults from the community. CFS allowed children to participate in activities where they could play, express their feelings, thoughts and opinions, and learn from adults and other children, providing a sense of normality in an otherwise abnormal situation. These activities helped to trigger positive coping mechanisms, minimize the consequences of deprivation and traumatic experiences, and positively influence the children's resilience. The two locations were identified following consultation with the host communities, and addressed the security and accessibility requirements such as providing and open space with easy access for children, on a site that was ethnically neutral etc. The locations were then equipped with sport and non sport tools such as footballs, volleyballs kits, tennis balls, skipping ropes, darts board, chess sets, hula hoops, toys, pencils, crayons wax, mathematical sets, exercise books and so on. Committed volunteers were trained in sport and conflict resolution skills, and three psychosocial counsellors per centre assisted the two communities with implementing the activities.

According to age and gender, a weekly schedule was developed together with participants in order to best suit their free time. Each centre organized football and volleyball tournaments for the duration of 3 weeks.

1.Coalter, F. *"Sport-in-Development: A Monitoring and Evaluation Manual"* (2006), University of Stirling

The psychosocial team attempted to foster community re-interaction, especially between displaced and non-displaced people. Consequently, sharing experiences developed a sense of empathy between community members, and with this followed forgiveness: the first step to achieving reconciliation.

Methodology

With the essential assistance of very committed psychosocial counsellors, a first evaluation of this project was carried out just before Christmas 2008 to analyze the impact of sport on youth involved in football and volleyball tournaments.

The data required was collected through focus group discussions (FGD) and questionnaires. Focus group discussions were prepared considering three different target groups: children, youth and adults, and were held in Illula and Seregeya, reaching almost 150 people. For children in particular a problem tree approach was used.

Structured questionnaires were adjusted according to an early analysis of FGD, and then re-administered in Illula to fifty youth between 18 and 25 to gather more qualitative and quantitative data.

Analysis and interpretation of Focus Group Discussions

Through focus group discussions it was possible to identify some changes caused by sporting activities: we saw improvement in participants' relationships with their parents; we saw them use their idle time more meaningfully; and we saw higher levels of participation in both artistic and economic pursuits. For many, participating in sporting activities within the newly created social networks served as entry points to paying careers. Some youth were also been absorbed into the military and in companies such as Kenya Pipeline, AFC Leopards, and Gor Mahia FC. Furthermore, sport led to physical fitness and all its known benefits. More unusual plusses such as acquired skills in micro finance enterprises were also picked up by several participants as well. In sum, the results were as follows:

- CHILDREN: "Happy & sad face" exercises were used to analyze the impact of Child Friendly Spaces in their young lives. Participation in physical activities of all varieties were largely popular, even if not everyone was initially comfortable using new equipment like skipping ropes. Some parents did not allow their children to participate in activities involving different ethnicities: this was an ongoing but worrying problem.

- YOUTH: The main benefits to the youth participants were: introduction to new things; creativity; friendly competition; making friends; increased respect for different ethnicities; and the renewed hope for a better future. Youth appreciated the opportunity given by open discussions after activities, especially those directly about reconciliation, entrepreneurship, and health issues such as personal hygiene and sex. They became more tolerant towards each other, and they began to feel part of a group, sharing ideas and having similar goals. Children had the chance to be personally involved in the activities at the decision making level, increasing their sense of ownership for the centre. Challenges included lack of facilities and support, the risk of injury, and occasionally negative behaviour attributed to their past experiences.

• ADULTS: Adults were directly and indirectly involved in the activities: directly attending the official launching program and indirectly by allowing their children to attend. They appreciated the positive behaviour change seen in their children who, they said, were busier during the day and more relaxed in the evening, more positive in thinking about their future, and more active, filled with a new sense of hope. Parents benefited directly from Child friendly spaces since they stopped worrying about the children's where-abouts. Seeing the positive benefit in their children, they expressed their willingness to have something similar set-up for adults.

Analysis and Interpretation of the Questionnaire

Sport was not so common a past-time amongst females. Girls were more involved in both domestic work and looking after younger brothers and sisters, and as a result the majority of the respondents were males- 67%. However a solid effort was made by psychosocial counsellors to involve girls in dancing, volleyball and in football, and the feedback was very positive.

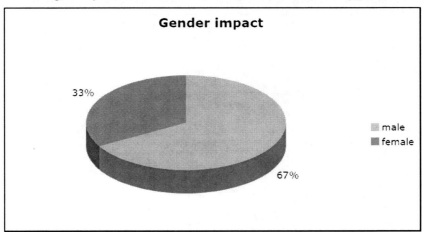

Figure 1: Graph "Gender distribution"

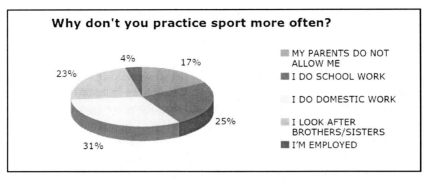

Figure 2: Graph "Why don't you practice sport more often?"

The most common sport practiced by respondents was football followed by volleyball and then running. Before coming to CFS respondents were, on average, involved in sport activities a few times a week. Some, however, were approaching sport for the first time. The main reason they were not playing sport more often was domestic work for both males and females- where domestic work represents harvesting for boys and housekeeping for girls. Sport was also not perceived as that important from parents who, at the beginning, were a bit reluctant to send their children to the centre. However, as highlighted in the focus group discussions, they soon began to see positive changes in their children's behaviour.

As indicated in the next graph, most people used their free-time to work or look for a job. Poverty remained the main problem and sport is not a panacea. It can only be used as to bring benefits that help the situation, such as instilling a sense of self-worth and respect, a sense of commitment, achievement, and self confidence, all of which are necessary to build a better future.

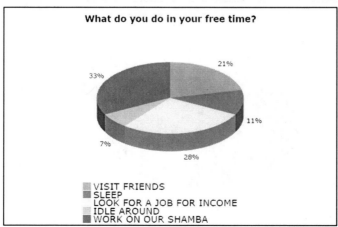

Figure 3: Graph "What do you do in your free time"?

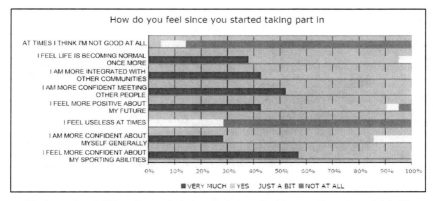

Figure 4: Graph "How do you feel since you started taking part in sport activities?"

Figure 4 shows that youth were more confident about themselves and more tolerant towards others. They were hopeful about the future, and believe that reconciliation is possible. In this case sport sped up trauma healing and overall resilience to difficult surroundings.

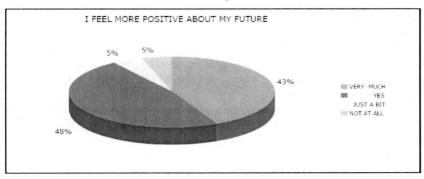

Figure 5: Graph "I feel more positive about my future"

Discussion groups and psychosocial sessions in which youth followed sport activities where possible. Individual sessions targeted youth not yet ready for an open discussion with others. This built a willingness to share and fostered and empathy to listen to others.

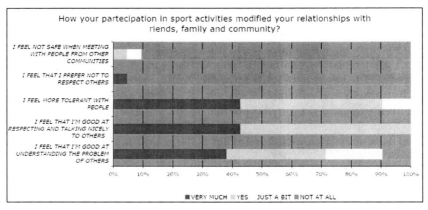

Figure 6: Graph "How your participation in sport activities modified your relationship
with friends, family and community?"

The results of the questionnaire were encouraging. Youth seemed not to mind where new friends originated from. Collectively, youth understood the fickleness and uselessness of the recent post-election violence. They seemed to realize that at the societal level there were no winners, and al of Kenya suffered. According to the Saturday Nation newspaper on January 10th 2009, one in three Kenyans was in danger of starvation owing to crop failure. The food shortages were partially caused by the post election violence that saw militia burn food stores, and also by the disruption the violence reaped upon agrarian cycles.

Furthermore almost a quarter of a million pupils who sat the Kenya Certificate of Primary Education (KCPE) examinations were not enrolled into secondary school as they had not expanded enough to respond to increased enrolment in primary schools. This was further aggravated by the destruction of many schools during clashes.

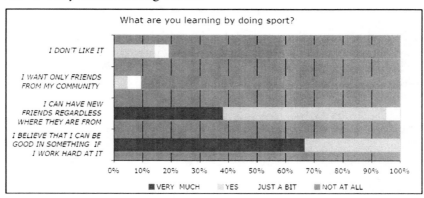

Figure 7: "What are you learning by doing sport?"

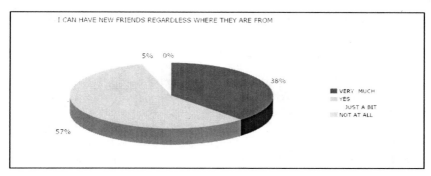

Figure 8: Graph "I can have new friends regardless where they are from"

Conclusions

For Galtung (1998), the vicious cycle of conflict and violence can be broken and turned into a virtuous cycle with a joint action of the '3 Rs': reconstruction of people and places, reconciliation of relationships, and resolution of issues and animosities. If you do only one of these three without the other two you will not even get that one. It is necessary to have synergy between these elements in order to achieve results that may better contribute towards a lasting peace.

Among the peace building initiatives carried out in a post conflict situation sport is a very powerful, neutral, simple, universal and useful means that can contribute, under certain conditions, to speed up each stage of the long process of especially reconciliation.

The difference between practicing sport in its simple form and using it to achieve much more ambitious goals, such as reconciliation and a peaceful coexistence, lies in structured and planned implementation. The trick is to focus and channel sport's innate benefits to yield even loftier ones. Furthermore, from this paper I think it is possible to draw some tentative suggestions and recommendations to be used in sport for reconciliation programs:

- Understand the conflict and the culture where the conflict takes places. There is not a one size fits all approach.
- Always use the very simple humanitarian intervention principle of "Do no harm."
- Be conscious of the distribution of services across conflicting lines. One-sided support might exacerbate the potential for conflict rather than reduce it.
- Base the activities on commonalities and mutual interest/identity that cut across horizontal inequalities.
- Use a participatory approach involving youth in the decision-making process in order to increase their stake in the program.
- Use peer educators and train them with sport, peace building and conflict management skills.

- Focus on daily activities at grassroots level, using events and elite athletes to gather more youth and to promote the idea of sport for reconciliation.
- Promote fair play rather than win at all costs.
- Be sensitive in understanding group dynamics, and immediately address possible conflicts arising amongst participants.
- Create a social network with other actors from all community levels.
- Focus on the process of healing, building relationship and empathy rather than sport itself.
- Develop a monitoring and evaluation mechanism able to proof the impact of sport in reconciliation with qualitative and quantitative indicators

The holistic approach must be used not only in peace building process but also in sport programs themselves. Through an adapted "Dugan Nested paradigm" this chapter also shows a mechanism that allows sport to have a better chance of success in social change. Healing is the first step to rebuilding relationships that contribute to wider social change, and sport is proven to be a very adept tool to achieve this difficult goal.

References

"Practical Guide to Multilateral Needs Assessments in Post-Conflict Situations", A Joint UNDG, UNDP and World Bank Guide, prepared by GTZ with the support of BMZ, Available at: www.reliefweb.int/rw/lib.nsf/db900SID/LHON64UGQZ/$FILE/Needs_Assess_Post_Conflict_UNDG_Aug_2004.pdf?OpenElement], (Accessed 12th March 2012).

"Reconciliation After Violent Conflict": (2003) A Handbook. International Institute for Democracy and Electoral Assistance (IDEA). Available at: www.idea.int/publications/reconciliation/upload/reconciliation_full.pdf] (Accessed 12th March 2012).

Armstrong, G. "Talking up the Game: Football and the Reconstruction of Liberia, West Africa" (2002) 9 Global Studies in Culture and Power, 471-494.

Bailey, R. "Evaluating the Relationship Between Physical Education, Sport and Social Inclusion" (2005), 57 Educational Review, 71-90.

Coalter, F. "Sport-in-Development: A Monitoring and Evaluation Manual" (2006), University of Stirling, Available at: www.uksport.gov.uk/assets/File/News/monitoring_and_evaluation_140906.pdf], (Accessed 12th March 2012).

Duncan, J; Arntson, L "Children in Crisis: Good Practices in Evaluating Psychosocial Programming" (2004). Available at: http://www.savethechildren.org/publications/Good_Practices_in_Evaluating_Psychosocial_Programming.pdf], (Accessed 12th March 2012).

European Commission. *"White Paper on Sport"* (Brussels: 2003) Available at:http://ec.europa.eu/sport/whitepaper/wp_on_sport_en.pdf] (Accessed 12th March 2012).

Fischer, M. *"Recovering from Violent Conflict: Regeneration and (Re-)Integration as Elements of Peacebuilding"* Berghof Handbook for Conflict Transformation, Available at: http://www.berghof-handbook.net], (Accessed 12th March 2012).

Galtung, J. "AFTER VIOLENCE: 3R, RECONSTRUCTION, RECONCILIATION, RESOLUTION Coping With Visible and Invisible Effects of War and Violence" (1998)

Galtung, J. *"Conflict Transformation by Peaceful Means (the Transcend Method)"*. (Geneva 1998) Participant`s Manual, the Mini-Version. Available at: http://www.undmtp.org/english/conflict_transform/ conflict.pdf] (Accessed 12th March 2012).

Gasser, P. & Levinsen, A. *"Breaking Post-War Ice: Open Fun Football Schools in Bosnia and Herzegovina"* (2004) 7:3 Sport in Society, 457-472.

Gasser, Patrick K. and Levinsen, Anders "Breaking Post-War Ice: Open Fun Football Schools in Bosnia and Herzegovina" (2006). In Giulianotti, Richard and Mcardle, David (eds). Sport in the Global Society.

Guest, A.M., *"Thinking both critically and positively about development through sport"*, (2005). Available at: http://archive.sportanddev.org/en/articles, (Accessed 12th May 2012).

Guest, Andrew M., PhD; *"What exactly does sport do? Thinking both critically and positively about development through sport "* (2005), University of Portland, US; published on: www.sad.ch/

Heiniger, J.P. & Meuwly, M. *"Movement, Games and Sports: Developing Coaching Methods and Practices for Vulnerable Children in the Southern Hemisphere"* (Lausanne: Foundation Terre des Hommes, 2005).

Henley, R. *"Helping Children Overcome Disaster Trauma Through Post-Emergency Psychosocial Sports Programs"* (Biel: Swiss Academy for Development, 2005), Available at:http://www.sportanddev.org/data/ document/document/209.pdf, (Accessed 12th March 2012).

Lea-Howarth, J. "Sport and Conflict: Is Football an Appropriate Tool to Utilise in Conflict Resolution, reconciliation or Reconstruction?" (2006) Contemporary War and Peace Studies MA Dissertation. University of Sussex.

Keetch, M. & Houlihan, B. *"Sport and the End of Apartheid"* (1999) 349 The Round Table, 109-121.

Keim, M. *"Nation Building at Play: Sport as a Tool for Social Integration in Post-Apartheid South Africa"* (Oxford: Meyer & Meyer Sport, 2003).

Keim, M. *"Sport as Opportunity for Community Development and Peace-Building in South Africa"* in Y. Vanden Auweele, C. Malcolm & B. Meulders, eds. Sport and Development (Leuven: Lannoo Campus, 2006).

Kriesberg, Louis *"Constructive Conflicts, From Escalation to Resolution"*. 2nd
ed. (2003) Rowman and Littlefield. Oxford.

Kunz, V. *"Sport and Play for Traumatized Children and Youth. An assessment of
a pilot-project in Bam, Iran"* (2006); published on: www.sad.ch/

Lederach, J.P. *"Building Peace: Sustainable Reconciliation in Divided Societies"*,
(1997). cf. Dugan, *"A Nested Theory of Conflict,"* Women in Leadership v..1 no..1

Pelle Kvalsund, *"Sport as a tool for peace-building and reconciliation"*, (2005) Input Paper for the Break-Out Session. 2nd Magglingen Conferen-
ce, Available at: www.magglingen2005.org/downloads/
05_peace_building.pdf] (Accessed 12th March 2012).

Refugee Studies Centre and UNICEF (Ed.) *"Working with children in un-
stable situations. A guiding manual for psychosocial interventions"*,
(2002). Oxford. Available at: http://psp.drk.dk/graphics/
2003referencecenter/Docman/Documents/2Childrenarmed/chil-
dren_in_unstable_situations.pdf, (Accessed 12th March 2012).

Richards, P. *"Soccer and Violence in War-Torn Africa: Soccer and Social Rehab-
ilitation in Sierra Leone"* in G. Armstrong & R. Giuliannotti, eds.
Entering the Field: New Perspectives on World Football (New
York: Berg, 1997).

SFCG/ECFCG *"Search for Common Ground in Sierra Leone. Program Overview"*. (2004). Washington, D.C./Brussels: Search for Common
Ground / European Centre for Common Ground. Available at:
http://www.sfcg.org/Documents/Programs/Sierra_Leone.pdf,
(Accessed 12th March 2012).

SFCG/ECFCG. *"Search for Common Ground in Burundi. Program Overview"*.
(2002) Washington, D.C./Brussels: Search for Common Ground /
European Centre for Common Ground. Available at:
http://www.sfcg.org/Documents/Programs/Burundi.pdf, (Accessed 12th March 2012).

Sport for Development and Peace International Working Group. *"From the
Field: Sport for Development and Peace in Action"* (Toronto: SDP
IWG Secretariat, 2007), Available at: http://iwg.sportanddev.org/
en/publications-key-documents/index.htm, (Accessed 12th March
2012)

Sport for Development and Peace International Working Group. *"Literature Reviews on Sport for Development and Peace* (Toronto: SDP
IWG Secretariat, 2007), Available at: http://iwg.sportanddev.org/
data/ht"mleditor/file/Lit.%20Reviews/literature%20re-
view%20SDP.pdf, (Accessed 12th March 2012).

Sport for Development and Peace International Working Group. *"Sport for
Development and Peace: From Practice to Policy—Preliminary Report"*
(Toronto: 2007), Available at: http://iwg.sportanddev.org/en/
publications-key-documents/index.htm, (Accessed 12th March
2012).

Sport for Development and Peace International Working Group. *"Sport for Development and Peace: Governments in Action"* (Toronto: SDP IWG Secretariat, 2008), Available at: http://iwg.sportanddev.org/en/publications-key-documents/index.htm, (Accessed 12th March 2012).

Sugden, J. *"Teaching and Playing Sport for Conflict Resolution and Co-existence in Israel"* (2006) 41:2 International Review for the Sociology of Sport, 221-240.

UNICEF. Sport, Recreation and Play (New York: 2004).

UNICEF. The State of the World's Children (New York: 2001).

1. KENYA PROFILE – AT A GLANCE

Table 1: Kenya profile

Full name:	The Republic of Kenya
Population:	38.5 million (UN, 2008)
Capital:	Nairobi
Government	Semi-presidential Republic
- President	Mwai Kibaki
- Prime Minister	Raila Odinga
Independence	From the United Kindom
- date	December 12, 1963
- Republic declared	December 12, 1964
Area:	582,646 sq km (224,961 sq miles)
Major languages:	Swahili, English
Major religion:	Christianity
Life expectancy:	53 years (men), 55 years (women) (UN)
Ethnicity	Majority Kikuyu, followed by Luya, Luo and Kalenjin
Monetary unit:	1 Kenya shilling = 100 cents
Main exports:	Tea, coffee, horticultural products, petroleum products
GNI per capita:	US $680 (World Bank, 2007)

Part VI
Reflections of Sport, Peace and Development

Chapter 36
Contemplating a Moral World

Keith Gilbert & Will Bennett

'Sport is a very powerful tool but is not a magic box; it is a neutral box that must be filled with the right ingredients to achieve the expected result considering the context and the need'. (Serena Borsani[1] 2012).

'The last thing on peoples' minds when they are homeless and hungry is the playing of sport; the last thing on peoples' minds when they are fighting for survival against torture is the playing of sport; the last thing on peoples' minds when women are being mutilated is the playing of sport; the last thing on severely disabled people's minds is the playing of sport. If you're a refugee, a survivor or steeped in poverty sport doesn't matter unless you're locked in an internment camp and you're looking to pass the time'. (Gilbert[2], 2006, p. 57)

Introduction

This chapter aims to analyse the previous thirty-four chapters in order to contribute to the theoretical and practical expansion of the processes, outcomes and experiences of the 'sport, peace and development' movement and its on-going debates. As such the metasynthesis conducted in this

---

1. Please see more about Selena Borsani on the following website and for further details of Sport2 Build and its great work in Africa and beyond: (http://www.sport2build.org/wp/?page_id=205).

2. Gilbert, K. (2006) The Wrong-Way Around, In Wolff, E., et. al. (2006), (Eds.) Sport and Human Rights - ICSSPE Bulletin. Edition 43 pp. 57-59.

chapter aims to build on the previous chapters and comments about 'sport, peace and development' and the successes and failures outlined and noted in the various chapters. Importantly, before embarking on this process it is necessary for us to share our thoughts on metasynthesis? We accept that this term is used to describe the compilation of numerous research studies or pieces of academic work into a single theoretical perspective. Typically this process involves working with quantitative data and its definition revolves around the quantitative analysis of research. A plausible definition is that 'meta-analysis provides a quantitative method of increasing sample size to enable a reliable estimate of the most likely effect of an intervention, particularly for studies involving randomized, clinically controlled trials' (Scholfield, 2004, p. 204). However, as the world shifts more towards the qualitative paradigm its researchers have moved towards the concept of the term 'metasynthesis' as a method of utilising qualitative data. As Thorne and colleagues (2004, p. 1346) note when referring to qualitative health research:

> '.....in qualitative health research, we have come to understand that metasynthesis must be quite different from simple accumulative logic or averaging across studies. The goal is clearly interpretive, not mere aggregation to achieve unity; it is not a summary portraying the lowest common denominator. Metasynthesis is not a method designed to produce oversimplification; rather, it is one in which difference is retained and complexity enlightened. The goal is to achieve more, not less. The outcome will be something like a common understanding of the nature of a phenomenon, not a consensual worldview'.

The aim in this chapter is to synthesize the findings of the various individual chapters into a comprehensive account of the phenomenon under investigation and provide a 'common understanding' – in this case of the 'sport, peace and development movement' and its problematics. In this manner, as mentioned previously, this chapter seeks to deconstruct and repackage the findings from the preceding chapters. However, the topics broached by the authors are too broad to allow a thorough exploration of 'sport, peace and development' for theory building or explicating approach. As such, a 'theory development' metasynthesis will be undertaken which will involve reanalysis of the original material and the use of an imposed structure to organise findings into processes, outcomes and experiences of 'sport, peace and development'. Where appropriate, establishing theories will be used to reflect on the findings and position them within the body of the new literature in the research to date. What follows then are thoughts and perspectives which have arisen from the aforementioned chapters.

Geopolitics and Sport for Development and Peace

As argued by Dodds (2007) 'Geopolitics is a way of looking at the world: one that considers the links between political power, geography, and cultural diversity. In certain places such as Iraq or Lebanon, moving a few feet either side of a territorial boundary can be a matter of life or death, dramatically highlighting the connections between place and politics'. Or more simply argued 'geopolitics is a study of the influence of such factors as geography, economics, and demography on the politics and especially the foreign policy of a state'[3].

However, there have been arguments as to whether there can be a full definition of geopolitics and certainly there have been few attempts to relate sport to geopolitical perspectives. Increasingly the nature of geopolitics seems to be important in the development of a nation state and more importantly the geopolitical nature of a country can have significant impacts on whether sport can be played or even used as a tool for reconciliation, or as Galtung (1998) suggests for 'societal re-building, re-habilitation, re-structuration and re-culturation'. Importantly, Flint (2006) when discussing the historical development of the concept of geopolitics noted that '...there was always a central role for the notion of power in its various definitions'. This is true as issues of governmental power, military power, gangland power and indeed power over women and other disadvantaged groups goes to the very core of the discipline of sport, peace and development. In short people need geopolitical space. This is supported by the work of 'The Sport for Development Platform'[4] who argue that 'the idea of the creation of safe and accessible social spaces can be innovative in broadening and deepening peace-building initiatives'. The quest for geopolitical power is therefore a central cause of problems within societies but 'on the flip side' a necessary evil which we cannot do without for the curing of some of the ills that beset people's lives.

As individuals working at the 'coal face' in countries and cities where inhabitants require support and development we understand that the power of sport becomes a central issue in the process of development. However, without an understanding of cultural diversity, the geography of the country and the politics behind the situation we cannot work effectively to support the disadvantaged, oppressed and marginalized without understanding and knowledge of the geopolitics of the region. The message here then is that we have to understand the very nature of the geopolitical influences of a region, country or state before we go blindly into the sport and development process. It's not simply a matter of sending people and materials to a country to support sport for development - it's about really understanding the historical and current geopolitical power and cultural diversity in that part of the world and we feel that up to now these considerations have not been fully explored in the research literature or indeed in practice. However, there is some light on the horizon as it is here that we begin to understand the notion of 'sport for diplomacy' as espoused by Joel Bouzou in the preface of this book and along with a grasp of geopolitics and diplomacy goes a better

---

3. See Wikipedia for further tangible definitions for the word 'geopolitics'.

4. The Sport for Development Platform is a great resource for all individuals who work in the area of Sport, Peace and Development and also university and college students. They have definitions, case studies and commentary on major organisations across the world. For more information see the following website: http://www.sport-anddev.org/en/learnmore/sport_and_peace_building/project_case_studies/

understanding of cultural doctrines, customs and behaviour. Basically then, all we want is for all governments across the globe to be cognizant of the influence of sport and its power to improve the lives of disadvantaged people and for people working in 'far regions of the globe' to be politically aware of how their actions can be perceived locally and globally. In order for this to occur we need to be more strategic and diplomatic and embrace geopolitics.

Culture

Never have people in different cultures across the globe looked over their shoulders with so much fear and in trepidation as 'do gooder westerners' swarm over their lands inculcating western culture and destroying theirs in the name of 'sport, peace and development'. This statement is not true in all contexts but we should be viewing other people's culture as sacred and not assume that all aspects of our culture can work in other societies. If we believe that culture is as Tylor (1871) first announced: "....that complex whole which includes knowledge, belief, art, law, morals, custom, and any other capabilities and habits acquired by man as a member of society". Then we have to understand that as a world peopled by different cultures that the advent of globalisation has endangered much of the dance, language, religion, art, food, customs, and social mores of people who have become disadvantaged, marginalized and cut off from contemporary society through war, famine, disaster and poverty. As individuals, NGO's and charity workers we are often guilty of not totally respecting peoples cultural norms when we go into a country to support development and peace-making initiatives. This can be from simply a lack of understanding or an ignorance of the way in which other people live their lives. However, we cannot argue against the fact that culture is a powerful social device which supports our very existence, but there needs to be a delicate almost diplomatic entry into the culture of others. Having access to someone's culture also belies a responsibility to work our magic with sports but within the constructs of the culture and to respect people's historiographical background and anthropology. Indeed, we need to be cognizant of the dangers of imparting our own morals, values and ethics on others cultural norms.

One way in which we can blend into other people's lives is to perhaps become a part of their subculture which means we support them and provide experiences which ease their plight and provide solid and fundamental ideas for their development without overpowering them with western sporting ideals. In this manner we can develop the shared cultural traits of subcultures which set us apart and assist in retaining and rebuilding their society. Luckily we are working within the sporting realm which as we all know is a subset and perhaps sub-culture of most societies. A good example of sport being a part of the culture of a country can be taken from the Australian perspective where 'sport rules'.

Culture then plays a very important role in the lives of people who are disadvantaged and relying on the support of the outside world for their very existence. As individuals working in sport, peace and development we must attempt to support cultural differences which include attitudes to race, disability and gender into our programme planning and development. We have to make an effort to understand other cultures and the very essence of '*multiculturalism*'. As Tomosello (1999) concludes '....the key feature of cultural learning is that it occurs only when an individual understands others as intentional agents, like the self, who have a perspective on the world that can be followed into, directed and shared'. In other words multiculturalism is the key to a better world and we need to understand that in some countries tribal cultures, family cultures and religion are difficult to tear down, break into and to understand. Along with this we need to comprehend different cultures and work with sensitivity within them and not assume that all societies are the same, because there are different subcultures within the cultural context of individual countries. These subcultures are often the cause of in-fighting, civil-war and discrimination and making an assumption that sport cuts across the different subcultures and social mores of people is as absurd as believing that 'sport can, on its own, change the whole world for the better'. This is perhaps where we need more education and also where a good solid degree in sport, peace and development might allow time for these sensitive cultural issues to be propagated into our work-force. Indeed, there is plenty of scope for future developmental understandings of differing cultures, sub cultures and customs to be researched and this knowledge transferred to the individuals working at the coalface thereby assisting them to better control the context of their work in multicultural environments across the world. Education thus appears to be the key to further improvement of our work practices; further understanding of cultural norms and further expansion of sport, peace and development initiatives and the enlisting of higher education institutions in provision of these courses on culture can only benefit the cause. Why then are the world powers not spending more money and time on education for people who are in HIV/AIDS infected areas? Why are they not supporting children and youth in disadvantaged countries and educating them to a better standard? These are questions which need to be answered and can only be achieved by further 'on the ground research'.

Morality, ethics and values

We recognise that in any project which works directly with human beings there needs to be moral and ethical practices put into place in order to maintain some form of life values to which we all adhere. For example as argued by Lister (2005, p.1) when referring to poverty that there are' various moral and political claims' which are not necessarily correct and the study and work with the poor does not take into account individuals inherent feelings and pride. In other words we need to avoid just treating people as objects and review our own moral and ethical values. Imposing sport on the poor, disadvantaged, marginalised, traumatised, hungry and war torn requires in most cases a rebuilding of their societies, cultural values and social mores. Without a measured response to the deep philosophical underpinnings of society itself we cannot expect to make significant changes for the better and changing individual's morality, ethical understanding and life values are important to the betterment of humankind. Throughout the writing of this book we have come to understand that the incorporation of the perspectives of all people involved in the 'sport, peace and development movement' is a priority and if we leave out the recipients of the program in our thinking then we open ourselves to long term failure. We also realise that there are metaphorically speaking 'no magic bullets' to escape the human factor as most 'sport, peace and development' projects lack support from the societies which have been traumatised and most countries lack 'modern values' and as argued by Sachs (2005, p.309) 'Africa's morals are so broken down that it is no surprise AIDS has run out of control'. We all know that one of the main problems within countries where we organise 'sport, peace and development' programs is the corruption of senior officials and tribal leaders and that the values of many leaders are morally destitute. This may be a reflection of the fact 'that poverty and wealth are simply a reflection of global societal values'? That is why it is important to attempt to instil morality and ethics and values through our program planning in 'sport, peace and development' projects across the world. Surely the lack of morals, ethics and values in some countries is a direct rebuttal to the notion of the most fundamental human right – that of 'freedom of expression and peaceful assembly' – why is it that we have to experience through our television sets the suffering of others from a distance? – Where are our own moral values? Indeed, how do we change others morals and values in order to respect life and family through the medium of sport in an ethical manner? These and other questions need to be debated in order for our profession and our movement to go forward.

Building Capacity and Social Capital through Sport

Capacity building is an important aspect of our work in 'sport, peace and development' programming and should be high on our outcomes list. Indeed, the United Nations Development Program (UNDP) has placed a high emphasis on the building of capacity which it defines as '...the ability of individuals, institutions and societies to perform functions, solve problems, and set and achieve objectives in a sustainable manner'[5]. If we further break the term down then we realise that 'capacity building' relates significantly to the development of individuals and institutional capacity. In other words community training which involves increasing and supporting health, environ-

---

5. Please see the UNDP website for more information regarding the building of 'capacity' in developing nations. (http://www.undp.org/content/undp/en/home.html)

ment and local government initiatives. In organising a 'sport, peace and development' mission it has become increasingly clear to us that the notion of capacity building can be enhanced by the sustainability of a programme over time. The development of management structures which train and educate individuals to organise sport and physical activity can only be beneficial to the community whether in the sport or political community contexts. Because 'sport, peace and development' programs are about education, organisation and skill development it would be relatively easy to provide capacity building exercises into the curriculum. For example lessons could be taught regarding health, disability, gender and environmental sustainability through the medium of sport through teambuilding, governance and confidence fostering activities. In short then we need to debate and come up with solutions which are specific to individuals - gender and disability - or community based – relationship and shared norms – when capacity building through sport. Perhaps the main way in which sports programs can assist is in the development of strategies which emphasis management and quality of life issues. If we argue that the definition of capacity building is: 'The societal activities and resources that strengthen the skills, abilities of people and community groups to take effective action and leading roles in development of their communities' then sport has all the attributes to support this definition[6].

Hand in hand with the notion of capacity building goes the building of potential in people known as 'social capital' (Bourdieu, 1983; Putman, 1993) which has been defined by Bourdieu (1983, p.249) as:

'Social capital is the aggregate of the actual or potential resources which are linked to possession of a durable network of more or less institutionalized relationships of mutual acquaintance and recognition'.

And by Putman (2000, p. 19) as:

'Whereas physical capital refers to physical objects and human capital refers to the properties of individuals, social capital refers to connections among individuals – social networks and the norms of reciprocity and trustworthiness that arise from them. In that sense social capital is closely related to what some have called "civic virtue." The difference is that "social capital" calls attention to the fact that civic virtue is most powerful when embedded in a sense network of reciprocal social relations. A society of many virtuous but isolated individuals is not necessarily rich in social capital'.

Sport and physical activity lends itself to the social aspects of development and in particular the development of social capital and in Putman's mind 'social capital allows citizens to resolve collective problems more easily' thus the development of social capital through sport seems a forgone conclusion. Nothing could be easier perhaps? However what we find is that the social capital of many 'sport, peace and development programs' occurs simply through osmosis and not as a planned and developed outcome of the project. We feel that the aspects of capacity building and social capital

---

6. Definition taken from (http://en.wikipedia.org/wiki/Capacity_building).

can be further explored through sport and requires further research in order to provide supplementary support to the individuals in disadvantaged situations.

Sustainable Programming

As mentioned in the beginning chapter of this book we firmly believe that sport is not a panacea but we also have come to understand that in actuality sport can cover a multitude of problems and adversities by providing many solutions to seemingly insurmountable difficulties. As such we also realise that the problems associated with sustaining a 'sport, peace and development program' are immense. In this regard we caution anyone who wishes to start a program to understand the notion of sustainability before they embark on the task because without a rudimentary understanding then the project is almost doomed to failure even before it begins. What do we mean by sustainability of 'sport, peace and development programs'? When defining sustainability (Savery & Gilbert, 2011, p. 5-6) argue that 'sustainability is a holistic concept with much more depth than just environmental considerations alone. In a broad sense, sustainability refers to a holistic perspective that harmonizes social, economic and environmental dimensions and systems, and balances opportunities and constraints'. Indeed, The World Commission on Environment and Development, a body derived from the United Nations, created a report entitled *Our Common Future*. It was submitted to the General Assembly of the United Nations in August of 1987 (The 42nd Session of the General Assembly of the United Nations, August 4th 1987). *The Brundtland Report*[7] outlined global environmental concerns and related *development challenges*, and attempted to address these issues relative to necessary future actions to promote an improved quality of life while protecting the planet's ecosystems. The link between sustainability and development was emphasized repeatedly, noting the particular interrelation between poverty and the environment. Most importantly, the report became known for its definition of sustainable development which argues that:

> 'Humanity has the ability to make development sustainable to ensure that it meets the needs of the present without compromising the ability of future generations to meet their own needs. The concept of sustainable development does imply limits – not absolute limits but limitations imposed by the present state of technology and social organization on environmental resources and by the ability of the biosphere to absorb the effects of human activities'.
>
> *Brundtland Report*[8]

---

7. Brundtland, G. (1987). (Eds.) Our Common Future: The World Commission on Environment and Development. Oxford: Oxford University Press. p. 24.

8. ibid

Interestingly, we agree that: 'sport becomes sustainable when it meets the needs of today's sporting community while contributing to the improvement of future sport opportunities for all and the improvement of the integrity of the natural and social environment on which it depends' (Chernushenko in Savery, J. & K. Gilbert, 2012 p.7).

Consequently, sustainable program development is intrinsically linked to capacity building and the development of social capital. Also sustainability is not only one of the principles of commitment fundamental to the identity of the 'sport, peace and development program' but it is also a significant task for all global development organisations. There are four areas of sustainability according to the International Fund for Agricultural Development (IFAD[9]) and these are:

1. Institutional sustainability – functional institutions will be self-sustaining after the project ends.

2. Community resilience – resilient communities are readily able to anticipate and adapt to change through clear decision-making processes, collaboration, and management of resources internal and external to the community.

3. Environmental sustainability – an environmentally sustainable system must maintain a stable resource base, avoid over-exploitation of renewable resources and preserve biodiversity.

4. Structural change – the structural dimensions of poverty are addressed through the empowerment of poor and marginalized rural households.

We suggest that these and other similar aspects of sustainability be built into the 'sport, peace and development' program specifications in the development stages of the documentation. Of course we are not naïve enough to think that along with the sustainability ideals of a project must come the funding to ensure the project is sustainable. The aspect of funding is of course central to the development process and all programs require extended funding lines and support from various factions of society including local government, national government and business. This programming cost can be offset by the notion of corporate social responsibility.

Corporate Social Responsibility

Increasingly, as argued by Gilbert[10] (2012) '...the issue of corporate social responsibility (CSR) is becoming more and more oriented towards the development process and 'sport, peace and development' programmes need to

---

9. Sustainability of Rural Development Projects (2009). 8th series of discussion papers IFAD Asia Pacific

10. Gilbert, K. (2011). CSR and Sport: The Case of Premiership Rugby – unpublished Keynote paper presented to the 16th International Scientific Congress 'Olympic Sport and Sport for All' - Sophia, Bulgaria – 17th -19th May 2012.

quickly capitalise on this business trend'. Indeed, they appear to be a great source of revenue for the expansion of 'sport, peace and development' work and as yet are not fully exploited by the sport, peace and development program developers. There is a generally held belief that corporate social responsibility relates specifically to '....the ethical and legal behaviour by organisations in the workplace and the wider community[1]' or as Carroll (2000 p.284) comments:

'Corporate social responsibility is the notion that corporations have an obligation to constituent groups in society other than stockholders and beyond that prescribed by law and union contract'.

(Carroll, A. 2000 p. 284)

Whatever the definition, corporate social responsibility programs have more than one goal. These goals as related to 'sport, peace and development' initiatives have the double focus of 'enhancing the commercial functioning of the organisation' and more importantly for sport, peace and development, 'providing much needed social recognition in the local, national and international communities'[12]. The following extract and adaptations from a diagram by Smith and Westerbeek (2007, p. 3) provides a clearer understanding of the relationship between corporate social responsibility and sport.

However, we could easily transpose 'sport, peace and development' agency for the sport organisation and go directly to business for corporate social responsibility support. One thing that is obvious from figure 1 is that the work from Carroll (1979) cannot be ignored as it contains four important elements which he describes as 1. Economic (the basic responsibility to make a profit and, thus, be viable), 2. Legal (the duty to obey the law), 3. Ethical (responsibility to act in a manner consistent with societal expectations), and 4. Discretionary (activities that go beyond societal expectations). What the fourth column attempts to explain is the that these four aspects can be manifested in certain ways through the development of programs which are geared towards health, education, grass roots participation and social inclusion which incorporate matters of disability, gender, culture and race etc. Clearly persuading corporations to part with money or provide expertise whether sporting or business is not an easy task but this aspect of a company's corporate life is very important. Indeed, to be seen to be putting something tangible back into the community is valuable in terms of a business reputation and stakeholder pride.

---

11. Unknown author

12. For further description please see the following paper: Porter M. E. and M.R. Kramer (2006). Strategy and Society: The link between competitive advantage and corporate social responsibility. *Harvard Business Review*, Vol. 84, No. 12, pp. 78-92.

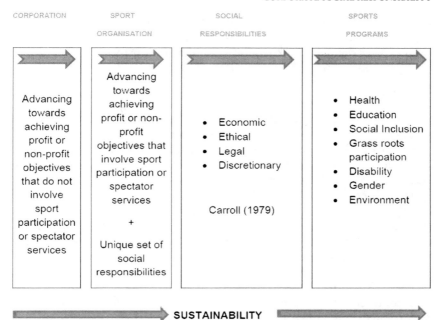

Figure 1: Deploying Corporate Social Responsibility[13] within a Sustainability Framework

Some examples of this form of corporate support can be found through the work of companies who are investing heavily in order to improve their image and reputation such as Nike who run programs for disadvantaged youth, and invest 1.5% of their pre-tax income annually in sustainable development projects as part of their initiatives to prevent energy wastage, slash water use, empower workers, reject toxins and reduce waste and Barclays bank who plough £11 million a year into their education, disability, social inclusion, arts and environment programs. There are also sports organisations such as FIFA, UEFA, the IOC and other individual sports federations and organisations which contribute to the worldwide corporate social responsibility agenda.

Increasingly, the individual sports organisations such as the English Rugby Union, Premiership Rugby, UK Triathlon and some football clubs in Europe have realised the opportunities to raise their profile and are using Corporate Social Responsibility projects to deliver their moral viewpoint to the local and international 'sport, peace and development' communities. For example the work of the Swiss group SCORE is a prime example of enthusiastic individuals combining with football clubs to deliver a strong

---

13. Adapted from the following work: Smith, A.C.T. & H. Westerbeek (2007). Sport as a vehicle for deploying corporate social responsibility, *Journal of Corporate Citizenship* Vol. 25 Spring 2007 pp. 43-54

program and message for youth in Palestine and other countries. We believe that the development of strong *'partnerships'*[14] is another key to the success of sport, peace and development programming for the future.

Benchmarking

The study and practice of benchmarking has seen significant attention over the past decade however, few have examined this practice within sport peace and development spectrum and fewer still have attempted to examine it within the arena of sport peace and development programming initiatives. As an example we might recall when on October 1st 2000 Juan Antonio Samaranch brought the Olympic Games of the 27th Olympiad in Sydney to a close proclaiming them as the "best ever". Ever since it has been imperative for organizing committees including, AOGOC, (Athens Olympic Games organizing Committee), and LOCOG (London Olympic Games Organizing Committee) to produce events, to increase the size and scope of major events and as a consequence the expected service levels have continued to increase. As a result of the evolution in the sports industry the expectations have continued to grow from the media, host community and governments for organizing committees to produce an event that is deemed to be better than any previous. In the same way we need to be raising our expectation and be analyzing other successful programs in order to benchmark and arrive at quality standards across the 'sport, peace and development movement'. Despite the complexity of this task most often achieving the title of best ever - often comes down to the view of the leadership within the governing body proclaiming such a triumph. In this way we need to be wary of organizations trumpeting their successes without some form of sustainability of programming in place. Contrastingly, within the public sector the government generally uses economic impact as the basis for comparing events. However, these methods provide little guidelines for comparison guidelines between and amongst events.

Importantly then, to this point there has been no universally accepted method of benchmarking 'sport, peace and development' initiatives. Here we need to perhaps travel back to where benchmarking originated in the Xerox Corporation (1979) with their recognition of the need to improve performance in the face of increasing international competition. Xerox was forced to go down the benchmarking path to reverse its performance and competitive stance. Faced with loss of market share, increased and heightened competition from national and Japanese competitors, Xerox sought a methodology for examining unit manufacturing costs and making product quality and feature comparisons. The results of this first benchmarking study provided the blueprint for Xerox's future business plans (Camp, 1989). Similarly the publication of a number of influential compar-

---

14. See Chapter 15 on partnerships, in this book, by Kylie Bates 'Creating win-win partnerships for sport, peace & development'.

ative studies of industrial performance demonstrated clearly the greater effectiveness of many Japanese and non-US/European industries (Camp, 1989 & Cook, 1995). Since then benchmarking has becoming an increasingly popular tool throughout a variety of industries including various business functions, law, and environment and banks (Dattakumar & Jagadeesh, 2003). So what is the purpose of benchmarking against other successful worldwide 'sport, peace and development' initiatives?

The Purpose of Benchmarking with Sport, Peace & Development programmes

Benchmarking has become the catch word for sport managers [however not as yet for sport, peace and development managers] because people at the top are constantly on the lookout for techniques to enable quality improvement. It is one such technique that has become popular in the recent times[15]. Though benchmarking is not new, it has now found more subscribers, and occupies a prominent place, helping quality upgrades. Quite often, the benchmarking concept is understood to be an act of imitating or copying. But in reality this proves to be a concept that helps in innovation rather than imitation (Thompson & Cox, 1997).

Benchmarking uses standard measurements in an industry for comparison to other organizations in order to gain perspective on organizational performance. Questions need to be asked of sport, peace and development organisations themselves. It seems alright for them to monitor and evaluate programmes but how many are actively reviewing their own business practices? It provides a new vision or perspective on traditional management concerns (Leibfried & McNair, 1994). Management has traditionally relied on internal expertise, bolstered by occasional outside intervention, to establish strategic objectives, and monitor performance (Leibfried & McNair, 1994). Benchmarking promotes superior performance by providing an organised framework where organisations can learn how the best carry out their practices and implement change to improve performance (Besterfield et. al, 1999). The ultimate purpose is to generate action and improvement that will enhance the value of the organization to its stakeholders (Ettore, 1993).

Benchmarking helps a company define its objectives, shedding new light on issues important to the organization and placing a critical examination on what needs to be done in the first place (Liebfried & McNair, 1992). Therefore, benchmarking places the focus on the core issues, suggesting creative, novel ways to approach them while highlighting value added activities and eliminating non-value added activities. (Camp, 1989). Whatever

---

15. We would like to thank Kipp Kaufmann [A past masters student of Dr. Gilbert] for agreeing to allow us to utilise some work from a study which he produced on benchmarking while a student at Deakin University in Melbourne, Australia. His insight and passion have been instrumental in our thinking re benchmarking in sport and he remains one of the brightest young individuals in world sport/cycling today.

the underlying purpose, or target, of the benchmarking process the ultimate goal is to generate action and trigger improvements by changing the way a role is performed, processes are undertaken, or strategic issues are defined. Benchmarking, then, can be used to focus the individual, organisation, or NGO on the opportunities for improvement; to benchmark is to explicitly decide that the process of implementation of sports development programming is going to change. These changes are undertaken carefully, using objective, externally based information that pinpoints weaknesses and suggests solutions (CHEMS, 1989). For example benchmarking efforts could be directed initially towards the standards and quality of teachers and coaches who are already in sport, peace and development systems and determinations made to improve their delivery and pastoral care.

Revisiting Daily Physical Activity

There are many statements made about the relationship between physical activity a.k.a. sport and the perceived benefits for children and youth in disadvantaged countries. Indeed, statements like 'Sport has the capacity to transform the lives of individuals' or '....it bolsters physical, psychological, emotional, and social well-being and development'. At the same time sport plays a significant role in cultures and communities around the world. These factors alone justify investment in sports programming. But there is also a growing understanding that sports programs merit support because they are powerful vehicles for achieving broader goals, particularly in advancing development and peace agendas' (USAID, 2009 p.4). However, they rarely back up the claims with solid research and *it appears as though anything can be said in the name of sport and its benefits to society'*. We need to start arguing for the benefits from a scientific perspective so that we have hard data to show the politicians and business people who we are attempting to influence and who pay for our programmes. Then let's take a step backwards in time and remember that physical educators have been arguing the benefits of daily physical activity for years. For example if we take the work of (Dodd, 1983) in the early 1980's who discovered through research and practical 'daily physical education' in schools that sport on a daily basis improves youngsters concentration, behaviour, self-esteem, motor skills, fitness, social skills and overtime results indicated that regular exercise improves examination results. So as early as 1982, over thirty years ago, researchers and physical educators were arguing for more quality sports and physical activities in schools.

These arguments can still be picked up and are valid in relation to 'sport, peace and development' programming. *Why are we reinventing the wheel?* What's needed are a series of systematic research projects looking into the benefits of physical activity in sport, peace and development programmes across the world. We need positive proof that all the programmes which are undertaken are achieving some aims and objectives and achieving positive results. Similarly there are many claims for sport and its benefits but few actually look at the negative aspects of sport in communities or indeed the overall picture. It's easy to pick out the positives that you want and need for further funding or to justify your programmes and in some cases your very existence – it's harder to criticise your own and others programmes.

We urge groups and organisations to go back to review physical education teaching and then ask questions as to how many of the managers, coaches, teachers and assistants actually have the required skills in order to take on the tasks of educating children and youth through the medium of games and sport. It's a complex and difficult task which is often left to the 'western do gooder' with little or no teaching or coaching skills. People should perhaps not be allowed into foreign schools and into difficult teaching situations without the necessary skills which can only be obtained by the gaining of physical education and sport coaching qualifications. The *feel good factor* is no longer enough. Our argument is therefore that minimum teaching and coaching standards must be achieved across the programmes and in our experience they are not being met.

Monitoring and Evaluation

Increasingly, monitoring and evaluation is becoming more important as we try to understand the worth of our 'sport, peace and development' schemes in the field. In- fact having an understanding of the effectiveness and impact of our programs on the youth and a quality assessment through a performance report is as necessary as the delivery of the program itself. How can we decide if we are capacity building if there is no starting point or end point to our work in the field? How do we build trust in our sponsors, stakeholders, governments and indeed program recipients without evidence of the hard results of our labours? How do we explain the potential for 'sport for good' if we have no proof of program development and strategies? How do we know that we need change? How can we evaluate our partnership arrangements? These and other questions can be easily answered if we have the proof of the 'sport, peace and development' program successes and failures and monitoring and evaluation (M & E) provides the key to the delivery of our programs in a professional and calculated manner. This can perhaps be best explained by the following diagram which indicates how monitoring and evaluation contributes to improved results and accountability in programme planning.

495

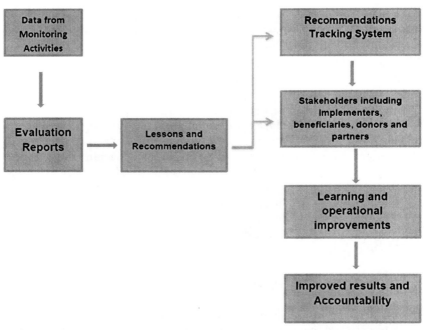

Diagram 2: Indicates how Monitoring and Evaluation contributes to Improved Results and Accountability in Programme Planning

There have however, been some good attempts at solving the above problems already and the work of (SAD[16], Baker 2000; Hauge & Mackay 2004; Coalter 2006; Morra-Imas & Rist 2006) is particularly good in assisting us with the important task of monitoring and evaluating our 'sport, peace and development' programs.

Monitoring and evaluation of programmes can be put into place through a co-ordination with groups like SAD [see footnote 16] and in future perhaps advice from the United Nations. Guidance from any university would be good in supporting research into your own programmes of 'sport, peace and development' and the employment of graduates with statistical knowledge and general research skills is now becoming more and more important. We cannot emphasise the importance of M & E programming being built into your business plan as without it your programmes are worthless.

---

16. Swiss Academy of Development: See www.http://www.sad.ch/

Millennium Development Goals & 'Sport for Peace and Development'

There has been a great amount of writing and debate about the United Nations Millennium Development Goals known as (MDG's)[17]. These goals are designed to:

1. Eradicate extreme poverty and hunger
2. Achieve universal primary education
3. Promote gender equality and empower women
4. Reduce child mortality
5. Improve maternal health
6. Combat HIV/AIDS, malaria and other diseases
7. Ensure environmental sustainability
8. Develop global partnership for development

However, to be fair the jury is still out as to whether many of these goals will be fully achieved by the date of 2015 and even more interesting is: How far the 'sport for peace and development movement' has come and how much it can contribute significantly towards these United Nations Millennium Goals? For example, the latest report from the UNOSDP[18] [United Nations Office for Sport Development and Peace; 2012] and the comment by Ban Ki-moon the United Nations Secretary-General suggests that: 'Sport has become a world language, a common denominator that breaks down all the walls, all the barriers. It is a worldwide industry whose practices can have a widespread impact. Most of all, it is a powerful tool for progress and development'. This statement clearly highlights the significance of sport in the UN. This message is clearly supported by the words of Wilfried Lemke the Special Adviser to the United Nations Secretary-General on Sport for Development and Peace who wrote that:

> 'The United Nations considers sport to be a powerful tool to promote education, health, development and peace. Sport unites people of all social classes, cultures, religions and backgrounds in a positive and educational way'[19].
>
> (U.N.O.S.D.P. Annual Report, 2012 p. 36).

It is clear that from the stated outcomes of this report that programmes of 'sport for peace and development' are increasing in their scope and range throughout the world and continuing to make, albeit mostly by osmosis, positive inroads in support of the United Nations Millennium Development Goals. In actuality at the time of writing there are four years to go in order to reach the stated objectives of the Millennium Development Goals.

---

17. Please see the following website for further understanding of the United Nations Millennium Development Goals: http://www.un.org/millenniumgoals/. (Accessed 7th June 2012).

18. UNOSDP Annual Report [Ten Years of Action] June 2011. Available at www.un.org/sport/. (Accessed 7th June 2012).

19. For further information please see the following website: http://dfsu.sportaccord.com/en/news/index.php?idContent=16309

There are according to some sources some disadvantages of the notion of the development of the Millennium Development Goals which according to (Deneulin Shahani, 2009) include the absence of systematic investigation and reasoning behind the intentions of the MDG's. Indeed the four issues of poverty, racism, gender inequality and disability are not dealt with significantly in the documentation regarding the MDG's and sport. *In fact, the issues of gender really need highlighting and badly require greater efforts in academic research.* However, if for example, we take a closer look at the issue of MDG's sport and disability we find it also lacks development. There are some really good programmes out there, like 'PlayAble' and we admire what they are trying to achieve. However, programmes like this are few and far and away in the minority. We however, have long been advocates of sport for individuals with a disability (Schantz & Gilbert 2012., Legg & Gilbert, 2011., Gilbert & Schantz 2009) and we argue along with Givens (2012) that:

> 'Although there has been progress, much work remains to be done if persons with disabilities are to have full access to human rights and the stigmatisation, disempowerment, and social, political, and economic marginalisation they face at present are to be a thing of the past'.

In short we need to re-evaluate the needs of marginalised individuals and more especially those individuals with disability. For more information re gender and youth the work of Givens (2012) is a good start to your research. Please see the excellent chapters by Amy Farkas et al and Ian Brittain in this book for further insights into disability and the marginalised.

We feel strongly that in future perhaps there needs to be a programme of accountability and monitoring put into action by the UN or International Paralympic Committee or the International Olympic Committee in order to satisfy the needs of the disparate groups across the world. However, it must be noted that the UNSODP and sport NGO's are making valiant efforts to reach the MDG targets set by the United Nations. However, we are not entirely sure how this is being achieved. We believe that these could be better met if there were a summit organised to discuss the relationship between NGO's and the gaining of the new structure of goals after 2015 so that we might go forward in a positive light over the next four years and maximise the potential of the UN objectives. An important question might be: What are the UNSODP going to do after the time period of the Millennium Goals is over? What will everyone be working towards? It seems like we will be working towards a similar set of goals but with better monitoring and evaluation procedures which we feel should be put in place by the UN as an overseeing organisation. As argued by Givens[20] (2012):

> 'As 2015 fast approaches, so too does the end of the current cycle of development objectives, the MDGs. With the end of the MDGs comes the end of a 15 year cycle in which governments, NGOs, UN Agencies, Funds and Systems,

---

20.(See) David Givens (2012). http://davidgivenblogs.wordpress.com/2012/04/05/the-future-of-sport-for-development-and-peace/ [Accessed 12th October 2012]. These are an excellent set of papers reviewing up-to-date aspects of Sport, Peace and Development.

and academics have all been focused and aligned by a common goal. The results and full effects of the MDGs, and the success of each nation's attempts to achieve the MDGs, are yet to be seen. However, it is clear that come 2015, poverty will not have been eradicated, HIV/AIDS will still be a global pandemic, and inequality will persist throughout the world. What is known is that there will be no repeat of the MDGs, that was a once off occurrence that will forever be remember as the first framework that brought together the development world under a common banner'. (Givens 2012)

Givens (2012) is also right in his assumptions that we have little understanding of the direction of the 'sport, peace and development movement' once the 2015 MDG's deadline date is past. We need to be thinking now about where we go as a 'Movement' and the future role of 'sport, development and peace' initiatives. Over the past ten years we have fostered 'sport, peace and development' programmes and come together 'in an ad hoc and loosely amalgamated universal sporting structure' which is not clearly defined. It is disparate in nature and has NGO's, sports federations, private suppliers and others fighting for scarce private and even governmental resources and now is the time to push our efforts with business and government to develop our universality because as each week goes by we are losing potential funding and partnership potential which more than likely will not be available after 2015. Indeed, we feel that the 'Right to Play' (2008) recommendation to governments was correct in that:

> 'The potential contribution that sport can make, combined with the fundamental urgency underlying the MDG targets, unites Sport for Development and Peace proponents in their efforts to engage and mobilize Governments in developing nations to include Sport for Development and Peace in their national development frameworks and strategies and to encourage governments in donor nations to integrate sport into their international assistance strategies.'

This report was good quality document which we feel needs to be revisited in terms of its usefulness at this juncture by larger organisations, as was the Sport for Development and Peace International Working Group (SDP IWG), document *'Sport for Development and Peace: Governments in Action*[21].' We wonder why these documents are not promoted more in the university and government contexts. We badly need more dialogue between the 'SPD big players', 'governments', 'International sporting bodies', 'Sports Federations' and the United Nations. We argue here that it is perhaps time for the big 'sport, peace and development' agencies and organisations like 'Right to Play, SAD and Peace and Sport' to come together more often in order to promote sport, peace and development. If they came together with others and pooled their resources, then we could really make a difference to people's lives. We need less micro-politics and more action.

---

21. Please see the following website for the full PDF text from Right to Play: http://www.un.org/wcm/webdav/site/sport/shared/sport/pdfs/SDP%20IWG/Governments%20in%20Action%20Part1-Table%20of%20Contents_Foreword_Introduction%20and%20Summary.pdf

Does sport really make a difference to the marginalised?

The short answer is: 'yes - **sport makes a difference**'. Participation in sport provides outlets for frustration, alleviates boredom, provides skill development, and sport links strongly with desired traits such as leadership and presents opportunities for individuals to better themselves and their families through improved fitness and health as participation in sport is clinically proven to ease some forms of anxiety and lessen depression. Indeed, UNICEF as far back as 2004 was quick to point out that 'In many countries, sport is being used to raise awareness of HIV/AIDS and to target vulnerable groups such as orphans and out-of-school youth. Sport can tackle factors that contribute to the spread of HIV/AIDS by providing knowledge, life skills, access to services, and safe and supportive environments.' In fact, it can provide for individual difference like: gender, race, and disability but as previously mentioned more work needs to be done in these areas. Sport provides an escape from the real world, an opportunity to work together in a peaceful, secure, playful environment and most importantly sport empowers people to make a difference and change in their lives and those of others through the sport-education nexus. As argued by the United States Agency for International Development (2010)[22]: 'People who participate in sport have the opportunity to improve their communication skills and gain valuable experience in collaboration and teamwork. Sport brings people together who might not otherwise have a chance to meet and allows them an opportunity to share their experiences and work together toward a common goal'. In order to achieve this form of positive output with individuals in the future organisations will need to lobby the governments across the world and at the grass roots level produce quality teachers and coaches who are culturally aware and have the ability to deliver their programmes in areas of extreme poverty, disaster and danger. This standardization of delivery would aid in supporting cultures and subcultures and provide some form of 'social stability'. We would like to see more students taking masters and PhD degrees in the area (especially gender issues) so that they are better informed before taking time to go into the field and support change. We believe that all these things can be achieved through the medium of sport but we wish for more credibility and sustainability of programmes. We also believe that sports programmes are only one kind of programme which should be integrated into a package of programmes which makes change in people's lives and the introduction of the arts, music, dance and suchlike can also make a valuable contribution to the education process and well-being of people across the world.

22.USAID (2009). <u>The Role of Sport as a Development Tool</u>, Displaced Children's Fund Publication, December. Silver Spring MD.

Conclusive statement

This chapter synthesised many of the ideas and perspectives put forward by the various authors and makes an attempt to highlight some new and recurring issues of which we need to be aware in the 'sport, peace and development movement'. These included the notions of geopolitics, culture, morality, ethics, values, capacity building, social capital, sustainable programming, corporate social responsibility, and the building of partnerships, benchmarking, benefits of daily physical activity, monitoring and evaluation, Millennium Development Goals and the benefits of sport to individuals and communities.

Finally, like sport, this book is not a panacea but perhaps is the starting point for many and hopefully it will provide a sound basis of practice and theory and innovative ideas that might bring about the beginnings of a new chapter in the lives of others.

References

Baker, J.L. (2000). Evaluating the Impact of Development Projects on Poverty: A Handbook for Practitioners, the World Bank, Washington D.C.

Besterfield, D. H., Besterfield-Michna, C., & M. Besterfield-Sacre (1999). Total Quality Management, Prentice Hall, USA

Bourdieu, P. (1983) The Forms of Capital. In J. Richardson (Ed.) Handbook of Theory and Research for the Sociology of Education (New York, Greenwood), pp. 241-258

Brundtland, G. (1987). (Eds.) Our Common Future: The World Commission on Environment and Development. Oxford: Oxford University Press. p. 24.

Camp, R.C. (1980). Benchmarking: The search for industry best practices that lead to superior performance Quality Press, Michigan, USA

Carroll A. B. (2000). A commentary and an overview of key questions on corporate social performance measurement. *Business and Society*, 39, 4, pp.466-478.

Carroll, A.B. (1979) 'A Three-dimensional Conceptual Model of Corporate Performance', *Academy of Management Review* 4.4: 497-505.

Carroll, A. B. (2000) 'Corporate Social Responsibility: the evolution of a definitional construct' *Business and Society* 38(3): 268-295.

Carroll, A. and G. Beiler (1977) "Landmarks in the Evolution of the Social Audit" in Carroll, A. (Eds.). 1978. Managing Corporate Social Responsibility. Boston: Little, Brown and Co.

Case, A. (2005) 'Playgrounds for Peace', *Parks*

Castka, P. et al & D. Givens, (2012). Future of SDP [Available at: http://davidgivenblogs.wordpress.com/2012/04/05/the-future-of-sport-for development-and-peace/], [Accessed 12th October 2012].

Chernunshenko, D. (2011). Promoting Sport through Sport: An Industry Professional looks back and forward and issues a challenge. In Savery, J. & K. Gilbert (2011) Sport and Sustainability, Commonground Publishing, Illinois, USA

Coalter, F. (2006). A Monitoring and Evaluation Manual, Sterling University and UK Sport).Evaluation the impact of development projects, a handbook for Practitioners, © 2000 The International Bank for Reconstruction and Development, Judy L. Baker (pdf)

Cook, H.E. (1995). Benchmarking in Hospitality and Tourism, Routledge, London

Deneulin, S., & L. Shahani (2009). An Introduction to the Human Development and Capability Approach: Freedom and Agency. Sterling, VA: Earthscan.

Dodd G.D. (1983). (Eds.) Daily Physical Education - Level 4, ACHPER Publications, Kingswood, South Australia; 1-7.

Dodds, K. (2007). Global Geopolitics: A Critical Introduction, Prentice Hall Publishing.

Duttakumar, R. & R. Jagadeesh (2003). A review of literature on benchmarking, *Benchmarking: An International Journal* Vol. 10 No. 3, 2003 pp. 176-209

Ettorre, B. (1993), ªBenchmarking: the next generation°, Management Review, June, pp. 10-16

Fingeld, D.L. (2003). Metasynthesis: The state of the art – so far, *Qualitative Health Research,* vol.13, no. 7 pp. 893-904

Flint, C. (2006). Introduction to Geopolitics: tensions, conflict and resolutions, Taylor and Francis Publishing, London.

Galtung, J. (1998). Following Violence, 3R: reconstruction, reconciliation, resolution. Facing the visible and invisible effects of war and violence. Bilbao, Gernika Gogoratuz Publishing

Gilbert, K. & O.J. Schantz (2009). The Paralympics: Empowerment or Sideshow, Meyer – Meyer Verlag, Aachen, Germany

Gilbert, K. (2006) The Wrong-Way Around, In Wolff, E., et. al. (2006),(Eds.) Sport and Human Rights - *ICSSPE Bulletin.* Edition 43 pp. 57-59.

Hauge A.O. & K. Mackay (2004). Monitoring and Evaluation for Results: Lessons from Uganda. Capacity Development Brief 3, World Bank (pdf).

Holden, M; Mackenzie, J. & R. VanWynberghe (2008). Vancouver's promise of the world's first sustainable Olympic Games. *Environment & Planning C: Government and Policy,* Vol.26, pp 882-905.

Legg, D. & K. Gilbert (2011). Paralympic Legacies, Commonground publishing, Illinois, USA

Leifried, K.H.J. & C.J.McNair (1994). A Tool for Continuous Imporovement, Harper Collins, USA.

Lister, R. (2005). Being Feminist (Politics of Identity – VIII). Government Opposition , Vol. 40, Issue 3, pp. 442-463 Summer 2005.

Morra-Imas, L. & R.C. Rist (2006). The Capacity to Evaluate: Why Countries Need It. Capacity Development Brief 17, World Bank (pdf)

Morse, L.M. (2000). Editorial: Theoretical Congestion, Qualitative Health Research, Vol.10 no. 6 pp. 715-716

Morse J.M. & Richards, L (2002). *Readme first for users guide to qualitative research methods*. Thousand Oaks, California, Sage Publications.

Porter M. E. and M.R. Kramer (2006). Strategy and Society: The link between competitive advantage and corporate social responsibility. *Harvard Business Review*, Vol. 84, No. 12, pp. 78-98

Putnam, R. D. (1993) 'The prosperous community: social capital and public life' in the *American Prospect*, 4:13

Sachs, G. (2005). The End of Poverty: Economic Possibilities for our time. Penguin Press

Savery, J. & K. Gilbert (2011). Sustainability and Sport, Commonground Publishing, Illinois, USA.

Schantz, O.J. & K. Gilbert (2012). Heroes or Zeros: The Medias Perceptions of the Paralympics, Commongroundpublishing, Illinois, USA

Scholfield, M. (2004). Sampling in quantitative research. In Minichiello (et al) *Research Methods for Nursing and Health Sciences* (2nd Ed.) Prentice Hall, N.S.W. Frenches Forest.

Schrieber, R; Crooks, D. & N. Stern (2007). Qualitative Meta – analysis, In J.M.Morse (2nd Eds) *Research Methods for Nursing and Health Sciences*, Prentice Hall, N.S.W. Frenches Forest.

Smith, A.C.T. & H. Westerbeek (2007). Sport as a vehicle for deploying corporate social responsibility, *Journal of Corporate Citizenship* Vol. 25 Spring 2007 pp. 43-54

The Measuring Volunteering Toolkit is a practical guide on the study of volunteer behaviour, UN and Independent International platform for sport and development http://www.sportanddev.org/en/about_this_platform/vision_mission_goals22/sector (pdf)

Thompson, I. and Cox, A. (1997), Don't imitate, innovate, *Supply Management*, pp. 40-3

Thorne, S; Jenson. K; Kearney, L; Noblit, G; & M. Sandelowski (2004). Qualitative metasynthesis: reflections on methodological orientation and ideological agenda; *Qualitative Health Research*; Vol. 14, no. 10 pp. 1342-1365.

Tomasello, M. (1999). "The Human Adaptation for Culture" in *Annual Review of Anthropology* vol. 28: p.514

Tylor, E. B. (1871) *Primitive Culture*, Harper & Row. New York 1958 p.16

USAID (2009). The Role of Sport as a Development Tool, Displaced Childrens Fund Publication, December. Silver Spring MD.

Contributors

Gary Armstrong PhD is a Reader in the School of Sport and Education, Brunel University, London. He is a prolific author and among his many books he has written 'Football in Africa: Conflict, Conciliation and Community', published by Palgrave, 2003.

Maria Rato Barrio is a researcher and academic at the CiTDH & Group for Cooperation DIM, Technical University of Madrid, Spain, and postdoctoral scholar of the Ministry of Foreign Affairs and Cooperation (MAEC) and the Spanish Agency for International Cooperation for Development (AECID).

Kylie Bates specialises in partnership development. Her understanding of sport, government and United Nations systems enables her to connect sport agencies with development agencies in way that creates authentic, transformational relationships.

James Beale is a British Psychological Society Chartered & BASES Accredited Sport & Exercise Psychologist and Senior Lecturer in the Applied Sport Sciences within the School of Health, Sport and Bioscience at the University of East London.

Will Bennett is Research and Development Consultant at Generations for Peace based in Jordan but previously worked for Right to Play as Director of the Education Department in the UK. He has written on sport as a vehicle to identify and address stigma surrounding HIV/AIDS in Rwanda and also on promoting youth citizenship in Uganda. He holds degrees in

History from Bristol University and a Master's degree in War Studies from King's College, The University of London.

Bojana Blagojevic is an Assistant Professor of Political Science at LaGuardia Community College, City University of New York. During the Bosnian war she worked for the International Committee of the Red Cross (ICRC) in Gorazde and Pale. Bojana holds a PhD and her research and writing focuses on the causes of war, peace building, and the role of sport in development and peace.

Kristina Bohnstedt is the Head of Projects for the SCORT Foundation. She is very experienced in conducting Sport Development and Peace programmes and holds a master's degree from the University of Mainz in Sport Science. Kristine has been successful in working over the past years on projects involving football in the Sudan, Kosovo, Sri Lanka, and Palestine and more recently in Uganda.

Vladimir Borkovic is co-founder, Network Director and Chief Operating Officer at streetfootballworld. He holds a Doctorate in Human Science from the University of Potsdam, Germany, and his expertise lies in 'applied socialization theory', as well as 'monitoring & evaluation' of community sports programs. Vladimir is lecturer and tutor at the FIFA Master in Management, Law and Humanities of Sport and guest lecturer at several universities.

Serena Borsani is the founder and director of the organization Sport2build. She earned her Master's degree in economics from University of Sacred Heart, Milan, Italy and her Master of Arts in Human Rights and conflict management from Scuola Superiore S'Anna, Pisa, Italy.

Joel Bouzou is the President and Founder of the organisation 'Peace and Sport'. He is also the Secretary General of the Modern Pentathlon International Federation (ex- world champion), advisor to HSH Prince Albert II of Monaco and has recently been elected to President of the World Olympians Association (WOA).

Ian Brittain is the Project Manager for 'Peace, Olympics, Paralympics' in the Centre for Peace and Reconciliation Studies at Coventry University, United Kingdom. He holds a PhD and has written extensively in the field of disability and Paralympic sport including 'The Paralympic Games Explained' published by Routledge in 2009.

Marc-Andre Buchwalder is the Chief Executive and founder of the SCORT Foundation. He holds a Master's degree in Sport Science from the University of Mainz and is responsible for SCORT's many international programmes based around Football as an initiative for Sport, Development and Peace.

Jamie Bull is a past student of Exercise and Sport Science Faculty in the University of East London and is currently working on projects within the context of development and sport.

Karen Chad is the Vice-President of Research and a Professor in the College of Kinesiology at the University of Saskatchewan. Her research interests centre on health promotion, the prevention of lifestyle-related diseases and program development to empower individuals to make positive choices. Karen has a Master's degree in Physiology from the University of Victoria and a PhD from the University of Queensland, Australia.

Emma Colucci works for Right to Play Canada and holds a Master of Arts degree in the Communication and Culture program from Ryerson University and York University in Toronto, Canada.

Eric Dienes is the Liaison Officer at the United Nations Office on Sport for Development and Peace, New York.

Amy Farkas works as a Sport for Development Specialist for UNICEF in New York and has more than 15 years of experience in using sport, recreation and play to address the needs of youth and marginalized populations. She has been a lead contributor to the work of the Sport for Development and Peace International Working Group, and the National Centre on Physical Activity and Disability in the University of Illinois, U.S.A.

Keith Gilbert PhD is Professor in the School of Health, Sport and Bioscience at the University of East London, United Kingdom. Keith was first introduced to issues relating to sport, development and peace on a visit to Kosovo in 2004. His recent books (2011-2012) include 'Paralympic Legacies', 'Sustainability and Sport', and 'Heroes or Zeros: The media and the Paralympics'.

Lori Hansen is an Associate Professor in Community Health and Epidemiology in the College of Medicine at the University of Saskatchewan. Lori has a PhD from the University of Saskatchewan and is an international researcher with projects in global health and development.

Ludovic Hubler is the Head of Programmes and Field Operations at Peace and Sport: '*L'Organisation pour la Paix per la Sport*'. Ludovic has worked for Peace for over 10 years and has made over 500 presentations to various associations and schools during and after his 5 year tour of the world by hitchhiking (see www.ludovichubler.com). He is the author of the prize-winning book '*Le Monde en Stop, 5 années à l'école de la vie*'.

Mary A. Hums obtained her Ph.D. from Ohio State University, and M.A./M.B.A. from the University of Iowa. Mary is an experienced academic who has co-authored/co-edited five sport management textbooks, over 30 journal articles, and made over 150 presentations to various scholarly associations both in the United States and abroad.

Valerie Karr currently works as an Assistant Professor at Adelphi University and serves as the Director for Research Programs for the Victor Pineda Foundation, which is the only youth-focused international disability rights organization. She is the author of UNICEF's Human Rights Education Manual for Youth with Disabilities which is based on the UN Convention on the Rights of Persons with Disability.

Marion Keim is an Associate Professor at the University of the Western Cape, South Africa and Director of its Interdisciplinary Centre of Excellence for Sports Sciences and Development. She is well published and an Advocate of the High Court of South Africa and certified in Sports Law and in Mediation. Marion is also the Chairperson of the Western Cape Network for Community Peace and Development.

Michael Kleiner holds a Master's degree in Political Science from the University of Geneva and professional training as a journalist. He was previously manager of the United Nations office of the Special Adviser for Sport, then former Swiss President Adolf Ogi, to the UN Secretary General Kofi Annan. He now works for the Geneva State Administration as Deputy Director for Sport.

Pelle Kvalsund is a sports development professional, currently based out of Nashville, Tennessee, United States. His experience includes five years in Southern Africa working for local Sport and Development organizations and National Sport Governing bodies. He now works as a consultant, focusing primarily on sport as a response to conflict and disaster.

Anna Lachowska holds an LLM degree in International Human Rights Law. She is the Legal Advisor with ATLAS Council, a leading NGO with a global mandate to promote the protection of the rights of persons with disabilities and the ratification and full implementation of the Convention on the Rights of Persons with Disabilities.

Glenn Laverack has worked in public health, social development, and research in developing countries for more than 20 years. Previously, Glenn worked as the Coordinator (Empowerment) at the Special Programme for Research and Training in Tropical Diseases/World Health Organization, in Geneva and is currently a Research Fellow at Flinders University Prevention, Promotion and Primary Health Care unit in Adelaide, Australia.

Wilfried Lemke is the Special Adviser to the United Nations Secretary-General on Sport for Development and Peace.

Clemens Ley is a researcher and academic at the Institute of Sport Science, University of Vienna, Austria and a member of the CiTDH & Group for Cooperation DIM, Technical University of Madrid, Spain. He earned his PhD from Universidad Politécnica de Madrid (Spain) and his research focusses on the relationship between sport, health, HIV/AIDS, psychosocial intervention, participatory tools and project evaluation.

Andrei S. Markovits is Arthur F. Thurnau Professor and the Karl W. Deutsch Collegiate Professor of Comparative Politics and German Studies at the University of Michigan in Ann Arbor. He is well published for example: Offside: Soccer and American Exceptionalism (Princeton University

Press, 2001); and Gaming the World: How Sports Are Reshaping Global Politics and Culture (Princeton University Press, 2010) are two of his best known works

Amber Morris is from Virginia Beach, Virginia, U.S.A. and attended Princess Anne High School. She graduated from Virginia Commonwealth University before earning a law degree from North Eastern University in Boston where she interned at the Centre for Sport and Society.

Bob Munro is the Managing Director of XXCEL Africa Ltd. He works in Africa as a Senior Policy Adviser on Sustainable Development for the United Nations and African governments. He is the founder (1987) and Chairman of the Board of Trustees of the Mathare Youth Sports Association (MYSA) and Chairman of Mathare United FC as well as a founding Director (2003) and Vice Chairman of the Kenyan Premier League Ltd.

Oscar Mwaanga is Senior Lecturer and course leader of the MA Sport and Development in the Faculty of Sport, Business and Enterprise at Southampton Solent University in the UK. He holds a Diploma in Physical Education and Geography from the University of Zambia, and an MA in Sport Studies and Sport Psychology from the Norwegian University of Sport Science. He is currently completing his PhD.

Chiaki Okada is an Associate Professor in the Department of Global Human Sciences in the Graduate School of Human Sciences at Osaka University, Japan. She earned her Doctor of Arts degree from the Graduate School of Human Development and Environment at Kobe University and her M'Ed degree from the Graduate School of International Development and Cooperation at Hiroshima University, Japan.

Ian Pickup is Director of Student Development at Roehampton University, having previously worked as Director of Sport and Wellbeing and Principal Lecturer in Physical Education. In 2006 Ian founded 'Move', an innovative sports-based social inclusion project which transfers life skills from the sports context to empower young people to engage with educational and vocational opportunities.

Daniela Preti was a Project Manager at the Swiss Academy for Development where she specialised in capacity building of grassroots organisations in the field of project planning, monitoring & evaluation and is currently Programme Coordinator at 'Oxfam Germany'. She holds a Master of Advanced Studies in Secondary and Higher Education. Daniela has worked in multilateral diplomacy at the Permanent Mission of Switzerland to the United Nations in New York.

Dean Ravizza is an Assistant Professor and Physical Education Program Director in the Department of Health and Sport Sciences and Research Practitioner for the Centre for Conflict Resolution at Salisbury University. He was the creator of the Peaceful Play programme for children and youth in armed conflict. He earned his bachelor's and master's degrees from George Mason University and Ph.D. from Virginia Tech University with an emphasis on psychosocial aspects of sport and physical activity.

Sebastian Rockenfeller has ten years' experience working in sport and sport for development across Australasia, Africa and Europe. He recently worked for the German Olympic Sport Confederation and managed sport for development projects for Jambo Bukoba in Tanzania.

Kazuhiko Saito is an Associate Professor in the Department of Teacher Education in the College of Human and Social Sciences at Kanazawa University, Japan. He has a Doctor of Education degree from the Graduate School of Education at Hiroshima University and a M.Ed. from the Graduate School of International Development and Cooperation at Hiroshima University, Japan.

Geoff Thompson was the founder and Executive Chairman of the U.K. based charity and United Nations Non-Governmental Organisation, Youth Charter. In 2008 he was awarded an Honorary Doctorate of Law (honoris causa) from the University of Roehampton for his work in this domain. His current work includes the 'Olympic Citizenship in Action' legacy project for the 2012 Olympic and Paralympic Games.

Emily Vest is currently living in Oxford and completing her PhD at Brunel University. Her research, an Ethnographic study of a Bosnian Muslim village in the Bosnian Serb area of Bosnia Herzegovina, examines the impact football has upon reconciliation. Her interest in sport as a vehicle for peace stems from her previous work for NGOs in Bosnia and Sierra Leone.

Ben Weinberg is a lecturer at the Institute of European Sport Development and Leisure Studies at the German Sport University Cologne, Germany. He is currently participating in a research project covering the sport-in-development initiative Jambo Bukoba in Tanzania. Ben holds a PhD and read American Studies, History and Law at the Universities of Bonn and Cologne (Germany) and the University College Cork (Ireland).

Eli A. Wolff is currently the Co-Director of the Sport for Development Fellowship program at Brown University U.S.A. From 2001 - 2010, he was the Director of Research and Advocacy at the Centre for Sport in Society at North-eastern University in Boston for many years where he established many programmes. He is well known for his advocacy programmes and co-incidentally, Eli is a graduate of Brown University.

Mia Caroline Wyszynski studied political science at the University of Bremen, Germany and at the Coastal Carolina University, South Carolina, U.S.A. She is currently working as Network Manager at streetfootballworld and coordinating all network member activities on the online donation platform UNITED. Mia's professional interests lie in examining the role that football plays as a catalyst for social change, with a focus on gender equality.

CPSIA information can be obtained at www.ICGtesting.com
Printed in the USA
LVOW07s0755070913

351414LV00004B/162/P